# 21ST CENTURY

# SPANISH-ENGLISH ENGLISH-SPANISH DICTIONARY

LAUREL

Produced by The Philip Lief Group, Inc.

Published by
Dell Publishing
a division of
Bantam Doubleday Dell Publishing Group, Inc.
1540 Broadway
New York, New York 10036

Published by arrangement with
The Philip Lief Group, Inc.
6 West 20th Street
New York, NY 10011

ISBN: 0-440-22087-4
Printed in the United States of America

Published simultaneously in Canada

September 1996

10   9

OPM

# Contents

# Introduction

The *21st Century Spanish-English/English-Spanish Dictionary* is an invaluable reference source for today's students, business people, and travelers. Rather than wasting space on verbose, overly complicated definitions, the *21st Century Spanish-English/English-Spanish Dictionary* provides essential information in a brief, easy-to-use format.

The dual format of the *21st Century Spanish-English/English-Spanish Dictionary* eliminates the need to use two dictionaries: one volume for looking up words in Spanish; and a separate one for looking up words in English. A student, for example, can use this dictionary to find the English translation to an unfamiliar Spanish word—*and* to discover the correct way to express a certain English phrase in Spanish. Because each entry is listed in both Spanish and English, this dictionary is useful for every situation. Whether you are a business person checking the terms of a contract on an international deal, a foreign exchange student getting settled into a Spanish dormitory, or a tourist trying to understand the items on a menu, the *21st Century Spanish-English/English-Spanish Dictionary* will help you find quick, clear translations from Spanish to English—*and* from English to Spanish.

Each entry in the *21st Century Spanish-English/English-Spanish Dictionary* appears in a concise, easy-to-follow format. The headwords are listed in alphabetical order, with a separate A-to-Z section for both the Spanish-English and the English-Spanish. The pronunciation, complete with syllable markings, appears in brackets after each headword, followed by its part of speech. (See Pronunciation Guide.) Entries for nouns also include an indication of gender, with *M* signifying a masculine word, *F* indicating a feminine word, and *N* representing a neuter word. Verbs are marked either *vt* (verb transitive) or *vi* (verb intransitive). Finally, a clear, succinct translation of each word appears, followed by a list of related forms and common phrases.

Reflecting current attitudes and ever-changing sensitivities in its choice of word list, definitions, translations, and pronunciations, the *21st Century Spanish-English/English-Spanish Dictionary* provides the most reliable and up-to-date information available. Whether for speaking, writing, or understanding, the *21st Century Spanish-English/English-Spanish Dictionary* successfully combines a simple, concise format with a contemporary slant, and will serve as an indispensable tool for every occasion.

# Pronunciation Guide

This dictionary represents a unique approach to phonetic pronunciation. It relies on plain, or readily understood, symbols and letters. There are no Greek symbols, and most people, whether English-speaking or Spanish-speaking should be able to easily sound out the words using this guide.

For English words, the pronunciation is based on conventional (unaccented) American English. The most common pronunciation has been chosen in any instance where there is more than one acceptable pronunciation.

The Spanish language is very consistent with the sounds of its vowel groupings as well as consonants. This outline has very few, if any, exceptions. Vowel sounds are generally pure. The groupings in the left column are the Spanish language; their English counterparts are in the right hand column.

| VOWELS | | ENGLISH EQUIVALENT |
|--------|---|---|
| a = ah | | cop, mop |
| e = eh | | eh, hefty, heather |
| I = ee | | seen, keen, mean |
| o = oh | | phone, hope |
| u = oo | | hoop, loop, soup |

| CONSONANTS | | ENGLISH EQUIVALENT |
|------------|---|---|
| b | b | bat, be, able |
| c | c | cat |
| d | d | dip, seed |
| f | f | fall, physic, laugh |
| g | g | gap, big |
| h | h | heat |

CONSONANTS                                    ENGLISH EQUIVALENT

|        |      |                              |
|--------|------|------------------------------|
|        | j    | *job*, e*dge*                |
| k      | k    | *c*at, ti*ck*, *k*in, *q*uit |
| l      | l    | *l*ip, pu*ll*, he*l*p        |
| m      | m    | ha*m*, *m*at, li*m*p         |
| n      | n    | *n*o, ha*n*g, bi*n*          |
| p      | p    | *p*ut, u*p*                  |
| r      | r    | ta*r*, *r*ipe, pa*r*t        |
| s      | s    | *s*it, *c*ite, hi*ss*        |
| t      | t    | ha*t*, *t*in, bu*tt*er       |
| v      | v    | *v*ine, ha*v*e               |
| w      | w    | *wh*y, *w*it                 |
| y      | y    | *y*es                        |
| z      | z    | *z*oo, hi*s*, read*s*        |
|        | ch   | *ch*in, i*tch*               |
|        | sh   | a*sh*, a*c*tion              |
|        | th   | *th*e, *th*at                |
|        | zh   | vi*s*ion                     |
|        | ng   | ba*n*k, a*n*ger              |

## *SPANISH PRONUNCIATION GUIDE*

Spanish has the following vowel sounds, with the corresponding English equivalents noted.

| *SPANISH*                | *ENGLISH EQUIVALENT*                      |
|--------------------------|-------------------------------------------|
| a = ah                   | ah, as in far, father                     |
| e = ai                   | ai, as in pay, say, day, hay              |
| I = ee                   | ee, as in feet, heat, beat, meet          |
| o = oh, long             | oh, as in obey, Oklahoma, only            |
| u = oo                   | oo, as in boot, hoot, loot                |
| y = Spanish I, or ee     | see, he, be                               |

The diphthongs in Spanish are pronounced as follows:

| *SPANISH* | *ENGLISH*                                            |
|-----------|------------------------------------------------------|
| ai, ay    | = English I in light, fight, sight                   |
| au        | = English ou in sound, bound, hound                  |
| ei, ey    | = English ai in they, say, may                       |
| eu        | = English combination of a in pay with ew of mew     |
| oi, oy    | = English oy as in boy, toy, soy                     |
| ia, ya    | = English ya like yarn, yard                         |

| | |
|---|---|
| ua | = English wa as in wand, want, will |
| ie, ye | = English yet, yearn, yore |
| ue | = English wa as in wake, woke, weather |
| io, yo | = English yo in yoke, yellow• |
| uo | = English uo in quote, quick, quite |
| iu, you | = English Yule, yoke |
| ui | = English wee in week, weak |

Triphthongs are a combination of three vowels together. They are pronounced as follows:

*iai* is pronounced somewhat like yah with ai = yah-eii, as is estudiáis in Spanish pronounced eh•stoo•dee•yai•ihs

*iei* is pronounced like the English yea, as in ah•ih, the Spanish example being estudiéis, pronounced eh•stoo•dee•ah•ihs

*uai, uay* sounds like the English wi, as in wide, the Spanish word guay would be pronounced gwai

*uei, uey* sounds like wei, as in the English weigh, the Spanish example being buey, pronounced bwei

Consonants that are exceptions to the way they are pronounced in English are as follows:

c: before a, o, u, or a consonant sounds like the English c as in cook, but before e or I, it sounds like the English s, as soon, see

d: when at the end of a word, it has the slight sound of Th, as in this, but it is very subtle and difficult to place in a pronunciation of a word, but could be the Spanish word usted, pronounced oo•tehd(th)

g: before a, o, and u, ue, and ui, or a consonant, it sounds like the g in English in gain, give, go. Before e or I, it hounds like the English "H".

h: in Spanish is usually silent

j: sounds like the English "h"

ll: the double ll in Spanish sounds like the English "y", like yet

ñ: this n sounds like the ni or ny combination in English of onion (on•yohn)

q: sounds like the English "c" in coat or cool

rr: this is a strongly trilled sound with the front of the tongue trilling against the teeth

v: can have a very subtle "b" intonation, but not enough to be the predominant sound, as in the Spanish "mover" could be pronounced moh•bair, but still with the v sound there as well.

y: sounds like the English y when at the beginning of words, or between two vowels

z: sounds like the English "s"

*Basic pronunciation in this dictionary*

| *Traditional English phonetics* | *Becomes* | *As in* |
|---|---|---|
| **VOWELS** | | |
| æ | a | cat, ask |
| e | ai | gate, they, air |
| a, a: | ah | hot, father |
| | au | bought, haunt, war, fall |
| | e | fell, head |
| I, I: | ee | see, tea |
| | I | lid, damage |
| aï | uy | buy, lie, height, I |
| o | o | no, foe, road |
| u | oo | loop, chute, poor |
| | ou | now, out, town |
| | oi | boy, void |
| | uh | but, mother, hunt |
| | u | bird, aloof, alert, debris |
| | | book, put, could |

This neutral *u* sound is one of the most common vowel sounds in English, and it is used for many unstressed syllables.

# Introducción

El *Diccionario español-inglés e inglés-español del siglo XXI* es una fuente invaluable de consulta para los modernos estudiantes, comerciantes y viajeros. En vez de desperdiciar espacio en definiciones verbosas y extremadamente complicadas, el *Diccionario español-inglés e inglés-español del siglo XXI* ofrece información esencial en un formato breve y de fácil uso.

El doble formato del *Diccionario español-inglés e inglés-español del siglo XXI* elimina la necesidad de utilizar dos diccionarios: un volumen para buscar las palabras en español y otro para buscarlas en inglés. Por ejemplo, un estudiante puede utilizar este diccionario para hallar la traducción inglesa de una palabra española desconocida y para descubrir la forma correcta de decir cierta frase inglesa en español. Debido a que cada anotación se hace en español y en inglés, este diccionario es útil para cualquier situación. Sea usted un comerciante que busca los términos del contrato de un negocio internacional, un estudiante de divisas extranjeras que está instalándose en un dormitorio universitario en España o un turista que trata de comprender el contenido de un menú, el *Diccionario español-inglés e inglés-español del siglo XXI* le ayudará a encontrar traducciones rápidas y claras del español al inglés y del inglés al español.

Cada anotación en el *Diccionario español-inglés e inglés-español del siglo XXI* aparece en un formato conciso y fácil de seguir. Las palabras principales se enuncian en orden alfabético, con una sección distinta de la A a la Z, tanto para la parte de español a inglés como para la de inglés a español. La pronunciación, con la separación de las sílabas, aparece entre corchetes después de cada palabra principal, seguida por el lugar que ocupa en la oración. (Remítase a la Guía de pronunciación). Las anotaciones de sustantivos también comprenden el género, indicado por una M (masculino), una F (femenino) o una N (neutro). Respecto a los verbos, se indica vt (verbo transitivo) o vi (verbo intransitivo). Finalmente, aparece una traducción clara y sucinta de cada palabra, seguida de una lista de formas afines y frases comunes.

El *Diccionario español-inglés e inglés-español del siglo XXI* (que refleja las actitudes y sentimientos siempre cambiantes en la elección de las palabras, las definiciones, las traducciones y las pronunciaciones) ofrece la información más digna de confianza y más actualizada que puede obtenerse. Sea para hablar, escribir o comprender, el *Diccionario español-inglés e inglés-español del siglo XXII* combina con éxito un formato sencillo y conciso con un concepto moderno, y será un instrumento indispensable para toda ocasión.

# Guía de Pronunciación

Este diccionario representa un enfoque único de la pronunciación fonética. Se funda en símbolos y letras sencillos o rápidamente comprensibles. No contiene caracteres griegos y la mayoría de los usuarios de habla inglesa o italiana pueden pronunciar fácilmente las palabras utilizando esta guía.

La pronunciación de las palabras inglesas se funda en el inglés americano convencional, sin acentos. En todos los casos se ha escogido la pronunciación más común cuando hay varias aceptables.

La lengua española es muy constante en los sonidos de sus grupos de vocales y sus consonantes. Esta regla tiene pocas excepciones, si es que las tiene. Generalmente, las vocales son sonidos puros. Los grupos de la columna de la izquierda pertenecen a la lengua española; sus equivalentes ingleses se encuentran en la columna de la derecha.

| VOCALES | | EQUIVALENTE INGLES |
|---|---|---|
| a = ah | | gorra, mapa |
| e = eh | | eh, fuerte |
| i = ee | | visto, listo |
| | | malévolo |
| o = oh | | teléfono, esperanza |
| u = oo | | zuncho, bucle |

| CONSONANTES | | |
|---|---|---|
| b | b | bate, sea, capaz |
| c | c | gato |
| d | d | sumergir, semilla |
| f | f | caída, físico, risa |
| g | g | brecha, grande |

| h | h | calor |
| | j | trabajo, borde |
| k | k | gato, garrapata, linaje, dejar |
| l | l | labio, halar, ayuda |
| m | m | jamón, estera, cojear |
| n | n | no, colgar, arcón |
| p | p | poner, arriba |
| r | r | brea, maduro, parte |
| s | s | sentar, citar, silbar |
| t | t | sombrero, lata, mantequilla |
| v | v | vid, tener |
| w | w | por qué, ingenio |
| y | y | sí |
| z | z | zoológico, suyo, lee |
| | ch | barbilla, picazón |
| | sh | ceniza, acción |
| | th | el, que |
| | zh | visión |
| | ng | banco, enojo |

## GUIA DE LA PRONUNCIACION ESPAÑOLA

Las vocales españolas tienen los siguientes sonidos, cuyos equivalentes ingleses se enuncian:

| ESPAÑOL | EQUIVALENTE INGLES |
|---|---|
| a = ah | ah, como en lejos, padre |
| e = ai | ai como en pago, decir, día, heno |
| i = ee | ee, como en pies, calor, apalear, encontrarse |
| o = oh, largo | oh, como en obedecer, Oklahoma, sólo |
| u = oo | oo, como en bota, ruido, botín |
| y = i española o ee | ver, él, ser |

Los diptongos españoles se pronuncian así:

| ESPAÑOL | INGLES |
|---|---|
| ai, ay | = e inglesa en luz, pelea, vista |
| au | = ou inglesas en sonido, atado, sabueso |
| ei, ey | = ai inglesas en ellos, decir, puede |
| eu | = combinación inglesa de la a en pago, con la ew en maullar |
| oi, oy | = oy inglesas como en niño, juguete, soya |

| | |
|---|---|
| ia, ya | = ya inglesas, como en madeja, yarda |
| ua | = wa inglesas, como en vara, querer, voluntad |
| ie, ye | = aún, anhelar, antaño, en inglés |
| ue | = wa inglesas, como en velorio, despertó, tiempo |
| io, yo | = yo inglesas en horquilla, amarillo |
| uo | = uo inglesas en citar, rápido, bastante |
| iu, you | = como Natividad y horquilla, en inglés |
| ui | = wee inglesas en semana y débil |

Los triptongos son combinaciones de tres vocales juntas. Se pronuncian así:

iai se pronuncia de una forma parecida a "yah" con ai = yah-eii, como estudiáis, que en español se pronuncia ch-stoo-dee-yai-ihs.

iei se pronuncia como "yea" en inglés, como en ah-ih, que en el ejemplo español es estudiéis, pronunciado eh-stoo-dee-ah-ihs.

uai, uay, suena como las letras wi en inglés, como en ancho. La palabra española ¡guay!, se pronuncia "gwai"

uei, uey, suena como "wei", como en la palabra inglesa peso. Como el ejemplo español es buey, se pronuncia bwei.

Las consonantes que son excepciones a la forma como se pronuncian en inglés son las siguientes:

c: antes de a, o, u ó una consonante, suena como la c inglesa en cocinera; pero antes de e ó i, suena como la s inglesa, en pronto y vea.

d: al final de una palabra, tiene el sonido ligero de la th como en esto; pero es muy sutil y difícil de colocar en la pronunciación de una palabra, aunque podría ser la palabra española usted, que se pronuncia oo-tehd(th).

g: antes de a, o, u y ue ó una consonante, suena como la g inglesa en ganancia, dar, ir. Antes de e ó i, suena como la h inglesa.

h: en español es siempre muda.

j: suena como la h inglesa.

ll: la elle española suena como la y inglesa en aunque.

ñ: esta letra suena como la combinación ni ó ny en inglés, como en cebolla (ce-bo-lla).

# A

**a** [ah] *prep* to; in; at; until
(time)

**abajo** [ah•BAH•ho] *adv* down;
below; calle ~\ down the
street; más ~\ below

**abandonado**
[ah•BAN•do•NAH•do] *adj*
forsaken

**abandonar**
[ah•BAHN•doh•NAHR] *vt*
abandon; forgo; relinquish;
neglect; discard; release

**abanico** [ah•BAHN•EE•koh] *n*
M fan

**abaratar** [ah•BAHR•ah•TAHR]
*vt* cheapen

**abastecer** [ah•BAH•steh•SAIR]
*vt* cater (banquet etc)

**abatimiento**
[ah•BAH•tee•MEE•EN•to] *n*
M stoop

**abdomen** [ahb•DOH•men] *n* M
abdomen

**abedul** [ah•BEH•dool] *n* M
birch

**abeja** [ah•BAI•ha] *n* F bee

**abejarrón** [ah•BAI•hahr•OHN]
*n* M bumblebee

**abertura** [ah•BAIR•toor•ah]
*n* F opening; vent; loophole;
slit

**abeto** [ah•BAI•to] *n* M fir

**abiertamente**
[ah•BEE•air•tah•MEN•tai] *adv*
openly

**abierto** [ah•BEE•AIR•to] *adj*
open

**abigarrado**
[ahb•EEG•ahr•RAH•do] *adj*
variegated; multicolored

**abismo** [ah•BEES•moh] *n* M
abyss

**ablandar** [ah•BLAN•dahr] *vt*
soften

**ablandarse**
[ah•BLAHN•DAHR•sai] *vi*
relent

**abogado** [AH•boh•GAH•do] *n*
M lawyer

**abolir** [AH•boh•LEER] *vt*
abolish

**abominable** [AH•
boh•mih•NAHB•lai] *adj*
abominable; ~cion\
abomination *n*

**abono** [ah•BOH•no] *n* M
manure

**abordar** [ah•BOR•dahr] *vt*
board (on board)

**aborrecer**
[ah•BOHR•reh•SAIR] *vt*
abhor; loathe

**aborrecible**
[ah•BOR•reh•SEEB•lai] *adj*
loathsome

**aborto** [ah•BOHR•toh] *n* M
abortion; miscarriage

**abra** [AH•brah] *n* F cove; creek

**abrazadera**
[AH•brah•sah•DAIR•ah] *n* F
brace

**abrazo** [ah•BRAH•soh] *n* M
embrace; hug

**abrazo estrecho** [ah•BRAH•so
eh•STREH•cho] *n* M cuddle

**abreviación**
[AH•brai•VEE•ah•SEE•ohn] *n*
abbreviation

**abreviar** [AH•brai•VEE•ahr] *vt*
abbreviate

**abrigo** [ah•BREE•go] *n* M
topcoat; coat

**abril** [ah•BRIL] *n* M April

**abrochar** [AH•broh•CHAHR] *vt*
clasp

**abrupto** [ah•BROOP•toh] *adj*
abrupt

**absolutamente**
[AHB•soh•LOO•tah•MEN•tai]
*adv* absolutely; (neg.) not at
all

**absoluto** [AHB•soh•LOO•toh]
*adj* absolute

**absorber** [AHB•sor•BAIR] *vt*
absorb

**abstenerse**
[AHB•steh•NAIR•sai] *vi*
abstain

**absurdo** [ahb•SOOR•doh] *adj*
absurd

**abuela** [ah•BWAI•lah] *n* F
grandma; grandmother

**abuelo** [ah•BWAI•lo] *n* M
grandpa; grandfather

**abuelos** [ah•BWAI•los] *npl*
grandparents

**abundancia**
[ah•BUHN•dan•SEE•ah] *n* F
plenty

**abundante 1**
[AH•buhn•DAHN•tai] *adj*
abundant

**abundante 2**
[AH•buhn•DAHN•tai] *adj*
plentiful

**aburrido** [AH•boor•EE•do] *adj*
boring; be bored

**aburrimiento**
[AH•boor•EE•MEE•EN•to] *n*
M boredom

**abusar de** [ah•BOO•sahr dai] *vt*
abuse

**abuso** [ah•BOO•soh] *n* M
abuse; misuse

**acaballadero**
[AH•kah•BAH•yah•DAIR•oh]
*n* M stud (animal)

**academia**
[AH•kah•dai•MEE•ah] *n* F
academy

**acalorado**
[AH•kah•lo•RAH•doh] *adj*
excited; heated; acalorarse *vi\*
get hot/excited

**acamar** [AH•kah•MAHR] *v* lay

**acampamento**
[a•KAHMP•ah•MEN•toh] *n* M
encampment

**acanalar** [AH•kahn•AH•lahr] *vt*
channel

**acariciar**
[AH•kahr•EE•SEE•ahr] *vt*
fondle; caress

**acarrear** [AH•kahr•EE•ahr] *vt* transport; accareo *n* M transport

**a cause de** [ou KOU•seh dai] *prep* because of

**acceder** [AK•sai•DAIR] *vi* agree

**acceso** [ak•SEH•so] *n* M access

**accidental** [AHK•see•DEHN•tahl] *adj* accidental

**accidente** [AHK•see•DEHN•tai] *n* M accident

**acción** [ahk•SEE•OHN] *n* F action; deed

**acción de matricularse** [ahk•SEE•OHN DAI MAH•trihk•you•LAHR•sai] *n* matriculation

**accionista** [ahk•SEE•ON•EE•stah] *n* F stockholder

**acebo** [ah•SAI•bo] *n* M holly

**acechar** [ah•SAI•char] *vi* pry

**aceite** [ah•SAI•tai] *n* M oil

**aceitoso** [ah•SAI•TOH•so ] *adj* oily

**acento** [ah•SEN•toh] *n* M accent

**aceptar** [ah•SEH•tahr] *vt* accept

**acera** [ah•SAIR•ah] *n* F sidewalk

**acercarse** [AH•sair•KAHR•sai] *vt* accost; *vi* stalk

**ácido** [ah•SEE•doh] *n* M acid; *adj* sour

**aclaramiento 1** [ah•KLAHR•ah•MEE•EN•to] *n* M clearance; clearing

**aclaramiento 2** *n* M clearing

**aclarar 1** [AH•klah•RAR] *vt* rinse

**aclarar 2** [ah•KLAHR•rahr] *vt* clear

**acolchado** [AHL•koh•CHAH•do] *n* M padding

**acometedor** [AH•koh•mai•TAI•dor] *adj* aggresive; enterprising

**acometer** [AH•koh•MAI•tair] *vt* attack; acometida *n* F attack

**acomodado** [ah•KOH•moh•DAH•do] *adj* well-to-do

**acomodar** [AH•kohm•OH•dahr] *vt* accommodate

**acompañante** [ah•KOHM•pan•YAHN•tai] *n* M escort

**acompañar** [ah•KOHM•pahn•YAHR] *vt* accompany

**acongojado** [ah•KOHN•go•HAH•doh] *adj* heartbroken; dejected

**aconsejar** [uh•KOHN•sai•HAHR] *vt* advise

**acordar** [ah•KOR•dahr] *vt* remind; agree upon; decide

**acorde** [ah•KOHR•dai] *prep* according

**acornear** [AH•kor•NAI•ahr] *vt* gore

**acortar 1** [ah•KOHR•tahr] *vt* curtail

**acortar 2** [ah•KOR•tahr] *vt* shorten

**acorzado** [AH•kor•SAH•do] *n* M battleship

**acosar** [ah•KOH•sahr] *vt* accost;
besiege

**acostumbrado**
[AH•koh•STOOM•BRAH•do]
*adj* custom; wont

**acostumbrar**
[AH•koh•STOOM•brahr] *vt*
accustom

**acre 1** [AH•krai] *n* M acre

**acre 2** [AH•krai] *adj* tart

**actitud** [AHK•tee•TOOD] *n* F
attitude

**actividad** [AHK•tee•VEE•dahd]
*n* F activity; fuss

**activo** [ahk•TEE•voh] *adj* active

**activo rápido** [ahk•TEE•vo
RAH•pee•doh] *adj* brisk

**acto** [AHK•toh] *n* M act

**actor** [AHK•tohr] *n* M actor

**actriz** [ahk•TREES] *n* F actress

**acuarela** [AH•kwah•RAI•lah] *n*
F watercolor

**acuchillar**
[AH•koo•CHEE•yahr] *vt* slash

**acuerdo 1** [ah•KWAIR•doh] *n*
M accord

**acuerdo 2** [ah•KWER•doh] *n* M
agreement

**acumulamiento**
[AH•koo•moo•LAH•mee•EN•
to] *n* M hoard

**acunar** [ah•KOO•nahr] *vt* rock

**acuoso** [AH•koo•OH•so] *adj*
watery

**acusado** [AH•koo•SAH•doh] *n*
M defendant

**acusar** [ah•KOO•sahr] *vt* indict;
accusse; acusarse *vt* confess;
acusación *n* F accusation

**adaptar** [ah•DAHP•tahr] *vt*
adapt

**adaptarse**
[AH•dahp•TAHR•sai] *vi*
temporize

**adelantado**
[AH•deh•LAHN•tah•doh] *adj*
fast; further

**adelantar** [AH•dai•LAN•tahr]
*vt* advance; move forward,
thrive

**adelante** [AH•deh•LAHN•tai]
*adv* onward

**adelanto** [AH•dai•LAN•to] *adj*
advanced; *n* M advance,
progress

**además** [AH•dai•MAHS] *adv*
*prep* besides; furthermore;
moreover

**adeudado** [AH•doi•DAH•do]
*adj* indebted

**adherir** [AHD•hair•EER] *vt*
attach

**adherirse** [AHD•air•EER•sai] *vi*
abide (by); cling

**adhesión a un partido**
[AD•ai•see•OHN ah oon
par•TEE•do] *n* F siding

**adición** [AH•dee•SEE•ohn] *n* F
addition

**adicional**
[ah•DEE•see•oh•NAHL] *adj*
additional

**adicto** [ah•DEEK•toh] *n* M drug
addict

**adiestar** [ah•DEE•eh•STAHR]
*vi* spar

**adiós** [ah•DEE•ohs] *n* M
farewell

**adivinanza**
[AH•dih•VEEN•ahn•zah] *n* F
riddle

**adivino** [AH•dih•VEEN•oh] *n*
M soothsayer; fortune-teller

**adjetivo** [AHD•he•TEE•voh] *n*
M adjective

**adjudicar** [ad•HOO•dee•KAHR]
*vt* award

**administración**
[ad•MIHN•ih•STRAH•see•
OHN] *n* F management;
administration

**administrador**
[ad•MIHN•ih•STRAH•dohr] *n*
M administrator; manager

**administrar**
[ahd•MEEN•ee•STRAHR] *vt*
administer; manage

**admirable** [ahd•MEER•ab•LAI]
*adj* wonderful

**admiración**
[ahd•MEER•ah•SEE•OHN] *n*
F wonder; admiration

**admirar** [ahd•MEER•ahr] *vt*
admire

**admisión** [ahd•MEE•see•OHN]
*n* F admission

**admitir** [AHD•mih•TEER] *vt*
admit

**adobo** [ah•DOH•boh] *n* M
pickle

**adoctrinar**
[AH•dohk•TREEN•ahr] *vt*
indoctrinate

**adolescencia**
[AH•doh•leh•SEN•SEE•ah] *n*
F adolescence

**adopción** [AH•dop•SEE•ohn] *n*
F adoption

**adoptar** [ah•DOP•tahr] *vt* adopt

**adorador** [AH•dor•AH•dor] *n*
M worshipper

**adorar** [ah•DOHR•ahr] *vt* adore

**adormecido**
[AH•dor•MEH•SEE•doh] *adj*
drowsy; tired; sleepy

**adornado** [AH•dor•NAH•doh]
*adj* ornate

**adornar** [ah•DOR•nahr] v
garnish

**adquirir** [ahd•KVEER•eer] *vt*
acquire

**adulación**
[AH•doo•lah•see•OHN] *n* F
flattery

**adulado** [AH•doo•LAH•dor]
*adj* flattering

**adular** [ah•DOO•lahr] *vt* flatter

**adulterio**
[AH•duhl•TAIR•EE•oh] *n* M
adultery

**adulto** [ah•DOOL•toh] *n* M
adult

**advenedizo**
[AHD•ven•eh•DEE•so] *n* M
upstart

**advenimiento**
[AD•ven•TEE•mee•EN•toh] *n*
M Advent

**adverbio** [ahd•VAIR•BEE•oh]
*n* M adverb

**adversidad**
[AHD•vair•see•DAHD] *n* F
adversity

**advertir** [ahd•VAIR•teer] *vt*
admonish

**aerodinámico**
[AI•oh•dee•NAH•MEE•koh]
*adj* streamlined

**aeroplano** [AI•ro•PLAH•noh] *n*
M airplane

**aeropuerto** [AI•ro•PWAIR•toh]
*n* M airport

**afán** [ah•FAHN] *n* M hard work

**afanar** [ah•FAHN•ahr] *vt* pinch

**afanarse** [ah•FAHN•AHR•sai] *vi* strive; plod

**afanoso** [AH•fah•NO•so] *adj* painstaking

**afectar** [ah•FEHK•tahr] *vt* affect

**afectuoso** [ah•FEHK•too•OH•so] *adj* kindly

**aferrar** [ah•FAIR•rahr] *vt* grapple; grasp

**Afganistan** [AHF•gahn•EE•stahn] *n* Afghanistan

**afición** [ah•FIHKS•ee•OHN] *n* F addiction

**aficionado 1** [ah•FIHK•see•ohn•AH•doh] *n* M amateur

**aficionado 2** [ah•FIHK•see•ohn•AH•doh] *adj* fond

**aficiónado 3** [ah•FIHK•see•oh•NAH•doh] *n* M addict

**afilado** [AH•fee•LAH•doh] *adj* keen

**afilar** [ah•FEE•lahr] *vt* whet

**afinación** [AH•fih•nah•SEE•ohn] *n* F tuning

**afinado** [AH•fih•NAH•doh] *adj* finished

**afirmar** [ah•FEER•mahr] *vt* fasten

**afligido** [AH•flih•HEE•do] *adj* sorrowful

**aflojar** [ah•FLO•har] *vt* slacken

**afluir** [ah•FLOO•eer] *vt* flush

**afortunadamente** [ah•FOR•too•NAH•dah• MEN•tai] *adv* fortunately; luckily

**afortunado** [ah•FOR•too•NAH•do] *adj* fortunate; lucky

**afrecho** [ah•FRAI•cho] *n* M bran

**Africa** [ah•FREE•kah] *n* Africa

**afrontar** [ah•FRON•tahr] *vt* face; be brave

**agacharse** [AH•gah•CHAR•sai] *vi* cower; squat

**agarrar** [ah•GAHR•rahr] *vt* grab; grasp; *vi vi* clutch, claw (at)

**agarro 1** [ah•GAHR•roh] *n* M handle; grip; tenere agarraderos\ have influence

**agarro 2** [ah•GAHR•ro] *n* M gripe; complaint

**agaunieve** [ah•GWAH•nee•AI•vai] *n* F sleet

**agazapar** [ah•GAH•sah•PAHR] *vt* nab

**agazaparse** [ah•GAH•sah•PAHR•sai] *vt* hide

**agencia** [ah•HEN•SEE•ah] *n* F agency

**agencia de viajes** [ah•HEN•SEE•ah dai vee•AH•hais] *n* F travel agency

**agente** [ah•HEN•tai] *n* M agent; broker

**ágil** [AH•heel] *adj* nimble

**agitador** [ah•HEE•TAH•dor] *n* M trouble maker

**agitar** [ah•HEE•tahr] *vt* fluster; rattle

**agitarse** [ah•HEE•tahr•SAI] *vi*
fidget

**agosto** [ah•GO•stoh] *n* M
August

**agotador** [AH•ho•TAH•dor]
*adj* grueling

**agotamiento**
[AH•goh•TAH•mee•EN•toh] *n*
M exhaustion

**agotar** [ah•GO•tahr] *vt* harass

**agraciado**
[ah•GRAH•see•AH•doh] *adj*
engaging

**agradable**
[AH•grah•DAHB•lai] *adj*
agreeable; enjoyable; pleasant;
pleasing

**agradar** [ah•GRAH•dahr] *vt*
please

**agradecido**
[ah•GRAH•deh•SEE•doh] *adj*
grateful; thankful

**agrandar** [ah•GRAHN•dahr] *vt*
enlarge; magnify

**agrandarse**
[AH•gran•DAHR•seh] *vt*
grow; get bigger (person)

**agravar** [ah•GRAH•vahr] *vt*
aggravate

**agravio** [ah•GRAH•VEE•oh] *n*
M grievance

**agregar** [ah•GREH•gahr] *vt* add

**agresivo** [AH•greh•SEE•voh]
*adj* aggressive

**agricolo** [AH•gree•KOH•loh] *n*
farmer; *adj* agricultural

**agricultura**
[AH•gree•kuhl•TOOR•ah] *n* F
agriculture

**agua** [AH•gwah] *n* M water; al
~n M\ overboard; de ~ dulce
*n* M\ freshwater

**aguacero** [ah•GWA•SAIR•oh]
*n* M downpour

**aguardar** [ah•GWAH•DAHR]
*vt* wait for; *vi* wait

**aguardar emboscado**
[ah•GWAH•DAHR
EM•boh•SKAH•do] *vt* waylay

**agudeza** [AH•goo•DAI•sah] *n*
F wisecrack; witticism

**águila** [AH•GWEE•lah] *n* F
eagle

**aguja** [ah•GOO•ha] *n* F needle

**ahí** [ah•HEE] *adv* there; de ~
que\ so that; por ~\ over
there; thereabouts

**ahijada** [AH•hee•HA•dah] *n* F
goddaughter

**ahogar** [AH•oh•gahr] *vt* choke

**ahogar sumergir** [AH•oh•gahr]
[soo•MAIR•heer] *vt* drown

**ahora** [ah•OR•ah] *adv* now; ~
bien\ but; ~ mismo\ right
now; de ~ en adelante\ from
now on; in the future; por ~\
for the time being

**ahorrar de reserva** [ah•OR•ahr
dai rai•sair•vah] *vt adj* spare

**aire** [AI•rai] *n* M air; el ~ libre\
*adv* outdoors

**aire acondicionado**
[-AH•kohn•DIH•see•on•AH•
doh] *adj* air•conditioned

**aislamiento**
[AIS•lah•mee•EN•toh] *n* M
isolation

**aislar** [AIS•lahr] *vt* insulate;
isolate

**ajedrez** [AH•hai•DRAIS] *n* M
chess

**ajeno** [ah•HAI•noh] someone
else's; other people's; foreign

**ajo** [AH•ho] *n* M garlic

**ajuar de novia** [ah•HWAHR dai noh•VEE•ah] m M trousseau

**ajustar** [ah•HOO•stahr] *vt* adjust; readjust; accommodate

**ala** [AH•lah] *n* F wing

**alado** [ah•LAH•do] *adj* winged

**alambre** [ah•LAHM•brai] *n* M wire; de ~\ wiry

**alameda** [AH•lah•MAI•dah] *n* F avenue

**álamo** [ah•LAH•mo[ *n* M poplar

**alardear** [AH•lahr•DAI•ahr] *vi* boast

**alargar** [ah•LAHR•gahr] *vt* lengthen; *vi* protract

**alarma** [ah•LAHR•mah] *n* F alarm; alarmar *vt* alarm; alarmante *adj* \ alarming

**alba** [AHL•bah] *n* M dawn

**albahaca** [AHL•bah•HAH•kah] *n* F basil

**albania** [AHL•bah•NEE•ah] *n* Albania

**albaricoque** [AL•bahr•ih•KOH•kai] *n* M apricot

**albedrío** [AHL•bai•DREE•o] *n* M will; libre~\ free will

**alberca** [ahl•BAIR•kah] *n* F pond

**albergue** [ahl•BAIR•hai] *n* M housing

**albóndiga** [AHL•bon•DIH•gah] *n* F meatball

**albornoz** [al•BOR•nos] *n* M bathrobe

**álbum** [AHL•boom] *n* M album

**alcalde** [ahl•KAHL•dai] *n* M mayor

**alcance** [ahl•KAHN•sai] *n* M extent; scope

**alcanzar** [ahl•KAHN•sahr] *vt* overtake

**alcaudón** [ahl•KOU•don] *n* M shrike

**alcohol** [ahl•KOH•hol] *n* M alcohol

**alcohólico** [ahl•KOH•hol•EE•koh] *n adj* M alcoholic

**aldea** [ahl•DAI•ah] *n* M hamlet

**alegación** [AH•leh•gah•SEE•ohn] *n* F allegation

**alegrador** [AH•lai•GRAH•dor] *adj* exhilarating

**alegrar** [ah•LAI•grahr] *vt* cheer; rejoice; make happy

**alegrarse** [AH•lai•GRAHR•sai] *vi* cheer up

**alegre** [ah•LAIG•grai] *adj* cheerful; glad; merry

**alegremente** [ah•LEH•greh•MEN•tai] *adv* gladly

**alegría** [AH•leh•GREE•ah] *n* F glee

**Alemán** [AH•leh•MAN] *adj* German

**alemanía** [AH•leh•MAHN•ee•ah] *n* F Germany

**alentar** [ahl•EN•tahr] *vt* encourage; abet

**alergia** [AH•lair•HEE•ah] *n* F allergy

**alérgico** [ah•LAIR•HEE•koh] *adj* M allergic

**alerta** [ah•LAIR•tah] *adj* alert;
alertar *vt* alert

**aleta** [ah•LAI•tah] *n* F fin

**aletear** [ah•LAI•TAI•ahr] *vi*
flutter

**alfabeto** [AHL•fah•BAI•toh] *n*
M alphabet

**alfombra** [ahl•FOHM•brah] *n* F
carpet

**alforza** [ahl•FOR•sah] *n* F tuck

**alfrombra** [ahl•FOM•brah] *n* F
rug

**álgebra** [AHL•hai•BRAH] *n* F
algebra

**algo** [AHL•go] *pron* something;
anything; *adv* somewhat

**algodón** [AHL•goh•DOHN] *n*
M cotton

**algoso** [al•GO•so] *adj* weedy

**alguien** [ahl•GEE•ehn] *pron*
somebody; someone; anyone;
anybody

**algún** [AHL•GOON] *adv* some;
de ~ modo\ somehow

**alguna cosa** [ahl•GOON•ah
KOH•sah] *pron* anything; *adv*
somewhat

**algún día** [ahl•GOON DEE•ah]
*n* M sometime

**alguno** [ahl•GOO•no] *pron*
anyone (anybody)

**alhelí** [AHL•eh•LEE] *n* M
wallflower

**alianza** [AH•lee•AHN•sah] *n* F
alliance

**alicates** [AH•lee•KAH•tais] *npl*
pliers

**aliento** [AH•lee•EN•toh] *n* M
encouragement; sin ~ *adj*
breathless

**alimentar** [AH•lee•MEN•tahr]
*vt* cherish

**alimento** [ah•LEE•MEN•toh] *n*
M feed

**alisador** [ah•LEE•SΛH•dor] *n*
M slicker

**alistar** [ah•LEE•stahr] *vt* muster

**alistar enrolar** [ah•LEE•stahr]
[en•ROH•lahr] *vt* enlist

**alistar matricular**
[ah•LEE•stahr]
[MAH•TREEK•oo•LAHR] *vt*
enroll

**aliviar** [ah•LEE•VEE•ahr] *vt*
soothe

**aljofifa** [AHL•ho•FEE•fah] *n* F
mop

**allí** [aiy•YEE] *prep* there; por ~\
thereabouts; thereby

**alma** [AL•mah] *n* F soul

**almacén 1** [ahl•MAH•sen] *n* M
department store

**almacén 2** [ahl•MAH•sen] *n* M
stockroom; warehouse

**almacenamiento**
[AHL•mah•SEN•ah•MEE•EN•
to] *n* M storage

**almeja** [ahl•MAI•hah] *n* F clam

**almidón** [ahl•MEE•dohn] *n* M
starch

**almohada** [AHL•mo•AH•dah] *n*
F pillow

**almohadilla**
[AHL•moh•ha•DEE•yah] *n* F
pad

**almuerzo** [ahl•MWAIR•so] *n*
M lunch

**alojamiento**
[AH•loh•HAH•MEE•en•toh] *n*
M lodgings

**alondra** [ah•LON•drah] *n* F lark

**al por mayor** [AL por mai•YOR] *n* M wholesale

**alquila** [al•KEE•lah] *n* rent

**alquilar** [ahl•KEE•lahr] *vt* let; hire

**alrededor** [AL•rai•DAI•dohr] *adv* around

**altamente** [ahl•TAH•MEN•tai] *adj* highly

**altavoz** [AHL•tah•VOHS] *n* F loudspeaker

**altercado** [AHL•tair•KAH•do] *n* M haggle; quarrel

**altercar** [ahl•TAIR•kahr] *vi* wrangle

**alternar** [al•TAIR•nahr] *vt* alternate (with)

**alto 1** [AHL•to] *n* M halt

**alto 2** [AHL•to] *adj* high; tall (person); steep (geog); en lo~\ on the top of

**alto 3** [AHL•toh] *adv* aloud

**alto el fuego** [AHL•to ehl FOO•AI•go] *n* M cease-fire

**alto superior** [AHL•to] [soo•PAIR•EE•ohr] *adj* upper

**altura** [ahl•TOOR•ah] *n* F highness; height

**alucinación** [ah•LOO•sin•AH•SEE•øhn] *n* F hallucination

**alumbramiento** [ah•LOOM•brah•MEE•EN•toh] *n* M childbirth

**alusión** [ah•LOO•see•OHN] *n* F allusion

**allanar** [ay•YAHN•ahr] *vt* flatten

**allí** [aiy•YEE] *prep* there

**allí dentro** [aiy•YEE DEN•troh] *prep* therein

**ama** [AH•mah] *n* F mistress

**amabilidad** [AH•mah•BIHL•ih•DAHD] *n* F kindness

**amable** [ah•MAHB•lai] *adj* kind; likable; lovable

**ama de casa** [AH•mah dai•KAH•sah] *n* F housewife

**amaestrado** [AH•mai•eh•STRAH•dor] *n* M trainer

**amanecer** [ah•MAHN•eh•SAIR] *n* M daybreak

**amante** [ah•MAHN•tai] *n* M lover

**amapola** [AH•mah•POH•lah] *n* F poppy

**amargo** [ah•MAHR•go] *adj* bitter

**amargón** [ah•MAHR•gohn] *n* M dandelion

**amargor** [ah•MAHR•gor] *n* M bitterness

**amarillo** [AH•mahr•EE•yo] *adj* *n* M yellow

**amartillar** [AH•mahr•TEE•yahr] *vt* cock (a gun)

**amasar** [ah•MAH•sahr] *vt* knead

**ambiente** [ahm•BEE•EN•tai] *n* M environment

**ambientarse** [ahm•BEE•en•TAHR•sai] *vt* adapt

**ambiguo** [ahm•BEEG•wo] *adj* ambiguous

**ambos** [AHM•bohs] *adj* both

**amenaza** [AH•men•AH•sah] *n* F menace; threat; *adj* threatening

**amenazador**
[ah•MEN•ah•SAH•dor] *adj*
menacing

**amenazar** [ah•MEN•ah•SAHR]
*vt* threaten

**ameno** [ah•MAIN•oh] *adj*
delightful

**ameno grato** [ah•MEN•oh]
[grah•to] *adj* agreeable;
pleasant; comfortable

**a menudo** [ah meh•NOO•do]
*adv* often

**América** [ah•MAIR•EE•kah] *n*
America

**América latina**
[ah•MAIR•ih•KAH
lah•TEEN•ah] *n* F Latin
America

**América del Sur**
[ah•MAIR•IH•kah del SOOR]
*n* F South America

**ametrallar**
[ah•MEH•trai•YAHR] *n* F
machine gun

**amigdalitis**
[ah•MIHG•dah•LEE•tihs] *n* M
tonsillitis

**amigo** [ah•MEE•go] *n* friend

**amiláceo**
[ahl•MEE•LAH•kai•oh] *adj*
starchy

**aminorar**
[ah•MEEN•oh•RAHR] *vt*
lessen

**amistad** [ah•MEE•stahd] *n* F
friendship

**amistoso** [AH•mee•STO•so] *adj*
friendly

**amnistia** [AHM•nee•STEE•ah]
*n* F amnesty

**amontado**
[AH•mohn•TAH•doh] *vt*
accumulate

**amontonar**
[AH•mohn•TON•ahr] *vi*
huddle

**amo patrón** [AH•mo]
[pah•TRON] *n* M master

**amor** [AH•mor] *n* M love; hacer
el ~\ make love; por (el) ~ de
Dios\ for God's sake

**amor cariño** [AH•mohr]
[kah•REEN•yo] *n* M affection

**amores** [ah•MOR•ais] *n* M love
affair

**amortajar** [AH•mor•TAH•har]
*vt* shroud

**ampolla** [am•POI•yah] *n* F
blister

**año** [AN•yo] *n* M year

**año bisiesto** [AHN•yo
BEE•see•EH•stoh] *n* M leap
year

**año nuevo** [AHN•yo
noo•AI•vo] *n* New Year

**anadeo** [AHN•ah•DAI•oh] *n* M
waddle

**analfabetismo**
[AHN•ahl•FAH•beh•TEES•mo]
*n* M illiteracy

**analfabeto**
[AHN•ahl•fah•BEH•toh] *adj*
illiterate

**análisis** [ahn•AHL•ih•SEES] *n*
F analysis

**analizar** [AHN•ahl•IH•sahr] *vt*
analyze

**analogía** [AHN•ah•loh•HEE•ah]
*n* F analogy

**ananás** [AH•nah•NAHS] *n* F
pineapple

**anaquel** [an•AH•kehl] *n* M
ledge

**anarquía** [AHN•ahr•KEE•ah] *n*
F anarchy

**ancha escarpa** [AHN•cha]
[eh•SKAHR•pah] *n* F bluff

**ancho** [AHN•cho] *adj* broad;
wide

**anchura** [ahn•CHOOR•ah] *n* F
breadth; width

**ancia** [ahn•SEE•ah] *n* F anchor

**anciano** [AHN•see•AH•noh] *adj*
aged

**anciar** [ahn•SE•ahr] *vi* anchor;
drop anchor

**áncora** [ahn•KOHR•ah] *n* F
anchor

**andar 1** [AHN•dahr] *n* M gait;
*vt* trudge

**andar 2** [AHN•dahr] *vi* walk; ~
por\ be about

**andar detrás de** [AHN•dahr
dai•TRAHS dai] *vi* tag along

**andar sobre agua** [AN•dahr
SO•brai AH•gwah] *vi* wade

**aneblado** [AH•neh•BLAH•do]
*adj* hazy

**anejo** [ah•NAI•ho] *n* M
outhouse

**ángel** [AHN•hel] *n* M angel

**anguila** [ahn•GWEE•lah] *n* F
eel

**ángulo** [AHN•goo•loh] *n* M
angle

**anhelante** [AN•eh•LAHN•tai]
*adj* wistful

**anhelar** [ahn•HAI•lahr] *vi* yearn

**anhelo** [ahn•EH•lo] *n* M
yearning

**anillo rodear** [ah•NEE•yo
ro•DAI•ahr] *n vi* M ring

**animado 1** [AH•nee•MAH•doh]
*adj* animated; sprightly

**animado 2** [AH•nih•MAH•do]
*adj* lively; gay

**animador** [AH•nih•MAH•dor] *n*
M host

**animal** [ah•NEE•mahl] *n* M
animal

**animal doméstico**
[ah•NEE•mahl•do•MEH•
STEE•koh] *n* M pet

**aniversario**
[AHN•ee•vair•SAHR•ee•oh] *n*
M anniversary

**annotar** [AH•no•TAHR] *vt*
record

**anochecer** [ah•NOH•che•SAIR]
*n* M evening; nightfall

**anormal** [ah•NOR•mahl] *adj*
abnormal

**ansia** [ahn•SEE•ah] *n* F greed

**ansiedad** [AHN•see•EH•dahd]
*n* F anxiety

**ansioso 1** [AHN•see•OH•soh]
*adj* eager; greedy

**ansioso 2** [AHN•see•OH•soh]
*adj* anxious

**anta** [AHN•tah] *n* F elk

**ante Cristo** [AN•tai KREE•sto]
BC

**antebrazo** [AHN•tai•BRAH•so]
*n* M forearm

**antepasado**
[AN•tai•PAH•sah•doh] *n* M
ancestor; forefather

**antepecho** [AN•tai•PEH•cho] *n*
M windowsill

**anterior** [AHN•tair•EE•or] *adj*
prior

**anterior pasado**
[AHN•tair•EE•ohr
pah•SAH•do] *adj* former

antes / apellido de soltera    13

**antes** [AHN•tais] *adv* before; ~
de\ before; lo ~ posible\ as
soon as possible

**antesala** [AN•tai•SAH•la] *n* F
waiting-room

**antever** [an•TAI•vair] *vt* foresee

**anticuado**
[AHN•tee•KWAH•do] *adj*
obsolete; old-fashioned;
outmoded; outdated

**antifaz** [ahn•TEE•fahs] *n* F
mask

**antiguo** [ahn•TEE•gwo] *adj*
ancient; antique

**antisocial**
[AHN•tee•soh•SEE•ahl] *adj*
antisocial

**antojo 1** [an•TO•ho] *n* M
birthmark

**antojo 2** [ahn•TOH•ho] *n* M
whim

**antologia**
[ahn•TOH•loh•HEE•ah] *n* F
anthology

**antorcha** [an•TOR•cha] *n* F
torch

**anual** [ah•NOO•ahl] *adj* M
annual

**anublado** [ah•NOO•BLAH•do]
*adj* overcast

**anular** [ah•NOO•lahr] *vt* nullify

**anunciar** [AH•nuhn•SEE•ahr] *vt*
announce

**anuncio** [AH•nuhn•SEE•oh] *n*
M advertisement; classified
ad; commercial

**ánuo** [AHN•oo•oh] *adj* M
annual

**ansiar** [ahn•SEE•ahr] *vt vi* crave

**ansiedad** [AHN•see•EH•dahd]
*n* F concern

**antipatia**
[AHN•tee•pah•TEE•ah] *n* F
dislike; reluctance;
unwillingness

**apalear** [AH•pah•LAI•ahr] *vt*
bludgeon; club

**aparador** [AH•pah•RAH•dohr]
*n* M cupboard

**aparato de señales**
[AH•pah•RAH•to dai
sen•YAL•ais] *n* M blinker
(car)

**aparecer** [ah•PAIR•eh•sair] *vi*
appear

**aparejo** [AH•pah•RAI•ho] *n* M
gear

**aparentar** [AH•pahr•REN•tahr]
*vi* pretend

**aparición**
[ah•PAH•rih•SEE•ohn] *n* F
appearance

**apartadero**
[ah•PAHR•tah•DAIR•oh] *n* M
sidetrack

**apartado 1** [AH•pahr•TAH•do]
*n* M mailbox

**apartado 2** [AH•pahr•TAH•do]
*adj* off; removed

**apartamento**
[ah•PAHR•tah•MEHN•toh] *n*
M apartment

**apartar** [ah•PAHR•tahr] *vt*
seclude; deter; hold off; keep
off

**apasionado**
[ah•PAH•see•ohn•AH•doh]
*adj* impassioned; passionate

**apellido de soltera**
[AH•peh•YEE•doh dai
sol•TAIR•ah] *n* M maiden
name

**apenas** [ah•PAIN•ahs] *adv* hardly

**aperitivo** [ah•PAIR•ih•TEE•voh] *n* M appetizer

**apetito** [AH•peh•TEE•toh] *n* M appetite

**ápice** [AH•pee•sai] *n* M tip

**apilar** [ah•PEE•lahr] *vt* mow

**aplacar** [ah•PLAH•kahr] *vt* placate

**aplastante** [ah•PLAH•stahn•TAI] *adj* overwhelming

**aplastar** [ah•PLAH•stahr] *vt* squelch

**aplaudir** [ah•PLOU•deer] *vt vi* applaud; *vi* clap

**aplazar** [ah•PLAH•sahr] *vi* procrastinate

**aplicación** [ah•PLIH•kah•see•OHN] *n* F application

**aplicar** [ah•PLEE•kahr] *vt* apply

**apodo** [ah•POH•do] *n* M nickname

**aporrear** [ah•POHR•rai•AHR] *vi* thump

**apostar** [ah•PO•stahr] *vt* wager

**apoyo** [ah•POY•yo] *n* M headrest

**apreciar** [ah•PRAI•SEE•ahr] *vt* appraise

**aprehensión** [ah•PREH•hen•SEE•ohn] *n* F seizure

**aprender** [ah•PREN•dair] *vt vi* learn

**aprender de memoria** [ah•PREN•dair dai MEM•or•EE•ah] *vt* memorize

**apresuradamente** [ah•PREH•soor•AH•dah•MEN•tai] *adv* hurriedly

**apresurar** [AH•preh•SOOR•ahr] *vt* hasten

**apretar** [ah•PREH•tahr] *vt* squeeze; stow; strangulate; untie

**apretón de manos** [AH•preh•TON dai mahn•os] *n* M handshake

**apretura** [ah•PRAI•toor•AH] *n* F press

**aprobación** [AH•pro•BAH•SEE•ohn] *n* F approval

**aprobar** [ah•PROH•bahr] *vt* approve

**apropriado** [AH•pro•PREE•AH•doh] *adj* appropriate

**aprovechable** [ah•PRO•veh•CHAB•lai] *adj* available

**aproximadamente** [ah•PROHKS•ee•MAH•dah•MEN•tai] *adv* approximately

**aptitud** [ahp•TEE•tood] *n* F flair; suitability

**aptitudo** [ahp•TEE•tood•o] *adj* capable

**apuesta** [ah•PUE•stah] *n* F bet

**apuntador** [ah•PUHN•tah•DOR] *n* M pointer

**apuntar** [ah•PUHN•tahr] *vi* aim; *vt* jot

**apuro** [ah•POOR•oh] *n* M pinch

**aquel 1** [AH•kehl] *adv* yonder

**aquel 2** [AH•kehl] that

**aquí** [ah•KEE] *adv* here; de ~\
from here; de ~ para allí\ to
and fro; de ~ que\ so that;
hasta ~\ until now; por ~\
around; de ~\ henceforth

**arado** [ah•RAH•do] *n* M plow

**araña 1** [ah•RAHN•yah] *n* F
penchant; inclination

**araña 2** [ah•RAN•yah] *n* F
spider

**arándano** [ah•RAHN•dah•NO]
*n* M blueberry; cranberry

**arbitrar** [ahr•BEE•trahr] *n* M
referee

**árbitro** [AHR•bee•troh] *n* M
umpire

**árbol** [AHR•bol] *n* M tree

**árbol geneslógico**
[HEN•ais•LOH•HEE•koh] *n*
M tree (family)

**arbusto** [ahr•BOO•stoh] *n* M
bush; shrub

**arbustos** [ahr•BOO•stohs] *npl*
shrubbery

**arcaico** [ahr•KAI•koh] *adj*
archaic

**arce** [AHR•sai] *n* M maple

**arcilla** [ahr•SEE•yah] *n* F clay

**arco 1** [AHR•koh] *n* M bow

**arco 2** [AHR•koh] *n* M arch

**arco iris** [ahr•KOH EER•ihs] *n*
M iris; rainbow

**ardid** [ahr•DEED] *n* M ruse

**ardiente** [AHR•dee•EN•tai] *adj*
fiery; zealous

**ardilla** [ahr•dee•yah] *n* F
squirrel

**área** [ah•RAI•alı] *n* F area

**arena 1** [ah•RAI•nah] *n* F arena

**arena 2** [ah•RAI•nah] *n* F grit;
gravel; sand

**arena movediza** [ah•RAI•nah
MOH•veh•DEE•sah] *n* F
quicksand

**arenque** [ahr•EN•kai] *n* M
herring

**Argelia** [AHR•gai•LEE•ah] *n* M
Algeria

**argumentar**
[AHR•goo•MEN•tahr] *vi*
argue

**argumento** [ahr•GOO•MEN•to]
*n* M argument

**árido** [AHR•ee•doh] *adj* arid

**arma** [AHR•mah] *n* F weapon

**armada** [ahr•MAH•dah] *n* F
fleet; navy

**armadura 1**
[AHR•mah•DOOR•ah] *n* F
armor

**armadura 2**
[AHR•mah•DOOR•ah] *n* F
frame

**armario** [AHR•mahr•EE•oh] *n*
M wardrobe

**armonía** [AHR•mohn•EE•ah] *n*
F harmony

**armónica** [ahr•MOH•nee•KAH]
*n* F harmonica

**armonioso**
[AHR•moh•nee•OH•so] *adj*
harmonious

**armonizar**
[AHR•mohn•EE•sahr] *vt*
harmonize

**arneses** [ahr•NAI•sais] *n* M
harness

**aro** [AH•roh] *n* M bail

**aroma** [ah•ROH•mah] *n* F
aroma

**arpa** [AHR•pah] *n* F harp

**arpía** [ahr•PEE•ah] *n* F shrew

**arpón** [ahr•POHN] *n* M
harpoon

**arqueologia**
[AHR•kai•oh•loh•HEE•ah] *n* F
archaeology

**arqueta** [ahr•KEH•tah] *n* F
casket

**arquitecto**
[AHR•kee•TEHK•toh] *n* M
architect

**arquitectura**
[AHR•kee•tehk•TOOR•ah] *n*
F architecture

**arrancar 1** [ah•RAHN•sahr] *vt*
extort

**arrancar 2** [ahr•RAHN•kahr] *vt*
pluck

**arranque** [ahr•RAHN•kai] *n* M
outburst

**arrastrar prolongar**
[ahr•RAH•strahr
proh•LON•gahr] *vt vi* drag

**arrastrarse**
[AHR•rah•STRAHR•sai] *vi*
crawl; sprawl

**arrebatado**
[AHR•reh•bah•TAH•do] *adj*
rapt

**arrebatador**
[AHR•reh•bah•TAH•dor] *adj*
sweeping

**arrebatar** [AHR•rai•BAH•tahr]
*vt* ravish

**arreglar 1** [ah•RAI•glahr] *vt*
arrange

**arreglar 2** [ahr•RAIG•lahr] *vt*
straighten

**arremetida**
[AHR•reh•meh•TEE•dah] *n* F
onslaught

**arremolinarse**
[AHR•reh•moh•LEEN•AHR•
sai] *vi* swirl

**arrendar** [ah•REN•dahr] *vt* rent

**arrendatario**
[AHR•ren•DAH•tahr•EE•oh] *n*
M tenant

**arrepentirse**
[ahr•REHP•en•TEER•sai] *vi*
repent

**arrestar** [AH•reh•STAHR] *vt*
arrest

**arriba 1** [ahr•REE•bah] *adv* up;
upstairs

**arriba 2** [ahr•REE•bah] *adj*
over; calle ~\ up the street; de
~ abajo\ from top to bottom;
la parte de ~\ the top part;
más ~\ above; lo de ~ abajo\
topsy-turvy

**arricés** [AHR•ree•SAIS] *n* M
buckle

**arriendo** [AHR•ree•EN•doh] *n*
M lease

**arriesgado aventurero**
[ah•REES•GAH•doh]
[ah•ven•too•rair•oh] *adj*
adventurous

**arriesgar** [AHR•ree•EHS•gahr]
*vt* jeopardize; endanger

**arrodillarse**
[ahr•ROH•DEE•yahr•sai] *vi*
kneel

**arrogante** [AH•roh•GAHN•tai]
*adj* arrogant

**arrogarse** [AH•roh•GAHR•sai]
*vt* assume

**arrojadizo**
[AHR•roh•ha•DEE•so] *n* M
missile

**arrojarse** [ahr•ROH•har•sai] *vi*
rush

**arrojo** [ahr•ROH•ho] *n* M
boldness

**arrollamiento**
[AHR•roh•yah•MEE•EN•to] *n*
M winding

**arrollar** [ah•ROY•yahr]
*vt* coil

**arroyo** [ah•ROI•yo] *n* M
stream; brook; gutter

**arroz** [ahr•ROHS] *n* M rice

**arruga** [ahr•ROO•gah] *n* F
wrinkle

**arrugar** [ahr•ROO•gahr] *vt*
rumple; shrivel

**arrullar** [ahr•ROO•yahr] *vi* M
coo; lull to sleep

**arrullo** [ahr•ROO•yo] *n* M
lullaby

**arte** [AHR•tai] *n* M art; craft

**arte en el trabajo** [AHR•tai en
el] *n* M workmanship

**articulación**
[AHR•tih•KOO•lah•SEE•ohn]
*n* F utterance

**articular** [AR•tihk•YOO•lahr] *vt*
articulate

**artículo** [AR•TEE•koo•lo] *n* M
article

**artificial**
[AHR•tih•FIII•SEE•ahl] *adj*
artificial

**artista** [ar•TEE•stah] *n* F artist

**asa** [AH•sah] *n* F handle

**asad** [ah•SAHD] *n* M roast
(mcat)

**asamblea** [ah•SAHM•BLAI•ah]
*n* F assembly

**asar** [ah•SAIIR] *vt* broil; roast

**asado** [ah•SAH•do] *adj* roasted

**ascendente** [AH•sen•DEN•tai]
*adv* upward

**ascua** [ah•SKOO•ah] *n* F
cinder

**ascuas** [AH•skwahs] *npl*
embers

**aseado** [AH•sai•AH•do] *adj*
tidy; trim

**aseguranción**
[AH•seh•goor•AHN•see•OHN]
*n* F insurance

**asegurar** [AH•seh•GOOR•ahr]
*vt* ensure; insure; secure

**asentada** [AH•sen•TAH•dah] *n*
F sitting

**asentar** [ah•SEN•tahr] *vi* sit

**asentir** [ah•SEN•teer] *vi* agree;
~ con la cabeza *vi* \ nod

**asesinar** [AH•sehs•EEN•ahr] *vt*
assassinate

**asesinato**
[ah•SEHS•ee•NAH•to] *n* M
assassination; murder

**asesino** [AH•seh•SEE•noh] *n* M
murderer

**así** [ah•SEE] *adv* thus; so; like
this; ~ ~\ such; ~ asá; ~
asado so-so; ~ como\ just as;
~ sea\ so be it; ~ y todo\ even
so; aun ~\ even so

**asiento** [AH•see•EN•to] *n* M
seat

**asignar** [ah•SIG•nahr] *vt* assign

**asimiento**
[ah•SEE•MEE•EN•toh] *n* M
grasp

**asmático** [ahs•MAH•TEE•ko]
*adj* wheezy

**asna** [AHS•nah] *n* F rafter
(building)

**asnilla** [ahs•NEE•yah] *n* F
trestle

**asociación**
[ah•SO•see•AH•see•OHN] *n* F
association

**asociación de obreros**
[ah•SOH•see•AH•see•OHN
dai ob•RAIR•ohs] *n* F
trade-union

**asociación obrera**
[ah•SO•see•AH•see•OHN
oh•BRAIR•ah] *n* F labor
union

**asociarse**
[ah•SOH•see•AHR•sai] *vt*
associate

**asolador** [AH•soh•LAH•dor]
*adj* wasteful

**asolar 1** [ah•SOH•lahr] *vt*
ravage; destroy

**asolar 2** *vi* dry up (plants)

**asomar** [ah•SOH•mahr] *vi* peep

**asombrar 1** [ah•SOHM•brahr]
*vt* astonish

**asombrar 2** [ah•SOM•brahr] *vt*
overshadow

**aspa** [AH•spah] *n* F reel

**aspecto** [ah•SPEK•to] *n* M
aspect

**aspirina** [AH•speer•EEN•ah] *n*
F aspirin

**asquerosamente**
[ah•SKAIR•oh•sah•MEN•tai]
*adj* nauseous

**asta** [AH•stah] *n* F pole

**astilla** [ah•STEE•yah] *n* F
splint; splinter

**astrologia**
[AH•stroh•loh•HEE•ah] *n* F
astrology

**astronauta**
[AH•stroh•NOW•tah] *n* M
astronaut

**astronomía**
[AH•strah•no•MEE•ah] *n* F
astronomy

**astucia** [AH•stoo•SEE•ah] *n* F
guile; cleverness; cunning

**astuto** [ah•STOO•toh] *adj*
crafty; wily

**asunto** [ah•SUHN•to] *n* M
topic; affair

**asustadizo**
[ah•SUHS•tah•DEE•so] *adj*
skittish

**asustar** [ah•SUHS•tahr] *vt*
scare; *vi* startle

**atacar** [ah•TAH•kahr] *vt* attack

**atado 1** [ah•TAH•do] *adj* bound

**atado 2** [ah•TAH•do] *n* M
bundle

**atajo** [ah•TAH•ho] *n* M shortcut

**ataque** [ah•TAH•kai] *n* M
stroke (medical)

**ataque cardíaco** [ah•TAH•kai
KAHR•DEE•ahk•oh] *n* M
heart attack

**ataque de nervios**
[ah•TAH•kai dai
nair•VEE•ohs] *n* hysterics

**atar 1** [AH•tahr] *vi* tackle; *vt*
tie-up

**atar 2** [AH•tahr] *vt* attach

**ataúd** [ah•TAUD] *n* M coffin

**atención** [ah•TEN•see•OHN] *n*
F attention

**atender** [ah•TEN•dair] *vt*
attend; vr heed

**atento** [ah•TEN•to] *adj*
attentive; courteous; mindful;
observant

**aterrar** [ah•TAIR•rahr] *vt* terrify
**aterrorizar**
[AH•tair•ROHR•ih•SAHR] *vt*
terrorize
**atezado** [AH•teh•SAH•do] *adj*
swarthy
**ático** [ah•TEE•koh] *n* M loft;
attic
**atiesar** [AH•tee•EH•sahr] *vt*
stiffen
**atisbo** [ah•TEES•boh] *n* M peek
**atizador** [AH•tee•SAH•dor] *n*
M poker
**atizat** [ah•TEE•sahr] *vt* stoke
**atoño** [ah•TON•yo] *n* M
autumn
**atontarse** [AH•ton•TAHR•sai]
*vi* stupefy
**atormentador**
[AH•tor•men•TAH•dor] *n* M
tormentor; torturer
**atormentar**
[AH•tor•MEHN•tahr] *vi*
tantalize; *vt* torment
**atracción**
[ah•TRAHK•see•OHN] *n* F
attraction
**atractivo**
[ah•TRAHK•TEE•voh] *adj*
attractive; inviting
**atraer 1** [ah•TRAI•air] *vt* attract
**atraer 2** [ah•TRAI•air] *vt* wile;
deceive
**atrás** [ah•TRAHS] *adv*
backward
**atrasado mental**
[ah•TRAH•SAH•do men•tahl]
*n* M moron
**atravesar 1** [AH•trah•VAI•sahr]
*vt* pierce

**atravesar 2**
[AH•trah•VEH•stahr] *vt*
traverse; cross; go through
**atrevido 1** [AH•trai•VEE•doh]
*n* M daredevil; *adj* daring
**atrevido 2** [AH•treh•VEE•doh]
*adj* impudent
**atronador** [AH•troh•NAH•dor]
*adj* thundering; thunderous
**atropello** [ah•TROH•PAI•yo] *n*
M outrage
**atroz horrible** [ah•TROHS]
[tair•EEB•lai] *adj* awful
**aturdimiento**
[ah•TOOR•dee•MEE•EN•to] *n*
M daze
**aturdir** [ah•TOOR•deer] *vt* stun
**audición** [ou•DIH•see•OHN] *n*
F audition
**aullido** [ou•YEE•do] *n* M howl
**aumentar 1** [ou•MEN•tahr] *vt*
hike; increase; step up
(manufacturing)
**aumentar 2** [ou•MEN•tahr] *vi*
zoom
**aumento** [ou•MEN•toh ] *n* M
increase; en ~\ increasingly
**aun** [aun] *adv* even; ~ así\ even
so; ~ cuando\ although; más ~
even more; ni~\ not even
**aún** [oun] *adv* still; yet
**aunque** [OUN•kai] *conj*
although; though
**auricular** [ou•RIH•KOO•lahr] *n*
M receiver (telephone)
**ausente** [ou•SEN•tai] *adj*
absent
**Australia** [au•STRAH•LEE•ah]
*n* F Australia
**Austria** [ou•STREE•ah] *n* F
Austria

**auténtico** [ou•TEN•tee•KOH]
*adj* authentic

**autobiografía**
[OU•to•BEE•oh•grah•FEE•ah]
*n* F autobiography

**autobús** [OU•to•BOOS] *n* M
bus

**autodidacto**
[OU•to•dih•DAHK•to] *adj*
self-taught

**autógrafo** [ou•TO•grah•FO] *n*
M autograph

**automático**
[OU•to•MAH•tee•KOH] *adj*
automatic

**automóvil** [OU•to•MOH•veel]
*n* M car

**autopista** [OU•to•PEE•stah] *n*
F speedway

**autor** [OU•tor] *n* M author

**autor dramático** [OU•tor
drah•MAH•tee•ko] *n* M
playwright

**autor romántico** [OU•tor
roh•MAHN•tee•koo] *n* M
romanticist

**autoridad** [OU•tor•ih•DAHD] *n*
F authority

**autorización**
[OU•tor•ih•SAH•SEE•OHN] *n*
F warrant

**avancar** [ah•VAHN•sahr] *vt*
advance

**avanzo** [ah•VAHN•so] *n* M
balance-sheet

**avaricia** [AH•vahr•EE•SEE•ah]
*n* F stinginess

**avaro** [ah•VAH•ro ] *adj*
miserly; stingy; *n* M skinflint

**a veces** [ah VAI•sais] *adv*
sometimes; at times

**avellana** [AH•veh•YAHN•ah] *n*
F hazelnut

**avenas** [ah•VAI•nahs] *npl* oats

**avenida** [AH•ven•EE•dah] *n* F
avenue

**aventajar** [AH•ven•TAH•hahr]
*vi* excel

**aventura** [AH•ven•TOOR•ah] *n*
F adventure

**avergonzado**
[AH•vair•gon•SAH•do] *adj*
ashamed (to be)

**averiguar** [AH•vair•EE•gwar]
*vt* detect

**aversión** [AH•vair•SEE•OHN]
*n* F dislike; reluctance;
unwillingness

**avestruz** [AH•veh•STROOHS]
*n* M ostrich

**avíos de pescar** [ah•VEE•ohs
dai peh•SKAHR] *n* M tackle
(fishing)

**avisado** [AH•vee•SAH•doh] *adj*
clever

**avisar** [ah•VEE•sahr] *vt* warn

**avisar anunciar** [ah•VEE•sahr
ah•NUHN•see•AHR] *vt*
advertise

**aviso** [ah•VEE•so] *n* M warning

**avispa** [ah•VEE•spah] *n* F wasp

**avispón** [ah•VEE•spohn] *n* F
hornet

**avivar** [ah•VEE•vahr] *vt*
quicken

**axis** [AHKS•ees] *n* M axis

**ay!** [ai] *excl* alas; ouch; ~ de\
poor

**ayer** [ai•YAIR] *adv* yesterday; ~
por la mañana; ~ noche\ last
night

**ayuda** [ai•YOO•dah] *n* F help; aid

**ayuda asistencia** [ai•YOO•dah] [AH•sih•STEN•see•AH] *n* F aid

**ayudador** [AI•yoo•DAH•dor] *n* M helper

**ayudar** [ai•YOO•dahr] *vi* help

**azafrán** [AH•sah•FRAHN] *n* M saffron

**azar** [AH•sahr] *n* M chance; misfortune; al ~\ at random; por ~\ by chance

**azotamiento** [AH•soh•TAH•mee•EN•to] *n* M whipping

**azotar** [ah•SO•tahr] *vt* flog

**azote 1** [ah•soh•tai] *n* M scourge

**azote 2** [ah•SOH•tai] *n* M spanking

**azotes** [ah•SO•tais] *n* M flogging

**azucar 1** [ah•SOO•kahr] *n* M candy

**azúcar 2** [ah•SOO•kahr] *n* M sugar

**azucarera** [ah•SOO•kahr•RAIR•ah] *n* F sugar bowl

**azúl** [ah•SOOL] *adj n* M blue

# B

**baba** [BAH•bah] *n* F drivel; spittle; slime

**babador** [bah•BAH•dor] *n* M bib

**babar** [BAH•bahr] *vi* slobber

**babor** [BAH•bor] *n* M port a ~\ on the port side

**bacalao** [bah•KAH•lau] *n* M cod

**bache** [BAH•chai] *n* M pothole

**bahía** [bah•HEE•ah] *n* F bay

**bailador** [bai•LAH•dor] *n* M dancer

**bailarina** [BAI•lah•REE•nah] *n* F ballerina

**baile** [BAI•lai] *n* M dance

**baile de espectáculo** [BAI•lai dai EH•spchk•TAHK•oo•lo] *n* M ballet

**bajada** [bah•HAH•dah] *n* F dip; slope

**baha** [BAH•ha] *n* F drop, fall

**bajar** [BAH•har] *vi* slither

**bajar corriendo** [bah•HAHR KOR•ree•EN•do] *adj* run-down

**bajío** [bah•HEE•yo] *n* M reef; sand bank

**bajo 1** [BAH•ho] *n* M bass (mus)

**bajo 2** [BAH•ho] *adj* low; lower; *adv* below; *prep* under

**bajón** [bah•HON] *n* M bassoon

**bala** [BAH•lah] *n* F hale

**balada** [bah•LAH•dah] *n* F ballad

**balandra** [bah•LAHN•drah] *n* F sloop

**balanza** |bah•LAHN•sah| *n* F
balance

**balceon** |bal•KOHN| *n* M
balcony

**baloncesto**
|BAHL•ohn•SEHS•to| *n* M
basketball

**balota** |bah•LO•tah| *n* F ballot

**balsa** |BAHL•sah| *n* F raft

**ballena** |bay•YAIN•ah| *n* F
whale

**bambú** |bahm•BOO| *n* M
bamboo

**banda** |BAHN•dah| *n* F
band

**bañera** |bahn•YAIR•ah| *n* F
bathtub

**bañista** |bahn•YEE•stah| *n* F
bather

**baño** |BAHN•yo| *n* M bath;
toilet

**banco** |BAHN•koh| *n* M bank;
bench

**banco de iglesia** |BAHN•koh
dai ihg•LAI•see•ah| *n* M
pew

**bandada** |bahn•DAH•dah| *n* F
flock

**banda transportadora**
|BAHN•dah TRAHNS•
pohr•tah•DOHR•ah| *n* F
conveyer belt

**bandeja** |bahn•DAI•ha| *n* F
tray

**bandera** |bahn•DAIR•a| *n* F
banner; flag

**bandido** |bahn•DEE•do| *n* M
outlaw

**banquero** |bahn•KAIR•oh| *n* M
banker

**banquete** |ban•KEH•tai| *n* M
banquet

**barajar** |bahr•AH•hahr| *vi*
shuffle

**barandilla**
|BAHR•rahn•DEE•yah| *n* F
curb

**barato 1** |bah•RAH•toh| *adj*
cheap; inexpensive

**barba** |BAHR•bah| *n* F
beard

**barbado** |bahr•BAH•do| *adj*
barbed

**barba mentón** |BAHR•bah|
|men•TOHN| *n* F chin

**bárbaro** |bahr•BAH•ro| *adj n*
M barbarian

**barbero** |bahr•BAIR•oh| *n* M
barber

**barca** |BAHR•kah| *n* F ferry; M
boat

**barcaza** |bahr•KAH•sah| *n* F
barge

**barniz** |bahr•NEES| *n* M
varnish

**barómetro** |BAH•roh•MAI•tro|
*n* M barometer

**barquillo** |bahr•KEE•yo| *n* M
waffle

**barra 1** |BAHR•rah| *n* F
hanger

**barra 2** |BAHR•rah| *n* F rail;
rod; staff

**barranco** |bahr•RAHN•ko| *n* M
ravine

**barrendero**
|BAHR•ren•DAIR•oh| *n* M
sweeper

**barrer 1** |BAHR•rair| *vt* sweep
**barrer 2** |BAHR•rair| *vi* swoop

**barrera** [bah•RAIR•ah] *n* F
barrier; ~ del sonido\ sound
barrier

**barricada** [BAHR•ih•KAH•da]
*n* F barricade

**barril** [BAHR•reel] *n* M barrel;
keg

**barrilete** [BAHR•ree•LEH•tai]
*n* M jack

**barrio** [bahr•REE•oh] *n* M
borough; neighborhood

**barrita de color** [bahr•REE•tah
dai KOH•lor] *n* F crayon

**barro 1** [BAHR•roh] *n* M mud

**barro 2** [BAHR•roh] *n* M
pimple

**barro 3** [BAHR•roh] *n* M pug

**barroco** [bar•ROH•koh] *adj*
baroque

**barroso** [bahr•ROH•so] *adj*
muddy

**basa** [BAH•sah] *n* F base; basis;
foundation a ~ de\ thanks to;
a ~ de bien\ very well; de la
~ de\ on the basis of

**basamento** [BAH•sah•MEN•to]
*n* M basement

**base fundamento** [BAH•seh]
[FUHN•dah•MEN•to] *n* M
basis

**básico** [bah•SEE•koh] *adj* basic

**¡basta!** *excl* that's enough!

**bastante** [bah•STAN•tai] *adj*
enough; *adv* rather

**bastar** [BAH•stahr] *vi* suffice

**bastardo** [bah•STAHR•do] *n* M
bastard

**bastear** [bah•STAIR•ahr] *vt*
baste

**bastón** [BAH•ston] *n* M baton

**basura 1** [bah•SOOR•ah] *n* F
garbage; rubbish; waste; trash

**basura 2** [bah•SOOR•ah] *n* F
descent

**basurero** [BAH•soor•AIR•oh] *n*
M scavenger

**batalla** [bah•TAI•yah] *n* F battle

**batallón** [BAH•tah•YON] *n* F
battalion

**batata** [bah•TAH•tah] *n* F
sweet potato

**batea** [bah•TAI•ah] *n* F tub

**batería** [BAH•tair•EE•ah] *n* F
battery

**batido 1** [bah•TEE•doh] *n* M
icing

**batido 2** [bah•TEE•do] *n* M
batter

**batidor** [bah•TEE•dohr] *n* M
scout

**batir** [bah•TEER] *vt* beat
(cooking); churn

**bautismo** [bou•TEES•mo] *n* M
baptism

**bautizar** [bou•TEE•sahr] *vt*
baptize; christen

**baya** [BAI•yah] *n* F berry

**bayoneta** [BAI•yon•EH•tah] *n*
F bayonet

**bazar** [bah•SAHR] *n* F bazaar

**bazo** [BAH•so] *n* M spleen

**bebé** [BEH•bch] *n* M baby

**beber a sorbos** [bai•BAIR a
SOR•bos] *vt* sip

**bebida** [bai•BEE•dah] *n* F
beverage; drink

**bebido borracho**
[bai•BEE•doh bor•RAH•cho]
*adj* M drunk

**becerro** [beh•SAIR•oh] *n* M
calf

**béisbol** [BAIS•bol] *n* M
baseball

**belga** [BEL•gah] *adj* Belgian

**Bélgica** [behl•HEE•kah] *n* F
Belgium

**belicoso** [BEH•lee•KOH•so] *adj*
warlike

**belleza** [beh•YAI•sah] *n* F
beauty

**bello** [BAI•yo] *adj* lovely

**bendecir** [BEN•DAI•seer] *vt*
bless

**bendició** [BEN•dik•SEE•on] *n*
F benediction

**bendición** [BEN•dihk•SEE•ohn]
*n* F blessing

**beneficio**
[BEHN•eh•FIH•SEE•oh ] *n* M
benefit

**beneficios**
[BEHN•eh•fee•SEE•ohs] *npl*
proceeds

**beneficioso**
[BEN•eh•fih•SEE•OH•so] *adj*
beneficial

**benigno** [ben•IG•no] *adj* benign

**berenjena** [BAIR•en•HAI•nah]
*n* F eggplant

**bermejo** [bair•MAI•ho] *n* M
red; russet

**beso** [BEH•so] *n* M kiss

**bestia** [bai•STEE•ah] *n* F beast

**bestial** [bai•STEE•ahl] *adj*
beastly

**Biblia** [BIB•lee•AH] *n* F Bible

**biblioteca**
[BIHB•lee•oh•TAI•kah] *n* F
library

**bibliotecario**
[BIHB•lee•oh•TEH•KAHR•
ee•oh] *n* M librarian

**bicicleta** [BEE•see•KLAI•tah] *n*
F bicycle; bike

**bicho** [BEE•cho] *n* M vermin

**bien** [BEE•en] *adj* well; ~ que\
although; ¡está ~!\ fine!; más
~\ rather; muy ~\ very good;
no ~\ as soon as; qué ~\
marvelous, great; si ~\
although

**bienaventuranza gloria**
[BEE•en•ah•VEN•toor•AN•
sah GLO•ree•ah] *n* F bliss

**bienestar** [BEE•en•EH•stahr] *n*
M welfare; well-being

**bienhechor** [BEE•en•AI•chor]
*n* M benefactor

**bien venido** [BEE•en
veh•NEE•do] *n* welcome

**biftec** [BEEF•tehk] *n* steak

**bigamia** [BI•ha•MEE•ah] *n* F
bigamy

**bigote** [bih•HO•tai] *n* M
mustache

**bilingüe** [bee•LEEN•gwe] *adj*
bilingual

**bilis** [BEE•lis] *n* M bile

**billar** [bee•YAHR] *n* M billiards

**billete** [bee•YEH•tai] *n* M bill;
M ticket

**billón** [bee•YON] *n* M billion

**binocular** [BEE•nok•OO•lar]
*adj* binoculars

**biografía**
[BEE•oh•grah•FEE•ah] *n* F
biography

**biología** [BEE•oh•lo•HEE•ah] *n*
F biology

**Birmania** [BEER•mahn•EE•ah]
*n* Burma

**birmano** [beer•MAHN•oh] *adj*
Burmese

**bisabuela** [BEES•ah•BWAI•la]
*n* F great-grandmother

**bisabuelo** [BEES•ah•BWAI•lo]
*n* M great-grandfather

**bisabuelos**
[BEES•ah•BWAI•los] *npl*
great-grandparents

**bisnieta** [bees•NEE•EH•tah] *n* F
great-granddaughter

**bisnieto** [BEES•nee•EH•to] *n*
M great-grandson

**bizcar** [BEES•kahr] *vi* squint

**bizcochito**
[BIS•koh•CHEE•toh] *n* M
cookie

**bizcocho** [bees•KOH•cho] *n* M
scone; sponge cake

**bizna** [BEES•nah] *n* F zest

**blanco 1** [BLAHN•koh] *n* M
target

**blanco 2** [BLAN•koh] *adj*
white; blano y negro\ black
and white; dejar en blanco\
leave white/blank

**blanco espacio** [BLAHN•ko
EH•spah•SEE•oh] *n* M blank;
blank space

**blancura** [blahn•KOOR•ah] *n* F
whiteness

**blando** [BLAHN•do] *adj* mild;
mellow

**blandura** [blahn•DOOR•ah] *n* F
softness

**blanquear** [blan•KAI•ahr] *vi*
whiten

**blanqueo** [blan•KAI•oh] *n* M
bleach

**blasfemar de**
[BLAHS•feh•MAHR dai] *vt*
blaspheme

**bloque** [BLO•kai] *n* M block

**bloqueo** *n* M blockade

**blusa** [BLOO•sah] *n* F blouse

**boca** [BOH•kah] *n* F mouth

**boca de agua** [BOH•kah dai
AH•gwah] *n* F hydrant

**bocado** [boh•KAH•do] *n* M
morsel; mouthful

**boceto** [boh•SEH•to] *n* M
sketch

**boda 1** [BOH•dah] *n* F floor

**boda 2** [BOH•dah] *n* F wedding

**bodega** [boh•DAI•gah] *n* F
grocery

**bódega** [boh•DAI•gah] *n* F
wine cellar

**boicot** [BOI•koht] *n* M boycott

**boina** [BOI•nah] m F beret

**boina escocesa** [BOI•nah
EHS•koh•SEH•sah] *n* F tam-
o'-shanter

**bola** [BOH•lah] *n* F ball

**bola de nieve** [BOH•lah dai] *n*
F snow ball

**boletin** [BOH•leh•TEEN] *n* M
bulletin

**bolita** [bo•LEE•tah] *n* F bullet

**bolsa** [BOHL•sah] *n* F handbag;
pocketbook; purse

**Bolsa de valores** [BOHL•sah
dai vah•LOR•ais] *n* F Stock
Exchange

**bolsillo** [bohl•SEE•yo] *n* M
pocket

**bolsista** [bohl•SEE•stah] *n* F
stockbroker

**bollo** [BOI•yo] *n* M bun

**bomba 1** [BOHM•bah] *n* F
bomb

**bomba 2** [BOIIM•bah] *n* F
pump

**bombardear** [BOHM•bahr•DAI•ahr] *vt* bombard

**bombardeo** [BOM•bahr•DA[•oh] *n* M bombing; bomber

**bombero** [bom•BAIR•øh] *n* M fireman

**bonito** [boh•NEE•to] *adj* pretty

**boquear** [boh•KAI•ahr] *vi* gasp

**boquete** [boh•KEH•tai] *n* M gap

**borbolleo** [BOR•boy•AI•oh] *n* M gurgle

**borbotón** [bor•BOH•ton] *n* M spurt

**bordado** [bor•DAH•doh] *n* M embroidery

**borde 1** [BOR•dai] *n* M border; outskirts; rim

**borde 2** [BOR•dai] *n* M verge

**bordear** [bohr•DAI•ahr] *vi* coast

**borla** [BOR•lah] *n* F tassel

**borrachera** [BOR•rah•CHAIR•ah] *n* F drunkenness

**borracho** [bohr•RAH•cho] *adj* intoxicated

**borrajear** [BOR•rah•HAI•ahr] *vi vt* doodle

**borrar** [BOHR•rahr] *vt* delete; erase; obliterate

**Bosnia** [bohs•NEE•ah] *n* Bosnia

**bosnio** [bohs•NEE•oh] *adj* Bosnian

**bosque** [BOH•skai] *n* M forest; woodland

**bosquecillo** [BOH•skai•SEE•yo] *n* M grove

**bostezado** [BOH•steh•SAH•do] *adj* gaping

**bostezar** [boh•STEH•sahr] *vi* gape; yawn

**bota** [BOH•tah] *n* F boot

**botánica** [BOH•tahn•EE•kah] *n* F botany

**bote 1** [BAHR•kah] *n* M boat

**bote 2** [BOH•tai] *n* M can

**bote salvavidas** [BOH•tai SAHL•vah•VEE•dahs] *n* M lifeboat

**botella** [boh•TAI•yah] *n* F bottle

**botín** [boh•TEEN] *n* M booty

**botón** [boh•TOHN] *n* M bud; button

**bóveda** [BOH•veh•dah] *n* F vault

**bovino** [boh•VEEN•oh] *adj* bovine

**boxeador** [BOKS•air•AH•dor] *n* M boxer

**boxeo** [boks•SAI•o] *n* M boxing

**boya** [BOI•ya] *n* F buoy

**bragas** [BRAH•has] *npl* panties

**brama** [BRAH•mah] *n* F rut

**bramido** [brah•MEE•do] *n* M bellow

**bravo** [BRAH•vo] *adj* fearless

**bravura** [brah•VOOR•ah] *n* F bravery

**braza** [BRAH•sah] *n* F fathom

**brazalete** [BRAH•sah•LEH•tai] *n* M bracelet

**brazo** [BRAH•so] *n* M arm

**brea** [BRAI•ah] *n* F tar

**brecha** [BRAI•cha] *n* F breach (in wall); flaw

**breve** [BRAI•vai] *adj* brief

**brevedad** [breh•VAI•dahd] *n* F
brevity

**brevemente**
[BREH•veh•MEN•tai] *adv*
briefly; shortly

**brezo** [BREH•so] *n*.M heather

**bribón 1** [bree•BOHN] *n* M
rascal; scoundrel

**bribón 2** [bree•BON] *n* M
villain

**bribonzuelo**
[BREE•bon•SWAI•lo] *n* M
urchin

**brillante** [bree•YAN•tai] *adj*
bright; brilliant; glaring

**brillar** [BREE•yahr] *vi* glisten

**brillo** [BREE•yo] *n* M
brilliance; radiance; splendor

**brincar** [BRIHN•kar] *vi* M skip

**brisa** [BREE•sa] *n* F breeze

**británico** [BRIH•tahn•EE•koh]
*adj* British

**brocado** [broh•KAH•do] *n* M
brocade

**bróculi** [broh•KOO•lee] *n* M
broccoli

**brocha** [BROH•cha] *n* F
paintbrush

**broche** [BROH•chai] *n* M
brooch; *vt* clasp

**brocheta** [broh•CHE•tah] *n* F
skewer

**broma** [BROH•mah] *n* F hoax;
jest; practical joke

**bromista** [brohm•EE•stah] *n* M
joker

**bronce** [BROHN•sai] *n* M
bronze

**broquelillo**
[BROH•kai•el•EE•yo] *n* M
earring

**bruja** [BROO•hah] *n* F witch

**brujo** [BROO•ho] *n* M wizard

**brumoso** [broo•MO•so] *adj*
misty

**Bruselas** [broo•SAI•lahs] *n*
Brussels

**brusquedad**
[BRUH•skai•DAHD] *n* F
suddenness

**brutal** [BROO•tahl] *adj* brutal

**bruto** [BROO•toh] *n* M brute

**bu** [boo] *vt vi* boo

**budismo** [buh•DEES•mo] *n* M
Buddhism

**buen negocio** [BOO•en
neh•GOH•see•OH] *n* M
bargain

**bueno** [BWAIN•oh] *adj* good;
*int* well; buenas dias/ tardes/
noches\ good day/afternoon/
night; por la buenas\ be in a
good mood

**buena voluntad** [BWAIN•ah
vol•UHN•tahd] *n* F
willingness

**buey** [BOO•ai] *n* M ox; steer

**búfalo** [BUH•fah•loh] *n* M
buffalo

**bufanda** [boo•FAHN•dah] *n* F
scarf

**bufón** [boo•FOHN] *n* M clown

**búho** [BOO•ho] *n* M owl

**bujia** [boo•HEE•ah] *n* F spark
plug

**bulbo** [BUHL•boh] *n* M bulb

**Bulgaria** [BUHL•gahr•EE•ah] *n*
Bulgaria

**bulto** [BUHL•toh] *n* M bulge;
knob

**bullicioso**
[BUH•yee•see•OH•so] *adj*
hilarious

bullir 1 [BOO•yeer] vt stir

bullir 2 [BOO•yeer] vi n M bustle

bumerang [boom•AIR•ahng] n M boomerang

buque cisterna [BOO•kai sih•STAIR•nah] n M tanker

buque de vapor [BOO•kai dai VAH•por] n M steamboat; steamship

buque de vela [BOO•kai dai VAI•lah] n M sailboat

burbuja [boor•BOO•ha] n F bubble

burbujear [BOOR•boo•HAI•ahr] n F bubble

burdel [BOOR•del] n M brothel

burla [BOOR•lah] n F mockery

burlar [BOOR•lahr] vt balk

burlarse [buhr•LAHR•sai] vt deride; vi jeer

burocracia [BOOR•oh•krah•SEE•ah] n F bureaucracy

burro [BOOR•oh] n M donkey; mule

busca [BOO•skah] n F quest

buscar [BOO•skahr] vt search; seek

busto [BUH•sto] n M bust (of statue)

buzo [BOO•so] n M plunger

# C

cabalgar [kahl•BAH•gahr] vi ride

caballería 1 [KAH•bah•yair•EE•yah] n F cavalry

caballería 2 [KAH•bah•yair•EE•ah] n F chivalry

caballero [KAH•bah•YAIR•oh] n M gentleman; knight

caballo [kah•BAI•yo] n M horse; a ~ adv\ horseback

caballo padre [kah•BAI•yo pah•DRAI] n M stallion

cabaña 1 [kah•BAHN•ya] n F cabin; tent

cabaña 2 [kah•BAN•yah] n F cot

cabaret [KAH•bah•RAI] n F nightclub

caballero [KAH•bai•YAIR•oh] n M rider

cabelludo [KAH•beh•YOO•do] adj hairy

cabestro [kah•BEH•stroh] n M halter

cabeza [kah•BAI•sah] n F head; andar de ~ have a lot to do; dar una ~da nod off

cable [KAH•blai] n M cable

cabo 1 [KAH•bo] n M end; butt (of cigarette)

cabo 2 [KAH•boh] n M cape (geog)

cabra [KAH•brah] m F goat

cabriola [KAH•bree•OH•lah] n F caper

cabriolar [KAH•bree•OH•lahr] vi prance

**cabrito** [kah•BREE•toh] *n* M
kid

**cacahuete**
[KAH•kah•HWEH•tai] *n* M
peanut

**cacao** [KAH•kau] *n* M cocoa;
confusion (figurative)

**cacareo** [KAH•kah•RAI•oh] *n*
M cackle

**cacho** [KAH•cho] *n* M bit;
piece

**cacto** [KAHK•toh] *n* M cactus

**cada** [KAH•dah] *adj* each; ~
uno\ each one; everyone

**cada todo** [KAH•dah] [toh•doh]
*adj* every

**cada uno** [KAH•dah OON•oh]
*pron* everybody

**cadáver** [kah•DAH•vair] *n* M
carcass; cadaver; corpse

**cadena** [kah•DAI•nah] *n* F
chain

**cadera** [kah•DAIR•ah] *n* F hip

**café 1** [KAH•fai] *n* M coffee

**café 2** [KAH•fai] *n* M coffee
shop

**cafetera** [KAH•feh•tair•ah] *n* F
coffee pot

**cafetería**
[KAH•feh•TAIR•ee•ah] *n* F
cafeteria

**caída** [kai•EE•dah] *n* F fall

**caído** [kai•EE•do] fell

**caja** [KAH•ha] *n* F box; cash
register; container; ~ a fuerte\
safe; ~ de ahorros\ savings
bank

**caja arca** [KAH•ha] [AHR•kah]
*n* F bin (for garbage)

**caja de cartón** [KAH•ha dai
kahr•TOHN] *n* F carton

**cajón 1** [kah•HON] *n* F drawer;

**cajón 2** [kah•HON] *n* M till

**calabaza** [KAH•lah•BAH•sah] *n*
F gourd; pumpkin

**calabozo** [KAH•lah•BOH•soh]
*n* M dungeon

**calambre** [kah•LAHM•brai] *n*
M cramp

**calamocano**
[KAH•lah•moh•KAHN•oh]
*adj* tipsy

**calceta 1** [kah•SEH•tah] *n* F
knitting

**calceta 2** [kahl•SAI•tah] *n* F
stocking

**calcetería**
[KAH•seh•tair•EE•ah] *n* F
hosiery

**calcetín** [kahl•SEH•TEEN] *n* M
sock

**calcio** [kahl•SEE•oh] *n* M
calcium

**calculador**
[KAHL•koo•LAH•dor] *n* M
calculator

**calcular** [KAHL•koo•LAHR] *vt*
calculate

**caldera** [kahl•DAIR•ah] *n* F
kettle

**caldo** [KAHL•do] *n* M broth

**calefacción**
[KAH•leh•fahk•SEE•ohn] *n* F
heating

**calendario**
[KAHL•en•dahr•EE•oh] *n* M
calendar

**calentador**
[KAH•lehn•TAH•dor] *n* M
heater

**calidad** [kahl•EE•dahd] *n* F
quality

**calidoscopio**
[kah•LEE•dah•skoh•PEE•oh] *n*
M kaleidoscope
**caliente** [kah•LEE•en•TAI] *adj*
hot; warm; angry (figurative)
**calificación**
[kah•LIH•fih•KAH•see•OHN]
*n* F qualification
**calificar** [kahl•EE•fih•kahr] *vi*
qualify
**calina** [kah•LEE•nah] *n* F haze
**calma** [KAL•mah] *n* F
composure
**calmar** [KAHL•mahr] *vt* calm
down
**calor** [KAH•lor] *n* M heat;
warmth; anger (figurative)
**calvo** [KAHL•vo] *adj* bald;
hairless
**calza** [KAHL•sah] *n* F wedge
**calzo** [KAHL•so] *n* M skid
**callado** [kai•YAH•do] *adj* quiet;
secretive
**calle** [KAI•yai] *n* F street; ~
mayor\ main street; abrir ~\
make way
**callejear** [KAH•yeh•HAI•ahr] *vi*
ramble
**cama** [KAH•mah] *n* F bed
**camafeo** [KAH•mah•FAI•yo] *n*
M cameo
**camaleón** [KAH•mah•LAI•on]
*n* F chameleon
**cámara 1** [KAH•mahr•rah] *n* F
camera
**cámara 2** [KAH•mah•rah] *n* F
chamber
**camarera**
[KAH•mah•RAIR•rah] *n* F
cleaning lady; housekeeper;
stewardess

**camarero** [KAH•mah•RAIR•oh]
*n* M steward
**camarón** [KAH•mah•ROHN] *n*
M shrimp
**camarote** [KAH•mah•ROH•tai]
*n* M stateroom
**cambiar** [kahm•BEE•ahr] *vt*
swap; change
**cambio** [kahm•BEE•oh] *n* M
exchange; change
**camello** [kah•MAI•yo] *n* M
camel
**caminar** [kah•MEEN•ahr] *vi*
walk
**camino** [kah•MEEN•oh] *n* M
lane; path; road
**camino real** [kah•MEE•no
rai•AHL] *n* M highway
**camino transveral**
[kah•MEE•no TRANS•
vair•SAHL] *n* M crossroads
**camiseta** [KAH•mee•SEH•tah]
*n* F undershirt
**campamento**
[KAHM•pah•MEN•toh] *n* M
camp; campground
**campaña** [kahm•PAN•ya] *n* F
campaign; *vi* salir a ~
[sah•leer ah ~] campaign
**campana** [kam•PAHN•ah] *n* F
bell
**campaneo**
[KAHM•pahn•AI•oh] *n* M
chime
**campanil** [kam•PAHN•eel] *n* M
belfry; bell tower
**campeón** [kahm•PAI•ohn] *n* M
champion
**campo** [KAHM•poh] *n* M field
**caña** [KAHN•yah] *n* F cane;
reed

**canción** |kahn•SEE•ohn| *n* F
song

**candela** |kahn•DAI•lah| *n* F
candle

**cañón 1** |KAHN•yon| *n* M
canyon

**cañón 2** |KAHN•yon| *n* M
flue

**Canadá** |kah•NAH•DAH| s
Canada

**canal** |KAH•nahl| *n* M
waterway; canal; F
channel

**canalete** |KAH•nahl•EH•tai| *n*
M paddle

**canario** |KAHN•ahr•EE•oh| *n*
M canary

**canasta** |kah•NAH•stah| *n* F
crate

**cancelar** |kahn•SEH•lahr| *vt*
cancel; call off

**cáncer** |KAHN•sair| *n* M
cancer

**canciller** |kahn•SEE•yair| *n* M
chancellor

**candado** |kahn•DAH•do| *n* M
padlock

**candidato**
|KAHN•dee•DAH•toh| *n* M
candidate

**cándido** |kahn•DEE•do| *adj*
candid

**canela** |kah•NAI•lah| *n* F
cinnamon

**cangrejo** |kahn•GRAI•ho| *n* M
crab

**canguro** |kahn•GOO•roh| *n* M
kangaroo

**canibal** |kah•NEE•bahl| *n* M
cannibal

**canilla** |kah•NEE•yah| *n*
F tap

**canino** |kah•NEE•noh| *adj*
canine

**canoa** |kah•NO•ah| *n* F canoe

**canoa automóvil** |kah•NO•ah
OU•toh•moh•VEEL| *n* F
motorboat

**cañon** |KAHN•yon| *n* M gun;
cannon

**canónigo** |kah•NOHN•ee•GO|
*n* M canon

**cansado** |kahn•SAH•do| *adj*
tired; tiresome; weary

**cansancio**
|KAHN•sahn•SEE•oh| *n* M
tiredness; weariness

**cansar** |KAN•sahr| *vt vi* tire;
bore

**cantar** |KAHN•tahr| *vt vi*
sing

**cante** |KAHN•tai| *n* M folk
song

**cantera** |kahn•TAIR•ah| *n* F
quarry

**cantidad** |kahn•TEE•dahd| *n* F
quantity; amount

**canto** |KAHN•toh| *n* M chant;
song

**cantonero**
|KAHN•to•NAIR•oh| *n* M
loafer

**caoba** |kah•OH•bah| *n* F
mahogany

**caos** |KAH•ohs| *n* M chaos

**capa** |KAH•pah| *n* F cloak;
layer

**capacidad**
|KAH•pah•see•DAHD| *n* F
capacity

**capacitar** |KAH•pah•SEE•tahr|
*vt* enable

**capellán** |KAH•peh•YAHN| *n*
M chaplain

**capilla** |kah•PEE•yah| *n* F
chapel

**capital** |kah•PEE•TAHL| *n* F
capital

**capitalismo**
|KAH•pee•tahl•EES•moh| *n*
M capitalism

**capitán** |kah•PEE•tahn| *n* M
captain

**capitel** |kah•PEE•tel| *n* M
steeple

**capítulo** |KAH•pee•TOO•loh| *n*
M chapter

**caponera** |KAH•pon•AIR•ah| *n*
F coop

**capota** |kah•POH•tah| *n* F
bonnet; sliding roof
(automotive)

**capotillo** |KAHP•oh•TEE•yoh|
*n* M cape (clothing)

**caprichoso**
|KAH•pree•CHO•so| *adj*
whimsical

**cápsula** |kahp•SOO•lah| *n* F
capsule; pod

**captura 1** |kahp•TOOR•ah| *n* F
caption

**captura 2** |kahp•TOOR•ah| *n* F
capture

**capturar** |kahp•TOOR•ahr| *vt*
capture

**capucha** |kah•POO•cha| *n* F
hood

**capuchina**
|KAH•poo•CHEE•nah| *n* F
nasturtium

**capullo** |kah•POO•yo| *n* M
cocoon

**caqui** |KAH•kee| *n* M khaki

**cara** |KAH•rah| *n* F face; ~ a\
facing; towards; ~ a ~\ face to
face; dar la ~\ face up to;
tener ~ de\ look; seem to be;
de ~ a frente\ facing

**carácter** |kah•RAHK•tair| *n* M
character

**característica**
|kah•RAHK•tair•IH•STI•kah|
*n* F feature

**característico -a**
|KAHR•ahk•TAIR•IST•ee•koh|
|-kah| *adj n* F characteristic

**carbón** |kahr•BOHN| *n* M coal

**carbón de leña** |kahr•BOHN
dai lain•YAH| *n* M charcoal

**carbono** |kahr•BOH•no| *n* M
carbon

**cárcava** |kahr•KAH•vah| *n* F
gully

**cárcel** |KAHR•sel| *n* M jail;
prison

**cardenal** |kahr•DAI•nahl| *n* M
cardinal

**cardíaco** |kahr•DEE•ahk•OH|
*adj* cardiac

**cardo** |KAHR•do| *n* M thistle

**carestía** |KAH•reh•STEE•ah| *n*
F famine

**carga 1** |KAHR•gah| *n* M
burden; cargo; freight; load;
levar la ~ de algo\ be
responsible for something

**carga 2** |KAHR•gah| *n* F charge

**cargar** |KAHR•gahr| *vt vi*
charge

**cargo** |KAHR•goh| *n* M care

**caribe** [kah•REE•bai] *n* M
Caribbean (Sea)

**caricatura**
[KAHR•ree•kah•TOOR•ah] *n*
F cartoon

**caricia** [KAHR•ee•SEE•ah] *n* F
caress

**caridad** [kahr•ee•DAHD] *n* F
charity

**cariñoso** [KAHR•reen•YO•soh]
*adj* endearing

**carmesí** [kahr•MEH•see] *adj* M
crimson

**carnada** [kahr•NAH•dah] *n* F
bait

**carnal** [KAHR•nahl] *adj* carnal

**carnaval** [kahr•NAH•vahl] *n* M
carnival

**carne** [KAHR•nai] *n* F flesh; M
meat

**carne de vaca** [KAR•nai dai
VAH•kah] *n* F beef

**carne dura** [KAHR•nai
DOO•rah] *n* F brawn

**carnero** [kahr•NAIR•oh] *n* M
mutton

**carnicería**
[KAHR•nih•sair•EE•yah] *n* F
butcher (shop)

**carnicero**
[KAHRN•ih•SAIR•oh] *n* M
butcher

**carnívoro**
[KAHR•nee•VOHR•oh] *adj*
carnivorous

**carnoso** [kahr•NO•so] *adj*
fleshy

**caro** [KAH•roh] *adj* expensive;
dear

**carpa** [KAHR•pah] *n* F carp

**carpa dorada** [KAHR•pah
dor•AH•da] *n* F goldfish

**carpintero**
[KAHR•peen•TAIR•oh] *n* M
carpenter

**carramato**
[KAHR•rah•MAH•to] *n* M
van

**carrera 1** [kahr•RAIR•ah] *n* F
career

**carrera 2** [kahr•RAIR•ah] *n* F
running

**carreta** [kahr•REH•tah] *n* F
wagon

**carrete** [kahr•REH•tai] *n* M
spool

**carretilla** [KAHR•reh•TEE•yah]
*n* F truck

**carretilla de mano**
[KAHR•reh•tee•yah] *n* F
wheelbarrow

**carril** [KAHR•reel] *n* M track

**carro** [CAHR•roh] *n* M car

**carromato**
[KAHR•roh•MAH•toh] *n* M
cart

**carruaje** [KAHR•roo•AH•hai] *n*
M carriage

**carta** [KAHR•tah] *n* F card;
letter; chart; ~ de crédito\
credit card

**cartel** [KAHR•tel] *n* M placard

**cartel** KAHR•tel *n* M poster

**cartela** [kahr•TAI•lah] *n* F
bracket (in writing)

**cartera** [kahr•TAIR•ah] *n* F
briefcase

**cartero** [kahr•TAIR•oh] *n* M
mailman; postman

**cartílago** [kahr•TEE•LAH•go] *n*
M gristle

**cartón** [kahr•TOHN] *n* M
cardboard

**casa** [KAH•sah] *n* F house; ir a
~\ go home; salir de ~\ go
out; en la ~ de al lado de\
next-door; de fuera de ~\
outdoors

**casa de empeños** [KAH•sah
dai em•PAIN•yos] *n* F
pawnshop

**casa del Ayuntamiento**
[KAH•sah del
ai•YOON•ah•MEE•EN•toh] *n*
F city hall

**casado** [kah•SAH•do] *adj*
married; wedded

**casar** [KAH•sahr] *vt* marry

**casarse** [kah•SAHR•sai] *vt* wed

**cascada** [kah•SKAH•dah] *n* F
chute; waterfall

**cascanueces**
[KAH•skah•noo•EH•sais] *npl*
nutcrackers

**cáscara** [kah•SKAHR•ah] *n* F
husk

**casco 1** [KAH•skoh] *n* M cask

**casco 2** [KAHS•koh] *n* M hoof

**casco 3** [KAH•sko] *n* M helmet

**caseta 1** [kah•SEH•tah] *n* F
cassette

**caseta 2** [kah•SAI•tah] *n* F hut

**casí** [KAH•see] *adv* almost; ~ ~\
very nearly; ~ nada\ hardly
any; ~ nunca\ hardly ever

**casilla** [kah•SEE•yah] *n* F booth

**casita** [kah•SEE•tah] *n* F
cottage; lodge

**caso** [KAH•soh] *n* M case;
instance; event; en ~ de\ in
the event of; el ~ es que\ the
fact is that; hacer ~ de\ take
notice of

**caspa** [KAH•spah] *n* F dandruff

**castaña** [kah•STAHN•yah] *n* F
chestnut

**castaño** [kah•STAHN•yo] *adj*
maroon

**castidad** [KAH•stee•DAHD] *n*
F chastity

**castigar** [KAH•stee•GAHR] *vt*
chastise; punish

**castigo** [kah•STEE•go] *n* M
punishment

**castillo** [kah•STEE•yo] *n* M
castle

**casto** [KAH•stoh] *adj* chaste

**castor** [KAH•stor] *n* M beaver

**casual** [kah•SOO•ahl] *adj* casual

**casualidad**
[KAH•swahl•IH•dahd] *n* F
haphazard

**casucha** [kah•SOO•cha] *n* F
shack

**catálogo** [KAH•tah•LOH•goh]
*n* M catalogue

**catapulta** [KAH•tah•PUHL•tah]
*n* F catapult; *vt* lanzar con ~

**catarata** [KAH•tahr•AH•tah] *n*
F cataract

**catastrófico**
[KAH•tah•STROH•FEE•koh]
*n* M catastrophe

**catedral** [kah•TEH•drahl] *n* M
cathedral

**categoria**
[KAH•teh•gohr•EE•ah] *n* F
category; rank

**categórico**
[KAH•teh•GOHR•EE•koh] *adj*
categorical

**católico** [KAH•toh•LIH•koh]
*adj* Catholic

**catorce** [kah•TOR•sai] *num*
fourteen

**caución** [KOU•see•OHN] *n* F
caution

**causa** [KOU•seh] *n* F cause;
sake; a ~ de\ because of; por~
de\ because of

**cáustico** [KOU•stih•koh] *adj*
caustic

**cautelosamente**
[KOU•teh•lo•sah•MEN•tai]
*adv* gingerly

**cautivo** [kow•TEE•vo] *n* M
captive

**cauto 1** [KOU•toh] *adj* cautious

**cauto 2** [KOU•to] *adj* wary

**cavar** [KAH•vahr] *vt* dig

**caverna** [kah•VAIR•nah] *n* F
den; cavern

**cavidad** [KAH•vee•DAHD] *n* F
cavity

**caza 1** [KAH•sah] *n* F hunt

**caza 2** [KAH•sah] *n* F chase

**cazador** [kah•SAH•dor] *n* M
hunter

**cazar** [KAH•sahr] *vt* chase

**cazo** [KAH•so] *n* M pan; skillet

**cebada** [sai•BAH•da] *n* F barley

**cebolla** [seh•BOI•yah] *n* F bulb;
onion

**cebollana** [SEH•boi•YAHN•ah]
*n* F chive

**cebra** [SEH•brah] *n* F zebra

**cedazo** [seh•DAH•so] *n* M
sieve

**ceder** [SEH•dair] *vt* cede; *vt vi*
concede

**cedilla** [seh•DEE•yah] *n* F
cedilla

**cedro** [SEH•droh] *n* M cedar

**céfiro** [seh•FEER•oh] *n* M
zephyr

**ceja** [SAI•ha] *n* F eyebrow

**cejar** [SAI•har] *vi* wince

**celda** [SEHL•dah] *n* F cell

**celebración**
[seh•LEH•brah•see•OHN] *n* F
celebration

**celebrar** [seh•LEH•brahr] *vt*
celebrate

**celebridad**
[SEH•leh•BRIH•dahd] *n* F
celebrity

**celestial** [SEH•leh•STEE•ahl]
*adj* heavenly

**célibe** [SEH•leeb] *adj* M
celibate

**celo** [SAI•lo] *n* M zeal

**celos** [SAI•los] *n* M jealousy

**celosía** [SEH•loh•SEE•ah] *n* F
lattice

**celoso** [SEH•LOH•soh] *adj*
jealous

**céltico** [SEHL•tee•KOH] *adj*
Celtic

**cementerio**
[SEH•men•TAIR•EE•oh] *n* M
cemetery

**cemento** [seh•MEN•toh] *n* M
cement

**cenagal** [SEH•nah•GAHL] *n* M
quagmire

**cendal** [SEN•dal] *n* M gauze

**cenicero** [SEN•ih•SAIR•oh] *n*
M ashtray

**Cenicienta** [lah
SEHN•ee•SEE•EN•tah] *n* F
Cinderella

**ceniza** [sen•EE•sah] *n* F ash

**ceño** [SAIN•yo] *n* M frown; *vt* funicir el ~

**censo** [SEN•so] *n* M census

**censor** [SEHN•sohr] *n* M censor

**censura** [sen•SOOR•ah] *n* F censorship

**centavo** [sen•TAH•vo] *n* M penny

**centella** [sen•TAI•yah] *n* F thunderbolt

**centelleante** [SEN•tai•YAHN•tai] *n* M twinkling; flash

**centelleo** [SEN•teh•YAI•oh] *n* M twinkle; flash

**centenario** [SEN•ten•AHR•EE•oh] *n* M centennial

**centeno** [sen•TEN•oh] *n* M rye

**centésimo** [sen•TEH•SEE•mo] *num* M hundredth

**centígrado** [sen•TEE•GRAH•doh] *adj* centigrade

**centímetro** [sen•TEE•MAI•troh] *n* M centimeter

**centinela** [SEN•tin•AI•lah] *n* F sentinel

**centípedo** [sen•TEE•PEH•doh] *n* M centipede

**central** [SEN•trahl] *adj* central

**centro** [SEN•troh] *n* M center; midst

**centuria** [SEN•toor•EE•ah] *n* F century

**cepillar** [seh•PEE•yahr] *vt* brush

**cepillo** [seh•PEE•yo] *n* M brush; hairbrush; *vt* whisk; sweep

**cera** [SAIR•ah] *n* F wax

**cerámico** [sair•AH•MEE•koh] *n* M ceramic

**cerca 1** [SAIR•kah] *prep* by (near to); *adj* nearby; ~ de *prep\* near; de ~\ from close up, closely

**cerca 2** [SAIR•kah] *prep* beside; besides

**cercanamente** [SAIR•kahn•ah•MEN•tai] *adv* nearly

**cercano** [sair•KAH•no] *adj* near; local

**cercar** [SAIR•kahr] *vt* encompass

**cerda 1** [SAIR•dah] *n* F bristle

**cerda 2** [SAIR•dah] *n* F sow

**cerdo** [SAIR•do] *n* M hog

**cereal** [sair•AI•ahl] *n* M cereal

**cerebro** [sair•AI•bro] *n* M brain

**ceremonia** [SAIR•eh•moh•NEE•ah] *n* F ceremony

**ceresa** [sair•AI•sah] *n* F cherry

**cernerse** [sair•NAIR•sai] *vi* hover

**cernícalo** [sair•NEE•kah•LOH] *n* M hawk

**cero** [SAIR•oh] *n* M zero

**cerrado** [sair•RAH•do] *adj adv* closed; shut; ~ dura\ locked

**cerrador** [sair•RAH•dor] *n* M shutter

**cerrar** [SAIR•ahr] *vt* close; shut

**certeza** [sair•TAI•sah] *n* F certainty

**certificar** [SAIR•tih•FEE•kahr] *vt* certify

**cervato** [sair•VAH•to] *n* M fawn

**cervecería** [SAIR•veh•sair•EE•ah] *n* F brewery

**cervecero** [SAIR•veh•SAIR•oh] *n* M brewer

**cerveza** [sair•VAI•sah] *n* F beer

**cesación** [SEH•sah•see•OHN] *n* F cease

**césped** [SEH•sped] *n* M lawn; sod; turf

**cesta** [SEH•stah] *n* F hamper

**cesto** [SEH•sto] *n* M basket; waste-paper basket

**cetro** [SEH•troh] *n* M scepter

**cianotipia** [SEE•ahn•oh•TEE•PEE•ah] *n* F blueprint

**cicatero** [SIH•kah•TAIR•oh] *n* M tightwad

**cicatriz** [see•KAH•TREES] *n* F scar

**ciclista** [see•KLEE•stah] *n* F rider

**ciclo** [SEEC•loh] *n* M cycle

**ciclòn** [see•KLON] *n* M cyclone

**ciego** [see•AI•go] *adj* blind

**cielo** [see•AI•loh] *n* M sky; heaven

**cien ciento** [SEE•ehn] [-to] *n* M hundred

**ciencia 1** [SEE•en•SEE•ah] *n* F finance

**ciencia 2** [SEE•en•SEE•ah] *n* F science

**científico** [SEE•en•TEE•FEE•koh] *adj* scientific

**ciero** [see•AIR•o] *adv* some

**ciervo** [see•AIR•voh] *n* M deer; stag

**cifrar** [SIH•frahr] *vt* code; encode

**cigarrillo** [SIH•gahr•REE•yoh] *n* M cigarette

**cigarro** [sih•GAHR•roh] *n* M cigar

**cigüeña** [sih•GWAIN•yah] *n* F stork

**cima** [SEE•mah] *n* F hilltop

**cinc** [sink] *n* M zinc

**cincel** [SIHN•sel] *n* M chisel

**cincelar** [SIN•sai•LAHR] *vt* chisel

**cincha** [SEEN•cha] *n* F girth

**cinco** [SEEN•ko] *num* five

**cincuenta** [seen•KWEN•tah] *num* fifty

**cine** [SEE•nai] *n* M cinema

**cinfianza** [KON•fee•AHN•sah] *n* F confidence

**cínico** [sin•EE•koh] *n* M cynic

**cinico** *adj* cynical

**cinta 1** [SEEN•tah] *n* F ribbon

**cinta 2** [SIN•tah] *n* F tag; band

**cinto** [SEEN•toh] *n* M girdle

**cinturón** [sin•TOOR•ON] *n* M belt

**cinturón salvidas** [sin•TOOR•OHN sahl• VEE•dahs] *n* M life jacket

**ciprés** [see•PREHS] *n* M cypress

**circo** [SEER•koh] *n* M circus

**circuito** [seer•KWEE•toh] *n* M circuit

**circulación** [SEER•koo•lah•SEE•ohn] *n* F circulation

**circular** [SEER•koo•LAHR] *adj* circular; *vi* circulate

**círculo** [SEER•koo•LOH] *n* M
circle

**circuncisión**
[SEER•kuhn•see•SEE•OHN] *n*
F circumcision

**circunferencia**
[SEER•kuhn•FAIR•ehn•
SEE•ah] *n* F circumference

**circunflejo**
[SEER•kuhn•FLAI•ho] *adj*
circumflex

**circunstancias**
[SEER•kuhn•STAHN•see•
AHS] *npl* circumstances

**ciruela** [see•WAI•lah] *n* F plum

**ciruela pasa** [see•WAI•lah
PAH•sah] *n* F prune

**cisma** [SIHS•mah] *n* F schism

**cisne** [SEES•nai] *n* M swan

**cita 1** [SEE•tah] *n* F excerpt

**cita 2** [SEE•tah] *n* F
appointment; convenida tener
una ~\ to have an appointment
w/someone

**citación 1** [SIH•tah•SEE•ohn] *n*
F quotation

**citación 2** [SIH•tah•SEE•ohn] *n*
F subpoena

**citar** [SEE•tahr] *vt* cite; quote

**cítara** [see•TAHR•ah] *n* F zither

**ciudad** [SEE•oo•DAHD] *n* F
city; town

**ciudadano**
[SEE•oo•dah•DAHN•oh] *n* M
citizen

**cívico** [SEE•vee•koh] *adj* civic

**civil** [sih•VEEL] *adj* civil

**civilización**
[SIH•vil•ih•ZAH•see•OHN] *n*
F civilization

**civilizar** [SIH•vee•LIH•zahr] *vt*
civilize

**clamor** [KLAH•mohr] *n* M
clamor; racket; noise

**clan** [klahn] *n* M clan

**clandestino**
[KLAHN•deh•STEEN•oh] *adj*
clandestine

**claramente**
[KLAHR•ah•MEN•tai] *adv*
clearly; plainly

**claridad 1** [klahr•EE•dahd] *n* F
clarity

**claridad 2** [klahr•IH•dahd] *n* F
lightness

**clarificar**
[KLAHR•ee•FEE•kahr] *vt*
clarify

**clarinete** [KLAHR•ih•NEH•tai]
*n* M clarinet

**claro 1** [KLAHR•oh] *adj*
outspoken

**claro 2** [KLAHR•oh] *adj* clear

**clase 1** [KLAH•sai] *n* M
classroom

**clase 2** [KLAH•sai] *n* F class;
sort; type; de al ~ media\
middle class

**clásico** [klah•SEE•koh] *adj n* M
classic; classical

**clasificado**
[KLAH•see•fih•KAH•doh] *adj*
classified

**clasificar** [KLAH•see•FIH•kahr]
*vt* classify; especie ~\ sort

**claustro** [KLOU•stroh] *n* M
cloister

**cláusula** [klou•SOO•lah] *n* F
clause

**clava** [KLAH•vah] *n* F club

**clavar 1** [KLAH•vahr] *vt* clench

**clavar 2** [KLAH•vahr] *vt* break in; knock in

**clavel** [KLAH•vehl] *n* M carnation

**clavero** [klah•VAIR•oh] *n* M clove

**clavicordio** [KLAH•vee•kor•DEE•øh] *n* M harpsichord

**clavija** [klah•VEE•hah] *n* F peg

**clavillo** [klah•VEE•yo] *n* M pin

**clavo** [KLAH•vo] *n* M nail

**clerical** [klair•IH•kahl] *adj* clerical

**clero** [KLAIR•oh] *n* M clergy

**cliente** [klee•EHN•tai] *n* M client; customer

**clientela** [KLEE•ehn•TAI•lah] *n* F clientele

**clima** [KLEE•mah] *n* F climate

**clínica** [KLIH•NEE•kah] *n* F clinic

**clínico** [KLIH•NEE•koh] *adj* clinical

**cloaca** [klo•AH•kah] *n* F sewer

**cloquear 1** [klo•KAI•ahr] *vi* cluck; chuckle

**cloquear 2** [kloh•KAI•ahr] *vt* chuck; toss

**clorifila** [KLOHR•oh•FEE•lah] *n* F chlorophyll

**coadjutor** [KOH•ahd•HOO•tor] *n* M curate

**coartada** [KO•ahr•TAH•dah] *n* F alibi

**cobarde** [KOH•BAHR•dai] *n* M coward; quitter; *adj* cowardly

**cobardia** [KOH•bahr•DEE•ah] *n* F cowardice

**cobertizo** [KOH•bair•TEE•so] *n* M hovel

**cobertura** [KOH•bair•TOOR•ah] *n* F coverage

**cobre** [KOH•brai] *n* M copper

**cocaína** [KOH•kai•EEN•ah] *n* F cocaine

**cocer** [KOH•sair] *vt* bake

**coche** [KOH•chai] *n* M coach

**coche fúnebre** [KOH•chai fuh•NAI•brai] *n* M hearse

**coche usado** [KOH•chai oo•SAH•do] *n* M used car

**cociente** [KOH•see•EN•tai] *n* M quotient

**cocina** [koh•SEE•nah] *n* M cooking; F kitchen

**cocinero** [KOH•seen•AIR•oh] *n* M chef; cook

**coco** [KOH•koh] *n* M coconut

**cocodrilo** [KO•koh•DREE•lo] *n* M crocodile

**còctel** [KOHK•tehl] *n* M cocktail

**codazo** [koh•DAH•so] *n* M nudge

**codiciar** [KO•dee•SEE•ahr] *vt* covet; envy

**código** [koh•DEE•go] *n vt* M code; ~ de la circulación\ traffic code

**codo** [KOH•doh] *n* M elbow

**codorniz** [kor•DON•nees] *n* M quail

**coercer** [KOH•air•SAIR] *vt* coerce

**coetáneo** [KOH•tah•NAI•o] *adj* contemporary

**cofre** [KOH•frai] *n* M hutch; chest

**coger** [KOH•hair] *vt* catch; seize

**coherente** [KOH•air•EHN•tai] *adj* coherent

**cohete** [koh•HE•tai] *n* M rocket

**cohombro** [KOH•OHM•broh] *n* M cucumber

**coincidencia** [KOH•in•SI•dehn•SEE•ah] *n* F coincidence

**coincidir** [KOH•in•SIH•deer] *vi* coincide

**cojear** [koh•HAI•ahr] *vi* hobble

**cojera** [koh•HAIR•ah] *adj* limp

**cojín** [koh•HEEN] *n* M cushion

**cojo** [KOH•ho] *n* M cripple; *adj* lame

**cola 1** [KOH•lah] *n* F glue

**cola 2** [KOH•lah] *n* F tail

**colaborar** [KOH•lah•BOR•ahr] *vi* collaborate

**coladero** [KOH•lah•DAIR•oh] *n* M strainer

**colcha** [KOHL•cha] *n* F quilt

**colchón** [KOHL•chon] *n* M mattress

**colección** [KOH•lehk•SEE•ohn] *n* F set

**colega** [koh•LAI•hah] *n* F colleague

**colegio** [KOH•lai•HEE•oh] *n* M college

**cólera** [koh•LAIR•ah] *n* F cholera

**colgar** [KOHL•gahr] *vi* dangle; hang; *vt* drape

**colibrí** [koh•LIH•bree] *n* M humming-bird

**coliflor** [koh•LEE•flor] *n* M cauliflower

**colina** [koh•LEE•nah] *n* F hill

**colmena** [kohl•MAIN•ah] *n* F beehive; hive

**colmillo** [kohl•MEE•yo] *n* M fang; tusk

**colmo** [KOHL•mo] *n* M heyday

**colocar 1** [koh•LOH•kahr] *vt* pose

**colocar 2** [koh•LOH•kahr] *vt* settle

**colodra** [koh•LOH•drah] *n* F pail

**colon** [KOH•lohn] *n* M colon

**colonia** [KOH•lon•EE•ah] *n* F colony

**color** [KOH•lohr] *n* M color; hue; de ~ escarlata\ scarlet

**color de canela** [KO•lor dai ka•NAI•lah] *n* M beige

**colosal** [koh•LOH•sahl] *adj* colossal

**columna** [koh•LOOM•nah] *n* F column

**columpio** [KOH•loom•PEE•oh] *n* M seesaw

**coma 1** [KOH•mah] *n* F comma

**coma 2** [KOH•mah] *n* F coma

**comadreja** [kohm•AH•DRAI•ha] *n* F weasel

**comandante** [KOH•mahn•DAHN•tai] *n* M commander

**combar** [KOM•bahr] *vi* sag

**combate** [kohm•BAH•tai] *n* M combat; battle

**combinación** [KOHM•bih•nah•SEE•ohn] *n* F combination

**combinar** [kohm•BEE•nahr] *vt* combine

**combustible** [KOHM•boo•STEEB•lai] *n* M fuel

**comedero 1**
[KOH•meh•DAIR•oh] *n* M
crib

**comedero 2**
[KOHM•eh•DAIR•oh] *n* M
trough

**comedia** [koh•MAI•DEE•ah] *n*
F comedy

**comedor** [koh•MAI•dor] *n* M
dining room

**comensal** [koh•MEHN•sahl] *n*
M diner

**comentar** [koh•MEN•tahr] *vi*
comment

**comento** [koh•MEN•to] *n* M
comment

**comenzar** [koh•MEN•sahr] *vt*
commence; *vt vi* begin

**comer** [KOH•mair] *vi* dine; *vt vi*
eat; dar de ~ a\ feed

**comerciante 1**
[KOH•mair•SEE•AHN•tai] *n*
M dealer

**comerciante 2**
[KOM•mair•SEE•AHN•tai] *n*
M trader

**comercio** [koh•MAIR•see•oh] *n*
M commerce; trading; trade

**comestible**
[koh•MEH•steeb•lai] *adj*
edible

**comestibles**
[koh•MEH•stee•blais] *npl*
groceries

**cometa 1** [koh•MAI•tah] *n* F
comet

**cometa 2** [koh•MAI•tah] *n* F
kite

**cometer** [koh•MEH•tair] *vt*
commit; make a commitment

**cómicas** [koh•MEE•kahs] *npl* F
comics (comic strip)

**cómico** [koh•MEE•koh] *n* M
comedian; *adj* funny;
humorous; ludicrous

**comida** [koh•MEE•dah] *n* F
dinner; food; meal; M buffet

**comienzo** [KOH•mee•EN•so] *n*
M outset; beginning

**comisaría de policía**
[KOH•mih•sahr•EE•ah dai] *n*
F police station

**comisión** [KOH•mih•see•OHN]
*n* F commission; committee

**comisionado**
[KOH•mih•see•OHN•AH•doh]
*n* M commissioner

**comitiva** [KOH•mih•TEE•vah]
*n* F retinue

**como** [KOH•moh] as; like; ~
quieras\ as you like; ~ sabes\
as you know; ~ si\ as if

**cómo** [KOH•moh] *adv* how; ¿~
está Vd?\ how are you; ¡ ~
no!\ of course\ ¿~ te llamas?\
what's your name; ¡y ~!\ and
how!

**cómoda** [KOH•MOH•dah] *n* F
dresser; chest of drawers

**comodidad**
[KOH•mo•DEE•dahd] *n* F
comfort

**cómodo** [KOH•MOH•doh] *adj*
cozy; snug; comfortable

**como quiera** [KOH•moh
kee•AIR•ah] *conj* however

**compañero**
[KOHM•pan•YAIR•oh] *n* M
companion; fellow; mate; pal

**compañia**
[KOHM•pahn•YEE•ah] *n* F
company; en ~ de\ with

**comparación**
[KOHM•pahr•AH•see•OHN] *n*
F comparison

**comparar** [kohm•PAHR•ahr] *vt*
compare

**compartimiento**
[KOHM•pahr•TEE•mee•EN•toh]
*n* M compartment; division

**compás** [KOHM•pahs] *n* M
compass

**compasivo 1**
[KOHM•pah•SEE•voh] *adj*
compassionate

**compasivo 2**
[KOM•pah•SEE•vo] *adj*
pitiful

**compatible**
[KOHM•pah•TEEB•lai] *adj*
compatible

**compeler** [kohm•PAI•lair] *vt*
compel; force

**compensar** [kohm•PEN•sahr] *vt*
compensate

**competencia**
[KOHM•peh•TEHN•see•ah] *n*
F competence

**competente capaz**
[KOHM•peh•TEN•tai]
[kah•pahs] *adj* competent

**competición**
[KOHM•peh•tih•SEE•OHN] *n*
. F competition

**competir** [kohm•PEH•teer] *vi*
compete

**complacido**
[KOHM•plah•SEE•doh] *adj*
complacent

**complaciente**
[KOM•plah•SEE•en•TAI] *adj*
obliging

**complejo** [kohm•PLAI•ho] *adj*
complex

**complemento**
[KOHM•pleh•MEN•toh] *n* M
complement

**completamente**
[KOHM•pleh•tah•MEN•tai]
*adj* thoroughly

**completar** [kohm•PLEH•tahr]
*vt* complete

**completo 1** [kom•PLEH•to] *adj*
thorough

**completo 2** [kohm•PLEH•to]
*adj* overall; complete

**complicado**
[KOHM•plee•KAH•doh] *adj*
complicated

**complicar** [kohm•PLEE•kahr] *vt*
complicate

**cómplice** [kohm•PLEE•sai] *n* M
accomplice

**componente**
[KOHM•po•NEN•tai] *n* M
component

**componer 1** [kom•POH•nair] *vt*
compose

**componer 2** [kom•POH•nair] *n*
*vt* compromise

**composición**
[KOHM•po•zih•SEE•OHN] *n*
F composition

**compositor**
[KOHM•po•ZEE•tor] *n* M
composer

**compota** [kom•POH•tah] *n* F
jam

**compra** [KOHM•prah] *n* F
purchase

**comprador 1**
[kohm•PRAH•dor] *n* M buyer

**comprador 2**
[kohm•PRAH•dor] *n* M
shopper

**comprar** [KOHM•prahr] *vt* buy

**compras** [KOM•prahs] *npl* F
shopping

**comprender** [kom•PREN•dair]
*vi* understand

**comprender incluir**
[kom•PREN•dair]
[in•KLOO•eer] *vt* comprise

**comprender realizar**
[kom•PREN•dair]
[RAI•ahl•IH•sahr] *vt* realize

**comprensible**
[KOM•pren•SEE•blai] *adj*
understandable

**comprensión**
[KOHM•pren•SEE•ohn] *n* F
comprehension

**comprensivo**
[KOHM•pren•SEE•vo] *adj*
comprehensive

**compresión**
[KOHM•preh•SEE•ohn] *n* F
crush

**comprimir** [kom•PRIH•meer] *vt*
compress

**comprometer**
[KOHM•proh•MEH•tair] *vt*
endanger

**compromiso**
[KOM•pro•MEE•so] *n* M
compromise

**compuesto**
[kohm•POO•ES•toh] *adj*
compound

**compulsivo**
[KOM•puhl•SEE•vo] *adj*
compulsive

**computadora**
[KOM•pew•tah•DOR•ah] *n* F
computer

**común** [koh•MOON] *adj* M
common; en ~\ common; por
lo ~\ generally

**comúnamente**
[koh•MOON•ah•MEN•tai] *adv*
commonly

**comunicar**
[KOH•moon•ih•KAHR] *vt*
communicate

**comunidad**
[koh•MOON•I•dahd] *n* F
community

**comunión**
[koh•MOON•ee•OHN] *n* F
communion

**comunismo**
[KOH•moon•EES•moh] *n* M
communism

**comunista**
[KOH•moon•EE•stah] *adj n* F
communist

**con** [kon] *prep* with; ~ que\ so;
~'tal que\ as long as

**coñac** [KOHN•yahk] *n* M
brandy

**concebir** [kohn•SEH•beer] *vt vi*
conceive

**conceder 1** [kon•SEH•dair] *vt*
award

**conceder 2** [kohn•SEH•dair] *vt*
*vi* concede

**conceder la extradición**
[kon•SEH•dair lah
EK•strah•DIH•see•OHN] *vt*
extradite

**concentrado en sí mismo**
[KON•sen•TRAH•do en see
mees•mo] *adj* self-centered

**concentrar(se)**
[KOHN•sen•TRAHR•sai] *vt vi*
concentrate

**concepto** [kohn•SEP•toh] *ñ* M
concept

**con certeza** [kohn
sair•TAI•sah] *adv* certainly

**concerto** [kohn•SAIR•toh] *n* M
concert

**concesión**
[KOHN•seh•SEE•OHN] *n* F
concession; grant

**conciencia**
[KON•see•EN•SEE•ah] *n* F
conscience

**concienzudo**
[KON•see•EN•SOO•doh] *adj*
conscientious

**concilio** [KON•see•LEE•oh] *n*
M council

**conciso** [kohn•SEE•soh] *adj*
concise

**concluir** [kon•KLOO•eer] *vt vi*
conclude

**concreto** [kon•KREE•toh] *adj*
concrete; lo ~ *n* M\ concrete

**concurrencia**
[KOHN•koor•EN•SEE•ah] *n* F
audience

**condado** [kon•DAH•doh] *n* M
county

**condena** [kon•DAI•nah] *n* F
doom; sentence

**condena a cadena perpetua**
[kon•DAI•nah ah
kah•DAI•nah
PAIR•peh•TOO•ah] *n* F life
sentence

**condenado**
[KON•den•AH•doh] *n* M
convict

**condena perpetual**
[kon•DAIN•ah
PAIR•peh•TOO•ahl] *n* F
sentence (death)

**condenar** [CON•den•AHR] *vt*
condemn

**condensar(se)**
[KOHN•den•SAHR•sai] *vt vi*
condense

**condesa** [kon•DEH•sah] *n* F
countess

**condescendiente**
[KON•deh•SEN•dee•EN•tai]
*adj* condescending

**condición**
[KON•dih•SEE•OHN] *n* F
condition

**condicionar**
[KON•dih•SEE•ohn•AHR] *vt*
condition

**condiciones de tiempo**
[kon•DIH•see•OHN•ais dai]
*npl* weather conditions

**cóndor** [KON•dor] *n* M vulture

**conducir** [kon•DOO•seer] *vt*
tend (a machine)

**conducirse mal**
[KON•doo•SEER•sai mahl] *vi*
misbehave

**conducta** [kon•DUHK•tah] *n* F
conduct; demeanor

**conducto** [kon•DOOK•to] *n* M
duct

**conductor** [kon•DUHK•tohr] *n*
M conductor; driver

**conectar** [KOHN•ehk•TAHR]
*vt* connect

**conejera** [KOHN•ai•HAIR•ah]
*n* F burrow

**conejillo** [KOHN•eh•HEE•yo] *n*
M guinea pig

**conejo** [koh•NAI•ho] *n* M
rabbit

**confederación**
[kon•FED•air•AH•see•OHN] *n*
F confederation

**conferencia**
[kon•FAIR•en•SEE•ah] *n* F
conference

**conferir** [KON•fair•EER] *vt*
confer

**confesar(se)**
[KON•fehs•AHR•sai] *vt vi*
confess; admit

**confesión** [kon•FEH•see•OHN]
*n* F confession

**confiable** [KON•fee•AHB•lai]
*adj* reliable

**confiante** [KON•fee•AHN•tai]
*adj* confident

**confianza** [KON•fee•AHN•sah]
*n* F reliance; trust

**confiar 1** [kon•FEE•ahr] *vi*
confide; ~ en\ trust

**confiar 2** [kon•FEE•ahr] *vi* rely

**confidencial**
[kon•FEE•den•SEE•ahl] *adj*
confidential

**confidente** [KON•fee•DEN•tai]
*n* M confidant

**confinar** [kon•FEE•nahr] *vt*
confine

**confirmación**
[KON•feer•MAH•see•OHN] *n*
F confirmation

**confirmar** [KON•feer•MAHR]
*vt* confirm

**confiscar** [KON•fee•SKAHR] *vt*
seize; confiscate

**confitado** [KON•fee•TAH•doh]
*adj* confectionery

**conflicto** [kon•FLEEK•to] *n* M
conflict

**conformarse**
[KON•for•MAHR•sai] *vi*
conform

**conformista**
[KON•for•MEE•stah] *n* F
conformist

**confortable**
[KOHN•for•TAHB•lai] *adj*
comfortable

**confortar** [KOHN•for•TAHR]
*vt* comfort

**confraternidad**
[KOHN•frah•TAIR•nih•
DAHD] *n* F fellowship

**confrontar** [KON•fron•TAHR]
*vt* confront

**confundir** [KON•fuhn•DEER]
*vt* confound; dumbfound;
perplex

**confús** [kon•FOOS] *adj*
confusing

**confusión** [kon•FOO•see•OHN]
*n* F confusion

**congestión**
[kohn•HEHS•tee•OHN] *n* F
congestion

**con gratitud** [kon
grah•TIH•tood] thankfully

**congratular**
[kon•GRAH•too•LAHR] *vt*
congratulate

**congregación**
[kon•GREH•gah•SEE•OHN] *n*
F congregation

**congregar** [KON•greh•GAHR]
*vt* congregate; assemble;
collect

**conjetura**
[KOHN•heh•TOOR•ah] *n* F
guess

**conjunción**
[kon•HUHNK•see•OHN] *n* F
conjunction; conjugation

**conjunto** [[kon•HUHN•toh] *adv*
altogether

**con lo qual** [kon lo kwahl] *n*
wherewithal

**conmemorativo**
[KON•mem•OR•ah•TEE•voh]
*adj* memorial

**conmoción** ·
[KOHN•moh•SEE•OHN] *n* F
commotion

**conmutar** [kohn•MOO•tahr] *vt*
commute

**cono** [KOH•no] *n* M cone

**conocedor** [KON•oh•SAI•dohr]
*n* M conversant

**conocimiento 1**
[KOH•no•SEE•mee•EN•toh] *n*
M acquaintance

**conocimiento 2**
[KOH•no•SEE•mee•EN•toh] *n*
M knowledge

**conocimiento 3**
[KON•oh•SEE•mee•EN•to] *n*
M understanding

**conquista** [kon•KEE•stah] *n* F
conquest

**conquistador**
[KON•kee•STAH•dohr] *n* M
conqueror

**conquistar** [kon•KEE•stahr] *vt*
conquer

**consagrado**
[KOHN•sah•GRAH•doh] *adj*
devoted

**consagrar** [KON•sah•GRAHR]
*vt* consecrate

**consciente** [KON•see•EN•tai]
*adj* conscious; ~ de sí mismo\
self-conscious; ~ de\ aware

**consecuencia 1**
[KON•se•KWEN•SEE•ah] *n* F
consequence

**consecuencia 2**
[KON•seh•KWEN•SEE•ah] *n*
F issue

**consecutivo**
[kon•SEK•oo•TEE•vo] *adj*
consecutive

**consejero** [KON•sai•HAIR•oh]
*n* M counselor

**consejo** [kohn•SAI•ho] *n* M
advice; counsel

**consentir** [KOHN•sen•TEER]
*vi* acquiesce; consent; *vt* allow

**consentimiento**
[KON•sen•TEE•mee•EN•toh]
*n* M consent

**conservación**
[KON•sair•VAH•see•OHN] *n*
F conservation

**conservativo**
[KON•sair•vah•TEE•vo] *adj*
conservative

**considerable**
[kon•SIH•dair•AHB•lai] *adj*
considerable

**consideración**
[kon•SIH•dair•AH•see•OHN]
*n* F thoughtfulness

**considerando**
[kon•SIH•dair•AHN•doh] *prep*
considering; whereas

**considerar**
[kon•SEE•dair•AHR] *vt*
consider

**considerado**
[kon•SIH•dair•AH•doh] *adj*
considerate

**consistencia**
[kon•SIH•sten•SEE•ah] *n* F
consistency

**consistente**
[kon•SIH•STEN•tai] *adj*
consistent

**consistir** [KON•sihs•TEER] *vi*
consist

**consocio** [KON•soh•SEE•oh] *n*
M partner

**consola** [KON•soh•LAH] *n* F
console

**consolación**
[KON•soh•LAH•see•OHN] *n*
F consolation

**consolar** [KON•soh•LAHR] *vt*
console

**consolidar** [KON•sahl•IH•dahr]
*vt* consolidate

**consonante**
[KOHN•soh•NAHN•tai] *adj*
consonant

**consorcio** [KON•sor•SEE•oh] *n*
M partnership

**conspicuo**
[KON•spihk•YOO•oh] *adj*
conspicuous

**conspiración**
[KOHN•speer•ah•SEE•OHN]
*n* F conspiracy; plot

**constante** [kohn•STAHN•tai]
*adj n* M constant

**constelación**
[KON•stchl•AH•see•OHN] *n*
F constellation

**constitución**
[KON•stih•TOO•see•OHN] *n*
F constitution; temperament

**constitutivo**
[KON•stih•TOO•tee•VOH] *n*
M constituent

**constreñimiento**
[KON•stren•YEE•MEE•en•toh]
*n* M constraint

**constructor**
[kohn•STRUHK•tor] *n* M
builder

**construir** [KOHN•stroo•EER] *vt*
build; construct

**consuelo** [kon•SWAI•lo] *n* M
solace; consolation

**consulado**
[KON•soo•LAH•doh] *n* M
consulate

**consultar** [kon•SOOL•tahr] *vt*
*vi* consult

**consumar** [kon•SOO•mahr] *vt*
consummate

**consumidor**
[KON•soo•MEE•dor] *n* M
consumer

**consumir** [kon•SOO•meer] *vt*
consume

**consunción**
[KON•suhn•SEE•ohn] *n* F
consumption

**contacto** [kon•TAHK•toh] *n vt*
M contact

**contador** [kon•TAH•dor] *n* M
timer

**contagioso**
[kon•TAH•hee•OH•soh] *adj*
contagious

**contaminar**
[kon•TAH•meen•AHR] *vi*
contaminate

**contar** [KON•tahr] *vt* count

**contemplar** [kon•TEM•plahr] *vt*
contemplate; regard

**contender 1** [kon•TEN•dair] *vi*
contend; cope (with)

**contender 2** [kohn•TEN•dair]
*vi* compete

**contener 1** [kon•TEN•air] *vt*
contain

**contener 2** [kon•TEN•air] *n vt* M contact

**contener comprobar verificar** [KOHN•ten•AIR] [KOHM•proh•BAHR] [VAIR•ih•FEE•kahr] *vt* check

**contenido** [KON•ten•EE•doh] *n* M contents

**contento** [kon•TEN•toh] *adj* content; pleased

**contestar** [kohn•TEHST•ahr] *vt* answer

**contexto** [kon•TEHKS•toh] *n* M context

**contienda** [KON•tee•EN•dah] *n* F contest

**continente** [KON•tih•NEN•tai] *n* M continent; mainland

**contingencia** [kon•TIN•hen•SEE•ah] *n* F contingency

**continuación** [kon•TIN•yoo•AH•see•OHN] *n* F continuation

**continuar** [KON•tin•YOO•ahr] *vt* continue

**continuo** [KON•teen•OO•oh] *adj* M continual

**contonearse** [KON•toh•NAI•AHR•sai] *vi* swagger

**contra** [KOHN•trah] *prep* against; en ~\ against

**contracción** [kon•TRAHK•see•OHN] *n* F contraction

**contrachapado** [kon•TRAH•cha•PAH•do] *n* M plywood

**contradecir** [KON•trah•DAI•seer] *vt* contradict

**contradicción** [KON•trah•DIHK•see•OHN] *n* F contradiction

**contraer** [KON•trai•AIR] *vt* contract

**contragolpe** [KOHN•trah•GOL•pai] *n* M backlash

**contrario** [KON•trahr•EE•oh] *adj* untrue; contrary; *n* M lo ~\ contrary

**contrarrestar** [KON•trah•REH•stahr] *vt* counteract

**contraseña** [KON•trah•SAIN•yah] *n* F password

**contraste** [kon•TRAH•stai] *n* M contrast

**contrato** [kon•TRAH•toh] *n* M contract

**contribución** [KON•trih•BYOO•see•OHN] *n* F contribution

**contribuir** [KON•trih•BYOO•eer] *vt vi* contribute

**contribuyente** [kon•TRIH•boo•YEHN•tai] *n* M taxpayer

**controversia** [kon•TRO•vair•SEE•ah] *n* F controversy

**convalecencia** [KON•vah•LEH•sen•SEE•ah] *n* F convalescence

**convaleciente** [KON•vahl•EH•sen•SEE•ah] *adj* convalescent

**convencer** [KON•ven•SAIR] *vt* convince

**conveniencia**
[KON•ven•EE•en•SEE•ah] *n* F
convenience

**conveniente**
[KON•ven•EE•EHN•tai] *adj*
convenient

**convenio** [KON•vain•EE•oh] *n*
M agreement; covenant

**convento** [kon•VEN•toh] *n* M
convent

**converger** [kon•VAIR•hair] *vi*
converge

**conversación**
[KON•vair•sah•SEE•OHN] *n*
F conversation; parlance

**conversar** [kon•VAIR•sahr] *vi*
converse

**conversión**
[KOHN•vair•SEE•ohn] *n* F
conversion

**converso** [kon•VAIR•soh] *n* M
convert

**convertir** [kon•VAIR•teer] *vt*
convert

**convexo** [kon•VEHKS•oh] *n* M
convex

**convincente**
[KON•vin•SEN•tai] *adj*
convincing

**convocación**
[KON•voh•KAH•see•OHN] *n*
F convention

**convocar** [KOHN•voh•KAHR]
*vt* assemble; convene

**convoy** [KON•voi] *n* M convoy

**cooperación**
[KOH•op•AIR•ah•SEE•OHN]
*n* F cooperation

**cooperar** [KOH•op•AIR•ahr] *vi*
cooperate

**coordinación**
[KOH•or•DIH•nah•see•OHN]
*n* F coordination

**coordinar** [KOH•or•DIH•nahr]
*vt* coordinate

**copañero de cuarto**
[KOM•pahn•YAIR•oh dai
KWAHR•to] *n* M roommate

**copero** [koh•PAIR•oh] *n* M
sideboard

**copía** [koh•PEE•ah] *n* F copy

**copioso** [KOH•pee•OH•soh] *adj*
copious

**copo** [KOH•poh] *n* M flake

**copo de nieve** [KOH•poh dai]
*n* M snowflake

**coral** [KOH•rahl] *n* M coral

**corazòn** [koh•RAH•SON] *n* F
heart

**corbata** [kor•BAH•tah] *n* F tie

**corbata de lazo** [kor•BAH•tah
dai•LAH•so] *n* F bow tie

**Córcega** [KOR•sai•HA] *n*
Corsica

**corcel** [KOR•sel] *n* M steed

**corcho** [KOR•cho] *n* M cork

**cordel** [KOR•del] *n* M twine;
cord; thin rope

**cordero** [kor•DAIR•oh] *n* M
lamb

**cordón 1** [kohr•DOHN] *n* M
chord

**cordón 2** [kohr•DOHN] *n* M
cord; lace; string; ~ de zapato\
shoelace

**Corea** [kor•RAI•ah] *n* M Korea

**cornisa** [kor•NEE•sah] *n* F
cornice

**coro** [KOH•roh] *n* M choir;
chorus

**corona** [kohr•OH•nah] *n* F
crown; wreath

**coronación**
[KOR•oh•NAH•see•OHN] *n* F
coronation

**corporación**
[KOR•por•AH•see•OHN] *n* F
corporation

**corporal** [kor•POR•ahl] *adj*
corporal

**correa** [kor•RAI•ah] *n* F thong;
leash

**corrección**
[kohr•REHK•see•OHN] *n* F
correction

**correctamente**
[kor•REHK•tah•MEN•tai] *adv*
correctly

**correcto** [kor•REHK•toh] *adj*
correct

**corredor 1** [kor•REH•dor] *n* M
corridor

**corredor 2** [kohr•REH•dor] *n* M
racer; runner

**corregir** [kohr•REH•heer]
correct; ammend (law)

**correo** [kor•RAI•oh] *n* M mail

**correr** [KOHR•rair] *vi* jog; run

**correr a toda velocidad**
[KOR•rair ah TOH•dah
VEH•lo•SEE•dahd] *vi* sprint

**correr regatear raza**
[kor•RAIR rai•GAH•tai•AHR
RAH•sa] *vi* race

**correspondencia**
[KOR•reh•SPON•den•SEE•ah]
*n* F correspondence

**corresponder**
[KOR•reh•SPON•dair] *vi*
correspond; belong

**correspondiente**
[KOR•reh•SPON•dee•EN•tai]
*n* M correspondent

**corriente 1** [KOR•ree•EN•tai]
*adj* current

**corriente 2** [KOR•reh•EN•tai] *n*
M stream

**corroer** [kor•RO•air] *vt* corrode;
erode

**corrosión** [kor•ROH•see•OHN]
*n* F corrosion; erosion

**corrosivo** [KOH•roh•SEE•voh]
*adj* acrid; corrosive

**corrspondiente**
[KOR•reh•SPON•dee•EN•tai]
*adv* corresponding

**corrupción**
[kor•ROOHP•see•ohn] *n* F
corruption; taint

**corrupto** [kohr•ROOP•toh] *adj*
corrupt

**cortadora de césped**
[KOR•tah•DOR•ah dai] *n* F
lawn mower

**cortapluma**
[KOR•tah•PLOO•mah] *n* F
pocketknife

**cortar** [KOHR•tahr] *vt* cut; chop

**corte 1** [KOR•tai] *n* M court;
edge

**corte 2** [KOHR•tai] *n* M chop;
cut; nick

**corte el pelo** [KOR•tai el
PAI•lo] *n* M haircut

**cortesía** [KOR•teh•SEE•ah] *n* F
courtesy; politeness

**corteza** [kor•TAI•sah] *n* F crust;
hull; rind; bark (of tree)

**cortina** [kor•TEE•nah] *n* F
curtain

**corto** [KOR•to] *adj* short; brief; quedarse ~\ fall short; ~ de alances\ dim; thick

**corto de vista** [KOR•toh dai VEE•stah] *adj* near-sighted

**cosa** [KOH•sah] *n* F thing; ~ de\ about; dome si tal ~\ just like that

**coser** [KOH•sair] *vt* sew

**cosmético** [kohs•MEH•tee•KOH] *n* M cosmetic

**cosmopolita** [KOHS•MOH•pol•EE•tah] *n adj* F cosmopolitan

**cosquillear** [KOHS•kee•YAI•ahr] *vt* tickle

**costa 1** [KOH•stah] *n* F coast

**costa 2** [KOH•stah] *n* F strand

**coste** [KOH•stai] *n* M cost

**costo** [KOH•stoh] *n* M cost

**costilla** [koh•STEE•yah] *n* F rib

**costumbre** [koh•STOOM•brai] *n* M custom

**costura** [koh•STOOR•ah] *n* F seam; sewing

**costurera** [KOH•stoor•AIR•ah] *n* F seamstress

**cráneo** [krah•NAI•oh] *n* M skull

**crápula** [krah•POO•lah] *n* F debauchery

**cráter** [KRAH•tair] *n* M crater

**creación** [KRAI•ah•SEE•ohn] *n* F creation

**creado** [krai•AH•dohr] *n* M creator

**creador** [krai•AH•dohr] *adj* creative

**crear** [KRAI•ahr] *vt* create

**crecer** [KRAI•sair] *vi* flourish; *vt* grow

**crecimiento** [KRAI•see•MEE•EN•toh] *n* M growth

**crédito** [krai•DEE•toh] *n* M credit

**credo** [KRAI•doh] *n* M creed

**creencia** [KRAI•en•SEE•ah] *m* F belief

**creer** [KRAI•air] *vt vi* believe

**creíble** [krai•EEB•lai] *adj* credible

**crema** [KRAI•mah] *n* F cream

**cremoso** [krai•MOH•soh] *adj* creamy

**crepúscolo** [KREH•puh•SKOH•lo] *n* M twilight

**crespo** [KRES•poh] *adj* crisp

**crespón** [krehs•POHN] *n* M crape

**cresta** [KREH•stah] *n* F crest

**creta** [KRAI•tah] *n* chalk

**criadero** [KREE•ah•DAIR•oh] *n* M nursery

**criatura** [KREE•ah•TOOR•ah] *n* F creature

**crimen** [KREE•men] *n* M crime

**criminal** [KRIH•mee•NAHL] *n* M thug; criminal

**crin** [krihn] *n* M mane

**crisantemo** [KREE•sahn•TAI•moh] *n* M chrysanthemum

**crisis** [KREE•sis] *n* M crisis

**cristal** [KRIH•stahl] *n* M crystal

**cristalino** [KRIII•stah•LEF•no] *adj* glassy

**cristiandad** [krih•STEE•ahn•DAHD] *n* F Christianity

**cristiano** [KRIH•stee•AHN•oh] *adj n* M Christian

**Cristo** [KREE•stoh] *n* M Christ

**criterio** [KREE•tair•EE•oh] *n* M criterion

**crítica** [krih•TEE•kah] *n* F criticism

**criticar** [krih•TEE•kahr] *vt vi* criticize

**crítico 1** [krih•TEE•koh] *n* M critic

**crítico 2** [krih•TEE•koh] *adj* crucial

**crómico** [kroh•MEE•koh] *n* M chronic

**cromo** [KROH•moh] *n* M chrome

**crónica** [kroh•NEE•kah] *n* F chronicle

**cronógafo** [KRON•oh•GAH•fo] *n* M stopwatch

**cronológico** [kroh•NOH•loh•HEE•koh] *adj* chronological

**crótalo** [kroh•TAH•lo] *n* M rattlesnake

**crucero 1** [kroo•SAIR•oh] *n* M cruise

**crucero 2** [kroo•SAIR•oh] *n* M transept

**crucifijo** [KROO•sih•FEE•ho] *n* M crucifix

**crucigrama** [KROO•see•GRAHM•ah] *n* F crossword (puzzle)

**crudo** [KROO•doh] *adj* crude; raw

**cruel** [KROO•el] *adj* cruel; ruthless

**crujido** [kroo•HEE•doh] *n* M crack

**crujir** [KROO•heer] *vi* creak

**cruz** [kroos] *n* F cross

**cruzada** [kroo•SAH•dah] *n* F crusade

**cruzado** [kroo•SAH•doh] *adj* double-breasted

**cruzar** [KROO•sahr] *vt* intersect

**cuadrado** [kwah•DRAH•do] *n* M square

**cuadrante** [kwah•DRAHN•tai] *n* M quadrant

**cuadrilátero** [KWAH•DREE•lah•TAIR•oh] *adj* quadrilateral

**cuadro de actores** [KWAH•droh dai•ahk•TOHR•ais] *n* M cast

**cuadro de distribución** [KWAH•droh dai DIH•strih•BOO•see•OHN] *n* M switchboard

**cuajar** [KWAH•har] *vt* curdle

**cual** [kwahl] *pron* el ~, la ~ etc that which; who; that; *adv* as; like; ~ si\ as if

**cuál** [kwahl] *pron* which

**cualitativo** [KWAHL•ih•TAH•tee]•vo *adj* qualitative

**cualquier** [kwahl•KEE•air] *adj* any; *pron* whatever

**cualquiera** [KWAHL•kee•AIR•ah] *pron* whichever; anyone, anybody

**cuando** [KWAHN•do] *adv* when; ~ más\ at the most; ~ menos\ at the least; ~ no\ if not; aun ~\ even if; de ~ en ~\ from time to time

**cuándo** [KWAHN•do] *adv* & *conj* when; ¿desde ~?\ since when?

**cuando quiera** [KWAN•do kee•AIR•ah] *adv* whenever

**cuantitativo** [kwan•TIH•tah•TEE•vo] *n* M quantitative

**cuánto** [KWAHN•to] how much? how many: ¿~ tiempo?\ how long; ¿a ~ ?\ how much?

**cuarenta** [kwah•REN•tah] *num* forty

**cuarentena** [KWAHR•en•TEN•ah] *n* F quarantine

**cuaresma** [kwahr•EHS•mah] *n* F Lent

**cuartel** [KWAR•tel] *n* M barracks

**cuartel general** [KWAHR•tel hen•AIR•ahl] *n* M headquarters

**cuartillo** [kwahr•TEE•yo] *n* M pint

**cuarto 1** [KWAHR•to] *num* fourth

**cuarto 2** [KWAHR]•to *n* M quart; quarter

**cuarto 3** [KWAHR•to] *n* M room

**cuarto de baño** [KWAR•to dai BAHN•yo] *n* M bathroom

**cuarto de prueba** [KWAR•to dai proo•AI•bah] *n* M fitting room

**cuarto de respeto** [KWAHR•toh dai reh•SPEH•to] *n* M guestroom

**cuarzo** [KWAHR•so] *n* M quartz

**cuatro** [KWAH•tro] *num* four

**Cuba** [KOO•bah] *n* Cuba

**cubano** [koo•BAN•oh] *adj* Cuban

**cúbico** [koo•BIH•koh] *n* M cubic

**cubierta** [KOO•bee•AIR•tah] *n* F covering; wrapping paper

**cubierto** [KOO•bee•AIR•toh] *adj* covert

**cubito de hielo** [koo•BEE•toh dai] *n* M ice cube

**cubo 1** [KOO•boh] *n* M bucket

**cubo 2** [KOO•bo] *n* M cube

**cubo 3** [KOO•boh] *n* M hub pivot

**cubrir** [KOO•breer] *vt* cover; coat

**cucaracha** [KOO•kah•RAH•cha] *n* F cockroach

**cuchara** [koo•CHAR•ah] *n* F spoon

**cucharada** [KOO•char•AH•dah] *n* F spoonful

**cucharilla** [KOO•chahr•EE•yah] *n* F teaspoon

**cucharón** [koo•CHAR•OHN] *n* F ladle; scoop

**cuchilla de carnicero** [koo•CHEE•yah dai KARN•ih•SAIR•oh] *n* F cleaver

**cuchillería** [KOO•chee•air•EE•ah] *n* F cutlery

**cuchillo** [koo•CHEE•yo] *n* M knife

**cuello 1** [KWAI•yo] *n* M collar

**cuello 2** [KWAI•yo] *n* M neck

**cuenta 1** [KWEN•tah] *n* F account; check (bill)

**cuenta 2** [KWEN•tah] *n* F score

**cuenta colectivo** [KWEN•tah KOH•lehk•TEE•vah] *n* F joint account

**cuento** [KWEN•toh] *n* M tale

**cuento de hadas** [KWEN•to dai AH•dahs] *n* M fairy tale

**cuentos para niños** [KWEN•tos PAH•rah NEEN•yos] *npl* nursery rhyme

**cuerda** [KWAIR•dah] *n* F rope; tether

**cuerno** [KWAIR•no] *n* M horn

**cuerpo** [KWAIR•poh] *n* M body

**cuerpo legisladores** [KWAI•po lai•HEES•lah•DOR•ais] *n* M legislature

**cuervo** [KWAIR•vo] *n* M raven

**cuesta** [KWEH•stah] *n* F upgrade

**cuesta arriba** [KWEH•stah ahr•REE•bah] *adj* uphill

**cuestionable** [KWEH•stee•ohn•AH•blai] *adj* questionable

**cuestionario** [KWEH•stee•OHN•ahr•EE•oh] *n* M questionnaire

**cueva** [koo•AI•vah] *n* F cave

**cuidado** [kwee•DAH•doh] *n* M care

**cuidadoso** [KWEE•dah•DOH•so] *adj* M careful

**cuidar** [KWEE•dahr] *vi* tend; *vi* care (about)

**culminación** [KUHL•mih•NAH•see•OHN] *n* F climax

**culminar** [KUHL•mee•NAHR] *vi* culminate

**culpa** [KUHL•pah] *n* F guilt

**culpable 1** [kuhl•PAHB•lai] *n* M culprit

**culpable 2** [kuhl•PAH•blai] *adj* guilty; criminal

**culpar** [KUHL•pahr] *vt* accuse

**cultivar** [kuhl•TEE•VAHR] *vt* cultivate; grow; raise

**cultivo** [kuhl•TEE•voh] *n* M crop; farming

**culto** [KUHL•to] *n* M cult

**cultura** [KUHL•toor•AH] *n* F culture

**cultural** [KUHL•toor•AHL] *adj* cultural

**cumpleaños** [KOOM•plai•AN•yos] *n* M birthday

**cumplimiento** [KOOM•plee•MEE•EN•toh] *n* M compliment; fulfillment

**cumplir** [KOOM•pleer] *vi* comply; *vt* fulfill

**cumulativo** [koo•MOO•lah•TEE•voh] *adj* cumulative

**cuñada** [koon•YAH•dah] *n* F sister-in-law

**cuñado** [koon•YAH•do] *n* M brother-in-law

**cuna** [KOO•nah] *n* F cradle

**cuota** [KWOH•tah] *n* F quota; part; portion

**cúpon** [KOO•pon] *n* F coupon

**cúpula** [kuh•POO•lah] *n* F dome

**cura** [KOOR•ah] *n* F cure

**curar** [KOOR•ahr] *vt* heal

**curiosidad**
[KOOR•ee•OH•sih•DAHD] *n*
F curiosity

**curioso** [KOOR•ee•OH•so] *adj*
curious; nosy

**curso 1** [KOOR•soh] *n* M
course

**curso 2** [KOOR•soh] *n* M
currency

**curtir** [[KOOR•teer] *vt* bark

**curva** [KOOR•vah] *n* F crook;
curve

**custodio** [KUH•stoh•DEE•oh] *n*
M custodian

**cuyo cuya** [KOO•yo] [KOO•ya]
*pron* whose; of whom

**chabacano**
[CHAH•bah•KAH•no] *adj*
scurrilous

**chacal** [CHAH•kahl] *n* M jackal

**chaleco** [cha•LAI•ko] *n* M vest

**champaña** [cham•PAHN•ya] *n*
F champagne

**chantaje** [chan•TAH•hai] *n* M
blackmail

**chapa** [CHA•pa] *n* F veneer

**chapucear**
[CHAH•poo•SAI•ahr] *vt*
fumble

**chaqueta** [chah•KAI•tah] *n* F
jacket; coat; cardigan

**charlar** [CHAR•lahr] *vi* babble;
chat

**charol** [CHAHR•ohl] *n* M
patent leather

**checo** [CHEH•koh] *adj* Czech

**Checoslovaquia**
[che•KOH•slo•VAH•KEE•ah]
*n* M Czechoslovakia

**cheque** [CHEH•kai] *n* M check
(currency)

**chiflado** [cheef•LAH•doh] *adj*
kinky

**Chile** [CHEE•lai] *n* M Chile

**chillar** [chee•YΛHR] *vi* squeak;
squeal

**chillido** [chee•YEE•do] *n* M
screech; shriek

**chimenea** [CHIM•en•AI•ah] *n*
F chimney; fireplace

**chimpancé** [CHIM•pahn•SAI] *n*
M chimpanzee

**China** [CHEE•nah] *n* China

**chinchorro** [chin•CHOR•roh] *n*
M dinghy; small boat

**chino** [CHEE•noh] *adj* Chinese

**chiquitín** [CHI•kih•TEEN] *n* M
tot

**chiripa** [CHEER•ee•PAH] *n* F
godsend

**chirriar** [CHEER•ee•AHR] *vi*
-chirp

**chismear** [CHEES•mai•AHR] *vt*
blab

**chismografía**
[chees•MO•grah•FEE•ah] *n* F
gossip

**chismoso** [chees•MOH•so] *n* M
telltale

**chispa** [CHEE•spa] *n* F spark

**chispeante**
[CHIHS•pai•AHN•tai] *adj*
sparkling

**chispear** [CHIH•spai•AHR] *vi*
sparkle

**chiste** [CHEE•stai] *n* M joke

**chistoso** [chee•STOH•soh] *adj*
facetious

**chocar 1** [CHO•kahr] *vt*
conflict; *vi* vi clash

**chocar 2** [CHO•kahr] *vi* collide
(with); bump

**chocolate** [CHOK•oh•LAH•tai] *n* M chocolate

**chófer** [CHOH•fair] *n* M chauffeur

**choque 1** [CHO•kai] *n* M impact; shock; bump

**choque 2** [CHO•kai] *n* M wreck

**choque 3** [CHOH•kai] *n* M clash

**chorro** [CHOR•roh] *n* M jet; gush

**chuleta** [choo•LAI•tah] *n* F cutlet

**chunga** [CHUN•gah] *n* F banter

**chupar** [CHOO•pahr] *vt* suck

**chusma** [CHUHS•mah] *n* F rabble

# D

**dadivoso** [DAH•dee•VOH•soh] *adj* lavish

**dado** [DAH•doh] *prep* given; ~ que\ given that

**dados** [DAH•dohs] *npl* dice

**daltoniano** [DAHL•ton•ee•AHN•oh] *n* M color-blind

**dama** [DAH•mah] *n* F lady

**dama de honor** [DAH•mah dai ON•or] *n* F bridesmaid

**dañar** [DAHN•yahr] *vt* injure

**daño** [DAN•yo] *n* M damage; harm; injury

**dañoso** [dahn•YO•so] *adj* harmful

**dañoso** [dahn•YO•so] *adj* hurtful

**dar** [dahr] *vt* give; ~ con\ meet; find; ~ por\ assume

**dar conceder** [dahr] [kon•SAI•dair] *vt* bestow

**dardo** [DAHR•do] *n* M dart

**dar énfasis a** [dahr ah] *vt* emphasize

**dar forma** [dahr FOR•mah] *vt* whittle

**dar fuerza a** [dahr FWAI•sah ah] *vt* enforce

**dar gracias** [dahr grah•SEE•ahs] *vt* thank

**dar miedo** [dahr mee•AID•oh] *vt* frighten

**dar náuseas** [dahr NOW•SAI•ahs] *vt* nauseate

**dar saltos.mortales** [dahr SAHL•tohs MOR•tahl•AIS] *v* somersault

**dar un tirón** [dahr oon TEER•on] *vt* yank

**datos** [DAH•tos] *npl* data

**de a en** [dai] [ah en].*prep* of; ~ dios\ by day

**debajo** [dai•BAH•ho] *adv* beneath; *prep* underneath; ~ de\ underneath; por ~ de\ below

**debate** [dai•BAH•tai] *n* M debate

**debe** [DAI•bai] *n* M debit

**deber 1** [DAI•bair] *n* M duty

**deber 2** [DAI•bair] *aux v* ought; should

**deber 3** [DAI•bair] *vt* owe

**debido** [dai•BEE•doh] *adj* due

**débil** [deh•BEEL] *adj* faint; feeble; flimsy; weak; *adv* weakly

**debilitar** [DEH•bih•LIH•tahr] *vt* impair; weaken

**debilitarse** [DEH•bee•LIH•TAHR•sai] *vi* fade

**década** [dai•KAH•dah] *n* F decade

**decadencia** [deh•KAH•den•SEE•ah] *n* F decadence

**decadente** [DEH•kah•DEN•tai] *adj* decadent

**decaimiento** [deh•KAI•mee•EN•to] *n* M decay

**decano** [dai•KAHN•oh] *n* M dean

**decapitar** [DAI•kah•PEE•tahr] *vt* behead

**decencia** [DAI•sen•SEE•ah] *n* F decency

**decente** [dai•SEN•tai] *adj* decent

**decepcionante** [DEH•sep•SEE•ohn•AHN•tai] *adj* disappointing

**deceptionar** [DEH•sehp•SEE•ohn•AHR] *vt* disappoint

**decidir** [dai•SIH•deer] *vt* decide

**decimal** [dai•SEE•mahl] *adj* decimal

**décimo** [deh•SEE•mo] *num* tenth

**decimoquinto** [deh•SEE•mo•KEEN•toh] *num* fifteenth

**decimoséptimo** [DEH•see•MOH•sehp•TEE•moh] *num* seventeenth

**décimosexto** [deh•SEE•moh•SEHKS•to] *num* sixteenth

**décimotercio** [DEH•see•MOH•tair•SEE•oh] *num* thirteenth

**decir** [DAI•seer] *vt* tell

**decir menos de lo que hay** [DAI•seer MAIN•oh dai loh kai ai] *vt* understate

**decisión** [DAI•sih•see•OHN] *n* F decision

**decisivo** [DAI•sih•SEE•voh] *adj* decisive

**declaración** [DEHK•lahr•AH•see•OHN] *n* F statement

**declarar** [dai•KLAHR•ahr] *vt* declare

**declarar culpable** [DEH•klahr•AHR kuhl•PAHB•lai] *v* convict

**declive** [dai•KLEE•vai] *n* M decline

**declive** [deh•KLEE•vai] *n* M incline

**decoración** [DEH•kohr•AH•see•OHN] *n* F decoration

**decorar** [deh•KOHR•ahr] *vt* decorate

**decoro** [dai•KOR•oh] *n* M decorum

**decrecer** [DAI•crai•SAIR] *vt*
decrease

**decrépito** [DAI•kreh•PEE•toh]
*adj* decrepit

**decreto** [dai•CREH•toh] *n* M
decree; statute

**dedal** [DAI•dahl] *n* M thimble

**dedicación**
[DEH•dih•KAH•see•ON] *n* F
dedication

**dedicar** [DEH•dee•KAHR] *vt*
dedicate; devote

**dedo** [DAI•do] *n* M finger; digit

**dedo del pie** [DAI•do dai
PEE•ai] *n* M toe

**deducción**
[dai•DOOK•see•OHN] *n* F
deduction; withdrawal; retreat

**deducir** [DAI•doo•SEER] *vt*
deduct

**defecto** [dai•FEHK•toh] *n* M
defect; shortcoming

**defectuoso**
[deh•FEHK•too•OH•so] *adj*
faulty

**defender** [DAI•fen•DAIR] *vt*
defend; *vi* fend

**defender en juicio**
[DAI•fen•DAIR en
HOO•ee•SEE•oh] *vt* plead

**defensa** [dai•FEN•sah] *n* F
defense; plea

**defensa propia** [dai•FEN•sah
proh•PEE•ah] *n* F self-defense

**defensivo** [DAI•fen•SEE•voh]
*adj* defensive

**defensor** [DAI•fen•SOHR] *n* M
champion

**deficiencia**
[DAI•fih•SEE•en•SEE•ah] *n* F
deficiency

**deficiente**
[DAI•fih•SEE•EHN•tai] *adj*
deficient

**definición**
[DEH•fin•IH•see•OHN] *n* F
definition

**definidamente**
[DEH•fihn•EE•dah•MEN•tai]
*adv* definitely

**definidio** [DEH•fin•EE•doh] *adj*
definite

**definir** [DEH•fin•EER] *vt* define

**deformado**
[DAI•for•MAH•doh] *adj*
deformed

**defraudar** [DAI•frou•DAHR] *vt*
cheat; defraud

**degenerado**
[dai•HEN•air•AH•doh] *adj*
degenerate

**degenerar** [DE•hen•AIR•ahr]v
degenerate

**deglución**
[deh•GLOO•see•OHN] *n* F
swallow

**degradante**
[DEH•grah•DAHN•tai] *adj*
degrading

**deidad** [DAI•eh•DAHD] *n* F
deity

**dejar** [dai•HAHR] *vt* leave;
bequeath; quit

**dejar de cumplir** [dai•HAHR
dai koom•PLEER] v default

**delante** [deh•LAHN•tai] *adv*
forth; *prep* ahead of; delante
~\ in front of; de ~\ front

**delantero 1**
[DEH•lahn•TAIR•oh] *adj*
foremost

**delantero 2**
[DEH•lahn•TAIR•oh] *adj*
forward

**delegación**
[DEH•leh•GAH•see•OHN] *n*
F delegation

**delegado** [DEH•leh•GAH•doh]
*n* M delegate

**deletreo** [DEH•leh•TRAI•oh] *n*
M spelling

**delfín** [dehl•FEEN] *n* M dolphin

**delgadamente**
[dehl•GAH•dah•MEN•tai] *adv*
thinly

**delgadez** [DEHL•gah•DEHS] *n*
F thinness

**delgado** [del•DAH•doh] *adj*
slim; thin; gaunt

**deliberado**
[DAI•lihb•air•AH•doh] *adj*
deliberate

**deliberar** [dai•LIHB•air•AHR]
discuss; debate

**delicadeza**
[deh•LEE•kah•DAI•sah] *n* F
delicacy

**delicado** [DEH•lee•KAH•doh]
*adj* delicate; delicious;
luscious

**delincuente**
[DEH•lihn•KWEN•tai] *adj n*
M delinquent

**delinear** [DEH•lihn•AI•ahr] *vt*
trace

**delirante** [DEH•leer•AHN•tai]
*adj* delirious

**delirar** [deh•l EER•ahr] *vt* rant,
rave

**delusión** [DEH•loo•SEE•OHN]
*n* F delusion

**demacrado**
[DEH•mah•KRAH•doh] *adj*
emaciated; shrunken

**demagogo** [DEH•mah•GO•go]
*n* M demagogue

**de mala gana** [dai MAH•lah
GAH•nah] *adv* reluctantly

**demanda 1** [deh•MAHN•dah] *n*
F demand

**demanda 2** [dai•MAN•dah] *n* F
claim

**demandante 1**
[DAI•man•DAN•tai] *n* M
plaintiff

**demandante 2**
[DAI•man•DAN•tai] *n* M
prosecutor

**demandar** [dai•MAN•DAHR]
*vt* sue

**demente 1** [deh•MEN•tai] *n* M
lunatic

**demente 2** [deh•MEN•tai] *adj*
demented; mad; angry

**demérito** [deh•MAIR•IH•toh] *n*
M demerit

**democracia**
[deh•MOH•krah•SEE•ah] *n* F
democracy

**demócrata**
[deh•MOH•krah•tah] *n* F
democrat

**democratico**
[deh•MOH•krah•TEE•koh] *adj*
democratic

**demoler** [DEH•moh•LAIR] *vt*
demolish

**demonio** [DEH•mon•EE•oh] *n*
M fiend

**demorar** [dai•MOR•ahr] *vi*
linger

**demostración**
[DEH•moh•STRAH•see•OHN]
*n* F demonstration

**demostrar**
[DEH•moh•STRAHR] *vt*
demonstrate

**demostrativo**
|deh•MOH•strah•TEE•voh|
*adj* demonstrative

**densidad** |DEHN•see•DAHD| *n*
F density

**denso** |DEHN•soh| *adj* dense

**dental** |DEN•tahl| *adj* dental

**dentista** |dehn•TEE•stah| *n* M
dentist

**dentro** |DEN•troh| *prep* within;
~ in\ in; ~ de poco\ soon; por
~\ inside; en ~\ into

**denunciar**
|DEH•nuhn•SEE•ahr| *vt*
denounce

**departamento**
|deh•PAHR•tah•MEN•toh| *n*
M department

**deplorable**
|DEH•plohr•AHB•lai| *adj*
deplorable

**deplorar** |deh•PLOR•ahr| *vt*
deplore

**deponer** |dai•PON•air| *vt*
depose

**deportar** |dai•POR•tahr| *vt*
deport; banish

**deporte** |dai•POR•tai| *n* M
sport; hacer ~\ play sports

**deporte de bochas**
|dai•POR•tai dai BOH•chahs|
*n* M bowling

**deportes acuatícos**
|dai•POR•tais ah•KWAH•
TEE•kohs| *npl* water sports

**deportista** |DAI•por•TEE•stah|
*n* F sportsman

**depósito** |DEH•poh•SEE•toh| *n*
M deposit

**depósito de cadaveres**
|deh•POH•sih•to dai
KAH•dah•VAIR•ais| *n* M
morgue

**depreciar**
|deh•PREH•see•AHR| *vt*
depreciate

**depresión**
|deh•PREH•see•OHN| *n* F
depression

**deprimido**
|DEH•prih•MEE•doh| *adj*
depressed; downcast

**deprimir** |DEH•pri•MEER| *vt*
depress

**de puntillas** |dai
puhn•TEE•yahs| *adj* tiptoe

**derecha** |deh•RAI•cha| *adj*
right; a la ~\ on the right

**derecho** |deh•RAI•cho| *adj*
straightforward; upright; erect

**derechos de propiedad**
|deh•RAI•chos dai
PROH•PEE•eh•DAHD| *npl*
copyright

**derechos humanos**
|deh•RAI•chos oo•
MAHN•ohs| *npl* human rights

**deriva** |dair•EE•vah| *n* F drift

**derivar** |DAIR•ih•VAHR| *vt*
derive

**derogar** |DAIR•oh•GAHR| *vt*
repeal

**derribar** |DEH•ree•BAHR| *vi*
topple; *v* lay

**derrochar** |DEHR•roh•CHAR|
*vt* squander

**derrochardor**
|DAIR•roh•CHA•dor| *n* M
spendthrift

**derrota** [dair•ROH•tah] *n* F
defeat

**derrumbamiento 1**
[DAI•room•BAH•mee•EN•to]
*n* M breakdown (machine);
collapse

**derrumbamiento 2**
[DEHR•room•BAH•mee•EN•
to] *n* M landslide

**derrumbarse**
[DAIR•ruhm•BAHR•sai] *vi*
collapse

**des** [dehs] un- (used to convey
negative)

**desabotonar**
[DEHS•ah•BOH•ton•AHR] *vt*
unbutton

**desacato** [dehs•SAH•KAH•toh]
*n* M disrespect

**desacostumbrado**
[dehs•AH•kohs•toom•BRAH•
do] *adj* unaccustomed

**desacreditado**
[DEHS•ah•KREH•dee•DAH•
toh] *adj* disreputable

**desafiar 1** [DEHS•ah•fee•AHR]
*n* F defiance

**desafiar 2** [DEHS•ah•fee•AHR]
*vt* defy; challenge

**desafio** [DEH•sah•FEE•oh] *n* M
dare; challenge

**desagradable**
[dehs•AH•grah•DAHB•lai] *adj*
displeased

**desagradecido**
[dehs•AH•grah•deh•SEE•doh]
*adj* thankless

**desagradecimiento**
[DEHS•ah•GRAHD•eh•SEE•
mee•EN•to] *n* M thanklessness

**desalentado**
[DEHS•ah•len•TAH•doh] *adj*
despondent

**desalentar**
[DEH•sah•len•TAHR] *vt*
discourage

**desalojar**
[DEHS•ah•loh•HAHR] *vt* oust

**desamparar**
[DEHS•ahm•pahr•AHR] *vt*
forsake

**desaparecer**
[DEHS•ah•pah•ah•SAIR] *vi*
disappear; *vt* vanish

**desapasionado**
[DEHS•ah•PAH•see•ohn•AH•
doh] *adj* dispassionate

**desaprobar**
[DEHS•ah•PROH•bahr] *vi*
disapprove; condemn

**desar** [deh•SAI•ahr] *vt* covet;
envy

**desarmado**
[DEHS•ahr•MAH•do] *adj*
unarmed

**desarmar** [DEH•sahr•MAHR]
*vt vi* disarm

**desarreglado**
[dehs•AH•reh•GLAH•doh] *adj*
messy; deranged

**desarrollar**
[DEHS•ahr•ROY•yahr] *vi*
evolve

**desarrolo** [DEHS•ah•ROY•yo]
*n* M development

**desaseo** [DEHS•ahs•AI•oh] *n*
M untidiness

**desastre** [deh•SAHS•trai] *n* M
disaster

**desastroso**
[DEH•sah•STROH•so] *adj*
disastrous

**desatar** [DEH•sah•TAHR] *vt*
detach; untie

**desatender**
[DEHS•sah•TEN•dair] *vt*
disregard

**desayuno** [DEH•sai•OON•oh] *n*
M breakfast

**desbandarse**
[DEHS•bahn•DAHR•sai] *vi*
straggle

**desbaratar**
[DEHS•bahr•AH•tahr] *vt*
thwart

**descalzo** [dehs•KAHL•so] *adj*
barefoot

**descanso** [dehs•KAHN•so] *n* M
rest; ease; recess

**descarga 1** [dehs•KAHR•ga] *n*
F discharge; exhaust

**descarga 2** [dehs•KAHR•gah] *n*
F volley

**descargar 1**
[DEHS•kahr•GAHR] *vt* acquit

**descargar 2**
[DEHS•kahr•GAHR] *vi* dump;
unload; discharge; *vt* unburden

**descarrilar**
[DEHS•kahr•ee•LAHR] *vi*
derail

**descartarse**
[DEHS•kahr•TAHR•sai] *vt*
discard; release

**descendente**
[DEH•sen•DEN•tai] *adj*
downward

**descender** [DEH•sen•DAIR] *vi*
descend

**descendiente**
[deh•SEN•dee•EN•tai] *n* M
descendant

**descenso** [deh•SEHN•soh] *n* M
descent

**descifrar** [DEH•see•FRAHR] *vt*
decipher; decode

**disciplina** [DIH•sih•PLEEN•ah]
*n* F discipline

**descomponer**
[DEHS•kohm•POHN•air] *vi*
decompose

**desconfiado**
[dehs•KON•fee•AH•doh] *adj*
distrustful

**desconfianza**
[dehs•KOHN•fee•AHN•sah] *n*
F distrust; mistrust

**desconocer**
[dehs•KOH•noh•SAIR] *vt*
ignore

**descontentar**
[dehs•KON•ten•TAHR] *vt*
dissatisfy

**descontento**
[dehs•KOHN•ten•TOH] *adj*
disgruntled

**desconvenir**
[dehs•KOHN•ven•EER] *vi*
disagree

**descorazonar**
[DEHS•kor•ah•SON•ahr] *vt*
dishearten; discourage

**descorchar** [DEHS•kor•CHAR]
*vt* uncork

**descraciado**
[DEHS•grah•SEE•AH•do] *adj*
hapless

**describir** [deh•SKREE•beer] *vt*
describe

**descripción**
[DEH•skrihp•SEE•ohn] *n* F
description

**descubrimiento**
[deh•SKOO•bree•MEE•EN•
toh] *n* M discovery;
disclosure; detection

**descubrir** [deh•SKOO•breer] *vt*
discover; uncover; unveil;
disclose

**descuento** [dehs•KWEN•toh] *n*
M discount

**descuidado 1**
[DEHS•kwee•DAH•do] *adj*
careless; reckless; slattern

**descuidado 2**
[DEHS•kwee•DAH•do] *adj*
unsuspecting; unwary; estar ~\
not to worry; rest assured

**descuidar** [DEHS•kwee•DAHR]
*vt* neglect; disregard

**descuido** [dehs•KWEE•doh] *n*
M disregard

**desde** [DEHS•dai] *adv* hence;
since; ~ hace poco\ for a short
time; de ~\ from ~ luego\ of
course; ~\ Madrid hasta
Pamplona\ from Madrid to
Pamplona

**desdeñar** [dehs•DAIN•yahr] *vt*
scorn; spurn

**deseable** [DEH•sai•AHB•lai]
*udj* desirable

**desear** [DEH•sai•AHR] *vi* wish

**desechado**
[DEHS•ai•CHAH•do] *adj*
outcast

**desembarazar**
[DEHS•sem•BAR•ah•SAHR]
*vt* disengage

**desembarco**
[DEHS•em•BAHR•koh] *n* M
landing

**desencaminado**
[DEHS•en•KAH•mee•NAH•do]
*adj* misleading

**desengañar**
[dehs•EN•gahn•YAHR] *vt*
undeceive

**desenterrar**
[dehs•EN•tair•RAHR] *vt*
unearth

**desenvolver 1**
[dehs•EN•vohl•VAIR] *vt*
develop; *vi* evolve

**desenvolver 2**
[dehs•EN•vol•VAIR] *vt*
unwrap

**deseo** [deh•SAI•oh] *n* M desire;
wish; liking

**deseoso 1** [DEH•sai•OH•soh]
*adj* ambitious

**deseoso 2** [DEH•sai•OH•so]
*adj* willing

**desequilibrado**
[DEHS•eh•KEE•lee•BRAH•do]
*adj* unbalanced

**desertor** [DEH•sair•TOHR] *n*
M deserter

**desesperación**
[DEH•sehs•pair•AH•see•OHN]
*n* F despair; desperation

**desesperado**
[DEHS•eh•SPAIR•AH•doh]
*adj* desperate; hopeless

**desestimar**
[dehs•EH•stee•MAHR] *vt*
underestimate

**desfalcar** [DEHS•fal•SAHR] *vt*
embezzle

**desfigurar** [des•FIH•goo•AHR]
*vt* deface; disfigure

**desgajar** [DEHS•gah•HAR] *vt*
disrupt

**desgarbado**
[DEHS•gahr•BAH•do] *adj*
awkward

**desgarrar** [DEHS•gahr•RAHR]
*vt* shred; tear

**desgracia** [DEHS•grah•SEE•ah]
*n* F disgrace

**desgreñado**
[DEHS•gren•AH•doh] *adj*
dishevelled

**deshacer** [DEHS•ah•SAIR] *vt*
undo

**deshelar** [DEHS•ai•LAHR] *vi*
thaw

**deshidratar**
[dehs•EE•drah•TAHR] *vt*
dehydrate

**deshielo** [DEHS•ee•AI•loh] *n*
M debacle

**deshonor** [DEHS•on•OR] *n* M
dishonor

**deshonroso**
[DEHS•on•ROH•so] *adj*
disgraceful

**desierto** [DEH•see•AIR•toh] *n*
M desert

**desigual** [dehs•EE•gwahl] *adj*
unequal; inequal

**desigualdad**
[dehs•EE•gwahl•DAHD] *n* F
inequality

**desilusión**
[DEHS•ih•LOO•see•OHN] *n*
F disappointment; disillusion

**desinfectante**
[dehs•IN•fehk•TAHN•tai] *n* M
disinfectant

**desinfectar**
[dehs•IN•fehk•TAHR] *vt*
disinfect

**desinflar** [DES•in•FLAHR] *vt*
deflate

**desintegrar**
[dehs•IN•teh•GRAHR] *vi*
disintegrate

**desinteresado**
[DEHS•in•TAIR•eh•SAH•doh]
*adj* disinterested

**desistir** [DEH•sih•STEER] *vi*
desist

**desliz** [dehs•LEES] *n* F mishap;
accident

**deslizarse**
[DEHS•lee•SAHR•sai] *vi*
creep; glide

**deslumbrante**
[DEHS•loom•BRAHN•tai] *n*
M glare

**deslustrar**
[DEHS•loo•STRAHR] *vt*
tarnish

**desmayarse**
[DEHS•mai•YAHR•sai] *vi*
swoon

**desmayo** [dehs•MAI•yo] *n* M
dismay

**desmemoriado**
[dehs•mem•OR•ee•AH•do] *adj*
M oblivious

**desmenuzar**
[DEHS•men•OO•sahr] *vt*
mince

**desmontar**
[DEHS•mon•TAHR] *vt*
dismount

**desmoralizar**
[DES•mohr•ah•LEE•sahr] *vt*
demoralize

**desmovilizar**
[des•MOH•vih•lih•SAHR] *vt*
demobilize; disarm

**desnatar** [DEHS•nah•TAHR] *vt*
skim

**desnudar** [DEHS•noo•DAHR]
*vt* strip (clothes); *vi vt* undress

**desnudez** [DEHS•noo•DEHS] *n*
F nakedness; nudity

**desnudo** [dehs•NOO•do] *adj*
bare; naked

**desobedecer**
[DEHS•oh•beh•DAI•SAIR] *vt*
disobey

**desobediente**
[DEHS•oh•BAI•dee•EN•tai]
*adj* disobedient

**desocupación 1**
[dehs•OHK•oo•PAH•see•OHN]
*n* F leisure

**desocupación 2**
[dehs•OHK•oo•PAH•see•OHN]
*n* F unemployment

**desocupado**
[dehs•OHK•oo•PAH•do] *adj*
unemployed

**desolado** [DEH•soh•LAH•doh]
*adj* desolate; forlorn

**desorden** [dehs•ORD•en] *n* M
mess; disorder; disarray; poner
en ~\ clutter

**desordenar**
[DEHS•or•DEN•ahr] *vt*
confuse

**desorganizado**
[DEHS•or•GAHN•ih•SAH•doh]
*adj* disorganized

**desorientado**
[DEHS•or•EE•en•TAH•doh]
*adj* disoriented

**despacho** [dehs•PAH•cho] *n* M
transaction

**despacho de billetes**
[dehs•PAH•cho dai] *n* M
ticket office

**despechar**
[DEHS•peh•CHAHR] *vt* wean

**despecho** [dehs•PAI•cho ] *n* M
spite; a ~ de *prep*\ despite

**despedir 1** [DEHS•pai•DFER]
*vt* dismiss

**despedir 2** [DEHS•pai•DEER]
*vt* spill

**despedir plantado**
[DEHS•pai•DEER
plahn•TAH•do] *vt* jilt

**despejo** [dehs•PAI•ho] *n* M
clearance

**despensa** [deh•SPEN•sah] *n* F
pantry

**despensero**
[DEH•spen•SAIR•oh] *n* M
butler

**despertado**
[DEH•spair•TAH•do] *n* M
alarm clock

**despertar** [DEH•spair•TAHR]
*vt* rouse; *vi* wake; waken

**despiadado**
[dehs•PEE•ah•DAH•do] *adj*
pitiless

**despido** [dehs•PEE•doh] *n* M
dismissal

**despierto** [DEH•spee•AIR•to]
*adj* awake

**desplacer** [DEHS•plah•SAIR]
*vt* displease

**desplegar** [DEHS•plai•GAHR]
*vt* flaunt

**despojar 1** [DEHS•poh•HAHR]
*vt* deprive

**despojar 2** [DEHS•poh•HAR]
*vt* plunder

**desposeer** [DEHS•poh•SAI•air]
*vt* evict

**déspota** [DEH•SPOH•tah] *n* F
despot

**despótico** [dehs•POH•TEE•koh]
*adj* M arbitrary

**despreciable**
[dehs•PRAI•see•AB•lai] *adj*
contemptible; despicable

**despreciar**
[DEHS•prai•see•AHR] *vt*
despise

**desprecio**
[DEHS•preh•SEE•OH] *n* M
contempt

**desprevenido**
[dehs•PREH•ven•EE•do] *adj*
unaware

**después** [deh•SPOO•AIS] *prep*
*adv* after; thereafter; ~ de/que\
after; ~ de todo\ after all;
poco ~\ soon after

**desputar** [dehs•PEW•tahr] *v*
dispute; nip; cut off (a point);
be clear or witty; *n* F dispute;
argument

**desquitarse**
[DEHS•kee•TAHR•sai] *vi*
retaliate

**desquite** [dehs•KEE•tai] *n* M
retaliation

**destarar** [DEHS•tahr•AHR] *n*
tare; weed

**destello** [deh•STAI•yo] *n* M
flare; gleam; spangle

**desterrar** [DEHS•tair•RAHR] *vt*
banish

**destierro** [DEH•stee•AIR•øh] *n*
M exile

**destilar** [deh•STEEL•ahr] *vi vt*
distill

**destilería** [DEH•stihl•air•EE•ah]
*n* F distillery

**destinación**
[DEH•stee•NAH•see•OHN] *n*
F destination

**destino** [deh•STEE•noh] *n* M
destiny; fate

**destituido**
[deh•STIH•too•EE•doh] *adj*
destitute

**destornillador**
[DEHS•tor•NEE•yah•DOR] *n*
M screw-driver

**destral** [DEH•strahl] *n* M
hatchet

**destreza** [deh•STREH•sah] *n* F
sleight

**destrizar** [DEHS•tree•SAHR] *vt*
crumble

**destrucción**
[deh•STROOHK•see•OHN] *n*
F destruction

**destructivo**
[DEH•struhk•TEE•voh] *adj*
destructive

**destruido** [DEH•stroo•EE•doh]
*adj* extinct

**destruir** [DEH•stroo•EER] *vt*
destroy; raze

**desunir** [DEHS•oo•NEER] *vt*
disconnect; disunite

**desvalido** [DEHS•vah•LEE•do]
*adj* helpless

**desventaja**
[DEHS•ven•TAH‚ha] *n* F
disadvantage

**desviado** [DEHS•vee•AH•doh]
*adj* devious

**desviar 1** [DEHS•vee•AHR] *vtr*
deflect; turn away, aside or off

**desviar 2** [DEHS•vee•AHR] *vi*
deviate; go off; exit; swerve

**desviar 3** [DEHS•vee•AHR] *vt*
divert avert one's eyes

**desviarse** [DEHS•vee•AHR•šai]
*vi* digress; stray

**desvío** [dehs•VEE•oh] *n* M
detour; shunt

**detallado** [DAI•tai•YAH•doh]
*adj* elaborate

**detallar** [DEH•tai•YAHR] *vt*
itemize

**detalle** [deh•TAI•yea] *n* M
detail; al ~\ in detail; con todo
~\ in great detail

**detallista** [DEH•tai•YEE•stah]
*n* F retailer

**detención**
[DEH•ten•SEE•OHN] *n* F
detention; stoppage

**detener 1** [DEH•tchn•AIR] *vt*
detain; withhold; arrest; hinder

**detener 2** [DEH•ten•AIR] *vt*
deter; hold off; keep off

**detergente** [DAI•tair•HEN•tai]
*n* M detergent

**deteriorar**
[dai•TAIR•ee•oh•AHR] *vt*
deteriorate; spoil

**determinación**
[dai•TAIR•mihn•AH•see•OHN]
*n* F determination

**determinar**
[dai•TAIR•mee•NAHR] *vt*
determine

**detestar** [DAI•teh•STAHR] *vt*
detest

**de tiple** [dai TEP•lai] *n* M
treble clef

**detonar** [DEH•toh•NAHR] *vi*
detonate

**detractor** [DEH•trahk•TOHR]
*adj* disparaging

**detraer** [DEH•trai•AIR] *vt*
detract

**detrás** [dai•TRAHS] *prep adv*
behind; back; ~ de\ behind;
por ~\ on the back (of)

**detener** [DAI•ten•AIR] *vt* stop

**deuda** [DOI•dah] *n* F debt

**deudor** [DOI•dor] *n* M debtor

**devanar** [deh•VAHN•AHR] *vt*
unwind

**devastador**
[deh•VAH•stah•DOHR] *adj*
devastating

**devastar 1** [DEH•vah•STAHR]
*vt* devastate

**devastar 2** [DEH•vah•STAHR]
*vt* waste

**de viaje** [dai vee•AH•hai] *adv*
traveling

**devoción** [DEH•voh•see•OHN]
*n* F devotion

**devorar** [DEH•vor•AHR] *vt*
devour

**devoto** [DEH•VOH•toh] *adj*
devout

**día** [DEE•ah] *n* M day

**diabético**
[DEE•ah•BAI•tih•koh] *adj n*
M diabetic

**diabetis** [DEE•ah•BAI•tis] *n* M
diabetes

**diablillo** [DEE•ahb•LEE•yo] *n*
M imp

**diablo** [dec•AHB•loh] *n* M
devil

**diabólico**
[dee•AH•boh•LEE•koh] *adj*
fiendish

**diabtriba** [DEE•ah•TREE•bah]
*n* F tirade

**día de descanso** [DEE•ah dai
dehs•KAHN•so] *n* M Sabbath

**día de la semana** [DEE•ah dai
lah seh•MAHN•ah] *n* M
weekday

**día de trabajo** [DEE•ah dai] *n*
M workday

**día del juicio final** [DEE•ah del HWE•SEE•oh FEE•nal] *n* M doomsday

**diagnoal** [DEE•ah•GO•nahl] *adj* diagonal

**diagnosis** [DEE•ah•NO•sis] *n* M diagnosis

**diagnosticar** [DEE•ah•NOH•stee•KAHR] *vt* diagnose

**diagrama** [DEE•ah•GRAH•mah] *n* F diagram

**dialecto** [DEE•ah•LEHK•toh] *n* M dialect

**diálogo** [DEE•ah•LOH•goh] *n* M dialog

**diamante** [DEE•ah•MAHN•tai] *n* M diamond

**diámetro** [dee•AH•MEH•troh] *n* M diameter

**diario 1** [dee•AHR•EE•oh] *adj* daily; everyday

**diario 2** [dee•AHR•EE•oh] *n*.M diary; journal

**dibujante** [DIH•boo•HAHN•tai] *n* M designer

**dibujo** [dih•BOO•ho] *n* M drawing

**diccionario** [dih•SEE•ohn•AHR•EE•oh] *n* M dictionary

**diciembre** [DEE•SEE•em•brai] *n* M December

**dictado** [dihk•TAH•doh] *n* M dictation

**dictador** [DIHK•tah•DOR] *n* M dictator

**dictadura** [DIHKT•ah•DOOR•ah] *n* F dictatorship

**dictar** [DIHK•tahr] *vt* dictate

**diecinueve** [DEE•ais•EE•noo•AI•vai] *num* nineteen

**dieciocho** [DEE•ais•ee•OH•cho] *num* eighteen

**dieciseis** [DEE•ais•EE•SAIS] *num* sixteen

**diecisiete** [DEE•ais•EE•see•EH•tai] *num* seventeen

**diente** [dee•EN•tai] *n* M tooth

**diesmo** [dee•EHS•mo] *n* M tithe

**diestro** [dee•AI•stroh] *adj* deft

**diestro** [dee•AI•stroh] *adj* handy

**diestro** [dee•EH•stroh] *adj* skillful

**diestro** [dee•AI•stroh] *adj* slick

**dieta** [dee•EH•tah] *n* M diet

**diez** [dee•AIS] *num* ten

**diezmar** [DEE•ais•MAHR] *vt* decimate

**difamación** [DEE•fah•MAH•see•OHN] *n* F defamation; slander

**difamar** [DEE•fah•MAHR] *vt* defame; malign

**diferencia** [dih•FAIR•en•SEE•ah] *n* F difference

**diferenciar** [dih•FAIR•en•SEE•ahr] *vt* differentiate (between)

**diferente** [DIH•fair•EN•tai] *adj* different

**diferir 1** [DIH•fair•EER] *vt* defer

**diferir 2** [DIH•fair•EER] *vi* differ

**difícil** [dih•FEE•sil] *adj* difficult

**dificultad** [dih•FIH•kuhl•TAHD] *n* F difficulty

**difundir 1** [DEE•fuhn•DEER] *vt* broadcast

**difundir 2** [DIH•fuhn•DEER] *vt* diffuse

**digerir** [DIH•hair•EER] *vt* digest

**digestión** [dih•HEH•stee•OHN] *n* F digestion

**dignidad** [DIHG•nih•DAHD] *n* dignity

**dignificado** [dihg•NIH•fee•KAH•doh] *adj* dignified

**dignificar** [dihg•NIH•fee•KAHR] *vt* dignify

**dilatar 1** [DEE•lah•TAHR] *vt* delay; halt; stop; keep open

**dilatar 2** [DEE•lah•TAHR] *vt* dilate

**dilema** [dih•LAI•mah] *n* F dilemma

**diligencia** [dih•LIH•hen•SEE•ah] *n* F diligence

**diligente** [DIH•lih•HEN•tai] *adj* diligent

**diluir** [DIH•loo•EER] *vt* dilute

**diluvio** [DEH•loo•VEE•oh] *n* M deluge; flood

**dimensión** [DIH•men•SEE•OHN] *n* F dimension

**dimitir** [DIH•mih•TEER] *vt* resign

**Dinamarca** [DIHN•ah•MAHR•ka] *n* Denmark

**dinámico** [dee•NAH•MEE•koh] *adj n* M dynamic

**dinamita** [DEE•nah•MEE•tah] *n* F dynamite

**dinastía** [DEE•nah•STEE•ah] *n* F dynasty

**dinero** [dih•NAIR•oh] *n* M money; ~ effectivo\ cash; ~ suelto\ change

**dinsaurio** [DEE•no•SAU•REE•oh] *n* M dinosaur

**diócesis** [dee•OH•seh•SIS] *n* M diocese

**Dios** [DEE•ohs] *n* M God

**diosa** [dee•OH•sa] *n* F goddess

**diploma** [dih•PLOH•mah] *n* F diploma

**diplomacia** [dih•PLOH•mah•SEE•ah] *n* F diplomacy

**diplomado** [DIH•ploh•MAH•do] *adj* competent; qualified

**diplomático** *adj* diplomatic

**diplomático** [dih•PLOH•mah•TEE•koh] *n* M diplomat

**diputado** [DIH•poo•TAH•doh] *n* M deputy

**dique** [DEE•kai] *n* M dam

**dirección 1** [dee•REHK•see•OHN] *n* F address; direction; de una sola ~\ one-way

**dirección 2** [dihr•REHK•sec•OHN] *n* F leadership

**directamente** [dee•REHK•tah•MEN•tai] *adv* directly

**directo** [dee•REHK•toh] *adj*
direct; undeviating

**director 1** [DEE•rehk•TOHR] *n*
M director; manager;
controller

**director 2** [DEE•rehk•TOR] *n*
M editor

**directorio**
[DIH•rehk•TOHR•EE•oh] *n* M
directory

**dirigir 1** [DEER•ih•HEER] *vt*
address

**dirigir 2** [DEER•ih•HEER] *vt*
edit

**dirigir 3** [DEER•ih•HEER] *vt*
manage; operate

**discernimiento**
[dih•SAIR•nee•MEE•EN•to] *n*
M insight

**discernir** [DIH•sair•NEER] *vt*
discern; discriminate

**disminuirse**
[DIHS•min•WEER•sai] *vi*
dwindle

**disputa** [dihs•PEW•tah] *n* F
dispute

**disco** [DIH•sko] *n* M disk

**díscolo** [dee•SKOH•lo] *adj*
wayward

**discordancia**
[dihs•KOHR•dan•SEE•ah] *n* F
disagreement

**discordia** [DIHS•kor•DEE•ah] *n*
F discord

**discreción**
[dih•SKREH•see•OHN] *n* F
discretion

**discrédito** [DIH•krai•DEE•toh]
*n* M discredit

**discrepancia**
[dih•SKREH•pahn•SEE•ah] *n*
F discrepancy

**discreto** [dih•SKREH•toh] *adj*
discreet

**discución**
[dih•SKOO•see•OHN] *n* F
discussion

**disculpa** [dih•SKOOL•pah] *n* F
apology

**disculpar** [dih•SKOOL•pahr] *vi*
apologize

**discurso** [dih•SKOOR•soh] *n* M
discourse

**discutir** [DIH•skoo•TEER] *vt*
discuss

**disecar** [DEE•seh•KAHR] *vt*
dissect

**diseminar**
[dih•SEHM•ee•NAHR] *vt*
disseminate

**disenso** [dih•SEN•soh] *n* M
dissent

**disfraz1** [dihs•FRAHS] *n* M
disguise

**disfraz 2** [dihs•FRAHS] *n* M
travesty

**disgusto** [dihs•GOO•stoh] *n* M
distaste; disgust

**disidencia**
[dih•SIH•den•SEE•ah] *n* F
separatism

**disidente** [DIH•sih•DEN•tai] *n*
*adj* M nonconformist

**disimular**
[dih•SIHM•ew•LAHR] *vi* *vt*
dissimulate; dissemble

**disimulo** [DIHS•ih•MOO•lo] *n*
M stealth

**disípulo** [DIH•see•POO•loh] *n*
M disciple

**dislocar** [DIHS•lo•KAHR] *vt*
displace; dislocate

**disminuir** [dihs•MIHN•oo•EER]
   *vt vi* diminish; minimize;
   shrink; taper

**disociar** [dish•SOH•see•AHR] *vt*
   dissociate

**disoluto** [DIH•soh•LOO•toh]
   *adj* M dissolute

**disolver** [DIH•sohl•VAIR] *vt*
   dissolve

**disparate** [DIHS•pahr•AH•tai]
   *n* M blunder

**dispensador**
   [dih•SPEHN•sah•DOHR] *n* M
   dispenser

**dispensar** [DIH•spen•SAHR] *vt*
   dispense; dispel; disperse;
   dissipate; scatter

**disponer** [DIHS•pon•AIR] *vt*
   dispose

**disposición 1**
   [dih•SPOH•zih•see•ØHN] *n* F
   disposal

**disposición 2**
   [dih•SPOH•zih•see•ØHN] *n* F
   disposition

**dispositivo**
   [dihs•POH•see•TEE•vo] *n* M
   device

**disputa** [dihs•PEW•tah] *n* F
   dispute; argument; brawl;
   feud; squabble

**disputar 1** [DIS•pew•TAHR] *vi*
   bicker; argue; squabble

**disputar 2** [DIHS•pew•TAHR]
   *vt* contest; challenge

**distancia** [DIH•stahn•SEE•ah] *n*
   F distance

**distante** [DIH•STAHN•tai] *adj*
   distant

**distinguir** [DIH•sting•GWEER]
   *vt* distinguish

**distinto** [dih•STEEN•toh] *adj*
   distinct

**distraer** [DIS•trai•AIR] *vt*
   distract

**distraído 1** [DIH•strai•EE•doh]
   *adj* absent-minded

**distraído 2** [DIH•strai•EE•doh]
   *adj* distraught

**distribución**
   [DIH•strih•BEW•see•OHN] *n*
   F distribution

**distribuir** [DIH•strih•boo•EER]
   *vt* distribute

**distrito** [dih•STREE•to] *n* M
   district

**disturbio** [DIH•stoor•BEE•oh] *n*
   M trouble; disturbance

**disuadir** [DIH•swa•DEER] *vt*
   dissuade

**divergir** [DEE•vair•HEER] *vi*
   diverge

**diversidad**
   [DEE•vair•SEE•dahd] *n* F
   diversity

**diversificar**
   [DEE•vair•sih•FEE•kahr] *vt*
   diversify

**diversión** [DIH•vair•see•OHN]
   *n* F entertainment

**diverso** [dee•VAIR•soh] *adj*
   diverse

**divertido** [DEE•vair•TEE•do]
   *adj* fun; amusing

**divertir** [DEE•vair•TEER] *vt*
   amuse; entertain

**dividir** [DIH•vee•DEER] *vt*
   divide

**divinidad** [DIH•vih•nee•DAHD]
   *n* F divinity

**divino** [dih•VEEN•oh] *adj*
   divine

**división** [dih•VIH•see•OHN] *n*
F division; partition; cleavage

**divorcio** [DIH•vor•SEE•oh] *n* M
divorce

**divulgar** [DIH•vool•GAHR] *vt*
divulge

**doblar** [DOH•blahr] *vt vi* flex

**doble** [DO•blai] *adj* double

**doble vista** [DOH•blai
VEE•stah] *n* F double vision

**doblemente**
[DOH•bleh•MEN•tai] *adv*
doubly

**doblez** [doh•BLAIS] *n* M fold;
*n* F pleat

**doce** [DOH•sai] *num* twelve

**docena** [doh•SAI•nah] *n* F
dozen

**dócil** [DOH•seel] *adj* gentle;
docile; tame

**doctor** [DOHK•tor] *n* M doctor

**doctorado**
[DOHK•tor•AH•doh] *n*
doctorate

**doctrina** [DOHK•tree•NAH] *n*
F doctrine

**documento**
[DOHK•ew•MEN•toh] *n* M
document

**dogma** [DOHG•mah] *n* F
dogma

**doler** [DOH•lair] *vi* ache

**dolor** [DOH•lohr] *n* M grief;
pain; sorrow; woe; distress

**dolor de cabeza** [DOH•lor dai
kah•BAI•sah] *n* M headache

**dolor de diente** [DOH•lor dai]
*n* M toothache

**dolor del estómago** [DOH•lor
dai] *n* M stomachache

**doloroso** [DOH•loh•ROH•so]
*adj* painful; grievous

**dollar** [doy•YAHR] *n* M dollar

**doméstico**
[DOH•meh•STEE•koh] *adj*
domestic

**domicilio**
[DOH•mih•SEEL•EE•oh] *n* M
abode

**dominado**
[DOH•mee•NAH•doh] *adj*
compelling

**dominador**
[DOH•mee•NAH•dor] *adj*
overbearing

**dominante**
[DOH•mih•NAHN•tai] *adj*
dominant; domineering

**dominar** [DOH•mee•NAHR] *vi*
dominate; control

**Domingo de Ramos**
[doh•MING•go dai
RAH•mohs] *n* M Palm
Sunday

**dominio de sí mismo**
[DOH•min•EE•oh] *adj*
self-control

**donación** [doh•NAH•see•OHN]
*n* F donation

**donador** [DOH•nah•DOHR] *n*
M donor

**doña** [doh•NYAH] Mrs. — (in
address)

**donar** [DOH•nahr] *vt* donate

**doncella** [don•SAI•yah] *n* F
maid

**donde** [DON•dai] *prep* where

**dónde** [DON•dai] *prep* where;
¿hasta ~?\ where?; ¿por ~?\
whereabouts; ¿a ~ vas?\

where are you going?; ¿de ~
eras?\ where are you from?

**dondequiera**
[DOHN•dai•kee•AIR•ah] *adv*
everywhere; anywhere; *prep*
wherever; ~ que\ wherever;
por ~\ everywhere

**dorado** [dor•AH•do] *adj* gilded;
plated

**dormido** [dor•MEE•do] *adv*
asleep

**dormir** [dor•MEER] *vi* sleep;
echarse a ~\ go to bed

**dormitar** [DOR•mee•TAHR] *vi*
doze

**dormitorio**
[dor•MIH•tor•EE•oh] *n* M
bedroom; dormitory

**dos** [dohs] *num* two

**dos veces** [dohs VAI•sais] *num*
twice

**dosel** [DOH•sel] *n* M canopy

**dosis** [DOH•sis] *n* M dose

**dote** [DOH•tai] *n* M dowry

**dragón** [drah•GOHN] *n* M
dragon

**drama** [DRAH•mah] *n* M
drama

**dramático**
[DRAH•MAH•tee•koh] *adj*
dramatic

**dramatizar**
[DRAH•mah•TEE•sahr] *vt*
dramatize

**dramaturgo**
[DRAH•mah•TOOR•go] *n* M
dramatist

**drástico** [DRAH•stee•koh] *adj*
drastic

**droga** [DROH•gah] *n* F drug;
dope

**droguero** [droh•GAIR•oh] *n* M
druggist

**dual** [DOO•ahl] *adj* M dual

**ducha** [DOO•cha] *n* F shower

**duda** [DOO•dah] *n* F doubt;
misgivings

**dudoso** [doo•DOH•soh] *adj*
dubious; doubtful

**duelo** [dwai•loh] *n* M duel

**dueño** [DWAIN•yo] *n* M
owner; employer

**duende** [DWEN•dai] *n* M
goblin

**dueto** [doo•TEH•toh] *n* M duet

**dulce** [DUHL•sai] *adj* sweet

**dulce de chocolate** [DUHL•sai
dai CHOH•koh•LAH•tai] *n* F
fudge

**dulzura** [duhl•SOOR•ah] *n* F
sweetness

**duna** [DOO•nah] *n* F dune

**duodécimo**
[doo•OH•deh•SEE•mo] *num*
twelfth

**duplicado 1**
[DOOP•lih•KAH•doh] *n* M
counterpart

**duplicado 2**
[DOO•plih•KAH•doh] *adj n*
M duplicate

**duplicar** [DOO•plih•KAHR] *vt*
duplicate

**duplicidad**
[doo•PLIH•sih•DAHD] *n* F
duplicity

**duque** [DOO•kai] *n* M duke

**duquesa** [doo•KAI•sah] *n* F
duchess

**durable** [doo•RAHB•lai] *adj*
durable

**duración** [door•AH•see•OHN] *n* F duration

**duradero** [DOOR•ah•DAIR•oh] *adj* lasting; durable

**durante** [door•AHN•tai] *adv* while; during

**durazno** [door•AHS•no] *n* M peach

**durmiente** [DOOR•mee•EN•tai] *n* M sleeper; *adj* sleeping

**duro 1** [DOOR•oh] *adj* firm; hard

**duro 2** [DOO•ro] *adj* stern

# E

**e** [eh] *conj* and

**ébano** [EH•BAH•no] *n* M ebony

**eclesiástico** [eh•KLAI•see•AHS•TEE•koh] *adj* ecclesiastic

**eclipse** [eh•klihp•sai] *n* M eclipse

**eco** [EH•koh] *n* M echo

**ecología** [eh•KOH•loh•HEE•ah] *n* F ecology

**economía 1** [eh•KOHN•oh•MEE•ah] *n* F economics; economy; *adj* economic; economical

**economía 2** [eh•KON•oh•MEE•ah] *n* F thrift

**ecuación** [eh•KWAH•see•OHN] *n* F equation

**ecuador** [eh•KWAH•dohr] *n* M equator

**echada** [ai•CHA•dah] *n* F pitch

**echar** [ai•CHAR] *vt* cast off; eject; fling; pour

**echar a correr** [ai•CHAR ah KOR•rair] *vi* scurry; hasten

**echar el aire** [eh•CHAR el AI rai] *vt* toss

**echar fuera** [eh•CHAR FWAIR•ah] *vi* throw out

**edad** [ai•DAHD] *n* F age

**edición** [EH•dih•SEE•OHN] *n* F edition

**edicto** [eh•DEÉK•to] *n* M ban

**edificio** [EH•dih•FEE•SEE•oh] *n* M building

**editorial** [EH•dih•TOR•ee•AHL] *adj n* F editorial

**educación** [EH•doo•KAH•see•OHN] *n* F education

**educar** [EH•doo•KAHR] *vt* educate

**educativo** [eh•DOO•kah•TEE•voh] *adj* educational

**educir** [EH•doo•SEER] *vt* elicit

**efectivo 1** [EH•fehk•TEE•vo] *n* M cash

**efectivo 2** [EH•fehk•TEE•voh] *adj* effective

**efecto** [eh•FEHK•toh] *n* M effect

**efectuar** [eh•FEHK•too•AHR]
*vi* perform

**efervescencia**
[EH•fair•VEH•sen•SEE•ah] *n*
F fizz; effervescence

**eficiencia**
[eh•FIH•SEE•en•SEE•ah] *n* F
efficiency

**eficiente** [eh•FIH•see•EHN•tai]
*adj* efficient

**egipcio** [AI•gip•SEE•oh] *adj*
Egyptian

**Egipto** [ai•GIP•toh] *n* Egypt

**ego** [AI•goh] *n* M ego

**egoísmo** [AI•go•EES•moh] *n* M
selfishness

**egoísta** [AI•goh•EE•stah] *n* F
selfish

**egotista** [AI•go•TEE•stah] *n* M
egotist

**eh** [eh] *excl* hey

**eje** [AI•hai] *n* M axle

**ejecución 1**
[EH•he•KEW•see•OHN] *n* F
execution

**ejecución 2**
[EH•he•KOO•see•OHN] *n* F
performance

**ejecutar** [eh•HEK•yo•TAHR] *vt*
execute

**ejecutivo**
[EH•HEK•ew•TEE•voh] *adj*
executive

**ejecutor** [eh•HE•kew•TOHR] *n*
M executioner

**ejemplar** [EH•hem•PLAHR] *adj*
exemplary

**ejemplificar**
[eh•HEM•plih•fih•KAHR] *vt*
exemplify

**ejemplo 1** [eh•HEM•plo] *n* M
example; pattern

**ejemplo 2** [eh•HEM•ploh] *n* M
instance

**ejercer** [EH•hair•SAIR] *vt* exert;
wield

**ejercicio** [eh•HAIR•see•SEE•øh]
*n* M exercise

**ejército** [EH•hair•SEE•toh] *n* M
army

**él** [ehl] *pers pron* he

**él; él mismo** [ehl] [ehl
mees•moh] *pron* himself

**él; ella** [ehl] [AI•yah] *pron* it

**el; la; lo; los; las** [ehl] [lah] [lo]
[lohs] [lahs] the

**elástico** [ai•LAH•STEE•koh]
*adj n* M elastic

**elección 1** [eh•LEHK•see•OHN]
*n* F election

**elección 2** [eh•LEHK•see•OHN]
*n* F option

**electricidad**
[EH•lek•TREE•sih•DAHD] *n*
F electricity

**eléctrico** [EH•lehk•TREE•koh]
*adj* electric

**electrocutar**
[EH•lehk•TRO•kew•TAHR] *vt*
electrocute

**electrónico**
[EH•LEHK•tron•EE•koh] *adj*
electronic

**elefante** [EH•leh•FAN•tai] *n* M
elephant

**elegancia**
[EH•leh•HAHN•SEE•ah] *n* F
elegance

**elegante** [EH•leh•GAHN•tai]
*adj* elegant; stylish

**elegible** [EH•leh•HEEB•lai] *adj*
eligible

**elegir** [EH•leh•HEER] *vt* elect

**elemental** [EH•leh•MEN•tahl]
*adj* elementary

**elemento 1** [EH•leh•MEN•toh]
*n* M element

**elemento 2** [EH•leh•MEN•toh]
*n* M item

**elevador** [eh•LEH•vah•DOR] *n*
M elevator

**elevar** [EH•leh•VAHR] *vt*
heighten

**elevar levantar**
[EH•lai•VAHR]
[lai•VAHN•tahr] *vt* elevate

**eliminar** [eh•LIHM•ee•NAHR]
*vt* eliminate

**elocuencia**
[eh•LOH•kwen•SEE•ah] *n* F
eloquence

**elocuente** [EH•loh•KWEN•tai]
*adj* eloquent

**elogio** [EH•loh•HEE•oh] *n* M
eulogy

**eludir** [EH•loo•DEER] *vt* elude

**ella** [AI•ya] *pron* she; her; it

**ella misma** [AI•ya MEES•mah]
*pron* herself

**ello** [AI•yo] *pron* he his it

**ellos; ellas** [AIY•yos]
[AIY•yahs] they; theirs

**emanar** [EH•mahn•AHR] *vi*
emanate

**emancipación**
[eh•MAHN•sih•PAH•see•
OHN] *n* F emancipation

**embajada** [EHM•bah•HA•dah]
*n* F embassy

**embajador**
[ehm•BAH•hah•RAH•DOHR]
*n* M ambassador

**embarazada**
[em•BAHR•ah•SAH•dah] *adj*
pregnant

**embarazar 1**
[EM•bahr•ah•SAHR] *vt*
embarrass

**embarazar 2**
[EM•bahr•ah•SAHR] *vt vi*
clog

**embarazo** [EM•bahr•AH•so] *n*
M embarrassment

**embarazoso**
[em•BAHR•ah•ZO•soh] *adj*
embarrassed

**embarcadero**
[em•BAHR•kah•DAIR•oh] *n*
M pier; wharf

**embargo** [em•BAHR•go] *n* M
embargo

**embarrancar**
[em•BAHR•rahn•KAHR] *vi*
strand

**embellecer**
[em•BEH•yeh•SAIR] *vt*
embellish

**embestida** [EM•beh•STEE•dah]
*n* F attack

**embestidar**
[em•BEH•stee•DAHR] *vt vi*
attack

**embetunar**
[em•BAI•too•NAHR] *vt*
blacken

**emblema** [ehm•BLEM•ah] *n* F
emblem; badge; stripe

**embotado 1** [EM•bo•TAH•do]
*adj* blunt

**embotado 2**
[EM•boh•TAH•do] *adj* jaded

**embotado romo**
[EM•boh•TAH•doh]
[ROH•moh] *adj* dull

**embrague** [ehm•BRAH•hai] *n* M clutch

**embriagar** [em•BREE•ah•GAHR] *adj* inebriated

**embriaguez** [em•BREE•ah•GWAIS] *n* F drunkenness

**embrión** [EM•bree•OHN] *n* F embryo

**embrollar** [EM•broi•YAHR] *vt* mix up; involve

**embrollo** [em•BROI•yo] *n* M muddle

**emergencia** [eh•MAIR•hen•SEE•ah] *n* F emergency

**emerger** [EM•air•HAIR] *vi* emerge

**emigrante** [eh•MIH•GRAHN•tai] *n* M emigrant

**emigrar** [EH•mee•GRAHR] *vi* emigrate; migrate

**eminencia** [eh•MIH•nen•SEE•ah] *n* F eminence

**eminente** [EH•mih•NEN•tai] *adj* eminent

**emisario** [eh•MIH•sahr•EE•oh] *n* M emissary

**emisión** [eh•MIH•see•OHN] *n* F emission

**emitir** [eh•MIH•TEER] *vt* emit

**emocionante** [eh•MO•see•oh•NAN•tai] *n* M stirring

**empapar** [EM•pah•PAHR] *vt* soak; steep

**empaque** [ehm•PAH•kai] *n* M packing

**empeñado** [EM•pain•YAH•do] *adj* in debt; empeñadarse *vt \* get into debt

**empeñar** [EM•pain•YAHR] *vt* engage

**emperador** [em•PAIR•ah•DOHR] *n* M emperor

**emperatriz** [em•PAIR•ah•TREES] *n* F empress

**empesar** [EM•pai•SAHR] *vi* start

**empezar** [EM•pai•SAHR] *vt vi* begin; para ~\ to begin with

**empleado** [EHM•plai•AH•doh] *n* M clerk; employee

**emplear** [EM•plai•AHR] *vt* employ

**empleo** [em•PLAI•oh] *n* M employment

**emprenado** [EM•pren•AH•do] *pp* undertaken

**emprendedor** [em•PREHN•deh•DOHR] *n* M enterprise; *adj* enterprising

**emprender** [EM•pren•DAIR] *vt* undertake

**empresa** [em•PRAI•sah] *n* F undertaking

**empresario** [em•PREH•SAHR•EE•oh] *n* M undertaker

**empujar** [EM•poo•HAHR] *vt* push; shove; thrust; boost

**empujón** [EHM•poo•HON] *n* M hustle

**emular 1** [EM•yoo•LAHR] *vt* emulate

**emular 2** [EM•oo•LAHR] *vi* vie

**en** [en] *prep* in; on; inside; at ~ casa\ at home; ~ auto\ by car; en 5 días\ in five days

**enamorado** [en•AH•mor•AH•do] *adj* in love (with); enamored

**enano** [en•AHN•o] *n* M runt; dwarf

**encaje** [en•KAH•hai] *n* M socket

**encandilar** [en•CAHN•dee•LAHR] *vt* dazzle

**encantador** [en•KAHN•tah•DOHR] *adj* M charming

**encantamiento** [en•KAHN•tah•MEE•EN•toh] *n* M charm

**encantar** [EN•kahn•TAHR] *vt* enchant

**encanto 1** [en•KAHN•toh] *n* M delight

**encanto 2** [en•KAHN•to] *n* M glamor

**encarcelar** [EN•kahr•SEH•lahr] *vt* imprison

**encargado** [EN•kahr•GAH•do] *n* M foreman

**encarnar** [EN•kahr•NAHR] *vt* embody

**encendedor** [en•SEN•deh•DOR] *n* M lighter

**encender** [EN•sen•DAIR] *vt* ignite; kindle

**encerrar** [EN•sair•RAHR] *vt* enclose

**enciclopedia** [en•SEE•klo•pai•DEE•ah] *n* F encyclopedia

**encima** [en•SEE•mah] *adv* thereon; on top of; ~ de\ on, on top of; over; por ~\ on top; por ~ de todo\ above all; *prep* upon; *adv* above

**encogado** [EN•koh•HAH•do] *adj* shrunk

**encogerse** [EN•koh•HAIR•sai] *vi* cringe

**encogimiento** [EN•koh•EE•mee•EN•to] *n* M shrinkage

**encomendar** [en•KOH•men•DAHR] *vt* commend

**encontrado** *pp* [en•KOHN•TRAH•do] found

**encontrar** [EN•kohn•TRAHR] *vt* meet

**encontrarse** [en•KOHN•TRAR•sai] *vi* occur

**encorvar** [EN•kohr•VAHR] *vt* *vi* flex; *vt* bend

**encuentro** [en•KWEN•troh] *n* encounter; find; bout; affair

**endentecer** [EN•den•TEH•sair] *vi* teethe

**endosar** [EN•doh•SAHR] *vt* endorse

**endulzar** [EN•doohl•SAHR] *vt* sweeten

**endurecer** [EN•door•EH•sair] *vt* harden; toughen

**endurencimiento** [EN•door•EH•see•MEE•EN•toh] *n* M toughness

**enemigo** [EN•eh•MEE•go] *n* M enemy; foe

**energía** [EN•air•HEE•ah] *n* F energy

**enérgico** [en•AIR•GEE•koh]
*adj* energetic

**enero** [eh•NAIR•oh] *n* M
January

**enfado** [en•FAH•do] *n* M huff

**énfasis** [EIIN•fah•SIS] *n* M
emphasis

**enfermar** [EN•fair•MAHR] *vi*
sicken

**enfermedad 1**
[EN•fair•MIH•dahd] *n* F
disease

**enfermedad 2**
[EHN•fair•MEH•dahd] *n* F
illness; infirmity; sickness

**enfermero** [EN•fair•MAIR•oh]
*n* M nurse

**enfermizo** [EN•fair•MEE•so]
*adj* sickly

**enfermo** [en•FAIR•moh] *adj* ill;
sick

**enfriar** [en•FREE•ahr] *vt* chill

**enfurecer** [EN•foor•EH•sair] *vt*
enrage; infuriate

**engañar 1** [en•GAHN•yahr] *vt*
deceive; hoodwink

**engañar 2** [en•GAHN•yahr] *vt*
cheat

**engaño** [en•GAN•yo] *n* M
deceit; deception; lure

**engañoso** [EN•gahn•YO•so]
*adj* deceitful

**engendrar** [EN•hen•DRAHR]
*vt* teem

**engolfar** [EN•gohl•FAHR] *vt*
engulf

**engordar** [EN•gor•DAHR] *vt*
fatten

**engrandecer**
[EN•grahn•DEH•sair] *vt*
enhance

**engullir** [EN•goo•YEER] *vt*
gobble; guzzle

**enigma** [en•IG•mah] *n* F riddle;
enigma

**enjuague** [en•HWA•hai] *n* M
mouthwash

**enlace** [en•LAH•sai] *n* M
liaison

**enloquecer** [en•LOH•kai•SAIR]
*vt* madden

**enmaderamiento**
[EN•mah•DAIR•ah•MEE•EN•
to] *n* M woodwork

**enmienda** [EN•mee•EN•dah] *n*
F amendment

**ennegrecer**
[en•NAI•greh•SAIR] *vt*
blacken

**enojado furioso**
[EN•oh•HAH•doh]
[foor•ee•oh•so] *adj* angry

**enojo 1** [en•OH•ho] *n* M anger

**enojo 2** [ehn•OH•ho] *n* M
grouch

**enorme** [eh•NOR•mai] *adj*
enormous

**enredar** [EN•rai•DAHR] *vt*
tangle; confuse

**enriquecer** [en•REE•keh•SAIR]
*vt* enrich

**enrojecer** [en•ROH•he•SAIR] *vt*
redden

**ensalada** [en•SAH•lah•DAH] *n*
F salad

**ensalada de col picada**
[en•SAH•lah•DAH dai kohl
pee•KAH•dah] *n* F slaw

**ensayar** [EN•sai•YAHR] *vt*
rehearse; test

**ensayo 1** [en•SAI•yo] *n* M
essay

**ensayo 2** [en•SAI•yo] *n* M
rehearsal

**enseñado** [EN•sen•YAH•do] *pp*
taught

**enseñanza**
[EN•sen•YAHN•sah] *n* F
tuition

**enseñar** [EN•sen•YAHR] *vt*
teach

**enseros** [EN•sair•OHS] *n* M
paraphernalia

**ensopar** [EN•soh•PAHR] *vt* sop

**ensordecedor**
[EN•sor•DEH•seh•DOHR] *adj*
deafening

**ensordecer** [EN•sor•DEH•sair]
*vt* deafen

**ensuciamiento**
[EN•soo•SEE•ah•MEE•EN•to]
*n* M pollution

**ensueño** [en•SWEN•yo] *n* M
daydream

**entender** [EN•ten•DAIR] *vt*
comprehend; *vi* understand

**entender mal** [EN•ten•DAIR
mahl] *vt* misunderstand

**enteramente**
[en•TAIR•ah•MEN•tai] *adv*
entire; altogether

**enternidad**
[eh•TAIR•nih•DAHD] *n* F
eternity

**entero** [en•TAIR•oh] *adj* entire;
unbroken

**enterrar** [EN•tair•AHR] *vt* bury

**entidad** [EN•tee•DAHD] *n* F
entity

**entierro** [EN•tee•AIR•oh] *n* M
burial; funeral

**entonces** [EN•ton•SAIS] *adv*
then; en aquel ~, por aquel ~\
at that time, then

**entrada** [EN•trah•DAH] *n* F
entrance; entry; admission

**entrambos** [en•TRAHM•bos]
*adj* either

**entrar** [en•TRAHR] *vt* enter

**entre 1** [en•TRAI] *prep adv*
between; among; amongst

**entre 2** [en•TRAI] *n* M
entrance; ~ de las bastidores\
stage door

**entreabierto**
[EHN•trai•AH•bee•AIR•toh]
*adj* ajar

**entrega** [EN•trai•GAH] *n* F
delivery

**entregar** [EN•trai•GAHR] *vt*
render

**entremetido**
[en•TRAI•meh•TEE•doh] *n* M
busybody; intruder

**entrenador**
[en•TRAIN•ah•DOHR] *n* M
coach (sports)

**entrenar** [EN•train•AHR] *vt*
coach (sports)

**entretanto** [EN•trai•TAHN•to]
*adv* meantime

**entretejer** [en•TRAI•teh•HAIR]
*vt* intertwine

**entretenido**
[en•TREH•ten•EE•doh] *adj*
entertaining

**entrevista** [EN•trai•VEE•stah]
*n* F interview

**entristecer** [EN•tree•steh•SAIR]
*vi* mope

**entristecer**
[en•TREE•steh•SAIR] *vt*
sadden

**entrometerse**
[en•TRAI•meh•TAIR•sai] *vi*
meddle

**entumecido**
[en•TOO•meh•SEE•doh] *adj*
numb

**entusiasmo**
[en•TOO•see•AHS•moh] *n* M
enthusiasm

**entusiástico**
[en•TOO•see•ah•STIH•koh]
*adj* enthusiastic

**enumerar** [eh•NOO•mair•AHR]
*vt* enumerate

**enviado** [EN•vee•AH•doh] *n* M
envoy

**enviar** [EN•vee•AHR] *vt* send

**envidia** [EN•vee•DEE•ah] *n* F
envy

**envidioso**
[en•VEE•dee•OH•soh] *adj*
envious

**envoltura** [EN•vol•TOOR•ah] *n*
F envelope

**envolvedor** [en•VOL•vai•DOR]
*n* M wrapper

**envolver 1** [EN•vohl•VAIR] *vt*
envelope; involve; entail

**envolver 2** [EN•vol•VAIR] *vt*
wrap

**épico** [EHP•ee•koh] *adj* epic

**epidémico**
[eh•PIH•DEHM•EE•koh] *n* M
epidemic

**episodio** [eh•PIH•soh•DEE•oh]
*n* M episode

**epístola** [eh•PEE•stoh•LAH] *n*
F epistle

**epitafío** [eh•PIH•tah•FEE•oh] *n*
M epitaph

**epítome** [eh•PEE•to•MAI] *n* M
epitome; sketch; draft;
summary

**época** [EH•poh•KAH] *n* F
epoch; period (hist)

**equilibrio**
[eh•KEE•lee•BREE•oh] *n* M
poise

**equipaje** [EH•kee•PAH•hai] *n*
M baggage; luggage

**equipar** [EH•kee•PAHR] *vt*
equip

**equipo 1** [eh•KEE•poh] *n* M
crew; team

**equipo 2** [eh•KEE•poh] *n* M
equipment; outfit; rig

**equivalencia**
[eh•KEE•vah•LEHN•SEE•ah]
*n* F par

**equivalente**
[eh•KEE•vah•LEHN•tai] *adj*
equivalent

**equivocación**
[eh•KEE•voh•KAH•see•OHN]
*n* F mistake; misunderstanding

**equivocado**
[eh•KEE•vo•KAH•do] *adj*
mistaken

**era** [AIR•ah] *n* F era; period (hist)

**erección** [eh•REHK•see•OHN]
*n* F erection

**erizo** [air•EE•so] *n* M hedgehog

**ermitaño** [AIR•mih•TAN•yo] *n*
M hermit

**errada** [air•RAH•dah] *n* F miss

**erradicar**
[AIR•rah•DEE•KAHR] *vt*
eradicate

**errar** [AIR•rahr] *vi* err

**errata** [air•RAH•tah] *n* F
misprint

**erróneo** [AIR•roh•AI•oh] *adj*
wrong

**error** [air•ROHR] *n* M error

**error de cuenta** [air•ROHR dai KWEN•tah] *n* M miscount

**erudicion** [AIR•oo•DIH•see•OHN] *n* F scholarship

**erudito** [AIR•oo•DEE•toh] *adj* erudite; learned; scholarly

**erupción 1** [eh•ROOP•see•OHN] *n* F outbreak; erruption

**erupción 2** [eh•ROOP•see•OHN] *n* F rash

**escala** [eh•SKAH•lah] *n* F stepladder

**escalar** [eh•SKAH•lahr] *vt* escalate

**escalera** [eh•SKAH•lair•ah] *n* F escalator; staircase; ladder

**escalera abajo** [EH•skah•LAIR•ah ah•BAH•ho] *n* F downstairs

**escalfar** [EH•kahl•FAHR] *vt* poach

**escalón** [EH•skah•LOHN] *n* F doorstep

**escape 1** [eh•SKAH•pai] *n* M escape

**escape 2** [eh•SKAH•pai] *n* M exhaust

**escarabajo** [eh•SKAHR•ah•BAH•ho] *n* M scarab; beetle

**escena** [EH•sai•NAH] *n* F scene; stage

**escena retrospectiva** [SAI•nah reh•TROH•spehk•TEE•vah] *n* F flashback

**escenario** [eh•SEN•ahr•EE•oh] *n* M setting

**escéptico** [eh•SKEHP•TEE•ko] *adj* skeptic

**escarpa** [EH•skahr•PAH] *n* F cliff

**escisión** [eh•SIH•see•OHN] *n* F fission

**esclavitud** [eh•SKLAH•vih•TOOD] *n* F bondage; slavery

**esclavizar** [eh•SKLAH•vee•SAHR] *vt* enslave

**esclavo** [eh•SKLAH•vo] *n* M slave

**escoba** [eh•SKOH•bah] *n* F broom

**escocés** [EH•skoh•SAIS] *n* M Scot

**Escocia** [EH•skoh•SEE•ah] *n* F Scotland

**escoger** [EH•skoh•HAIR] *vt vi* choose; *vt* select

**escogimiento** [eh•SKOH•HEE•mee•EHN•toh] *n* M choice

**escolar** [EH•skoh•LAHR] *n* M scholar

**escolástico** [EH•skoh•LAH•STEE•koh] *adj* scholastic

**escollera** [EH•skoh•YAIR•ah] *n* F jetty

**escombro** [eh•SKOHM•broh] *n* M mackerel

**esconder** [eh•SKOHN•dair] *vt* conceal; hide

**esconderse** [EH•skon•DAIR•sai] *vi* lurk; skulk

**escondido** [EH•skohn•DEE•to] *adj* hidden

**escondimiento** [eh•SKON•dee•MEE•EN•to] *n* M hiding

**escondite** [EH•skon•DEE•tai] *n*
M hiding place

**escopeta de caza**
[EH•sko•PAI•tah dai
CAH•sah] *n* F shotgun

**escorpión** [EH•skor•PEE•OHN]
*n* F scorpion

**esquivar** [EHS•kee•VAHR] *vt*
avoid

**escribiente**
[eh•SKREE•BEE•en•TAI] *n*
M scribe; clerk

**escribir** [eh•SKREE•beer] *vt*
write

**escribir con mala ortografía**
[ehs•KREE•beer kon MAH•la
OR•toh•GRA•FEE•ah] *vt*
misspell

**escrito** [eh•SKREE•to] *n* M
writ; writing; poner por ~\ put
in writing

**escritor** [EH•skree•TOR] *n* M
writer; author

**escritorio**
[EH•SKREE•tor•EE•oh] *n* M
bureau; desk

**escritura** [EHS•kree•TOOR•ah]
*n* F handwriting; writing;
script

**escrúpulo**
[EH•SKROO•POO•lo] *n* M
scruple

**escrupuloso**
[eh•SKROO•poo•LO•so] *adj*
scrupulous

**escrutar** [EH•skroo•TAHR] *vt*
scrutinize

**escuadra** [eh•SKWAII•drah] *n*
F squadron

**escuálido** [EH•skwah•LEE•do]
*adj* squalid

**escuchar** [EH•skoo•CHAR] *vt*
*vi* listen (to)

**escudero** [EH•skoo•DAIR•oh] *n*
M squire

**escudete** [EH•skoo•DEH•tai] *n*
M gusset

**escudilla** [EH•skoo•DEE•yah] *n*
F bowl

**escueal de párvulos**
[eh•SKWAI•lah dai
pahr•voo•los] *n* F kindergarten

**escuela 1** [eh•SKWAI•lah] *n* F
grade school

**escuela 2** [eh•SKWAI•lah] *n* F
school

**escuela de derecho**
[eh•SKWAI•lah dai
deh•RAI•cho] *n* F law school

**escuela de internos**
[eh•SKWAI•lah dai
in•TAIR•nos] *n* F boarding
school

**escuela industrial**
[eh•SKWAI•lah
in•DOO•stree•AHL] *n* F trade
school

**escuela secondaria**
[eh•SKWAI•lah
seh•KUN•dahr•EE•ah] *n* F
high school

**escultor** [EH•skool•TOR] *n*
sculptor

**escultura** [EH•skool•TOOR•ah]
*n* F sculpture

**escurrir** [EH•skoo•REER] *vi*
trickle

**escurrirse** [EH•skoor•EER•sai]
*vi* slink

**ese; esa** [EH•sai] [EH•sah] *pron*
that

**ése; ésa; ésos; ésas** *pron* that one; those

**esencia** [EH•sen•SEE•ah] *n* F essence

**esencial** [EH•sen•SEE•ahl] *adj* essential

**esencialmente** [EH•sen•SEE•ahl•MEN•tai] *adv* essentially

**esfera** [ehs•FAIR•ah] *n* F sphere

**esférico** [EHS•fair•IH•koh] *adj* global; spherical

**esforzarse** [EHS•for•SAHR•sai] *vi* strive

**esfuerzo** [ehs•FWAIR•soh] *n* M effort; endeavor

**esgrima** [ehs•GREE•mah] *n* F fencing

**esguince** [ehs•GEEN•sai] *n* M dodge

**esmalte** [ehs•MAHL•tai] *n* M enamel

**esmeralda** [EHS•mair•AHL•dah] *n* F emerald

**eso** [EH•so] *pron* that; por ~ *prep\* therefore; de ~\ thereof

**esos; esas** [EH•sohs] [EH•sahs] *pron* those

**espacio** [EH•spah•SEE•oh] *n* M space; interval

**espacioso** [eh•SPAH•see•OH•so] *adj* roomy; spacious

**espada** [eh•SPAH•dah] *n* F sword

**espalda** [eh•SPAHL•da] *n* F back

**espaldera** [EH•spahl•DAIR•ah] *n* F trellis

**español** [eh•SPAHN•yol] *n* M Spaniard; *adj* Spanish

**esparadrapo** [eh•SPAHR•ah•DRAH•po] *n* M tape

**esparcido** [EH•spar•SEE•do] *adj* sparse

**esparcimiento** [eh•SPAHR•see•MEE•EN•toh] *n* M broadcast

**esparcir** [EH•spahr•SEER] *vt* spray; strew

**espárrago** [EH•SPAHR•ah•go] *n* M asparagus

**esparrancarse** [eh•SPAHR•ahn•KAHR•sai] *vi* straddle

**espasmo** [eh•SPAHS•mo] *n* M spasm

**especial** [eh•SPEH•see•AHL] *adj* special

**especialista** [EH•speh•SEE•ahl•EE•stah] *n* F specialist

**especializar** [EH•speh•SEE•ahl•IH•sahr] *vi* specialize

**especialmente** [EH•speh•SEE•ahl•MEN•tai] *adv* especially

**especie** [eh•SPAI•see•AI] *n* F species

**especificar** [EH•speh•SEE•fih•KAHR] *vt* specify

**específico** [EH•speh•SEE•fee•koh] *adj* specific

**espécimen** [eh•SPEH•sih•MEN] *n* M specimen

**especioso**
[eh•SPEH•see•OH•so] *adj*
specious

**espectacular**
[EH•spehk•TAHK•oo•LAHR]
*adj* spectacular

**espectáculo**
[eh•SPEHK•tahk•OO•lo] *n* M
spectacle

**espectador**
[eh•SPEHK•tah•DOR] *n* M
onlooker; spectator

**espectro 1** [eh•SPEHK•tro] *n*
M specter; ghost

**espectro 2** [eh•SPEHK•tro] *n*
M spectrum

**especulación**
[eh•SPEHK•oo•lah•SEE•OHN]
*n* F speculation

**especulador**
[eh•SPEHK•oo•lah•DOR] *n* M
speculator

**especular**
[eh•SPEHK•oo•LAHR] *vi*
speculate

**especulativo**
[eh•SPEHK•oo•lah•TEE•vo]
*adj* speculative

**espejo** [eh•SPAI•ho] *n* M
mirror

**espeluznante**
[eh•SPEH•loos•NAN•tai] *n* M
thrill

**espera** [eh•SPAIR•ah] *n* F
expectation; waiting

**esperanza** [EH•spair•AHN•sah]
*n* F hope

**esperanzado**
[eh•SPAIR•ahn•SAH•do] *adj*
hopeful

**esperar** [ch•SPAIR•ahr] *vt* wait;
expect

**espesar** [eh•SPEH•sahr] *vt*
thicken

**espeso** [eh•SPAI•so] *adj* thick

**espesor** [eh•SPEH•sor] *n* M
thickness

**espetar** [eh•SPEH•tahr] *vi* spit

**espía** [eh•SPEE•ah] *n* F spy

**espiar** [eh•SPEE•ahr] *vi* spy

**espiche** [eh•SPEE•chai] *n* M
spigot

**espiga** [eh•SPEE•gah] *n* F pivot

**espina** [eh•SPEE•nah] *n* F thorn

**espina dorsal** [DOR•sahl] *n* F
spinal column

**espinaca** [EH•spin•AH•kah] *n* F
spinach

**espinal** [EH•spee•NAHL] *adj*
spinal

**espinazo** [EH•spih•NAH•so] *n*
M ridge

**espionaje** [EH•spee•on•AH•hai]
*n* M espionage

**espira** [eh•SPEER•ah] *n* F spire

**espiral** [EH•speer•AHL] *adj*
spiral

**espirar** [EH•speer•AHR] *vi*
expire; wear out

**espíritu** [eh•SPEER•IH•too] *n*
M ghost; spirit; de ~ abierto\
open-hearted

**espiritual**
[eh•SPEER•ih•too•AHL] *adj*
spiritual

**espiritualidad**
[eh•SPEER•ih•too•AHL•ih•
DAHD] *n* F spirituality

**espiritualismo**
[eh•SPEER•ih•too•AHL•IHS•
mo] *n* M spiritualism

**espita** [eh•SPEE•tah] *n* F
faucet; plug

**espléndido**
[EH•splehn•DEE•do] *adj*
splendid

**esponja** [eh•SPOHN•ha] *n* F
sponge

**espontaneidad**
[EH•spon•TAH•nai•DAHD] *n*
F spontaneity

**espontáneo**
[eh•SPON•tahn•AI•oh] *adj*
spontaneous

**esposa** [eh•SPOH•sah] *n* F
wife

**esposo** [eh•SPOH•so] *n* M
spouse

**espuela** [eh•SPWAI•lah] *n* F
spur

**espuma** [eh•SPOO•mah] *n* F
foam; froth; lather; scum

**esqueleto** [EH•skeh•LEH•to] *n*
M skeleton

**esquema** [eh•SKAI•mah] *n* F
scene; scenario; scheme

**esquiar** [EH•skee•AHR] *vi* ski

**esquina** [eh•SKEE•nah] *n* F
corner

**esquito** [eh•SKEE•to] *n* M
schist

**esrutinio**
[eh•SKROO•tin•EE•oh] *n* M
scrutiny

**estabilidad**
[eh•STAH•bihl•EE•dahd] *n* F
stability

**estabilizar**
[eh•STAH•bih•LIH•sahr] *vt*
stabilize

**estable** [eh•STAHB •lai] *adj*
stable

**establecer**
[eh•STAHB•leh•SAIR] *vt*
enact; establish; appoint

**establecimiento**
[eh•STAHB•leh•SEE•mee•
EN•toh] *n* M establishment;
settlement

**establo** [eh•STAHB•lo] *n* M
stable; stall

**estaca** [eh•STAH•kah] *n* F
picket; stake

**estacada** [EH•stah•KAH•dah] *n*
F fence; stockade

**estación 1**
[EH•STAH•see•OHN] *n* F
depot; station

**estación 2**
[EH•STAH•see•OHN] *n* F
season

**estación de ferrocarril**
[eh•STAH•see•OHN dai] *n* F
railroad station

**estacionamiento**
[eh•STAH•see•OHN•ah•
MEE•EN•to] *n* M parking

**estacionario**
[eh•STAH•see•OHN•ahr•EE•
oh] *adj* stationary

**estadio** [eh•STAH•DEE•oh] *n*
M stadium

**estadista**
[eh•STAH•dee•STAH] *n* F
statesman

**estadísticas**
[EH•stah•DIH•stee•KOHS]
*npl* F statistics

**estado** [eh•STAH•doh] *n* M
estate; state; plight

**estado legal** [eh•STAH•do
LAI•gal] *n* M status

estafa [eh•STAH•fah] n F
swindle

estafador
[eh•STAH•fah•DOHR] n M
cheater

estafar [EH•stah•FAHR] vi
swindle

estampa [eh•STAM•pah] n F
stamp

estampación
[eh•STAHM•pah•see•OHN] n
F printing

estampar [eh•STAM•pahr] vt
stamp; print; imprint

estampica
[eh•STAHM•PEE•kah] n F
stampede

estampido
[eh•STAHM•PEE•do] n M
boom

estañado [EH•stan•YAH•do]
adj tinned

estaño [eh•STAN•yo] n M tin

estancado [EH•stahn•KAH•do]
adj stagnant

estancar [EH•stahn•KAHR] vt
stanch; stem

estancia 1 [EH•stahn•SEE•ah] n
F sojourn; stay

estancia 2 [eh•stahn•SEE•ah] n
F stanza

estanco 1 [eh•STAHN•koh] adj
staunch; watertight

estanco 2 [eh•STAN•koh] n M
tobacco shop

esta noche [EH•stah NO•chai]
adv tonight

estar [eh•STAHR] vi be; ~
para\ be about to; ~ por\
remain to be; be in favor of

estarcido [EH•stahr•SEE•doh] n
M stencil

estarcir [EH•stahr•SEER] vt
pounce

estático [EH•stah•TEE•koh] adj
static

estatua [eh•stah•TOO•ah] n F
statue

este [EH•stai] adj n M east; al
~\ eastward

este; esta [EH•stai] [eh•stah]
this

este mundo [EH•stai
MUHN•do] n M underworld

estela [eh•STAI•lah] n F
wake

estenógrafo
[EH•sten•OH•GRAH•fo] n M
stenographer

estera [eh•STAIR•ah] n F mat

estereotipo
[eh•STAIR•ai•oh•TEE•po] n
M stereotype

estéril [eh•STAIR•eel] adj
sterile; barren

esterilidad
[EH•stair•IH•lih•DAHD] n F
sterility

esterilizar
[EH•stair•IH•lih•SAHR] vt
sterilize

esterio [EH•stair•EE•oh] n M
stereo

esterlina [EH•stair•LEE•nah] n
F sterling

estetoscopio
[EH•steh•TOH•skoh•PEE•oh]
n M stethoscope

estibador [eh•STEE•BAH•dor]
n M stevedore

**estiércol** [EH•stee•AIR•kohl] *n*
M dung

**estigma** [eh•STIG•mah] *n* F
stigma

**estilo** [eh•STEEL•oh] *n* M style

**estima** [eh•STEE•mah] *n* F
esteem

**estimable**
[eh•STEE•MAHB•lai] *adj*
reputable

**estimacieon**
[EH•stih•MAH•see•OHN] *n* F
appraisal; estimate

**estimar** [EH•stee•MAHR] *vt*
deem; appraise

**estimulante**
[EH•stihm•oo•LAN•tai] *n* M
stimulant

**estimular**
[eh•STEE•moo•LAHR] *vt*
stimulate

**estímulo** [eh•STIH•moo•loh] *n*
M stimulation; stimulus

**estipendio**
[eh•STIH•pen•DEE•oh] *n* M
stipend

**estipulación**
[EH•stih•PEW•lah•see•OHN]
*n* F proviso; stipulation

**estipular** [eh•STEE•poo•LAHR]
*vt* stipulate

**estirador** [eh•STEER•ah•DOR]
*n* M stretcher

**esto** [EH•stoh] *pron* this; en ~\
at this point; en ~ de\ in this
matter of; por ~\ therefore

**esto es** [EH•stoh ehs] *adv*
namely

**estoico** [eh•STOI•koh] *n* M
stoic

**estola** [eh•STOH•lah] *n* F stole

**estómago** [eh•STOH•mah•GO]
*n* M belly; stomach

**estopa** [eh•STOH•pah] *n* F
tow

**estorbo** [eh•STOHR•boh] *n* M
hindrance; nuisance

**estrago** [eh•STRAH•go] *n* M
havoc

**estrangulación**
[eh•STRAHN•goo•LAH•see•
OHN] *n* F strangulation

**estrangular**
[eh•STRAHN•goo•LAHR] *vt*
strangle

**estrategia**
[eh•STRAH•teh•HEE•ah] *n* F
strategy

**estratégico**
[eh•STRAH•tai•HEE•koh] *adj*
strategic

**estratosfera**
[eh•STRAH•to•SFAIR•ah] *n* F
stratosphere

**estrecho 1** [eh•STREH•cho] *adj*
narrow

**estrecho 2** [eh•STREH•cho] *n*
M strait

**estrella** [eh•STRAI•yah] *n* F
star

**estrenar** [EH•streh•NAHR] *vt*
use for the first time; wear for
the first time

**estrenarse**
[EH•streh•NAHR•sai] *vi* make
one's debut

**estreno** [eh•STREH•no] *n* M
debut

**estrenuo** [EH•strehn•OO•oh]
*adj* strenuous

**estrepitoso**
[eh•SHTRAI•pih•TO•so] *adj*
boisterous

**estribo** [eh•STREE•boh] *n* M
stirrup

**estribor** [eh•STREE•bor] *n* M
starboard

**estricto** [eh•STREEK•to] *adj*
strict

**estridente** [EH•strih•DEN•tai]
*adj* shrill; strident

**estropajo** [EH•stroh•PAH•ho] *n*
M swab

**estropear**
[eh•STROH•pai•AHR] *vt* mar

**estructura**
[EH•struhk•TOOR•ah] *n* F
structure

**estructural**
[eh•STRUHK•toor•AHL] *adj*
structural

**estrujar** [EH•stroo•HAHR] *vt*
squash

**estuco** [eh•STOO•koh] *n* M
plaster; stucco

**estudiante**
[eh•STOO•dee•AHN•tai] *n* M
pupil; schoolboy; student

**estudiante de segundo año**
[eh•STOO•dee•AHN•tai dai
seh•GUHN•do AN•yo] *n* M
sophomore

**estudiante de universidad**
[eh•STOO•dee•AHN•tai dai
OON•ih•VAIR•sih•DAHD] *n*
M undergraduate

**estudiante del primer año**
[eh•STOO•dee•AHN•tai del
PREE•mair AHN•yo] *n* M
freshman

**estudiar** [eh•STOO•dee•AHR]
*vi* study

**estudio** [EH•stoo•DEE•oh] *n* M
studio

**estufa 1** [eh•STOO•fah] *n* F
stove; heater

**estufa 2** [eh•STOO•fah] *n* F
step

**estupendo** [EH•stoo•PEN•do]
*adj* stupendous

**estupefacción 1**
[eh•STOO•peh•fah•SEE•ON]
*n* F astonishment

**estupefacción 2**
[eh•STOO•peh•fah•SEE•ON]
*n* M narcotic

**estupidez** [EH•stoo•PEE•dehs]
*n* F stupidity; stupid act

**estúpido** [eh•STOO•PEE•do]
*adj* stupid; dumb

**estupor** [eh•STOO•por] *n* M
stupor

**esturión** [eh•stoor•EE•OHN] *n*
F sturgeon

**eterno** [eh•TAIRN•oh] *adj*
eternal

**ético** [EH•tee•KOH] *n* M ethic

**Etiopia** [eh•TEE•oh•PEE•ah] *n*
M Ethiopia

**etiqueta** [EH•tee•KAI•tah] *n* F
etiquette

**étnico** [EHT•nih•koh] *adj* ethnic

**eufemismo**
[OI•feh•MEES•moh] *n* M
euphemism

**Europa** [oi•ROH•pah] *n* F
Europe

**europeo** [OI•roh•PAI•oh] *adj*
European

**eutanasia**
[oi•TAH•nah•SEE•ah] *n* F
euthanasia

**evacuar** [eh•VAH•koo•AHR] *vt*
evacuate; vacate

**evadir** [EH•vah•DEER] *vt* evade

**evaluar** [eh•VAH''loo•AHR] *vt*
evaluate

**evangelio**
[eh•VAN•hai•LEE•oh] *n* M
gospel

**evantarse**
[LEH•vahn•TAHR•sai] *vi*
stand

**evaporado**
[eh•VAH•por•AH•do] *adj*
vapid

**evaporar** [eh•VAH•por•AHR]
*vt* evaporate

**evasivo** [EH•vah•SEE•voh] *adj*
evasive

**eventual** [eh•VEN•too•AHL]
*adj* eventual

**eventualmente**
[eh•VEN•twal•MEN•tai] *adv*
eventually

**evidencia** [eh•VIH•den•SEE•ah]
*n* F evidence

**evidente** [eh•VIH•den•TAI] *adj*
evident

**evidentemente**
[EH•vih•DEHNT•ih•MEN•tai]
*adv* apparently; evidently

**evitar** [AI•vee•TAHR] *vt* avoid;
spare; balk; shun

**evocar** [EH•voh•KAHR] *vt*
evoke

**evolución**
[EH•voh•LOO•see•OHN] *n* F
evolution

**exacto** [eks•AHK•toh] *adj*
exact; accurate

**exageración**
[EHKS•ah•hair•AH•see•OHN]
*n* F exaggeration

**exagerar** [ehks•AH•hair•AHR]
*vt vi* exaggerate

**exaltado** [EHKS•ahl•TAH•do]
*adj* hot-tempered

**exaltar** [EHKS•ahl•TAHR] *vt*
exalt

**exámen** [EHKS•AH•men] *n* M
exam; quiz

**examinar**
[EHKS•ahm•EE•nahr] *vt*
examine

**exasperar**
[EHKS•ah•SPAIR•ahr] *vt*
exasperate

**excavar** [ehks•KAH•vahr] *vt*
excavate; dig

**exceder** [EHKS•seh•DAIR] *vt*
exceed

**excederse**
[EHKS•seh•DAIR•sai] *vi*
overdo; go too far

**excelencia**
[ehks•SEL•en•SEE•ah] *n* F
excellence

**excelente** [EHKS•el•LEN•tai]
*adj* excellent

**excéntrico**
[EKS•sen•TREE•koh] *n adj* M
eccentric

**excepción**
[ehk•SEHP•see•OHN] *n* F
exception

**excepcional**
[EHK•sep•SEE•ohn•AHL] *adj*
exceptional

**excepto** [ehk•SEHP•toh] *prep*
*conj* except; but

**exceso** [ehks•SEH•soh] *n* M
excess; extravagance

**excitante**
[EHKS•see•TAHN•tai] *adj*
exciting

**excitar** [EHK•see•TAHR] *vt*
excite

**exclamar** [EHKS•klah•MAHR]
*vi* exclaim

**excluir** [EHKS•kloo•EER] *vt*
exclude

**excremento**
[EHKS•kreh•MEN•toh] *n* M
excrement

**excursión**
[ehks•KOOR•see•óHN] *n* F
excursion

**excusa** [ehks•KOO•sah] *n* F
excuse

**exhalación**
[ehks•HAH•lah•SEE•ON]n F
shooting star; como una ~\ at
top speed

**exhalar** [EHKS•hah•LAHR] *vt*
exhale

**exhibición**
[ehks•IH•bih•SEE•OHN] *n* F
display; exhibit

**exigente** [EKS•ih•HEN•tai] *adj*
demanding; fastidious; tener
mucas exigencias\ be very
demanding

**existencia**
[EHK•sih•STEN•SEE•ah] *n* F
existence

**existir** [EHK•ih•STEER] *vi* exist

**éxito** [ehk•SEE•to] *n* M success;
no tener ~\ fail; tener ~\ be
successful

**éxodo** [EHKS•OH•doh] *n* M
exodus

**exonerar** [EHKS•ohn•air•AHR]
*vt* exonerate

**exótico** [ehks•OH•tec•KOH] *adj*
exotic

**expansión**
[ehks•PAHN•see•OHN] *n* F
expansion

**expedición**
[ehks•SPEH•dih•see•OHN] *n*
F expedition

**expeler** [EHK•speh•LAIR] *vt*
expel

**expender** [EHK•spen•DAIR] *vt*
expend

**experiencia**
[ehks•PAIR•ee•en•SEE•ah] *n*
F experience

**experimentado**
[ehk•SPAIR•ih•men•TAH•doh]
*adj* experienced; skilled

**experimentar**
[ehks•PAIR•ih•MEN•tahr] *vt*
test; experiment (with);
undergo

**experimento**
[ehk•SPAIR•ih•MEN•toh] *n*
M experiment

**experto** [ehk•SPAIR•toh] *n adj*
M expert

**explicación**
[ehk•SPLIH•kah•SEE•OHN] *n*
F explanation

**explicar** [EHKS•plee•KAHR] *vt*
explain; construe

**exploración**
[ehk•SPLOR•ah•see•OHN] *n*
F exploration; probe

**explorador**
[ehk•SPLOR•ah•DOR] *n*
explorer

**explorar** [EHK•splor•AHR] *vt*
*vi* explore

**exponer** [EHKS•pon•AIR] *vt*
expose

**exportación**
[EHK•sport•tah•SEE•OHN] *n*
F export

**expresar con el ceño**
[EH•preh•SAHR kon el
sain•yo] *vt* scowl

**expresión**
[ehk•SPREH•see•óHN] *n* F
expression

**expresivo**
[ehk•SPREH•see•VOH] *adj*
expressive

**expreso** [ehk•SPREH•so] *adj*
express; nonstop

**expuesto** [ehks•PWE•stoh] *n* M
exposure

**exquisito** [EHKS•kee•SIH•toh]
*adj* exquisite

**éxtasis** [EHKS•tah•SIS] *n* M
ecstasy

**extático** [EHKS•tah•TEE•koh]
*adj* ecstatic

**extender** [EHKS•ten•DAIR] *vt*
expand; extend; reach; spread;
stretch

**extendido** [EHK•sten•DEE•do]
*adv* widespread

**extensamente**
[ehk•STEN•sah•MEN•tai] *adv*
widely

**extensión**
[EHK•sten•SEE•OHN] *n* F
extension; span

**extensivo**
[EHK•sten•SEE•VOH] *adj*
extensive

**exterior 1**
[ehk•STAIR•ee•OHR] *n* M
exterior; *adj* outer; outside;
exterior

**exterior** [ehks•TAIR•ee•OHR]
*adj* outside

**exteriormente**
[ehks•TAIR•ee•or•MEN•tai]
*adv* outwardly

**exterminar**
[ehk•STAIR•mee•NAHR] *vt*
exterminate

**externo** [ehk•STAIR•noh] *n* M
external; *adj* outward

**extinguir** [EHK•sting•GOO•eer]
*vt* extinguish; quench

**extra** [EHKS•trah] *adj* extra

**extracto** [ehk•STRAHK•toh] *n*
extract

**extrañado**
[EKS•trahn•YAH•doh] *adj*
estranged

**extrañeza** [EH•strahn•YAI•sah]
*n* F strangeness

**extraño** [ehks•TRAHN•yo] *adj*
strange; queer; *n* M stranger

**extranjero**
[EH•strahn•HAIR•oh] *adj*
foreign; *n* M foreigner

**extraordinario**
[ehk•STRAH•or•DIH•nar•
EE•oh] *adj* extraordinary

**extraviar**
[ehk•STRA•vee•AHR] *vt*
misplace

**extremista**
[ehk•STRAI•MIH•stah] *n* M
extremist

**extremo 1** [ehk•STRAIM•oh]
*adj n* M extreme

**extremo 2** [ehks•TRAIM•oh] *n*
M tip

**exuberante**
[ehk•SOO•bair•AHN•tai] *adj*
exuberant

**exudar** [EHKS•oo•DAHR] *vi*
sweat

**exultar** [EHK•sool•TAHR] *vi*
exult

# F

**fábrica** [FAH•BREE•kah] *n* F
factory; marca de ~\
trademark

**fabricante**
[FAH•bree•KAHN•tai] *n* M
manufacturer

**fabricante de tabaco**
[FAH•brih•KAN•tai dai ] *n* M
tobacconist

**fabricar** [FAH•bree•KAHR] *vt*
fabricate; manufacture

**fábula** [fah•BOO•lah] *n* F fable;
tale; myth

**fabuloso** [FAH•boo•LOH•soh]
*adj* fabulous

**faceta** [fah•SAI•tah] *n* F facet

**fácil** [FAH•seel] *adj* easy

**facilidad 1** [fah•SIH•lih•DAHD]
*n* F facilities

**facilidad 2**
[fah•SIHL•ih•DAHD] *n* F
knack

**fácilmente** [FAH•seel•MEN•tai]
*adv* easily

**factible** [FAHK•tee•BLAI] *adj*
feasible

**factor** [FAHK•tohr] *n* M factor

**facultad** [FAH•kuhl•TAHD] *n*
F faculty; ability; power

**facultativo**
[fah•KUHL•tah•TEE•vo] *adj*
optional

**facha** [FAH•cha] *n* F look

**fachada** [fah•CHA•dah] *n* F
facade; show

**faja** [FAH•ha] *n* F strip; swathe

**falbalá** [FAHL•bah•LAH] *n* F
flap

**falda 1** [FAHL•dah] *n* F lap

**falda 2** [FAHL•dah] *n* F skirt

**falda corta** [FAHL•dah
KOR•tah] *n* F kilt

**falsear** [FAHL•sai•AHR] *vt*
falsify

**falsificado**
[FAHL•see•FIH•kah•DOH]
*adj* counterfeit

**falso 1** [FAHL•soh] *adj* false;
lying

**falso 2** [FAHL•soh] *adj* shoddy

**falta 1** [FAHL•tah] *n* F fault

**falta 2** [FAHL•tah] *n* F lack;
shortage

**faltar** [FAHL•tahr] *vi* fail

**falto** [FAHL•toh] *adj* devoid

**fallar** [FAI•yahr] *vi* misfire

**fama** [FAH•mah] *n* F fame;
reputation; de mala ~\ of ill
repute; tene ~ de\ have the
reputation of

**famado** [fah•MAH•do] *adj*
famed

**familia** [FAH•mee•LEE•ah] *n* F
family

**familiar** [fah•MIHL•ee•AHR]
*adj* familiar, informal
colloquial

**familiarizar**
[FAH•mih•LEE•ahr•IH•sahr]
*vt* familiarize

**famoso** [fah•MOH•soh] *adj*
famous

**fanático** [fah•NAH•tee•KO] *n*
M zealot

**fanfarronear**
[FAHN•fahr•roh•NAI•ahr] *vi*
brag

**fantasía** [FAHN•tah•SEE•ah] *n*
F fantasy

**fantasma** [fahn•TAHS•mah] *n*
F phantom; spook

**fantástico**
[FAHN•TAH•STEE•koh] *adj*
fantastic

**farfulla** [fahr•FOO•yah] *n* M
gibberish

**farmacéutico**
[FAHRM•ah•SOO•tee•koh] *n*
M chemist

**farmacia** [FAHR•mah•SEE•ah]
*n* F pharmacy

**faro** [FAH•roh] *n* M lighthouse;
headlight (automotive)

**farsa** [FAHR•sah] *n* F farce; *adj*
phony

**fascinación**
[FAH•see•NAH•see•OHN] *n*
F fascination

**fascinando**
[FAH•see•NAHN•doh] *adj*
fascinating

**fascinador** [FAH•see•NAH•dor]
*adj* glamorous; bewitching

**fascinar** [fah•SEEN•ahr] *vt*
fascinate

**fascismo** [fah•SEES•moh] *n* M
fascism

**fase** [FAH•seh] *n* F phase

**fastidiar** [fah•STIH•dee•AHR]
*vi* tease

**fatal** [FAH•tahl] *adj* fatal

**fatiga 1** [fah•TEE•gah] *n* F
fatigue

**fatiga 2** [fah•TEE•gah] *n* F
harassment

**fatigado** [FAH•tee•GAH•doh]
*adj* exhausted

**fatigar** [FAH•tee•GAHR] *vt*
tire; overwork; exhaust

**fatuo** [fah•TOO•oh] *adj* fatuous

**fauna** [FAU•nah] *n* F fauna

**favor** [FAH•vor] *n* M favor; a ~
de, en ~ de\ in favor (of); por
~\ please

**favorable** [FAH•vor•AH•blai]
*adj* favorable

**favorecer** [fah•VOR•eh•SAIR]
*vt* befriend

**favorito** [FAH•vor•EE•toh] *adj*
M favorite

**fe** [fai] *n* F faith; dar ~ de\
certify; de buena ~\ in good
faith

**fealdad** [FAI•ahl•DAHD] *n* F
ugliness

**febrero** [feh•BRAI•roh] *n* M
February

**febricitante**
[feh•BREE•see•TAHN•tai] *adj*
feverish

**fecha** [FAI•cha] *n* F date; a
estas fechas\ now, still; hasta
la ~\ so far; poner la ~\ date

**fechoría** [FAI•chor•EE•ah] *n* F
misdeed

**federación**
[FEH•dair•AH•see•OHN] *n* F
federation

**federal** [feh•DAIR•AHL] *adj*
federal

**felicidad** [feh•LEE•see•DAHD]
*n* F happiness

**felíz** [feh•LEES] *adj* happy;
Felices Pascuas\ Merry
Christmas; Felices Año
Nuevo\ Happy New Year;
Felices cumpleaños\ happy
birthday

**felizmente** [FEH•lees•MEN•tai]
*adv* happily

**femenino**
[FEH•meh•NEEN•oh] *adj*
feminine; womanly

**feminidad** [fem•IH•nih•DAHD]
*n* F womanhood

**fenómeno** [FEH•noh•MEN•oh]
*adj* freak; *n* M phenomenon

**feo** [FAI•oh] *adj* homely; ugly

**feo horrible** [FAI•oh]
[o•REE•blai] *adj* hideous

**fermentar** [FAIR•men•TAHR]
*vi* ferment

**ferretería**
[FAIR•eh•TAIR•REE•ah] *n* F
hardware

**ferrocarril**
[FAIR•roh•kahr•REEL] *n* M
railroad; railway

**ferroviario**
[FAIR•roh•VEE•ahr•EE•oh] *n*
M trainman

**fértil** [FAIR•teel] *adj* fertile

**fertilidad**
[fair•TIHL•ee•DAHD] *n* F
fertility

**fertilizante**
[FAIR•til•IH•SAN•tai] *n* M
fertilizer

**fertilizar** [fair•TIL•ih•SAHR] *vt*
fertilize

**festivo** [feh•STEE•vo] *adj*
festive; jolly

**feto** [FEH•to] *n* M fetus

**feudal** [FOI•dahl] *adj* feudal

**feudo** [FOI•do] *n* M manor

**fiable** [fee•AHB•lai] *adj*
trustworthy

**fiambres** [fee•AHM•bres] *npl*
M delicatessen

**fianza** [fee•AHN•sah] *n* F bail

**fibra** [FEE•brah] *n* F fiber

**ficción** [FIHK•see•OHN] *n* F
fiction

**fideicomisario**
[FEE•dai•KOH•mih•SAHR•
EE•oh] *n* M trustee

**fidelidad**
[fee•DEHL•ee•DAHD] *n* F
fidelity; loyalty

**fiebre** [fee•AI•brai] *n* M fever

**fiel 1** [FEE•ehl] *adj* faithful;
loyal; trusty

**fiel 2** [FEE•ehl] *adj* accurate;
exact

**fiero** [fee•AIR•oh] *adj* fierce

**fiero; feroz** [fee•AIR•oh]
[fee•AIR•ohs] *adj* ferocious

**fiesta** [fee•EH•stah] *n* F
holiday; festival; feast

**figura** [fih•GOOR•ah] *n* F figure

**figurativo**
[fihg•OOR•ah•TEE•vo] *adj*
figurative

**fijación** [fee•HAH•see•OHN] *n*
F fixation

**fijar** [FEE•har] *vt* fix

**fijo** [FEE•ho] *adj* certain; fixed

**fila** [FEE•lah] *n* F row; range;
tier; file

**filete** |fih•LEH•tai| *n* M fillet;
tenderloin

**filo** |FEE•loh| *n* M edge

**filosifia** |fih•LOH•so•FEE•ah| *n*
F philosophy

**filosófico**
|fih•LOH•so•FIH•koh| *adj*
philosophical

**filósofo** |FIH•loh•SO•fo| *n* M
philosopher

**filtración** |fihl•TRAH•see•OHN|
*n* F leak

**filtrar** |FIHL•trahr| *vt* filter;
seep

**filtro** |FIL•troh| *n* M filter

**fin** |feen| *n* M end; ending; ~ de
semana\ weekend; a ~ de\ in
order to; a ~ de que\ in order
that; al ~\ finally; dar ~ a\
end, conclude; en ~\ in short;
por ~\ finally; sin ~\ endless

**fin objeto** |feen ob•HEH•to| *n*
M purpose

**final** |FEE•nahl| *adj* final; *n* M
ending

**finalmente**
|FEE•nahl•MEN•tai| *adj*
ultimately

**finamente** |FEEN•ah•MEN•tai|
*adv* nicely

**financiero**
|fih•NAHN•see•AIR•oh| *adj*
financial

**finca** |FINK•ah| *n* F farm;
property; estate

**finés** |FIN•AIS| *n* Finn

**fingir** |FING•eer| *vt* feign; *vt vi*
dissemble

**finlandés** |FIN•lan•DAIS| *adj*
Finnish

**Finlandia** |FIN•lan•DEE•ah| *n*
Finland

**fino** |FEE•no| *adj* fine

**firma 1** |FEER•mah| *n* F
signature

**firma 2** |FEER•mah| *n* F
subscription

**firmante** |feer•MAHN•tai| *n* M
subscriber

**firme** |FEER•mai| *adj* steadfast;
steady

**firmemente**
|FEER•meh•MEN•tai| *adj*
steadily

**firmes** |FEER•mais| *n* attention

**firmeza** |feer•MAI•sah| *n* F
steadiness

**fiscal** |FIH•skahl| *adj* fiscal

**física** |fih•SEE•kah| *n* F physics

**físico 1** |fih•SEE•koh| *adj*
physical; *n* M physician;
physicist

**físico 2** |fih•SEE•koh| *n* M
physique

**flaco** |FLAH•koh| *adj* lean;
skinny

**flaco** |FLAH•koh| *adj*
emaciated; shrunken

**flagrante** |flah•GRAHN•tai| *adj*
flagrant

**flama** |FLAH•mah| *n* F flame

**flamenco** |flah•MEN•koh| *n* M
flamingo

**flámeo** |flah•MAI•oh| *adj*
flammable

**flámula** |flah•MOO•lah| *n* F
pennant; streamer

**flan** |flahn| *n* M custard

**flauta** |FLOU•tah| *n* F flute

**flecha 1** |FLAI•cha| *n* F arrow

**flecha 2** |FLAI•cha| *n* F bolt

**flexible** [flehk•SEE•blai] *adj*
flexible; pliable

**flirteador**
[FLEER•tai•AH•dohr] *n* M
flirt

**flojamente**
[FLOH•hah•MEN•tai] *adv*
loosely

**flojo** [FLO•ho] *adj* loose; slack;
yielding

**flor** [flor] *n* F flower; blossom

**flora** [FLOR•ah] *n* F flora

**floración** [FLOR•ah•SEE•ON] *n*
F bloom

**florero** [flor•AIR•oh] *n* M vase

**floricultor**
[FLOR•ih•KUHL•tor] *n* M
florist

**flotar** [FLOH•tahr] *vt* float

**fluctuar** [flook•TOOR•AHR] *vi*
flicker; fluctuate

**fluidez** [FLOO•ih•DEHS] *n* F
fluency

**fluido 1** [FLOO•EE•doh] *adj n*
M fluid

**fluido 2** [FLOO•EE•doh] *adj*
fluent

**flujo** [FLOO•ho] *n* M flow;
influx

**fluorescente**
[floo•OR•eh•SEN•tai] *adj*
fluorescent

**fluoruro** [FLOO•or•OO•do] *n*
M fluoride

**foca** [FOH•kah] *n* F seal

**focal** [FOH•kahl] *adj* focal

**foco** [FOH•koh] *n* M focus;
limelight

**follaje** [foi•YAH•hai] *n* M
foliage

**folleto** [foi•YEH•to] *n* M
brochure; pamphlet

**fomentar** [FOH•men•TAHR] *vt*
foment

**fonda** [FON•dah] *n* F inn

**fondeadero**
[fon•DAI•ah•DAIR•oh] *n* M
haven

**fondista** [fon•DEE•stah] *n* F
innkeeper

**fondo 1** [FON•do] *n* M bottom;
background (in the)

**fondo 2** [FON•do] *n* M fund

**fonética** [FOH•neh•TEE•kah] *n*
F phonetics

**fonil** [FON•eel] *n* M funnel

**fontanería**
[FON•tan•air•EE•ah] *n* F
plumbing

**forastero** [FOR•ah•STAIR•oh]
*n* M outsider

**forcejeo** [FOR•seh•HAI•oh] *n*
M flounder

**fórceps** [FOR•sehps] *n* M
forceps

**forja** [FOR•ha] *n* F forge

**forma** [FOR•mah] *n* F form

**formal** [FOR•mahl] *adj* formal

**formalidad**
[FOR•mah•LEE•dahd] *n* F
formality

**formidable**
[FOR•mih•DAHB•lai] *adj*
formidable; grim

**fórmula** [for•MOO•lah] *n* F
formula

**fornido** [tor•NEE•doh] *adj*
stalwart; sturdy; well-built

**forrage** [for•RAH•hai] *n* M
forage

**forraje** [for•RAH•hai] *n* M hay; fodder

**fortalecer** [FOR•tah•LEH•sair] *vi* strengthen

**fortaleza 1** [FOR•tah•LAI•sah] *n* F fort (military); fortress; stronghold

**fortaleza 2** [FOR•tah•LAI•sah] *n* F fortitude; strength

**fortificación** [for•TIH•fih•KAH•see•OHN] *n* F fortification

**fortificar** [for•TIH•fee•KAHR] *vt* fortify

**fortuito** [FOR•too•EE•toh] *adj* fortuitous

**fortuna** [for•TOO•nah] *n* F fortune

**fósforo** [FOHS•for•oh] *n* M match

**fósil** [FOH•SEEL] *n* M fossil

**fosilizado** [foh•SEE•lih•SAH•do] *adj* petrified

**foso** [FOH•so] *n* M moat; trench

**fotografía** [foh•TOH•grah•FEE•ah] *n* F photo; photograph; photography

**fotógrafo** [FOH•TOH•GRAH•fo] *n* M photographer

**fracaso** [frah•KAH•so] *n* M failure

**fractura 1** [frahk•TOOR•ah] *n* F fracture

**fractura 2** [frahk•TOOR•ah] *n* F invoice

**fragancia** [FRAH•gan•SEE•ah] *n* F fragrance

**fragante** [frah•GAN•tai] *adj* fragrant

**frágil** [FRAH•heel] *adj* fragile

**fragmento** [frahg•MEN•to] *n* M fraction; fragment; scrap

**fragor** [FRAH•gohr] *n* M din

**framacéutico** [fahr•MAH•soi•TEE•koh] *n* M pharmaceutist

**frambuesa** [frahm•BWAI•sah] *n* F raspberry

**francés** [frahn•SEHS] *adj* French

**Francia** [FRAHN•SEE•ah] *n* France

**francmasón** [FRAHNK•mah•SON] *n* M mason

**franco** [FRAHN•koh] *n* M franc

**franela** [frah•NAI•lah] *n* F flannel

**franja** [FRAHN•ha] *n* F fringe

**franqueza** [frahn•KAI•sah] *n* F franchise

**frasco** [FRAH•skoh] *n* M flask

**frase** [FRAH•sai] *n* F phrase; slogan

**fraternal** [frah•TAIR•nahl] *adj* fraternal

**fraternidad** [frah•TAIR•nih•DAHD] *n* F fraternity

**fraude** [FROU•dai] *n* M fraud; trickery

**fraudulento** [FROU•doo•LEN•toh] *adj* dishonest; fraudulent

**frecuencia** [FREH•kwen•SEE•ah] *n* F frequency

**frecuentar**
[FREH•kwen•TAHR] *vt*
frequent; hang out; haunt

**frecuente** [freh•KWEN•tai] *adj*
frequent

**fregadero**
[FREH•gah•DAIR•oh] *n* M
sink; kitchen sink

**fregar** [FRAI•gahr] *vt* scour;
scrub

**freírse** [frair•EER•sai] *vi* sizzle

**frenético** [FREN•eh•TEE•koh]
*adj* frantic

**freno** [FREH•no] *n* M brake

**frente 1** [FREHN•tai] *n* M
forehead

**frente 2** [FREN•tai] *adj* front;
al frente *adv prep*\ ahead (of)

**fresa** [FREH•sah] *n* F
strawberry

**fresco** [FREHS•koh] *adj* cool;
fresh; *n* M coolness

**frescura** [freh•SKOOR•ah] *n* F
freshness

**fricción** [frihk•SEE•OHN] *n* F
friction

**frígido** [frih•HEE•doh] *adj*
frigid

**frijol** [FREE•hol] m M bean

**frío** [FREE•oh] *adj* chilly, cold;
*n* M cold, chill

**friolera** [FREE•oh•LAIR•ah] *n*
F trifle

**frívolo** [frec•VO•lo] *adj*
frivolous

**frontera** [fron•TAIR•ah] *n* F
frontier

**frotador** [FROH•tah•DOR] *n* M
wiper

**frotar de arriba abajo**
[FROH•tahr dai ahr•REE•bah
ah•BAH•ho] *vt* rub-down

**frustración**
[fruh•STRAH•see•OHN] *n* F
frustration

**frustrar** [FROO•strahr] *vt*
frustrate

**fruto; fruta** [FROO•to]
[froo•tah] *n* MF fruit

**fue** [fwai] been *pp* estar

**fuego** [FWAI•go] *n* M fire;
bonfire

**fuego cruzado** [FWAI•go
kroo•SAH•doh] *n* M crossfire

**fuego de artillería** [FWAI•go
dai ar•TIHL•lair•EE•ah] *n* M
gunfire

**fuegos artificiales** [FWAI•gos
AR•ti•FI•see•AHL•ais] *npl*
fireworks

**fuente 1** [FWEN•tai] *n* F fountain

**fuente 2** [FWEN•tai] *n* M well
(oil)

**fuera** [FWAIR•ah] *adv* out; ~
de\ outside; por ~\ on the
outside

**fuerte 1** [FWAIR•tai] *adj*
strong; tough; bright (color)
loud (sound); large; heavy

**fuerte 2** [FWAIR•tai] *n* M fort

**fuertemente**
[FWAIR•teh•MEN•tai] *adv*
strongly

**fuerza** [FWAIR•sah] *n* F force;
might; strength

**fuerza motriz ejercida por un
caballo** [fwair•sah moh•trees
ai•hair•see•dah por uhn ] *n* F
horsepower

**fugarse** [foo•GAHR•sai] *vi*
elope

**fugitivo** [FOO•hi•TEE•vo] *n* M
fugitive; runaway

**fumigar** [FOO•mee•GAHR] *vt*
fumigate
**función** [FUHNK•see•OHN] *n*
F function
**funda de almohada**
[FUHN•dah dai] *n* F
pillowcase
**fundación** [FUN•dah•see•OHN]
*n* F foundation
**fundador** [fuhn•DAH•DOR] *n*
M founder
**fundamental**
[fuhn•DAH•men•TAHL] *adj*
fundamental
**fundido** [fuhn•DEE•do] *adj*
melted; molten

**funesto** [fuh•NEH•stoh] *adj*
fateful
**furia** [foor•EE•ah] *n* F fury
**furioso** [FOOR•ee•OH•so] *adj*
mad; furious
**furtivo** [foor•TEE•vo] *adj*
furtive
**fusilar** [foo•SEE•lahr] *vt* shoot
**fusión** [FOO•see•OHN] *n* F
fusion
**fútbol** [FOOT•bol] *n* M football
**fútil** [FOO•teel] *adj* futile
**futuro** [foo•TOOR•oh] *n* M
future

# G

**gabán** [gah•BAHN] *n* M
overcoat
**gabardina**
[GAH•bahr•DEE•nah] *n* F
raincoat; gabardine (fabric)
**gabinete** [GAH•bee•NEH•tai] *n*
M cabinet; closet
**gaélico** [GAH•ai•LIH•koh] *adj*
Gaelic
**gafa** [GAH•fah] *n* F hook
**gafas** [GAH•fahs] *npl* F glasses;
spectacles
**gafas para el sol** [GAH•fahs
PAH•rah el sol] *n* F goggles
**gaita** [GAI•tah] *n* F bagpipes
**gajo** [GAH•ho] *n* M segment;
prong
**galante** [gah•LAHN•tai] *adj*
gallant

**galantear** [GAH•lahn•TAI•ahr]
*vt* woo
**galera** [gah•LAIR•ah] *n* F
galley
**galocha** [gah•LOH•cha] *n* F
patter
**galón** [GAH•LON] *n* F gallon
**galope** [gah•LOH•pai] *n* M
gallop
**gallería** [GAH•lair•EE•ah] *n* F
gallery
**galleta** [gai•YAI•tah] *n* F
gingerbread
**galletas** [GAI•ai•TAHS] *npl* F
cracker
**gallina** [gai•YEE•nah] *n* F hen
**gallinero** [GAI•yeen•AIR•oh] *n*
M hen-house
**gallo** [GAI•yo] *n* M cock

**gallo** [GAl•yo] *n* M fowl

**gama** [GAH•mah] *n* F doe

**ganado 1** [gah•NAH•doh] *n* M cattle; livestock

**ganado 2** [gah•NAH•do] won *pp* ganar

**ganador** [GAH•nah•DOR] *n* M winner

**ganancia** [GAH•nahn•SEE•ah] *n* F gain

**ganar** [GAH•nahr] *vt* earn; win

**ganchio** [gahn•CHEE•oh] *n* M stool pigeon

**gancho** [GAHN•cho] *n* M hook

**ganchudo** [gahn•CHOO•do] *n* hooky

**ganga** [GAHN•ja] *n* F bargain; easy job

**gangear** [GAHN•gai•AHR] *vi* snuffle

**gangster** [gahng•STAIR] *n* M gangster

**ganso** [GAHN•so] *n* M goose

**garabatear** [GAHR•ah•BAH•tai•AHR] *vt* scrawl

**garaje** [gah•RAH•hai] *n* M garage

**garante 1** [hah•RAHN•tai] *n* M sponsor

**garante 2** [gahr•AHN•tai] *n* M voucher

**garantía** [GAH•rahn•TEE•ah] *n* F guarantee

**garfa** [GAHR•fah] *n* F claw

**garganta** [gahr•GAN•tah] *n* F gorge; throat

**gargarizar** [gahr•GAHR•ih•SAHR] *vi* gargle

**gárgola** [GAHR•go•LAH] *n* F gargoyle

**garra** [GAHR•rah] *n* F paw

**garrafa** [gahr•RAH•fah] *n* F decanter

**garrapata** [GAHR•rah•PAH•tah] *n* F tick

**garrapatear** [GAHR•rah•PAH•TAI•ahr] *vt* scribble

**garrote** [gah•RO•tai] *n* M club, cudgel

**garrucha** [gahr•ROO•cha] *n* F pulley

**garza** [GAHR•sah] *n* F heron

**gaseoso** [GAH•sai•OH•so] *adj* gaseous

**gasolina** [GAH•so•LEE•nah] *n* F gas; gasoline

**gastado** [gah•STAH•doh] *adj* hackneyed; shabby

**gastador** [gah•STAH•DOHR] *adj* extravagant

**gastar** [GAH•stahr] *vt* spend

**gasto** [GAH•stoh] *n* M expenditure; expense

**gatear** [GAH•tai•AHR] *vt* scramble

**gatillo** [gah•TEE•yo] *n* M trigger

**gatito** [gah•TEE•toh] *n* M kitten

**gato** [GAH•toh] *n* M cat; tomcat

**gaznate 1** [gahs•NAH•tai] *n* M gullet

**gaznate 2** [gahs•NAH•tai] *n* M throttle

**gelatina** [GEHL•ah•TEE•nah] *n* F gelatin

**gema** [HAl•mah] *n* F gem

**gemelo** [geh•MEH•lo] *n* M
twin

**gemido** [heh•MEE•do] *n* M
groan; moan

**gemir** [HEM•eer] *vt* whimper;
whine

**gen** [hen] *n* M gene

**genealogía**
[HEN•ai•AH•loh•HEE•ah] *n* F
pedigree; geneology

**generación**
[HEN•air•AH•see•OHN] *n* F
generation

**generador** [hen•AIR•ah•DOR]
*n* M generator

**general** [HEN•eh•RAHL] *n* M
general

**generalización**
[HEN•air•AL•ih•SAH•see•
óHN] *n* F generalization

**generalizar**
[HEN•air•AHL•ih•SAHR] *vt*
generalize

**generalmente**
[hen•AIR•ahl•MEN•tai] *adv*
generally

**generar** [HEN•air•AHR] *vt*
generate

**género** [HEN•AIR•oh] *n* M
gender

**generosidad**
[HEN•air•OH•sih•DAHD] *n* F
generosity

**generoso** [HEN•air•OH•so] *adj*
generous

**genético** [HEN•eh•TEE•ko] *adj*
genetic

**genial** [HEN•ee•AHL] *adj*
genial

**genio** [hen•EE•oh] *n* M genius

**genital** [HEN•ee•TAHL] *adj*
genital

**gente** [HEN•tai] *n* F people;
folk

**gente culta** [HEN•tai
KUHL•ta] *n* gentry

**genuino** [hen•WEEN•o] *adj*
genuine

**geografía**
[HAI•oh•grah•FEE•ah] *n* F
geography

**geología** [HAI•oh•lo•HEE•ah]
*n* F geology

**geometría**
[HAI•oh•meh•TREE•ah] *n* F
geometry

**geométrico**
[HAI•oh•meh•TRIH•ko] *adj*
geometric

**germen** [HAIR•men] *n* M germ

**germinar** [GAIR•mee•NAHR]
*vi* germinate

**gesto** [HEHS•to] *n* M beckon

**giba** [GEE•bah] *n* F hump

**giga** [GEE•gah] *n* F jig

**gigante** [hee•GAHN•tai] *n adj*
M giant

**gigantesco**
[HEE•gan•TESK•oh] *adj*
gigantic

**gimnasio** [HIM•nah•SEE•oh] *n*
M gym; gymnasium

**gimnasta** [HIM•nah•STAH] *n* F
gymnast

**girar** [HEER•ahr] *vi* gyrate;
swivel; whirl

**gitano** [gee•TAH•noh] *n* M
gypsy

**glacial** [GLAH•see•AHL] *adj*
icy

**glaciar** [GLAH•see•AHR] *n* M glacier

**glándula** [glahn•DOO•lah] *n* F gland

**globo 1** [GLO•bo] *n* M balloon

**globo 2** [GLOH•bo] *n* M globe

**globo del ojo** [GLOH•boh del OH•ho] *n* M eyeball

**gloria** [glo•REE•ah] *n* F glory

**glorificar** [glo•RIH•fee•KAHR] *vt* glorify

**glorioso** [GLOR•ee•OH•so] *adj* glorious

**glosario** [GLO•sahr•EE•oh] *n* M glossary

**glotón** [GLOH•ton] *adj* gluttonous; *n* M glutton

**glotonería** [glo•TON•air•EE•ah] *n* F gluttony

**glucosa** [gloo•KOH•sah] *n* F glucose

**gobernador** [GO•bair•NAH•dor] *n* M governor

**gobernadora** [GO•bair•NAH•DOR•ah] *n* F governess

**gobernar** [GO•bair•NAHR] *vt* *vi* govern; *vt* steer

**gobierno** [GO•bee•AIR•no] *n* M government

**gocete** [goh•SEH•tai] *n* M palette

**goleta** [go•LEH•tah] *n* F schooner

**golfillo** [gol•FEE•yo] *n* M waif

**golfo** [GOHL•foh] *n* M gulf

**golfo Pérsico** [GOL•fo PAIR•sih•koh] *n* M Persian Gulf

**golpazo** [gohl•PAH•so] *n* M bounce; crash

**golpe** [GOL•pai] *n* M hit; blow; knock; stroke; ~ de fortuna\ stroke of luck; ~ de vista\ glance; de ~\ suddenly; de un ~\ in one try

**golpeador** [GOHL•pai•ah•DOHR] *n* M knocker; striker

**golpear** [GOL•pai•AHR] *vt* rap; strike; swat; swipe

**golpe meastro** [GOL•pai mai•AI•stroh] *n* M coup

**golpe vivo** [GOL•pai VEE•vo] *n* M flip

**goma** [GOH•mah] *n* F gum; rubber

**goma de borrar** [GOH•mah dai BOHR•rahr] *n* F eraser

**gong** [gong] *n* M gong

**gordinflón** [GOR•deen•FLOHN] *adj* chubby

**gorda** [GOR•dah] *n* F thick tortilla

**gordo 1** [GOR•do] *adj* fat; plump

**gordo 2** [GOR•do] *n* M first prize

**gorgojo** [gor•GOH•ho] *n* M weevil

**gorila** [gor•EE•lah] *n* F gorilla

**gorjeo** [hor•HAI•oh] *n* M twitter

**gorra** [GOHR•rah] *n* F cap

**gorrión** [GOR•ree•OHN] *n* F sparrow

**gota 1** [GO•tah] *n* F drop

**gota 2** [GO•tah] *n* F gout

**gota de lluvia** [GOH•tah dai
YOO•vee•AH] *n* F raindrop
**goteo** [goh•TAI•oh] *n* M drip
**gótico** [go•TEE•ko] *adj* gothic
**gozar** [GO•sahr] *vt* enjoy
**gozarse** [GO•sahr•SAI] *vi* gloat
**gozne** [GOHS•nai] *n* M hinge
**gozo** [GO•so] *n* M rejoicing
**gozoso** [go•ZO•so] *adj* elated;
delighted
**grabado** [GRAH•BAH•doh] *n*
M engraving
**grabar** [GRAH•bahr] *vt* engrave
**gracia 1** [grah•SEE•ah] *n* F
grace
**gracia 2** [grah•SEE•ah] *n* M
fool; comic; comic character
**gracias** [grah•SEE•ahs] *npl* F
thanks
**gracioso 1** [grah•SEE•oh•so]
*adj* graceful; gracious
**gracioso 2** [grah•SEE•oh•so]
*adj* funny
**grado** [GRAH•doh] *n* M
degree; grade; rate
**gradual** [GRAH•doo•AHL] *adj*
gradual
**graduar** [GRAH•doo•AHR] *v*
graduate
**gráfica** [grah•FEE•kah] *n* F
graph
**gráfico** [grah•FEE•koh] *adj*
graphic
**grajo** [GRAH•ho] *n* M crow
**gramática**
[grah•MAH•TEE•kah] *n* F
grammar
**gramatical**
[grah•MAH•TEE•kahl] *adj*
grammatical
**gramo** [GRAH•mo] *n* M gram

**gramófono**
[grahm•OH•FON•oh] *n* M
jukebox
**gran** [grahn] *adj* M great
**granada** [grah•NAH•dah] *n* F
grenade
**Gran Bretaña** [lah grahn
breh•TAHN•yah] *n* F Great
Britain
**grande** [GRAN•dai] *adj* big;
grand; large
**grande enorme** [GRAHN•dai
eh•NOR•mai] *adj* huge
**grandemente**
[GRAND•eh•MEN•tai] *adv*
largely
**grandeza** [GRAHN•dai•SAH] *n*
F grandeur; greatness
**grandioso** [GRAN•dee•OH•so]
*adj* grandiose
**granero** [grah•NAIR•o] *n* M
barn; granary
**granito** [grahn•EE•to] *n* M
granite
**granizo** [grah•NEE•so] *n* M hail
**granjero** [gran•HAIR•oh] *n* M
farmer
**grano** [GRAH•no] *n* M grain;
kernel
**gránulo** [grahn•OO•lo] *n* M
granule
**grasa 1** [GRAH•sah] *n* F grease
**grasa 2** [GRAH•sah] *n* F slag
**gratitud** [GRAH•tee•TOOD] *n*
F gratitude
**grave** [GRAH•vai] *adj* grave;
staid
**gravedad** [GRAH•veh•DAHD]
*n* F gravity
**graznar** [GRAHS•nahr] *vt*
quack; *vi* squawk

**graznido** [grahs•NEE•do] *n* M
croak

**Grecia** [grai•SEE•ah] *n* F
Greece

**gremio** [grai•MEE•oh] *n* M
guild; union

**griego** [gee•AI•go] *adj* Greek

**grillo 1** [GREE•yo] *n* M cricket

**grillo 2** [GREE•yo] *n* M shackle

**gripe** [GREE•pai] *n* M flu

**gris** [grees] *n adj* M gray

**gritar** [GREE•tahr] *vi* bawl;
scream; shout; yell

**gritería** [GREE•tair•EE•ah] *n* F
uproar

**grito** [GREE•toh] *n* M cry;
outcry; racket; hoot; whoop

**Groenlandia**
[GROHN•lahn•DEE•ah] *n*
Greenland

**grosella** [groh•SAI•yah] *n* F
currant

**gorsería** [GROH•sair•EE•ah] *n*
F coarseness; coarse remark

**grosero** [groh•SAIR•oh] *adj*
coarse

**grotesco** [groh•TEH•sko] *adj*
grotesque

**grueso** [groo•AI•so] *adj* thick

**grulla** [GROO•yah] *n* F crane

**gruñido** [groon•YEE•do] *n* M
growl; grunt

**grupo** [GROO•poh] *n* M gang;
group; cluster

**grupo de cinco** [GROO•poh
dai SEEN•ko] *n* M quintet

**grupo de cuatro** [GROO•po
dai KWAH•tro] *n* M quartet

**guadaña** [gwah•DAHN•yah] *n*
F scythe

**guante** [GWAN•tai] *n* M glove;
gage (archaic)

**guantes** [GWAN•tais] *npl* M
mittens

**guapo** [GWAʌ•po] *adj*
good-looking

**guarda 1** [GWAR•dah] *n* F
custody; keeping

**guarda 2** [GWAHR•dah] *n* F
ward

**guardafango**
[GWAR•dah•FAN•goh] *n* M
dashboard

**guardafuegos**
[GWAR•dah•FWAI•gos] *npl*
fender

**guardamlacén**
[GWAHR•dahl•MAH•sen] *n*
M storekeeper

**guardar** [GWAHR•dahr] *vt* keep

**guardarropa**
[GWAHR•dahr•RO•pah] *n* M
wardrobe; cloakroom

**guardarse** [GWAR•dahr•SAI]
*vi* beware (of)

**guardia** [gwar•DEE•ah] *n* F
guard; keeper

**guardia de corps**
[gwar•DEE•ah dai korps] *n* F
bodyguard

**guardián** [GWAHR•dee•AHN]
*n* M guardian; warden;
watchman

**guardián de un cafe**
[GWAR•dee•AHN dai oon
CAH•fai] *n* M bouncer

**guarida** [gwar•DEE•ah] *n* F den

**guerra** [GAIR•rah] *n* F war; dar
~ a\ annoy

**guerrero** [gair•RAIR•oh] *n* M
warrior

**guerrillero** [GAIR•ee•AIR•oh]
_n_ M guerrilla

**guía 1** [GEE•ah] _n_ F clue

**guía 2** [GEE•ah] _n_ F leader;
leading; guidance

**guiar** [GEE•ahr] _vt_ guide

**guijarro** [gwee•HAHR•oh] _n_ M
pebble

**guijarros** [gwee•HAHR•rohs]
_npl_ cobblestones

**guillotina** [GEE•oh•TEE•nah] _n_
F guillotine

**guión** [GEE•YON] _n_ M hyphen

**guirnalda** [GWEER•nahl•DAH]
_n_ F garland

**guisa** [GWEE•sah] _n_ F guise

**guisado** [gee•SAH•do] _n_ M
stew

**guisante** [gee•SAHN•tai] _n_ M
pea

**guitarra** [gee•TAHR•rah] _n_ F
guitar

**gusaniento**
[goo•SAHN•ee•EN•to] _adj_
grubby

**gusano** [goo•SAN•oh] _n_ M
worm

**gusto** [GOO•stoh] _n_ M taste;
pleasure; a ~\ comfortable; a
mi ~\ to my liking

# H

**haber** [AH•bair] aux verb have;
~ que\ must

**hábil** [AH•beel] _adj_ able;
suitable; cunning

**habilidad** [AH•bil•EE•dahd] _n_
F ability; know-how; skill

**habitación**
[ah•BEE•tah•see•OHN] _n_ F
dwelling

**habitante** [AH•bee•TAHN•tai]
_n_ M inmate

**habitante del oeste**
[AH•bih•TAN•tai del
OH•eh•STAI] _n_ M westerner

**habitar** [ah•BEE•tahr] _vi_ dwell;
_vt_ inhabit

**hábito** [hah•BEE•toh] _n_ M
habit

**habitual** [ah•BEE•too•ahl] _adj_
habitual

**habla** [AHB•lah] _n_ F speech; al
~\ speaking (on telephone);
ponerse al ~ con\ get in touch
with; se ~ español\ Spanish
spoken

**hablador** [ahb•LAH•dor] _adj_
talkative

**hablar** [AHB•lahr] _vi_ speak;
talk; ~ con\ talk to

**hace** [AH•sai] _adv_ ago

**hacendado** [AH•sen•DAH•do]
_n_ M landowner

**hacer** [AH•sair] _vt_ do; make; ~
de\ act as; hace poco\
recently; hace sol\ it's sunny;
hace viento\ it's windy; ¿que
le vamos a ~?\ what are we
going to do?

**hacer cerveza** [AH•sair
sair•VAI•sah] _vt_ brew

**hacer erupción** [AH•sair eh•ROOP•see•OHN] *n* F erupt

**hacer ganchillo** [HAH•sair gahn•CHEE•yo] *vi* crochet

**hacer mohínes** [ah•SAIR mo•EE•nais] *vi* pout

**hacer tictac** [AH•sair TIHK•tahk] *vi* tick (as clock); run; work (coll)

**hacer trampas** [AH•sair TRAHM•pahs] *vt* juggle

**hacer visible** [AH•sair vih•SEE•blai] *vt* visualize

**hacia** [ah•SEE•ah] *prep* towards; unto; ~ arriba\ upwards; ~ abajo\ downwards

**hacia casa** [ah•SEE•ah KAH•sah] *adv* homeward

**hacia el este** [ah•SEE•ah el EH•stai] *adv* eastward

**hacia el norte** [ah•SEE•ah el NOR•tai] *adv* northward(s)

**hacienda** [AH•see•EN•dah] *n* F farm; property; estate hacha [ah•cha] *n* F\ axe

**hada** [AH•dah] *n* F fairy

**Haiti** [HAI•tee] *n* M Haiti

**halcón** [ahl•KOHN] *n* M falcon

**halo** [AH•lo] *n* M halo

**hallarse** [ai•YAHR•sai] *vi* occur

**hamaca** [hah•MAH•kah] *n* F hammock

**hambre** [AHM•brai] *n* M hunger; starvation; tener ~\ to be hungry

**hambriento** [AHM•bree•EN•toh] *adj* famished; hungry; ravenous

**hamburguesa** [AHM•boor•GAI•sah] *n* F hamburger

**hangar** [AN•gahr] *n* M hangar

**harina** [ah•REE•nah] *n* F flour

**harina de avena** [ah•REEN•ah dai ah•VAI•nah] *n* F oatmeal

**hartazgo** [ar•TAHS•go] *n* M glut

**hasta** [AH•stah] *prep* till; until

**hasta ahora** [AH•stah AH•or•AH] *adv* thus far

**hasta aquí** [AH•stah ah•KEE] *adv* hitherto

**hasta la fecha** [AH•stah lah FAI•cha] *adj* up-to-date

**hasta la vista** [AH•stah lah VEE•stah] goodbye

**hasta luego** [AH•stah loo•WAI•go] until later; see you later

**hastial** [AH•stee•AHL] *n* F gable

**haya** [AI•ya] *n* F beech

**hazaña** [ah•SAHN•yah] *n* F stunt

**héctico** [HEHK•tee•koh] *adj* hectic

**hechicero** [ai•CHEE•SAIR•oh ] *adj* bewitching; *n* M sorcerer

**hechizado** [ai•CHEE•SAH•do] *adj* spellbound

**hechizar** [ai•CHEE•sahr] *vi* spell

**hecho 1** [AI•cho] *n* M fact

**hecho 2** [AI•cho] *n* M feat; act; event

**hecho a mano** [AI•cho ah MAH•no] *n* M handmade

**hecho en casa** [AI•cho en KAH•sah] *adj* homemade

**hechos** [AI•chos] *npl* M doings

**helado** [ai•LAH•do] *n* M
ice-cream

**helador** [ai•LAH•dor] *n* M
freezer

**helamiento**
[AI•lah•MEE•EN•to] *n* M
frost

**helar** [AI•lahr] *vt* freeze

**helecho** [eh•LAI•cho] *n* M fern

**helicóptero**
[eh•LEE•kohp•TAIR•oh] *n* M
helicopter

**hembra** [EHM•brah] *n* F female

**hemisferio**
[EM•ih•SFAIR•EE•oh] *n* M
hemisphere

**hemorragia**
[EHM•or•rah•GEE•ah] *n* F
hemorrhage

**hemorroides**
[EH•mor•ROI•dais] *npl* F
hemorrhoids

**hendidura**
[EHN•dee•DOOR•ah] *n* F
crevice; cleavage

**hendimiento**
[en•DEE•mee•EN•toh] *n* M
fissure

**heráldica** [air•AHL•dih•KAH] *n*
F heraldry

**heraldo** [air•AHL•doh] *n* M
herald

**herbario** [air•BAHR•EE•oh] *adj*
herbal

**herboso** [air•BOH•so] *adj*
grassy

**heredad** [AIR•eh•DAHD] *n* F
domain

**heredar** [AIR•eh•DAHR] *vt*
inherit

**heredera** [AIR•eh•DAIR•ah] *n*
F heiress

**heredero** [AIR•eh•DAIR•oh] *n*
M heir

**herediatrio**
[AIR•eh•DIH•tahr•EE•oh] *adj*
hereditary

**herejía** [AIR•eh•HEE•ah] *n* F
heresy

**herencia 1** [AIR•en•SEE•ah] *n*
F heredity; heritage;
inheritance

**herencia 2** [AIR•en•SEE•ah] *n*
F heirloom

**herir** [AIR•eer] *vt* hurt; stab

**hermana** [air•MAHN•ah] *n* F
sister

**hermano** [hair•MAHN•oh] *n* M
brother

**hermétticamente cerrado**
[air•MEH•tee•KAH•MEHN•tai
sair•RAH•doh] *adj* airtight

**hermosa** [air•MOH•sah] *adj*
beautiful; good-looking

**hernia** [air•NEE•ah] *n* F hernia

**héroe** [AIR•oh•ai] *n* M hero

**heroico** [air•OI•koh] *adj* heroic

**heroína** [air•OI•nah] *n* F
heroine

**heroìna** [AIR•oh•EE•nah] *n* F
heroin

**heroismo** [AIR•oh•EES•mo] *n*
M heroism

**herradura** [AIR•rah•DOOR•ah]
*n* F horseshoe

**herramiento**
[AIR•rah•MEE•EN•toh] *n* M
implement

**herrar** [AIR•ahr] *vt* brand

**herrero** [hair•AIR•oh] *n* M
blacksmith

**hervir** [AIR•veer] *vi* boil;
simmer; seethe

**heterosexual**
[eh•TAIR•oh•sehks•OO•AHL]
*n* M heterosexual.

**hexágono** [EHKS•ah•GON•oh]
*n* M hexagon

**híbrido** [ee•BRIH•do] *n adj* M
hybrid

**hice; hizo** [EE•sai] [EE•soh] did
*pp* hacer

**hidráulico** [EE•drah•LIH•koh]
*adj* hydraulic

**hidrógeno** [EE•droh•GEN•oh]
*n* M hydrogen

**hiedra** [ee•AI•drah] *n* F ivy

**hiel** [ee•EL] *n* M gall

**hielo** [ee•AI•lo] *n* M ice

**hiemación** [ee•MAH•see•OHN]
*n* F hibernation

**hiena** [ee•AI•nah] *n* F hyena

**hierba** [ee•AIR•bah] *n* F grass;
herb; weed

**hierro** [ee•AIR•oh] *n* M iron

**hierro forjado** [ee•AIR•roh
for•HAH•do] *n* M wrought
iron

**hígado** [ee•GAH•doh] *n* M liver

**higiene** [EE•gee•AI•nai] *n* F
hygiene

**higo** [HEE•go] *n* M fig

**hija** [EE•ha] *n* F daughter

**hijastra** [ee•HAH•strah] *n* F
stepdaughter

**hijastro** [ee•HAH•stroh] *n* M
stepchild; stepson

**hijo** [EE•ho] *n* M son

**hijo; hija** [EE•ho] [ee•hah] *n*
child

**hilado** [ee•LAH•do] *pp* spun

**hilador** [EE•lah•DOR] *n* M
spinner

**hilar** [EE•lahr] *vt* spin

**hilas** [EE•lahs] *npl* F lint

**hilo** [EE•loh] *n* M thread

**himnasia** [HIM•nah•SEE•ah] *n*
F gymnastics

**himno** [IHM•noh] *n* M hymn

**hinchado** [een•CHAH•do] *adj*
bloated; swollen

**hinchazón** [een•CHA•SON] *n*
M swelling

**hindú** [in•DOO] *adj* M Hindu

**hipnosís** [EEP•noh•SIS] *n* M
hypnosis

**hipnótico** [IHP•noh•TEE•koh]
*adj* hypnotic

**hipnotizar** [ihp•NO•tee•SAHR]
*vt* hypnotize

**hipo** [EE•poh] *n* M hiccup

**hipócrata** [IH•poh•KRAH•tah]
*n* F hypocrite

**hipocresía**
[ih•POH•krai•SEE•ah] *n* F
hypocrisy

**hipocrita** [IH•poh•KRIH•tah]
*adj* hypocritical

**hipopótamo**
[ee•PO•poh•TAH•moh] *n* M
hippopotamus

**hipotecar** [EE•po•TAI•kahr] *n*
M mortgage

**hipotésis** [IH•poh•TAI•sis] *n* M
hypothesis

**hipotético**
[ih•POH•tai•TEE•koh] *adj*
hypothetical

**hirviente** [EER•vee•EN•tai] *adj*
fervent

**hispánico** [EE•spahn•EE•koh]
*adj* Hispanic

**histérico** [ih•STAIR•EE•koh]
*adj* hysterical

**historia** [IH•stor•EE•ah] *n* F
history; story

**historiador**
[IH•stor•EE•AH•dor] *n* M
historian

**histórico** [IH•stor•EE•ko] *adj*
historic

**hocico** [oh•KEE•koh] *n* M
muzzle

**hockey** [OH•kee] *n* M hockey

**hogar** [OH•gahr] *n* M home

**hogar** [OH•gahr] *n* M hearth

**hoja** [OH•ha] *n* F blade

**hoja** [OH•ha] *n* F leaf

**hoja de estaño** [OH•ha dai ] *n*
F tinfoil

**hojuela** [oh•HWAI•lah] *n* F
pancake

**hola** [OH•lah] *excl* hello

**Holanda** [oh•LAHN•dah] *n*
Holland

**holandés** [OH•lahn•DAIS] *adj*
Dutch

**holgado** [ohl•GAH•do] *adj*
loose; comfortable

**holocausto** [OH•loh•KOU•sto]
*n* M holocaust

**hollín** [oy•YEEN] *n* M soot

**holliniento** [oy•YIN•ee•EN•to]
*adj* sooty

**hombre** [OM•brai] *n* M man

**hombre brutal** [OM•brai
BROO•tahl] *n* M ruffian

**hombre de ciencia** [OM•brai
dai SEE•ehn•SEE•a] *n* M
scientist

**hombre de cuevas** [OHM•brai
de coo•AI•vahs] *n* M caveman

**hombre de negocios; mujer
de negocios** [OM•brai dai-]
[MOO•hair] *n* businessman;
-woman

**hombre libre** [OM•brai
LEE•brai] *n* M yeoman

**hombro** [OM•broh] *n* M
shoulder

**homicida** [OHM•ih•SEE•dah]
*adj* murderous

**homicidio**
[oh•MIH•see•DEE•oh] *n* M
homicide

**homicidio**
[ohm•IH•see•DEE•oh] *n* M
manslaughter

**homosexual**
[oh•MOH•sehk•SOO•el] *adj n*
homosexual

**honda** [ON•dah] *n* F sling

**hondo** [ON•doh] *adj* deep

**hongo** [ON•go] *n* M fungus;
mushroom

**honor** [ON•ohr] *n* M honor

**honorable** [ON•or•AHB•lai]
*adj* honorable

**honorario** [ohn•OR•ahr•EE•oh]
*n* M fee; honorarium

**honradez** [ON•rah•DAIS] *n* F
honesty

**honrado** [on•RAH•doh] *adj*
honest

**hora** [OR•ah] *n* F hour; ¿a que
~?\ at what time?; de ~ en ~\
hourly; ¿qué ~ es?\ what time
is it?; ¿tiene Vd. ~?\ do you
have the time?;\ de cada ~
hourly

**hora del almuerzo** [OR•ah
dai] *n* F lunch hour

**hora punta** [OR•ah PUN•tah] *n* F rush-hour

**horario** [OR•ahr•EE•oh] *n* M schedule; timetable

**horca** [OR•kah] *n* F gallows

**horca** [OR•kah] *n* F pitchfork

**horizontal** [OR•ih•SON•tahl] *adj* horizontal

**horizonte** [OR•ih•SON•tai] *n* M horizon

**hormiga** [or•MEE•gah] *n* F ant

**hormiguear** [OR•mih•GAI•ahr] *vi* tingle

**hormiguero** [OR•mih•GAIR•oh] *n* M swarm

**hormón** [or•MOHN] *n* F hormone

**hornear** [or•NAI•ahr] *vt* bake

**hornero** [or•NAIR•oh] *n* M baker

**horno** [OR•no] *n* M oven; furnace; kiln

**horóscopo** [or•OH•SKOH•poh] *n* M horoscope

**horquilla** [or•KEE•yah] *n* F hairpin

**horrendo** [or•REN•doh] *adj* dire

**horrible** [or•REEB•lai] *adj* ghastly; horrible; awful

**hórrido** [or•REE•doh] *adj* horrid

**horror** [HOHR•rohr] *n* M horror

**horrorizar** [or•ROHR•ih•SAHR] *vt* horrify

**horroroso** [OR•ror•OH•so] *adj* grisly

**hospedero** [OH•speh•DAIR•oh] *n* M host

**hospital** [OH•spee•TAHL] *n* M hospital

**hospitalario** [OH•spih•TAH•lahr•EE•oh] *adj* hospitable

**hospitalidad** [OH•spee•TAHL•ih•DAHD] *n* F hospitality

**hostia** [oh•STEE•ah] *n* F wafer

**hostil** [oh•STEEL] *adj* hostile

**hostilidad** [OH•steel•IH•dahd] *n* F hostility

**hotel** [OH•tcl] *n* M hotel

**hoy** [oi] *adv* today; ~ dia\ nowadays; ~ mismo\ this very day; ~ por ~\ for the time being; de ~ en adleante\ from now on

**hoya** [OI•ah] *n* F hole; grave

**hoyuelo** [oi•WAI•low] *n* M dimple

**hueco** [WAI•koh] *adj* hollow

**huella** [oo•AI•yah] *n* F footprint

**huella digital** [OO•WAI•yah DIH•hee•TAHL] *n* F fingerprint

**huérfano** [WAIR•fah•noh] *n* M orphan

**huero** [WAIR•oh] *adj* empty

**huerta** [WAIR•tah] *n* F truck farm

**huerto** [WAIR•toh] *n* M orchard

**hueso** [HWAI•so] *n* M bone

**huésped** [oo•WEH•spehd] *n* M guest; lodger

**huevas** [oo•WAI•vahs] *npl* F spawn

**huevo** [OOWAI•vo] *n* M egg

**huevo hervido** [oo•WAI•vo air•VEE•do] *n* M boiled egg

**huida** [oo•EE•dah] *n* F flight;
    escape
**huir** [oo•EER] *vt vi* flee; *vi* run
    away
**humanidad**
    [oo•MAHN•ih•DAHD] *n* F
    humanity; mankind
**humanitario**
    [OO•man•IH•tahr•EE•oh] *adj*
    humanitarian
**humano** [oo•MAN•oh] *adj*
    human, humane; *n* M human
**humectar** [OO•mehk•TAHR] *vt*
    moisten
**humedad** [OO•meh•DAHD] *n*
    F humidity; moisture
**húmedo 1** [oo•MEH•doh] *adj*
    damp; humid; moist
**húmedo 2** [oo•MEH•do] *adj*
    marshy

**humildad** [OO•mihl•DAHD] *n*
    F humility
**humilde** [OO•mihl•DAI] *adj*
    humble; lowly; mean
**humillación**
    [OO•mee•YAH•see•OHN] *n* F
    humiliation
**humillar** [oo•MEE•yahr] v
    humiliate
**humor** [oo•MOHR] *n* M humor;
    mood
**humos** [OO•mos] *npl* fumes
**hundir** [uhn•DEER] *vt* sink
**húngaro** [uhn•GAHR•oh] *adj*
    Hungarian
**Hungría** [uhn•GREE•ah] *n*
    Hungary
**huracán** [OOR•ah•KAHN] *n* M
    hurricane
**hurón** [oor•OHN] *n* F ferret

# I

**iceberg** [ees•BAIRG] *n* M
    iceberg
**ictericia** [ees•TAIR•ee•SEE•ah]
    *n* F jaundice
**ida** [EE•dah] *n* F outward;
    journey; departure; de ~ y
    vuelta\ round trip
**idea** [ee•DAI•ah] *n* F idea
**ideal** [IH•dai•AHL] *adj n* F
    ideal
**idealismo**
    [ih•DAI•ahl•EES•moh] *n* M
    idealism
**idealista** [ih•DAI•ah•EE•stah]
    *adj* idealistic

**idear** [ih•DAI•ahr] *vi* contrive;
    conceive
**ídem** [EE•DEHM] *n* M ditto
**idéntico** [IH•den•TEE•koh] *adj*
    identical
**identificación**
    [IH•den•TIH•fih•KAH•see•
    OHN] *n* F identification
**ideologia**
    [IH•dai•OH•loh•HEE•ah] *n* F
    ideology
**idiota** [IH•dee•OH•tah] *adj*
    idiotic; *n* F idiot
**idolatrar** [ee•DOH•lah•TRAR]
    *vt* idolize

**ídolo** [ee•DOH•loh] *n* M idol

**iglesia** [IH•glai•SEE•ah] *n* F
church

**ignición** [ihg•NIH•see•OHN] *n*
F ignition

**ignorancia**
[IHG•nor•AHN•see•AH] *n* F
ignorance

**ignorante** [IG•nor•AHN•tai]
*adj* ignorant

**igual** [ee•GWAL] *adj* equal;
even; alike

**igualdad** [EE•gwal•DAHD] *n* F
equality

**igualmente**
[EE•gwal•MEN•tai] *adv*
equally

**ijada** [ee•HAH•dah] *n* F flank;
loin

**ilegal** [IHL•ai•GAHL] *adj*
illegal

**ilegítimo**
[ihl•EH•hee•TEE•moh] *adj*
illegitimate

**iliberal** [IH•lih•BAIR•ahl] *adj*
narrow-minded

**ilícito** [IHL•ih•SEE•to] *adj* illicit

**ilimitado** [ihl•IH•mee•TAH•do]
*adj* unbounded

**ilógico** [IHL•loh•HEE•koh] *adj*
illogical

**iluminación**
[IH•loo•mih•NAH•see•OHN]
*n* F lighting

**iluminar** [ih•LOO•mee•NAHR]
*vt* illuminate; lighten

**ilusión** [ih•LOO•see•OHN] *n* F
illusion

**ilustración**
[ihl•OO•strah•SEE•OHN] *n* F
illustration

**ilustrar** [IH•loo•STRAHR] *vt*
illustrate

**ilustre** [ihl•OO•strai] *adj*
illustrious

**imagen** [ee•MAH•hen] *n* M
image

**imaginación**
[ih•MAH•hee•NAH•see•OHN]
*n* F imagination

**imaginar** [ih•MAH•hee•NAHR]
*vt* imagine

**imaginario**
[IH•mah•HEE•nahr•EE•oh]
*adj* imaginary

**imaginativo**
[IH•mah•HEE•nah•TEE•vo]
*adj* imaginative

**imaginería**
[IH•mah•HIN•air•EE•ah] *n* F
imagery

**imán** [ee•MAHN] *n* M magnet

**imbécil** [ihm•BEH•seel] *n* M
imbecile

**imitación**
[IH•mih•TAH•see•OHN] *n* F
fake; imitation

**imitar** [IH•mee•TAHR] *vt*
imitate

**impaciencia**
[IM•pah•SEE•en•SEE•ah] *n* F
impatience

**impaciente**
[im•PAH•see•EHN•tai] *adj*
impatient

**impar** [IM•pahr] *adj* odd

**imparcial** [IM•pahr•see•AHL]
*adj* impartial; unbiased

**impartir** [IM•pahr•TEER] *vt*
impart; bestow

**impasible** [IM•pah•SEE•blai]
*adj* stolid

**impedido** |IM•peh•DEE•do| *adj*
handicapped

**impedimento**
|im•PEH•dih•MEN•toh| *n* M
impediment; obstacle

**impedir** |IM•peh•DEER| *vt*
impede

**impedir el crecimiento**
|IM•peh•deer el
KRAI•see•MEE•EN•to| *vt*
stunt

**impeditivo**
|im•PEH•dih•TEE•vo| *adj*
preventive

**impeler** |IM•peh•LAIR| *vt*
impel

**impenetrable**
|im•PEN•eh•TRAHB•lai| *adj*
impervious

**imperativo**
|im•PAIR•eh•TEE•vo| *adj*
imperative

**imperdible** |IM•pair•DEEB•lai|
*n* M safety pin

**imperecedero**
|IM•pair•EH•seh•DAIR•oh|
*adj* undying

**imperfecto** |IM•pair•FEHK•to|
*adj* imperfect

**imperial** |im•PAIR•EE•ahl| *adj*
imperial

**imperio** |IHM•pair•EE•oh| *n* M
empire

**imperioso** |im•PAIR•ee•OH•so|
*adj* imperious

**impermeabilidad**
|im•PAIR•mai•ah•BIHL•ih•
DAHD| *n* F tightness

**impermeable**
|im•PAIR•mai•AHB•lai| *adj*
waterproof

**impersonal**
|im•PAIR•so•NAHL| *adj*
impersonal

**impertinente 1**
|im•PAIR•tih•NEN•tai| *adj*
flippant; impertinent

**impertinente 2**
|im•PAIR•tih•NEN•tai| *adj*
irrelevant

**impetu** |im•PEH•too| *n* M
impetus

**impetuoso**
|im•PEH•too•OH•so| *adj*
brash; impetuous

**implacable**
|IM•plah•KAHB•lai| *adj*
merciless; relentless

**implantar** |IM•plahn•TAHR| *vt*
implant

**implicar 1** |IM•plee•KAHR| *vt*
implicate

**implicar 2** |IM•plee•KAHR | *vt*
imply

**implícito** |IM•plih•SEE•to| *adj*
implicit

**implorar** |IM•plohr•AHR| *vt*
implore

**impolítico**
|im•POH•lee•TEE•koh| *adj*
impolite

**imponer** |IM•poh•NAIR| *vt*
impose; *vi* intrude

**importación**
|IM•pohr•TAH•see•ON| *n* F
import

**importancia**
|im•POHR•tahn•SEE•ah| *n* F
importance; significance

**importante**
|IM•pohr•TAHN•tai| *adj*
important

**importante grave**
[IM•por•TAHN•tai
GRAH•vai] *adj* momentous

**imposible** [IM•poh•SEE•blai]
*adj* impossible

**imposición**
[IM•poh•SIH•see•OHN] *n* F
imposition; condition

**impostor** [IM•poh•STOHR] *n*
M impostor

**impotente** [IM•poh•TEN•tai]
*adj* impotent; powerless

**impresión 1**
[im•PREH•see•OHN] *n* F
impression; imprint

**impresión 2**
[im•PREH•see•OHN] *n* F
print

**impresionante**
[IM•preh•SEE•ohn•AHN•tai]
*adj* impressive

**impresor** [IM•preh•SOR] *n* M
printer

**imprimir** [IM•prih•MEER] *vt*
impress

**improbable**
[IM•proh•BAHB•lai] *adj*
improbable

**impropio** [IM•proh•PEE•oh]
*adj* improper; inappropriate;
unbecoming; unsuitable

**improvisar**
[im•PRO•vee•SAHR] *vt vi*
improvise; de improviso
offhand

**imprudente** [IM•proo•DEN•tai]
*adj* imprudent; unwise

**impuesto** [im•PWEH•stoh] *n* M
income tax; tax

**impuesto de utilidades** [dai
oo•TIH•lih•DAHD•ais] *n* M
tax (income)

**impulsivo** [IM•puhl•SEE•vo]
*adj* impulsive

**impunidad**
[im•POO•nih•DAHD] *n* F
impunity

**impureza** [IM•poor•EH•sah] *n*
F impurity

**impurificar**
[IM•poor•IH•fih•KAHR] *vt*
pollute

**impuro** [im•POOR•oh] *adj*
impure

**imputar** [IM•pew•TAHR] *vt*
impeach

**inacable** [IN•ah•KAH•blai] *adj*
unending

**inaccesible**
[in•AHK•seh•SEE•blai] *adj*
unapproachable

**inactivo** [IN•ahk•TEE•vo] *adj*
inactive

**inadecuado**
[in•AH•deh•KWAH•doh] *adj*
inadequate

**inadvertencia**
[IN•ahd•VAIR•ten•SEE•ah] *n*
F thoughtlessness

**inadvertidamente**
[in•AHD•vair•TIH•dah•MEN•
tai] *adv* unawares

**inadvertido**
[in•AHD•vair•DEE•doh] *adj*
inadvertent

**inalámbrico**
[in•AH•lahm•BREE•ko] *adj*
wireless

**inalterado**
[in•AHL•tair•AH•do] *adj*
unchanged

**inane** [in•AH•neh] *adj* inane

**inanimado**
[in•AHN•ih•MAH•doh] *adj*
inanimate

**inapreciable**
[IN•ah•PREH•see•AHB•lai]
*adj* priceless

**inauguración**
[in•AH•goor•AH•see•OHN] *n*
F inauguration

**incansable** [IN•kahn•SAH•blai]
*adj* tireless; untiring

**incapacidad**
[IN•kah•PAH•sih•DAHD] *n* F
inability

**incapaz** [IN•kah•PAHS] *adj*
incapable; unable

**incauto** [in•KOU•toh] *adj*
gullible

**incendio** [IN•sen•DEE•oh] *n* M
blaze

**incesante** [IN•seh•SAHN•tai ]
*adj* incessant; unceasing

**incesantemente**
[IN•seh•SANT•eh•MEN•tai]
*adj* continually

**incidental 1**
[in•SIH•den•TAHL] *adj*
incidental

**incidental 2**
[in•SIH•den•TAHL] *adj*
occasional

**incidente** [IN•sih•DEN•tai] *n* M
incident

**incienso** [IN•see•EN•so] *n* M
incense

**incierto** [IN•see•AIR•to] *adj*
uncertain

**incitar** [IN•see•TAHR] *vt* incite

**incitativo** [in•SIH•tah•TEE•vo]
*n* M incentive

**incivil** [IN•sih•VEEL] *adj*
uncivil

**inclinación**
[IN•kli•NAH•see•ON] *n* F
bend; tilt

**inclinar** [IN•klihn•AHR] *vt*
droop; tilt

**inclinarse** [IN•kli•NAHR•sai] *vt*
*vi* bow

**incluido** [IN•kloo•EE•doh] *adj*
including

**incluir** [in•KLOO•eer] *vt* include

**incluso** [in•KLOO•so] *adj*
included; herein

**incomodidad**
[IN•koh•MO•dee•DAHD] *n* F
discomfort

**incómodo** [in•KOH•MOH•do]
*adj* uncomfortable

**incomparable**
[in•KOHM•pahr•AHB•lai] *adj*
incomparable

**incompatible**
[in•KOHM•pah•TEEB•lai] *adj*
incompatible

**incompetente**
[in•KOHM•peh•TEN•tai] *adj*
incompetent

**incompleto** [IN•kohm•LEH•to]
*adj* incomplete

**inconcebible**
[in•KON•se•BEE•blai] *adj*
unthinkable

**inconcienia**
[in•KON•see•en•SEE•ah] *n* F
unconsciousness

**incondicional**
[in•KOHN•dih•SEE•ohn•AHL]
*adj* unconditional

**inconquistado**
[in•KON•kee•STAH•do] *adj*
unconquered

**inconsciente**
[in•KON•see•EN•tai] *adj*
unconscious
**inconsiderado**
[IN•kon•SIH•dair•AH•do] *adj*
inconsiderate; thoughtless
**inconsistente**
[in•KOHN•sis•TEN•tai] *adj*
inconsistent
**incontable** [IN•kon•TAHB•lai]
*adj* countless
**incorporar** [in•KOH•por•AHR]
*vt* incorporate
**incorrecto** [IN•kohr•REHK•to]
*adj* incorrect
**incoveniente**
[IN•kon•VEN•ee•EN•tai] *adj*
inconvenient
**incrédulo 1** [IN•kreh•DOO•lo]
*adj* incredulous
**incrédulo 2** [IN•kreh•DOO•lo]
*n* M unbeliever
**increíble** [IN•krai•EEB•lai] *adj*
incredible; unbelievable
**increpar** [IN•kreh•PAHR] *vi*
rebuke
**incriminar**
[in•KRIH•mee•NAHR] *vt*
incriminate
**incubar** [in•koo•BAHR] *vt*
hatch
**inculto** [in•KUHL•to] *adj*
uncultured; uneducated
**incurable** [IN•kewr•AHB•lai]
*adj* incurable
**incurrir** [IN•koor•EER] *vt* incur
**incursión** [in•KOOR•see•OHN]
*n* F incursion; raid
**indebido** [IN•dai•BIH•do] *adj*
undue

**indecente** [IN•deh•SEN•tai] *adj*
indecent
**indeciso** [IN•deh•SEE•so] *adj*
undecided
**indefinido**
[in•DEH•fihn•EE•doh] *adj*
indefinite
**indemnidad**
[in•DEM•nih•DAHD] *n* F
indemnity
**indentidad**
[ih•DEN•tee•DAHD] *n* F
identity
**indentificar**
[ih•DEN•tih•FIH•kahr] *vt*
identify
**independencia**
[IN•deh•PEN•den•SEE•ah] *n*
F independence
**independiente**
[IN•deh•PEN•dee•EN•tai] *adj*
independent
**indeseable**
[in•DEH•sai•AH•blai] *adj*
unwelcome
**indestructible**
[in•DEH•strook•TEE•blai] *adj*
indestructible
**India** [in•DEE•ah] *n* F India
**indicación**
[IN•dih•KAH•see•OHN] *n* F
cue; hint
**indicador** [in•DEE•kah•DOR] *n*
M indicator
**indicar** [ihn•DEE•kahr] *vt*
designate; indicate
**índice** [in•DEE•sai] *n* M index
**índice de longevidad**
[IN•DEE•sai dai
lon•HEH•vee•DAHD] *n* F life
expectancy

**indiferencia**
[IN•dih•FAIR•en•SEE•ah] *n* F
recklessness

**indiferente**
[in•DIH•fair•EN•tai] *adj*
half-hearted; indifferent;
nonchalant; unconcerned

**indigena** [IN•dih•HAI•nah] *adj*
indigenous

**indigestión**
[ihn•DIH•heh•STEE•OHN] *n*
F indigestion

**indignado** [in•DIHG•NAH•doh]
*adj* indignant

**indigno** [in•DIG•no] *adj*
unworthy

**indigo** [in•DEE•go] *adj n* M
indigo

**indio** [in•DEE•oh] *adj* Indian

**indirecto** [IHN•dih•REHK•to]
*adj* indirect

**indiscreto** [IN•dih•SKREH•to]
*adj* indiscreet

**indispensable**
[in•DIH•spen•SAHB•lai] *adj*
indispensable

**indispuesto**
[IN•dih•SPWEHS•toh] *adj*
indisposed

**indistinto** [IN•dih•STIN•toh]
*adj* indistinct

**individual**
[in•DIH•vih•DOO•ahl] *adj*
individual

**indolente** [IN•doh•LEN•tai] *n*
M slacker

**indoloro** [IN•doh•LOH•roh] *adj*
painless

**inducir** [IN•doo•SEER] *vt*
induce; force

**industria** [IN•doo•STREE•ah] *n*
F industry

**industrial** [IN•doo•STREE•ahl]
*adj* industrial

**industrioso**
[in•DOO•stree•OH•so] *adj*
industrious

**ineficaz** [in•EH•fee•KAHS] *adj*
ineffective

**inesperado**
[in•EH•spair•AH•do] *adj*
sudden

**inestimable**
[in•EH•stee•MAHB•lai] *adj*
invaluable

**inevitable**
[in•EH•vee•TAHB•lai] *adj*
inevitable; unavoidable

**inexacto** [IN•ehks•AHK•to] *adj*
inaccurate

**inexperto** [IN•ehk•SPAIR•toh]
*adj* inexperienced; untrained

**inexplicable**
[in•EHKS•plih•KAHB•lai] *adj*
unaccountable

**inexpugnable**
[in•EHKS•puhg•NAH•blai]
*adj* unassailable

**infalible** [IN•fah•LEE•blai] *adj*
infallible

**infame** [in•FAH•mai] *adj*
infamous

**infancia** [IN•fahn•SEE•ah] *n* F
infancy; childhood

**infante** [in•FAHN•tai] *n* M
infant

**infantería**
[in•FAHN•tair•EE•ah] *n* F
infantry

**infantil** [IHN•fahn•TEEL] *adj*
childish

**infección** [in•FEHK•see•OHN]
*n* F infection

**infeccioso**
[in•FEHK•see•OH•so] *adj*
infectious

**infectar** [IN•fehk•TAHR] *vt*
infect

**infeliz** [IN•feh•LEES] *adj*
wretched

**inferior** [in•FAIR•ee•OHR] *adj*
*n* M inferior

**inferir** [IN•fair•EER] *vt* infer

**infidelidad**
[IN•fee•DEHL•ee•DAHD] *n* F
infidelity

**infierno** [IHN•fee•AIR•no] *n* M
hell

**infinidad** [in•FIH•nih•DAHD] *n*
F infinity

**infinitivo** [in•FIH•nih•TEE•voh]
*adj* infinitive

**infinito** [IN•fih•NEE•toh] *adj*
infinite

**inflación** [in•FLAHK•see•OHN]
*n* F inflation

**inflamar** [IN•flah•MAHR] *vt*
inflame

**inflar** [in•FLAHR] *vt* inflate;
swell

**inflexible** [IN•flehk•SEE•blai]
*adj* unbending; uncompromising; unyielding

**inflexión** [in•FLEHK•see•OHN]
*n* F inflection

**infligir** [IN•flih•HEER] *vt* inflict

**influencia**
[in•FLOO•en•SEE•ah] *n* F
influence

**influenza** [IN•floo•EN•sah] *n* F
influenza; flu

**información**
[IN•for•MAH•see•OHN] *n* F
information

**informar** [IN•for•MAHR] *vt*
inform

**informar mal** [IN•for•MAHR
mahl] *vt* misinform

**infortunio** [IN•for•toon•EE•oh]
*n* M misfortune

**infracción1**
[in•FRAHK•see•OHN] *n* F
breach (of contract)

**infracción 2**
[in•FRAHK•see•OHN] *n* F
trespass

**infrascrito** [IN•frah•SKREE•to]
*n* M undersigned

**infringir** [IN•frin•GEER] *vt*
infringe

**infructífero**
[in•FRUHK•tee•FAIR•oh] *adj*
barren

**infructuoso**
[in•FRUHK•too•OH•so] *adj*
unsuccessful

**infundado** [IN•fuhn•DAH•do]
*adj* groundless; baseless

**ingeniería**
[in•HEN•ee•AIR•ee•ah] *n* F
engineering

**ingeniero** [in•HEN•ee•AIR•oh]
*n* M engineer

**ingenio** [IN•hen•EE•oh] *n* M
engine

**ingenio** [IN•hen•EE•oh] *n* M
wit

**ingenioso 1** [in•HEN•ee•OH•so]
*adj* ingenious

**ingenioso 2** [in•HEN•ee•OH•so]
*adj* witty

**Inglaterra**
[EENG•glah•TAIR•rah] *n* F
England

**ingle** [IN•glai] *n* M groin

**inglés** [in•GLAIS] *n* M English

**ingratitud**
[in•GRAH•tih•TOOD] *n* F
ingratitude

**ingrediente**
[in•GREH•dee•EN•tai] *n* M
ingredient

**ingreso** [in•GREH•so] *n* M
income

**inhabilitar**
[IN•ah•BEE•lee•TAHR] *vt*
disqualify

**inhabitable**
[in•AH•bih•TAHB•lai] *adj*
homeless

**inhalar** [IN•hah•LAHR] *vt*
inhale

**inherente** [IN•hair•EN•tai] *adj*
inherent

**inhumano** [IN•hoo•MAHN•oh]
*adj* inhuman

**inicial** [in•IH•see•AHL] *adj*
initial

**iniciar** [in•IH•see•AHR] *vt*
initiate

**injerto** [in•HAIR•to] *n* M graft

**injusticia**
[in•HOO•stee•SEE•ah] *n* F
injustice

**injustificado**
[IN•hoo•STEE•fih•DAH•do]
*adj* unwarranted

**inmaculado**
[in•MAH•koo•LAH•do] *adj*
immaculate

**inmaterial**
[in•MAH•tair•EE•ahl] *adj*
immaterial

**inmaturo** [IN•mah•TOOR•oh]
*adj* immature

**inmediamente**
[IN•mai•DEE•ah•MEN•tai]
*adv* immediately; right away

**inmediato**
[in•MAI•dee•AH•toh] *adj*
immediate

**inmenso** [in•MEN•so] *adj*
immense

**inmerecido**
[in•MAIR•eh•SEE•do] *adj*
unearned

**inmigración**
[IN•mee•GRAH•see•OHN] *n*
F immigration

**inmigrante**
[IN•mih•GRAHN•tai] *n* M
immigrant

**inminente** [IN•mihn•EN•tai]
*adj* imminent

**inmoral** [IN•mohr•AHL] *adj*
immoral

**inmortal** [IN•mor•TAHL] *adj*
immortal

**inmortalidad**
[IN•mor•TAHL•ih•DAHD] *n*
F immorality

**inmóvil** [IN•moh•VEEL] *adj*
immobile

**inmovilizar**
[IN•moh•VEE•lih•SAHR] *vt*
immobilize

**inmune** [in•MOO•nai] *adj*
exempt; immune

**inmunidad**
[in•MOO•nih•DAHD] *n* F
immunity

**inmunizar**
[in•MOON•ih•SAHR] *vt*
immunize

**inmutable** [IN•moo•TAH•blai] *adj* unchangeable

**innato** [in•NAH•to] *adj* innate

**innecesario** [IN•neh•SEH•sahr•EE•oh] *adj* needless

**innegable** [IN•neh•GAHB•lai] *adj* undeniable

**innovación** [in•NOH•vah•SEE•OHN] *n* F innovation

**inocencia** [in•OH•sen•SEE•ah] *n* F innocence

**inocente** [IN•oh•SEN•tai] *adj* innocent

**inocular** [IN•oh•KOO•LAHR] *vt* inoculate

**inorgánico** [IN•or•GAHN•ee•koh] *n* F inorganic

**inquietud** [in•KEE•eh•TOOD] *n* F restlessness

**inquirir** [in•KWEER•eer] *vi* inquire

**inquisición** [in•KWIH•zih•SEE•OHN] *n* F inquisition

**inquisitivo** [in•KIH•see•TEE•vo] *adj* inquisitive

**insaciable** [in•SAH•see•AHB•lai] *adj* insatiable

**insano** [in•SAHN•oh] *adj* insane

**inscripción** [in•SKRIHP•see•OHN] *n* F inscription

**insecticida** [in•SEHK•tih•SEE•dah] *n* F insecticide

**insecto** [in•SEHK•toh] *n* M bug; insect

**inseguro** [IN•seh•GOOR•oh] *adj* insecure

**insensible** [IN•scn•SEE•blai] *adj* insensitive; senseless

**inseparable** [in•SEH•pahr•AHB•lai] *adj* inseparable

**inserir** [IN•sair•EER] *vt* insert

**insignia** [IN•sig•NEE•ah] *n* F badge

**insignificante** [IN•sig•NIH•fee•KAHN•tai] *adj* insignificant; petty

**insinuación** [in•SIN•oo•ah•SEE•OHN] *n* F innuendo; hint; indication

**insípido** [IN•sih•PEE•doh] *adj* insipid

**insistente** [IN•sih•SEN•tai] *adj* insistent

**insistir 1** [IN•sis•TEER] *vi* insist

**insistir 2** [IN•sih•STEER] *vt* urge

**insolente** [IN•soh•LEN•tai] *adj* insolent

**insolvente** [IN•sol•VEN•tai] *adj* bankrupt

**insomne** [IN•som•NAI] *adj* sleepless

**insomnio** [IN•som•NEE•oh] *n* M insomnia

**insospechado** [IN•so•SPECH•AH•do] *adj* unsuspected

**inspección** [in•SPEHK•see•OHN] *n* F inspection

**inspeccionar** [in•SPEHK•see•oh•NAHR] *vt* inspect

**inspector** [IN•spehk•TOR] *n* M
inspector; overseer

**inspiración**
[IN•speer•AH•see•OHN] *n* F
inspiration

**inspirar** [IN•speer•AHR] *vt*
inspire

**instalación**
[IN•stah•LAH•see•OHN] *n* F
installation

**instalar** [IN•stah•LAHR] *vt*
induct; install

**instante** [in•STAHN•tai] *adj*
instant

**instigar** [IN•stee•GAHR] *vt*
instigate

**instilar** [IN•stee•LAHR] *vt*
instill

**instinto** [in•STIN•toh ] *n* M
instinct

**instituto** [IN•stih•TOO•toh] *n*
M institute

**instrucción**
[in•STROOK•see•OHN] *n* F
instruction; teaching; training

**instructor** [in•STROOK•tor] *n*
M instructor

**instruir** [in•STROO•eer] *vt*
instruct

**instrumento**
[IN•stroo•MEN•to] *n* M
instrument; tool

**insuficiencia**
[IN•SUH•fih•SEE•en•SEE•ah]
*n* F deficit

**insuficiente**
[IN•suh•FIH•see•EN•tai] *adj*
insufficient

**insufrible** [IN•suh•FREE•blai]
*adj* unbearable

**insuflación**
[IN•suhl•FLAHK•see•OHN] *n*
F insulation

**insulso** [in•SUHL•so] *adj*
tasteless

**insultar** [IN•sool•TAHR] *vt*
flout

**insulto** [in•SUHL•to] *n* M insult

**intacto** [in•TAHK•toh] *adj*
intact; untouched

**integración**
[IN•teh•GRAH•see•OHN] *n* F
integration

**integrante**
[IN•teh•GRAHN•tai] *adj*
integral

**integridad**
[in•TEH•grih•DAHD] *n* F
integrity

**intelectual**
[IN•teh•LEHK•too•AHL] *adj*
intellectual

**inteligencia**
[in•TEHL•ih•HEN•SEE•ah] *n*
F intelligence

**inteligente**
[in•TEHL•ih•HEN•tai] *adj*
intelligent

**intempestivo**
[in•TEM•peh•STEE•vo] *adj*
untimely

**intención** [in•TEN•see•OHN] *n*
F intention

**intencional**
[IN•ten•SEE•on•AHL] *adj*
intentional

**intensidad** [in•TEN•sih•DAHD]
*n* F intensity

**intensificar**
[in•TEN•sih•FEE•kahr] *vt*
intensify

**intenso** [in•TEN•so] *adj*
intense; intensive
**intentar** [IN•ten•TAHR] *vt*
intend
**intento 1** [in•TEN•to] *n* M
intent
**intento 2** [in•TEN•to] *n* M
endeavor
**intercambiar**
[in•TAIR•KAHM•bee•AHR]
*vt* exchange; interchange
**intercambio**
[in•TAIR•kahm•BEE•oh] *n* M
interchange
**interceptar**
[in•TAIR•sehp•TAHR] *vt*
intercept
**interés** [IN•tair•EHS] *n* M
interest; concern; en ~ a
beneficio de\ on behalf (of)
**interesante**
[in•TAIR•eh•SAHN•tai] *adj*
interesting
**interferencia**
[IN•tair•FAIR•en•SEE•ah] *n* F
interference
**interferir** [in•TAIR•fair•EER] *vi*
interfere
**interior** [in•TAIR•ee•OHR] *adj*
indoor; inner; inside; *n* M
interior
**intermedio**
[in•TAIR•mai•DEE•oh] *adj*
intermediate; interim
**interminable**
[in•TAIR•mee•NAHB•lai] *adj*
endless; interminable
**intermisión**
[in•TAIR•mih•SEE•OHN] *n* F
intermission

**internacional**
[in•TAIR•nah•SEE•oh•NAHL]
*adj* international
**interno 1** [in•TAIR•no] *n* M
intern
**interno 2** [in•TAIR•no] *adj*
internal; inward
**interponerse**
[in•TAIR•pon•AIR•sai] *vi*
go-between
**interpretación**
[in•TAIR•preh•TAH•see•OHN]
*n* F interpretation
**interpretado**
[IN•tair•PREH•tah•DORR] *n*
M interpreter
**interpretar**
[in•TAIR•preh•TAHR] *vt*
interpret
**interrogación**
[in•TAIR•roh•GAH•see•OHN]
*n* F interrogation
**interrogar**
[in•TAIR•roh•GAHR] *vt*
interrogate
**interrumpir**
[in•TAIR•room•PEER] *vt vi*
interrupt
**interrupción**
[IN•tair•RUHP•see•OHN] *n* F
interruption
**intersección**
[IN•tair•SEHK•see•OHN] *n* F
intersection
**intervención**
[IN•tair•VEN•see•OHN] *n* F
intervention
**intervenir** [in•TAIR•ven•EER]
*vt* intervene
**interventor**
[in•TAIR•ven•TOR] *n* M
controller

**intestino** |IN•teh•STEE•no| *n*
M intestine

**intestinos**
|IN•tehs•STEEN•ohs| *npl* M
bowels

**intimidad** |in•TEE•mih•DAHD|
*n* F intimacy; privacy

**intimidar** |in•TEE•mih•DAHR|
*vt* daunt

**íntimo** |in•TEE•mo| *adj* inmost;
intimate

**intitulado**
|in•TEE•too•LAH•doh| *adj*
entitled

**intolerable**
|in•TOH•lair•AHB•lai| *adj*
intolerable

**intolerancia**
|IN•toh•LAIR•ahn•SEE•ah| *n*
F intolerance

**intolerante**
|in•TOH•lair•AHN•tai| *adj*
intolerant

**intoxicar**
|in•TOHKS•ih•KAHR| *vt*
poison

**intoxicación**
|IN•tohks•ih•KAH•see•OHN|
*n* F poisoning

**intranquilo**
|in•TRAHN•KEE•lo| *adj*
restless; uneasy

**intriga** |in•TREE•gah| *n* F
intrigue

**intrincado** |IN•treen•KAH•do|
*adj* intricate

**introducción**
|IN•troh•DOOK•see•OHN| *n*
F introduction

**introducir**
|in•TROH•doo•SEER| *vt*
introduce

**introverso** |IN•troh•VAIR•soh|
*n* M introvert

**intrución** |in•TROO•see•OHN|
*n* F intrusion

**intuición** |IN•too•IH•see•OHN|
*n* F intuition

**inundado** |IN•uhn•DAH•do|
*adj* overrun

**inundar** |IN•uhn•DAHR | *vt*
inundate

**inútil** |in•OO•teel| *adj* fruitless;
useless

**inutilidad**
|IN•oo•TIHL•ih•DAHD| *n* F
uselessness

**inutilizado**
|IN•oo•TEE•lih•SAH•doh| *adj*
disabled

**invadir** |IN•vah•DEER| *vt*
invade

**invalidar** |in•VAH•lee•DAHR|
*vt* avoid

**inválido** |IN•vah•LEE•do| *adj*
invalid

**invariablemente**
|in•VAHR•ee•AHB•leh•MEN•
tai| *adv* invariably

**invasión** |in•VAH•see•OHN| *n*
F invasion

**invencible** |IN•ven•SEE•blai|
*adj* invincible

**invención** |in•VEN•see•OHN| *n*
F invention

**inventar** |IN•ven•TAHR| *vi*
contrive; invent

**inventario**
|in•VEN•tahr•EE•oh| *n* M
inventory

**inventivo** |IN•ven•TEE•vo| *adj*
inventive

**inventor** [IN•ven•TOHR] *n* M
inventor

**invernáculo para plantas**
[IN•vair•NAH•koo•lo
PAH•rah PLAHN•tahs] *n* M
greenhouse

**invernar** [IN•vair•NAHR] *vi*
hibernate

**inverso** [LO in•VAIR•so] *n* M
reverse

**investidura**
[in•VEH•stee•DOOR•ah] *n* F
investment

**investigación**
[in•VEH•stee•GAH•see•OHN]
*n* F investigation

**investigar**
[in•VEH•stee•GAHR] *vt*
investigate

**investir** [IN•veh•STEER] *vt vi*
invest

**invierno** [IN•vee•AIR•no] *n* M
winter; de ~\ *adj* wintry

**invisible** [IN•vih•SEE•blai] *adj*
M invisible

**invitación**
[IN•vih•TAH•see•OHN] *n* F
invitation

**invitar** [IN•vee•TAHR] *vt* invite

**invocar** [IN•voh•KAHR] *vt*
invoke

**involuntario**
[in•VOH•luhn•TAHR•EE•oh]
*adj* involuntary

**inyectar** [IN•yehk•TAHR] *vt*
inject

**ir** [eer] *vi* go; ~ a hacer\ to be
going to do; ~ a pie\ walk; ~
en coche\ go by care; no me
va ni me viene\ it's all the
same to me; ¡vete a saber!\

who knows; ¡ya voy!\ I'm
coming

**ira** [EER•ah] *n* F wrath; anger

**Irak** [EER•ahk] *n* M Iraq

**Irán** [eer•AHN] *n* M Iran

**iranio** [EER•ahn•EE•oh] *adj*
Iranian

**ir de compras** [eer dai
KOM•prahs] *vi* shopping (to
go)

**irlandés** [EER•lahn•DAIS] *adj*
Irish

**Irlanda** [EER•lahn•DEE•ah] *n* F
Ireland

**ironía** [EER•ohn•EE•ah] *n* F
irony

**irónico** [EER•ohn•EE•koh] *adj*
ironic

**ir por** [eer por] *vt* fetch

**irracional**
[eer•RAH•see•OHN•AHL] *adj*
irrational

**irreemplazable**
[EER•reh•EM•plah•SAHB•lai]
*adj* irreplaceable

**irreflexivo**
[eer•REH•flehks•EE•vo] *adj*
unthinking

**irrefrenable**
[eer•REH•fren•AHB•blai] *adj*
uncontrollable

**irregular** [eer•REH•goo•LAHR]
*adj* irregular

**irregularidad**
[eer•REH•goo•LAHR•ih•
DAHD] *n* F irregularity

**irreparable**
[eer•REH•pahr•AHB•lai] *adj*
irreparable

**irresistible**
[eer•REH•sis•TEEB•lai] *adj*
irresistible

**irresponsable**
[eer•REH•spon•SAHB•lai] *adj*
irresponsible

**irrigación**
[EER•rih•GAH•see•OHN] *n* F
irrigation

**irrigar** [EER•rih•GAHR] *vt*
irrigate

**irritable** [EER•ih•TAHB•lai]
*adj* cranky; irritable

**irritar** [EER•rih•TAHR] *vt*
irritate

**irrompible**
[EER•rohm•PEE•blai] *adj*
unbreakable

**irse** [EER•sai] *vr* go away

**irse a fondo** [EER•sai ah
FON•do] *vi* lunge

**isla** [EES•lah] *n* F island

**Islam** [ees•LAHM] *n* Islam

**Islandia** [EES•lahn•DEE•ah] *n*
Iceland

**italiano** [IH•tah•lee•AHN•oh]
*adj* Italian

**itálico** [IH•tahl•IH•koh] *adj*
italic

**itinerario**
[ih•TIHN•air•AHR•EE•oh] *n*
M itinerary

**izar** [ee•SAHR] *vt* hoist

**izquierdista**
[ihs•KEE•air•DEE•stah] *n* F
left; *n* MF leftist; a la ~ a\ on
the left, to the left; de ala ~\
left-wing

# J

**jabalina** [HAH•bah•LEEN•ah] *n*
F javelin

**jabón** [hah•BON] *n* M soap

**jabonaduras**
[hah•BON•ah•DOOR•ahs] *npl*
F suds

**jacinto** [hah•SEEN•to] *n* M
hyacinth

**jactancia** [HAHK•tan•SEE•ah]
*n* F vaunt

**jadeante** [HAH•dai•AHN•tai]
*adj* breathless

**jaeces** [HAI•ai•SAIS] *npl*
trappings

**jalea** [hah•LAI•ah] *n* F jelly

**jamón** [hah•MOHN] *n* M ham

**Japón** [hah•POHN] *n* M Japan

**japonés** [HAH•pohn•EHS] *adj*
Japanese

**jaquita** [hah•KEE•tah] *n* pony

**jarabe** [hah•RAH•bai] *n* M
syrup

**jarana** [hah•RAHN•ah] *n* F
revelry

**jardín** [har•DEEN] *n* M garden

**jarro** [HAHR•roh] *n* M mug;
jug; pitcher

**jaula** [HOU•lah] *n* F cage

**jazz** [yahz] *n* M jazz

**jefe** [HEH•fai] *n* M boss; chief

**jengibre** [hen•HEE•brai] *n* M
ginger

**jerarquía** [HAIR•ahr•KEE•ah] *n*
F hierarchy

**jerga** [HAIR•gah] *n* F jargon; lingo; slang

**jeringa** [HAIR•ing•GAH] *n* F syringe

**jeringar** [HAIR•ring•GAHR] *vi* squirt

**jersey** [HAIR•see] *n* M jersey

**jirafa** [HEER•ah•FAH] *n* F giraffe

**jockey** [YOH•kee] *n* M jockey

**joroba** [hor•OH•bah] *n* F hunch

**jorobado** [HOR•oh•BAH•doh] *n* M hunchback

**joven** [HO•ven] *adj* young; youthful; el más ~\ youngster

**joven rico** [HO•ven REE•koh] *n* M playboy

**jovenes** [HO•vehn•AIS] *npl* teens

**joya** [HOI•yah] *n* F jewel; trinket

**joyas** [HOI•yahs] *npl* F jewelry

**joyero** [hoi•YAIR•oh] *n* M jeweler

**júbilo** [hoo•BEE•loh] *n* M joy

**jubiloso** [HOO•bee•LOH•soh] *adj* joyful; jubilant; overjoyed

**judaico** [hoo•DAI•koh] *adj* Jewish

**judicial** [hoo•DIH•see•AHL] *adj* judicial

**judío** [hoo•DEE•oh] *n* M Jew

**juego 1** [HWAI•go] *n* M gamble; game; play

**juego 2** [HWAI•go] *n* M kit

**juego de palabras** [hoo•AI•go dai pah•LAH•brahs] *n* M pun

**juerga** [HWAIR•gah] *n* F spree

**jueves** [HWAI•vais] *n* M Thursday

**juez** [hwais] *n* M judge

**jugador** [hoo•GAH•dor] *n* M player

**jugar** [HOO•gar] *vt vi* play

**jugar al golf** [HOO•gar ahl golf] *n* M golf

**juglar** [HOOG•lahr] *n* M juggler

**jugo** [HOO•go] *n* M juice

**jugoso** [hoo•GO•so] *adj* juicy

**juguete** [hoo•GEH•teh] *n* M plaything; toy

**juguetear** [HOO•geh•TAI•ahr] *vi* frolic

**juguetón** [HOO•geh•TON] *adj* playful

**juicioso** [HWEE•see•OH•so] *adj* judicious

**julio** [hoo•LEE•oh] *n* M July

**junco** [HUHN•koh] *n* M junk

**junio** [hoon•EE•oh] *n* M June

**juntar 1** [huhn•TAHR] *vt* splice

**juntar 2** [huhn•TAHR] *vt vi* collect

**junto** [HUHN•to] *prep* together

**junto a** [HUHN•toh ah] *prep* about

**junto con esto** [HUHN•to kon EH•sto] *adv* herewith

**junto de** [HUII•to dai] *prep* by

**jurado** [hoor•AH•doh] *n* M juror

**jurado** *n* M jury

**juramento** [HOOR•ah•MEN•toh] *n* M oath

**jurar** [HOOR•ahr] *vi* swear

**jurisdicción 1** [HOOR•ihs•DIHK•see•OHN] *n* F jurisdiction

**jurisdicción 2** [HOOR•ihs•DIHK•see•OHN] *n* F venue

**justicia** [HOO•stee•SEE•ah] *n* F justice

**justificar**
  [hoo•STEE•fee•KAHR] *vt*
  justify
**justo** [HUH•stoh] *adj* just
**juvenil** [HOO•ven•EEL] *adj*
  juvenile

**juventud** [HOO•ven•TOOD] *n*
  F youth
**juzgar mal** [HOOS•gahr mahl]
  *vt* misjudge

# K

**Kenya** [KEHN•yah] *n* Kenya
**kilogramo**
  [KEE•loh•GRAHM•oh] *n* M
  kilogram

**kilometro** [KEE•lo•MAI•troh] *n*
  M kilometer
**kilovoltio**
  [kee•LO•vohl•TEE•oh] *n* M
  kilowatt

# L

**la; le** [lah] [lai] pers *pron* her; the
**laberinto** [LAH•bair•EEN•to] *n*
  M maze
**labio** [lah•BEE•oh] *n* M lip
**laboratorio**
  [LAH•bor•AH•tor•EE•oh] *n* M
  lab; laboratory
**labrador** [lah•BRAH•dor] *n* M
  peasant
**laca** [LAH•kah] *n* F lacquer
**ladera** [lah•DAIR•ah] *n* F
  hillside
**lado** [LAH•do] *n* M side; al ~\
  *adv* aside; *prep* beside; de ~\
  sideways; de un solo ~ *adj*
  one-sided
**lado superior** [LAH•do
  SOO•pair•EE•or] *n* M upside

**ladrillo** [lah•DREE•yo] *n* M brick
**ladrón** [lah•DRON] *n* M
  burglar; robber; thief
**lagarto** [LAH•gahr•TOH] *n* M
  lizard
**lago** [LAH•go] *n* M lake
**lágrima** [LAH•GREE•mah] *n* F
  tear
**laguna** [lah•GOON•ah] *n* F
  lagoon
**lama** [LAH•mah] *n* F tinsel
**lamentable**
  [LAH•men•TAHB•lai] *adj*
  rueful
**lamentar 1** [LAH•men•TAHR]
  *vt* mourn; regret
**lamentar 2** [LAH•men•TAHR]
  *vi* wail

**lamentarse**
[LAH•men•TAHR•sai] *vi*
complain; lament

**lamento** [lah•MEN•toh] *n* M
complaint; mourning

**lamer** [LAH•mair] *vt* lick

**laminar** [LAH•mee•NAHR] *vt*
laminate

**laminita** [LAH•mee•NEE•tah] *n*
F foil

**lampára** [lahm•PAHR•ah] *n* F
lamp

**lana** [LAHN•ah] *n* F wool; de
~\ woolly

**langosta** [LAHNG•go•STAH] *n*
F crayfish; lobster; locust

**lánguido** [lahng•GWEE•do] *adj*
languid

**lanilla** [lahn•EE•yah] *n* F fluff

**lanudo** [lah•NOO•do] *adj*
woolen

**lanza 1** [LAN•sah] *n* F lance;
spear

**lanza 2** [LAHN•sah] *n* F nozzle

**lanzadera**
[LAHN•sah•DAIR•ah] *n* F
shuttle

**lanzamiento**
[lahn•SAH•mee•EN•to] *n* M
launch; discharge; shoot
off

**lanzar** [LAN•sahr] *vt* bounce;
hurl

**lápiz** [LAH•pees] *n* F pencil

**lápiz labial** [LAH•pees
lah•BEE•ahl] *n* M lipstick

**lapso** [LAHP•soh] *n* M lapse

**largo** [LAHR•go] *adj* long; a lo
~ de\ along; tener 25 metros
de ~\ be 25 meters long; por
lo ~\ along

**larva** [LAHR•vah] *n* F grub

**lascivo** [lah•SEE•voh] *adj*
lewd

**lástima** [LAH•STEE•mah] *n* F
compassion

**lastimar** [LAH•stee•MAHR] *vt*
grieve; hurt

**lastimoso** [LAH•stee•MOH•so]
*adj* piteous

**lata** [LAH•tah] *n* F tin can

**latente** [lah•TEN•tai] *adj* latent

**latido** [lah•TEE•do] *n* M
heartbeat

**látigo** [lah•TEE•go] *n* M switch;
whip

**latino** [lah•TEEN•oh] *adj n* M
Latin

**latir** [lah•TEER] *vi* throb

**latitud** [LAH•tee•TOOD] *n* F
latitude

**laurel** [LOU•rehl] *n* M laurel

**lava** [LAH•vah] *n* F lava

**lavabo** [LAH•VAH•boh] *n* M
lavatory

**lavadero** [LAH•vah•DÁIR•oh]
*n* M laundry

**lavado** [lah•VAH•do] *n* M
washer; washing; ~ de
cerebro\ brainwashing; ~ en
seco\ dry cleaning

**lavadora** [LAH•vah•DOR•ah] *n*
F washing-machine

**lavaplatos**
[LAH•vah•PLAH•tos] *n* M
dishwasher

**lavar** [LAH•vahr] *vt* launder;
wash

**laxativo** [LAHKS•ah•TEE•vo]
*n* M laxative

**laxo** [LAHK•so] *adj* lax

**laya** [LAI•yah] *n* F spade

**lazo** [LAH•so] *n* M noose

**le** *pron* him; her; you

**lebrel** [LEH•brehl] *n* M hound

**lección** [LEHK•see•OHN] *n* F lecture; lesson

**lector** [LEHK•tor] *n* M reader; reading

**leche** [LEH•chai] *n* F milk

**lecheria** [LEH•chair•EE•ah] *n* F dairy

**lechuga** [leh•CHOO•gah] *n* lettuce

**lechuguilla** [LEH•choo•GWEE•yah] *n* F ruffle

**leer** [LAI•air] *vt* read

**legado** [lai•GAH•do] *n* M legacy

**legal** [LAI•gahl] *adj* lawful; *n* M legal

**legalizar** [lai•GAHL•ih•SAHR] *vt* legalize

**legendario** [leh•HEN•dahr•EE•oh] *adj* legendary

**legible** [leh•HEE•blai] *adj* legible

**legislación** [LEH•his•LAH•see•OHN] *n* F legislation

**legitimo** [LEH•hih•TEE•moh] *adj* legitimate

**lejos** [LAI•hos] *adj* far; ~ de\ far from; a lo ~\ in the distance; desde ~\ from a distance, from afar; a lo ~\ beyond; lo más ~\ farthest

**lejos fuera** [LAI•hos] [foo•AIR•ah] *adv* away

**leña** [LAIN•yah] *n* F firewood

**leñador** [LEHN•yah•DOR] *n* M lumberjack

**lengua** [LAING•gwah] *n* F tongue

**lenguaje** [lehn•GWAH•hai] *n* F language

**lentamente** [LEHN•tah•MEN•tai] *adv* heavily

**lente** [LEHN•tai] *n* M lens

**lente de aumento** [LEHN•tai dai ou•MEN•toh] *n* M magnifying glass

**león** [lai•OHN] *n* M lion

**leona** [lai•OH•nah] *n* F lioness

**leopardo** [lai•OH•pahr•DOH] *n* M cheetah; leopard

**lepra** [LEH•prah] *n* F leprosy

**leproso** [leh•PROH•so] *n* M leper

**lesbiano** [LEHS•bee•AHN•oh] *n* M lesbian

**lesión** [LEH•see•OHN] *n* F wound

**letal** [LEH•tahl] *adj* lethal

**letargo** [leh•TAHR•go] *n* M lethargy

**Letonia** [LEH•toh•NEE•ah] *n* M Latvia

**letra** [LEH•trah] *n* F script

**leva** [LAI•vah] *n* F levy

**levadura** [LEH•vah•DOOR•ah] *n* F yeast

**levantado** [LAI•van•TAH•doh] *adj* erect

**levantamiento** [LEH•vahn•TAH•mee•EN•toh] *n* M lift; uprising

**levantar** [LEH•vahn•TAHR] *vt* heave; raise; uplift; elevate

**ley** [lai] *n* F law; statute

**leyenda** [lai•EHN•dah] *n* F legend

**Líbano** [LEE•BAHN•oh] *n* M
Lebanon

**libelo** [lee•BEH•loh] *n* M
lampoon; libel

**libélula** [lee•BEH•LOO•lah] *n* F
dragonfly

**liberación**
[LEE•bair•AH•see•OHN] *n* F
liberation

**liberal** [LEE•bair•AHL] *adj n* M
liberal

**libertad** [LEE•bair•TAHD] *n* F
freedom; release; liberty

**libertad de palabra**
[LEE•bair•TAHD dai
pah•LAH•brah] *n* F free
speech

**libertar** [LEE•bair•TAHR] *vt*
deliver; liberate

**Libia** [lih•BEE•ah] *n* F Libya

**libra** [LEE•brah] *n* F pound

**librar** [LEE•brahr] *vt* rid

**libre** [LEE•brai] *adj* free

**librea** [lih•BRAI•ah] *n* F livery

**librecambio**
[lee•BRAI•kahm•BEE•oh] *n*
M free trade

**libre de cuidados** [LEE•brai
dai kwee•DAH•dos] *adj*
carefree

**libre de derechos** [LEE•brai
dai dair•AI•chos] *adj* duty-
free

**librería** [LEE•brair•EE•ah] *n* F
bookstore

**libreta** [lih•BREH•tah] *n* F
notebook

**libro** [LEE•bro] *n* M book

**libro de texto** [LEE•bro dai
TEHKS•toh] *n* M textbook

**licencia** [LIH•sen•SEE•ah] *n* F
leave; license

**licor** [LIH•kohr] *n* M liquor

**liebre** [lee•AI•brai] *n* M hare

**lienzo** [lee•EN•so] *n* M linen

**liga 1** [LEE•gah] *n* F garter

**liga 2** [LEE•gah] *n* F league

**ligadura** [LEE•gah•DOOR•ah]
*n* F ligament

**ligeramente**
[lee•HAIR•ah•MEN•tai] *adv*
lightly; slightly

**ligero 1** [lee•HAIR•oh] *adj*
slight

**ligero 2** [lee•HAIR•oh] *adj*
active

**lima** [LEE•mah] *n* F lime

**limitación**
[LIH•mih•TAH•see•OHN] *n* F
limitation

**limitación de la natalidad**
[LILH•mih•TAH•see•ON dai
lah nah•TAHL•ee•DAHD] *n* F
birth control

**límite** [lih•MEE•tai] *n* M
boundary; limit

**límite de velocidad**
[lih•MEE•tai dai
veh•LO•see•DAHD] *n* M
speed limit

**limón** [lee•MON] *n* M lemon

**limonada** [LEE•moh•NAH•dah]
*n* F lemonade

**limousine** [LIH•moo•SEEN•ai]
*n* M limousine

**limpiador**
[lihm•PEE•ah•DOHR] *n* M
cleaner

**limpianicves**
[lihm•PEE•ah•nee•AI•vais] *n*
M snowplow

**limpiar** [lihm•PEE•ahr] *vt* clean;
wipe

**limpieza** [lihm•PEE•ai•SAH] *n* F cleanliness

**limpio** [lihm•PEE•oh] *adj* clean; neat; stainless

**linaje** [lih•NAH•hai] *n* M breed (animals)

**linchar** [LIN•char] *vt* lynch

**lindo** [LEEN•do] *adj* cute

**lindo** [LEEN•do] adj pretty

**línea** [lin•AI•ah] *n* F line; perpendicular

**línea vedada** [lih•NAI•ah vai•DAH•dah] *n* F deadline

**lingüístico** [lin•GWIH•STEE•koh] *n* M linguistics

**lino** [LEE•no] *n* M flax

**linterna** [lihn•TAIR•nah] *n* F flashlight; headlight; lantern

**liquidar** [LIH•kwee•DAHR] *vt* liquidate; melt

**líquido** [lih•KEE•doh] *n* M liquid

**lírico** [leer•IH•koh] *adj* lyrical; *n* M lyric

**liso** [LEE•so] *adj* sleek

**lista** [LIH•stah] *n* F list

**litera** [lih•TAIR•ah] *n* F litter

**literal** [lih•TAIR•ahl] *adj* literal

**literario** [lih•TAIR•ahr•EE•oh] *adj* literary

**literatura** [lih•TAIR•ah•TOOR•ah] *n* F literature

**litigación** [LIH•tih•GAH•see•OHN] *n* F litigation

**lívido** [lih•VEE•doh] *adj* livid

**llegar** [YEAH•gahr] *vi* come

**lo; le** [loh] [leh] *pers pron* him

**lobo** [LOH•bo] *n* M wolf

**lóbulo** [loh•BOO•loh] *n* M lobe

**local** [LOH•kahl] *adj* local

**localizar** [loh•KAHL•ee•SAHR] *vt* locate

**locamente** [LOH•kah•MEN•tai] *adv* madly

**loción** [LOH•see•OHN] *n* F lotion

**loco** [LOH•koh] *adj* crazy; loony; *n* M madman; lunatic

**locomotor** [LOH•koh•MOH•tohr] *n* M locomotive

**locura** [loh•KOOR•ah] *n* F frenzy; insanity; madness

**lodo blando** [LOH•do BLAHN•do] *n* M slop

**lógica** [loh•HEE•kah] *n* F logic

**lógico** [loh•HEE•koh] *adj* logical

**logo** [LOH•goh] *n* M logo

**lona** [LOH•nah] *n* F canvas

**Londres** [LON•drais] *n* M London

**longitud** [lohn•GIH•tood] *n* F length; longitude

**longitud de onda** [lon•GI•tood dai ON•dah] *n* F wavelength

**loor** [lohr] *n* M praise

**los las les** [lohs] [lahs] [lais] them

**lote** [LOH•tai] *n* M lot

**lubricante** [LOO•brih•KAHN•tai] *n* M lubricant

**lubricar** [loo•BREE•KAHR] *vt* lubricate

**lúcido** [loo•SEE•do] *adj* lucid

**lucir** [loo•SEER] *vt* show off; *vi* shine; give off light; sparkle

**lucha** [LOO•cha] *n* F fight;
strife

**luchador** [loo•CHA•DOHR] *n* n
M figher

**luchar** [loo•CHAR] *vi* struggle;
wrestle

**lugar** [loo•GAHR] *n* M place;
location; locality; en segundo
~\ secondly; en tercer ~\
thirdly

**lugareño** [LOO•gahr•EN•yo] *n*
M villager

**lujo** [LOO•ho] *n* M luxury

**lujoso** [loo•HO•so] *adj*
luxurious

**lujurioso** [loo•JOOR•ee•OH•so]
*adj* lecherous

**luminoso** [LOO•min•OH•so]
*adj* luminous

**luna** [LOO•nah] *n* F moon

**luna de miel** [LOO•nah dai
MEE•ehl] *n* F honeymoon

**luna llena** [LOO•nah YAI•nah]
*n* F full moon

**lunar** [LOO•nahr] *adj* lunar

**lunes** [LOO•nais] *n* M Monday

**lustre** [LOO•strai] *n* M glaze;
gloss; uster

**lustroso** [luh•STROH•so] *adj*
glossy

**luz** [loos] *n* F glow; light

**luz de al luna** [loos dai lah
LOO•nah] *n* F moonlight

**luz del cielo** [loos del] *n* F
skylight

**llamada** [yah•MAH•dah] *n* F
phone call

**llamai** [YAH•mahr] *vt* call

**llamarada**
[YAH•mah•RAH•dah] *n* F
flash

**llanta** [YAHN•tah] *n* F tire

**llanta extra** [YAHN•tah
EHK•strah] *n* F tire (spare)

**llanto** [YAN•to] *adj* weeping

**llave** [YAH•vai] *n* M key

**llavero** [yah•VAIR•oh] *n* M key
ring

**llegada** [yai•GAH•dah] *n* F
arrival

**llegar** [YAI•gahr] *vi* arrive

**llenar** [YAI•nahr] *vt* fill;
replenish

**lleno** [YAI•no] *adj* full

**llevado** [yai•VAH•do] *pp* wore

**llevar 1** [YAI•vahr] *vt* wear

**llevar 2** [YAI•vahr] *vt* carry

**llevar 3** [YEAH•vahr] *vt* convey

**llorar** [YOR•ahr] *vi* weep

**llovizna** [yo•VEES•nah] *n* F
drizzle

**lluvia** [yoo•VEE•ah] *n* F rain;
rainfall

**lluvioso** [YOO•vee•OH•so] *adj*
rainy

# M

**maca** [MAH•kah] *n* F defect;
bruise

**macaco** [mah•KAH•koh] *adj*
ugly; *n* M monkey

**macarrohes**
[MAH•kah•ROHN•ais] *npl* M
macaroni

**macerar** [MAH•sair•AHR] *vt*
mash

**macilento**
[MAH•see•LEHN•toh] *adj*
haggard

**macho** [MAH•cho] *n* M male

**madeja** [mah•DAI•ha] *n* F
skein

**madera** [mah•DAIR•ah] *n* F
lumber; timber; wood

**madición** [mahl•DEE•see•OHN]
*n* F curse

**madrastra** [MAH•drah•STAH]
*n* F stepmother

**madre** [MAH•drai] *n* F mother

**madurez** [mah•DOOR•ais] *n* F
maturity

**maduro** [mah•DOOR•oh] *adj*
mature; ripe

**maestro** [mai•AI•stroh] *n* M
schoolteacher; teacher;
master

**maestro de escuela**
[mai•AI•stroh dai
eh•SWAI•lah] *n* M
schoolmaster

**magia** [mah•HEE•ah] *m* F
magic

**mágico** [mah•HEE•koh] *adj*
magical; *n* M magician

**magín** [mah•HEEN] *adj* fancy

**magistrado**
[MAH•hee•STRAH•do] *n* M
magistrate

**magnético**
[MAHG•neh•TEE•koh] *adj*
magnetic

**magnetizar**
[mahg•NEH•tee•SAHR] *vt*
mesmerize; hypnotize

**magnificencia**
[MAG•nih•FIH•sen•SEE•ah] *n*
F magnificence

**magnífico** [mahn•YEE•FEE•ko]
*adj* gorgeous; magnificent

**magnitud** [MAHG•nih•TOOD]
*n* F magnitude

**magro** [MAH•groh] *adj* meager

**magulladura**
[mah•GOO•yah•DOOR•ah] *n*
F bruise

**majestad** [MAH•hehs•TAHD] *n*
F majesty

**majestuoso**
[mah•HE•stoo•OH•so] *adj*
majestic; stately

**mal** [mahl] *adj* bad; badly; ~
que bien\ somehow or other;
de ~ en peor\ worse and
worse; hacer ~ en\ do badly
by

**mal olor** [mahl OH•lor] *n* M
reek

**mala conducta** [MAH•lah
kon•DUHK•tah] *n* F
misconduct; misdemeanor

**mala interpretación**
[MAH•lah
IN•tair•preh•TAH•see•OHN] *n*
F misconception

**maldad** [MAHL•dahd] *n* F
wickedness

**maleta** [mah•LAI•tah] *n* F
valise

**malevolencia**
[MAH•leh•VOH•len•SEE•ah]
*n* F malice

**malévolo** [MAHL•eh•VO•loh]
*adj* malicious

**maleza** [mah•LAI•sah] *n* F
underbrush

**malhumorado**
[mahl•OO•mor•AH•doh] *adj*
glum; grumpy; moody

**maligno** [mali•LIHG•no] *adj*
malignant

**malo** [MAH•loh] *adj* evil;
mischievous; naughty; wicked;
wrong; *n* M evil; harm; illness

**malquerencia**
[mahl•KAIR•en•SEE•ah] *n* F
ill will

**malsano** [mahl•SAHN•oh] *adj*
unwholesome

**maltratar** [MAHL•trah•TAHR]
*vt* mistreat

**malvado** [mahl•VAH•do] *n* M
felon

**malversación**
[MAHL•vair•SAH•see•OHN]
*n* F misappropriation

**malla** [MAI•yah] *n* F mesh

**mamífero**
[MAH•MEE•FAIR•oh] *n* M
mammal

**mamut** [MAH•moot] *n* M
mammoth

**mañana** [mahn•YAHN•ah] *adv*
tomorrow; *n* F morning; por
la ~\ in the morning

**manada** [mah•NAH•dah] *n* F
drove; herd; pack en ~\ in
crowds

**manco** [MAN•ko] *adj*
single-handed

**mancha** [MAN•cha] *n* F fleck;
spot; stain

**manchado** [mahn•CHA•do] *adj*
blurry; dingy; spotty

**manchar** [MAHN•char] *vt*
defile; speckle

**mandar 1** [MAN•dahr] *vt* send

**mandar 2** [MAN•dahr] *vt* leave;
bequeath

**mandato** [man•DAH•toh] *n* M
mandate

**mandíbula**
[MAHN•dee•BOO•lah] *n* F
jaw

**manejable**
[MAHN•eh•HAB•lai] *adj*
tractable

**manera** [mahn•AIR•ah] *n* F
manner; de ~ que\ so that; de
otra ~\ otherwise; de ninguna
~\ not at all

**maneras** [mah•NAIR•ahs] *npl* F
behavior; de todas ~\ anyway

**manga** [MAHN•gah] *n* F hose;
sleeve

**manía** [mah•NEE•ah] *n* F craze;
mania; fad

**manicura**
[MAHN•ee•KOOR•ah] *n* F
manicure

**manifiesto**
[mahn•EE•fee•EH•stoh] *adj n*
M manifest

**manigua** [mahn•EE•gwah] *n* F
jungle

**manilla** [mahn•EE•ya] *n* F
handcuff

**maniobra** [MAN•ee•OH•brah]
*n* F maneuver

**manipular** [MAN•ihp•OO•lahr]
*vt* manipulate

**mano** [MAH•no] *n* F hand; a ~\
by hand; de segunda ~\
second hand; echar una ~\
lend a hand; tener buena ~\

para to be good at; de la ~\
right-hand

**mano izquierda** [MAH•no
ihs•KEE•AIR•dah] *n* F
left-handed

**manojo** [mahn•OH•ho] *n* M
bunch; handful

**manopla** [man•OP•lah] *n* F
gauntlet

**manotear** [MAH•no•TAI•ahr]
*vi* gesticulate

**mansión** [MAHN•see•OHN] *n*
F mansion

**manso** [MAHN•so] *adj* meek

**manta** [MAHN•tah] *n* F blanket

**manteca** [man•TAI•kah] *n* F
butter; shortening

**mantener** [man•TEN•air] *vt*
maintain; uphold; preserve;
keep; maintain

**mantenimiento**
[man•TEN•ee•MEE•EN•toh] *n*
M maintenance

**mantequera**
[MAHN•teh•QAIR•ah] *n* F
churn

**mantequilla**
[MAHN•teh•KEE•ya] *n* F
butter

**manual** [MAHN•oo•AHL] *adj n*
M manual

**manubrio** [MAN•oo•BREE•oh]
*n* M crank; winch

**manuscrito**
[MAH•noo•SKREE•toh] *n* M
manuscript

**manutención**
[MAN•oo•TEN•see•OHN] *n* F
upkeep

**manzana** [mahn•SAHN•ah] *n* F
apple

**mapa** [MAH•pah] *n* M map; F
chart

**mapache** [mah•PAH•chai] *n* M
raccoon

**máquina** [mah•KEE•nah] *n* F
machine

**máquina de coser**
[mah•KEE•nah dai KOH•sair]
*n* F sewing machine

**máquina de escribir**
[mah•KEE•nah dai
eh•SKREE•beer] *n* F
typewriter

**máquina de vapor**
[mah•KEE•nah dai VAH•por]
*n* F steam engine

**maquinaria**
[mah•KEEN•ahr•EE•ah] *n* F
machinery

**mar** [mahr] *n* M sea; la ~ de\
lots of

**maratón** [mahr•AH•TON] *n* F
marathon

**maravilla** [MAH•rah•VEE•yah]
*n* F marigold; marvel

**maravillar** [MAH•rah•VEE•ahr]
*vt* amaze

**maravillosamente**
[mahr•AH•vee•YO•sah•MEN•
tai] *adv* wonderfully

**maravilloso**
[mah•RAH•vee•YOH•so] *adj*
amazing; marvelous;
wonderful

**marca** [MAHR•kah] *n* F brand;
label; mark

**marca de fábrica** [MAHR•kah
dai fah•BREE•kah] *n* F
trademark

**marcador** [MAHR•kah•DOR] *n*
M marker

marcar [MAHR•kahr] *vt* brand

marcha [MAHR•cha] *n* F headway

marchar [MAHR•char] *vt* march

marcial [mahr•SEE•AHL] *adj* martial

marea [mah•RAI•ah] *n* F tide

mareado [MAHR•ai•AH•doh] *adj* dizzy; giddy; seasick

marfil [MAHR•feel] *n* M ivory

margarina [MAHR•gar•EE•nah] *n* F margarine

margarita [MAHR•gahr•EET•tah] *n* F daisy

margen [MAHR•hen] *n* M margin

marginal [MAHR•hee•NAHL] *adj* marginal

marido [mah•REE•doh] *n* M husband

marihuana [mahr•IH•hoo•AHN•ah] *n* F marijuana

marinar [MAHR•ee•NAHR] *vt* marinate

marinero [MAH•ree•NAIR•oh] *n* M sailor

marino [mah•REEN•oh] *n* M marine

mariposa [MAHR•ee•POH•sah] *n* F butterfly

mariscal [MAHR•ee•SKAHL] *n* M marshal

marjal [MAHR•hahl] *n* M moor

mármol [MAHR•mohl] *n* M marble

Marruecos [mahr•RWAI•kohs] *n* Morocco

marsopa [mahr•SOH•pah] *n* F porpoise

Marte [MAHR•tai] *n* M Mars

martes [MAHR•tais] *n* M Tuesday

martes de carneval [MAHR•tais dai kar•NEH•val] *n* M Shrove Tuesday

martillo [mahr•TEE•yo] *n* M hammer

mártir [MAHR•teer] *n* M martyr

marzo [MAHR•so] *n* M march

más [mahs] *adj* more; most; ~ bien\ rather; ~ de\ more than; ~ o menos\ more or less; ~ y ~\ more and more; a lo ~\ at most; de ~\ too many; es ~\ moreover; no ~\ no more

más allá [mahs AI•yah] *adv prep* beyond

más alto [mahs AHL•to] *adv* topmost

más lejano [mahs lai•HAN•oh] *adj adv* furthest

más lejos [mahs LAI•hos] *adj* farther

más otro [mahs] [OH•troh] *adv* else

más reciente [mahs RAI•see•EN•tai] *adj* latter

masa [MAH•sah] *n* F clump; dough; M paste

masaico [moh•SAI•koh] *n* M mosaic

masaje [mah•SAH•hai] *n* F massage

masarada [MAH•skahr•AH•dah] *n* F masquerade

**mascar** [MAH•skahr] *vt* chew; crunch; *vt vi* munch

**masculino** [MAH•skoo•LEE•no] *adj* masculine

**masilla** [mah•SEE•yah] *n* F putty

**maslo** [MAHS•loh] *n* M dock

**mástil** [mah•STEEL] *n* M flagpole; mast

**matador** [mah•TAH•dor] *n* M killer

**matanza** [mah•TAHN•sah] *n* F massacre

**matar** [MAH•tahr] *vt* kill; slaughter; *vi* slay

**matemática** [mah•TEH•mah•TEE•kah] *n* F mathematics

**materia bruta** [mah•TAIR•EE•ah BROO•tah] *n* F raw material

**material** [MAH•tair•EE•ahl] *adj* material; *n* F stuff

**materialista** [MAH•tair•EE•ahl•EE•stah] *n* F materialist; *adj* materialistic

**maternal** [mah•TAIR•nahl] *adj* maternal; motherly

**maternidad** [mah•TAIR•nee•DAHD] *n* F motherhood

**matiz** [MAH•teez] *n* F nuance

**matón** [MAH•ton] *n* M bully; *n* F hoodlum

**matrimonio** [MAH•trih•mon•EE•oh] *n* M marriage; matrimony

**matriz** [mah•TREES] *n* F matrix

**maximum** [MAHKS•ee•MOOM] *n adj* M maximum

**mayo** [MAI•yo] *n* M May

**mayor 1** [MAI•yor] *adj n* M elder; senior; *adj* older; elderly

**mayor 2** [MAI•yor] *n* M ledger

**mayor 3** [MAI•yor] *adj* major

**mayor edad** [MAI•yor ai•DAHD] *n* M seniority

**mayoría** [MAI•yor•EE•ah] *n* F majority

**mazo** [MAH•so] *n* M mallet

**me; mí** [mai] [mee] *pers pron* me

**mecánico** [meh•KAHN•ih•KOH] *n* M mechanic; *adj* mechanical

**mecanismo** [MEH•kan•EES•mo] *n* M gadget; mechanism

**mecanógrafo** [MEH•kahn•OH•GRAH•fo] *n* M typist

**mecedora** [MEH•seh•DOR•ah] *n* F rocking chair

**mecer** [MEH•sair] *vt* waft

**mecha** [MAI•cha] *n* F fuse

**mecha** [MEH•cha] *n* F wick

**medalla** [meh•DAI•yah] *n* F medal

**medallón** [MEH•dai•YON] *n* F medallion; pendant

**media 1** [mai•DEE•ah] *n* F media

**media 2** [mai•DEE•ah] *n* F stocking

**media 3** [mai•DEE•ah] *n* F average

**media hora** [mai•DEE•ah OR•ah] *n* F half-hour

**media luna** [mai•DEE•ah LOO•nah] *n* F crescent

**mediador** [MAI•dee•ah•DOR] m M mediator

**medianoche** [mai•DEE•ah•NOH•chai] *n* F midnight

**mediar** [mai•DEE•AHR] *vi* mediate

**medicina** [MEH•dih•SEE•nah] *n* F medicine

**medicinar** [meh•DEE•sih•NAHR] *vt* medicate

**medición** [meh•DIH•see•OHN] *n* F measurement

**médico** [MEH•DEE•koh] *adj* M medical; *n* M doctor

**medida** [mai•DEE•dah] *n* F measure; size; a lal ~ de\ made to measure; a ~ a que\ as; en cierta ~ a\ to a certain point

**medida para áridos** [mai•DEE•dah pah•rah ah•ree•dos] *n* F bushel

**medidor** [mai•DEE•dor] *n* M meter

**medieval** [MEH•dee•VAHL] *adj* medieval

**medio** [mai•DEE•oh] *adj* halfway; mid; *n* M middle; medium; en ~\ in the middle, among; por ~ de\ through; por este ~\ hereby

**mediocre** [meh•DEE•oh•KRAI] *adj* mediocre

**mediodía** [mai•DEE•oh•DEE•ah] *n* M noon

**medio precio** [mai•DEE•oh prai•see•oh] *n* M half-price

**meditación** [MEH•dih•TAH•see•OHN] *n* F muse

**meditar** [MEH•dee•TAHR] *vi* meditate

**meditativo** [meh•DIH•tah•TEE•vo] *adj* thoughtful

**medroso** [meh•DROH•so] *adj* scary

**médula espinal** [meh•DOO•lah] *n* F spinal cord

**medusa** [mch•DOO•sah] *n* F jellyfish

**megáfono** [MEH•gah•FOH•no] *n* M megaphone

**mejicano** [MEH•hee•KAHN•oh] *adj* Mexican

**Méjico** [meh•HEE•koh] *n* M Mexico

**mejilla** [meh•HEE•yah] *n* F cheek

**mejillón** [meh•HEE•YON] *n* F mussel

**mejor** [MAI•hor] *adj* better; a lo ~\ perhaps; tanto ~\ so much the better; lo ~\ best, elite

**mejoramiento** [MAI•hor•ah•MEE•EN•to] *n* M improvement

**mejorar** [MAI•hor•AHR] *vt* improve

**melancolía** [meh•LAHN•koh•LEE•ah] *n* F melancholy

**melaza** [meh•LAH•sah] *n* F molasses

**melifluo** [MEH•lee•FLOO•oh] *adj* bland

**melodía** [MEH•loh•DEE•ah] *n* F melody; tune

**melón** [meh•LOHN] *n* F melon

**mella** [MAI•yah] *n* F dent

**mellado** [mai•YAH•doh] *adj* jagged

**mellar** [MAI•yahr] *vt* indent

**membrillo** [mehm•BREE•yo] *n* M quince

**memento de calma** [moh•MEN•to dai KAHL•mah] *n* M lull

**memoria** [MEH•mor•REE•ah] *n* F memoirs; memory

**mencionar** [men•SEE•ohn•AHE] *vt* mention

**mendigo** [men•DEE•go] *n* M beggar

**menear** [MEHN•ai•AHR] *vi* wag

**menguar** [men•GWAHR] *vi* subside; wane; decrease; lessen

**meno** [MAI•nor] *adj n* M minor

**menopausia** [men•OH•pou•SEE•ah] *n* F menopause

**menor** [MAI•nohr] *adj* junior; lesser

**menos** [MAI•nos] *adj* less; minus; a ~ que\ unless; al ~\ at least; ni mucho ~\ far from it; por lo ~\ at least

**menosprecio** [meh•NO•spreh•SEE•øh] *n* M disdain

**mensaje** [men•SAH•hai] *n* M message

**mensajero** [men•sah•HAIR•oh] *n* M courier; messenger

**menstruación** [MEN•stroo•AH•see•OHN] *n* F menstruation

**mensualmente** [MEN•swahl•MEN•tai] *adj* monthly

**menta** [MEN•tah] *n* F peppermint

**mental** [MEN•tahl] *adj* mental

**mentalidad** [men•TAHL•ih•DAHD] *n* F mentality

**mente** [MEN•tai] *n* F mind

**mentira** [men•TEER•ah] *n* F lie

**mentirilla** [MEN•teer•EE•yah] *n* F fib

**mentiroso** [MEN•teer•oh•so] *adj* lying; *n* M liar

**menú** [MEH•noo] *n* F menu

**meramente** [MAIR•ah•MEN•tai] *adv* merely

**mercader** [MAIR•kah•DAIR] *n* M merchant; tradesman

**mercadería** [mair•KAH•dair•EE•ah] *n* F commodity; merchandise

**mercado** [mair•KAH•do] *n* M market

**mercado de bolsas** [mair•KAH•do dai BOL•sahs] *n* M stock market

**mercado negro** [mair•KAH•do] *n* M black market

**mercador del tiempo** [mair•KAH•DOR dai tee•EM•poh] *n* M timekeeper

**mercancías**
[MAIR•kahn•SEE•ahs] *npl*
ware
**mercenario**
[mair•SEN•ahr•REE•oh] *adj n*
M mercenary
**mercurio** [MAIR•koor•EE•oh] *n*
M mercury; quicksilver
**merecedor**
[mair•EH•sai•DOHR] *adj*
deserving
**merecer** [MAIR•eh•SAIR] *vt*
deserve
**mérito** [MAIR•EE•toh ] *n* M
merit
**mermar** [MAIR•mahr] *vi*
dwindle
**mermelada**
[MAIR•meh•LAH•dah] *n* F
marmalade
**mes** [mehs] *n* M month
**mesa 1** [MAI•sah] *n* F plateau
**mesa 2** [MAI•sah] *n* F table
**mestizo** [meh•STEE•so] *n* M
mongrel
**meta** [MEH•tah] *n* F goal
**metáfora** [MEH•tah•FOR•ah] *n*
F metaphor
**metal** [MEH•tahl] *n* M metal
**metal bronce** [meh•TAHL]
[BROHN•sai] *n* M brass
**metálico** [MEH•tahl•EE•koh]
*adj* metallic
**meteoro** [MEH•tai•OR•oh] *n* M
meteor
**meteorología**
[MAI•tair•OH•lo•GEE•ah] *n* F
meteorology
**meter** [MEII•tair] *vt* tamper
**meticuloso**
[meh•TIH•koo•LOH•soh] *adj*
meticulous

**método** [meh•TOH•do] *n* M
method
**métrico** [meh•TREE•koh] *adj*
metric
**metropolitano**
[MEH•troh•POH•lee•TAHN•
oh] *adj* metropolitan; *n* M
subway
**mezcla** [MEHS•kla] *n* F mixture
**mezclar** [mehs•KLAHR] *vi*
mingle; *vt* mix; blend
**mezquita** [mehs•KEE•tah] *n* F
mosque
**mi; mis** [mee] [mees] *poss adj*
my
**micrófono**
[mee•KROH•FON•oh] *n* M
microphone
**microscópico**
[mee•KROH•skoh•PEE•koh]
*adj* microscopic
**microscopio**
[mee•KROH•skoh•PEE•øh] *n*
M microscope
**miedo** [mee•AI•doh] *n* M fear;
fright; dread
**miedo al público** [mee•AID•oh
al POOB•lih•koh] *n* M stage
fright
**miel** [MEE•ehl] *n* M honey
**miembro** [mee•EHM•broh] *n* M
limb; member
**mientras** [mee•EN•trahs] *adv*
meanwhile; ~ que\ whereas; ~
tanto\ in the meantime
**miércoles** [MEE•air•KOH•lais]
*n* Wednesday
**miga** [MEE•gah] *n* F crumb
**migraña** [mee•GRAHN•yah] *n*
F migraine
**mil** [meel] *num* thousand

**milagro** [mee•LAH•groh] *n* M
miracle

**milagroso** [MEE•lah•GROH•so]
*adj* miraclulous

**milenio** [MIH•len•EE•øh] *n* M
millenium

**milésimo** [MIHL•eh•SEE•moh]
*num* thousandth

**milicia** [MIH•lee•SEE•ah] *n* F
militia

**militante** [MIH•lih•TAN•tai]
*adj* militant

**militares** [lohs
MIH•lee•TAHR•ais] *npl*
military

**milla** [MEE•yah] *n* F mile

**millón** [MEE•YON] *n* M
million

**millonario**
[mee•YON•ahr•EE•oh] *n* M
millionaire

**mimar** [MEE•mahr] *vt* pamper

**mimbre** [MEEM•brai] *n* M
wicker

**mímico** [mih•MEE•koh] *n* M
mimic

**mina 1** [MEEN•ah] *n* F mine

**mina 2** [MEE•nah] *n* F mint

**minar** [MEEN•ahr] *vt* mine;
undermine

**mineral** [min•AIR•ahl] *adj* M
mineral; ore

**minería** [MIN•air•EE•ah] *n* F
mining

**miniatura**
[min•EE•ah•TOOR•ah] *n* F
miniature

**mínimo** [MIHN•ee•MOH] *adj*
least; *n* M minimum

**ministerio** [min•IH•stair•EE•øh]
*n* M ministry

**ministro** [min•EE•stroh] *n* M
minister

**minoridad**
[mee•NOR•ih•DAHD] *n* F
minority

**minuto** [min•TOO•to] *n* M
minute

**mirada** [meer•AH•dah] *n* F
look; glance; leer

**miraje** [meer•AH•hai] *n* M
mirage

**mirar** [MEER•ahr] v gaze; *vt*
look at; view

**mirilla** [meer•EE•yah] *n* F
peephole

**mirlo** [MEER•loh] *n* M
blackbird

**misa** [MEE•sah] *n* F mass

**misántropo**
[mihs•AHN•TROH•poh] *n* M
misanthropist

**misceláneo**
[MIH•sel•AH•nai•oh] *adj*
miscellaneous

**miserable** [MIH•sair•AHB•lai]
*adj* miserable; *n* M wretch

**miseria** [MIH•sair•EE•ah] *n* F
misery

**misericordia**
[MEE•sair•IH•kor•DEE•ah] *n*
F mercy

**misericordioso**
[mih•SAIR•ee•KOR•dee•OH•
so] *adj* merciful

**mísero** [mee•SAIR•oh] *n* M
miser

**misión** [MIH•see•OHN] *n* F
errand; mission

**misionario**
[MIH•see•OHN•ahr•EE•oh] *n*
M missionary

**mismo** [ehl MEES•mo] *adj*
same; ahora ~\ right now;
aquí ~\ right here; el ~\ itself

**misterio** [MIH•stair•EE•oh] *n*
M mystery

**misterioso**
[mih•STAIR•ee•OH•so] *adj*
mysterious; uncanny

**místico** [MIH•STEE•koh] *n* M
mystic; *adj* mystical

**mítico** [MIH•TEE•koh] *adj*
mythical

**mitigando**
[MIH•tee•GAHN•do] *adj*
mitigating

**mitología**
[mih•TOH•loh•GEE•ah] *n* F
mythology

**moco** [MOH•ko] *n* M snuff

**mocoso** [moh•KOH•so] *n* M
brat

**mochila** [moh•CHEE•lah] *n* F
knapsack; wallet

**moda** [MOH•dah] *n* F fad;
vogue; fashion; de este ~\ so,
in this fashion; a la ~\
fashionable; de todos modos\
anyway, in any fashion

**moda de vivir** [MOH•dah dai
VEE•veer] *n* F lifestyle

**modelar** [MOH•deh•LAHR] *vt*
remodel

**modelo** [moh•DEL•oh] *n* M
model

**moderación**
[MOH•dair•AH•see•OHN] *n* F
moderation

**moderado** [MO•dair•AH•do]
*adj n* M moderate

**modernizar**
[moh•DAIR•nee•SAHR] *vt*
modernize

**moderno** [mo•DAIRN•oh] *adj*
modern

**modesta** [moh•DEH•stah] *adj*
coy

**modestia** [MOH•deh•STEE•ah]
*n* F modesty

**modesto** [moh•DEH•sto] *adj*
modest; unassuming

**modificar**
[moh•DEE•fih•KAHR] *vt*
modify

**modo** [MOH•doh] *n* M fashion;
mode

**mofa** [MOH•fah] *n* F scoff

**mofar** [MOH•fahr] *vt* mock

**mofeta** [moh•FEH•tah] *n* F
skunk

**moho** [MOH•ho] *n* M mildew;
mold; rust

**mohoso** [moh•HO•so] *adj*
musty; rusty

**mojado** [moh•HA•do] *adj* wet

**mojar** [moh•HAHR] *vt* dampen

**mojellas** [moi•YAI•has] *n* F
sweetbreads

**mola** [MOH•lah] *n* F mole

**molar** [moh•LAHR] *n* M molar

**molendero**
[MOH•len•DAIR•oh] *n* M
grinder

**moler** [MOH•lair] *vt* grind

**molestar** [MOH•leh•STAHR] *vt*
annoy; worry; bother; molest;
pester; *n* M bother; no ~\ do
not disurb

**molesto 1** [moh•LEH•stoh] *adj*
annoying

**molesto 2** [moh•LEH•stoh] *adj*
ill at ease

**molino** [mo•LEE•no] *n* M mill

**molino de viento**
[moh•LEE•no dai vee•EN•tai]
*n* M windmill

**molusco** [moh•LOO•skoh] *n* M
mollusk

**mollar** [MOH•lahr] *adj* soft

**mollera** [moh•LAIR•ah] *n* F
crown (of head); brains (coll.)

**momentáneo**
[moh•MEN•tah•NAI•oh] *adj*
momentary

**momento** [mo•MEN•to] *n* M
moment

**momia** [moh•MEE•ah] *n* F
mummy

**monarca** [MON•ahr•KAH] *n* F
monarch

**monarquía**
[MOH•nahr•KEE•ah] *n* F
monarchy

**monasterio**
[moh•NAH•stair•EE•oh] *n* M
abbey; monastery

**mondadientes**
[MON•dah•DEE•en•TAIS] *n*
M toothpick

**moneda** [moh•NAI•dah] *n* F
coin

**monetario**
[mon•EH•tahr•EE•oh] *adj*
monetary

**monises** [MON•ee•SAIS] *npl* M
money; dough (coll.)

**monje** [MOHN•hai] *n* M friar;
monk

**mono** [MOH•noh] *n* M ape;
monkey

**monólogo** [MOH•no•LOH•go]
*n* M monologue

**monopolio**
[mohn•OH•poh•LEE•oh] *n* M
monopoly

**monopolizar**
[mohn•OH•poh•LEE•SAHR]
*vt* monopolize

**monotonía**
[mon•OH•ton•EE•ah] *n* F
monotony

**monótono** [MON•oh•TON•oh]
*adj* monotonous; *n* M
monotone

**monstro** [MON•stroh] *n* M
monster

**monstruosidad**
[MON•stroo•OH•sih•DAHD]
*n* F monstrosity

**monstruoso**
[MON•stroo•OH•so] *adj*
monstrous

**montañes** [MON•tan•YAIS] *n*
M mountaineer

**montañoso** [MON•tan•YO•so]
*adj* mountainous

**montar** [MON•tahr] *vi* ride
(horseback)

**monte** [MON•tai] *n* M mount

**montòn** [mohn•TON] *n* F heap

**montón** [mon•TON] *n* M
mound; F pile

**montón de heno** [mon•TON
dai AI•no] *n* M haystack

**montuoso** [MON•too•OH•so]
*adj* hilly

**monumental**
[mon•OO•men•TAHL] *adj*
monumental; *n* M monument

**monzón** [mon•SOHN] *n* F
monsoon

**moral** [MOH•rahl] *adj* ethical;
moral; *n* M morale

**moralidad**
[mohr•AHL•ih•DAHD] *n* F
morality

**mórbido** [MOR•bee•do] *adj*
morbid

**mordaza** [mor•DAH•sah] *n* F
gag

**morder** [MOR•dair] *vt* bite;
gossip about (coll.)

**mordiscar** [MOR•dee•SKAHR]
*vt* nibble

**moreno** [mohr•AI•no] *n* M
brunet

**moribundo**
[MOR•ee•BUHN•doh] *adj*
dying

**morir** [mohr•EER] *vi* die

**morir de hambre** [mor•EER
dai AHM•brai] *vi* starve

**moro** [MOR•oh] *n* M Moor

**mortaja** [mor•TAH•ha] *n* F
shroud

**mortal** [mor•TAHL] *adj* deadly;
mortal

**mortalidad**
[mor•TAHL•ih•DAHD] *n* F
mortality

**mortero** [mor•TAIR•oh] *n* M
mortar

**mortificar**
[mor•TIH•fee•KAHR] *vt*
mortify

**morueco** [mor•WAI•koh] *n* M
ram

**mosca** [MOH•skah] *n* F fly

**Moscú** [moh•SKOO] *n* M
Moscow

**mosquito** [moh•SKEE•to] *n* M
gnat; mosquito

**mostaza** [moh•STAH•sah] *n* F
mustard

**mostrar** [moh•STRAHR] *vi*
show

**mote** [MOH•tai] *n* M motto

**motín** [moh•TEEN] *n* M mutiny

**motivar** [MOH•tee•VAHR] *vt*
motivate

**motivo** [mo•TEE•voh] *n* M
motif; motive

**motivo** [moh•TEE•vo] *n* M
motivation

**motocicleta**
[moh•TO•see•KLAI•tah] *n* F
motorcycle

**motor** [MOH•tor] *n* M motor

**mover** [MOH•vair] *vt* move;
budge

**mover a sacudidas** [MOH•vair
ah SAH•koo•DEE•dahs] *vt*
jiggle

**moverse** [moh•VAIR•sai] *vi*
move; budge

**movible** [moh•VEEB•lai] *adj*
movable

**móvil** [moh•VEEL] *adj* mobile

**movilizar**
[moh•VEE•lih•SAHR] *vt*
mobilize

**movimiento**
[MOH•vee•MEE•EN•toh] *n* M
motion; move; movement; *adj*
moving; *vi* bustle

**movimiento filosòfico del
siglo xvii**
[moh•VEE•MEE•EN•to
FIII•loh•SOH•FEE•koh del
sig•loh xviii] *n* M
Enlightenment

**moza** [MOH•sah] *n* F waitress

**mozo** [MOH•so] *n* M waiter

**mucoso** [moo•KOH•so] *n* M
mucous

**mucho** [MOO•cho] *adj* much;
ni ~ menos\ hy no means; por
~ que\ however much

muchos [MOO•chos] *adj* many;
~ gracias\ many thanks

mudanza [moo•DAHN•sah] *n* F
removal

mudo [MOO•doh] *adj*
tongue-tied; *n* M dummy;
mute

muebles [MWAI•blais] *npl*
furniture

mueca [MWAI•kah] *n* F
grimace

muelle [MWAI•yai] *n* M quay

muerte [moo•AIR•tai] *n* M
death

muerto [moo•AIR•toh] *adj*
dead; *n* M dead person;
cadaver; corpse

muerto [moo•AIR•to] *adj* M
deceased

muesca [MWEH•skah] *n* F
notch

muestra [moo•EH•strah] *n* M
dial

mufla [MOOF•lah] *n* F muffle

mugido [moo•HEE•do] *n* M
moo

mugre [MOO•grai] *n* M grime

mujer [moo•HAIR] *n* F woman

mujer policía [moo•HAIR] *n* F
policewoman

muleta [moo•LAI•tah] *n* F
crutch

múltiple [MUHL•tee•plai] adj;
*n* M multiple

multiplicación
[muhl•TIH•plih•KAH•see•
OHN] *n* F multiplication

multiplicar
[muhl•TIH•plih•KAHR] *vt*
multiply

multitud [MUHL•tih•TOOD] *n*
F multitude; throng

muñeca 1 [moon•YAI•kah] *n* F
doll

muñeca 2 [moon•YAI•kah] *n* F
wrist

muñeco [moon•YAI•koh] *n* M
puppet

mundano 1 [muhn•DAN•oh]
*adj* mundane

mundano 2 [muhn•DAN•oh]
*adj* worldly

mundo [MUHN•do] *n* M world;
todo el ~\ everybody

municipal [muhn•IH•sih•PAHL]
*adj* municipal

municipalidad
[muh•NIH•sih•PAHL•ih•
DAHD] *n* F municipality

municipio
[moon•IH•sih•PEE•oh] *n* M
township

mural [MOOR•ahl] *n* M mural

murciélago
[moor•SEE•AI•lah•go] *n* M
bat

murmullo [moor•MOO•yo] *n* M
murmur

murmurar [MOOR•moor•AHR]
*vt vi* mumble; mutter;
warble

muscular [MOO•skoo•LAHR]
*adj* muscular

músculo [moo•SKOO•lo] *n* M
muscle

museo [moo•SAI•oh] *n* M
museum

musgo [MUHS•go] *n* M moss

música [moo•SEE•kah] *n* F
music

**musical** [MOO•see•KAHL] *adj*
musical
**músico** [MOO•SEE•koh] *n* M
musician
**muslime** [moos•LEE•mai] *adj*
Muslim
**muslo** [MOOS•lo] *n* M thigh

**mutilar** [MOO•tee•LAHR] *vt*
maim; mutilate
**mutuo** [moo•TOO•oh] *adj*
mutual
**muy** [MOO•ey] *adv* very; too
**muy despierto** [mwee
DEH•spee•AIR•to] *adj* wide
awake

# N

**nabo** [NAH•bo] *n* M turnip
**nacer** [nah•SAIR] *vi* be born;
volver a ~\ escape narrowly
**nacido** [nah•SEE•do] *adj* born
(to be)
**nacimiento**
[NAH•see•MEE•EN•to] *n* M
birth; dar ~ a\ give rise to;
de ~\ place of birth;
Nativity
**nación** [NAH•see•OHN] *n* F
nation
**nacional** [nah•SEE•oh•NAHL]
*adj* national
**nacionalidad**
[nah•SEE•ohn•AHL•ih•DAHD]
*n* F nationality
**nacionalizar**
[nah•SEE•oh•NAHL•ih•SAHR]
*vt* nationalize
**nada 1** [NAH•dah] *n* F
nonentity
**nada 2** [NAH•dah] *pron*
nothing; ~ de eso\ nothing of
the sort; antes de ~\ first of all
¡de ~!\ don't mention it; para
~\ not at all; por ~ del

mundo\ not for anything in
the world
**nadador** [NAH•dah•DOR] *n* M
swimmer
**nadar** [NAH•dahr] *vi* swim
**nadie** [nah•DEE•ai] *pron*
nobody; no one
**nafta** [NAHF•tah] *n* F gasoline
**nalga** [NAHL•gah] *n* F buttock
**naranja** [nah•RAHN•ha] *adj*
orange
**narciso** [nahr•SEE•soh] *n* M
daffodil
**narcótico**
[NAHR•koh•TEE•koh] *n adj*
M narcotic
**¡narices!** [NAHR•ee•SAIS] *excl*
rubbish!
**naríz** [nah•REES] *n* F nose;
nostril
**narración**
[NAHR•rah•sec•OHN] *n* F
narration
**narrador** [NAHR•rah•DOR] *n*
M narrator
**narrar** [nahr•RAHR] *vt* narrate

**narrativo** [NAHR•rah•TEE•vo] *adj* narrative

**nasal** [nah•SAHL] *adj* nasal

**natación** [nah•TAH•see•OHN] *n* F swimming

**natalidad** [nah•TAHL•ee•DAHD] *n* F birthrate

**nativo** [nah•TEE•vo] *adj* native

**natura** [nah•TOOR•ah] *n* F nature

**natural** [NAH•toor•AHL] *adj* natural

**naturalizar** [NAH•toor•AH•lih•SAHR] *vt* naturalize

**naturalmente** [nah•TOOR•ahl•MEN•tai] *adv* naturally

**náusea** [NOW•sai•ah] *n* F nausea

**nauseabundo** [NOU•sai•ah•BUHN•do] *adj* sickening

**náutica** [NOU•TEE•kah] *n* F sailing

**navaja** [nah•VAH•ha] *n* F penknife

**navaja de afeitar** [nah•VAH•ha dai ah•FAI•tahr] *n* F razor

**naval** [nah•VAHL] *adj* naval

**navegación** [NAH•veh•GAH•see•OHN] *n* F navigation

**navegante** [NAH•veh•GAHN•tai] *n* M navigator

**navegar** [NAH•vai•GAHR] *vt* navigate; *vi* sail

**nave spacial** [NAH•vai spah•SEE•ahl] *n* M flying saucer

**Navidad** [NAH•vee•DAHD] *n* F Christmas; ¡feliz ~!\ Merry Christmas; por ~\ at Christmas

**necesario** [neh•SEH•sahr•EE•oh] *adj* necessary

**necesidad** [neh•SEH•sih•DAHD] *n* F necessity; need

**necesitado** [neh•SEH•see•TAH•do] *adj* needy

**necio** [neh•SEE•oh] *adj* foolish; silly; absurd

**negación** [neh•GAH•see•OHN] *n* F denial

**negar** [nai•GAHR] *vt* deny

**negativo** [NEH•gah•TEE•voh] *adj* negative

**negligencia** [neh•GLIH•hen•SEE•ah] *n* F negligence

**negligente** [NEH•glih•HEN•tai] *adj* negligent

**negociación** [neh•GO•see•AH•see•OHN] *n* F deal; negotiation

**negociar 1** [neh•GO•see•AHR] *vt vi* negotiate

**negociar 2** [neh•GO•see•AHR] *vt* transact; terminate; conclude

**negocio** [neh•GOH•SEE•oh] *n* M business; trade

**negocios** [neh•GOH•SEE•ohs] *npl* M dealings; de ~\ business

**negro** [NAI•gro] *adj n* M black;
Negro

**Neptuno** [nehp•TOON•oh] *n* M
Neptune

**nervio 1** [nair•vee•oh] *n* M
nerve

**nervio 2** [nair•vee•oh] *n* M vein

**nervioso** [NAIR•vee•OH•so]
*adj* nervous; los ~s a uno\ get
on someone's nerves; ponerse
~\ get excited

**neto** [NAI•toh] *adj* clear

**neumonia** [NOI•mon•EE•ah] *n*
F pneumonia

**neurosis** [NOI•roh•SIS] *n* M
neurosis

**neurótico** [noi•ROH•TEE•koh]
*adj n* M neurotic

**neutral** [noi•TRAHL] *adj*
neutral

**neutralidad**
[noi•TRAHL•ih•DAHD] *n* F
neutrality

**neutralizar**
[noi•TRAHL•ih•SAHR] *vt*
neutralize

**neutro** [NOI•troh] *adj* neuter

**nevada** [nai•VAH•dah] *n* F
snowfall

**ni** [nee] con nor ~. ~\
neither.nor; ~ que\ as if; ~
siquiera\ not even

**nicotina** [NIH•koh•TEEN•ah] *n*
F nicotine

**nicho** [NEE•cho] *n* M niche

**nido** [NEE•do] *n* M nest

**niebla** [nee•AI•blah] *n* F fog;
mist

**nieta** [nee•AI•tah] *n* F
granddaughter

**nieto** [nee•AI•toh] *n* M
grandson

**nieve** [nee•AI•vai] *n* F snow

**nieve acumulada** [nee•AI•vai
ah•KOOM•oo•LAH•dah] *n* F
snowdrift

**nilón** [nee•LON] *n* F nylon

**niña** [NEEN•yah] *n* F girl

**niño** [NEEN•yo] *n* M boy;
child; desde ~\ from
childhood; de ~\ as a child

**niñez** [NEEN•yez] *n* F
childhood

**ninfa** [NIN•fah] *n* F nymph

**ninguno** [neeng•OO•no] *adj*
neither; *pron adj* none; en
ninguna parte \ nowhere

**norte** [NOR•tai] *n* M north; del
~\ northern

**nitrógeno**
[nee•TROH•HEN•oh] *n* M
nitrogen

**nivel** [NEE•vehl] *n* M level

**no** [no] *adv* no; not; ~ más\
only; ¡a que ~!\ I bet!; cómo
~\ of course; ¡que ~!\
certainly not

**noble** [NOH•blai] *adj* noble

**nobleza** [noh•BLAI•sah] *n* F
nobility

**noción** [NOH•see•OHN] *n* F
notion

**nocivo** [noh•SEE•vo] *adj*
noxious

**nocturno** [nok•TOOR•no] *adj*
nightly

**nocturno** [nohk•TOOR•no] *adj*
nocturnal

**noche** [noh•chai] *n* F night; de
~\ at night; ~ vieja\ New

Year's Eve; **hacer ~\** spend
the night; **por la ~\** at night
**no dicho** |no DEE•cho| *adj*
untold
**no disponible** |no
dihs•PON•ee•BLAI| *adj*
unavailable
**nogal** |NOH•gahl| *n* M walnut
**nombrar** |nom•BRAHR| *vt*
nominate
**nombre** |NOHM•brai| *n* M
name; noun
**nombre de familia**
|NOHM•brai dai
fah•MEE•LEE•ah| *n* M last
name
**nombre de pila** |NOHM•brai
dai PEE•lah| *n* M first name
**nominación**
|NOH•mee•NAH•see•OHN| *n*
F nomination
**nominal** |NO•mee•NAHL| *adj*
nominal
**no probado** |no proh•BAH•do|
*adj* untried
**no reclamado** |no
RAI•klah•MAH•do| *adj*
unclaimed
**no reconocido** |no
rai•KON•oh•SEE•do| *adj*
unacknowledged
**norma** |NOR•mah| *n* F norm
**normal** |nor•MAHL| *adj* normal
**normalmente**
|NOR•mahl•MEN•tai| *adv*
normally
**norte** |NOR•tai| *adj* north
**Norte América** |NOR•tai
ah•MAIR•IH•kah| *n* North
America

**Nortes Irlandés** |NOR•tes
eer•LAHN•dais| *n* Northern
Ireland
**Noruega** |nor•WAI•gah| *n*
Norway
**noruego** |nor•WAI•go| *adj*
Norwegian
**nosotros** |noh•SOH•trohs| *per*
*pron* us; we
**nosotros** |no•SO•tros| *pers*
*pron* we
**nosotros mismos**
|noh•SOH•tros MEES•mohs|
*pron pl* ourselves
**nostalgia** |NOH•stahl•HEE•ah|
*n* F nostalgia
**nostálgico**
|NOH•stahl•HEE•koh| *n* M
homesick
**nota** |NO•tah| *n* F note; memo
**notable** |noh•TAH•blai| *adj*
notable; noteworthy; striking;
telling
**notablemente**
|noh•TAHB•leh•MEN•tai| *adv*
notably
**notario** |noh•TAHR•EE•oh| *n*
M notary
**noticia** |noh•TEE•SEE•ah| *n* F
news; notice
**noticiario**
|NOH•tee•SEE•ahr•EE•oh| *n*
M newscast
**notificar** |no•TEE•fee•KAHR|
*vt* notify
**notoriedad**
|NOH•tor•EE•eh•DAHD| *n* F
notoriety
**notorio** |NOH•tor•EE•oh| *adj*
notorious

**novatada** [NOH•vah•TAH•dah] *n* F hazard

**no usado** [no oo•SAH•do] *adj* unused

**novedad** [NOH•veh•DAHD] *n* F novelty

**novia** [noh•VEE•ah] girlfriend; fiancée; de la ~\ bridal

**novela** [no•VAI•lah] *n* F novel

**novelista** [noh•VEL•ee•STAH] *n* F novelist

**noveno** [noh•VEN•oh] *num* ninth

**noventa** [noh•VEN•tah] *num* ninety

**novia** [noh•VEE•ah] *n* F bride; girlfriend

**noviazgo** [NOH•vee•AHS•go] *n* M engagement

**novicio** [NO•vee•SEE•oh] *n* M beginner; novice

**noviembre** [noh•VEE•EM•brai] *n* M November

**novillero** [noh•VEE•YAIR•oh] *n* M truant

**novio** [no•VEE•oh] *n* M bridegroom; groom

**nube** [NOO•bai] *n* F cloud

**nuboso** [noo•BOH•soh] *adj* cloudy

**nuca** [NOO•kah] *n* F scruff; back of the neck

**nuclear** [NOO•klai•AHR] *adj* nuclear

**núcleo** [NOO•KLAI•oh] *n* M nucleus

**nudillo** [noo•DEE•yo] *n* M joint; knuckle

**nudista** [noo•DEF•stah] *n* F nudist

**nudo 1** [NOO•do] *n* M bow (knot); knot

**nudo 2** [NOO•do] adj; *n* M nude

**nudoso** [noo•DO•so] *adj* gnarled

**nuera** [noo•AIR•ah] *n* F daughter-in-law

**nuestro** [noo•AI•stroh] *poss adj* our; el ~\ ours

**nuevamente** [noo•AI•vah•MEN•tai] *adv* newly

**nuevas** [noo•AI•vahs] *npl* F tidings

**nueve** [noo•AI•vai] *num* nine

**nuevecito** [noo•AI•vai•SEE•toh] *adj* M brand-new

**nuevo** [noo•AI•vo] *adj* new; de ~\ again

**nuez** [noo•AIS] *n* F nut

**nulo** [NOO•lo] *adj* null

**numeral** [noo•MAIR•AHL] *n* F numeral

**numerar** [NOO•mair•AHR] *vt* count

**número** [NOO•MAIR•oh] *n* M number

**número de teléfono** [NOO•MAIR•oh dai ] *n* M telephone number

**numeroso** [NOO•mair•OH•so] *adj* numerous

**nunca** [NUHN•kah] *adv* never; ~ más\ never again; ~ casi\ hardly ever; más que ~\ more than ever

**nupcial** [NOOP•see•AHL] *adj* nuptial

**nutrición** [noo•TRIH•see•OHN]
*n* F nourishment
**nutrir** [noo•TREER] *vt* nourish;
nurture

**nutritivo** [noo•TRIH•TEE•voh]
*adj* nourishing; nutritious

# O

**o** [oh] *conj* or; ~ bien\ rather;
~.~\ either. or; ~ sea\ in other
words
**oasis** [oh•AH•sis] *n* M oasis
**obedecer** [oh•BEH•deh•SAIR]
*vt* obey
**obediencia**
[OH•beh•DEE•en•SEE•ah] *n* F
obedience
**obediente**
[oh•BAI•dee•EHN•tai] *adj*
obedient
**obeso** [oh•BEH•so] *adj* obese;
fat
**obispillo** [ob•EESP•EE•yo] *n* M
rump
**obispo** [ob•EES•poh] *n* M
bishop
**obituario**
[oh•BIH•too•AHR•EE•oh] *n*
M obituary
**objeción** [ob•HEK•see•OHN] *n*
F objection
**objetivo** [ob•HET•EE•vo] *n adj*
M objective
**objeto** [ohb•HEH•to] *n* M
object
**oblicuo** [ob•LEE•KOO•oh] *adj*
oblique
**obligación**
[OHB•lih•GAH•see•OHN] *n* F
obligation

**obligado** [OB•lee•GAH•doh]
*adj* liable; bound
**obligar** [OB•lee•GAHR] *vt*
oblige; compel; obligate
**obligatorio**
[ob•LEE•gah•TOR•EE•oh] *adj*
obligatory
**obligatorio**
[ob•LIHG•ah•TOR•EE•oh] *adj*
mandatory
**obra de sillería** [OH•bra dai
SEE•yair•EE•ah] *n* F
stonework
**obra maestra** [OH•brah
mai•AI•stra] *n* F masterpiece
**obrar conducirse** [OH•brahr]
[KON•doo•SEER•sai] *vi*
behave
**obrero 1** [oh•BRAIR•oh] *n* M
employer
**obrero 2** [oh•BRAIR•oh] *n* M
workman
**obscenidad**
[ob•SEN•ih•DAHD] *n* F
obscenity
**obsceno** [ob•SAIN•o] *adj*
bawdy; obscene
**obscurecer**
[ob•SKOOR•eh•SAIR] *vt*
darken

**obscuridad**
[ob•SKOOR•ih•DAHD] *n* F
darkness; obscurity

**obscuro** [ob•SKOOR•oh] adj; *n*
M dark; *adj* dim; gloomy;
murky

**observable**
[OB•sair•VAHB•lai] *adj*
remarkable

**observación**
[OB•sair•VAH•see•OHN] *n* F
observation; remark

**observador**
[ohb•SAIR•vah•DOR] *n* M
observer

**observancia**
[ob•SAIR•vahn•SEE•ah] *n* F
observance

**observante de la ley**
[OB•sair•VAHN•tai dai lah
lai] *adj* law-abiding

**observar** [OB•sair•VAHR] *vt*
observe

**observatorio**
[ob•SAIR•vah•TOR•EE•oh] *n*
M observatory

**obsesión** [ob•SEH•see•OHN] *n*
F obsession

**obsesionar**
[ob•SEH•see•OHN•ahr] *vt*
obsess

**obsesivo** [OB•seh•SEE•vo] *adj*
obsessive

**obstinación**
[OB•stih•NAH•see•OHN] *n* F
obstinacy; stubbornness

**obstinado** [ob•STEE•NAH•do]
*adj* obstinate; opinionated;
stubborn

**obstrucción**
[ob•STRUHK•see•OHN] *n* F
obstruction

**obstruir** [OB•stroo•EER] *vt*
block; obstruct; clog

**obtener** [ob•TEN•air] *vt* obtain;
procure

**obtener adquirir** [ob•TEN•air]
[ad•KVEER•eer] *vt* get

**obturador**
[ob•TOOR•ah•DOHR] *n* M
choke (of car)

**obtuso** [ob•TOO•so] *adj* obtuse

**obviamente**
[ob•VEE•ah•MEN•tai] *adj*
obviously

**obvio** [ob•VEE•oh] *adj* obvious

**ocasión** [oh•KAH•see•OHN] *n*
F occasion

**occidental**
[ohk•SEE•den•TAHL] *adj*
western

**océano** [OH•sai•AH•no] *n* M
ocean

**ocioso** [OH•see•H•so] *adj* idle

**octágono** [OHK•tah•GON•oh]
*n* M octagon

**octavo** [ohk•TAH•vo] *num*
eighth

**octogésimo**
[OHK•toh•HES•ee•MOH]
*num* eighteenth

**octubre** [ohk•TOO•brai] *n* M
October

**ocultar** [oh•KUHL•tar] *vt* hide

**oculto 1** [oh•KOOL•to] *adj*
occult

**oculto 2** [oh•KUHL•toh] *adj*
hidden

**ocupación**
[oh•KOO•pah•SEE•OHN] *n* F
occupation

**ocupado** [OHK•oo•PAH•do]
*adj* busy (person); occupied

**ocupante** [OH•koo•PAN•tai] *n*
M occupant

**ocupar** [OH•koo•PAHR] *vt*
occupy

**ocurrencia**
[oh•KUHR•en•SEE•ah] *n* F
occurence

**ocurrir** [OH•koor•EER] *vi*
happen

**ochenta** [oh•CHEN•tah] *num*
eighty

**ocho** [OH•cho] *num* eight

**odio** [oh•DEE•oh] *n* M hate;
hatred

**odioso** [OH•dee•OH•so] *adj*
hateful; odious

**oeste** [oh•EH•stai] *n* M west; al
~ *adj* \ westward

**ofender** [OH•fen•DAIR] *vt*
offend

**ofensa** [OH•FEN•sah] *n* F
offense

**ofensivo** [OH•fen•SEE•vo] *adj*
offensive; obnoxious

**oferta** [oh•FAIR•ta] *n* F bid;
offer; tender

**oficial** [oh•FIH•see•AHL] *n* M
officer; *adj* official

**oficina 1** [OH•fih•SEEN•ah] *n* F
office

**oficina 2** [OH•fih•SEE•nah] *n* F
orifice

**oficina de correos**
[OH•fih•SEE•nah dai
kohr•RAI•os] *n* F post office

**ofrecer** [oh•FREH•sair] *vt*
tender

**ofrenda** [oh•FREN•dah] *n* F
offering

**oído** [oh•EE•doh] *n* M hearing

**oír** [oh•EER] *vt* hear; overhear;
¡oiga!\ listen!; hello! (on
telephone)

**ojeada** [oh•HAI•AH•dah] *n* F
glimpse

**ojo** [OH•ho] *n* M eye; a ~ de
buen cubero\ rough estimate

**ola** [OH•lah] *adj* tidal; *n* F wave

**oler** [oh•LAIR] *vi* stink

**olivo** [oh•LEE•vo] *n* M olive

**olmo** [OHL•moh] *n* M elm

**olor** [OH•lor] *n* M odor

**olvidado** [OL•vee•DAH•do] *adj*
forgetful

**olvidarse** [OL•vee•DAHR•sai]
*vt vi* forget

**olvido** [ohl•VEE•do] *n* M
oblivion

**ollar** [oi•YAHR] *n* M nostril

**ollería** [oi•YAIR•EE•ah] *n* F
pottery

**ombligo** [ohm•BLEE•go] *n* M
navel; umbilicus

**ominoso** [OH•mih•NO•so] *adj*
ominous

**omisión** [oh•MIH•see•OHN] *n*
F omission

**omitir** [OH•mih•TEER] *vt* omit

**omnipotente**
[om•NIH•poh•TEN•tai] *adj*
omnipotent

**omnisciencia**
[OM•nih•SEE•ehn•SEE•ah] *n*
F omniscience

**once** [ON•sai] *num* eleven

**onceno** [on•SAI•noh] *num*
eleventh

**onda** [ON•dah] *n* F ripple;
wave; ~ corta\ short wave; ~
larga\ long wave; longitud de
~\ wavelength

**ondoso** [on•DOH•so] *adj* wavy

**ondulación permanente**
[on•DOO•lah•see•OHN
PAIR•man•EN•tai] *n* F
permanent wave

**ondular** [on•DOO•lar] *vi*
undulate

**onza** [on•SAH] *n* F ounce

**opaco** [oh•PAH•ko] *adj* opaque

**ópalo** [oh•PAH•lo] *n* M opal

**ópera** [oh•PAIR•ah] *n* F opera

**operación**
[OH•pair•AH•see•OHN] *n* F
operation

**operador** [oh•PAIR•ah•DOR] *n*
M operator

**operador de tomavistas**
[oh•PAIR•ah•DOR dai
toh•MAH•vee•STAHS] *n* M
cameraman

**opinión** [oh•PIN•ee•OHN] *n* F
opinion

**oponente** [OH•poh•NEN•tai] *n*
M opponent

**oponer** [oh•PON•air] *vt* oppose

**oportunidad**
[OH•por•TOON•ih•DAHD] *n*
F opportunity

**oportunista**
[oh•POR•toon•EE•stah] *n* F
opportunist

**oportuno** [OH•por•TOO•no]
*adj* opportune

**oposición**
[OH•poh•SIH•see•OHN] *n* F
opposition

**opresión** [oh•PREH•see•OHN]
*n* F hardship; oppression

**opresivo** [oh•PREH•SEE•vo]
*adj* oppressive

**oprimir** [OH•prih•MEER] *vt*
oppress

**optar** [OHP•tahr] *vi* opt; choose

**óptico** [ohp•TEE•koh] *adj*
optical; *n* M optician

**optimismo**
[OHP•tee•MIHS•mo] *n* M
optimism

**optimista** [OP•tec•MEES•tah] *n*
F optimist; *adj* optimistic

**opuesto** [oh•PWEH•sto] *adj*
opposite; opposed; *n* M rival

**opulencia** [op•OO•len•SEE•ah]
*n* F opulence

**opulento** [OP•oo•LEN•to] *adj*
opulent

**oración** [or•AH•see•OHN] *n* F
sentence

**oráculo** [ohr•AH•KOO•lo] *n* M
oracle

**orador** [OHR•ah•DOR] *n* M
orator; speaker; talker

**oratoria** [or•RAH•tor•EE•ah] *n*
F oratory

**órbita** [OHR•BIH•tah] *n* F orbit

**orden** [OR•den] *n* M
commitment; order; tidiness;
en ~\ in order; por ~\ in turn

**ordenado** [OR•deh•NAH•do]
*adj* orderly

**orden del día** [OR•den ehl
DEE•ah] *n* M agenda

**orden de registro
domiciliario** [OR•den dai
reh•HEE•stroh
do•MIH•sihl•EE•ahr•EE•oh] *n*
M search warrant

**orden mandato** [OR•den
mahn•DAH•toh] *n* M
command

**ordinariamente**
[or•DIH•nahr•EE•ah•MEN•tai]
*adv* ordinarily

**oregano** [OR•ai•GAH•no] *n* M
oregano

**oreja** [or•AI•ha] *n* F ear

**orfandad** [OR•fahn•DAHD] *n*
F orphanage

**orgánico** [or•GAHN•EE•koh]
*adj* organic

**organismo**
[or•GAHN•IHS•moh] *n* M
organism

**organizacíon**
[or•GAHN•ih•SAH•see•OHN]
*n* F organization

**organizar**
[or•GAHN•ee•SAHR] *vt*
organize

**órgano** [OHR•gah•no] *n* M
organ

**orgasmo** [OHR•gahn•EES•mo]
*n* M orgasm

**orgía** [or•HEE•ah] *n* F orgy

**orgullo** [or•GOO•yo] *n* M pride

**orgulloso** [OR•gew•OH•so] *adj*
conceited; haughty; proud

**oria** [ohr•REE•ah] *n* F hem

**orientación**
[or•EE•en•TAH•see•OHN] *n* F
orientation

**oriental** [or•EE•en•TAHL] *adj*
eastern; *n* M oriental

**orientar** [or•EE•ehn•TAHR] *vt*
orientate

**orificio** [or•IH•fee•SEE•oh] *n* M
hole

**origen** [or•EE•hen] *n* M origin;
source

**original 1** [or•EEH•hih•NAHL]
*adj n* M original

**original 2** [or•IH•hee•NAHL]
*adj* unconventional

**originalidad**
[or•IH•hi•NAHL•ee•DAHD] *n*
F originality

**originalmente**
[OHR•ih•HEE•nahl•MEN•tai]
*adv* originally

**originar** [ohr•IH•hee•NAHR] *vt*
originate

**orilla** [or•EE•yah] *n* F shore

**orina** [or•EE•nah] *n* F urine

**orinar** [OR•ee•NAHR] *vi*
urinate

**ornamental**
[OR•nah•MEN•TAHL] *adj*
ornamental

**ornamento** [OR•nah•MEN•toh]
*n* M ornament

**oro** [OR•oh ] *n* M gold; hacerse de
~\ make a fortune; prometer el ~
y el moro\ promise the moon; de
~\ golden

**orquesta** [ohr•KAI•stah] *n* F
orchestra; de ~\ orchestral

**orquidea** [or•KIH•DAI•ah] *n* F
orchid

**ortiga** [or•TEE•ga] *n* F nettle

**ortodoxo** [OR•toh•DOHKS•oh]
*adj* orthodox

**oruga 1** [ohr•OO•gah] *n* F
caterpillar

**oruga 2** [or•OO•gah] *n* F otter

**orzuelo** [or•SWAI•lo] *n* M sty

**oscilar** [OH•see•LAHR] *vi*
oscillate; sway; swing

**oso** [OH•so] *n* M bear

**ostensible** [OH•sten•SEE•blai]
*adj* ostensible

**ostentoso** [OH•sten•TOH•so]
*adj* flashy; gaudy; ostentatious

**ostra** [OH•strah] *n* F oyster

**otramente** [OH•trah•MEN•tai] *adv* otherwise

**otro** [OH•troh] *adj* another; other; el ~\ the other; el uno al ~\ one another, each other

**otro tiempo** [oh•TROH tee•EM•po] *adv* yore

**ovación** [oh•VAH•see•OHN] *n* F ovation

**oval** [oh•VAHL] *adj n* M oval

**ovario** [OH•vahr•EE•oh] *n* M ovary

**oveja** [oh•VAI•ha] *n* F ewe

**oxigeno** [OHKS•ih•HEN•oh] *n* M oxygen

**oyente** [oi•YEN•tai] *n* M listener

# P

**pabellón** [PAH•beh•YON] *n* F pavilion

**paca** [PAH•kah] *n* F pack

**paciencia** [pah•SEE•en•SEE•ah] *n* F patience

**paciente** [pah•SEE•en•TAI] *adj n* M patient

**pacificar** [pah•SEE•fih•KAHR] *vt* pacify

**pacifico** [pah•SIH•FEE•koh] *adj* peaceful; *n* M Pacific

**pacto** [PAHK•to] *n* M bond; pact; *adj* compact

**padrastro** [pah•DRAH•stoh] *n* M stepfather

**padre** [PAH•drai] *n* M father; parent

**padrina** [pah•DREEN•ah] *n* F godmother

**padrino** [pah•DREE•no] *n* M godfather

**paga** [PAH•gah] *n* F wage

**pagable** [pah•GAHB•lai] *adj* payable

**pagado por adelantado** [pah•GAH•do por ah•DEH•LAHN•tai] *adj* prepaid

**pagano** [pah•GAH•no] *adj n* M pagan

**pagar de un buque** [PAH•gahr dai oon BOO•kai] *vt* pay off dismiss

**pagar poco** [PAH•gahr POH•koh] *vt* underpay

**pagina** [pah•HEE•nah] *n* F page

**pago** [PAH•go] *n* M pay; payment

**pago al contado** [PAH•go ahl kon•TAH•doh] *n* M down payment

**país** [pai•EES] *n* M country

**paisaje** [pai•SAH•hai] *n* M scenery

**paisano** [pai•SAH•noh] *n* M countryman

**Países Bajos** [pai•EE•sais BAH•hos] *npl* M Netherlands

**paja** [PAH•ha] *n* F straw (drinking)

**pájaro** [PAH•ha•ro] *n* M bird; song-bird

**pala** [PAH•lah] *n* F dustpan; shovel

**palabra** [pah•LAH•brah] *n* F word

**palabra de honor** [pah•LAH•brah dai ON•or] *n* F parole

**palacio** [PAH•lah•SEE•oh] *n* M palace

**paladar** [PAH•lah•DAHR] *n* M palate

**palanca** [PAH•lahn•KAH] *n* F crowbar; lever

**Palestina** [PAH•leh•STEE•nah] *n* F Palestine

**pálido** [PAH•lee•do] *adj* pale; wan

**palito** [pah•LEE•toh] *n* M lollipop

**paliza** [pah•LEE•sah] *n* F beating

**palma** [PAHL•mah] *n* F palm

**palmada** [pal•MAH•da] *n* F slap

**palmadita** [PAHL•mah•DEE•tah] *n* F pat

**palo** [PAH•lo] *n* M stick

**palomo** [pah•LOH•moh] *n* M dove

**palpable** [pahl•PAHB•lai] *adj* palpable

**pan** [pahn] *n* M bread; loaf

**paño** [PAHN•yo] *n* M tweed

**pañuelo** [pahn•WAI•lo] *n* M handkerchief

**pana** [PAH•nah] *n* F corduroy

**panacea** [PAH•nah•SAI•ah] *n* F panacea

**panadería** [pah•NAH•dair•EE•ah] *n* F bakery

**panadero** [PAH•nah•DAIR•oh] *n* M baker

**Panama** [PAH•NAH•mah] *n* M Panama

**panda** [PAHN•dah] *n* F panda

**pandilla** [pahn•DEE•yah] *n* F crowd

**panecillo** [PAN•eh•SEE•yo] *n* M muffin

**pánico** [PAH•nee•koh] *n* M panic

**pantalia** [PAHN•tal•EE•ah] *n* F sconce

**pantalones** [PAHN•tah•LOHN•ais] *npl* M jeans; pants

**pantalones de trabajo** [PAHN•tah•LON•ais dai trah•BAH•ho] *npl* M overalls

**pantalla** [pahn•TAI•yah] *n* F screen; movie screen

**pantano** [pahn•TAN•o] *n* M bog; marsh; swamp

**pantera** [pahn•TAIR•ah] *n* F panther

**papà** [PAH•PAH] *n* M dad; papa; pope

**papagayo** [PAH•pah•GAI•yo] *n* M parrot

**papal** [pah•PAHL] *adj* papal

**papas fritas** [PAH•pahs FREE•tahs] *npl* M french fries

**papél** [pah•PEHL] *n* M paper

**papel de seda** [pah•PEHL dai SAI•dah] *n* M tissue-paper

**papel higiénico** |pah•PEHL ih•HEE•ain•IH•ko| *n* M toilet paper

**papelería** |pah•PEL•air•EE•ah| *n* F stationery

**paperas** |pah•PAIR•ahs| *npl* F mumps

**paquete** |pah•KEH•tai| *n* F package; packet; M parcel

**par** |pahr| *n* M peer

**para** |PAH•rah| *prep* for; ¿~ qué?\ why?; ~ que\ so that

**parábola** |pah•RAH•BOH•lah| *n* F parable

**parabrisas** |PAHR•rah•BREE•sahs| *npl* M windshield

**paracaídas** |pah•RAH•kai•EE•dais| *npl* M parachute

**parada 1** |pah•RAH•dah| *n* F stand

**parada 2** |pah•RAH•dah| *n* F relay

**parador** |pah•RAH•DOR| *n* M stopper

**paradero** |PAHR•ah•DAIR•oh| whereabouts

**paradoja** |PAHR•rah•DOH•ha| *n* F paradox

**paraguas** |PAH•rah•GWAHS| *n* F umbrella

**Paraguay** |PAH•rah•GWAI| *n* M Paraguay

**paraiso** |pah•RAI•so| *n* M paradise

**paralelo** |PAH•rah•LAI•loh| *adj* parallel

**parálisis** |pah•RAH•lih•SEES| *n* F paralysis

**paralizar** |pah•RAH•lih•SAHR| *vt* paralyze

**paranoid** |PAH•rah•NOID| *adj* paranoid

**parar** |PAHR•ahr| *vt* stop

**parásito** |PAH•rah•SEE•toh| *n* M parasite; sponger

**parcial** |pahr•SEE•ahl| *adj* partial

**parcialidad** |PAHR•see•AHL•ih•DAHD| *n* F partiality

**parcialmente** |pahr•SEE•ahl•MEN•tai| *adv* partially

**pardo** |PAHR•do| *adj* brown

**parecer** |pahr•EH•sair| *vi* seem; *vt* resemble

**parecidamente** |PAH•reh•SEE•dah•MEN•tai| *adv* likewise

**parecido 1** |PAH•reh•SEE•do| *n* M resemblance

**parecido 2** |PAH•reh•SEE•do| *adj* like

**pared** |pah•REHD| *n* F wall

**pareja** |pah•RAI•ha| *n* F couple; pair

**paréntesis** |pah•REN•teh•SIS| *n* M parenthesis

**parientes** |pahr•EE•en•TAIS| *npl* kin

**parlamentario** |pahr•LAH•men•TAHR•EE•oh| *adj* parliamentary

**parlamento** |PAHR•lah•MEN•to| *n* M parliament

**parlanchín** |PAHR•lahn•CHEEN| *n* M chatterbox

**parlante** [pahr•LAHN•tai] *n* M
talking

**parloteo** [PAHR•loh•TAI•oh ]
*n* M tattle-tale

**parodia** [PAH•roh•DEE•ah] *n* F
parody; skit

**parpadear**
[PAHR•pah•DAI•AHR] *vi*
blink

**párpado** [PAHR•pah•doh] *n* M
eyelid

**parque** [PAHR•kai] *n* M park

**parque de estacionamiento** *n*
M parking lot

**parque zoológico** [PAHR•kai
SOH•oh•LOH•hee•ko] *n* M
zoo

**parra** [PAHR•rah] *n* F vine

**párrafo** [PAH•rah•foh] *n* M
paragraph; break; pause

**parrillas** [pahr•REE•yahs] *npl* F
grill

**párroco** [PAHR•roh•koh] *n* M
parson

**parroquia** [PAH•roh•KEE•ah] *n*
F parish

**parroquial**
[pahr•ROH•kee•AHL] *adj*
parochial

**parte 1** [PAHR•tai] *n* F part;
role; en ~\ partly; en alguna
~\ somewhere; en ninguna ~\
nowhere; en otra ~\
elsewhere; en su mayor ~\
mostly; en todas partes *adv*\
anywhere

**parte 2** [PAHR•tai] *n* M
message; report; dar ~\ report;
de me ~\ for me; de ~ de\
from; en cualquier ~\
anywhere; en ~\ partly; la

mayor ~\ the majority;
ninguna ~\ nowhere; por otra
~\ on the other hand

**parte iluminada** [PAHR•tai
ihl•LOO•mih•NAH•dah] *n* F
highlight

**partera** [pahr•TAIR•ah] *n* F
midwife

**participación**
[pahr•TIH•sih•PAH•see•OHN]
*n* F participation

**participante**
[pahr•TIH•sih•PAHN•tai] *n* M
participant

**participar**
[pahr•TIH•see•PAHR] *vi*
participate

**partícula** [PAHR•tee•KOO•lah]
*n* F particle

**particular**
[PAHR•tih•KOO•lahr] *adj*
particular

**particularmente**
[PAHR•tih•KOO•lahr•MEN•
tai] *adv* particularly

**partida** [pahr•TEE•dah] *n* F
certificate

**partida del campo**
[pahr•TEE•dah del
KAHM•po] *n* F picnic

**partidario**
[pahr•TEE•dahr•EE•oh] *n adj*
M partisan

**partido** [pahr•TEE•do] *n* M
party; *adj* divided

**partido laborista**
[pahr•TEE•do LAH•
bor•EE•stah] *n* M Labor Party

**partir 1** [PAHR•teer] *vt* halve;
sever; split

**partir 2** [PAHR•teer] *vi* depart; leave; set out

**pasa** [PAH•sah] *n* F raisin

**pasado** [pah•SAH•do] *adj* gone; past; stale; *n* M past; el miercoles ~\ last Wednesday; *adv* ago

**pasaje** [pah•SAH•ha] *n* M passage

**pasajero** [PAH•sah•HAIR•oh] *n* M fare; passenger

**pasaporte** [PAH•sah•POR•tai] *n* F passport

**pasar** [PAH•sahr] *vt* pass; put; overlook; overstep; ~ de\ have no interest in; ~ lo bien\ have a good time; ~ por alto\ leave out; lo que pasa es que\ the fact is that; ¡pase Vd.!\ come in!, go in!; ¿qué pasa?\ what's happening?

**pasar la noche** [PAH•sahr lah•NOH•chai] *vi* overnight

**pasatiempo** [PAH•sah•tee•EM•poh] *n* M pastime

**Pascua de Navidad** [pah•SKWAH dai nah•VEE•dahd] *n* F Yuletide

**Pascua de Pentecostés** [pah•SKWAH dai PEN•teh•KOST•ais] *n* F Whitsuntide

**pasea en botes** [pah•SAI•ah en BOH•tais] *n* boating

**pasear** [PAH•sai•AHR] *vi* stroll

**paseo 1** [pah•SAI•oh] *n* M drive; outing; promenade

**paseo 2** [pah•SAI•oh] *n* M lounge

**pasillo** [pah•SEE•yo] *n* M lobby; aisle; hallway; gangway (ship)

**pasión** [PAH•see•OHN] *n* F passion

**pasivo** [pah•SEE•voh] *adj* passive

**paso** [PAH•so] *n* M footstep; pace; pass; tread; a pasos largos\ stride

**pasta** [PAH•stah] *n* F pasta; *n* M batter

**pasta de cacahuete** [PAH•stah dai ] *n* F peanut butter

**pasta dentífrica** [PAH•stah DEN•TEE•FRIH•kah] *n* F toothpaste

**pastel 1** [PAH•stel] *n* M pie

**pastel 2** [PAH•stehl] *adj n* M pastel

**pastel de carne** [PAH•stehl dai KAR•nai] *n* M pâté

**pastelería** [pah•STEH•lair•EE•ah] *n* F pastry; pastry shop

**pasterizar** [pah•STAIR•ih•SAHR] *vt* pasteurize

**pastinaca** [PAH•see•NAH•kah] *n* F parsnip

**pasto** [PAH•stoh] *n* M pasture

**pastor** [PAH•stor] *n* M pastor

**pastura** [pah•STOOR•ah] *n* F pasture

**patada** [pah•TAH•dah] *n* F kick

**pataleta** [PAH•tah•LEH•tah] *n* F tantrum; fit

**patán** [pah•TAHN] *n* M lout

**patata** [pah•TAH•tah] *n* F potato

**patente** [pah•TEN•tai] *n* M
patent

**paternal** [PAH•tair•NAHL] *adj*
fatherly

**paternal** [PAH•tair•NAHL] *adj*
paternal

**paternidad**
[pah•TAIR•nih•DAHD] *n* F
paternity

**paterno** [pah•TAIR•no] *adj*
paternal

**patético** [PAH•tai•TIH•koh] *adj*
pathetic

**patilla** [pah•TEE•yah] *n* F
whisker

**patín** [pah•TEEN] *n* M ice
skating; skate (ice)

**patín de ruedas** [dai
roo•AI•dahs] *n* M skate
(roller)

**patinadero**
[pah•TEE•nah•DAIR•oh] *n* M
rink

**patinar** [PAH•tee•NAHR] *vi*
ice-skate; skate

**patio** [pah•TEE•oh] *n* M
backyard; courtyard

**patio de recreo** [pah•TEE•oh
dai reh•KRAI•oh] *n* M
playground

**pato** [PAH•toh] *n* M duck

**patología**
[pah•TOH•loh•HEE•ah] *n* F
pathology

**patria** [pah•TREE•ah] *n* F
fatherland; homeland

**patriota** [pah•TREE•oh•TAH] *n*
F patriot

**patriótico**
[PAH•tree•OH•tih•KOH] *adj*
patriotic

**patriotismo**
[pah•TREE•oh•TIHS•mo] *n* M
patriotism

**patrocinar**
[pah•TROH•see•NAHR] *vt*
patronize

**patrono** [pah•TROH•no] *n* M
patron

**patrulla** [pah•TROO•yah] *n*
patrol

**pausa** [POU•sah] *n* F pause;
coffee break (coll)

**pavimentar**
[pah•VEE•men•TAHR] *vt*
pave

**pavimento** [PAH•vee•MEN•to]
*n* M pavement

**pavo** [PAH•voh] *n* M turkey

**pavón** [PAH•VON] *n* M
peacock

**paz** [pahs] *n* F peace

**peaje** [pai•AH•hai] *n* M toll

**pecado** [peh•KAH•do] *n* M sin

**pecador** [PEH•kah•DOR] *n* M
sinner

**pecisión** [prai•SIH•see•OHN] *n*
F precision

**peculiar** [peh•koo•lee•AHR] *adj*
peculiar

**peculiaridad**
[peh•KEW•lee•AHR•ih•
DAHD] *n* F oddity

**pecho** [PAI•cho] *n* M bosom;
breast; chest

**pedacito** [PAI•dah•SEE•toh] *n*
M chip

**pedal** [peh•DAHL] *n* M pedal

**pedante** [peh•DAN•tai] *n* M
pedant

**pedantesco**
[PEH•dahn•TEH•skoh] *adj*
pedantic

**pedazo** [peh•DAH•so] *n* M bit;
chunk

**pedazo; peiza** [peh•DAH•so]
[pee•AI•sah] *n* MF piece

**pedernal** [PEH•dair•NAHL] *n*
M flint

**pedestal** [PEH•deh•STAHL] *n*
M pedestal

**pedestre** [peh•DEH•strai] *n* M
pedestrian

**pedir** [pai•DEER] *vt* beg

**pedir prestado** [pai•DEER
preh•STAH•do] *vt* borrow

**pedregoso** [PEH•dreh•GO•so]
*adj* stony

**pegar** [PAI•gahr] *vt* beat;
wallop; whack

**pegarse** [peh•GAHR•sai] *vi*
cling

**peinado** [pai•NAH•do] *n* M
hairstyle

**peinar** [pai•NAHR] *vt* comb

**peine** [PAI•nai] *n* M comb

**película** [PEH•lee•KOO•lah] *n*
F film; movie

**peligro** [peh•LEE•gro] *n* M
danger; peril

**peligroso** [PEH•lee•GROH•soh]
*adj* dangerous; hazardous

**pelo** [PAI•lo] *n* M hair

**pelota** [peh•LOH•tai] *n* F wad

**pelotilla** [PEH•loh•TEE•yah] *n*
F pellet

**peluca** [peh•LOO•kah] *n*
F wig

**peluche** [peh•LOO•chai] *n* M
plush

**peludo** [peh•LOO•do] *adj* furry

**peluquero** [PEH•loo•KAIR•oh]
*n* M hairdresser

**pellejo** [peh•YAI•ho] *n* M pelt

**pena 1** [PAI•nah] *n* F distress

**pena 2** [PAI•nah] *n* F penalty

**penacho** [peh•NAH•cho] *n* M
tuft

**penal** [pai•NAHL] *adj* penal

**pender depender** [pen•DAIR]
[dai] *vi* depend

**pendiente** [PEN•dee•EHN•tai]
*adj* pending

**péndulo** [pen•DOO•loh] *n* M
pendulum

**pene** [PEH•nai] *n* M penis

**penetrar** [PEN•eh•TRAHR] *vt*
penetrate

**penetrar** [PEN•eh•TRAHR] *vt*
permeate

**penicilina**
[PEN•ih•SIH•lee•NAH] *n* F
penicillin

**península** [pen•EEN•soo•LAH]
*n* F peninsula

**penitencia**
[pehn•IH•ten•SEE•ah] *n* F
penance

**penoso** [pen•OH•so] *adj* sore;
troublesome

**pensador** [PEN•sah•DOR] *n* M
thinker

**pensamiento**
[pen•SAH•mee•EN•toh] *n* M
thinking; thought

**pensar** [pen•SAHR] *vi* think

**pensativo** [PEN•sah•TEE•vo]
*adj* pensive

**pensión** [PEN•see•OHN] *n* F
pension

**penumbra** [peh•NUHM•brah] *n*
F gloom

**peón** [pai•OHN] *n* M pawn

**peor** [pai•OR] *adj* worse; lo ~\
worst

**pequeñito** [PEH•kain•YEE•to]
*adj* tiny

**pequeño** [peh•KAIN•yo] *adj*
little; undersized

**pera** [PAIR•ah] *n* F pear

**perca** [PAIR•cah] *n* F perch

**percepción**
[pair•SEHP•see•OHN] *n* F
perception

**percibir** [PAIR•see•BEER] *vt*
perceive

**percha** [PAIR•cha] *n* F roost

**perder** [pair•DAIR] *vt* lose

**perder el tiempo** [PAIR•dair el
tee•EM•po] *vi* dawdle

**pérdida** [pair•DEE•dah] *n* F
forfeit; loss; *adj* missing; *adj*
lost

**perdiz** [pair•DEES] *n* M
partridge

**perdón** [pair•DOHN] *n* F
pardon

**perdonar** [PAIR•don•AHR] *vt*
condone; forgive

**perecer** [PAIR•eh•SAIR] *vi*
perish; die

**peregrinación**
[pair•EH•green•AH•see•OHN]
*n* F pilgrimage

**peregrinar**
[PAIR•eh•GREEN•AHR] *n* M
pilgrim

**perejil** [PAIR•eh•HEEL] *n* M
parsley

**perennal** [PAIR•en•NAHL] *adj*
perennial

**perezoso** [PAIR•eh•ZO•so] *adj*
lazy; shiftless

**perfección**
[pair•FEHK•see•OHN] *n* F
perfection; a la ~\ perfectly, to
perfection

**perfectamente**
[pair•FEHK•tah•MEN•tai] *adv*
perfectly

**perfecto** [pair•FEHK•to] *adj*
perfect

**pérfido** [pair•FEE•do] *adj* M
disloyal

**perfil** [pair•FEEL] *n* M outline;
profile

**perforar** [PAIR•for•AHR] *vt*
perforate

**perfume** [pair•FOO•mai] *n* M
perfume

**pergamino**
[PAIR•gah•MEE•no] *n* M
parchment

**pericia** [PAIR•ee•SEE•ah] *n* F
proficiency

**perímetro** [PAIR•ee•MAI•troh]
*n* M perimeter

**periódica**
[pair•EE•oh•DEE•kah] *n* F
periodical

**periódico 1**
[PAIR•ee•OH•DIH•koh] *n* M
gazette; newspaper

**periódico 2**
[PAIR•ee•OH•DEE•koh] *adj*
periodic

**periodismo**
[pair•EE•oh•DIHS•moh] *n* M
journalism

**periodistico**
[PAIR•ee•OH•dih•STEE•koh]
*n* M journalist

**periquito** [PAIR•ee•KEE•to] *n*
M parakeet

**perjudicar**
[pair•HOO•dee•KAHR] *vt*
harm; scathe

**perjudicial**
[PAIR•hoo•DEE•see•AHL]
*adj* detrimental

**perjudicial**
[PER•hoo•DIH•see•AHL] *adj*
prejudiced

**perjurio** [pair•HOOR•EE•oh] *n*
M perjury

**perla** [PAIR•lah] *n* F bead;
pearl

**permanente**
[PAIR•mah•NEN•tai ] *adj*
permanent

**permiso** [pair•MEE•so] *n* M
permission; permit

**permitir** [PAIR•mih•TEER] *vt*
let; allow

**pernera** [pair•NAIR•ah] *n* F
trousers

**pero** [PAIR•oh] *conj* but; *n* M
fault

**perpendicular**
[PAIR•pen•DIHK•oo•LAHR]
adj; *n* F perpendicular

**perpetrar** [PAIR•peh•TRAHR]
*vt* commit (an act); perpetrate

**perpetuo** [PAIR•peh•TOO•oh]
*adj* perpetual

**perplejidad**
[pair•PLEH•hee•DAHD] *n* F
puzzle

**perplejo** [pair•PLAI•ho] *adj*
perplexed

**perra** [PAIR•ah] *n* F bitch

**perrera** [pair•RAIR•ah] *n* F
kennel

**perrito** [pair•REE•to] *n* M pup;
puppy

**perro** [PAI•roh] *n* M dog;
spaniel

**perro de lanas** [PAIR•roh dai
LAHN•ahs] *n* M poodle

**perseguir 1**
[PAIR•seh•GWEER] *vt*
persecute

**perseguir 2**
[PAIR•seh•GWEER] *vt* pursue

**perseverancia**
[PAIR•seh•VAIR•ahn•SEE•ah]
*n* F perseverance

**perseverar**
[pair•SEH•vair•AHR] *vi*
persevere

**pérsico** [PAIR•sih•koh] *n* M
peach

**persistencia**
[pair•SIH•sten•SEE•ah] *n* F
persistence

**persistente**
[PAIR•sih•STEN•tai] *adj*
persistent

**persistir** [PAIR•sih•STEER] *vi*
persist

**persona** [pair•SON•ah] *n* F
person

**persona intolerante**
[pair•SON•ah
in•TOL•air•AHN•tai] *n* F
bigot

**personal 1** [PAIR•so•NAHL]
*adj* personal

**personal 2** [PAIR•son•AHL] *n*
F personnel

**personalidad**
[PAIR•son•AIIL•ih•DAHD] *n*
F personality

**personificar**
[PAIR•son•IH•fee•KAHR] *vt*
impersonate

**perspectiva**
[PAIR•spehk•TEE•vah] *n* F
perspective; prospect

**persuadir** [PAIR•swah•DEER]
*vt* coax; persuade

**persuasivo**
[PAIR•swah•SEE•vo] *adj*
persuasive

**pertenecer**
[pair•TEN•eh•SAIR] *vi*
pertain; belong

**perteneciente**
[PAIR•ten•EH•see•EHN•tai]
*adj* titular

**pertinente** [PAIR•tih•NEN•tai]
*adj* pertinent; relevant

**perturbación**
[PAIR•toor•BAH•see•OHN] *n*
F disturbance

**perturbador**
[pair•TOOR•bah•DOHR] *adj*
disturbing

**perturbar** [PAIR•toor•BAHR]
*vt* perturb; bother

**perverso** [pair•VAIR•so] *adj*
perverse

**pervertido** [PAIR•vair•TEE•do]
*n* M pervert

**pesadilla** [PEH•sah•DEE•ya] *n*
F nightmare

**pesado** [peh•SAH•do] *adj*
heavy; unwieldy; weighty

**pésame** [peh•SAH•mai] *n* M
condolences

**pesar** [PAI•sahr] *vt* weigh; a ~
de eso\ *adv* still

**pesaroso** [PEH•sah•ROH•so]
*adj* sorry

**pesca** [PEH•skah] *n* F fish;
fishing

**pescado** [peh•SKAH•do] *n* M
fish

**pesimismo**
[PEH•sih•MEES•moh] *n* M
pessimism

**pesimista** [PEH•sih•MEE•stah]
*adj* pessimistic; *n* F pessimist

**peso** [PAI•so] *n* M weight

**pesquero** [pe•SKAIR•oh] *n* M
fisherman

**pestaña 1** [peh•STAHN•yah] *n*
F eyelash; lash

**pestaña 2** [peh•TAHN•yah] *n* F
tab

**pestañear**
[peh•STAHN•yai•AHR] *vi*
wink

**peste 1** [PEH•steh] *n* M pest

**peste 2** [PEH•stai] *n* M stench

**pestillo** [peh•STEE•yo] *n* M
latch

**pesuasión**
[pair•SWAH•see•OHN] *n* F
persuasion

**pétalo** [peh•TAH•lo] *n* M petal

**petición** [peh•TIH•see•OHN] *n*
F petition

**petirrojo** [PEH•tee•ROH•ho] *n*
M robin

**petróleo** [PEH•troh•LAI•oh] *n*
M kerosene; petroleum

**pez** [pehs] *n* M fish

**pianista** [pee•HAN•ee•STAH] *n*
F pianist

**piano** [pee•AH•no] *n* M piano

**picadura** [PEE•kah•DOOR•ah]
*n* F bite (insect, snake)

**picante** [pih•KAHN•tai] *n* M
spice

**picaposte** [PEE•kah•POH•stai]
*n* M woodpecker

**picar** [PEE•kahr] *vt* poke; sting

**picazón** [PEE•kah•SON] *n* F itch

**picea** [pih•SAI•ah] *n* F spruce

**pico** [PEE•ko] *n* M beak; peak; pick

**picotazo** [PEE•koh•TAH•so] *n* M peck

**pichón** [pee•CHON] *n* M pigeon

**pie** [PEE•ai] *n* M foot

**piedad** [PEE•eh•DAHD] *n* F pity

**piedra** [pee•AI•drah] *n* F stone

**piedra de granizo** [pee•AI•drah dai grahn•EE•so] *n* F hailstone

**piedra pómez** [pee•AI•drah POHM•ehs] *n* F pumice

**piedra sepulcral** [pee•AI•drah SEH•puhl•KRAHL] *n* F tombstone

**piel** [PEE•el] *n* M fur

**piel** [PEE•ehl] *n* M leather; skin; articulos de ~\ leather goods

**pierna** [pee•AIR•nah] *n* F leg

**pigmento** [pig•MEN•to] *n* M pigment

**pigmeo** [pig•MAI•oh] *n* M dwarf

**pijama** [pee•HAH•mah] *n* F pajamas

**pila** [PEE•lah] *n* F stack

**pilar** [PEE•lahr] *n* M pillar; prop

**píldora** [pihl•DOR•ah] *n* F pill

**pilón** [pee•LON] *n* F pylon

**piloto** [pee•LOH•to] *n* M pilot

**pillaje** [pee•YAH•hai] *n* M loot

**pimienta** [PEE•mee•EN•tah] *n* F pepper

**pináculo** [pee•NAH•KOO•lo] *n* M pinnacle

**pinchar** [pin•CHAR] *vt* prick

**pinchazo** [peen•CHAH•зo] *n* M jab

**pincho** [PEEN•cho] *n* M spike

**pingüino** [pin•GWEE•no] *n* M penguin

**pino** [PEE•no] *n* M evergreen; pine

**pintor** [PIN•tor] *n* M painter

**pintoresco** [PIN•tor•ESK•oh] *adj* colorful; picturesque; quaint

**pintura 1** [pin•TOOR•ah] *n* F paint

**pintura 2** [pihn•TOOR•ah] *n* F picture; painting

**pinza** [PEEN•sah] *n* F clip

**pinzas** [PIN•sahs] *npl* F tweezers

**pinzón** [pin•SOHN] *n* M finch

**pío** [PEE•oh] *adj* pious

**piojo** [pee•OH•jo] *n* M louse

**pique** [PEE•kai] *n* M pique

**pirámide** [peer•AH•MEE•dai] *n* M pyramid

**pirata** [peer•AH•tah] *n* F pirate

**pisada** [pee•SAH•dah] *n* F trace

**pisar** [PEE•sahr] *vi* trample

**piscina** [pih•SEE•nah] *n* F pool

**piscina** [pih•SEEN•ah] *n* F swimming pool

**piso** [PEE•so] *n* M story (of house)

**piso bajo** [PEE•so BAH•ho] *n* M ground floor

**pista** [PEE•stah] *n* F trail

**pistola** [pih•STOH•lah] *n* F pistol

**pistolera** [PEE•sto•LAIR•ah] *n*
F holster
**pistón 1** [pih•STOHN] *n* F
piston
**pistón 2** [pih•STON] *n* F primer
**pizarra** [pee•SAHR•ah] *n* F
blackboard; slate
**pizca** [PEES•kah] *n* F whit
**placa** [PLAH•kah] *n* F plaque
**placa giratoria** [PLAH•sah
heer•AH•tor•EE•ah] *n* F
turntable
**placer** [PLAH•sair] *n* M
pleasure; me ~\ I like
**plácido** [plah•SEE•do] *adj*
placid
**plaga** [PLAH•gah] *n* F plague
**plan** [plahn] *n* M design
**plancha** [PLAHN•cha] *n* F
hot-plate
**planchado** [plahn•CHA•doh] *n*
M ironing
**planchador**
[PLAHN•cha•DOR] *n* M valet
**plan de acción** [plahn dai
akh•SEE•ohn] *n* M policy
**planeamiento**
[PLAHN•ai•ah•MEE•EN•toh]
*n* M layout
**planear** [PLAHN•ai•AHR] *vt*
devise
**planeta** [plah•NEH•tah] *n* F
planet
**plano 1** [PLAH•no] *adj* flat;
plain
**plano 2** [PLAH•no] *n* M plan
**plano llano** [PLAH•no
YAH•no] *n* M plane
**planta** [PLAHN•tah] *n* F plant
**plantación**
[PLAHN•tah•see•OHN] *n* F
plantation

**plástico** [plah•STEE•ko] *n* M
plastic
**plata** [PLAH•tah] *n* F silver
**plata labrada** [PLAH•tah
lah•BRAH•dah] *n* F
silverware
**plataforma**
[PLAH•tah•FOR•mah] *n* F
platform
**plátano** [plah•TAH•no] *n* M
banana
**platel** [PLAH•tel] *n* M platter
**platero** [plah•TAIR•oh] *n* M
silversmith
**platino** [plah•TEE•no] *n* M
platinum
**plato** [PLAH•toh] *n* M dish;
plate; course (of meal)
**playa** [PLAI•ya] *n* F beach
**plegar** [plai•GAHR] *vt* ply;
pucker
**plomero** [ploh•MAIR•oh] *n* M
plumber
**plomo 1** [PLOH•moh] *n* M lead
**plomo 2** [PLOH•mo] *n* M
sinker (fishing)
**pluma 1** [PLOO•mah] *n* F
feather; plume; quill
**pluma 2** [PLOO•mah] *n* F pen
**plural** [PLOOR•ahl] *adj n* F
plural
**plus** [ploos] *n* M plus; bonus
**población**
[pohb•LAH•see•OHN] *n* F
population
**poblar** [POHB•lahr] *vt* populate
**pobre** [POH•brai] *adj* paltry;
poor; ¡pobrecito!\ poor little
one ¡~ de mi!\ poor me
**pobreza** [poh•BRAI•sah] *n* F
poverty

**poción** [poh•SEE•OHN] *n* F
potion

**poco** [POH•koh] *adj* few; a ~\
little by little, gradually; a ~
de\ soon after; dentro de ~\
soon; hace ~\ not long ago;
poca cosa\ nothing much; por
~\ nearly (coll)

**poco atractivo** [POH•koh
AH•trahk•TEE•vo] *adj*
unattractive

**poco común** [POH•koh
koh•MOON] *adj* uncommon

**poco visible** [POH•koh
vih•SEEB•lai] *adj*
inconspicuous

**poder 1** [POH•dair] *vi aux* can;
*modal v* may; might

**poder 2** [POH•dair] *n* M power

**poder humano** [POH•dair
oo•MAHN•oh] *n* M
manpower

**poderoso** [POH•dair•OH•soh]
*adj* forceful; mighty; powerful

**poema** [POH•ai•MAH] *n* F
poem

**poesía** [POH•eh•SE•ah] *n* F
poetry

**poeta** [poh•EH•tah] *n* F poet

**poético** [POH•eh•TEE•koh] *adj*
poetic

**polaco** [poh•LAH•ko] *adj*
Polish; Pole

**polar** [POH•lahr] *adj* polar

**polen** [POH•len] *n* M pollen

**policía** [POH•lih•SEE•ah] *n* F
cop; policeman; *npl* police

**polilla** [POHL•ee•YAH] *n* F
moth

**Polinesia** [poh•LIH•nai•SEE•ah]
*n* Polynesia

**política** [POH•lih•TEE•kah] *n* F
politics

**político** [POH•lee•TEE•ko] *adj*
political; *n* M politician

**polo** [POH•lo] *n* M polo

**polo norte** [POH•lo NOR•tai] *n*
M North Pole

**Polonia** [POH•loh•NEE•ah] *n*
Poland

**pólvera** [pol•VAIR•ah] *n* F
gunpowder

**polvo** [POHL•voh] *n* M dust;
powder

**pollería** [POY•yair•EE•ah] *n* F
poultry

**pollo** [POI•yoh] *n* M chicken

**polluelo** [POI•yoo•AI•loh] *n* M
chick

**pompa** [POM•pah] *n* F parade

**pompa** [POM•pa] *n* F pomp

**pomposo** [pom•POH•so] *adj*
pompous

**ponderar** [pon•DAIR•ahr] *vt*
ponder

**ponedor** [PON•ai•DOR] *n* M
putter

**poner** [PON•air] *vt* put; ~ en
con\ put through (on the
telephone); ~ enclaro\ clarify;
~ por escrito\ put in writing;
~ una multa\ fine

**poner a media asta** [PON•air
ah mai•DEE•ah AH•stah] *adj*
half-mast

**poner áspero** [POH•nair
ah•SPAIR•oh] *vt* roughen

**ponerse** [poh•NAIR•sai] *vt*
put; get; put on; set

**pontazgo** [pon•TAHS•go] *n* M
toll

**populacho**
[POH•poo•LAH•cho] *n* M
populace

**popular** [POH•poo•LAHR] *adj*
popular

**popularidad**
[POH•poo•LAHR•ih•DAHD]
*n* F popularity

**popularizar**
[POP•oo•LAHR•ih•SAHR] *vt*
popularize

**por** [por] *prep* per; through; ~ la
calle\ on the street; ~ mi\ as
for me; ~ si\ in case; 45
kilómetros ~ hora\ 45
kilometers per hour

**por avión** [POHR
ah•VEE•OHN] *n* F airmail

**porcelana**
[POHR•seh•LAHN•ah] *n* F
china; porcelain

**porcentaje** [POR•sen•TAH•hai]
*n* M percentage

**por ciento** [por see•EN•to] *adv*
percent

**porción** [POHR•see•OHN] *n* F
helping; portion

**porche** [POR•chai] *n* M porch

**pornografía**
[por•NO•grah•FEE•ah] *n* F
pornagraphy

**poro** [POR•oh] *n* M pore

**poroso** [por•OH•so] *adj* porous

**porque** [POR•kai] *con* because

**porta** [POR•tah] *n* F porthole

**portátil** [POR•tah•TEEL] *adj*
portable

**portavoz** [POR•tah•VOZ] *n* F
spokesperson

**portero** [por•TAIR•oh] *n* M
janitor; porter; usher

**pórtico** [por•TIH•koh] *n* M
verandah; porch

**portilla** [por•TEE•yah] *n* F
portfolio

**Portugal** [POR•too•GAHL] *n*
Portugal

**portugués** [POR•too•GAIS] *adj*
Portuguese

**posadera** [POH•sah•DAIR•ah]
*n* F hostess

**poseer** [POH•sai•AIR] *vt*
possess

**posesión** [poh•SEH•see•OHN]
*n* F possession

**posfecha** [pohs•FAI•cha] *n* F
post date

**posibilidad**
[POH•see•BIH•lee•DAHD] *n*
F possibility

**posible** [poh•SEE•blai] *adj*
possible

**posiblemente**
[poh•SEE•bleh•MEN•tai] *adv*
possibly

**posición** [poh•SIH•see•OHN] *n*
F position; standing

**positivo** [POH•sih•TEE•vo] *adj*
positive

**postal** [POH•stahl] *adj* postal

**poste** [POH•stai] *n* M
lamp-post; post; stud
(architecture)

**posterior** [poh•STAIR•ee•OHR]
*adj n* M posterior

**postigo** [poh•STEE•go] *n* M
wicket

**postrado** [proh•strah•do] *adj*
prostrate

**postres** [POH•strais] *npl* M
dessert

**póstumo** [POHST•oo•mo] *adj*
posthumous

**postura** [poh•STOOR•ah] *n* F
posture

**potaje** [poh•TAH•hai] *n* M
porridge

**potasio** [POH•tah•SEE•oh] *n* M
potassium

**pote** [POH•tai] *n* M pot

**potencial** [poh•TEN•see•AHL]
*adj n* F potential

**potencialmente**
[POH•ten•SEE•ahl•MEN•tai]
*adj* potentially

**potente** [poh•TEN•tai] *adj*
potent

**potro** [POH•troh] *n* M colt

**poza** [POH•sah] *n* F puddle

**práctica** [prahk•TEE•kah] *n* F
practice

**práctico** [prahk•TEE•koh] *adj*
practical

**pradera** [prah•DAIR•ah] *n* F
prairie

**prado** [PRAH•do] *n* M meadow

**preámbulo**
[PRAI•AHM•BOO•loh] *n* M
foreword

**preboste** [prai•BOH•stai] *n* M
provost

**precario** [PREH•kahr•EE•oh]
*adj* precarious

**precaución**
[prai•KOU•see•OHN] *n* F
precaution

**precedencia**
[preh•SEH•den•SEE•ah] *n* F
precedence

**preceder** [PREH•seh•DAIR] *vt*
forego; precede

**precendente**
[PREH•seh•DEN•tai] *n* M
precedent

**preceptor** [PREH•sehp•TOR] *n*
M tutor

**precio** [prai•SEE•oh] *n* M price;
cost

**precioso** [PREH•see•OH•so] *adj*
precious

**precipitación**
[preh•SIH•pih•TAH•see•OHN]
*n* F precipitation

**precipitado**
[preh•SIH•pih•TAH•do] *adj*
hurried

**precipitar**
[prai•SIH•pee•TAHR] *vt*
precipitate

**precisamente**
[prai•SEES•ah•MEN•tai] *adv*
precisely

**preciso** [prai•SEE•so] *adj*
precise

**precoz** [prai•KOS] *adj*
precocious

**predecesor**
[preh•DEH•seh•SOHR] *n* M
forerunner; predecessor

**predecir** [PRAI•dai•SEER] *vt*
foretell; predict

**predestinado**
[prai•DEH•steen•AH•doh] *adj*
doomed

**predestino**
[PRAI•deh•STEEN•oh] *adj*
predestined

**predicado** [PRAI•dih•KAH•do]
*adj n* M predicate

**predicador**
[PRAI•dih•KAH•dor] *n* M
preacher

**predicamento**
[prai•DIH•kah•MEN•to] *n* M
predicament

**predicar** [PRAI•dih•KAHR] *vt*
*vi* preach

**predicción**
[prai•DIHK•see•OHN] *n* F
prediction

**predisponado**
[prai•DIHS•pon•AH•do] *adj*
predisposed

**predominante**
[prai•DOM•ih•NAN•tai] *adj*
predominant

**predominar**
[prai•DOH•mih•NAHR] *vt*
overpower

**prefacio** [PREH•fah•SEE•oh] *n*
M preface

**preferencia**
[preh•FAIR•en•SEE•ah] *n* F
preference

**preferente** [PREH•fair•EN•tai]
*adj* preferential

**preferible** [PREH•fair•EE•blai]
*adj* preferable

**preferiblemente**
[PREH•fair•EE•bleh•MEN•tai]
*adv* preferably

**preferir** [PRAI•fair•EER] *vt*
prefer

**prefigurar**
[prai•FIH•goor•AHR] *vt*
foreshadow

**prefijo** [prai•FEE•ho] *n* M
prefix

**pregunta** [prai•GUHN•tah] *n* F
question; query; inquiry

**preguntar** [PRAI•guhn•TAHR]
*vt* ask

**prejuicio** [PREH•hwee•SEE•oh]
*n* M prejudice

**preliminar**
[PREH•lih•MEE•NAHR] *adj*
preliminary

**preludio** [PRAI•loo•DEE•oh] *n*
M prelude

**prematuro**
[PRAI•mah•TOOR•oh] *adj*
premature

**premio** [prai•MEE•oh] *n* M
premium; prize; reward; bonus

**premisa** [prah•MEE•sah] *n* F
premise

**preñez** [prehn•YEHS] *n* F
pregnancy

**prenda** [PREN•dah] *n* F pledge

**prenuncio**
[PRAI•nuhn•SEE•oh] *n* M
premonition

**preocupado**
[prai•OH•koo•PAH•do] *adj*
preoccupied

**preocuparse**
[PRAI•oh•KOO•pahr•SAI] *vi*
worry

**preparación**
[PREH•pahr•AH•see•OHN] *n*
F preparation

**preparado** [PREH•pahr•AH•do]
*adj* ready

**preparar** [PREH•pahr•AHR] *vt*
prepare

**preponderar sobre**
[preh•PON•dair•AHR
SO•brai] *vt* outweigh

**preposición**
[PREH•poh•SIH•see•OHN] *n*
F preposition

**prepóstero**
[preh•POH•STAIR•oh] *adj*
preposterous

**presa 1** [PREH•sah] *n* F hold
**presa 2** [PREH•sah] *n* F prey
**presagio** [preh•SAH•jo] *n* M omen
**prescribir** [PRAI•skree•BEER] *vt* prescribe
**prescripción** [prai•SKRIHP•see•OHN] *n* F prescription
**presecución** [PROH•seh•KEW•see•OHN] *n* F prosecution
**presencia** [PREH•sen•SEE•ah] *n* F presence
**presentable** [PREH•sen•TAHB•lai] *adj* presentable
**presentación** [PREH•sen•TAH•see•OHN] *n* F presentation
**presente** [preh•SEN•tai] *adj* present; los ~s\ those present; tener ~\ remember
**presentemente** [preh•SEN•teh•MEN•tai] *adv* presently
**preservar** [PRAI•sair•VAHR] *vt* preserve
**presidente** [PREH•si•DEN•tai] *n* M chairman; president
**presidio** [PREH•sih•DEE•oh] *n* M garrison
**presión** [PREH•see•OHN] *n* F pressure; stress
**presor** [PREH•sor] *n* M professor
**préstamo** [PREH•stah•mo] *n* M loan
**prestar** [PREH•stahr] *vt* lend
**prestigio** [PREH•stee•HEE•oh] *n* M prestige

**presto** [PREH•sto] *adv* quick
**presumiblemente** [preh•SOOM•ee•blai•MEN•tai] *adj* presumably
**presumir** [PRAI•soo•MEER] *vt* presume
**presunción** [preh•SUHN•see•OHN] *n* F presumption
**presunto** [preh•SUHN•to] *adj* prospective
**presupuesto** [PRAI•soo•PWEH•stoh] *n* M budget
**pretencioso** [preh•TEN•see•OH•so] *adj* pretentious
**pretensión** [preh•TEN•see•OHN] *n* F pretension
**pretexto** [prai•TEHKS•to] *n* M pretext
**prevalecer** [preh•VAH•leh•SAIR] *vi* prevail
**prevaleciente** [PREH•vahl•EH•see•EN•tai] *adj* prevailing
**prevenir** [PRAI•ven•EER] *vt* prevent; preclude
**previo** [prai•VEE•oh] *adj* previous
**previsión** [preh•VIH•see•OHN] *n* F foresight
**prima** [PREE•mah] *adj* prime
**primado** [prec•MAH•do] *n* M primate
**primariamente** [PREE•mahr•EE•ah•MEN•tai] *adv* primarily

**primario** [PREE•mahr•EE•oh]
*adj* primary

**primavera**
[PREE•mah•VAIR•ah] *n* F
spring

**primera** [pree•MAIR•ah] *n* F
premiere; first; de ~ clase\
first-class; de ~ mano\
firsthand

**primer lugar** [pree•MAIR
loo•GAHR] *n* M lead

**primero** [pree•MAIR•oh] *adj*
first; main; premier

**primeros auxilios**
[pree•MAIR•ohs
auks•IHL•EE•ohs] *npl* M first
aid

**primer plano** [PREE•mair
PLAH•no] *n* M foreground

**primitivo** [PRIH•mih•TEE•vo]
*adj* primitive

**primo prima** [PREE•mo]
[-mah] *n* M cousin

**princesa** [prihn•SAI•sah] *n* F
princess

**principal 1** [PRIHN•sih•PAHL]
*adj* principal

**principal 2** [PRIN•see•PAHL]
*adj* staple

**príncipe** [prihn•SEE•pai] *n* M
prince

**principio** [PRIN•see•PEE•oh] *n*
M principle

**principio** [PRIN•see•PEE•oh] *n*
M beginning

**prioridad** [pree•OR•ih•DAHD]
*n* F priority

**prisa** [PREE•sah] *n* M flurry; F
hurry; haste

**prisionero**
[prih•SEE•ohn•AIR•oh] *n* M
prisoner

**prisma** [PREES•mah] *n* F prism

**privación** [prih•VAH•see•OHN]
*n* F privation

**privado** [pree•VAH•do] *adj*
private

**privilegiado**
[PRIH•vih•LEH•hee•AH•do] *n*
M prerogative

**privilegio**
[prih•VIH•lai•HEE•oh] *n* M
privilege

**pro** [pro] *n* M pro; advantage; el
~ y el contra\ the pros and
cons; en ~ de\ on behalf of

**proa** [PROH•ah] *n* M prow

**probabilidad**
[PROH•bah•DIHL•ee•DAHD]
*n* F probability

**probable** [proh•BAHB•lai] *adj*
likely; probable

**probablemente**
[pro•BAHB•leh•MEN•tai] *adv*
probably

**probar** [PROH•bahr] *vt* prove;
try; attempt (to)

**prueba** [proo•AI•bah] *n* F try;
de ~\ trying; a ~ de sonido\
soundproof

**problema** [proh•BLAIM•ah] *n*
M problem

**proceder** [PROH•seh•DAIR] *n*
M procedure; *vi* proceed; *adj*
proceeding

**procesión** [proh•SEH•see•OHN]
*n* F procession

**proceso** [proh•SEH•so] *n* M
lawsuit; process

**proclamar**
[PROH•klah•MAHR] *vt*
proclaim

**procuración**
[PRO•koor•AH•see•OHN] *n* F
proxy

**procurador**
[pro•KOOR•ah•DOR] *n* M
solicitor; lawyer

**procurar** [PRO•koor•AHR] *vt*
attempt (to)

**prodigio** [PROH•dee•HEE•oh]
*n* M prodigy

**pródigo** [proh•DEE•go] *adj*
prodigal

**producción**
[proh•DUHK•see•OHN] *n* F
production

**productivo**
[PROH•duhk•TEE•vo] *adj*
productive

**producto** [proh•DUHK•to] *n* M
product; produce

**productor** [PROH•duhk•TOR]
*n* M producer

**proeza** [pro•AI•sah] *n* F exploit

**profano** [proh•FAHN•oh] *adj*
profane

**profecia** [proh•fai•SEE•ah] *n* F
prophecy

**profesión** [proh•FEH•see•OHN]
*n* F calling; profession

**profesional**
[PROH•feh•SEE•ohn•AL] *adj*
*n* M professional

**profeta** [proh•FAI•tah] *n* F
prophet; seer

**profetizar**
[proh•FEH•tee•SAHR] *vt*
prophesy

**profundidad**
[pro•FUHN•dee•DAHD] *n* F
depth

**profundizar**
[pro•FUN•dee•SAHR] *vt*
deepen

**profundo** [proh•FUN•doh] *adj*
profound; deep

**profuso** [proh•FOO•so] *adj*
profuse

**programa** [proh•GRAHM•ah] *n*
M program

**progresivo**
[PROH•greh•SEE•vo] *adj*
progressive

**progresar** [PROH•grai•SAHR]
*n* M progress

**progreso** [proh•GRAI•so] *n* M
progress

**prohibición**
[PROH•ih•BIH•see•OHN] *n* F
prohibition

**prohibir** [PRO•ih•BEER] *vt*
forbid; prohibit

**prohibir** [PROH•ih•BEER] *vt*
inhibit

**proletariado**
[PROH•leh•TAHR•ee•AH•do]
*n* M proletariat

**prolongar** [PROH•long•AHR]
*vt* prolong

**promedio** [pro•MAI•DEE•oh]
*adj; n* M average

**promesa** [proh•MAI•sah] *n* F
promise; vow

**prometida**
[PROH•meh•TEE•dah] *n* F
fiancée

**prometido**
[PROH•meh•TEE•doh] *adj*
engaged

**prometido**
[PROH•meh•TEE•doh] *n* M
fiancé

**prometiente**
[proh•MEH•tee•EN•tai] *adj*
promising

**prominente**
[PROH•mih•NEN•tai] *adj*
prominent

**promiscuo**
[PRO•mih•SKEW•oh] *adj*
promiscuous

**promoción**
[proh•MOH•see•OHN] *n* F
promotion

**promotor** [pro•MOH•tor] *n* M
promoter

**promover** [PRO•mo•VAIR] *vt*
promote

**prono** [PROH•no] *adj* prone

**pronombre** [proh•NOM•brai] *n*
M pronoun

**pronóstico**
[PROH•no•STEE•koh] *n* M
forecast

**prontamente**
[PROHN•tah•MEN•tai] *adv*
promptly; readily

**prontitud** [PRON•tih•TOOD] *n*
F readiness

**pronto** [PRON•to] *adj* prompt;
soon

**pronunciación**
[pro•NUHN•see•AH•see•OHN]
*n* F pronunciation

**pronunciado**
[pro•NUHN•see•AH•do] *adj*
pronounced

**pronunciar**
[pro•NUHN•see•AHR] *vt*
pronounce

**propaganda**
[PRO•pah•GAHN•dah] *n* F
propaganda

**propiamente**
[pro•PEE•ah•MEN•tai] *adv*
properly

**propicio** [PROH•pee•SEE•oh]
*adj* M fair

**propiedad**
[proh•PEE•eh•DAHD] *n* F
ownership; property

**propiertario**
[PROH•pee•EH•tahr•EE•oh] *n*
M proprietor; landlord

**propietaria**
[PROH•pee•EH•tahr•EE•ah] *n*
F landlady

**propina** [pro•PEE•nah] *n* F
gratuity; tip

**propio** [pro•PEE•oh] *adj*
becoming; fit; proper

**propio mismo** [proh•PEE•oh
MEES•mo] *adj* own

**proponer** [pro•PON•air] *vt*
propose

**proporción**
[proh•POR•see•OHN] *n* F
proportion

**proposición**
[PROH•po•SIH•see•OHN] *n* F
proposition

**propuesta** [pro•PWEH•stah] *n*
F proposal

**propulsar** [PRO•puhl•SAHR] *vt*
propel

**propulsor** [PROH•puhl•SOR] *n*
M propeller

**prosa** [PROH•sah] *n* F prose

**proseguir** [PROH•seh•GWEER]
*vt* prosecute

**prosperar** [proh•SPAIR•ahr] *vt*
prosper

**prosperidad**
[prohs•PAIR•ih•DAHD] *n* F
prosperity

**próspero** [proh•SPAIR•oh] *adj*
prosperous; successful

**prostituta**
[PROH•stih•TOO•tah] *n* F
prostitute

**protección**
[proh•TEHK•see•OHN] *n* F
protection

**protector** [PROH•tehk•TOR]
*adj* protective; *n* M protector

**proteger** [proh•TEH•hair] *vt*
protect

**proteína** [proh•TEEN•ah] *n* F
protein

**protestante**
[PROH•teh•STAHN•tai] *n* M
Protestant

**protestar** [PROH•teh•STAHR]
*vt* protest

**protoplasma**
[PRO•to•PLAHS•mah] *n* F
protoplasm

**protuberancia**
[PROH•too•BAIR•ahn•SEE•ah]
*n* F protuberance

**prouesta** [proh•PWEH•stah] *n*
F overture

**provecho** [proh•VAI•cho] *n* M
profit

**provechoso** [PRO•vai•CHO•so]
*adj* profitable

**proveedor** [PRO•vai•EH•do] *n*
M provider

**proveer 1** [proh•VAI•air] *vt*
cater (banquet etc)

**proveer 2** [proh•VAI•air] *vt*
furnish; provide; supply

**provenier** [PROH•vai•NEER]
*vi* come; ~ de\ come from

**provento** [pro•VEN•to] *n* M
revenue

**proverbio** [PRO•vair•BEE•oh]
*n* M proverb

**providencia**
[proh•VIH•den•SEE•ah] *n* F
providence

**provincia** [PROH•vin•SEE•ah]
*n* F province

**provincial**
[PROH•vin•SEE•AHL] *adj*
provincial

**provisión** [proh•VIH•see•OHN]
*n* F provision

**provocar** [PROH•vo•KAHR] *vt*
provoke; taunt

**proximidad**
[prohks•IH•mee•DAHD] *n* F
proximity; closeness; nearness

**próximo** [PROHKS•ee•moh]
*adj* coming; next; near

**proyección**
[proh•YEHK•see•OHN] *n* F
projection

**proyectar** [PRO•yehk•TAHR]
*vt* project

**proyecto** [pro•YEHK•to] *n* M
project

**prudencia** [PROO•den•SEE•ah]
*n* F prudence

**prudente** [proo•DEN•tai] *adj*
prudent

**prueba** [proo•AI•bah] *n* F
proof; test; trial probation

**prunciar** [proh•NUN•see•AHR]
*vi* utter

**psicología**
[psih•KOH•loh•HEF•ah] *n* F
psychology

**psicológico**
[psih•KOH•LOH•HEE•ko] *adj*
psychological

**psicólogo** [psih•KOH•lo•go] *n*
M psychologist
**psiquiartra**
[PSEE•kee•AHR•tah] *n* F
psychiatrist
**psiquiatría**
[psee•KEE•ah•TREE•ah] *n* F
psychiatry
**publicación**
[POOB•lih•KAH•see•OHN] *n*
F publication
**publicador**
[POOB•lee•KAH•DOR] *n* M
publisher
**publicar** [POOB•lee•KAHR] *vt*
publicize; divulge; publish
**público** [POOB•lih•ko] *n* M
public; audience; dar al ~\
publish
**puchero** [poo•CHAIR•oh] *n* M
cooking pot
**pudín** [puh•DEEN] *n* M
pudding
**pudrir** [POOD•reer] *vt* putrefy
**pudrirse** [POO•DREER•sai] *vi*
rot
**pueblo** [PWEHB•lo] *n* M
village
**puente** [PWEN•tai] *n* M bridge;
deck
**puente donde se paga
pontazgo** [PWEN•tai
DON•dai sai PAH•gah] *n* M
toll-bridge
**puerco** [PWAIR•koh] *n* M pig;
pork
**puerco espín** [PWAIR•koh
eh•SPEEN] *n* M porcupine
**puerro** [PWAIR•roh] *n* M leek
**puerta** [PWAIR•tah] *n* F door;
gate

**puerta por donde entran**
[PWAIR•tah por DON•dai
EN•trahn] *n* F stage door
**puerta principal** [poo•AIR•tah
PRIN•see•PAHL] *n* F front
door
**puerto** [PWAIR•toh] *n* M
harbor
**puerto** [PWAIR•to] *n* M port
**puesto** [PWEH•stoh] *pp* left;
left behind
**puesto de bomberos**
[PWAI•stoh dai
bom•BAIR•ohs] *n* M fire
station
**puesto lado a lado** [PWAI•sto
LAH•doh a LAH•doh] *n* M
collateral
**pulga** [PUHL•gah] *n* F flea
**pulgada** [puhl•GAH•dah] *n* F
inch
**pulgar** [puhl•GAHR] *n* M
thumb
**pulimento** [POO•lee•MEN•to]
*n* M polish
**pulmón** [puhl•MOHN] *n* M
lung
**pulpa** [PUHL•pah] *n* F pulp
**púlpito** [PUHL•PEE•to] *n* M
pulpit
**pulpo** [PUHL•po] *n* M octopus
**pulsación**
[PUHL•sah•see•OHN] *n* F
pulsation
**pulsar** [puhl•SAHR] *vi* pulsate
**pulso** [PUHL•so] *n* M pulse
**pulverizado**
[puhl•VAIR•ih•SAH•do] *adj*
powdered
**pulverizador**
[PUHL•vair•EE•sah•DOR] *n*
M sprayer

**pulverizar**
[puhl•VAIR•ih•SAHR] *vt*
pulverize; crush

**puño** [POON•yo] *n* M cuff; fist;
hilt

**punta** [PUHN•tah] *n* F dash

**puntada** [puhn•TAH•dah] *n* F
stitch

**puntiagudo**
[puhn•TEE•ah•GOO•doh] *adj*
acute; pointed

**punto** [PUHN•toh] *n* M dot;
point

**punto de ebullición** [PUHN•to
dai EH•boo•LIH•see•OHN] *n*
M boiling point

**punto de exclamación**
[PUHN•toh deh
EHKS•klah•MAH•see•OHN]
*n* F exclamation point

**punto de partida** [PUHN•to
dai pahr•TEE•dah] *n* M
starting point

**punto de unión** [PUHN•toh
dai OO•nee•OHN] *n* M
junction

**punto de vista** [PUHN•to dai
VEE•stah] *n* M point of
view

**punto y coma** [PUHN•to ee
KOH•mah] *n* M semicolon

**puntuación**
[PUHN•too•ah•SEE•OHN] *n*
F punctuation

**puntual** [PUHN•too•ΛIIL] *adj*
punctual

**puntura** [puhn•TOOR•ah] *n* F
puncture

**punturar** [PUHN•toor•AHR] *vt*
*vi* puncture

**punzada** [puhn•SAH•dah] *n* F
pang; twinge

**punzar** [PUHN•sahr] *vt* prod

**pureza** [POOR•ai•SAH] *n* F
purity

**purgar** [poor•GAHR] *vt* purge

**purgatorio**
[poor•GAH•tor•EE•oh] *n* M
purgatory

**purificar** [poor•IH•fee•KAHR]
*vt* purify

**puro** [POOR•oh] *adj* pure;
sinless; chaste

**purpúreo** [POOR•poor•AI•oh]
*adj* purple

**puta** [POO•tah] *n* F whore

**puta** [POO•tah] *n* F bitch (zool)

**putfrefacto**
[POO•treh•FAHK•to] *adj*
rotten

**pútrido** [poo•TREE•do] *adj*
putrid

# Q

**que** [kai] *pron* who; whom;
which; that; *conj* that; than

**qué** [kai] *adj* what how; i

**queda toque de queda**
[kai•da TOH•kai dai KAI•dah]
*n* curfew

**quedar** [KAI•dahr] *vi* remain; ~
en nada\ come to nothing
**quehacer** [kai•AH•sair] *n* M job
**quehaceres domésticos**
[KAI•ah•SAIR•ais
DOH•meh•STEE•kohs] *npl* M
housekeeping; housework
**queja** [kai•HAH] *n* F complaint
**quemador** [KAI•mah•DOR] *n*
M burner
**quemadura**
[KAI•mah•DOOR•ah] *n* F
burn
**que parece vivo** [kai
pah•RAI•sai VEE•vo] *adj*
lifelike
**querer** [KAIR•air] *aux verb*
want; need
**querer voluntad** [KAIR•air]
[VOL•uhn•TAHD] *vi n* F will
**querido** [kair•EE•do] *adj; n* M
darling; beloved; *adj* dear
**que se repita** [kai sai
rai•PEE•tah] *n* encore
**queso** [KAI•soh] *n* M cheese
**quid** [kwid] *n* M quid
**quiebra 1** [kee•AI•brah] *n* F
bankruptcy
**quiebra 2** [kee•AI•brah] *n* F
chasm
**quien** [KEE•en] *pron* who; whom

**quienesquiera**
[KEE•en•ehs•KEE•AIR•ah]
*pron* whomever
**quieto** [kee•AI•to] *adv* still;
quite; untroubled
**quietud** [KEE•eh•TOOD] *n* F
quiet; stillness; quiescence
**quijotesco**
[KEE•ho•TEHS•koh]adj
quixotic
**química** [KEE•mee•kah] *n* F
chemistry
**químico** [KEE•mee•koh] *n* M
chemical
**quince** [KEEN•sai] *num* fifteen
**quincena** [keen•SAI•nah] *n* F
fortnight
**quincuagésimo**
[KEEN•kwa•HES•ee•moh]
*num* fiftieth
**quinina** [kee•NEE•nah] *n* F
quinine
**quintiplo** [kwin•TEEP•lo] *n* M
quintuplet
**quinto** [KEEN•toh] *num* fifth
**quiste** [KEE•stai] *n* M cyst
**quitar el hielo** [KEE•tahr el
ee•AI•loh] *vt* defrost
**quizás** [KEE•sahs] *adv* perhaps
**quórum** [KWOR•um] *n* M
quorum

# R

**rábano** [rah•BAH•no] *n* M
radish; horseradish
**rabia** [rah•BEE•ah] *n* F rage;
dar ~\ infuriate

**rabiar** [RAH•bee•AHR] *vt* rage;
long for; ~ por algo\ long for
something
**rabino** [rah•BEE•no] *n* M rabbi

**rabioso** [RAH•bee•OH•so] *adj* rabid

**racional** [rah•SEE•ohn•AHL] *adj* rational; reasonable

**racha** [RAH•cha] *n* F gust; squall

**radiador** [RAH•dee•AH•dor] *n* M radiator

**radiante** [rah•DEE•AHN•tai] *adj* radiant

**radical** [RAH•dee•KAHL] *adj* radical

**radio 1** [rah•DEE•oh] *n* M radio

**radio 2** [rah•DEE•oh] *n* M radius

**radiográfico** [RAH•dee•oh•GRAH•FEE•ko] *n* M X-ray

**ráfaga** [RAH•fah•gah] *n* F blast

**raído** [RAI•do] *n* M threadbare

**raíz** [rai•EES] *n* F root

**raja** [RAH•ha] *n* F sliver

**rallador** [RAI•yah•DOR] *n* M grater

**rama** [RAH•mah] *n* F branch; en ~\ raw

**ramita** [rah•MEE•tah] *n* F twig

**rana** [RAH•nah] *n* F frog

**rancio** [rahn•SEE•oh] *adj* rancid

**ranura** [rah•NOOR•ah] *n* F groove

**rápidamente** [rah•PEE•dah•MEN•tai] *adv* speedily

**rapidez** [RAH•pee•DEHS] *n* F speed

**rápido** [RAH•pee•do] *adj* rapid

**rápido** [RAH•pee•do] *adv* speedy

**rapto 1** [RAHP•toh] *n* M kidnaping

**rapto 2** [RAHP•to] *n* M rapture; trance

**raptor** [RAHP•tohr] *n* M kidnapper

**raramente** [RAHR•ah•MEN•tai] *adv* seldom; rarely

**rareza** [rahr•AI•sah] *n* F rarity

**raro** [RAHR•o] adj rare; scarce

**rascacielos** [rah•SKAH•see•AI•los] *n* M skyscraper

**rascadura** [RAHSK•ah•DOOR•ah] *n* F scratch

**rascar** [RAHS•kahr] *vi vt* claw (at)

**rasgar** [RAHS•gahr] *vt* tear

**rasgo** [RAHS•go] *n* M trait

**raso** [RAH•so] *adj* flat; smooth

**raspador** [rahs•PAH•dor] *n* M scraper

**raspar** [rah•SPAHR] *vt* rasp; scrape

**rastrillar** [RAH•stree•YAHR] *vt* heckle

**rastrojo** [rah•STROH•ho] *n* M stubble

**ratero** [rah•TAIR•oh] *n* M pickpocket

**ratificar** [rah•TEE•fih•KAHR] *vt* ratify

**rato** [RAH•to] *n* M while; short time; moment a ~s\ at times; ~s libres\ free time; hace un ~\ a moment ago; ¡hast otro ~!\ see you soon!; pasar mal~\ have a difficult time

**ratón** [rah•TON] *n* M mouse; rat

**ratones** |RAH•ton•AIS| *npl*
mice

**rauco** |ROU•koh| *adj* raucous

**raya** |RAI•ya| *n* F streak; stripe;
M ray

**rayo** |RAI•yo| *n* M spoke

**rayón** |RAI•yon| *n* M rayon

**raza** |RAH•sah| *n* F breed
(race); de pura ~\
thoroughbred

**razón** |rah•SON| *n* F reason

**razonablemente**
|RAH•son•AHB•leh•MEN•tai|
*adv* reasonably

**razonamiento**
|RAH•son•AH•mee•EN•to| *n*
M reasoning

**reacción** |rai•AHK•see•OHN| *n*
F reaction

**reaccionar**
|RAI•ahk•SEE•ohn•AHR| *vi*
react

**reaccionario**
|rai•AHK•see•ON•ahr•EE•oh|
*adj* reactionary

**reacio** |RAI•ah•SEE•oh| *adj*
unwilling

**real 1** |rai•AHL| *adj* real; *n* M
real (old Spanish coin)

**real 2** |rai•AHL| *adj* royal

**realidad** |rai•AHL•ih•DAHD| *n*
F reality

**realismo** |RAI•ahl•IS•mo| *n* M
realism

**realista** |RAI•ahl•EE•stah| *n* F
realist; *adj* realistic

**realización**
|RAI•ahl•ih•SAH•see•OHN| *n*
F realization

**realizar** |rai•AHL•ee•SAHR| *vt*
accomplish

**realmente** |RAI•ahl•MEN•tai|
*adv* actually; indeed; really

**reanudar** |rai•AH•noo•DAHR|
*vt* reopen

**reaparecer**
|RAI•ah•PAIR•ah•SAIR| *vt*
reappear

**reasumir** |rai•AH•SOO•MEER|
*vt* resume

**reavivamento**
|RAI•ah•VEE•vah•MEN•to| *n*
M revival

**rebaja** |rai•BAH•ha| *n* F rebate

**rebajar** |RAI•bah•HAHR| *vt*
abase; debase

**rebaño** |rai•BAN•yo| *n* M herd

**rebanada** |RAI•bahn•AH•dah|
*n* F slice

**rebelarse** |REH•behl•AHR•sai|
*vi* revolt

**rebelde** |rai•BEHL•dai| *adj*
rebellious; *n* M rebel

**rebelión** |reh•BEHL•ee•OHN| *n*
F rebellion

**rebosar** |RAI•boh•SAHR| *vt*
overflow

**rebosadero**
|rai•BOH•sah•DAIR•oh| *n* M
overflow

**rebotar** |RAI•bo•TAHR| *vt*
rebound

**rebusca** |rai•BOO•skah| *n* F
research

**rebuscar** |REH•boo•SKAHR| *vt*
glean

**rebuznar** |RAI•boos•NAHR| *vi*
bray

**recaída** |rai•KAI•dah| *n* F
relapse

**recepción** |rai•SEHP•see•OHN|
*n* F reception

**receptáculo**
[REH•sep•TAHK•OO•lo] *n* M
receptacle

**receptor 1** [REH•sehp•TOHR]
*n* M receiver; recipient

**receptor 2** [REH•sehp•TOHR]
*n* M headphones

**receta** [reh•SEH•tah] *n* F recipe

**recibir** [RAI•see•BEER] *vt*
receive

**recibo** [rai•SEE•bo] *n* M receipt

**reciente** [RAI•see•EN•tai] *adv*
recent

**reciproca** [rai•SEE•pro•KAH] *n*
F converse

**reciprocar**
[rai•SEE•proh•KAHR] *vt*
reciprocate

**recíproco** [rai•SEE•PRO•ko] *n*
M reciprocal

**recital** [REH•see•tahl] *n* M
recital

**recitar** [RAI•see•TAHR] *vt*
recite

**reclamación**
[RAI•klah•MAH•see•OHN] *n*
claim

**reclamar** [RAI•klah•MAHR] *vt*
reclaim; claim

**reclamo** [rai•KLAH•mo] *n* M
decoy

**reclinar** [rai•KLEEN•ahr] *vi*
recline

**reclutar** [RAI•kloo•TAHR] *vt*
recruit

**recobrar** [RAI•koh•BRAHR] *vt*
recover

**recobro** [rai•KOH•bro] *n* M
recovery

**recoger** [REH•koh•HAIR] *vi*
gather

**recolección**
[REH•koh•LEHK•see•OHN] *n*
F gathering

**recomendación**
[REH•kohm•en•DAH•see•
OHN] *n* F recommendation

**recomendar**
[rai•KOH•men•DAHR] *vt*
recommend

**recompensar**
[rai•KOM•pen•SAHR] *vt*
recompense

**reconciliación**
[RAI•kon•SIHL•ee•AH•see•
OHN] *n* F reconciliation

**reconciliar**
[RAI•kon•SIH•lee•AHR] *vt*
reconcile

**reconocer**
[rai•KOHN•oh•SAIR] *vt*
acknowledge; recognize

**reconocimiento 1**
[rai•KOHN•oh•see•MEE•EN•
to] *n* M recognition

**reconocimiento 2**
[rai•KON•oh•see•MEE•EN•to]
*n* M reconnaissance

**reconstruir**
[rai•CON•stroo•EER] *vt*
reconstruct

**recontar** [RAI•kon•TAHR] *vt*
recount

**reconvenir** [rai•KON•ven•EER]
*vt* upbraid; scold

**recordar** [RAI•kor•DAHR] *vi*
recollect; remember; que yo
recuerde\ as far as I remeber;
si mal no recuerdo\ if I
remember correctly

**recordativo**
[rai•KOR•dah•TEE•vo] *n* M
reminder

**recreación**
[RAI•krai•AH•see•OHN] *n* F
recreation

**rectángulo**
[REHK•tahn•GOO•lo] *n* M
rectangle

**rectificar** [rehk•TEE•fih•KAHR]
*vt* rectify

**rectitud** [REHK•tih•TOOD] *n* F
righteousness; straightness;
honesty

**recto** [REHK•to] *adj* righteous;
straight; todo ~\ straight on

**rector** [REHK•tor] *n* M rector

**recuerdo** [rai•KWAIR•doh] *n*
M keepsake; recollection;
souvenir; remembrance

**recuperar** [RAI•koo•PAIR•ahr]
*vt* recuperate; regain; retrieve

**recurrir** [RAI•koor•EER] *vt*
recur

**recurso 1** [rai•KOOR•so] *n* M
recourse; resort

**recurso 2** [rai•KOOR•so] *n* M
resource

**recusar** [RAI•koo•SAHR] *vt*
refuse

**rechazamiento**
[RAI•cha•SAH•mee•EN•to] *n*
M refusal

**rechazar** [RAI•cha•SAHR] *vt*
reject

**rechinante**
[REH•cheen•AN•tai] *adj*
grating

**rechinar** [RAI•chee•NAHR] *vt*
gnash (teeth); grind; squeak

**rechoncho** [rai•CHON•cho] *adj*
stocky; stout

**red 1** [rehd] *n* M net; network

**red 2** [rehd] *n* M luggage rack

**redención** [rai•DEN•see•OHN]
*n* F redemption

**redentor** [RAI•den•TOR] *n* M
redeemer

**redimir** [rEH•dee•MEER] *vt*
redeem; take off; detach

**redoma** [rai•DOH•mah] *n* F
vial

**redondo** [rai•DON•do] *adj*
round; a la redonda\ around;
en ~\ round

**reducción**
[reh•DOOK•see•OHN] *n* F
standardization

**reducir** [RAI•doo•SEER] *vt*
reduce

**reedificar**
[RAI•eh•DEE•fih•KAR] *vt*
rebuild

**reembolsar**
[rai•EM•bol•SAHR] *vt*
reimburse

**reembolso** [RAI•em•BOL•so] *n*
M refund; rebate

**referencia**
[reh•FAIR•en•SEE•ah] *n* F
reference

**referir** [RAI•fair•EER] *vt* tell;
refer; por lo que se refiere a\
as regards

**refinado** [RAI•feen•AH•do] *adj*
polite; refined

**refinamiento**
[rai•FIN•ah•MEE•EN•to] *n* M
refinement

**refinar** [RAI•fee•NAHR] *vt*
refine

**refinería** [rai•FIN•air•EE•ah] *n*
F refinery

**reflector** [reh•FLEHK•tor] *n* M
floodlight

**reflejar** [RAI•flai•HAHR] *vt*
reflect

**reflexión**
[rai•FLEHK•see•OHN] *n* F
reflection

**reflexionar**
[RAI•flehks•SEE•ohn•AHR] *vt*
deliberate; reflect (upon)

**reflexivo** [RAI•flehks•EE•vo]
*adj* reflexive

**reflujo** [rai•FLOO•ho] *n* M ebb

**reforma** [RAI•for•MAH] *n* F
reform

**reforzar** [RAI•for•SAHR] *vt*
reinforce

**refracción**
[rai•FRAHK•see•OHN] *n* F
refraction

**refrenar** [rai•FREN•ahr] *vt*
refrain; restrain

**refrescadura**
[rai•FREH•skah•DOOR•ah] *n*
F refreshment

**refrescante**
[RAI•freh•SKAHN•tai] *adj*
refreshing

**refrescar** [REH•frehs•KAHR] *vt*
freshen; refresh

**refrigeración**
[RAI•frih•hair•AH•sce•OHN]
*n* F refrigeration

**refugio** [RAI•foo•HEE•oh] *n* M
refuge

**refundir** [REH•fun•DEER] *vt*
rewrite; revise; rehash

**refunfuñar**
[rch•FUHN•foon•YAHR] *vi*
grumble

**refutar** [RAI•few•TAHR] *vt*
disprove; refute

**refutar** [RAI•foo•TAHR] *vi*
refute

**regalías** [rai•GAH•lee•AHS] *n*
F regalia

**regalo** [rai•GAH•loh] *n* M gift;
present

**regañar** [RAI•gan•YAHR] *vt*
nag

**regaño** [rai•GAN•yo] *n* M
scolding

**regañon** [RAI•gahn•YON] *adj*
shrewish

**regate** [rai•GAH•tai] *n* M
dodge

**regatar** [RAI•gah•TAHR] *vt*
haggle over; economize on

**régimen** [RAI•hee•MEN] *n* M
regime

**regimiento**
[rai•HEE•mee•EN•to] *n* M
regiment

**regio** [rai•HEE•oh] *adj* regal

**región** [rai•HEE•on] *n* F region

**registrar** [REH•hee•STRAHR]
*vt* register; record

**registro** [reh•HEE•stro] *n* M
registration

**regla** [RAI•glah] *n* F ruler; rule;
law; en ~\ in order; por ~\
general as a rule

**regresar** [RAI•greh•SAHR] *vi*
comeback

**regulación**
[rai•goo•LAH•see•OHN] *n* F
regulation

**regular** [RAI•goo•LAHR] *adj*
regular; *vt* regulate

**regularmente**
[reh•GOO•lahr•MEN•tai] *adv*
regularly

**rehén** [reh•HEN] *n* M hostage

**reina** [RAI•nah] *n* F queen
**reinante** [rai•NAN•tai] *adj* prevalent
**reinar** [rai•NAHR] *vt* reign
**reingresar** [rai•IN•greh•SAHR] *vt* F re-enter
**reino** [RAI•no] *n* M kingdom; realm
**reír** [rai•EER] *vi* laugh; chuckle; ~ se de\ laugh at; echarse a ~\ burst out laughing
**reír a carcajadas** [rai•EER ah KAHR•kah•HA•dahs] *vi* guffaw
**reírse** [rai•EER•sai] *vi* giggle
**reiterar** [RAI•tair•AHR] *vt* reiterate
**reja** [rai•HA] *n* F grate; grid
**rejuvenecer** [rai•HOO•ven•EH•sair] *vi* rejuvenate
**relación** [reh•LAH•see•OHN] *n* F relation; relationship; ratio
**relajación** [RAI•lah•HAH•see•OHN] *n* F relaxation
**relajar** [RAI•lah•HAR] *vt* relax
**relamido** [RAI•lah•MEE•do] *adj* prim
**relámpago** [RAI•LAHM•PAH•go] *n* M lightning
**relatado** [RAI•lah•TAH•do] *adj* related
**relatar** [RAI•lah•TAHR] *vt* relate; tell
**relativo** [REH•lah•TEE•vo] *adj* relative
**relator** [RAI•lah•TOR] *n* M teller; storyteller

**releampago** [RAI•lai•AM•PAH•go] *n* M zipper
**religión** [rai•LIH•hee•OHN] *n* F religion
**religioso** r[ai•LIH•hee•OH•so] *adj* religious
**relinchar** [REH•leen•CHAR] *vi* neigh
**reloj** [RAI•loh] *n* M clock; watch; timepiece; en el sentido de las saetas del ~\ clockwise
**reloj de arena** [RAI•loh dai ah•RAI•nah] *n* M hourglass
**reluctante** [RAI•luhk•TAN•tai] *adj* reluctant
**rellenar** [RAI•yai•NAHR] *vt* cram; refill
**relleno** [reh•YAI•no] *n* M filling; stuffing
**remachar 1** [RAI•mah•CHAR] *vt* punch; drive home (coll)
**remachar 2** [RAI•mah•CHAR] *vt* rivet
**remanente** [REH•mah•NEN•tai] *n* M remnant
**remediar** [rai•MAI•dee•AHR] *vt* reliever; mend
**remedio** [REH•mai•DEE•oh] *n* M remedy
**remiendo** [RAI•mee•EN•do] *n* M patch
**remilgada** [RAI•mihl•GAH•dah] *n* F prude
**remilgado** [RAI•mihl•GAH•do] *adj* squeamish
**reminiscencia** [REH•mih•NIHN•sen•SEE•ah] *n* F reminiscence

**remisión** [rai•MIH•see•OHN] *n*
F remission

**remiso** [rai•MEE•so] *adj* remiss

**remitente** [RAI•mih•TEN•tai ]n
M sender

**remitir** [RAI•mih•TEER] *vt*
remit; *vi* diminish

**remo** [RAI•mo] *n* M oar

**remojar** [RAI•moh•HAR] *vt*
drench

**remolacha** [RAI•mo•LAH•cha]
*n* F beet

**remolcar** [RAI•mohl•KAHR] *vt*
tow

**remolque** [RAI•mohl•KAI] *n*
M towing; trailer

**remordimiento**
[RAI•mor•DEE•mee•EN•toh]
*n* M qualm; remorse

**remoto** [rai•MOH•to] *adj*
remote

**remover** [RAI•moh•VAIR] *vt*
remove

**reñado** [rehn•YAH•doh] *adj*
frayed

**reñir** [rehn•YEER] *vt* scold

**renacimiento**
[RAI•nah•see•MEE•EN•to] *n*
M rebirth; renaissance

**renacuajo**
[REH•nah•KWAH•ho] *n* M
tadpole

**rencor** [REN•kor] *n* M rancor

**rendimiento**
[REHN•dee•MEE•EN•toh] *n*
M output

**rendir** [ren•DEER] *vt* yield

**reno** [RAI•no] *n* M reindeer

**renocación**
[REH•noh•VAH•sce•OHN] *n*
F renewal

**renombre** [reh•NOHM•brai] *n*
M renown; fame

**renovar** [REH•no•VAHR] *vt*
reñew; renovate

**renta** [REN•tah] *n* F rental

**renuencia**
[REH•noo•en•SEE•ah] *n* F
unwillingness

**renunciar**
[rai•NUHN•see•AHR] *vt* quit;
renounce; waive

**reparación**
[REH•pahr•AH•see•OHN] *n* F
compensation; reparation

**reparar** [RAI•pah•RAHR] *vt*
overhaul; repair; mend

**repasar** [RAI•pah•SAHR] *vt*
overlook

**repelente** [RAI•peh•LEHN•tai]
*adj* repulsive; repellant;
disgusting

**repeler** [REH•peh•LAIR] *vt*
repel; refuse; turn down

**repensar** [RAI•pen•SAHR] *vt*
reconsider

**de repente** [DAI rai•PEN•tai]
*adv* suddenly

**repetición**
[REH•peh•TIH•see•OHN] *n* F
repetition

**repetir** [REH•peh•TEER] *vt*
repeat

**repicar** [RAI•pee•KAHR] *vt*
ring; peal

**repisa de chimenea**
[rai•PEE•sa dai
CHIH•men•AI•ah] *n* F
mantelpiece

**réplica** [rehpl•IH•kah] *n* F
answer; replica

**repollo** |rai•POY•yo| *n* M
cabbage

**reponer** |RAI•pon•AIR| *vt*
replace

**reportaje** |RAI•por•TAH•hai| *n*
M report

**reportero** |RAI•por•TAIR•oh| *n*
M reporter

**reposado** |RAI•poh•SAH•do|
*adj* restful

**reposo** |rai•POH•so| *n* M
repose

**repración** |rai•PRAH•see•OHN|
*n* F reproof

**reprender** |RAI•pren•DAIR| *vi*
snub

**representación**
|REH•preh•sen•TAH•see•OHN|
*n* F representation

**representar**
|rai•PREH•sen•TAHR| *vt*
depict; represent

**representate**
|reh•PREH•sen•TAHN•tai| *n*
M representative

**reprimenda**
|REH•pree•MEN•dah| *n* F
reprimand

**reprimir** |RAI•prih•MEER| *vt*
quell; put down; suppress

**reprobar** |RAI•pro•BAHR| *vt*
blame; reprove

**reproche** |rai•PROH•chai| *n* M
reproach

**reprodución**
|RAI•proh•DOOK•see•OHN|
*n* F reproduction

**reproducir**
|rai•PRO•doo•SEER| *vt*
reproduce

**reptil** |rehp•TEEL| *n* M reptile

**república** |rai•POOB•lee•KAH|
*n* F republic

**republicano**
|rai•POOB•lee•KAHN•oh| *n*
M republican

**repudiar** |rai•POO•dee•AHR| *vt*
disavow; disown

**repudiar** |rai•POO•dee•AHR| *vt*
repudiate

**repugnancia**
|reh•PUHG•nahn•SEE•ah| *n* F
disgust

**repugnante**
|reh•PUHG•NAHN•tai| *adj*
disgusting; foul; repugnant

**repulsar** |RAI•puhl•SAHR| *vt*
repulse

**reputación**
|REH•poo•TAH•see•OHN| *n*
F reputation

**reputar** |RAI•poo•TAHR| *vi*
repute

**requerido** |REH•kair•EE•do| *n*
M prerequisite

**requerir** |reh•QWAIR•eer| *vt*
require

**requeta** |rah•KAI•tah| *n* F
racket

**requisito** |RAI•kee•SEE•to| *n*
M requirement

**res** |rais| *n* F animal; ~ lanar\
sheep; ~ vacuna\ cow, bull,
ox; carne de ~\ beef

**resaca** |reh•SAH•kah| *n* F
undertow

**resarcir** |REHS•ahr•SEER| *vt*
redress

**resbaladizo**
|rais•BAH•lah•DEE•so| *adj*
slippery

**resbalar** [RAIS•bah•LAHR] *vi*
slide

**resbalón** [REHS•bah•LOHN] *n*
M slip; skid

**rescatar** [REH•skah•TAHR] *vt*
rescue

**rescate** [rehs•KAH•tai] *n* M
ransom

**resentido** [REH•sen•TEE•do]
*adj* resentful

**resentimiento**
[reh•SEN•tee•MEE•EN•to] *n*
M grudge

**resentirse** [REH•sen•TEER•sai]
*vt* resent

**reservación**
[REH•sair•VAH•see•OHN] *n*
F reservation

**reservar** [REH•sair•VAHR] *vt*
reserve

**residencia**
[reh•SIH•den•SEE•ah] *n* F
residence

**residir** [REH•sih•DEER] *vi*
reside

**residuo** [REH•sih•DOO•oh] *n*
M residue

**resignación**
[REH•sig•NAH•see•OHN] *n* F
resignation

**resistencia**
[reh•SIH•sten•SEE•ah] *n* F
endurance; resistance

**resistir** [REH•sihs•TEER] *vt*
resist; withstand

**resolución**
[REH•soh•LOO•see•OHN] *n*
F resolution

**resolver** [RAI•sohl•VAIR] *vt*
solve; resolve

**resollar** [RAI•soi•YAHR] *vi*
pant

**resonancia**
[reh•SOH•nahn•SEE•ah] *n* F
resonance

**resonante**
[REH•soh•NAHN•tai] *adj*
resonant

**resoplar** [RAI•sohp•LAHR] *vt*
snort

**resoplido** [RAI•so•PLEE•do] *n*
M puff

**respaldar** [RAI•spahl•DAHR]
*vt* back; back up

**respectivo**
[REH•spehk•TEE•vo] *adv*
respective

**respecto de** [REH•SPEHK•to
dai] *adj* regarding

**respetable**
[RAI•speh•TAHB•lai] *adj*
respectable

**respeto** [reh•SPEH•to] *n* M
respect

**respeto de sí mismo** [-dai see
MEEZ•moh] *n* M self-respect

**respetuoso**
[reh•SPEH•too•OH•so] *adj*
respectful

**respiración**
[reh•SPEER•ah•SEE•ON] *n* F
breath

**respirar** [REH•speer•AHR] *vi*
breathe

**respiro** [reh•SPEER•oh] *n* M
respite; breather

**resplandeciente**
[reh•SPLAHN•deh•SEE•EN•
tai] *adj* glowing

**resplandor** [REH•splahn•DOR]
*n* M glimmer; glitter

**responder** [REH•spon•DAIR]
*vi* reply; respond; answer

**responsabilidad**
[reh•SPON•sah•BIHL•ih•
DAHD] *n* F responsibility

**responsable**
[RAI•spon•SAHB•lai] *adj*
responsible

**respuesta** [reh•SPWEH•stah] *n*
F response

**restablecer**
[reh•STAHB•leh•SAIR] *vt*
re-establish

**restauración**
[REH•stou•RAH•see•OHN] *n*
F restoration

**restaurante**
[REH•stau•RAHN•tai] *n* M
restaurant

**restaurar** [REH•stour•AHR] *vt*
restore

**restitución**
[REH•stih•TOO•see•OHN] *n*
F restitution

**restituir** [reh•STIH•too•EER] *vt*
repay

**resto** [REH•sto] *n* M remainder

**restos** [reh•STOHS] *npl* M
remains

**restricción**
[reh•STRIHK•see•OHN] *n* F
handicap; restriction

**restringir** [RAI•strin•GEER] *vt*
restrict

**resucitar** [rai•SUH•sih•TAHR]
*vt* resuscitate

**resuelto** [reh•SWEHL•to] *n* M
resolute

**resultado** [RAI•suhl•TAH•do] *n*
M outcome; result

**resultado final**
[RAI•sool•TAH•do FEE•nahl]
*n* M upshot

**resultados**
[REH•suhl•TAH•dos] *npl* M
returns (election)

**retardar** [RAI•tahr•DAHR] *vt*
retard; delay; halt; stop; keep
open

**retener** [rai•TEN•air] *vt*
recoup

**retiñir** [REH•tin•YEER] *vi* ring;
tinkle

**retirada** [REH•teer•AH•dah] *n*
F withdrawal; retreat

**retirado** [REH•teer•AH•do] *n*
M recluse; *adj* withdrawn;
secluded; retired

**retirar** [REH•teer•AHR] *vt*
withdraw

**retirarse** [REH•teer•AHR•sai] *vi*
retire

**retiro** [reh•TEER•oh] *n* M
retirement; withdrawal

**retoño** [reh•TON•yo] *n* M
sprout

**retorcer** [RAI•tor•SAIR] *vt*
twirl; wring

**retorcerse** [RAI•tor•SAIR•sai]
*vi* squirm

**retórica** [REH•tor•IH•kah] *n* F
rhetoric

**retornar** [REH•tor•NAHR] *vt vi*
return

**retorta** [rai•TOR•tah] *n* F
retort

**retozar 1** [RAI•to•SAHR] *vt*
romp; frolic

**retozar 2** [RAI•to•SAHR] *vt*
frisk

**retractar** |RAI•trahk•TAHR| vt
retract

**retraimiento**
|RAI•trai•MEE•EN•to| n M
seclusion

**retratar** |RAI•trah•TAHR| vt
portray

**retrato** |rai•TRAH•to| n M
portrait; portrayal

**retreta** |reh•TRAI•tah| n F
tattoo

**retroactivo**
|reh•TRO•ahk•TEE•vo| adj
retroactive

**retroceder**
|rai•TROH•seh•DAIR| vt
recede; recoil

**retrógrado**
|RAI•troh•GRAH•do| adj
backward

**retumbar** |RAI•toom•BAHR| vi
rumble

**reumatismo**
|ROI•mah•TIS•mo| n M
rheumatism

**reunión** |rai•OON•ee•OHN| n F
rally; reunion

**reunir** |RAI•oo•NEER| vt
rejoin; reunite; convene

**revelación**
|REH•veh•LAH•see•OHN| n
F revelation

**revelar** |REH•veh•LAHR| vt
reveal; tattle (coll)

**reventar** |RAI•ven•TAHR| vt
burst

**reverencia**
|reh•VAIR•en•SEE•ah| n F
reverence

**reverenciar**
|reh•VAIR•en•SEE•ahr| vt
revere; worship

**reverendo** |REH•vair•EN•do|
adj reverend

**reverente** |REH•vair•EN•tai|
adj reverent

**revertir** |RAI•vair•TEER| vt
revert

**revisar** |RAI•vee•SAHR| vt
revise

**revisión** |rai•VIH•see•OHN| n F
revision

**revista** |reh•VEE•stah| n F
magazine; review

**revivir** |RAI•vee•VEER| vi
recall

**revocar** |RAI•voh•KAHR| vt
revoke

**revolcarse**
|RAI•vohl•KAHR•sai| vi
wallow

**revolución**
|REH•voh•LOO•see•OHN| n
F revolution

**revolucionario**
|REH•voh•LOO•SEE•ohn•
AHR•EE•oh| adj
revolutionary

**rey** |rai| n M king

**reyes** |RAI•ais| npl king and
queen

**rezagarse**
|REH•sah•GAHR•sai| vi lag;
loiter

**rezno** |REHS•no| n M tick
(insect)

**rezumarse**
|REH•soo•MAHR•sai| vi
ooze

**ribete** |rih•BEH•tai| n M welt

**rico** |REE•ko| adj rich; wealthy;
n M rich person

**ridiculizar**
[RIH•dih•KOO•lee•SAHR] *vi*
ridicule

**ridículo** [ree•DEE•KOO•lo] *adj*
ridiculous

**rienda** [REE•en•DAH] *n* F
rein

**riesgo** [ree•EHS•go] *n* M
liability; risk; a ~ de\ at the
risk of; correr el ~ de\ run the
risk of

**rifa** [REE•fah] *n* F raffle

**rifle** [REEF•lai] *n* M rifle

**rigidez** [rih•GIH•dehs] *n* F
rigidity; rigor

**rígido** [rih•HEE•do] *adj* rigid;
stiff

**rima** [REE•mah] *n* F rhyme

**riñon** [reen•YON] *n* M kidney

**rinoceronte**
[ree•NO•sair•OHN•tai] *n* M
rhinoceros

**río** [REE•oh] *n* M river

**riostra** [REE•oh•STRAH] *n* F
strut

**ripio** [rih•PEE•oh] *n* M rubble

**riqueza** [ree•KAI•sah] *n* F
wealth; richness

**risa** [REE•sah] *n* F laughter;
laugh

**risco** [REES•koh] *n* M cliff

**ritmo** [RIHT•mo] *n* M rhythm

**rito** [REE•to] *n* M rite

**ritual** [rih•TOO•AHL] *n* M
ritual

**rivalidad**
[ree•VAHL•ih•DAHD] *n* F
rivalry

**rizado** [ree•SAH•do] *adj*
curly

**rizo** [REE•so] *n* M curl; lock

**robar** [roh•BAHR] *vt* rob;
steal

**roble** [ROH•blai] *n* M oak

**robo** [ROH•bo] *n* M larceny;
robbery; theft

**robusto** [roh•BUH•sto] *adj*
hardy; robust

**roca** [ROH•kah] *n* F rock

**rociar** [ROH•see•AHR] *vt*
douse; spray

**rocío** [roh•SEE•oh] *n* M dew

**rocoso** [roh•KOH•so] *adj*
rocky

**rodado** [roh•DAH•do] *n* M
boulder

**rodilla** [roh•DEE•yah] *n* F
knee

**roer** [RO•air] *vt* gnaw

**rogar** [roh•GAHR] *vi* pray

**rojez** [ROH•hes] *n* F redness

**rojo** [ROH•ho] *adj* red

**rollo** [ROI•yo] *n* M roll; scroll;
coil

**romance** [roh•MAHN•sai] *n* M
romance

**romano** [roh•MAN•oh] *adj*
Roman

**romanticismo**
[roh•MAN•tih•SEES•mo] *n* M
romanticism

**romántico**
[roh•MAHN•TEE•koh] *adj*
romantic

**romper 1** [ROM•pair] *vt* M
break

**romper 2** [ROHM•pair] *vt*
disrupt

**romperse** [rom•PAIR•sai] *vi*
rupture

**rompimiento**
[ROHM•pee•MEE•EN•to] *n*
M break

**ron** [rohn] *n* M rum

**ronco** [RON•ko] *adj* hoarse;
husky

**rondar** [ron•DAHR] *vt* prowl

**ronronear** [ron•ROH•nai•AHR]
*vt* purr

**ropa** [ROH•pah] *n* F clothes

**ropa blanca** [ROH•pah
BLAN•kah] *n* F lingerie

**ropa interior** [ROH•pah
IN•tair•EER•ohr] *n* F
underclothes; underwear

**ropaje 1** [roh•PAH•hai] *n* M
drapes

**ropaje 2** [roh•PAH•hai] *n* M
robe

**rosa** [ROH•sah] *adj n* F pink;
rose

**rosado** [roh•SAH•do] *adj*
rosy

**rosario** [ROH•sahr•EE•oh] *n* M
rosary

**rostro** [ROH•stroh] *n* M visage

**rotación** [roh•TAH•see•OHN] *n*
F rotation

**rotario** [ROH•tahr•EE•oh] *n* M
rotary

**roto** [ROH•to] *adj* broken;
ragged; tattered

**rótula** [roh•TOO•lah] *n* F
kneecap

**rozar 1** [roh•SAHR] *vi* fret

**rozar 2** [roh•SAHR] *vt* graze

**rozar 3** [roh•SAHR] *vt* rub
against; brush against; touch
upon (coll)

**rubí** [roo•BEE] *n* M ruby

**rubio** [roo•BEE•OH] *adj* blonde

**ruborizarse**
[roo•BOR•ih•SAHR•sai] *vi*
blush

**rudamente**
[ROO•dah•MEN•tai] *adv*
roughly

**rudimentario**
[ROO•dih•MEN•tahr•EE•oh]
*adj* vestigial

**rudo** [ROO•do] *adj* rude; gruff;
harsh

**rueda** [roo•AI•dah] *n* F wheel

**ruego** [roo•AI•go] *n* M prayer;
request

**rufián** [ROO•fee•AHN] *n* M
pimp

**rugir** [roo•HEER] *vi* roar

**rugoso** [roo•GO•so] *adj* rough;
rugged

**ruibarbo** [ROO•ee•BAHR•bo] *n*
M rhubarb

**ruido** [roo•EE•do] *n* M noise

**ruidoso** [ROO•ee•DOH•so] *adj*
noisy; loud

**ruina** [roo•EE•nah] *n* F ruin

**ruiseñor** [roo•EE•scn•YOR] *n*
M nightingale

**rumiar** [roo•MEE•ahr] *vt*
ruminate

**rumor** [roo•MOHR] *n* M rumor;
hearsay

**rural** [ROOR•ahl] *adj* rural

**Rusia** [roo•SEE•ah] *n* Russia

**ruso** [ROO•so] *adj* Russian

**rústico** [roo•STEE•koh] *adj*
rustic

**ruta** [ROO•tah] *n* F route

**rutina** [roo•TEEN•ah] *n* F rote;
routine

# S

**sábado** [sah•BAH•do] *n* M
Saturday

**sábalo** [sah•BAH•lo] *n* M shad

**sabedor** [SAH•bai•DOR] *adj*
aware

**saber 1** [sah•BAIR] *vt* know; be
able to; know how

**saber 2** [SAH•bair] *n* M
knowledge; lore

**sabidillo** [SAH•bih•DEE•yo] *n*
M know-it-all

**sabiduría**
[sah•BEE•door•EE•ah] *n* F
wisdom

**sabihondo** [SAH•bee•OHN•do]
*n* M wiseacre

**sable** [SAHB•lai] *n* M saber

**sabor** [sah•BOR] *n* M flavor

**saborear** [SAH•bor•AI•ahr] *vt*
taste; relish

**sabotaje** [SAH•bo•TAH•hai] *n*
M sabotage

**sabroso** [sah•BROH•so] *adj*
palatable; tasty

**sabueso** [sah•BWEH•so] *n* M
sleuth

**sacacorchos**
[SAH•kah•KOR•chos] *n* M
corkscrew

**sacapuntas**
[SAH•kah•PUN•tahs] *n* F
pencil sharpener

**sacar 1** [SAH•kahr] *vt* protrude

**sacar 2** [SAH•kahr] *vt* tap;
disengage; elicit

**sacerdocio**
[sah•KAIR•doh•SEE•oh] *n* M
priesthood

**sacerdote** [SAH•kair•DOH•tai]
*n* M priest

**saco** [SAH•koh] *n* M sack; bag

**sacramento**
[SAHK•rah•MEN•toh] *n* M
sacrament

**sacrificio**
[sah•KRIH•fee•SEE•oh] *n* M
sacrifice

**sacristán** [SAH•kree•STAHN] *n*
M sexton

**sacristía** [SAH•krih•STEE•ah] *n*
F vestry

**sádico** [SAH•dee•koh] *adj*
sadistic

**sagacidad**
[sah•GAH•sih•DAHD] *n* F
widsom; sagacity

**sagaz** [SAH•gahs] *adj* wise;
sagacious; shrewd

**Sagrada Escritura**
[sah•GRAH•dah
EH•skree•TOOR•ah] *n* F
scripture

**sagrado** [sah•GRAH•do] *adj*
sacred

**sala** [SAH•lah] *n* F sitting-room

**sala de recibimiento** [SAH•lah
dai rai•see•BEE•MEE•EN•to]
*n* F parlor

**salchicha** [sahl•CHEE•cha] *n* F
hot dog

**salida** [sah•LEE•dah] *n* F
departure; exit; outlet

**salida de emergencia**
[sah•LEE•dah dai ] *n* F
emergency exit

salidizo [SAHL•ee•DEE•so] *adj*
outstanding

saliente [SAH•lee•EN•tai] *adj*
outgoing

salir [sah•LEER] *vi* depart;
leave; set out

salmo [SAHL•mo] *n* M psalm

salpicar [SAHL•pee•KAHR] *vt*
spatter; spalsh; sprinkle

salsa [SAL•sah] *n* F gravy

salsa de tomate [SAHL•sah
dai toh•MAH•tai] *n* F ketchup

salsa mahonesa [SAHL•sah
MAH•oh•NAI•sah] *n* F
mayonnaise

saltador [SAHL•tah•dor] *n* M
skipper

saltamontes
[sahl•TAH•mon•TAIS] *n* M
grasshopper

saltar [sahl•TAHR] *vt* hop;
jump

salteamiento
[sahl•TAI•ah•MEE•EN•toh] *n*
M holdup

saltear [SAHL•tai•AHR] *vt vi*
fry

salto [SAHL•toh] *n* M dive;
leap; jump

salud [sah•LOOD] *excl* cheers

salud [sah•LOOD] *n* F health

saludar [SAH•loo•DAHR] *vt*
greet; bow

saludo [sah•LOO•do] *n* M
greeting; nod

salvaje [sahl•VAH•hai] *adj*
wild; savage

salvia [sal•VEE•ah] *n* F sage
(plant)

salvo [SAHL•vo] *adj* harmless;
safe

sangrar 1 [san•GRAHR] *vi*
bleed

sangrar 2 [sahn•GRAHR] *vt* tap

sangre [SAHN•grai] *n* M blood;
de ~ fría\ cold-blooded

sangriento
[SAHN•gree•EN•toh] *adj*
bloody; gory

sanguijuela
[sahn•GWEE•hoo•AI•lah] *n* F
leech

sano [SAH•no] *adj* M healthy;
wholesome

santamente
[SAHN•tah•MEN•tai] *adv*
saintly

santidad [SAHN•tee•DAHD] *n*
F holiness

santo 1 [SAHN•to] *adj* holy;
hallowed

santo 2 [SAHN•to] *n* M saint

sapo [SAH•po] *n* M toad

saquear [SAH•kai•AHR] *vt*
ransack

saquito [sah•KEE•toh] *n* M
pouch

sarampión
[SAHR•rahm•PEE•YON] *n* F
measles

sarcasmo [sahr•KAHS•mo] *n* M
quip

sargento [sahr•HEN•to] *n* M
sergeant

sarnoso [sahr•NOH•so] *adj*
itchy

sastre [SAHS•trai] *n* M tailor

satisfacción
[SAHT•is•FAHK•see•OHN] *n*
F gratification

satisfacer [sah•TEES•fah•SAIR]
*vt* indulge

**sauce** [SOU•sai] *n* M willow
**sazonamiento**
[sah•SON•ah•MEE•EN•to] *n*
M seasoning
**se** [sai] *pron* him; her; himself;
herself; oneself; yourself;
themselves
**se si uno mismo si mismo**
[sai] [see] [oo•no] [mees•mo]
[see] *pron* oneself
**sebo** [SAI•bo] *n* M suet; tallow
**secador** [SAI•kah•DOHR] *n* M
dryer
**secar** [SAI•kah]r *vt* sear; wilt;
wither
**sección** [SEHK•see•OHN] *n* F
section
**secesión** [seh•SEH•see•OHN] *n*
F secession
**seco** [SAI•koh] *adj* dried; dry
**secreción**
[seh•KREH•see•OHN] *n* F
secretion
**secretar** [SEH•kreh•TAHR] *vt*
secrete
**secretario**
[seh•KREH•tahr•EE•oh] *n* M
secretary
**secreto 1** [seh•KREH•to] *n* M
secret; secrecy
**secreto 2** [seh•KREH•to] *adj*
underhanded
**secta** [SEHK•tah] *n* F sect
**sectario** [sehk•TAHR•EE•oh]
*adj* sectarian
**sector** [SEHK•tor] *n* M sector
**secuela** [seh•KWAI•lah] *n* F
sequel
**secuestrar 1**
[SAI•kwehs•TAHR] *vt* abduct;
kidnap

**secuestrar 2**
[SAI•kweh•STRAHR] *vt*
sequester
**secuestro** [seh•KWEH•stroh] *n*
M sequestration
**secular** [SEHK•oo•LAHR] *adj*
secular
**secularizar**
[SEHK•oo•LAHR•ee•SAHr]
*vt* secularize
**secundario**
[SEH•kuhn•DAHR•ee•oh] *adj*
secondary
**sed** [sehd] *n* M thirst; tener~\ be
thirsty; tener ~ de\ be hungry
for something
**seda** [SAI•dah] *n* F silk; de ~
*adj* \ silken
**seda floja** [SAI•dah FLOH•ha]
*n* F floss
**sedán** [seh•DAHN] *n* M sedan
**sedativo** [SEH•dah•TEE•vo] *n*
M sedative
**sedentario**
[seh•DEN•TAHR•ee•oh] *adj*
sedentary
**sedicioso** [seh•DIH•see•OH•so]
*adj* seditious
**sedimentación**
[seh•DIH•men•TAH•see•OHN]
*n* F sedition
**sedimento** [SEHD•ih•MEN•to]
*n* M deposit; sediment; silt
**seducción**
[seh•DOOK•see•OHN] *n* F
seduction
**seducir** [SEH•doo•SEER] *vt*
seduce
**seductivo** [SEH•dook•TEE•vo]
*adj* seductive

**seductor** [SEH•dook•TOR] *n* M
seducer

**segar** [SAI•gahr] *vt* reap

**segmento** [seg•MEN•to] *n* M
segment

**segregar** [SEHG•greh•GAHR]
*vt* segregate

**seguidor** [seh•GWEE•dor] *n* M
follower

**seguimiento**
[SEH•gwee•MEE•EN•to] *n* M
pursuit

**seguir** [seh•GEER] *vt vi* follow

**según** [sai•GOON] *prep*
according

**segundo** [seh•GOON•do] *adj*
second; de ~ clase\
second-rate; de ~ mano\
second-hand

**segundón** [SEH•goon•DOHN]
*n* M cadet

**segur** [seh•GOOR] *n* M sickle

**seguramente**
[seh•GOOR•ah•MEN•tai] *adv*
safely

**seguridad**
[seh•GOOR•ih•DAHD] *n* F
safety; security

**seguro** [seh•GOOR•oh] *adj*
secure; dependable; safe

**seguro de sí mismo**
[seh•GOOR•oh dai see
MEES•mo] *adj* self-confident

**seis** [sais] *num* six

**selección** [seh•LEHK•see•OHN]
*n* F selection; choice

**selectivo** [SEH•lehk•TEE•voh]
*adj* selective

**selenciador**
[sih•LEN•see•AH•dor] *n* M
silencer

**sello 1** [SAI•yo] *n* M postage

**sello 2** [SAI•yo] *n* M signet

**semana** [seh•MAN•ah] *n* F
week

**semanal** [SEH•mah•NAHL] *adj*
weekly

**semejantemente**
[SEH•meh•HAN•tch•MEN•tai]
*adv* similarly

**semejanza**
[SEH•meh•HAN•sah] *n* F
semblance; likeness

**semestral** [SEH•meh•STRAHL]
*adj* semiannual

**semilla** [seh•MEE•yah] *n* F
corn; seed

**seminario**
[seh•MIHN•ahr•EE•oh] *n* M
seminary

**señal 1** [sen•YAHL] *n* M
landmark

**señal 2** [sen•YAHL] *n* M signal

**señal** [sen•YAHL] *n* M token

**señalar 1** [SAIN•yah•LAHR] *vt*
appoint

**señalar 2** [SAIN•yah•LAHR] *vi*
signalize

**señas del remitente**
[SAIN•yahs del REH•
mih•TEN•tai] *npl* return
address

**señor** [sen•YOR] *n* M mister;
sir; lord

**señora** [sen•YOR•ah] *n* F
madam; Miss

**senado** [seh•NAH•do] *n* M
senate

**senador** [SEH•nah•DOR] *n* M
senator

**sencillo** [sen•SEE•yo] *adj* naive;
unaffected

**senda** [SEN•dah] *n* F footpath;
pathway

**senectud** [SEN•ehk•TOOD] *n* F
senility

**senil** [sehn•EEL] *adj* senile

**seno** [SAI•no] *n* M sinus

**sensación** [sen•SAH•see•OHN]
*n* F sensation

**sensato** [sen•SAH•to] *adj* wise

**sensibilidad**
[SEN•sih•BIHL•ih•DAHD] *n*
F sensibility; sensitivity

**sensible** [sen•SEE•blai] *adj*
sensible

**sensitivo** [SEN•sih•TEE•vo] *adj*
sensitive

**sensual** [sen•SWAHL] *adj*
sensual

**sensualidad**
[sen•SOO•ahl•ih•DAHD] *n* F
lust

**sentar** [sen•TAHR] *vi* sit; place;
establish; suit

**sentido** [sen•TEE•doh] *n* M
sense; feeling

**sentido común** [-koh•MOON]
*n* M sense (common)

**sentimentalismo**
[SEN•tee•MEN•tahl•EES•mo]
*n* M sentimentality

**sentimiento**
[SEN•tee•MEE•EN•to] *n* M
sentiment

**separable** [SEH•pahr•AHB•lai]
*adj* separable

**separacíon**
[SEH•pahr•AH•see•OHN] *n* F
parting; separation

**separadamente**
[SEH•pahr•AH•dah•MEN•tai]
*adv* separately

**separado** [SEH•pahr•AH•do]
*adj* separate

**separar** [SEH•pah•RAHR] *vt*
separate; disconnect

**separarse** [seh•PAHR•ahr•SAI]
*vi* secede; come away; get
away; take off

**sepear** [SAIR•pai•AHR] *vi*
grovel

**séptico** [sep•TEE•koh] *adj*
septic

**septiembre**
[SEHP•tee•EM•brai] *n*
September

**séptimo** [sehp•TEE•mo] *num*
seventh

**septuagésimo**
[SEHP•twah•HEH•SEE•moh]
*num* seventieth

**sepulcro** [seh•PUHL•kroh] *n* M
sepulcher

**sequedad** [SEH•kai•DAHD] *n*
F drought

**ser 1** [sair] *aux v* be; ~ de\
made of, come from, belong
to

**ser 2** [sair] *n* M being

**ser convenir** [sair]
[KON•ven•EER] *vi* become

**serenata** [SAIR•eh•NAH•tah] *n*
F serenade

**serenidad**
[sair•EHN•ih•DAHD] *n* F
serenity

**sereno** [seh•RAIN•oh] *adj*
sedate; serene

**ser humano** [sair
oo•MAHN•oh] *n* M human
being

**seria** [sair•EE•ah] *n* F serial;
series

**seriamente**
  [sair•EE•ah•MEN•tai] *adv*
  seriously
**serie** [sair•EE•ah] *n* F sequence
**seriedad** [sair•EE•eh•DAHD] *n*
  F seriousness
**serio 1** [sair•EE•oh] *adj* demure
**serio 2** [sair•EE•oh] *adj* earnest;
  serious
**ser más que** [sair mahs kai] *vt*
  outnumber
**sermón** [sair•MON] *n* M
  sermon
**serpiente** [sair•PEE•EN•tai] *n*
  M serpent
**servible sair•VEE•blai]** *adj*
  serviceable
**servicio** [SAIR•vee•SEE•oh] *n*
  M stead
**servicio de mesa**
  [SAIR•vee•SEE•oh dai
  MAI•sah] *n* M tableware
**servidumbre**
  [SAIR•vih•DOOM•brai] *n* M
  servitude
**servil** [sair•VEEL] *adj* menial;
  servile; slavish
**servilleta** [SAIR•vee•YEH•tah]
  *n* F napkin
**servir** [sair•VEER] *vt* serve; no
  ~ de nada\ be useless; para
  servirle\ at your service
**sesenta** [seh•SEHN•tah] *num*
  sixty
**sesgo** [SES•go] *n* M bias; slant
**sesión** [SEH•see•OHN] *n* F
  session; meeting
**setenta** [seh•TEN•tah] *num*
  seventy
**seudónimo** [SOI•doh•NEE•mo]
  *n* M pseudonym

**severo** [seh•VAIR•oh] *adj*
  severe
**sexagésimo**
  [sehk•AH•he•SEE•mo] *num*
  sixtieth
**sexo** [SEHKS•oh] *n* M sex
**sexto** [SEHKS•to] *num* sixth
**sexual** [sehk•SWAHL] *adj*
  sexual
**si 1** [see] *conj* if; *adv* whether
**sí 2** [see] yes; yeah
**sibila** [sih•BIH•lah] *n* F sibyl
**sicómoro** [SIH•koh•MOR•oh] *n*
  M sycamore
**SIDA** [SEE•dah] *n* AIDS
**sidra** [SEE•drah] *n* F cider
**siega** [see•AI•gah] *n* F harvest
**siempre** [see•EHM•prai] *adv*
  ever; forever; always; ~ que\
  if; como ~\ as usual; lo de ~\
  the same old story; para ~\
  forever
**sierra** [see•AIR•ah] *n* F chain
  saw
**siervo** [see•AIR•voh] *n* M
  servant (civil)
**siesta** [see•EH•stah] *n* F nap
**siete** [see•EH•tai] *num* seven
**sifón** [see•FON] *n* M siphon
**significación**
  [sihg•NIH•fih•KAH•see•OHN]
  *n* F meaning
**significante**
  [sig•NIH•fih•KAHN•tai] *adj*
  significant
**significar** [sig•NIH•fee•KAHR]
  *vt* purport; signify
**signo** [SIHG•no] *n* M gesture;
  sign
**siguiente** [SEE•gee•EHN•tai]
  *adj* ensuing; following

**sílaba** [SIH•lah•bah] *n* F
syllable

**silbar 1** [sihl•BAHR] *vi* whistle

**silbar 2** [sil•BAHR] *vt* zip

**silencio** [SIH•len•SEE•oh] *n* M
silence; hush

**silenciosamente**
[SIH•len•SEE•oh•sah•MEN•tai]
*adv* silently

**silencioso** [sih•LEN•see•OH•so]
*adj* soundless

**silogismo** [SIH•loh•HEE•smoh]
*n* M syllogism

**silueta** [SIH•loo•EH•tah] *n* F
silhouette

**silla** [SEE•yah] *n* F chair;
armchair; saddle

**silla de ruedas** [SEE•yah
roo•AI•dahs] *n* F wheelchair

**simbólico** [sihm•BOH•lee•koh]
*adj* symbolic

**símbolo** [SIHM•boh•loh] *n* M
symbol

**simétrico** [sih•MEH•TREE•koh]
*adj* symmetrical

**similar** [SIH•mee•LAHR] *adj*
similar

**similitud** [sih•MIHL•ih•TOOD]
*n* F similitude

**simpatía** [SIM•pah•TEE•ah] *n*
F sympathy

**simpático** [sim•PAH•TEE•koh]
*adj* nice; sympathetic

**simpite** [sihm•PEE•tai] *n* M
boar

**simple** [SIHM•plai] *adj* simple;
mere

**simplicidad**
[sim•PLIH•sih•DAHD] *n* F
simplicity

**simplificación**
[SIM•plih•fih•KAH•see•OHN]
*n* F simplification

**simplificar** [SIM•plee•FIH•kahr]
*vt* simplify

**simplón** [sim•PLON] *n* M
simpleton

**simular** [sim•oo•LAHR] *vt*
simulate

**simultáneo**
[SIHM•ool•tan•AI•oh] *adj*
simultaneous

**sin** [seen] *prep* without; ~ que\
without

**sinagoga** [SIH•noh•GOH•gah]
*n* F synagogue

**sinceridad**
[sihn•SAIR•ee•DAHD] *n* F
sincerity; candor

**sincero** [sin•SAIR•oh] *adj*
frank; outright; sincere

**sin corazón** [seen kor•AH•son]
*adj* heartless

**sincronizar**
[sin•KROH•nih•SAHR] *vi*
synchronize

**sindicatura**
[sin•DIH•kah•TOOR•ah] *n* F
syndicate

**sin dinero** [seen dee•NAIR•oh]
*adj* penniless

**sin Dios** [seen dee•OHS] *adj*
godless

**sin embargo** [seen
em•BAHR•go] *adv*
nevertheless; notwithstanding

**sinfonía** [SIN•foh•NEE•ah] *n* F
symphony

**sin freno** [seen FREH•no] *adj*
uncontrolled

**singular** [SEEN•goo•LAHR]
*adj* singular

**siniestro** [SIN•ee•EH•stroh] *adj*
sinister

**sino** [SEE•no] *conj* but, except;
*n* M fate

**sinónimo** [sin•OH•NIH•moh] *n*
M synonym

**sinónimo** [SIH•noh•NEE•mo]
*adj* synonymous

**sin punta** [seen PUHN•tah] *adj*
pointless

**sintaxis** [sin•TAHKS•ihs] *n* F
syntax

**sintesis** [sin•TEH•sihs] *n* F
synthesis

**síntoma** [SIN•TOH•mah] *n* F
symptom

**sintomático**
[SIN•to•MAH•TEE•koh] *adj*
symptomatic

**sin valor** [seen VAH•lor] *adj*
worthless

**sin vida** [seen VEE•dah] *adj*
lifeless

**sirena** [seer•AI•nah] *n* F
mermaid; siren

**Siria** [seer•EE•ah] *n* F Syria

**sirio** [seer•EE•oh] *n* M Syrian

**sirviente** [SEER•vee•EN•tai] *n*
M servant

**sisear** [SIH•sai•AHR] *vi* hiss

**sistema** [sih•TAI•mah] *n* M
system; del ~ *adj* \ systematic

**sitiar** [SIH•tee•AHR] *vt* besiege;
surround

**sitio 1** [sih•TEE•oh] *n* M siege

**sitio 2** [sih•TEE•oh] *n* M site

**situación**
[SIH•too•AH•see•OHN] *n* F
situation

**situado** [SIH•too•AH•do] *adj*
situate

**situado hacia el sur**
[SIH•too•AH•dah ah•SEE•ah
al soor] *adv* southward

**soberano** [SOH•bair•AHN•oh]
*n* M sovereign

**sobornar** [SO•bor•NAHR] *vt*
bribe

**soborno** [so•BOR•no] *n* M
bribe

**sobrante** [soh•BRAHN•tai] *n*
M left-overs

**sobre** [SO•brai] *prep*
concerning; about; upon; *adv*
above

**sobre esto** [SOH•brai EH•stoh]
*adv* thereupon

**sobrecargar**
[SOH•brai•kahr•GAHR] *vt*
overcharge

**sobregirar**
[soh•BRAI•heer•AHR] *vt*
overdraw

**sobrepeso** [SOH•brai•PAI•so]
*adj* overweight

**sobrepujar 1**
[SOH•brai•poo•HAHR] *vi*
excel

**sobrepujar 2**
[SOH•brai•poo•HAHR] *vt*
transcend

**sobretodo** [SOH•brai•TOH•do]
*n* M overcoat

**sobreviviente**
[SOH•brai•VEE•vee•EN•tai] *n*
M survivor

**sobrevivir**
[soh•BRAI•vee•VEER] *vt*
outlive; survive

**sobriamente**
[soh•BREE•ah•MEN•tai] *adv*
soberly

**sobriedad**
[soh•BREE•eh•DAHD] *n* F
sobriety

**sobrina** [soh•BREEN•ah] *n* F
niece

**sobrino** [so•BREE•no] *n* M
nephew

**sobrio** [so•BREE•oh] *adj* sober

**socarrar** [SOH•kahr•RAHR] *vt*
scorch; singe

**sociable** [SOH•see•AHB•lai]
*adj* sociable

**social** [so•SEE•ahl ] *adj* social

**socialismo**
[soh•SEE•ahl•EES•mo] *n* M
socialism

**socialista**
[soh•SEE•ahl•EE•stah] *n* F
socialist

**sociedad** [soh•SEE•eh•DAHD]
*n* F society; membership

**sociología**
[SOH•see•OH•loh•HEE•ah] *n*
F sociology

**socorro** [soh•KOR•roh] *n* M
relief; succor

**soda** [SO•dah] *n* F soda

**sodio** [soh•DEE•oh] *n* M
sodium

**sofa** [SOH•fah] *n* M couch; sofa

**sofisticación**
[SOH•FIH•stih•KAH•see•
OHN] *n* F sophistication

**sofisticado**
[SOH•FIH•stih•KAH•do] *adj*
sophisticated

**sofocación**
[SOH•fo•KAH•see•OHN] *n* F
suffocation

**sofocante** [SOH•fo•KAHN•tai]
*adj* stuffy

**sofocar** [SOH•fo•KAHR] *vt*
stifle; suffocate; *vi* swelter;
choke

**sojuzgar** [SOH•hoos•GAHR] *vt*
subdue

**solapa** [soh•LAH•pah] *n* F lapel

**solar** [SOH•lahr] *adj* solar

**soldado** [sohl•DAH•do] *n* M
soldier; trooper

**soldadura**
[SOHL•dah•DOOR•ah] *n* F
solder

**soldar** [sol•DAHR] *vt* weld

**solecismo** [SOH•leh•SIHS•mo]
*n* M solecism

**soledad** [SOH•leh•DAHD] *n* F
loneliness; solitude

**solemne** [soh•LEM•nai] *adj*
solemn

**solemnidad**
[SOH•LEHM•nih•DAHD] *n* F
solemnity

**solemnizar**
[SOH•LEM•nih•SAHR] *vi*
solemnize

**solevamiento**
[soh•LEH•vah•MEE•EN•to] *n*
M upheaval

**solicitación**
[soh•LIH•sih•TAH•see•OHN]
*n* F solicitation

**solicitar** [soh•LEE•sih•TAHR]
*vt* solicit

**solícito** [SOH•lee•SEE•to] *adj*
solicitous

**solidaridad**
[SOH•lih•DAHR•ih•DAHD] *n*
F solidarity

**solidez** [SOH•lih•DEHS] *n* F
solidity

**solidificar**
[soh•LIH•dih•FIH•car] *vt*
solidify

**sólido** [SOH•lee•do] *adj* solid;
stout

**soliloquio**
[soh•LIL•oh•KEE•oh] *n* M
soliloquy

**solitario** [soh•LIH•tahr•EE•oh]
*adj* solitary

**sollozar** [SOl•yo•SAHR] *vi* sob

**solo** [SOH•loh] *adj* lone; lonely;
solo; alone

**solo único** [SOH•lo]
[OON•ee•ko] *adj* only; single

**solomillo** [SOH•loh•MEE•yo] *n*
M sirloin

**solsticio** [SOHL•stee•SEE•oh] *n*
M solstice

**soltar 1** [sol•TAHR] *vt* slam

**soltar 2** [sol•TAHR] *vt* loosen;
let go of

**soltero** [sohl•TAIR•oh] *n* M
bachelor

**solterona** [sol•TAIR•oh•NAH]
*n* F spinster

**solución** [soh•LOO•see•OHN] *n*
F solution

**solvente** [sol•VEN•tai] *n* M
solvent

**sombra 1** [SOM•brah] *n* F
shade

**sombra 2** [SOM•brah] *n* F
umbrage

**sombrero** [sohm•BRAIR•oh] *n*
M hat

**sombrilla** [som•BREE•yah] *n* F
parasol

**sombrío 1** [sohm•BREE•oh] *adj*
dreary; sombre; dismal

**sombrío 2** [sohm•BREE•oh] *n*
M dusk

**someter** [SOH•mal•TAIR] *vt*
submit

**sometimiento**
[soh•MAI•tee•MEE•EN•to] *n*
M subjection

**somnolencia**
[som•NO•len•SEE•ah] *n* F
sleepiness

**soñador** [SON•yah•DOHR] *adj*
dreamy

**soñoliento**
[SON•yo•LEE•EN•to] *adj*
sleepy; somnolent

**sonado** [son•AH•do] *pp* sonar
rang

**sonar** [SOH•nahr] *vi* vi ring;
clash

**sonata** [so•NAH•tah] *n* F
sonata

**soneto** [son•EH•to] *n* M
sonnet

**sonido** [son•EE•do] *n* M tone

**sonido vibrante** [son•EE•do
vih•BRAHN•tai] *n* M twang

**sonoro** [son•OR•oh] *adj*
sonorous

**sonrisa** [son•REE•sah] *n* F grin

**sopa** [SOH•pa] *n* F soup

**sopechar** [soh•SPAI•char] *vt*
suspect

**soplar** [so•PLAHR] *vt* blow

**soplo** [SOP•lo] *n* M whiff

**soporífero**
[soh•PO•ree•FAIR•oh] *adj*
soporific

**soporte** [soh•POR•tai] *n* M
support hold; footing

**soporte inferior** [soh•por•TAI in•FAIR•ee•OHR] *n* M undercarriage

**soprano** [soh•PRAHN•oh] *n* M soprano

**sórdido** [sor•DEE•do] *adj* sordid

**sordo** [SOR•doh] *adj* deaf

**sosiego** [SO•see•AI•go] *n* M composure

**sospecha** [sohs•PAI•cha] *n* F suspicion

**sostén** [SOHS•ten] *n* M bra; holder

**sostener** [soh•STEN•AIR] *vi* stay; sustain

**sostenible** [SOH•sten•EE•blai] *adj* tenable

**sostenimiento** [soh•STEN•ee•MEE•EN•to] *n* M sustenance

**sotabanco** [SO•tah•BAHN•koh] *n* M attic

**sótano** [SOH•TAH•noh] *n* M cellar

**soviet** [soh•vee•EHT] *adj* Soviet

**soy** [soi] *v first pers.* I am

**stoicismo** [STOH•ih•SEES•mo] *n* M stoicism

**su; sus; suyo; suyos** [soo] [soos] [soo•yo] [soo•yos] *poss pron* their; theirs; its

**suave** [SWAH•vai] *adj* soft; bland; suave

**suavemente** [SWAH•vah•MEN•tai] *adv* gently

**subarrendar** [soob•AH•ren•DAHR] *vt* sublet

**subcomisión** [suhb•KOH•mih•SEE•OHN] *n* F subcommittee

**subconsciente** [SUHB•kon•SEE•EN•tai] *adj* subconscious

**subdivisión** [suhb•DIH•vih•SEE•OHN] *n* F subdivision

**subida** [soo•BEE•dah] *n* F climb

**subir** [soo•BEER] *vt vi* rise; hoist; climb

**subjetivo** [SUHB•heh•TEE•vo] *adj* subjective

**subjuntivo** [SUHB•huhn•TEE•vo] *adj* subjunctive

**sublime** [suhb•LEE•mai] *adj* sublime

**submarino** [SUHB•mah•REE•no] *n* M submarine

**subordinado** [SUHB•or•dih•NAH•do] *adj* subordinate; subservient

**subrayar** [SUHB•rai•AHR] *vt* underline

**subscribir** [soob•SKRIH•beer] *vt* subscribe; underwrite

**subsecuente** [SUHB•seh•KWEN•tai] *adj* subsequent

**subsidiario** [SOOB•si•DEE•ahr•EE•oh] *adj n* M auxiliary

**subsistir** [SUHB•sih•STEER] *vt* subsist

**substancia** [SOOB•stan•SEE•ah] *n* F matter; substance; gist

**substancial**
[sub•STAN•SEE•ahl] *adj*
substantial

**substantivo**
[SUB•stan•TEE•vo] *adj*
substantive

**substracción**
[sub•STRAHK•see•OHN] *n* F
subtraction

**substraer** [SUHB•strai•AIR] *vt*
subtract; pull down; deduct

**subterráneo**
[suhb•TAIR•rah•NAI•oh] *adj*
subterranean; underground

**suburbano**
[SUH•boor•BAH•no] *adj*
suburban

**suburbio** [SUH•boor•BEE•oh] *n*
M suburb

**subvencionar**
[SUHB•ven•SEE•OHN•ahr] *vt*
subsidize

**subversivo**
[SOOB•vair•SEE•vo] *adj*
subversive

**subyacente**
[SUHB•yah•SEN•tai] *adj*
underlying

**subyugar** [SUHB•hoo•YAHR]
*vt* overcome; subjugate

**succión** [SUHK•see•OHN] *n* F
suction

**suceder** [SUH•seh•DAIR] *vi*
succeed

**sucesión** [suhk•SEH•see•OHN]
*n* F succession

**suceso** [suh•SEH•so] *n* M
happening

**suciedad** [suh•SEE•ch•DAHD]
*n* F filth

**sucio** [suh•SEE•oh] *adj* dirty;
filthy; nasty; unclean;
unwashed

**suculento** [SUH•koo•LEN•to]
*adj* succulent

**sucumbir** [SUH•koom•BEER]
*vi* succumb

**sudeste** [sood•EH•stai] *adj*
southeast

**sudoeste** [SUHD•oh•AI•stai]
*adv* southwest

**Suecia** [SWAI•see•ah] *n* F
Sweden

**sueco** [SWAI•koh] *n* M Swede;
*adj* Swedish

**suegra** [SWAI•grah] *n* F
mother-in-law

**suegro** [SWAI•gro] *n* M
father-in-law

**suela** [SWAI•lah] *n* F sole (of
shoe)

**suelo** [SWAI•lo] *n* M ground

**suelto** [SWEL•to] *adj* glib

**sueño 1** [SWAIN•yo] *n* M
dream

**sueño 2** [SWAIN•yo] *n* M
sound

**suero** [SWAIR•oh] *n* M
serum

**suerte** [SWAIR•tai] *n* F luck;
windfall; chance

**suéter** [SWEH•tair] *n* M
sweater

**suficiencia**
[suh•FIH•see•EN•SEE•ah] *n* F
sufficiency

**suficiente**
[suh•FIH•see•EHN•tai] *adj*
adequate; sufficient

**sufragio** [SUH•frah•HEE•oh] *n*
M suffrage

**sufrimiento**
[SOO•free•MEE•EN•to] *n* M
suffering

**sufrir** [soo•FREER] *vi* suffer

**sugerir** [soo•HAIR•eer] *vt*
suggest

**sugestión** [suh•HEH•stee•OHN]
*n* F suggestion

**sugestivo** [SUH•heh•STEE•vo]
*adj* suggestive

**suicidio** [soo•IH•see•DEE•oh] *n*
M suicide

**Suiza** [SWEE•sah] *n* F
Switzerland

**suizo** [SWEE•so] *n* M Swiss

**sujetar 1** [SOO•heh•TAHR] *vt*
staple

**sujetar 2** [SOO•heh•TAHR] *vt*
control

**sujeto** [soo•HEH•to] *n* M
subject

**suma** [SOO•mah] *n* F amount

**sumar** [soo•MAHR] *vt* tally

**sumergir** [SOO•mair•HEER] *vt*
immerse; submerge;
overwhelm

**sumersión**
[soo•MAIR•see•OHN] *n* F
plunge

**sumidero** [SUH•mee•DAIR•oh]
*n* M drain

**suministrar**
[soo•MIHN•ee•STRAHR] *vt*
afford

**sumisión** [suh•MIH•see•OHN]
*n* F submission

**sumo** [SOO•moh] *adj* utmost

**superficial**
[soo•PAIR•fih•SEE•AHL] *adj*
skin-deep

**superintender**
[soo•PAIR•in•TEN•DAIR] *vt*
oversee

**supervivencia**
[SOO•pair•VEE•VEN•see•ah]
*n* F survival

**suplente** [suh•PLEN•tai] *n* M
understudy

**suplicar** [SOOP•lee•KAHR] *vt*
*vi* crave

**suponer** [soo•PON•air] *vt*
reckon

**suprimir** [suh•PRIH•meer] *vt*
inhibit

**sur** [soor] *adj* south; del ~\
southerner

**surtir** [soor•TEER] *vt* furnish

**susceptibilidad**
[suh•SEHP•tih•BIHL•ih•
DAHD] *n* F susceptibility

**susceptible**
[SUH•sep•TEE•blai] *adj*
susceptible; touchy

**suspendedores**
[suh•SPEN•dai•DOR•ais] *npl*
M suspenders

**suspender 1**
[SUHS•spen•DAIR] *vt* hang

**suspender 2**
[SUHS•pen•DAIR] *vt*
postpone; suspend

**suspensión**
[suh•SPEN•see•OHN] *n* F
suspense

**suspirar** [SOO•speer•AHR] *vi*
sigh

**susurrar** [SUHS•oor•RAHR] *vi*
whisper

**sutil** [soo•TEEL] *adj* subtle

**sutilizar** [soo•TIH•lee•SAHR] *vi*
quibble

**sutura** [soo•TOOR•ah] *n* F
suture

**suyo; suya** [SOO•yo]
[SOO•yah] *poss pron* hers;
his; theirs

# T

**tabaco** [tah•BAH•ko] *n* M
tobacco

**taberna** [tah•BAIR•nah] *n* F
bar; tavern

**tabia** [tah•BEE•ah] *n* F slab

**tabililla** [TAH•bil•EE•yah] *n* F
slat

**tabla** [TAH•blah] *n* F
board

**tablero** [tah•BLAIR•oh] *n* M
counter; panel

**tableta** [tah•BLEH•tah] *n* F
tablet; tabloid

**tablón** [tahb•LOHN] *n* F
plank

**tabular** [TAH•boo•LAHR] *adj*
tabular

**taburete** [TAH•boor•EH•tai] *n*
M stool

**tácito** [TAH•see•toh] *adj* tacit

**taciturno**
[TAH•sih•TOORN•oh] *adj*
taciturn

**tacómetro**
[TAH•koh•MEH•troh] *n* M
tachometer

**táctica** [TAHK•TEE•kah] *n* F
tactics

**táctico** [TAHK•TEE•koh] *adj*
tactical

**táctil** [TAHK•teel] *adj* tactile

**tacto** [TAHK•toh] *n* M tact

**tachuela** [TAH•choo•AI•lah] *n*
F tack

**tafetán** [TAH•feh•TAHN] *n* M
taffeta

**tajar** [TAH•har] *vt* hack

**tal** [tahl] *adv* such; *pron*
someone; such a thing; *adv*
so; ~ como\ the way; con ~
que\ as long as; ¿qué ~ ?\
how are you; un ~ a\ certain

**taladrar** [TAHL•ah•DRAHR] *vt*
M bore

**taladro** [tah•LAHD•roh] *n* M
drill

**talco** [TAHL•koh] *n* M talcum

**talento** [tah•LEN•toh] *n* M
talent

**talentoso** [TAH•len•TOH•so]
*adj* gifted

**talonario de cheques**
[tahl•OHN•ahr•EE•oh dai] *n*
M checkbook

**tallar** [tai•YAHR] *vt* carve

**tallarines** [TAI•yahr•EEN•ais]
*npl* noodles

**talle** [TAI•yai] *n* M waist

**taller** [TAI•yair] *n* M workshop

**tallo** [TAI•yo] *n* M stalk; stem

**también** [tahm•BEE•EHN] *adv*
also; too

**tambor** [TAHM•bor] *n* M
drum; tympani

**tamizar** [TAH•mee•SAHR] *vt*
sift

**tándem** [TAHN•dem] *n* M
tandem

**tañer** [tan•YAER] *vt* chime

**tangente** [tahn•HEN•tai] *n* M
tangent

**Tánger** [TAHN•gair] *n* Tangiers

**tangerino** [TAHN•gair•EE•no]
*n* M tangerine

**tangible** [tahn•HEE•blai] *adj*
tangible

**tanino** [tah•NEE•no] *n* M tan

**tanque** [TAHN•kai] *n* M tank

**tapa** [TAH•pah] *n* F lid

**tapicería** [tah•PEE•sair•EE•ah]
*n* F upholstery

**tapiz** [tah•PEES] *n* M tapestry

**tapizar** [TAH•pee•SAHR] *vt*
upholster

**taquigrafía**
[tah•KEE•grah•FEE•ah] *n* F
shorthand

**taquilla** [tah•KEE•yah] *n* F box
office

**tara** [TAH•rah] *n* F tare

**tardanza** [tahr•DAHN•sah] *n* F
delay

**tardar** [TAHR•dahr] *vi* tarry

**tarde** [TAHR•dai] *n* F afternoon;
*adj* late

**tardío** [tahr•DEE•oh] *adj*
belated

**tardo** [TAHR•do] *adj* tardy

**tarea** [tah•RAI•ah] *n* F
homework; task

**tareas** [TAH•rai•AHS] *npl* F
chores

**tarifa** [tah•REE•fah] *n* F tariff

**tarjeta de crédito**
[tahr•HAI•tah dai
KREH•dee•toh] *n* F credit
card

**tarro** [TAHR•roh] *n* M jar

**tarta** [TAHR•tah] *n* F tart

**tartamudear**
[tahr•TAH•moo•DAI•ahr] *vi*
stammer; stutter

**tartán** [tahr•TAHN] *n* M plaid

**tártaro** [TAHR•tah•roh] *n* M
tartar

**taxi** [tahks•ee] *n* M cab; taxi

**taza** [tah•sah] *n* F cup

**taza de café** [TAH•sah dai
kah•FAI] *n* F coffee cup

**taza de té** [TAH•sah deh tai] *n*
F teacup

**taza de vino** [TAH•sah dai
VEEN•oh] *n* F wineglass

**té** [teh] *n* M tea; tea party

**teatral** [TAI•ah•TRAHL] *adj*
theatrical

**teatro** [tai•AH•troh] *n* M theater

**teclado** [teh•KLAH•doh] *n* M
keyboard

**técnico** [TEHK•nee•koh] *adj*
technical; *n* M technician

**techo** [TEH•cho] *n* M thatch

**tedioso** [TEH•dee•OH•soh] *adj*
tedious

**teja** [TAI•ha] *n* F tile

**tejer** [tai•HAIR] *vt vi* knit;
weave

**tejido** [teh•HEE•do] *n* M web;
webbing

**tela** [TAI•lah] *n* F cloth; fabric

**tela embreada** [TAI•lah
EM•brai•AH•dah] *n* F
tarpaulin

**telar** [TAI•lahr] *n* M loom

**telaraña** [TAI•lah•RAHN•yah]
*n* F cobweb

**teléfonico interior**
[tehl•EH•fohn•EE•koh
in•TAIR•ee•OR] *n* M
intercom

**telefonista**
[teh•LEH•fon•EE•stah] *n* F
telephone operator

**teléfono** [tehl•EH•FOH•no] *n*
M phone; telephone

**teléfono público**
[teh•LAI•FOH•no
POO•blih•ko] *n* M pay phone

**telégrafo** [teh•LEH•GRAH•fo]
*n* M telegraph

**telegrama**
[TEH•leh•GRAHM•ah] *n* M
telegram

**telescopio**
[teh•LEH•skoh•PEE•oh] *n* M
telescope

**televisar** [TEH•leh•VEE•sahr]
*vi* televise

**televisión**
[TEH•leh•VIH•see•OHN] *n* F
television; television set

**televisión de color**
[TEH•leh•VIH•see•OHN dai]
*n* F color television

**telilla** [TEH•lee•YAH] *n* F peel

**tema 1** [TAI•mah] *n* F hobby

**tema 2** [TAI•mah] *n* F theme

**temblar** [TEM•blahr] *vi* quake;
quaver; shiver; shudder;
tremble

**temblor** [TEM•blor] *n* M twitch

**temeridad**
[teh•MAIR•ih•DAHD] *n* F
temerity

**temeroso** [TEH•mair•OH•soh]
*adj* afraid (to be); fearful

**temperamento color**
[tem•PAIR•ah•MEN•toh]
[KOH•lohr] *n* M complexion

**temperatura**
[tem•PAIR•ah•TOOR•ah] *n* F
temperature

**tempestad** [TEM•peh•STAHD]
*n* F storm; tempest

**tempestad de nieve**
[TEM•peh•STAHD dai
nee•AI•vai] *n* F blizzard

**tempestivo**
[TEHM•peh•STEE•vo] *adj*
seasonable

**tempestuoso 1**
[tem•PEH•stoo•OH•so] *adj*
lurid

**tempestuoso 2**
[tem•PEH•stoo•OH•so] *adj*
stormy; tempestuous

**templado** [tem•PLAH•do] *adj*
temperate

**templanza** [tem•PLAHN•sah] *n*
F temperance

**temple** [TEM•plai] *n* M temper

**templo** [TEM•plo] *n* M temple

**temporal** [TEM•por•AHL] *adj*
temporal; temporary

**temprano** [tehm•PRAH•no] *adj*
early; timely

**teñir** [ten•YEER] *vt* suffuse;
tinge

**tenacidad**
[teh•NAH•see•DAHD] *n* F
tenacity

**tenaz** [TEH•nahs] *adj* tenacious

**tenazas** [ten•AH•SAHS] *npl* F
tongs

**tendencia** [TEN•den•SEE•ah] *n*
F tendency; trend

**tendero** [ten•DAIR•oh] *n* M
shopkeeper

**tendón** [ten•DON] *n* M sinew;
tendon

**tenedor** [tehn•EH•dor] *n* M
fork; holder

**tenedor de libros** [tehn•AI•dor
dai LEE• bros] *n* M
bookkeeper

**teneduría de libros**
[tehn•AI•door•ee•ah dai
LEE•bros] *n* F bookkeeping

**tenencia** [TEHN•en•SEE•ah] *n*
F holding

**tener** [TEH•nair] *vt* have; hold;
be; ~ al dia\ keep up to date;
~ a uno por\ consider
someone

**tener interés** [TEH•nair
in•tiar•AIS] *vi* care (about)

**tener que** [TEH•nair kai]
*modal v* must

**tenería** [TEH•nair•EE•ah] *n* F
tannery

**teniente** [TEHN•ee•en•tai] *n* M
lieutenant

**tenis** [TEH•nihs] *n* M tennis

**tenor** [TEH•nor] *n* M tenor

**tensión** [TEN•see•OHN] *n* F
tension

**tenso** [TEN•so] *adj* tense

**tentación** [ten•TAH•see•OHN]
*n* F temptation

**tentador** [TEN•tah•DOHR] *adj*
enticing

**tentador** [TEN•tah•DOR] *adj*
tempting

**tentalear** [TEN•tah•LAI•AHR]
*vi* grope

**tentar** [TEN•tahr] *vt* tempt

**tentativo** [TEN•tah•TEE•voh]
*adj* tentative

**tenue** [ten•OO•ai] *adj* tenuous

**teología** [tai•OH•loh•HEE•ah] *n*
F theology

**teorema** [TAI•oh•RAI•mah] *n*
F theorem

**teoría** [TAI•oh•REE•ah] *n* F
theory

**teórico** [TAI•oh•REE•koh] *adj*
theoretical

**teraéutica**
[TAIR•ah•POI•TIH•kah] *adj*
therapeutic

**tercero** [tair•SAIR•oh] *num*
third

**terco** [TAIR•so] *adj* pig-headed

**teritorio** [tair•RIH•tor•EE•oh] *n*
M territory

**termal** [TAIR•mahl] *adj*
thermal

**terminar** [TAIR•mee•NAHR] *vt*
terminate

**término 1** [tair•MEEN•oh] *n* M
term

**término 2** [tair•MEEN•oh] *n* M
end; terminal; dar ~ a\ finish
off; poner ~ a\ put an end to

**término final** [tair•MEEN•oh]
[fee•nahl] *n* M finish

**termómetro**
[TAIR•moh•MEH•tro] *n* M
thermometer

**termostato**
[TAIR•moh•STAH•to] *n* M
thermostat

**ternera** [tair•NAIR•ah] *n* F
veal

**terneza** [tair•NAI•sah] *n* F
tenderness

**terraplén** [TAIR•rah•PLEHN] *n* M embankment

**terraza** [tair•AH•sah] *n* F terrace

**terremoto** [TAIR•reh•MOH•toh] *n* M earthquake

**terreno** [tair•REHN•oh] *n* M terrain; tract

**terrestre** [TAIR•reh•STRAI] *adj* terrestrial

**terrible** [tair•REE•blai] *adj* terrible; dreadful

**terrífico** [TAIR•rih•FEE•koh] *adj* terrific

**terror** [tair•ROHR] *n* M terror

**terso** [TAIR•so] *adj* terse

**tesis** [TAI•sihs] *n* M thesis

**tesorero** [TEH•sor•AIR•oh] *n* M treasurer

**tesoro** [teh•SOR•oh] *n* M treasure; treasury

**testamento** [TEH•stah•MEN•to] *n* M testament

**testarudo** [TEH•stah•ROO•do] *adj* headstrong

**testificar** [TEH•stee•FIH•KAHR] *vt* testify; *vi* vouch (for)

**testigo** [teh•STEE•goh] *n* M eyewitness; witness

**testimonio** [teh•STIH•moh•NEE•oh] *n* M testimony

**tetera** [teh•TAIR•ah] *n* F teakettle; teapot

**tetilla** [teh•TEE•yah] *n* F nipple

**textil** [TEHKS•teel] *adj* textile

**texto** [TEHKS•to] *n* M text

**textura** [tehks•TOOR•ah] *n* F texture

**tía** [TEE•ah] *n* F aunt

**tiara** [tee•AHR•ah] *n* F tiara

**tibia** [tih•BEE•ah] *n* F tibia

**tibio** [tih•BEE•oh] *adj* lukewarm; tepid

**tiempo 1** [tee•EHM•poh] *n* M tense

**tiempo 2** [tee•EM•poh] *n* M time

**tiempo 3** [tee•EM•po] *n* M weather

**tiempo de Pascua** [tee•EHM•poh dai PAH•skwah] *n* M Easter

**tiempo incompleto** [tee•EHM•poh in•kom•PLAI•to] *n* M part-time

**tiempo suplementario** [tee•EHM•po SUHP•lch•MEN•tar•EE•oh] *n* M overtime

**tienda** [TEE•EN•dah] *n* F shop

**tienda** [TEE•EN•dah] *n* F store

**tierno** [tee•AIR•no] *adj* tender

**tierra** [tee•AIR•ah] *n* F dirt; earth; land; soil

**tieso** [tee•OH•so] *adj* tight; stuck-up

**tiesura** [TEE•eh•SOOR•ah] *n* F stiffness

**tifo** [TEE•fo] *n* M typhus

**tifoideo** [tee•foi•DAI•oh] *n* M typhoid

**tifón** [tee•FOHN] *n* M typhoon

**tigre** [TEE•grai] *n* M tiger

**tigresa** [tee•GREH•sah] *n* F tigress

**tijeras** [tee•HAIR•ahs] *npl* F
scissors; clippers

**timidez** [TIH•mih•DEHS] *n* F
shyness

**tímido** [TIH•mee•do] *adj* shy;
timid

**timón** [tee•MON] *n* M helm;
rudder

**tina** [TEE•nah] *n* F vat

**tinta** [TIHN•tah] *n* F ink

**tinte** [TIN•tai] *n* M tint

**tinte para las pestañas**
[TIHN•tai PAH•rah lahs
peh•STAHN•yahs] *n* M
mascara

**tintín** [tin•TEEN] *n* M jingle

**tintura** [tin•TOOR•ah] *n* F dye;
tincture

**tío** [TEE•oh] *n* M uncle

**tiovivo** [TEE•oh•VEE•vo] *n* M
merry-go-round

**típico** [TIH•pee•koh] *adj*
typical

**tipo 1** [TEE•po] *n* M guy

**tipo 2** [TEE•po] *n* M type

**tipografía**
[tih•PO•grah•FEE•ah] *n* F
typography

**tira** [TEER•ah] *n* F strap

**tirador** [TEER•ah•DOR] *n* M
shooter

**tiranía** [TEER•ahn•EE•ah] *n* F
tyranny

**tiránico** [TEER•ahn•IH•ko] *adj*
tyrannical

**tirano** [tihr•AHN•oh] *n* M
tyrant

**tirantez** [TEER•ahn•TEHS] *n* F
strain

**tirar** [TEER•ahr] *vt* haul; pull;
throw; tug

**tiro 1** [TEER•oh] *n* M draft;
draw

**tiro 2** [TEE•roh] *n* M gunshot;
pop; shooting; shot

**tirón 1** [teer•OHN] *n* M hitch

**tirón 2** [teer•OHN] *n* F jerk

**tiso** [TEE•so] *adj* stark

**tisú** [TIH•soo] *n* M tissue

**titulares** [tee•TOO•lahr•RAIS]
*n* M headline

**título** [TEE•TOO•lo] *n* M
title

**tiznado** [tees•NAH•do] *adj*
grimy

**toalla** [to•AI•yah] *n* F towel

**tobogán** [TO•boh•GAHN] *n* M
toboggan

**tocante** [toh•KAHN•tai] *adj*
touching

**tocar** [toh•KAHR] *vi* feel;
touch; honk

**tocino** [to•SEE•no] *n* M
bacon

**tocino gordo** [toh•SEEN•oh
GOR•doh] *n* M lard

**tocón** [toh•KOHN] *n* M stub;
stump

**todavía** [TO•dah•VEE•yah] *adv*
yet

**todo** [TOH•doh] *pron*
everything; *adj* whole

**todo; toda; todos** [TOH•do]
[dah] [dos] *adj* all

**todos** [TOH•dohs] *pron*
everybody

**tolerable** [TOH•lair•AHB•lai]
*adj* tolerable

**tolerancia**
[toh•LAIR•ahn•SEE•ah] *n* F
tolerance

**tolerante** [TOH•lair•AHN•tai] *adj* tolerant

**tolerar** [TOH•lair•AHR] *vi* tolerate

**tomador** [toh•MAH•dor] *n* M gasket

**tomar** [toh•MAHR] *vi* take; ~ bien\ take well; ~ mal\ take badly; ~ en serio\ take seriously; ~ por\ take for; ~ y daca\ give and take ¿qué va a ~?\ what would you like?

**tomate** [toh•MAH•tai] *n* M tomato

**tomillo** [toh•MEE•yo] *n* M thyme

**tonel** [TON•ehl] *n* M tun

**tonelada** [TON•ai•LAH•dah] *n* F ton

**tonelaje** [TON•eh•LAH•hai] *n* M tonnage

**tónico** [ton•EE•ko] *n* M tonic

**tonsila** [ton•SEE•lah] *n* F tonsil

**tonsura** [ton•SOOR•ah] *n* F tonsure

**tontería** [TON•tair•EE•ah] *n* F folly; nonsense

**tonto** [TON•toh] *n* M dunce; fool; *adj* silly; stupid

**topacio** [TOH•pah•SEE•oh] *n* M topaz

**tope** [TOH•pai] *n* M bumper (of car)

**topetar** [TOH•pai•TAHR] *vt* buck

**topografía** [to•PO•grah•FEE•ah] *n* F topography

**torbellino** [TOR•beh•YEEN•oh] *n* M whirlwind

**torcedura** [TOR•seh•DOOR•ah] *n* F sprain

**torcer** [tor•SAIR] *vt* distort; twist; wrest; writhe

**torcer el sentido** [tor•SAIR el sen•TEE•do] *vt* M misconstrue

**torcido** [tor•SEE•do] *adj* bent; biased, crooked; wry

**torcimiento** [TOR•see•MEE•EN•to] *n* M wrench

**tordo** [TOR•do] *n* M thrush

**tormento** [tor•MEN•to] *n* M anguish

**tornado** [tor•NAH•do] *n* M tornado

**torneo** [tor•NAI•oh] *n* M tournament

**tornillo** [tohr•NEE•yoh] *n* M clamp; screw

**torno para hilar** [TOR•no PAH•rah ee•LAHR] *n* M spinning-wheel

**toro** [TOH•roh] *n* M bull

**toronja** [tor•ON•hah] *n* F grapefruit

**torpe** [TOR•pai] *adj* clumsy; awkward

**torpedo** [tor•PAI•do] *n* M torpedo

**torpeza** [tor•PAI•sah] *n* F turpitude

**tórpido** [tor•PEE•do] *adj* torpid

**torre** [TOR•rai] *n* M tower

**torrecilla** [TOR•reh•SEE•yah] *n* F turret

**torrente** [tor•REHN•tai] *n* M torrent

**tórrido** [tor•REE•do] *adj* torrid

**torta** [TOHR•tah] *n* F cake

**tortilla de huevos**
[tor•TEE•yah dai WAI•vos] *n*
F omelet

**tortuga** [tor•TOO•gah] *n* F
tortoise; turtle

**tortuoso** [TOR•too•OH•so] *adj*
tortuous

**tortura** [tor•TOOR•ah] *n* F
torture

**tos** [tohs] *n* M cough

**toscamente**
[TOH•skah•MEN•tai] *adj*
uncouth

**tostada** [toh•STAH•dah] *n* F
toast

**total** [TOH•tahl] *adj n* M total

**totalidad**
[TOH•tahl•IH•DAHD] *n* F
entirety

**totalitario**
[TOH•tahl•IH•tahr•EE•oh] *adj*
totalitarian

**totalización**
[toh•TAHL•ih•SAH•see•OHN]
*n* F totality

**totalmente**
[TOH•tahl•MEN•tai] *adv*
quite; totally; wholly

**tóxico** [TOHK•see•koh] *adj* M
toxic

**toxina** [tohks•EE•nah] *n* F toxin

**trabajador**
[trah•BAH•HAH•dor] *n* M
laborer; worker

**trabajar** [trah•BAH•har] *vi* toil

**trabajo** [trah•BAH•ho] *n* M job;
labor; work; working

**trabajo de equipo**
[trah•BAH•ho dai] *n* M
teamwork

**tracción** [TRAHK•see•OHN] *n*
F traction

**tractor** [TRAHK•tor] *n* M
tractor

**tradición** [trah•DIH•see•OHN]
*n* F tradition

**traducción**
[trah•DUHK•see•OHN] *n* F
translation

**traducir** [TRAH•doo•SEER] *vt*
translate

**traductor** [trah•DUHK•tor] *n* M
translator

**traer** [TRAI•air] *vt* bring; carry

**tráfico** [trah•FEE•ko] *n* M
traffic

**tragar** [trah•GAHR] *vt* swallow

**tragedia** [TRAH•hai•DEE•ah] *n*
F tragedy

**trágico** [trah•HEE•koh] *adj*
tragic

**trago** [TRAH•go] *n* M gulp

**traición** [TRAI•see•OHN] *n* F
betrayal; treachery; treason

**traicionar**
[TRAIK•see•on•AHR] *vt*
betray

**traidor** [TRAI•dor] *n* M traitor;
betrayer; *adj* treacherous

**traje** [TRAH•hai] *n* M costume

**traje de baño** [TRAH•hai dai
BAHN•yo] *n* M bathing suit

**traje de baño** [TRAH•hai dai
BAHN•yo] *n* M swimsuit

**traje de esmoquing**
[TRAH•hai dai
EHSMOH•keeng] *n* M tuxedo

**trama** [TRAH•mah] *n* F woof
(wool)

**trambor** [TRAM•bohr] *n* M
drummer

**trampa** [TRAM•pah] *n* F trap;
trap-door

**tranquilamente**
[trahn•KEE•lah•MEN•tai] *adv*
quietly

**tranquilidad**
|tran•KEE•lih•DAHD] *n* F
tranquillity; ease

**tranquilizar**
[trahn•KEEL•ih•SAHR] *vt*
reassure

**tranquilo** [trahn•KEE•lo] *adj*
calm; tranquil

**transcendente**
[TRAN•sen•DEN•tai] *adj*
transitive

**transcribir**
[trahn•SKRIH•BEER] *vt*
transcribe

**transeúnte** [trahn•SOIN•tai] *n*
M passerby

**transferir** [TRANS•fair•EER] *vt*
transfer

**transformación**
[TRAHNS•for•MAH•see•OHN]
*n* F transformation

**transformador**
[trahns•FOR•mah•DOR] *n* M
transformer

**transformar**
[TRAHNS•FORM•ahr] *vt*
transform

**transfusión**
[trahns•FOO•see•OHN] *n* F
transfusion

**transgredir**
[TRAHNS•greh•DEER] *vt*
transgress

**transgresión**
[trahns•GREH•see•OHN] *n* F
transgression

**transgresor**
[TRAHNS•greh•SOR] *n* M
trespasser; interloper

**transición** [tran•SIH•see•OHN]
*n* F transition

**tránsito** [TRAHN•sih•to] *n* M
transit

**transitorio**
[TRAN•sih•TOR•EE•oh] *adj*
transient

**transmisión**
[TRAHNS•mih•SEE•OHN] *n*
F transmission

**transmisor**
[TRAHNS•mee•SOR] *n* M
transmitter

**transmitir**
[TRAHNS•mih•TEER] *vt*
transmit; convey

**transparente**
[TRAHNS•pahr•EN•tai] *adj*
transparent; *n* M window
shade

**transpiración**
[TRAHNS•peer•AH•see•OHN]
*n* F perspiration; transpiration

**transpirar**
[TRAHNS•peer•AHR] *vi*
perspire; transpire

**transponer**
[TRAHNS•pon•AIR] *vt*
transpose

**transportar**
[TRAHNS•por•TAHR] *vt*
transport

**transverso** [trahns•VAIR•so]
*adj* transverse

**tranvia** |trahn•VEE•ah] *n* F
streetcar; tram; trolley

**trapacero**
[TRAH•pah•SAIR•oh] *adj*
tricky

**trapecio** [TRAH•pai•SEE•oh] *n* M trapeze

**trapo** [TRAH•poh] *n* M rag

**tráque** [TRAH•kai] *n* M trachea

**trasero** [trah•SAIR•oh] *adj* hind; rear; *n* M rear

**trasladar** [TRAHS•lah•DAHR] *vt* adjourn

**traslapar** [TRAHS•lah•PAHR] *vt* overlap

**trasluciente** [trahs•LOO•see•EN•tai] *adj* translucent

**trasplantar** [TRAHS•plahn•TAHR] *vt* transplant

**tratado 1** [trah•TAH•do] *n* M treatise; dissertation; essay

**tratado 2** [trah•TAH•do] *n* M treaty

**tratamiento erróneo** [TRAH•tah•MEE•EHN•to AIR•roh•NAI•oh] *n* M malpractice

**tratar** [TRAH•tahr] *vt* treat

**tratar de coger** [TRAH•tahr dai KOH•hair] *vt vi* clutch

**trato1** [TRAH•to] *n* M treatment

**trato 2** [TRAH•to] *n* M usage

**trato carnal** [TRAH•to kahr•NAHL] *n* M intercourse (sexual)

**través** [trah•VAIS] *n* M slant; a ~ de\ through; a ~\ across

**travesura** [TRAH•veh•SOOR•ah] *n* F mischief; prank

**traviesa** [TRAH•vee•AI•sah] *n* F transom

**travieso** [TRAH•vee•EH•so] *adj* wanton

**trayectoria** [trai•YEHK•tor•EE•ah] *n* F trajectory

**trazador** [TRAH•sah•DOR] *n* M tracer

**trébol 1** [TRAI•bohl] *n* M clover

**trébol 2** [TREH•bohl] *n* M trefoil

**trece** [TREH•sai] *num* thirteen

**tregua** [treh•GOO•ah] *n* F truce

**treinta** [TRAIN•tah] *num* thirty

**tremendo** [treh•MEN•do] *adj* tremendous

**trementina** [TREM•en•TEE•nah] *n* F turpentine

**tremor** [TREH•mor] *n* M tremor

**trémulo** [TREH•MOO•lo] *adj* tremulous

**tren** [trehn] *n* M train

**tren rápido** [RAH•pee•do] *n* M train (express)

**trenza** [TREN•sah] *n* F braid; tress

**trenzar** [TREHN•sahr] *vt* braid

**trepar** [TREH•pahr] *vt vi* climb

**tres** [trehs] *num* three

**tres veces** [trais VAI•sais] *adv* thrice; three times

**treta** [TREH•tah] *n* F trick

**triángulo** [tree•AHN•GOO•lo] *n* M triangle

**tribu** [TREE•boo] *n* M tribe

**tribulación** [TRIH•boo•LAH•see•OHN] *n* F tribulation

**tribunal** [TRIH•BOO•nahl] *n* M
tribunal

**tribuno** [trih•BOON•oh] *n* M
tribune

**tributario**
[trih•BOO•tahr•EE•oh] *n* M
tributary

**trigésimo**
[TREE•heh•SEE•moh] *num*
thirtieth

**trigo** [TREE•go] *n* M wheat

**trilla** [TREE•yah] *n* F threshing

**trillado** [tree•YAH•do] *adj* trite

**trillar** [tree•YAHR] *vt* thrash

**trimestral**
[TREE•meh•STRAHL] *adj*
quarterly

**trinar** [TREE•nahr] *vi* trill

**trinchera 1** [treen•CHAIR•ah] *n*
F ditch

**trinchera 2** [trihn•CHAIR•ah] *n*
F trench coat

**trineo** [tree•NAI•oh] *n* M
sledge; sleigh

**trinitaria**
[TRIHN•ee•TAHR•EE•ah] *n* F
pansy

**trío** [TREE•oh] *n* M trio

**tripa** [TREE•pah] *n* F gut

**triple 1** [TREE•plai] *adj* treble;
treble voice

**triple 2** [TREEP•lai] *adj* triple

**trípode** [tree•POH•dai] *n* M
tripod

**triste** [TREE•stai] *adj* sad;
dismal

**tristeza** [tree•STAI•sah] *n* F
sadness

**triunfal** [TREE•uhn•FAHL] *adj*
triumphant

**triunfalmente**
[TREE•uhn•FAHL•MEN•tai]
*adv* triumphantly

**triunfar** [TREE•uhn•FAHR] *vt*
trump

**triunfo** [tree•UHN•fo] *n* M
triumph; *adj* winning

**trivial** [TRI•vee•AHL] *adj*
commonplace; trivial; banal

**trofeo** [troh•FAI•oh] *n* M
trophy

**trombón** [TROM•BOHN] *n* M
trombone

**trompa** [TROM•pah] *n* F
snout

**trompeta** [trohm•PAI•tah] *n* F
bugle; trumpet

**tronada** [troh•NAH•dah] *n* F
thunderstorm

**tronco** [TRON•koh] *n* M stock;
trunk

**trono** [TROH•no] *n* M throne

**tropa** [TROH•pah] *n* F troop

**tropel** [troh•PEHL] *n* M mob

**tropezar** [TROH•peh•SAHR] *vi*
stumble

**tropical** [TROH•pih•KAHL] *adj*
tropic

**trópico** [troh•PEE•koh] *adj*
tropic

**trotar** [TROH•tahr] *vi* trot

**trote** [TROH•tai] *n* M trot

**troza** [TROH•sah] *n* F log

**trozo** [TROH•so] *n* M lump

**trueno** [troo•EH•no] *n* M
thunder

**trueno gordo** [troo•EN•no
GOR•do] *n* M thunderclap

**trulla** [TROO•yah] *n* F trowel

**trullo** [TROO•yo] *n* M teal

**tú** [too] you; thou (sing. familiar)

**tú, ti, usted** [too] [tee] [oo•stehd] yourself

**tu, tus, de, usted de ustedes** [too] [toos] [dai OO•stehd] [-ais] your yours

**tú, usted** [too] [oo•STEHD] you

**tuberculosis** [too•BAIR•koo•LOH•sis] *n* M tuberculosis

**tuberculoso** [too•BAIR•koo•LOH•so] *adj* tubercular

**tubería** [TOO•bair•EEH•ah] *n* F tubing

**tubo** [TOO•bo] *n* M pipe; tube; duct

**tubo de ensayo** [TOO•boh dai en•SAI•yo] *n* M test tube

**tul** [tool] *n* M tulle

**tulipán** [TOO•lee•PAHN] *n* M tulip

**tumba** [TUHM•bah] *n* F tomb

**tumbar** [toom•BAHR] *vt* lay; overthrow

**tumbo** [TUHM•boh] *n* M jolt; lurch; tumble

**tumor** [too•MOR] *n* M tumor

**tumulto** [too•MUHL•to] *n* M tumult; turmoil

**tumultuoso** [tuh•MOOL•too•OH•so] *adj* tumultuous

**tuna** [TOO•nah] *n* F tuna

**túnel** [TOO•nel] *n* M tunnel

**túnica** [too•NIH•kah] *n* F tunic

**tupir** [TOO•peer] *vt* tighten

**turba** [TOOR•bah] *n* F peat

**turbar** [TOOR•bahr] *vt* disturb

**turbio** [toor•BEE•oh] *adj* turbid

**turbulento** [TOOR•boo•LEN•to] *adj* turbulent

**turco** [TOOR•koh] *n* M Turk; *adj* Turkish

**turquesco** [toor•KEHS•ko] *adj* Turkish

**turgente** [toor•GEN•tai] *adj* turgid

**turismo** [toor•EES•mo] *n* M tourism; sightseeing

**turista** [toor•EE•stah] *n* F tourist

**turnbina** [toor•BEE•nah] *n* F turbine

**turquesa** [toor•KAI•sah] *n* F turquoise

**Turquia** [toor•KEE•ah] *n* F Turkey

**tuyo** [TOO•yo] *adj pron* yours; un amigo ~\ a friend of yours

# U

**ubre** [OO•brai] *n* M udder

**úlcera** [uhl•SAIR•ah] *n* F ulcer

**ulceración** [UHL•sair•AH•see•OHN] *n* F ulceration

**ulterior** [uhl•TAIR•ee•OHR] *adj*
ulterior

**último** [UHL•tee•moh] *adj* last;
ultimate

**ultrajante** [UHL•trah•HAN•tai]
*adj* outrageous

**ultrajar** [UHL•trah•HAHR] *vt*
revile

**ultramarino**
[uhl•TRAH•mah•REE•no] *adj*
*adv* overseas

**umbral** [UHM•brahl] *n* M sill;
threshold

**un 1** [oon] *adv* some

**un 2; una** [oon] [-oon•ah] *art* a

**uña** [OON•yah] *n* F fluke

**uña de un dedo** [OON•yah dai
oon DAI•do] *n* F toenail

**una vez** [OO•nah vais] *adv*
once

**unánime** [un•AH•NEE•mai] *adj*
unanimous

**unanimidad**
[UHN•ah•NIM•ih•DAHD] *n* F
unanimity

**unción** [UHNK•see•OHN] *n* F
unction

**unificar** [oon•EE•fee•KAHR] *vt*
standardize

**unión** [OON•ee•OHN] *n* F
merger; conjugation

**unir** [oo•NEER] *vi* interlock; *vt*
join; merge; connect

**uno** [OO•no] *num* one

**uno y otro** [OO•no ee OH•troh]
*adj* either

**untuoso** [UHN•too•OH•so] *adj*
unctuous

**untura** [UHN•TOOR•ah] *n* F
ointment

**uranio** [OOR•ahn•EE•oh] *n* M
uranium

**urbano** [oor•BAHN•oh] *adj*
urban

**urdir** [oor•DEER] *vt* warp

**urgencia** [OOR•gen•SEE•ah] *n*
F urgency

**urgente** [oor•GEN•tai] *adj*
urgent; pressing

**urgentemente**
[oor•HEN•tah•MEN•tai] *adv*
urgently

**urna 1** [OOR•nah] *n* F shrine

**urna 2** [OOR•nah] *n* F urn

**uso** [OO•so] *n* M use

**usual** [oo•SWAHL] *adj*
ordinary; usual

**usura** [oo•SOOR•ah] *n* F usury

**usurero** [OO•soo•AIR•oh] *n* M
usurer; loan shark

**usurpar** [YOO•soor•PAHR] *vi*
encroach; *vt* usurp

**ususalmente**
[oo•SOO•al•MEN•tai] *adv*
usually

**utensilio** [oo•TEN•see•LEE•oh]
*n* M utensil

**útero** [oo•TAIR•oh] *n* M womb

**útil** [OO•teel] *adj* useful

**utilidad** [oo•TIH•lih•DAHD] *n*
F usefulness; utility

**utilizar** [oo•TIH•lih•SAHR] *vt*
utilize

**uva** [OO•vah] *n* F grape

**úvula** [oo•VOO•lah] *n* F uvula

# V

**vaca** [VAH•kah] *n* F cow

**vacación** [vah•KAH•see•OHN] *n* F vacation

**vacancia** [vah•KAHN•SEE•ah] *n* F vacancy

**vacante** [vah•KAHN•tai] *adj* vacant

**vaciar** [VAH•see•AHR] *vt* deplete

**vacilación** [VAH•sih•LAH•see•OHN] *n* F hesitation

**vacilante** [VAH•see•LAHN•tai] *adj* fickle; hesitant

**vacilar** [VAH•see•LAHR] *vi* falter; hesitate; flinch; stagger; totter; vacillate

**vacío** [vah•SEE•oh] *adj* empty; void

**vacunar** [VAH•koon•AHR] *vt* vaccinate

**vacuno** [vah•KOO•no] *n* M vaccine

**vacuo** [vah•KOO•oh] *n* M vacuum

**vado** [VAH•doh] *n* M ford

**vagabundo** [VAH•gah•BUN•doh] *n* M hobo; tramp; vagabond

**vagar** [vah•GAHR] *vi* roam; wander

**vago** [VAH•go] *adj* vague

**vainilla** [vai•NEE•yah] *n* F vanilla

**vajilla de oro** [vah•HEE•yah dai OR•oh] *n* F gold-plated

**valentía** [VAH•len•TEE•ah] *n* F valor

**Valentín** [VAH•len•TEEN] *n* M valentine

**valentón** [VAH•lehn•TOHN] *n* M bulldozer

**valeroso** [VAH•lair•oh•soh] *adj* courageous; valorous

**validez** [VAH•lee•DEHS] *n* F validity

**válido** [VAH•LEE•do] *adj* valid

**valiente** [VAH•lee•EN•tai] *adj* bold; valiant; brave

**valioso** [VAH•lee•OH•so] *adj* valuable; worthy

**valor 1** [VAH•lor] *n* M courage; prowess

**valor 2** [VAH•lor] *n* M value; worth

**valor mercadíl** [VAH•lor del mair•KAH•DEEL] *n* M value (market)

**vals** [vahls] *n* M waltz

**valuación** [VAH•loo•AH•see•OHN] *n* F rating; evaluation

**valuar apreciar** [VAH•loo•AHR] *vt* appreciate

**válvula** [VAHL•VOO•lah] *n* F valve

**valla 1** [VAI•yah] *n* F hurdle

**valla 2** [VAI•yah] *n* F hedge

**valle** [VAI•yai] *n* M valley

**vanidad** [VAH•nee•DAHD] *n* F conceit; vanity

**vano** [VAHN•oh] *adj* vain

**vapor** [VAH•por] *n* M steam;
steamer; vapor

**vaporizar** [VAH•por•IH•SAHR]
*vt* vaporize

**vaquero** [vah•KAIR•oh] *n* M
cowboy

**vara** [VAHR•ah] *n* F wand

**vara de medir** [VAH•rah dai
MEH•deer] *n* F yardstick

**variable** [VAHR•ee•AH•blai]
*adj* variable

**variación**
[vahr•EE•AH•see•OHN] *n* F
variance; variation

**variar** [VAHR•ee•AHR] *vt* vary

**variedad** [vahr•EE•eh•DAHD]
*n* F variety

**vario** [vahr•EE•oh] *adj* varied;
various

**varios** [vahr•EE•ohs] *adj* several

**vasija** [vah•SEE•hah] *n* F vessel

**vaso** [VAH•so] *n* M can

**vástago** [vah•STAH•go] *n* M
offspring

**vastedad** [VAH•steh•DAHD] *n*
F vastness

**vasto** [VAH•stoh] *adj* vast

**vecindad** [VEH•seen•DAHD] *n*
F neighborhood; vicinity

**vecino** [veh•SEEN•oh] *n* M
neighbor

**vegetación**
[VEH•he•TAH•sec•OHN] *n* F
vegetation

**vegetal** [VEH•he•TAHL] *n* M
vegetable

**vegetar** [VEH•geh•TAHR] *vi*
vegetate

**vegetariano**
[VEH•he•TAHR•ee•ahn•oh] *n*
M vegetarian

**vehemencia**
[veh•HF•men•SEE•ah] *n* F
vehemence

**vehículo** [veh•HEE•KOO•lo] *n*
M vehicle

**veinte** [VAIN•tai] *num* twenty

**vejar** [vai•HAHR] *vt* vex;
irritate

**vejiga** [veh•HEE•gah] *n* F
bladder

**vela** [VAI•lah] *n* F candle

**vela mayor** [VAI•lah•MAI•yor]
*n* F main course

**veleta** [veh•LEH•tah] *n* F vane

**velo** [VAI•lo] *n* M veil

**velocidad**
[VEH•loh•see•DAHD] *n* F
swiftness; speed; velocity; rate

**veloz** [VAI•lohs] *adj* swift

**vellón** [veh•YON] *n* F fleece

**vellorita** [VAI•yor•EE•tah] *n* F
primrose

**velloso** [vail•YO•so] *adj* fuzzy

**velludo** [veh•YOO•do] *n* M
velvet

**vena** [VAIN•ah] *n* F vein;
artery; vessel (blood)

**venado** [ven•AH•do] *n* M
venison

**vencedor** [VEN•seh•DOR] *n* M
victor

**vencer** [ven•SAIR] *vt* vanquish

**venda** [VEN•dah] *n* F bandage

**vendado de ojos** [ven•DAH•do
dai•OH•hos] *n* M blindfold

**vendedor** [ven•DEH•dor] *n* M
vendor, street vendor

**vender** [ven•DAIR] *vt* sell

**vender a bajo precio**
[ven•DAIR a BAH•ho
prai•SEE•oh] *vt* undersell

**vender de puerta a puerta**
|ven•DAIR dai PWAIR•tah
ah| *vt* peddle; sell door to
door

**vendimia** |VEN•dee•MEE•ah| *n*
F vintage

**veneno** |ven•EN•oh| *n* M
poison; venom

**venenoso** |VEN•en•OH•so| *adj*
poisonous; venomous

**venerable** |VEN•air•AHB•lai|
*adj* venerable

**veneración**
|ven•air•AH•see•OHN| *n* F
veneration

**venerar** |VEN•air•AHR| *vt*
venerate

**venganza** |ven•GAHN•sah| *n* F
revenge; vengeance

**vengar** |ven•GAHR| *vt* avenge

**venidero** |VEN•ih•DAIR•oh|
*adj* forthcoming

**venir** |veh•NEER| *vi* come

**venta al por menor** |VEN•tah
al por MAI•nor| *n* F retail

**ventada** |VEN•TAH•dah| *n* F
blast

**ventaja** |vehn•TAH•ha| *n* F
advantage; vantage

**ventajoso** |vehn•TAH•HO•soh|
*adj* advantageous

**ventalle** |ven•TAY•yai| *n* M
fan

**ventana** |ven•TAHN•ah| *n* F
window

**ventilación**
|VEN•tih•LAH•see•OHN| *n* F
ventilation

**ventilador** |ven•TEE•lah•DOR|
*n* M ventilator

**ventilar** |VEN•tee•LAHR| *vt*
ventilate

**ventoso** |ven•TOH•so| *adj*
windy

**ventura** |ven•TOOR•ah| *n* F
venture; business venture;
chance

**ver** |vair| *vi* see

**veracidad** |vair•AH•see•DAHD|
*n* F reliability; truthfulness

**veraz** |VAIR•ahs| *adj* truthful

**verbal** |VAIR•bahl| *adj* verbal

**verbo** |VAIR•bo| *n* M verb

**verboso** |vair•BOH•so| *adj*
verbose

**verdad** |vair•DAHD| *n* F truth

**verdaderamente**
|VAIR•dah•DAIR•ah•MEN•tai|
*adv* truly

**verdadero**
|VAIR•dah•DAIR•oh| *adj* true

**verdadero**
|VAIR•dah•DAIR•oh| *adj*
veritable

**verde** |VAIR•dai| *n adj* green

**veredicto** |VAIR•eh•DIHK•to|
*n* M verdict

**vergonzoso**
|VAIR•gon•ZOH•so| *adj*
bashful

**verificación**
|VAIR•ih•FIH•KAH•see•OHN|
*n* F verification

**verificar** |vair•IH•fih•KAHR| *vt*
verify

**verja** |ver•HAH| *n* F grille

**vernáculo**
|VAIR•NAH•KOO•lo| *adj*
vernacular

**verraco** |vair•AH•ko| *n* M boar

**verruga** [vair•ROO•gah] *n* F wart

**versado** [vair•SAH•do] *adj* versed

**versión** [VAIR•see•OHN] *n* F version

**verso** [VAIR•so] *n* M verse

**vértebra** [vair•TEH•brah] *n* F vertebra

**vertical** [vair•TIH•KAHL] *adj* vertical

**vértigo** [vair•TEE•go] *n* M vertigo

**Véspero** [veh•SPAIR•oh] *n* M vespers

**vestíbulo** [VEH•STEE•BOO•lo] *n* M hall; vestibule

**vestido** [veh•STEE•doh] *n* M dress; clothing; garment; gown

**vestido de noche** [veh•STEE•doh deh•NOH•chai] *n* M evening gown

**vestidos** [VEH•STEE•dohs] *npl* M clothing

**vestidura** [VEH•STEE•door•ah] *n* F vestment; official attire

**vestigio** [VEH•stih•GEE•oh] *n* M vestige

**vestir** [veh•STEER] *vt* clothe

**veterano** [VEH•tair•AHN•oh] *n* M veteran

**veterinario** [VEH•tair•IH•nahr•EE•oh] *n* M veterinarian

**veterinario** [VEH•tair•IHN•ahr•EE•oh] *adj* veterinary

**veto** [VEE•to] *n* M veto

**vez** [vais] *n* F time; turn; a la ~\ at the same time; otra ~\ again; de ~ en cando;\ occasionally; en ~ de\ instead; cada — más\ more and more; de una ~\ at one shot; de una ~ para siempre\ once and for all; hablú un ~\ once upon a time; rara ~\ rarely; una ~\ once

**vía** [vee•ah] *prep* via; *n* F way

**vía pública** [VEE•ah POOB•lih•kah] *n* F thoroughfare

**viaducto** [VEE•ah•DUHK•to] *n* M viaduct

**viajar** [vee•AH•har] *vi* travel

**viajar en bicicleta** [vee•AH•har en bee•SEE•KLAI•tah] *vi* ride (bicycle)

**viaje 1** [vee•AH•hai] *n* M journey

**viaje 2** [vee•AH•hai] *n* M tour; trip

**viaje por mar** [vee•AH•hai por mahr] *n* M voyage; cruise

**viajero** [VEE•ah•HAIR•oh] *n* M traveler; wanderer

**vianda** [vee•AHN•dah] *n* F viands

**viático** [VEE•ah•TEE•ko] *n* M viaticum

**víbora** [vee•BOR•ah] *n* F viper

**vibración** [vih•BRAH•see•OHN] *n* F vibration

**vibrar** [VEE•brahr] *vt* quiver; vibrate

**vicio** [vih•SEE•oh] *n* M vice

**vicioso 1** [VIH•see•OH•so] *adj* overgrown

**vicioso 2** [VIH•see•OH•so] *adj* vicious

**víctima** [vihk•TEE•mah] *n* F victim

**victoria** [VIHK•tor•EE•ah] *n* F victory

**victorioso** [VIHK•tor•EE•OH•so] *adj* victorious

**vida** [VEE•dah] *n* F life; de por ~\ for life; en mi ~\ never (in my life; en ~ de\ during the lifetime of; estar en ~\ be alive; de toda la ~\ lifelong

**vidrio 1** [vee•DREE•oh] *n* M glass

**vidrio 2** [vee•DREE•oh] *n* M pane

**viejo** [vee•AI•ho] *adj* old, *n* M old person

**viento** [VEE•EN•toh] *n* M gale; wind

**viernes** [vee•AIR•nais] *n* M Friday

**viga** [VEE•gah] *n* F beam; girder

**vigésimo** [VIH•heh•SEE•mo] *num* twentieth

**vigilante** [VIH•hil•AHN•tai] *adj* vigilant

**vigilia** [VIH•hee•LEE•ah] *n* F vigil

**vigor** [VIH•gor] *n* M vigor

**vigorizador** [VIH•gor•IH•sah•DOR] *adv* invigorating

**vigoroso** [VIH•go•RO•so] *adj* hearty

**vigoroso** [VIH•go•ROH•so] *adj* vigorous

**vil** [vihl] *adj* vile

**villa** [VEE•yah] *n* F villa; borough

**villanía** [VEE•yahn•EE•ah] *n* F villainy

**villano** [vee•YAHN•oh] *adj* villainous

**viña** [VEEN•yah] *n* F vineyard

**vinagre** [VIN•ah•GRAI] *n* M vinegar

**vínculo** [VEENK•yoo•loh] *n* M link

**vindicar** [vin•DIH•kahr] *vt* vindicate; avenge

**vindicativo** [vin•DIH•kah•TEE•vo] *adj* vindictive

**vino** [VEE•no] *n* M wine

**violación** [VEE•oh•LAH•see•OHN] *n* F rape; violation

**violar** [VEE•oh•LAHR] *vt* rape; violate

**violencia** [VEE•oh•LEN•SEE•ah] *n* F violence

**violento** [VEE•oh•LEN•to] *adj* violent

**violeta** [VEE•oh•LEH•tah] *n* F violet

**violín** [VEE•oh•LEEN] *n* F fiddle; violin

**violinista** [vee•OH•lihn•EE•stah] *n* F violinist

**violoncelo** [VEE•ohn•CEL•oh] *n* M cello

**virar** [VEER•ahr] *vi* veer

**virgen** [VEER•hen] *n* F virgin

**virginidad** [VEER•hin•IH•DAHD] *n* F virginity

**viril** [VEER•ihl] *adj* virile
**virilidad 1** [veer•IH•lee•DAHD]
*n* F manhood
**virilidad 2** [veer•IH•lih•DAHD]
*n* F virility
**virtual** [veer•TOO•ahl] *adj*
virtual
**virtualmente**
[VEER•too•AHL•MEN•tai]
*adj* virtually
**viruelas locas**
[VEER•oo•AI•lahs LOH•kahs]
*npl* F chicken pox
**virulencia**
[VEER•oo•LEN•SEE•ah] *n* F
virulence
**virus** [VEER•oos] *n* M virus
**visado** [vee•SAH•do] *n* M visa
**vísceras** [vih•SAIR•ahs] *npl* F
viscera
**viscosidad**
[vih•SKOH•sih•DAHD] *n* F
viscosity
**visera vista** [vih•SAIR•ah
VEE•stah] *n* F visor; vista
**visibilidad**
[vih•SIH•bil•IH•DAHD] *n* F
visibility
**visible** [vih•SEE•blai] *adj*
visible
**visionario**
[VIH•see•OHN•ahr•EE•oh]
*adj* visionary
**visita** [vih•SEE•tah] *n* F visit
**visitación**
[vih•SIH•tah•SEE•OHN] *n* F
visitation
**visitante** [VIH•sih•TAHN•tai] *n*
M visitor
**visón** [vee•SON] *n* F mink
**víspera** [VEE•spair•ah] *n* F eve

**víspera de todos los santos**
[VEE•spair•ah dai TOH•dohs
los SAHN•tohs] *n* F
Halloween
**vista 1** [VEE•stah] *n* F eyesight;
sight; view; vision;
appearance
**vista 2** [VEE•stah] *n* F outlook
**vista antemano** [VEE•stah
AN•tai•MAH•no] *n* F preview
**vistoso** [vee•STOH•so] *adj*
showy
**visual** [VIH•soo•AHL] *adj*
visual
**vital** [VEE•tahl] *adj* M vital
**vitalidad** [VEE•tahl•ih•DAHD]
*n* F stamina; vitality
**vitamina** [vee•TAH•MEEN•ah]
*n* F vitamin
**vitreo** [vih•TRAI•oh] *adj*
vitreous
**vitriolo** [VIH•tree•OH•lo] *n* M
vitriol
**vitualla** [VIH•too•AI•yah] *n* F
victuals
**viuda** [vee•OO•dah] *n* F widow
**viudo** [vee•OO•do] *n* M
widower
**vivacidad**
[vee•VAH•sih•DAHD] *n* F
quickness; vivacity
**vivamente** [VEE•vah•MEN•tai]
*adv* hastily; quickly
**vivaz** [VEE•vahs] *adj* vivacious;
lively
**vívido** [vih•VEE•do] *adj* vivid
**vivienda** [VEE•vee•EHN•dah] *n*
F tenement
**viviente** [VEE•vee•EN•tai] *adj*
living

**vivo** [VEE•vo] *adj* alive; live; spirited; gay

**vocabulario** [voh•KAH•boo•LAHR•EE•oh] *n* M vocabulary

**vocación** [voh•KAH•see•OHN] *n* F vocation

**vocal 1** [VOH•kahl] *adj* vocal

**vocal 2** [VOH•kahl] *n* M vowel

**vocingiero** [VOH•seen•HIER•o] *adj* blatant

**volar** [VO•lahr] *vi* soar

**volar estallar** [VOH•lahr] [eh•STAY•yahr] *vt vi* explode

**volátil** [vohl•AH•teel] *adj* volatile

**volcán** [vol•KAHN] *n* M volcano

**volcánico** [vohl•KAHN•IH•koh] *adj* volcanic

**volcar** [vol•KAHR] *vt* upset

**voltaje** [vohl•TAH•hai] *n* M voltage

**volteador** [vol•TAI•ah•DOR] *n* tumbler

**voltear** [VOL•tai•AHR] *vi* revolve

**voltereta** [vol•TAIR•ai•TAH] *n* F turnover

**voltio** [vohl•TEE•oh] *n* M volt

**volumen** [voh•LOO•men] *n* M volume

**voluminoso** [vol•OO•min•OH•so] *adj* massive; portly

**voluntariamente** [vol•UHN•tahr•EE•ah•MEN•tai] *adv* willingly

**voluntario** [vohl•UN•tahr•EE•oh] *adj* voluntary; *n* M volunteer

**voluntarioso** [vol•UHN•tahr•EE•OH•so] *adj* willful

**voluptuoso** [vol•UHP•TOO•oh•so] *adj* voluptuous

**volver** [vol•VAIR] *vi* return; turn

**vomitar** [VOH•mee•TAHR] *vi* spew; throw up; *vt* vomit

**vorágine** [VOR•ah•HEE•nai] *n* M whirlpool

**voraz** [vor•AHS] *adj* voracious

**votación** [voh•TAH•see•OHN] *n* F poll; voting

**votante** [voh•TAHN•tai] *n* M voter

**voto** [VOH•to] *n* M vote

**voz** [vohs] *n* F voice

**vuelo** [VWAI•loh] *n* M flight

**vuelta** [VWEL•tah] *n* F loop

**vuelto** [VWEL•toh] flown

**vulgar** [vuhl•GAHR] *adj* vulgar; blatant

**vulgaridad** [vuhl•GAHR•ih•DAHD] *n* F vulgarity

**vulnerable** [VUHL•nair•AH•blai] *adj* vulnerable

# W

**whisky** [WIS•kee] *n* M whiskey

# X

**xenófobo** [KSEN•OH•FO•bo] *n* M xenophobe

**xilófono** [KSEE•LOH•FON•oh] *n* M xylophone

**xilografía** [ksee•LO•grah•FEE•ah] *n* F xylography

# Y

**y** [ee] *conj* and

**ya** [yah] *adv* already

**yacija** [yah•SEE•ha] *n* F lair

**yarda** [YAHR•dah] *n* F yard

**yate** [YAH•tai] *n* M yacht

**yegua** [he•GOO•ah] *n* F mare

**yema** [YAI•mah] *n* F yolk

**yerno** [YAIR•no] *n* M son-in-law

**yesca** [YEH•skah] *n* F tinder

**yo** [yoh] pers *pron* I; *n* MF self

**yo mismo** [yoh MEES•mo] *pron* myself

**yodo** [YO•do] *n* M iodine

**yugo** [YOO•go] *n* M yoke

**yuxtaponer** [YUHK•stah•PON•air] *vt* juxtapose

# Z

**zagal** [SAH•gahl] *n* M swain

**zahurda** [sah•OOR•dah] *n* F pigsty

**zanahoria** [SAHN•ah•OR•EE•ah] *n* F carrot

**zanco** [SAN•koh] *n* M stilt

**zapador** [SAH•pah•DOR] *n* M pioneer

**zapatero** [SAHP•ah•TAIR•oh] *n* M shoemaker

zapatilla [SAH•pah•TEE•yah] *n* F slipper

zapato [sah•PAH•to] *n* M shoe

zar [sahr] *n* M czar

zarcillo [sahr•SEE•yo] *n* M tendril

zarzamora [SAHR•sah•MOR•ah] *n* F blackberry

zenit [seh•NIHT] *n* M zenith

zepelín [SEH•peh•LEEN] *n* M zeppelin

zigzag [SIHG•sahg] *n* M zigzag

zodiacal [SOH•dee•AH•kahl] *adj* zodiacal

zodíaco [SOH•dee•AH•ko] *n* M zodiac

zona [SO•nah] *n* F zone

zoología [soh•OH•loh•HEE•ah] *n* F zoology

zoológico [SOH•oh•LO•HIEE•kah] *adj* zoological

zorro [SOR•roh] *n* M fox

zumbar [SOOM•brahr] *vi* hum; whir; whiz

zumbido [soom•BEE•doh] *n* M buzz (of insect)

zurcir [soor•SEER] *vt* darn

zurrar [SOOR•ahr] *vt* spank

# A

**a** [u or ai ] (before vowel or
silent 'h' ) an [en] art un una
**abandon** [u•BAN•dun] *vt*
abandonar; *n* abandono;
desenfado M
**abase** [u•BAIS] *vt* rebajar;
degrader; *n* degradacion F
**abbey** [a•BEE] *n* monasterio M
**abbreviate** [u•BREE•vee•AIT]
*vt* abreviar
**abbreviation**
[u•BREE•vee•AI•shn] *n*
abreviación; *vt* abreviar
**abdomen** [AB•du•men] *n*
abdomen M
**abduct** [ub•DUHKT] *vt*
secuestrar; ~ion *n* secuestro M
**abet** [u•BET] *vt* alentar; ser
complice de
**abhor** [ub•HAUR] *vt* aborrecer
**abide (by)** [u•BUYD] *vi*
adherirse
**ability** [u•BI•li•tee] *n*
habilidad F
**able** [AI•bl] *adj* hábil ; be ~\
poder
**abnormal** [ab•NAUR•ml] *adj*
anormal
**abode** [u•BOD] *n* domicilio M
**abolish** [u•BAH•lish] *vt* abolir
**abominable** [u•BAH•mi•nu•bl]
*adj* abominable

**abortion** [u•BAUR•shn] *n*
aborto M
**about** [u•BOUT] *prep* sobre;
cerca; de junto a; ~ here\ por
aquí; be ~ to\ estar a punto
do; be up and ~\ estar
levantado; ~ face; ~ turn\
cambio rotundo
**above** [u•BUHV] *adv* arriba;
sobre; encima de
**abrupt** [u•BRUHPT] *adj*
abrupto; brusco
**absent** [AB•sunt] *adj* ausente
**absent-minded** [-MUYN•did]
*adj* distraído
**absolute** [AB•su•LOOT] *adj*
absoluto
**absolutely** [AB•su•LOOT•lee]
*adv* absolutamente
**absorb** [ub•ZAURB] *vt*
absorber
**abstain** [ab•STAIN] *vi*
abstenerse
**abstract** [ab•STRAKT] *adj*
abstracto; *n* abstracto M
**absurd** [ub•SURD] *adj* absurdo
**abundant** [u•BUHN•dunt] *adj*
abundante
**abuse** [u•BYOOS] *n* abuso M;
*vt* abusar de
**abyss** [u•BIS] *n* abismo M

**academy** [u•KA•du•mee] *n*
academia F; ~ of music *n*\
conservatorio M

**accent** [AK•sent] *n* acento M; *vt*
accentuar

**accept** [ak•SEPT] *vt* aceptar

**access** [AK•ses] *n* acceso M

**accident** [AK•si•dunt] *n*
accidente M

**accidental** [AK•si•DEN•tl] *adj*
accidental

**accommodate**
[uh•KAH•mu•DAIT] *vt*
acomodar; ajustar; alogar

**accompany** [u•KUHM•pu•nee]
*vt* acompañar

**accomplice** [u•KAHM•plis] *n*
cómplice MF

**accomplish** [u•KAHM•plish] *vt*
realizar

**accord** [u•KAURD] *n* acuerdo
M; *vi* concordar

**according** [u•KAUR•ding] *prep*
acorde; ~ to\ según

**accost** [u•KAUST] *vt* acercarse;
abordar

**account** [u•KOUNT] *n* cuenta
F; on ~ of\ a cause de; on no
~\ de ninguna manera; take
into ~\ tener en cuenta

**accumulate**
[u•KYOO•myu•LAIT] *vt*
amontado; *vi* acumularse

**accurate** [A•kyu•ret] *adj* exacto;
fiel

**accuse** [u•KYOOZ] *vt* acusar;
culpar

**accustom** [u•KUH•stum] *vt*,
acostumbrar

**acid** [A•sid] *adj n* ácido M

**acknowledge** [ek•NAH•lij] *vt*
reconocer

**acquaintance** [u•KWAIN•tuns]
*n* conocimiento M

**acquiesce** [a•kwee•YES] *vi*
consentir

**acquire** [u•KWUYUR] *vt*
adquirir

**acquit** [u•KWIT] *vt* descargar

**acquital** [u•KWIT•ahl] *n*
absolución F

**acre** [AI•kur] *n* acre M

**acrid** [A•krid] *adj* corrosivo

**across** [u•KRAUS] *adv* a través;
de un lado al otro; go ~\
atravesar

**act** [akt] *n* acto; hecho M;
acción F; *vt* hacer; *vi* actuar;
~ as\ actuar de; ~ for\
representar

**action** [AK•shn] *n* acción F

**active** [AK•tiv] *adj* ligero;
activo

**actor** [AK•tur] *n* actor M

**actress** [AK•tris] *n* actriz F

**actually** [AK•chu•lee] *adv*
realmente

**acute** [u•KYOOT] *adj*
puntiagudo

**ache** [aik] *n* doler

**adapt** [u•DAPT] *vt* adaptar

**add** [ad] *vt* agregar; ~ up\
sumar; ~ up to\ equivaler a

**addict** [A•dikt] *n* aficiónado M

**addiction** [u•DIK•shn] *n* afición
F; adicto M

**addition** [u•DI•shn] *n* adición;
suma F

**additional** [u•DI•shun•ul] *adj*
adicional

**address** [n. A•dres v. u•DRES]
  *n* dirección F; *vt* dirigir; *n*
  discurso (speech) M

**adequate** [A•de•kwet] *adj*
  suficiente

**adjective** [A•jik•tiv] *n*
  adjetivo M

**adjourn** [u•JURN] *vt vi*
  trasladar

**adjust** [u•JUHST] *vt* ajustar

**administer** [ud•MI•ni•stur] *vt*
  administrar

**admire** [ud•MUYR] *vt* admirar

**admission** [ud•MI•shun] *n*
  entrada; admisión F

**admit** [ud•MIT] (let enter)
  laisser entrerl *vt* admitir;
  confesar

**admonish** [ud•MAH•nish] *vt*
  advertir

**adolescence** [A•du•LE•suns] *n*
  adolescencia F

**adopt** [u•DAHPT] *vt* adoptar

**adoption** [u•DAHP•shun] *n*
  adopción F

**adore** [u•DAUR] *vt* adorar

**adult** [u•DUHLT] *n* adulto M

**adultery** [u•DUHL•tu•ree] *n*
  adulterio M

**advance** [ed•VANS] *vt/vi*
  avancar; *n* adelanto M; in ~\
  con anticipation

**advantage** [ed•VAN•tej] *n*
  ventaja F; take ~ of\ abusar

**advantageous**
  [AD•VUN•TAI•jus] *adj*
  ventajoso

**Advent** [AD•vent] *n*
  advenimiento M

**adventure** [ed•VEN•chur] *n*
  aventura F

**adventurous** [ed•VEN•chu•rus]
  *adj* arriesgado; aventurero

**adverbe** [AD•vurb] *n*
  adverbio M

**adversity** [ad•VUR•si•tee] *n*
  adversidad F

**advertise** [AD•vur•TUYZ] *vt*
  avisar; anunciar

**advertisement**
  [AD•vur•TUYZ•munt] *n*
  anuncio M

**advice** [ad•VUYS] *n* consejo M

**advise** [ad•VUYZ] *vt* aconsejar

**affair** [u•FAIR] *n* asunto;
  encuentro M; ~s *npl* \
  negocios (business)

**affect** [u•FEKT] *vt* afectar

**affection** [u•FEK•shn] *n* amor;
  cariño M

**afford** [uh•FAWRD] *vt*
  suministrar

**Afghanistan** [af•GA•ni•STAN]
  *n* afganistan

**afraid** (to be) [u•FRAID] *adj*
  temeroso; tener meido de

**Africa** [A•fri•ku] *n* Africa

**after** [AF•tur] *prep adv* después;
  *prep* después de; *conj* después
  de que; *adj* posterior

**afternoon** [AF•tur•NOON] *n*
  tarde F

**again** [uh•GEN] *adv* de nuevo;
  otra vez ; ~ and ~\ una y otra
  vez

**against** [uh•GENST] *prep adv*
  contra

**age** [aij] *n* edad F; of ~\ mayor
  de edad; under~\ menor de
  edad

**aged** [AI•jud / aij'd] *adj*
  anciano

**agency** [AI•jun•cee] *n* agencia F; organismo M

**agenda** [uh•JEN•duh] *n* orden del dìa M

**agent** [AI•junt] *n* agente M

**aggravate** [A•gru•VAIT] *vt* agravar

**aggressive** [u•GRE•siv] *adj* agresivo

**ago** [uh•GO] *adv* pasado; hace; a long time ~\ hace mucho tiempo

**agree** [uh•GREE] *vi* asentir; acordar; acceder; estar de acuerdo

**agreeable 1** [u•GREE•u•bl] *adj* agradable

**agreeable 2 (pleasant comfortable)** [u•GREE•u•bl] *adj* ameno grato

**agreement** [u•GREE•munt] *n* acuerdo; convenio M; in ~\ estar de acuerdo

**agriculture** [A•gri•CUL•chur] *n* agricultura F

**ahead (of)** [uh•HED] *adv* (prep) delante; al frente; be ~\ ir delante

**aid** [aid] *n* ayuda; asistencia F

**AIDS** [aids] *n* SIDA

**aim** [aim] *n* apuntar

**air** [air] *n* aire M

**air•conditioned** [-kuhn•DI•shuh•nd] *adj* aire acondicionado

**airmail** [AIR•mail ] (*by* ~) *n* por avión F

**airplane** [AIR•plain] *n* aeroplano M

**airport** [AIR•paurt] *n* aeropuerto M

**airtight** [AIR•tuyt] *adj* hermétticamente cerrado

**aisle** [uyl] *n* pasillo M

**ajar** [uh•JAHR] *adj* entreabierto

**alarm** [u•LAHRM] (*vt:* alarmer) *n* alarma F; *vt* asustar

**alarm clock** [u•LAHRM CLAHK] *n* despertado M

**alas** [uh•LAS] *excl* ¡ay!

**Albania** [al•BAI•nee•yuh] *n* albania F

**album** [AL•bum] *n* álbum M

**alcohol** [AL•ku•HAL] *n* alcohol M

**alcoholic** [AL•ku•HAU•lik] *adj* *n* alcohólico M

**alert** [uh•LUHRT] *adj* alerta; *vt* alertar

**algebra** [AL•je•bru] *n* álgebra F

**Algeria** [AL•jee•ree•yu] *n* Argelia F

**alibi** [A•li•BUY] *n* coartada F

**alike** [uh•LUYK] *adj* igual; a parecido; be ~\ parecerse; *adv* de la misma manera

**alive** [uh•LUYV] *adj* vivo

**all** [awl] *adj* *pron* todo; toda; todos;~ but one\ todo excepto uno~ of it\ todo; ~ but\ casi; *adv* completamente

**allegation** [A•lu•GAI•shun] *n* alegación F

**allergic** [u•LUR•jik] *adj* alérgico M

**allergy** [A•luhr•jee] *n* alergia F

**alliance** [u•LUY•yuns] *n* alianza F

**allow** [uh•LOU] *vt* permitir consentir

**allusion** [u•LOO•zhuhn] *n* alusión F

**allow** [uh•LAU] *vt* permitir;
condeder; ~ for\ tener en
cuenta
**almost** [AWL•most] *adv* casí
**alone** [uh•LON] *adj adv* solo;
sola; *adv* solo; solamente
**along** [uh•LAUNG] *prep* por; lo
largo
**aloud** [uh•LOUD] *adv* alto
**alphabet** [AL•fu•BET] *n*
alfabeto M
**already** [aul•RE•dee] *adv* ya
**also** [AHL•so] *adv* también
**alternate (with)**
[AUL•tur•NAIT] *vi* alternar
**although** [ahl•THO] *conj*
aunque
**altogether**
[AHL•too•GE•thuhr] *adv*
enteramente; conjunto; en
todo
**always** [AHL•waiz] *adv*
siempre
**(I) am** [am] — *v* soy
**amateur** [A•mu•CHUR] *adj n*
aficionado M
**amaze** [u•MAIZ] *vt* maravillar;
be ~ed\ atquedarse asombrado
**amazing** [u•MAI•zing] *adj*
maravilloso
**ambassador** [am•BA•su•dur] *n*
embajador M
**ambiguous** [am•BI•gyoo•wus]
*adj* ambiguo
**ambitious** [am•BI•shus] *adj*
deseoso
**amend** [u•MEND] (law)
amendment: amendment M *vt*
corregir; *n* enmienda F
**America** [u•ME•ri•ku] *n*
América

**amnesty** [AM•ni•stee] *n*
amnistia F
**among** [u•MUHNG] *prep* entre;
en medio de
**amount** [u•MOUNT] *n*
cantidad; suma F
**amuse** [u•MYOOZ] *vt* divertir
**amusement**
[u•MYOOZ•muhnt] *n*
diversión F
**analogy** [u•NA•lu•jee] *n*
analogía F
**analysis** [u•NA•lu•sis] *n*
análisis F
**analyze** [A•nu•LUYZ] *vt*
analizar
**anarchy** [A•nahr•kee] *n*
anarquía F
**ancestor** [AN•SE•stur] *n*
antepasado M
**anchor** [AN•kur] *n* ancia;
áncora F
**ancient** [AIN•shunt] *adj*
antiguo
**and** [and] or [end] *conj* y; more
~ more\ siempre más
**angel** [AIN•jul] *n* ángel M
**anger** [ANG•gur] *n* ira F;
enojo M
**angle** [ANG•gl] *n* ángulo M;
punto de vista (coll)
**angry** [ANG•gree] *adj* enojado;
furioso
**anguish** [AN•gwish] *n* tormento
M; angustia F
**animal** [A•ni•ml] *n* animal M
**animated** [A•ni•mut] *adj*
animado
**anniversary** [A•ni•VUR•su•ree]
*n* aniversario M

**announce** [u•NOUNS] *vt*
anunciar

**announcement**
[u•NOUNS•muhnt] *n*
annoncio M

**annoy** [u•NOI] *vt* molestar

**annoying** [u•NOI•ying] *adj*
molesto

**annual** [A•nyoo•ul] *adj* anua; *n*
ánuo M

**another** [u•NUH•thur] *adj* otro

**answer** [AN•sur] *vt* responder;
contestar; *n* repuesta;
solución F

**ant** [ant] *n* hormiga F

**anthology** [an•THAH•lu•jee] *n*
antologia F

**antique** [an•TEEK] *adj* antiguo

**antisocial** [AN•ti•SO•shul] *adj*
antisocial

**anxiety** [ang•ZUY•yu•tee] *n*
ansiedad F

**anxious** [ANK•shus] *adj*
ansioso

**any** [E•nee] *adj* cualquier;
algún; ningun (neg); at ~
moment\ en cualquier
momento; do you have
any . . .\ ¿tienes .?

**anyone** (anybody)
[E•nee•WUHN] *pron* alguien;
alguno

**anything** [E•nee•THING] *pron*
algo; alguna cosa

**anyway** [E•nee•WAI] *adv* de
todos modos

**anywhere** [E•nee•WAIR] *adv*
en todas partes

**apart** [u•pahrt] *adj* aparte;
apartado; separado; come ~\
romperse; take ~\ desmontar

**apartment** [u•PAHRT•munt] *n*
apartamento M

**ape** [aip] *n* mono M; *vt* imitar

**apologize** [u•PAH•lu•JUYZ] *vi*
disculpar

**apology** [u•PAH•lu•jee] *n*
disculpa F

**apparently** [u•PA•runt•lee] *adv*
evidentemente

**appear** [u•PEER] *vi* aparecer

**appearance** [u•PEER•uns] *n*
aparición; vista F

**appetite** [A•pu•TUYT] *n*
apetito M

**appetizer** [A•pu•TUY•zur] *n*
aperitivo M

**applaud** [u•PLAUD] *vt* aplaudir

**apple** [A•pl] *n* manzana F; ~
tree\ manzano M

**application** [A•pli•KAI•shn] *n*
aplicación F

**apply** [uh•PLUY] *vt* aplicar

**appoint** [u•POINT] *vt*
establecer; señalar

**appointment** [u•POINT•ment]
*n* cita; convenida F; to have
an ~ w/someone\ tener una
cita

**appraisal** [u•PRAI•zul] *n*
estimacieon F

**appraise** [u•PRAIZ] *vt* estimar;
apreciar

**appreciate** [u•PREE•shee•AIT]
*vt* valuar; apreciar

**approach** [u•PROCH] *vt*
acercarse; aproximarse

**appropriate** [u•PRO•pree•IT]
*adj* apropriado

**approval** [u•PROO•vl] *n*
aprobación F

**approve** [u•PROOV] *vt* aprobar

**approximately**
[u•PRAHK•su•mit•lee] *adv*
aproximadamente

**apricot** [A•pri•KAHT] *n*
albaricoque M

**April** [AI•pril] *n* abril M

**arbitrary** [AHR•bi•TRE•ree]
*adj* despótico M

**arch** [ahrch] *n* arco M

**archaeology**
[AHR•kee•AH•lu•jee] *n*
arqueologia F

**archaic** [ahr•KAI•ik] *adj* arcaico

**architect** [AHR•ki•TEKT] *n*
arquitecto M

**architecture**
[AHR•ki•TEK•chur] *n*
arquitectura F

**area** [A•ree•u] *n* área; zona F

**argue** [AHR•gyoo] *vi*
argumentar

**argument** [AHR•gyu•mint] *n*
argumento M

**arid** [A•rid] *adj* árido

**arm** [ahrm] *n* brazo M

**armchair** [AHRM•chair] *n*
silla F

**armor** [AHR•mur] *n* armadura F

**army** [AHR•mec] *n* ejército M

**aroma** [u•RO•mu] *n* aroma F

**around** [u•ROUND] *adv*
alrededor; cerca; all ~\ por
todas parted; *prep* alrededor
de

**arrange** [u•RAINJ] *vt* arreglar

**arrest** [u•REST] *vt* detener;
arrestar

**arrival** [u•RUY•vl] *n* llegada F

**arrive** [u•RUYV] *vi* llegar

**arrogant** [A•ru•gent] *adj*
arrogante

**arrow** [A•ro] *n* flecha F

**art** [ahrt] *n* artc M; fine ~s\
bellas artes *npl* F

**article** [AHR•ti•kl] *n* artículo M

**articulate** [ahr•Tl•cyu•LAIT] *vt*
*vi* articular

**artificial** [AHR•ti•FI•shl] *adj*
artificial

**artist** [AHR•tist] *n* artista F

**as** [az] *adv conj pron prep*
como; ya que (since); ~ big
~\ tan grande como; ~ far ~\
hasta; ~ if\ como si; ~ soon
~\ tan pronto como; ~ well\
tambien

**ash** [ash] *n* ceniza F

**ashamed** (to be) [u•SHAIMD]
*adj* avergonzado

**ashtray** [ASH•trai] *n* cenicero M

**aside** [u•SUYD] *adv* al lado

**ask** [ask] *vt* preguntar; ~ about\
enterarse de; ~ for help\ pedir
ayuda; ~ someone in\ invitar a
uno a pasar

**asleep** [u•SLEEP] *adj* dormido
durmiendo

**asparagus** [u•SPA•ru•gus] *n*
espárrago M

**aspect** [A•spekt] *n* aspecto M

**aspirin** [A•sprin] *n* aspirina F

**assassinate** [u•SA•si•NAIT] *vt*
asesinar

**assassination**
[u•SA•si•NAI•shun] *n*
asesinato M

**assemble** [u•SEM•bl] *vt*
congregar; convocar

**assembly** [u•SEM•blcc] *n*
asamblea F

**assign** [u•SUYN] *vt* asignar

**associate** [u•SO•shee•AIT] *vt*
asociarse

**association** [u•SO•see•AI•shn]
*n* asociación F

**assume** [u•SOOM] *vt* arrogarse;
suponer

**assumption** [u•SUHMP•shun]
*n* suposición F

**astonish** [u•STAH•nish] *vt*
asombrar

**astrology** [u•STRAH•lu•jee] *n*
astrologia F

**astronaut** [A•stru•NAHT] *n*
astronauta M

**astronomy** [a•STRAH•nu•mee]
*n* astronomía F

**at** [at] *prep* en; a; ~ home\ en
casa; ~ night\ por la noche; ~
Juan's\ en casa de Juan; ~
once\ en seguida; ~ times\ a
veces; not ~ all\ nade

**attach** [u•TACH] *vt* atar;
adherir

**attack** [u•TAK] *vt* atacar

**attempt (to)** [u•TEMPT] *vt*
procurar; probar

**attend** [u•TEND] *vt* atender

**attention** [u•TEN•shn] *n*
atención F

**Attention!** [u•TEN•shn] *excl*
firmes!

**attentive** [u•TEN•tiv] *adj*
atento

**attic** [A•tik] *n* sotabanco M

**attitude** [A•ti•TOOD] *n*
actitud F

**attract** [u•TRAKT] *vt* atraer

**attraction** [u•TRAK•shn] *n*
atracción F

**attractive** [u•TRAK•tiv] *adj*
atractivo

**audience** [AU•dee•uns] *n*
concurrencia F; púbilcio M

**audition** [au•DI•shun] *n*
audición F

**August** [AU•gust] *n* agosto M

**aunt** [ant or ahnt] *n* tía F

**Australia** [au•STRAIL•yu] *n*
Australia F

**Austria** [AU•stree•u] *n*
Austria F

**authentic** [au•THEN•tik] *adj*
auténtico

**author** [AU•thur] *n* auto
escritor M

**authority** [u•THAU•ri•tee] *n*
autoridad F

**autobiography**
[AU•to•buy•AH•gru•fee] *n*
autobiografía F

**autograph** [AU•to•GRAF] *n*
autógrafo M

**automatic** [AU•to•MA•tik] *adj*
automático

**autumn** [AU•tum] *n* atoño M

**auxiliary** [aug•ZIL•yu•ree] *adj*
*n* subsidiario M

**available** [u•VAI•lu•bl] *ðadj*
aprovechable

**avenge** [u•VENJ] *vt* vengar;
vindicar

**avenue** [A•vu•NOO] *n*
avenida F

**average** [A•vur•ij] *adj n*
promedio; medio M

**avoid** [u•VOID] *vt* invalidar;
esquivar

**awake** [u•WAIK] *adj* despierto;
*vt vi* despertar

**award** [u•WAURD] *vt*
conceder; adjudicar

aware [u•WAIR] *adj* sabedor;
consciente de

away [u•WAI] *adv* lejos; fuera

awful [AU•ful] *adj* atroz
horrible

awkward [AU•kwurd] *adj*
torpe; desgarbado

axe [aks] *n* hacha F

axis [AK•sis] *n* axis M

axle [AK•sl] *n* ejc M

# B

babble [BA•bl] *vi* charlar;
balbucir

baby [BAI•bee] *n* bebé M

bachelor [BA•chu•lur] *n*
soltero M

back [bak] *adv adj n vt* espalda
F; detrás; respaldar; ~ down\
*vi* volverse atrás; back out *vi*\
retirarse; ~ biting\ *n*
maledicencia F; ~stage\ a
debastidores

background (in the)
[BAK•ground] *n* fondo M

backlash [BAK•lash] *n*
contragolpe M

backward [BAK•wurd] *adv adj*
retrógrado atrás

backyard [bak•YAHRD] *n*
patio M

bacon [BAI•kun] *n* tocino M

bad [bad] *adj* mal

badge [baj] *n* insignia F

badly [BAD•lee] *adv* mal

bag [bag] *n* saco bolsa M

baggage [BA•gij] *n* equipaje M

bagpipes [BAG•puyps] *npl*
gaita F

bail 1 [bail] *n* fianza F

bail 2 [baiul] *n* aro M

bait [hait] *n* carnada F

bake [baik] *vt* cocer; hornear

baker [BAI•kur] *n* hornero;
panadero M

bakery [BAI•ker•ee] *n*
panadería F

balance [BA•lens] *n* balanza F

balance sheet [BA•lens
SHEET] *n* avanzo M

balcony [BAL•ku•nee] *n*
balceon M

bald [bauld] *adj* calvo

bale [baiul] *n* bala F

balk [bauk] *vi* evitar; burlar

ball 1 [bawl] *n* bola F

ball 2 [bawl] *n* baile M (dance)

ballad [BA•lud] *n* balada F

ballerina [BA•lu•REE•nu] *n*
bailarina F

ballet [BA•lai] *n* baile de
espectáculo M

balloon [bu•LOON] *n* globo M

ballot [BA•lut] *n* balota F

bamboo [bam•BOO] *n* bambú M

ban [ban] *n* edicto M

banal [bu•NAL] *adj* trivial;
común

banana [bu•NA•nu] *n* plátano M

band 1 [band] *n* cinta; banda F

band 2 [band] *n* orquesta F

bandage [BAN•dij] *n* venda F

**banish** [BA•nish] *vt* desterrar;
  deportar
**bank 1** [bank] *n* banco M; *vt*
  depositar; ~ on\ contar con
**bank 2** [bank] *n* orilla (river); *vt*
  cubir
**banker** [BANG•kur] *n*
  banquero M
**bankrupt** [BANK•ruhpt] *adj*
  insolvente
**bankruptcy**
  [BANK•RUHPT•see] *n*
  quiebra F
**banner** [BA•nur] *n* bandera F
**banquet** [BANG•kwet] *n*
  banquete M
**banter** [BAN•tur] *n* chunga F
**baptism** [BAP•tizm] *n*
  bautismo M
**baptize** [bap•TUYZ] *vt* bautizar
**bar** [bahr] (pub) *n* taberna F
**barbarian** [bahr•BE•ree•un] *adj*
  *n* bárbaro M
**barbed** [bahrbd] *adj* barbado
**barber** [BAHR•bur] *n* barbero M
**bare** [bair] *adj* desnudo (without
  clothes); vacio (empty);
  mostrar las dentes (teeth)
**barefoot** [BAIUR•fut] *adj adv*
  descalzo
**barely** [BAIR•lee] *adv* a penas
**bargain** [BAHR•gin] *n vi* buen
  negocio M
**barge** [bahrj] *n* barcaza F
**bark 1** [bahrk] n; ~ at\ *vi* curtir;
  *n* ladrido M
**bark 2** [bahrk] *n* corteza F
**barley** [BAHR•lee] *n* cebada F
**barn** [bahrn] *n* granero M
**barometer** [bu•RAH•mi•tur] *n*
  barómetro M

**baroque** [bu•ROK] *adj n*
  barroco
**barracks** [BA•ruks] *npl*
  cuartel M
**barrel** [BA•rul] *n* barril M
**barren** [BA•run] *adj* estéril;
  infructífero
**barricade** [BA•ri•KAID] *n*
  barricada F
**barrier** [BA•ree•ur] *n* barrera F
**base** [bais] *n* basa F; *vt* basar
**baseball** [BAIS•bawl] *n*
  béisbol M
**basement** [BAIS•munt] *n*
  basamento M
**bashful** [BASH•ful] *adj*
  vergonzoso
**basic** [BAI•sik] *adj* básico;
  fundamental
**basil** [baizl] *n* albahaca F
**basis** [BAI•sis] *n* base;
  fundamento M
**basket** [BA•skit] *n* cesto M
**basketball** [BA•skit•BAWL] *n*
  baloncesto M
**bass 1** [bais] *n* bajo M (mus)
**bass 2** [bas] *n* róbalo M (fish)
**bassoon** [bu•SOON] *n* bajón M
**bastard** [BA•sturd] *n* bastardo M
**baste** [baist] *vt* bastear
**bat 1** [bat] *n* murciélago M
**bat 2** [bat] *n* bate M; *vt* goplear
**bath** [bath] *n* baño M
**bather** [BAI•thur] *n* bañista F
**bathing suit** [BAI•thing ~ ] *n*
  traje de baño M
**bathrobe** [BATH•rob] *n*
  albornoz M
**bathroom** [BATH•room] *n*
  cuarto de baño M

**bathtub** [BATH•tuhb] *n*
bañera F

**baton** [bu•TAHN] *n* bastón M

**battalion** [bu•TA•lyun] *n*
batallón F

**batter 1** [DA•tur] *n* pasta;
batido M (baking)

**batter 2** [BA•tur] *vt* apalear

**battery** [BA•tu•ree] *n* batería F

**battle** [batl] *n* batalla combate
(m) F

**battleship** [BA•tl•SHIP] *n*
acorzado M

**bawdy** [BAU•dee] *adj*
obsceno M

**bawl** [baul] *vt vi* gritar

**bay** [bai] *n* bahía F

**bayonet** [BAI•u•net] *n*
bayoneta F

**bazaar** [bu•ZAHR] *n* bazar F

**BC** (before Christ) ante Cristo

**be** [bee] *aux v* ser; estar; ~ that
as it may\ sea como fuere;
how are you?\ ¿comó está?;
~ cold/hot\ tener frio; calor

**beach** [beech] *n* playa F

**bead** [beed] *n* perla; cuenta F;
abolorio (glass) M

**beak** [beek] *n* pico M

**beam** [beem] *n* viga F; rayo M
(*of light*) *vt* emitir

**bean** [been] *n* frijol M

**bear 1** [bair] *n* oso M

**bear 2** [bair] *vt* llevar; sportar

**beard** [beerd] *n* barba F

**beast** [beest] *n* bestia F

**beastly** [BEEST•lee] *adj* bestial

**beat** [beet] *vt* pegar; golpear; *vi*
latir (heart);~ it\ largarse
(coll)

**beating** [BEE•ting] *n* paliza F

**beautiful** [BYOO•ti•ful] *adj*
hermosa

**beauty** [BYOO•tee] *n* belleza F;
~ parlor\ salón de belleza M

**beaver** [BEE•vur] *n* castor M

**because** [bi•CUHZ] *conj*
porque; ~ of\ a cause de

**beckon** [BE•kun] *vt* gesto M

**become** [bi•KUHM] *vi* ser
convenir; llegar a ser;
volverse; convertirse en

**becoming** [bi•KUH•ming] *adj*
propio

**bed** [bed] *n* cama F

**bedroom** [BED•room] *n*
dormitorio M

**bee** [bee] *n* abeja F

**beech** [beech] *n* haya F

**beef** [beef] *n* carne de vaca F;
*vi* quejarse (*coll*)

**beehive** [BEE•huyv] *n*
colmena F

**been** [bin] *pp* fue

**beer** [bee'ur] *n* cerveza F

**beet** [beet] *n* remolacha F

**beetle** [beetl] *n* escarabajo;
cucaracha F

**before** [bi•FAUR] *adv* antes
(de); delante de; a week ~\ un
semana antes; ~ he leaves\
antes de que ser vaya

**befriend** [bu•FREND] *vt*
favorecer

**beg** [beg] *vt* pedir; I ~ your
pardon! ¡perdone Vd.!

**beggar** [BE•gur] *n* mendigo M

**begin** [bi•GIN] *vt vi* empezar;
comenzar

**beginner** [bu•GI•nur] *n*
novicio M

**beginning** [bi•GI•ning] *n*
principio comienzo M
**behalf** [bi•HAF] *n* en interés a
beneficio de
**behave** [bi•HAIV] *vi* obrar;
conducirse
**behavior** [bi•HAI•vyur] *n*
maneras
**behead** [bi•HED] *vt* decapitar
**behind** [bi•HUYND] *prep adv
n* detrás
**beige** [baizh] *adj n* color de
canela M
**being** [BEE•ing] *n* ser M; come
into ~\ nacer
**belated** [bi•LAI•tid] *adj* tardío
**belfry** [BEL•free] *n* campanil M
**Belgian** [BEL•jun] *adj* belga
**Belgium** [BEL•jum] *n* Bélgica F
**belief** [bi•LEEF] *n* creencia;
fe F
**believe** [bi•LEEV] *vt vi* creer
**belong** [bi•LAUNG] *vi*
pertenecer; corresponder
**beloved** [bi•LUVHVD] *adj*
querido
**below** [bi•LO] *adv* bajo; abajo
**belt** [belt] *n* cinturón M
**bell** [bel] *n* campana F
**bellow** [BE•lo] *vi* bramido M;
*vi* bramar
**belly** [BE•lee] *n* estómago M
**bench** [bench] *n* banco M
**bend** [bend] *vt* encorvar; *n*
inclinación F
**beneath** [bi•NEETH] *adv*
debajo; abajo
**benediction** [BE•ni•DIK•shun]
*n* bendició F
**benefactor** [BE•ni•FAK•tur] *n*
bienhechor M

**beneficial** [BE•nu•FI•shl] *adj*
beneficioso
**benefit** [BE•ni•FIT] *n*
beneficio M
**benign** [bi•NUYN] *adj* benigno
**bent** [bent] *adj* torcido;
encorvado
**bequeath** [bi•KWEETH] *vt*
dejar; mandar
**beret** [bu•RAI] *n* boina F
**berry** [BE•ree] *n* baya F
**beside** [bi•SUYD] *prep* cerca;
al lado
**besides** [bi•SUYDS] *adv prep*
además; excepto (exception)
**besiege** [bi•SEEJ] *vt* sitiar;
acosar
**best** [best] *adj adv* lo mejor; at
~\ a lo más; do one's ~\ hacer
todo lo posible; make the ~
of\ contentarse
**bestow** [bi•STO] *vt* dar
conceder
**bet** [bet] *n* apuesta F
**betray** [bi•TRAI] *vt* traicionar
**betrayal** [bi•TRAI•ul] *n*
traición F
**betrayer** [bi•TRAI•ur] *n*
traidor M
**better** [BE•tur] *adj* mejor; ~
off\ en mejores condiciones;
get ~\ mejorar; all the ~\ tanto
mejor; I'd ~\ más vale que;
the sooner the ~\ cuanto antes
mejor; *vt* mejorar; get the ~
of\ vencer a
**between** [bi•TWEEN] *prep adv*
entre; en medio
**beverage** [BE•vu•rij] *n*
bebida F

**beware** (of) [bi•WAIR] *vi*
guardarse

**bewitching** [bi•WI•ching] *adj*
hechicero fascinador

**beyond** [bi•YAHND] *adv prep*
más allá a lo lejos

**bias** [BUY•us] *n* sesgo M

**biased** [BUY•ust] *adj* torcido

**bib** *n* babador M

**Bible** [BUY•bl] *n* Biblia F

**bicker** [BI•kur] *vi* disputar

**bicycle** [BUY•si•kul] *n*
bicicleta F

**bid** [bid] *n* oferta F; *vi* hacer
una ofreta; *vt* ofrecer

**big** [big] *adj* grande

**bigamy** [BI•gu•mee] *n*
bigamia F

**bigot** [BI•gut] *n* persona
intolerante F

**bike** [buyk] *n* bicicleta F

**bile** [buyl] *n* bilis M

**bilingual** [BUY•LING•gwul]
*adj* bilingüe

**bill** [bil] *n* billete M; cuenta,
factura F; *vt* pasar la factura

**billiards** [BIL•yurdz] *n*
billar M

**billion** [BIL•yun] *num* billón M

**bin** [bin] *n* recipiente (for
garbage) caja; cubo F

**binoculars** [bi•NAH•kyu•lurz]
*npl* binocular

**biography** [buy•AH•gru•fee] *n*
biografía F

**biology** [buy•AH•lu•jee] *n*
biología F

**birch** [burch] *n* abedul M

**bird** [burd] *n* pájaro M

**birth** [burth] *n* nacimiento M

**birth control** [ ~ kuhn•TROL]
*n* limitación de la natalidad F

**birthday** [BURTH•dai] *n*
cumpleaños M

**birthmark** [BURTH•mahrk] *n*
antojo M

**birthrate** [BURTH•rait] *n*
natalidad F

**bishop** [BI•shup] *n* obispo M

**bit** *n* pedazo M

**bitch** [bich] *n* puta, muera
maligna, bruja; (zool) perra F

**bite** [buyt] *vt* morder; (insect,
snake) *n* picadura F

**bitter** [BI•tur] *adj* amargo

**bitterness** [BI•tur•NIS] *n*
amargor M

**blab** [blab] *vi vt* chismear

**black** [blak] *adj n* negro M

**blackberry** [BLAK•BU•ree] *n*
zarzamora F

**blackbird** [BLAK•burd] *n*
mirlo M

**blackboard** [BLAK•baurd] *n*
pizarra F

**blacken** [BLA•kun] *vt*
embetunar; ennegrecer

**blackmail** [BLAK•mail] *n*
chantaje M

**black market** [ ~ MAHR•kit] *n*
mercado negro M

**blacksmith** [BLAK•smith] *n*
herrero M

**bladder** [BLA•dur] *n* vejiga F

**blade** [blaid] *n* hoja F; (razor
blade) cuchilla

**blame** [blaim] *vt* reprobar; *n*
culpa F

**bland** [bland] *adj* suave;
melifluo

**blank** [blank] *n* blanco
espacio M

**blanket** [BLANG•kit] *n*
manta F

**blaspheme** [blas•FEEM] *vt vi*
blasfemar de

**blast** [blast] *n* ráfaga; ventada F;
*vt* volar

**blatant** [BLAI•tunt] *adj*
vocingiero; vulgar

**blaze** [blaiz] *n* incendio M;
llamarada F

**bleach** [bleech] *n* blanqueo M

**bleed** [bleed] *vi vt* sangrar

**blemish** [BLE•mish] *n* defecto
M; tacha F

**blend** [blend] *vt* mezclar;
combinar

**bless** [bles] *vt* bendecir

**blessing** [BLE•sing] *n*
bendición F

**blind** [bluynd] *adj* ciego; *vt*
cegar

**blindfold** [BLUYND•fold] *n*
vendado de ojos M

**blink** [blink] *vt* parpadear

**blinker** [BLING•kur] *n* (car)
aparato de señales M

**bliss** [blis] *n* bienaventuranza;
gloria F

**blister** [BLI•stur] *n* ampolla F

**blizzard** [BLI•zurd] *n* tempestad
de nieve F

**bloated** [BLO•tid] *adj* hinchado

**block** [blahk] *n* bloque M; ~ in
traffic\ embotellamiento; *vt*
obstruir

**blockade** [blah•KAID] *n*
bloqueo M

**blonde** [blahnd] *adj* rubio

**blood** [bluhd] *n* sangre M

**bloody** [BLUH•dee] *adj*
sangriento

**bloom** [bloom] *vi* floración F

**blossom** [BLAH•sum] *n* flor F

**blouse** [blous] *n* blusa F

**blow 1** [blo] *vt* soplar; fondar;
~ out\ apagar; ~ up\ inflar;
(explode) estallar

**blow 2** [blo] *n* golpe M

**bludgeon** [BLUH•jn] *vt* apalear

**blue** [bloo] *adj n* azúl M

**blueberry** [BLOO•BE•ree] *n*
arándano M

**blueprint** [BLOO•print] *n*
cianotipia F

**bluff** [bluhf] *n* ancha; escarpa F

**blunder** [BLUHN•dur] *n*
disparate M

**blunt** [bluhnt] *adj* embotado

**blurry** [BLU•ree] *adj* manchado

**blush** [bluhsh] *vi* ruborizarse

**boar** [baur] *n* verraco; simpite M

**board 1** [baurd] *n* tabla F;
tablero (bulletin board); above
~\ correcto; room and ~\ casa
y comida

**board 2** [baurd] *vt* abordar (on
board)

**boarding school** [BAUR•ding
~ ] *n* escuela de internos F

**boast** [bost] *vi* alardear

**boat** [bot] *n* bote; barca M

**boating** [BO•ting] *n* pasea en
botes

**body** [BAH•dee] *n* cuerpo M

**bodyguard**
[BAH•dee•GAHRD] *n* guardia
de corps F

**bog** [bahg] *n* pantano M

**boil 1** [boil] *vt* hervir; hacer
mucho calor (weather)

**boil 2** [boil] *n* furúnculo M
**boiled egg** [boild ~ ] *n* huevo hervido M
**boiling point** [BOI•ling ~ ] *n* punto de ebullición M
**boisterous** [BOI•ᴈtu•ɹus] *adj* estrepitoso
**bold** [bold] *adj* valiente
**boldness** [BOLD•nes] *n* arrojo M
**bolt** [bolt] *n* flecha F; lightning ~\ rayo; *vi* fugarse
**bomb** [bahm] *n* bomba F
**bombard** [BAHM•bahrd] *vt* bombardear
**bomber** [BAH•mur] *n* bombardero M
**bombing** [BAH•ming] *n* bombardeo M
**bond** [bahnd] *n* pacto M; obligación F
**bondage** [BAHN•dij] *n* esclavitud F
**bone** [bon] *n* hueso M
**bonfire** [BAHN•fuyur] *n* fuego M
**bonnet** [BAH•nit] *n* capota F
**bonus** [BO•nus] *n* premio; plus M
**boo** [boo] *vt vi* bu
**book** [bük] *n* libro M
**bookkeeper** [BÜK•KEE•pur] *n* tenedor de libros M
**bookkeeping** [BÜK•KEE•ping] *n* teneduría de libros F
**bookstore** [BÜK•staur] *n* librería F
**boom** [boom] *vi n* estampido M; *vt* retumbar; prosperar
**boomerang** [BOO•mu•RANG] *n* bumerang M

**boost** [boost] *vt* empuje M
**boot** [boot] *n* bota F
**booth** [booth] *n* casilla F
**booty** [BOO•tec] *n* botín M
**border** [BAUR•dur] *n* borde M
**bore 1** [baur] *vt* taladrar M; *vi* taladar
**bore 2** [baur] *vt* aburrir; *n* pelmazo M
**boredom** [BAUR•dum] *n* aburrimiento M
**boring** [BAU•ring] *adj* aburrido
**born** [baurn] *adj* nacido (to be)
**borough** [BUH•ro] *n* villa; barrio (m) F
**borrow** [BAH•ro] *vt* pedir; prestado
**Bosnia** [BAHZ•nee•u] *n* Bosnia
**Bosnian** [BAHZ•nee•un] *adj n* bosnio M
**bosom** [BU•zum] *n* pecho M
**boss** [baus] *n* jefe M; *vt* ~ around\ dar órdenes
**botany** [BAH•tu•nee] *n* botánica F
**both** [both] *pron adj* ambos; *adv* el mismo
**bother** [BAH•thur] *vt* molestar M
**bottle** [BAH•tl] *n* botella F
**bottom** [BAH•tum] *n* fondo M
**boulder** [BOL•dur] *n* rodado M
**bounce 1** [bouns] *vi vt* lanzar
**bounce 2** [bouns] *n* golpazo M
**bouncer** [BOUN•sur] *n* guardían de un cafe M
**bound** [bound] *adj* (to be ~ for) obligado atado con destino
**boundary** [BOUN•du•ree] *n* límite M

**bout** |bout| *n* encuentro

**bovine** |BO•vuyn| *adj* bovino

**bow 1** |bou| *vt vi n* saludar; inclinarse; arco M

**bow 2** |bo| *n* nudo (knot) M

**bow tie** |BOW tuy| *n* corbata de lazo F

**bowels** |boulz| *npl* intestinos M

**bowl** |bol| *n* escudilla F

**bowling** |BO•ling|| *n* deporte de bochas M

**box 1** |bahks| *n* caja F

**box 2** |bahks| *vt* boxear contra

**box office** | ~ AU•fis| *s* taquilla F

**boxer** |BAHK•sur| *n* boxeador M

**boxing** |BAHK•sing| *n* boxeo M

**boy** |boi| *n* niño M

**boycott** |BOI•kaht| *n vt* boicot M

**bra** |brah| *n* sostén M

**brace** |brais| *n* abrazadera F

**bracelet** |BRAI•slit| *n* brazalete M

**bracket (in writing)** |BRA•kit| *n* cartela F

**brag** |brag| *vi* fanfarronear

**braid** |braid| *n* trenza F *vt* trenzar

**brain** |brain| *n* cerebro M; *vt* romper la cabeza

**brake** |braik| *vi n* freno M; *vt vi* frenar

**bran** |bran| *n* afrecho M

**branch** |branch| *n* rama F

**brand 1** |brand| *n* marca F; *vt* marcar

**brand 2** |brand| *vt* (cattle etc) marcar; herrar

**brand-new** |brand•NOO| *adj* nuevecito M

**brandy** |BRAN•dee| *n* coñac M

**brash** |brash| *adj* impetuoso

**brass** |bras| *n* metal; bronce M

**brat** |brat| *n* mocoso M

**brave** |braiv| *adj* valiente; *vt* afrontar

**bravery** |BRAI•vu•ree| *n* bravura F

**brawl** |braul| *n* disputa F

**brawn** |braun| *n* carne dura F

**bray** |brai| *vi* rebuznar

**breach 1** |breech| *n vt* brecha F (*in wall*)

**breach 2** |breech| *n* infracción F (*of contract*)

**bread** |bred| *n* pan

**breadth** |bredth| *n* anchura F

**break 1** |braik| *vt vi* romper M

**break 2** |braik| *n* rompimiento M

**breakdown** |BRAIK•doun| *n* derrumbamiento M (machine)

**breakfast** |BREK•fust| *n* desayuno M

**breast** |brest| *n* pecho M

**breath** |breth| *n* respiración F

**breathe** |breeth| *vi* respirar

**breathless** |BRETH•lis| *adj* jadeante; sin aliento

**breed 1** |breed| *vt* linaje M (animals)

**breed 2** |BREE•ding| *n* raza F (race)

**breeze** |breez| *n* brisa F

**brevity** |BRE•vi•tee| *n* brevedad F

**brew** |broo| *vt* hacer; *vi* fermentar; *n* cerveza F

**brewer** [BROO•ur] *n*
cervecero M

**brewery** [BROO•u•ree] *n*
cervecería F

**bribe** [bruyb] *n* soborno M; *vt*
sobornar

**brick** [brik] *n* ladrillo M

**bridal** [BRUY•dl] *adj* de la
novia M

**bride** [bruyd] *n* novia F

**bridegroom** [BRUYD•groom]
*n* novio M

**bridesmaid** [BRUYDZ•maid] *n*
dama de honor F

**bridge** [brij] *n* puente M; *vt*
tender un puente sobre

**brief** [breef] *adj* breve; corto; *n*
maletin M; *vt* dar instrucciones a

**briefcase** [BREEF•kais] *n*
cartera F

**briefly** [BREE•flee] *adv*
brevemente

**bright** [bruyt] *adj* brillante; listo
(clever)

**brilliance** [BRIL•lyuns] *n*
brillo M

**brilliant** [bril•LYUNT] *adj*
brillante

**bring** [bring] *vt* traer; ~ about\
causar; ~ back\ devolver; ~
on\ causar

**brisk** [brisk] *adj* activo rápido

**bristle** [BRI•sl] *vi* cerda F

**British** [BRI•tish] *adj* británico

**broad** [braud] *adj* ancho; in ~
daylight\ en pleno día

**broadcast** [BRAUD•kast] *vt*
difundir; *n* esparcimiento M

**brocade** [bro•KAID] *n*
brocado M

**broccoli** [BRAH•klee] *n*
bróculi M

**brochure** [bro•SHUR] *n*
folleto M

**broil** [hroil] *vt* asar

**broker** [BRO•kur] *n* agente M

**bronze** [brahnz] *n adj* bronce M

**brooch** [broch] *n* broche M

**brook** [brük] *n* arroyo M

**broom** [broom] *n* escoba F

**broth** [brauth] *n* caldo M

**brothel** [BRAH•thl] *n* burdel M

**brother** [BRUH•thur] *n*
hermano M

**brother-in-law**
[BRUH•thur•in•LAU] *n*
cuñado M

**brown** [braun] *adj* pardo;
moreno

**bruise** [brooz] *n* magulladura F;
*vt* magulladurar

**brunette** [broo•NET] *n* moreno

**brush** [bruhsh] *vt* cepillar; *n*
cepillo M

**Brussels** [BRUH•slz] *n* Bruselas

**brutal** [BROO•tl] *adj* brutal

**brute** [broot] *n* bruto M

**bubble** [BUH•bl] *vi* burbujear;
*n* burbuja F

**buck** [buhk] *vi* topetar

**bucket** [BUH•kit] *n* cubo M

**buckle** [BUH•kl] *n vt* arricés M

**bud** [buhd] *n vi* botón M

**Buddhism** [BOO•DI•zm] *n*
budismo M

**budge** [buhj] *vi vt* mover;
moverse

**budget** [BUH•jit] *n* presupuesto
M; *vi* prepuestar

**buffalo** [BUH•fu•LO] *n*
búfalo M

**buffet** [buh•FAI] *n* comida M

**bug** [buhg] *n* insecto M

**bugle** [BYOO•gl] *n* trompeta F

**build** [bild] *vt* construir

**builder** [BIL•dur] *n* constructor M

**building** [BIL•ding] *n* edificio M

**bulb** [buhlb] *n* bulbo M; cebolla F

**Bulgaria** [BUHL•GAI•ree•u] *n* Bulgaria

**bulge** [buhlj] *n* bulto M

**bull** [bül] *n* toro M

**bulldozer** [BÜL•do•zur] *n* valentón M

**bullet** [BÜ•lit] *n* bolita F

**bulletin** [BÜ•lu•tin] *n* boletin M

**bully** [BÜ•lee] *n* matón M

**bumblebee** [BUHM•bl•BEE] *n* abejarrón M

**bump** [buhmp] *n* choque; *vt* chocar M

**bumper** [BUHM•pur] *n* tope M (of car)

**bun** [buhn] *n* bollo M

**bunch** [buhnch] *n* manojo M

**bundle** [BUHN•dl] *n* atado M

**buoy** [BOO•ee] *n* boya F; *vt* hacer flotar; animar (coll)

**burden** [BUR•dn] *n vt* carga M

**bureau** [BYÜ•ro] *n* escritorio M (furniture); officina F (office)

**bureaucracy** [byü•RAH•kru•see] *n* burocracia F

**burglar** [BUR•glur] *n* ladrón M

**burial** [BU•ree•ul] *n* entierro M

**Burma** [BUR•mu] *n* Birmania

**Burmese** [bur•MEEZ] *adj* birmano

**burn** [burn] *n* quemadura F; *vi* quemarse; ~ down\ destruir con fuego

**burner** [BUR•nur] *n* quemador M

**burrow** [BUH•ro] *n vt* conejera F

**burst** [burst] *vt* reventar

**bury** [BU•ree] *vt* enterrar

**bus** [buhs] *n* autobús M

**bush** [büsh] *n* arbusto M

**bushel** [BÜ•shul] *n* medida para áridos F

**business** [BIZ•nis] *n* negocio M; *adj* de negocios

**businessman; ~woman** [BIZ•nis•MAN] *n* hombre de negocios; mujer de negocios

**bust** [buhst] *n* busto M (of statue)

**bustle** [BUH•sl] *n* movimiento M; *vi* bullir

**busy** [BI•zee] *adj* ocupado M

**busybody** [BI•zee•BAH•dee] *n* entremetido M

**but** [buht] *conj* pero; sino; excepto

**butcher** [BU•chur] *n* carnicero M

**butcher shop** [BUTCH•ur SHAHP] *n* carnicería F

**butler** [BUHT•lur] *n* despensero M

**butt** (of cigarette) [buht] *n* cabo M

**butter** [BUH•tur] *n* mantequilla; manteca F

**butterfly** [BUH•tur•FLUY] *n* mariposa F

**buttock** |BUH•tuk| *n* nalga F
**button** |BUH•tn| *n* botón M
**buy** |buy| *vt* comprar; *n* compra F
**buyer** |BUY•ur| *n* comprador M

**buzz** |buhz| *n* zumbido M (of insect)
**by** |buy| *prep* junto; a cerca de; al lado de ; ~ and large\ en conjunto; ~ oneself\ por si solo

# C

**cab** |kab| *n* taxi M
**cabbage** |KA•bij| *n* repollo M
**cabin** |KA•bin| *n* cabaña F
**cabinet** |KA•bi•nit| *n* gabinete M; vitrina F
**cable** |KAI•bl| *n* cable M; vi/vt cablegrafiar
**cackle** |KA•kl| *n* cacareo M
**cactus** |KAK•tes| *n* cacto M
**cadaver** |ku•DA•vur| *n* cadáver M
**cadet** |ku•DET| *n* segundón M
**cafeteria** |KA•fi•TEE•ree•u| *n* cafetería F
**cage** |kaij| *n* jaula F; *vt* enjaular
**cake** |kaik| *n* torta F; pastel M
**calcium** |KAL•see•um| *n* calcio M
**calculate** |KAL•kyoo•LAIT| *vt* calcular
**calculator** |KAL•kyoo•LAI•tur| *n* calculador M
**calendar** |KA•lin•dur| *n* calendario M
**calf** |kaf| *n* becerro M
**call** |kaul| *n* llamada F *vt* llamar(by phone téléphoner)
**calling** |KAU•ling| *n* profesión F

**calm** |kahm| *adj* tranquilo; calmoso
**calm down** |KALM DOUN| *vt/vi* calmar
**camel** |KA•mul| *n* camello M
**cameo** |KA•mee•O| *n* camafeo M
**camera** |KA•mu•ru| *n* cámara F
**cameraman** |KA•mu•ru•MAN| *n* operador de tomavistas M
**camp** |kamp| *n vi* campamento M
**campaign** |kam•PAIN| *n* campaña F: *vi* salir a campaña
**campground** |KAMP•ground| *n* campamento M
**can 1** |kan| *n* vaso bote M
**can 2** *vi-aux* poder
**Canada** |KA•nu•du| *s* Canadá
**canal** |ku•NAL| *n* canal M
**canary** |ku•NA•ree| *n* canario M
**cancel (call off)** |KAN•suhl| *vt* décommander; cancelar (appointment)
**cancer** |KAN•sur| *s* cáncer M
**candid** |KAN•did| *adj* cándido
**candidate** |KAN•di•DUT| *n* candidato M

**candle** [KAN•dl] *n* vela; candela F

**candor** [KAN•dur] *n* sinceridad F

**candy** [KAN•dee] *n* azucar M

**cane** [kain] *n* caña F; *vt* castigar con palmeto

**canine** [KAI•nuyn] *adj* canino M

**cannibal** [KA•ni•bl] *n* canibal M

**cannon** [KA•nun] *s* cañon M

**canoe** [ku•NOO] *n* canoa F

**canon** [KA•nun] *s* canónigo M

**canopy** [KA•nu•pee] *n* dosel M

**canvas** [KAN•vus] *n* lona F

**canyon** [KA•nyun] *n* cañón M

**cap** [kap] *n* gorra F; *vt* tapar; poner cápsula

**capacity** [ku•PA•ci•tee] *n* capacidad F

**cape 1 (clothing)** [kaip] *n* capotillo M

**cape 2 (geog)** *n* cabo M

**caper** [KAI•pur] *n* cabriola F

**capital** [KA•pi•tl] *n* capital F

**capitalism** [KA•pi•tu•LI•zm] *n* capitalismo M

**capsule** [KAP•sul] *n* cápsula F

**captain** [KAP•tin] *n* capitán M; *vt* captanear

**caption** [KAP•shun] *n* captura F

**captive** [KAP•tiv] *n* cautivo M

**capture** [KAP•chur] *n* captura F; *vt* capturar

**car** [kahr] *n* automóvil carro M

**carbon** [KAHR•bun] *n* carbono M

**carcass** [KAHR•kus] *n* cadáver M

**card** [kahrd] *n* carta F

**cardboard** [KAHRD•baurd] *n* cartón M

**cardiac** [KAHR•dee•AK] *adj* cardíaco

**cardigan** [KAHR•di•gun] *n* chaqueta F

**cardinal** [KAHR•di•nl] *n* cardenal M

**care** [kair] *n* cuidado cargo M

**care (about)** [kair] tener interés; cuidar de

**career** [ku•REER] *n* carrera F

**carefree** [KAIR•free] *adj* libre de cuidados

**careful** [KAIR•ful] *adj* cuidadoso; prudente

**careless** [KAIR•lis] *adj* descuidado

**caress** [ku•RES] *vt* cariciar; *n* acaricia F

**cargo** [KAHR•go] *n* carga F

**Caribbean (Sea)** [KU•ri•BEE•un] *n* caribe M

**carnal** [KAHR•nul] *adj* carnal

**carnation** [kahr•NAI•shun] *n* clavel M

**carnival** [KAHR•nu•vl] *n* carnaval M

**carnivorous** [kahr•NI•vu•rus] *adj* carnivoro

**carp** [kahrp] *n* carpa F

**carpenter** [KAHR•pun•tur] *n* carpintero M

**carpet** [KAHR•put] *n* alfombra F

**carriage** [KA•rij] *n* carruaje M

**carrot** [KA•rut] *n* zanahoria F

**carry** [KA•ree] *vt* llevar; traer

**cart** [kahrt] *n* carromato M; *vt* acarrear; llevar

**carton** [KAHR•tn] *n* caja; de cartón F

**cartoon** [kahr•TOON] *n*
caricatura F

**carve** [kahrv] *vt vi* tallar

**case** [kais] *n* caso M; in ~ of\
en caso de; in any ~\ en todo
caso

**cash** [kash] *n* dinero; efectivo
M; *vt* cobrar

**cash register** [KASH
RE•jis•tur] *n* caja F

**cask** [kask] *n* casco M

**casket** [KA•skit] *n* arqueta F

**cassette** [ku•SET] *n* caseta F

**cast 1** [kast] *n* cuadro de
actores M

**cast 2** *vt* echar

**castle** [KA•sl] *n* castillo M

**casual** [KA•zhoo•ul] *adj* casual

**cat** [kat] *n* gato M

**catalogue** [KA•tu•LAHG] *n vt*
catálogo M

**catapult** [KA•tu•PUHLT] *n*
catapulta F; *vt* lanzar con
catapulta

**cataract** [KA•tu•RAKT] *n*
catarata F

**catastrophe** [ku•TA•stru•fee] *n*
catastrófico M

**catch** [kach] *vt* coger; asir;
tomar; ~ a cold\ resfirarse; ~
up\ poner al dia; ~ up with\
alcanzar

**categorical** [KA•tu•GAU•ri•kl]
*adj* categórico

**category** [KA•tu•GAU•ree] *n*
categoria F

**cater (banquet etc)** [KAI•tr]
*vt* abastecer; proveer

**caterpillar** [KA•tur•PI•lur] *n*
oruga F

**cathedral** [ku•THEE•drul] *n*
catedral M

**Catholic** [KATH•lik] *adj n*
católico

**cattle** [KA•tl] *npl* ganado M

**cauliflower**
[KAH•lee•FLOU•ur] *n*
coliflor M

**cause** [kauz] *vt n* causa F; *vt*
causar

**caustic** [KAU•stik] *adj* cáustico

**caution** [KAU•shun] *n vt*
caución F

**cautious** [KAU•shus] *adj* cauto

**cavalry** [KA•vl•ree] *n*
caballería F

**cave** [kaiv] *n* cueva F; ~ in\
hundirse

**caveman** [KAIV•man] *n*
hombre de cuevas M

**cavity** [KA•vi•tee] *n* cavidad F

**cease** [sees] *vt vi* cesación F

**cease-fire** [SEES•FUYUR] *n*
alto el fuego M

**cedar** [SEE•dur] *n* cedro M

**cede** [seed] *vt vi* ceder

**cedilla** [si•DI•lu] *n* cedilla F

**celebrate** [SE•li•BRAIT] *vt vi*
celebrar

**celebration** [SE•li•BRAI•shun]
*n* celebración F

**celebrity** [si•LE•bri•tee] *n*
celebridad F

**celibate** [SE•li•but] *adj* célibe M

**Celtic** [SEL•tik] *adj* céltico

**cell** [sel] *n* celda F; (biol)
célula F

**cellar** [SE•lur] *n* sótano M

**cello** [CHE•lo] *n* violoncelo M

**cement** [si•MENT] *vt n*
cemento M

**cemetery** [SE•mi•TE•ree] *n*
cementerio M

**censor** [SEN•sur] *n vt* censor M

**censorship** [SEN•sur•SHIP] *n*
censura F

**census** [SEN•sus] *n* censo M

**centennial** [sen•TEN•ee•ul] *n*
centenario M

**center** [SEN•tur] *n* centro M

**centigrade** [SEN•ti•GRAID]
*adj* centígrado M

**centimeter** [SEN•ti•MEE•tur] *n*
centímetro M

**centipede** [SEN•ti•PEED] *n*
centípedo M

**central** [SEN•trul] *adj* central

**century** [SEN•chu•ree] *n*
centuria F

**ceramic** [si•RA•mik] *adj*
cerámico M

**cereal** [SI•ree•ul] *n* cereal M

**ceremony** [SE•ri•MO•nee] *n*
ceremonia F

**certain** [SUR•tn] *adj* fijo; cierto;
for ~\ seguro

**certainly** [SUR•tn•lee] *adv* con
certeza

**certainty** [SUR•tn•tee] *n*
certeza F

**certificate** [sur•TI•fi•kut] *n*
partida F

**certify** [SUR•tu•FUY] *vt*
certificar

**chain** [chain] *n* cadena F

**chain saw** [CHAIN sau] *n*
sierra F

**chair** [chai'ur] *n* silla F; *vt*
presidir

**chairman** [CHAI'UR•mun] *n*
presidente M

**chalk** [chauk] *n* creta F

**challenge** [CHA•linj] *vt n*
desafío desafiar M

**chamber** [CHAIM•bur] *n*
cámara F

**chameleon** [ku•MEEL•yun] *n*
camaleón F

**champagne** [sham•PAIN] *n*
champaña F

**champion** [CHAM•pyun] *n*
defensor; campeón M; *vt*
defender

**chance** [chans] *n* suerte; ventura
M; *n* casualidad; opportunidad
F; by ~\ por casualidad; *vt*
arriesgar; *vi* suceder

**chancellor** [CHAN•su•lur] *n*
canciller M

**change** [chainj] *n vt vi* cambio
cambiar M

**channel 1 (TV radio)**
[CHA•nul] *n* canal F

**channel 2 (water)** *vt* acanalar

**chant (rel)** [chant] *n* canto M;
*vt vi* cantar

**chaos** [KAI•ahs] *n* caos M

**chapel** [CHA•pl] *n* capilla F

**chaplain** [CHA•plen] *n*
capellán M

**chapter** [CHAP•tur] *n* capítulo M

**character** [KA•ruk•tur] *n*
carácter M

**characteristic**
[KA•ruk•tu•RI•stik] *n adj*
característico -a F

**charcoal** [CHAHR•col] *n*
carbón de leña M

**charge** [charj] *n vi vt* carga;
cargar F; *vt* pedir (elec) in ~
of\ responsable de; take ~ of\
encargarse

**charity** [CHA•ru•tee] *n*
caridad F
**charm** [chahrm] *n vt*
encantamiento M
**charming** [CHAHR•ming] *adj*
encantador M
**chart** [chahrt] *n* carta F; mapa
M; *vt* poner en una carta
**chase** [chais] *n* caza F; *vt* cazar;
*vt* preseguir; *vi* correr; *n*
percución; F
**chasm** [KA•zm] *n* quiebra F
**chaste** [chaist] *adj* puro casto
**chastise** [cha•STUYZ] *vt*
castigar
**chastity** [CHA•sti•tee] *n*
castidad F
**chat** [chat] *vi* charlar
**chatterbox** [CHA•tur•BAHKS]
*n* parlanchín M
**chauffeur** [SHO•fur] *n*
chófer M
**cheap** [cheep] *adj* barato
**cheapen** [CHEE•pn] *vt* abaratar
**cheat** [cheet] *vt vi* engañar;
defraudar; *vi* hacer trampas; *n*
trampa F
**cheater** [CHEE•tr] *n* estafador M
**check 1** [chek] *vt* contener;
comprobar; verificar
**check 2** (bill) *n* cuenta F
**check 3** (currency) *n* cheque M
**checkbook** [CHEK•buk] *n*
talonario de cheques M
**cheek** [cheek] *n* mejilla F
**cheer** [cheer] *vt* alegrar
**cheer up** *vi* alegrarse
**cheerful** [CHEER•ful] *adj*
alegre
**cheers** (drinking toast) [cheerz]
*excl* salud

**cheese** [cheez] *n* queso M
**cheetah** [CHEE•tu] *n*
leopardo M
**chef** [shef] *n* cocinero M
**chemical** [KE•mi•kul] *adj n*
químico M; *n* product quimico
**chemist** [KE•mist] *n*
farmacéutico M
**chemistry** [KE•mi•stree] *n*
química F
**cherish** [CHE•rish] *vt* alimentar
**cherry** [CHE•ree] *n* ceresa F
**chess** [ches] *n* ajedrez M
**chest** [chest] *n* cofre pecho M
**chestnut** [CHEST•nuht] *n*
castaña F
**chest of drawers** [ ~
DRAW•urz] *n* cómoda F
**chew** [choo] *vt* mascar
**chick** [chik] *n* polluelo M·
**chicken** [CHI•kin] *n* pollo M
**chicken pox** [ ~ pahks] *n*
viruelas locas
**chief** [cheef] *n* jefe M
**child** [chuyld] *n* hijo; hija; niño
**childbirth** [CHUYLD•burth] *n*
alumbramiento M
**childhood** [CHUYLD•hud] *n*
infancia niñez F
**childish** [CHUYL•dish] *adj*
infantil
**Chile** [CHI•lee] *n* Chile
**chill** [chil] *n* frío M; *vi vt* enfriar
**chilly** [CHI•lee] *adj* frío
**chime** [chuym] *n* campaneo; M
*vi* tañer
**chimney** [CHIM•nee] *n*
chimenea F
**chimpanzee** [chim•PAN•ZEE]
*n* chimpancé M
**chin** [chin] *n* barba; mentón F

China [CHUY•nu] n China
china [CHUY•nu] n porcelana F
Chinese [chuy•NEEZ] adj chino
chip [chip] n pedacito M; vt
    cortar; picar
chirp [churp] vi chirriar
chisel [CHI•zl] n vt cincel;
    cincelar M
chitchat [CHIT•chat] n
    cháchara F
chivalry [SHI•vl•ree] n
    caballería F
chive [chuyv] n cebollana F
chlorophyll [KLAU•ru•FIL] n
    clorifila F
chocolate [CHAU•ku•lut] n
    chocolate M
choice [chois] n escogimiento;
    selección M; n elección F
choir [kwuyr] n coro M
choke 1 [chok] vt ahogar;
    sofocar
choke 2 (of car) n obturador M;
    n estrangulador
cholera [KAH•lu•ru] n cólera F
choose [chooz] vi vt escoger
chop 1 [chahp] vt cortar
chop 2 (of meat) n corte M
chord [kaurd] n cordón M
chores [chaurz] npl tareas
chorus [KAU•rus] n coro M
Christ [kruyst] n Cristo M
christen [KRI•sn] vt bautizar
Christian [KRI•schun] adj n
    cristiano M
Christianity
    [KRI•schee•A•nu•tee] n
    cristiandad F
Christmas [KRIS•mus] n
    Navidad F
chrome [krom] n cromo M

chronic [KRAH•nik] adj
    crómico M
chronicle [KRAH•ni•kl] n
    crónica F
chronological
    [KRAH•nu•LAH•ji•kl] adj
    cronológico
chrysanthemum
    [kri•SAN•thi•mum] n
    crisantemo M
chubby [CHUH•bee] adj
    gordinflón
chuck [chuhk] vt cloquear
chuckle [CHUH•kl] vi reír
    cloquear
chunk [chuhnk] n pedazo M
church [church] n iglesia F
churn (butter) [churn] vt n
    mantequera batir F
chute [shoot] n cascada F
cider [SUY•dur] n sidra F
cigar [si•GAHR] n cigarro M
cigarette [SI•gu•RET] n
    cigarrillo M
cinder [SIN•dur] n ascua F
Cinderella [SIN•du•RE•lu] n la
    Cenicienta F
cinema [SI•nu•mu] n cine M
cinnamon [SI•nu•mun] n
    canela F
circle [SUR•kl] n círculo M;
circuit [SUR•kit] n circuito M
circular [SUR•cyu•lur] adj
    circular
circulate [SUR•kyu•LAIT] vi vt
    circular
circulation
    [SUR•kyu•LAI•shun] n
    circulación F
circumcision
    [SUR•cuhm•SI•zhun] n
    circuncisión F

**circumference**
[sur•CUHM•fu•runs] *n*
circunferencia F
**circumflex** [SUR•cuhm•FLEKS]
*adj* circunflejo
**circumstances**
[SUR•cum•STANS] *n*
circunstancias
**circus** [SUR•kus] *n* circo M
**cite** [suyt] *vt* citar
**citizen** [SI•ti•zn] *n* ciudadano M
**city** [SI•tee] *n* ciudad F
**city hall** [SIT•tee HAL] *n* casa
del Ayuntamiento F
**civic** [SI•vik] *adj* cívico
**civil** [SI•vl] *adj* civil
**civilization** [SI•vi•li•ZAI•shun]
*n* civilización F
**civilize** [SI•vi•LUYZ] *vt*
civilizar
**claim** [klaim] *n* demanda;
reclamación F; *vt* reclamar
**clam** [klam] *n* almeja F
**clamor** [KLA•mur] *n* clamor;
grito M
**clamp** [klamp] *n vt* tornillo M
**clan** [klan] *n* clan M
**clandestine** [klan•DE•stin] *adj*
clandestino
**clap** [klap] *vi* aplaudir; *n*
palmada F; *n* trueno M
(thunder)
**clarify** [KLA•ri•FUY] *vt*
clarificar
**clarinet** [KLA•ri•NET] *n*
clarinete M
**clarity** [KLA•ri•tee] *s* claridad F
**clash** [klash] *vi* sonar; chocar; *n*
choque M
**clasp** [klasp] *n* broche M *vt*
abrochar

**class** [klass] *n* clase F; *vt*
clasificar
**classic** [KLA•sik] *adj n* clásico M
**classical** [KLA•si•kl] *adj* clásico
**classified** [KLA•si•FUYD] *adj*
clasificado
**classified ad** [KLASS•i•FUYD
AD] *n* anuncio M
**classify** [KLA•si•FUY] *vt*
clasificar
**classroom** [KLAS•rum] *n*
clase M
**clause** [klauz] *n* cláusula F
**claw** [klau] *n* garfa F; ~ at *vi* \
rascar; agarrar
**clay** [klay] *n* arcilla F
**clean** [kleen] *adj* limpio; *vt*
limpiar
**cleaner** [KLEE•nur] *n*
limpiador M
**cleaning lady** [KLEE•ning
LAI•dee] *n* camarera F
**cleanliness** [KLEN•lee•nis] *n*
limpieza F
**clear** [kleer] *adj* claro; *vt*
aclarar
**clearance** [KLEE•runs] *n*
despejo; aclaramiento M
**clearing** [KLEE•ring] *n*
aclaramiento M
**clearly** [KLEER•lee] *adv*
claramente
**cleavage** [KLEE•vij] *n*
hendidura; división F
**cleaver** [KLEE•vur] *n* cuchilla
de carnicero F
**clench** [klench] *vt* clavar
**clergy** [KLUR•jee] *n* clero M
**clerical** [KLE•ri•kl] *adj* clerical
**clerk** [klurk] *n* empleado M
**clever** [KLE•vur] *adj* avisado

**client** |KLUY•unt| *n* cliente M

**clientele** |KLUY•un•TEL| *n* clientela F

**cliff** |klif| *n* risco M; escarpa F

**climate** |KLUY•mit| *n* clima F

**climax** |KLUY•maks| *n* culminación F

**climb** |kluym| *n* subida F; *vt vi* trepar subir

**cling** |kling| *vi* adherirse; pegarse

**clinic** |KLI•nik| *n* clínica F

**clinical** |KLI•ni•kl| *adj* clínico

**clip 1** |klip| *n* pinza F; *vt* cortar golpear (coll)

**clip 2 (paper)** sujeta papeles M

**clippers** |KLI•purz| *npl* tijeras

**cloak** |klok| *n* capa F

**clock** |klahk| *n* reloj M

**clockwise** |KLAHK•wuyz| *adj adv* en el sentido de las saetas del reloj

**clog** |klahg| *vt vi* embarazar; obstruir

**cloister** |KLOI•stur| *n* claustro M

**close 1** |klos| *adj adv* cerrado; cerca

**close 2** |kloz| *vt vi* cerrar

**closet** |KLAH•zit| *n* gabinete M

**cloth** |klauth| *n* tela F

**clothe** |kloth| *vt* vestir

**clothes** |klothz| *npl* ropa F

**clothing** |KLO•thing| *n* vestidos

**cloud** |kloud| *n* nube F

**cloudy** |KLOU•dee| *adj* nuboso

**clove 1** |klov| *n* clavero; clavo M

**clove 2** |klov| (of garlic) *n* diente de ajo

**clover** |KLO•vur| *n* trébol M

**clown** |kloun| *n* bufón M

**club** |kluhb| *n* clava F; *vt* apalear

**cluck** |cluhk| *vi* cloquear

**clue** |kloo| *n* guía; pista F; not to have a ~\ no tener la menor idea

**clump** |kluhmp| *n* masa F

**clumsy** |KLUHM•zee| *adj* torpe

**cluster** |KLUH•stur| *n* grupo M

**clutch 1** |kluhch| *n* embrague M

**clutch 2** *vt* ( ~ at ) *vi* agarrar; tratar de coger

**clutter** |KLUH•tur| *vt* poner en desorden; *n* desorden M

**coach** |koch| *n* coche M

**coach** (sports) |koch| *n* entrenador M; *vt* entrenar

**coal** |kol| *n* carbón M

**coarse** |kaurs| *adj* grosero

**coast 1** |kost| *n* costa F

**coast 2** *vi* bordear

**coat** |kot| *n* chaqueta F; abrigo M; pelo M (animal); *vt* cubrir; revestir

**coax** |koks| *vt* persuadir; engastusar

**cobblestones** |KAH•bl•STONZ| *npl* guijarros M

**cobweb** |KAHB•web| *n* telaraña F

**cocaine** |ko•KAIN| *n* cocaína F

**cock 1** |kahk| *n* gallo M

**cock 2 (a gun)** *vt* amartillar

**cockroach** |KAHK•roch| *n* cucaracha F

**cocktail** |KAHK•tail| *n* cóctel M

**cocoa** |KO•ko| *n* cacao M

**coconut** |KO•ku•nuht| *n* coco M

**cocoon** |ku•KOON| *n* capullo M

**cod** |kahd| *n* bacalao M

**code** [kod] *n* código M; cifra F;
*vt* cifrar

**coerce** [ko•URS] *vt* coercer

**coffee** [KAU•fee] *n* café M

**coffee break** [KAU•fee
BRAIK] *n* pausa F

**coffee cup** [KAU•fee KUP] *n*
taza de café F

**coffee pot** [KAU•fee PAHT] *n*
cafetera F

**coffee shop** [KAU•fee
SHAHP] *n* café M

**coffin** [KAU•fin] *n* ataúd M

**coherent** [ko•HEE•runt] *adj*
coherente

**coil** [koil] *n* rollo; *vt* arrollar

**coin** [koin] *n* moneda F

**coincide** [ko•IN•suyd] *vi*
coincidir

**coincidence** [ko•IN•si•duns] *n*
coincidencia F

**cold** [kold] *adj n* frío M; be ~\
tener frío; it is ~\ hace frío;
have a ~\ estar constipado

**cold-blooded** [-BLU•did] *adj*
de sangre fría

**colon** [KO•lun] *n* colon M

**colony** [KAH•lu•nee] *n*
colonia F

**color** [KUH•lur] *n vt* color M

**color-blind** [KUH•lor bluynd]
*adj* daltoniano M

**colorful** [KUH•lur•ful] *adj*
pintoresco

**color television** [KUH•lor
TEL•i•VI•shn] *n* televisión de
color F

**colossal** [ku•LAH•sul] *adj*
colosal

**colt** [kolt] *n* potro M

**column** [KAH•luhm] *n*
columna F

**collaborate** [ku•LA•bu•RAIT]
*vi* colaborar

**collapse** [ku•LAPS] *n*
derrumbamiento; *vi*
derrumbarse

**collar** [KAH•lur] *n* cuello M

**collateral** [ku•LA•tu•rul] *n*
puesto lado a lado M

**colleague** [KAH•leeg] *n*
colega F

**collect** [ku•LEKT] *vt vi*
congregar; juntar

**college** [KAH•lij] *n* colegio M

**collide** (with) [ku•LUYD] *vi*
chocar

**colloquial** [ku•LO•kwee•ul] *adj*
familiar

**coma** [KAH•mu] *n* coma F

**comb** [kom] *n* peine M; *vt*
peinar

**combat** [KAHM•bat] *n* combate
M; *vt* combatir

**combination**
[KAHM•bi•NAI•shn] *n*
combinación F

**combine** [kum•BUYN] *vt*
combinar

**come** [cuhm] *vi* venir; llegar; ~
about\ ocurrir; ~ across\
encontrarse con; ~ back\
volver; ~ by\ obtener; ~
down\ bajar; ~ in\ entrar; ~
away\ separarse

**comeback** [KUHM•bak] *vi*
regresar

**comedian** [ku•MEE•dee•un] *n*
cómico M

**comedy** [KAH•mi•dee] *n*
comedia F

comet [KAH•mit] n cometa F

comfort [KUHM•furt] n
comodidad F vt confortar

comfortable [KUHMF•tur•bl]
adj confortable; comodo

comics (comic strip)
[KAH•miks] npl cómicas F

coming [KUH•ming] adj
próximo

comma [KAH•mu] n coma F

command [ku•MAND] n orden
mandato M

commander [ku•MAN•dur] n
comandante M

commence [ku•MENS] vt vi
comenzar

commend [ku•MEND] vt
encomendar

comment [KAH•ment] vi
comentar; n comento M

commerce [KAH•murs] n
comercio M

commercial [ku•MUR•shl] n
anuncio M

commission [ku•MI•shn] n
comisión F

commissioner [ku•MI•shu•nur]
n comisionado M

commit [ku•MIT] vt cometer;
perpetrar

committee [ku•MI•tee] n
comisión F

committment [ku•MIT•munt] n
orden M

commodity [ku•MAH•di•tee] n
mercadería F

common [KAH•mun] adj
común M

commonly [KAH•mun•lee] adv
comúnmente

commonplace
[KAH•mun•PLAIS] adj trivial

commotion [ku•MO•shn] n
conmoción F

communicate
[ku•MYOO•ni•KAIT] vt vi
comunicar

communion [ku•MYOO•nyun]
n comunión F

communism
[KAH•myu•NI•zm] n
comunismo M

communist [KAH•myu•nist]
adj n comunista F

community [ku•MYOO•nu•tee]
n comunidad F

commute [ku•MYOOT] vt/vi
conmutar

compact [kahm•PAKT] adj
pacto; compacto

companion [kum•PA•nyun] n
compañero M

company [KUHM•pu•nee] n
compañia; visita (guests)
sociedad (business) F

compare [kum•PAIR] vt
comparar

comparison [kum•PA•ri•sn] n
comparación F

compartment division
[kum•PAHRT•munt] n
compartimiento M

compass [KAHM•pus] n
compás M

compassion [kum•PA•shn] n
lástima F

compassionate
[kum•PA•shu•nit] adj
compasivo

compatible [kum•PA•ti•bl] adj
compatible

**compel** [kum•PEL] *vt* compeler;
obligar

**compelling** [kum•PE•ling] *adj*
dominado

**compensate**
[KAHM•pun•SAIT] *vt*
compensar

**compensation**
[KAHM•pun•SAI•shn] *n*
reparación F

**compete** [kum•PEET] *vi*
competi; contender

**competence** [KAHM•pi•tuns] *n*
competencia F

**competent** [KAHM•pi•tunt] *adj*
competente capaz

**competition**
[KAHM•pu•TI•shn] *n*
competición F

**complacent** [kum•PLAI•sunt]
*adj* complacido

**complain** [kum•PLAIN] *vi*
lamentarse

**complaint** [kuhm•PLAINT] *n*
lamento M

**complement** [KAHM•pli•munt]
*vt* complemento M

**complete** [kum•PLEET] *adj*
completo; *vt* completar

**complex** [kahm•PLEKS] *adj*
complejo

**complexion** [kum•PLEK•shn] *n*
temperamento; aspeto; color M

**complicate** [KAHM•pli•KAIT]
*vt* complicar

**complicated**
[KAHM•pli•kai•tid] *adj*
complicado

**compliment** [KAHM•pli•ment]
*n vt* cumplimiento M

**comply** [kum•PLUY] *vi* cumplir

**component** [kum•PO•nunt] *n*
componente M

**compose** [kum•POZ] *vt*
componer

**composer** [kum•PO•zur] *n*
compositor M

**composition**
[KAHM•pu•ZI•shn] *n*
composición F

**composure** [kum•PO•zhur] *n*
calma F; sosiego M

**compound** [KAHM•pound] *adj*
compuesto

**comprehend**
[KAHM•pree•HEND] *vt*
entender

**comprehension**
[KAHM•pree•HEN•shn] *vt*
comprensión F

**comprehensive**
[KAHM•pree•HEN•siv] *adj*
comprensivo

**compress** [kum•PRES] *vt*
comprimir; condensar

**comprise** [kum•PRUYZ] *vt*
comprender; incluir

**compromise**
[KAHM•pru•MUYZ] *n*
compromiso; *vt vi* componer

**compulsive** [kum•PUHL•siv]
*adj* compulsivo

**computer** [kum•PYOO•tur] *n*
computadora F

**comrade** [KAHM•rad] *n*
compañero M

**conceal** [kun•SEEL] *vt* esconder

**concede** [kun•SEED] *vt vi*
conceder; ceder

**conceit** [kun•SEET] *n*
vanidad F

**conceited** [kun•SEE•tid] *adj*
orgulloso

**conceive** [kun•SEEV] *vt vi*
concebir

**concentrate**
[KAHN•sun•TRAIT] *vt vi*
concentrar(se)

**concept** [KAHN•sept] *n*
concepto M

**concern** [kun•SURN] *n* interés;
asunto M; ansiedad F; as far
as it concerns me\ en cuanto
a mi

**concerning** [kun•SUR•ning]
*prep* sobre

**concert** [KAHN•surt] *n*
concerto M

**concession** [kun•SE•shn] *n*
concesión F

**concise** [kun•SUYS] *adj*
conciso

**conclude** [kun•KLOOD] *vt vi*
concluir dar fin a

**concrete** [*n.* KAHN•kreet *adj.*
kahn•KREET] *n* lo concreto
M; *adj* concreto

**condemn** [kun•DEM] *vt*
condena; desaprobar

**condense** [kun•DENS] *vt vi*
condensar(se)

**condescending**
[KAHN•di•SEN•ding] *adj*
condescendiente

**condition** [kun•DI•shn] *n*
condición F; *vt* condicionar

**condolences** [kun•DO•lun•ciz]
*npl* pésame M

**condone** [kun•DON] *vt*
perdonar

**conduct** [*n.* KAHN•duhkt *v.*
kun•DUHKT] *n* conducta F

**conductor** [kun•DUHK•tur] *n*
conductor M

**cone** [kon] *n* cono M

**confectionery**
[kun•FEK•shu•NE•ree] *adj*
confitado

**confederation**
[kun•FE•du•RAI•shn] *n*
confederación F

**confer** [kun•FUR] *vt vi* conferir

**conference** [KAHN•fu•runs] *n*
conferencia F

**confess** [kun•FES] *vt vi*
confesar(se)

**confession** [kun•FE•shn] *n*
confesión F

**confidant** [KAHN•fi•DAHNT]
*n* confidente M

**confide** [kun•FUYD] *vt/vi*
confiar

**confidence** [KAHN•fi•duns] *n*
cinfianza F

**confident** [KAHN•fi•dunt] *adj*
confiante

**confidential**
[KAHN•fi•DEN•shl] *adj*
confidencial

**confine** [kun•FUYN] *vt* confinar

**confirm** [kun•FURM] *vt*
confirmar

**confirmation**
[KAHN•fur•MAI•shn] *n*
confirmación F

**confiscate** [KAHN•fi•SKAIT]
*vt* confiscar

**conflict** [*n.* KAHN•flikt *v.*
kun•FLIKT] *n* conflicto M; *vi*
chocar

**conform** [kun•FAURM] *vt vi*
conformarse

**conformist** [kun•FAUR•mist]
*adj n* conformista F

**confound** [kun•FOUND] *vt*
confundir

**confront** [kun•FRUHNT] *vt*
confrontar

**confuse** [kun•FYOOZ] *vt*
desordenar

**confusing** [kun•FYOO•zing]
*adj* confús

**confusion** [kun•FYOO•zhn] *n*
confusión F

**congestion** [kun•JES•chn] *n*
congestión F

**congratulate**
[kung•GRA•chu•LAIT] *vt*
congratular

**congregate**
[KAHNG•gri•GAIT] *vi*
congregar

**congregation**
[KAHNG•gri•GAI•shn] *n*
congregación F

**conjugation**
[KAHN•joo•GAI•shn] *n*
unión; conjunción F

**conjunction** [kun•JUHNK•shn]
*n* conjunción F

**connect** [ku•NEKT] *vt* unir;
conectar

**conquer** [KAHGN•kur] *vt*
conquistar

**conqueror** [KAHNG•ku•rur] *n*
conquistador M

**conquest** [KAHNG•kwest] *n*
conquista F

**conscience** [KAHN•shuns] *n*
conciencia F

**conscientious**
[KAHN•shee•EN•shus]] *adj*
concienzudo

**conscious** [KAHN•shus] *adj*
consciente

**consecrate** [KAHN•se•KRAIT]
*vt* consagrar

**consecutive** [kun•SE•cyu•tiv]
*adj* consecutivo

**consent** [kun•SENT] *n*
consentimiento M; *vi*
consentir

**consequence**
[KAHN•si•KWENS] *n*
consecuencia F

**conservation**
[KAHN•sur•VAI•shn] *n*
conservación F

**conservative** [kun•SUR•vu•tiv]
*adj n* conservativo M

**consider** [kun•SI•dr] *vt*
considerar

**considerable** [kun•SI•du•ru•bl]
*adj* considerable

**considerate** [kun•SI•du•rit] *adj*
considerardo

**considering** [kun•SI•du•ring]
*prep* considerando

**consist** [kun•SIST] *vi* consistir

**consistency** [kun•SI•stun•see] *n*
consistencia F

**consistent** [kun•SIS•tunt] *adj*
consistente

**consolation**
[KAHN•su•LAI•shn] *n*
consolación F

**console** [*n*. KAHN•sol *v*.
kun•SOL] *vt* consolar; *n*
consola F

**consolidate**
[kun•SAH•lu•DAIT] *vt*
consolidar

**consonant** [KAHN•su•nunt] *n*
consonante

**conspicuous** [kun•SPI•kyoo•us] *adj* conspicuo

**conspiracy** [kun•SPI•ru•see] *n* conspiración F

**constant** [KAHN•stunt] *n adj* constante M

**constellation** [KAHN•stu•LAI•shn] *n* constelación F

**constituent** [kun•STI•choo•int] *n* constitutivo M

**constitution** [KAHN•sti•TOO•shn] *n* constitución F

**constraint** [kun•STRAINT] *n* constreñimiento M

**construct** [kun•STRUHKT] *vt* construir

**construe** [kun•STROO] *vt* explicar; interpretar

**consulate** [KAHN•su•lit] *n* consulado M

**consult** [kun•SUHLT] *vt vi* consultar

**consume** [kun•SOOM] *vt* consumir

**consumer** [kun•SOOM•ur] *n* consumidor M

**consummate** [KAHN•su•MAIT] *vt* consumar

**consumption** [kun•SUHMP•shn] *n* consunción F

**contact** [KAHN•takt] *n* contener M; *vt* contacto

**contagious** [kun•TAI•jus] *adj* contagioso

**contain** [kun•TAIN] *vt* contener

**container** [kun•TAI•nur] *n* caja F

**contaminate** [kun•TA•mi•NAIT] *vt* contaminar

**contemplate** [KAHN•tum•PLAIT] *vt vi* contemplar

**contemporary** [kun•TEM•pu•RE•ree] *adj n* coetáneo; colega F

**contempt** [kun•TEMPT] *n* desprecio M

**contemptible** [kun•TEMP•tu•bl] *adj* despreciable

**contend** [kun•TEND] *v* contender

**content** [kun•TENT] *adj* contento

**contents** [KAHN•tents] *npl* contenido M

**contest 1** [KAHN•test] *n* contienda F

**contest 2** [kun•TEST] *vt* disputar

**context** [KAHN•tekst] *n* contexto M

**continent** [KAHN•ti•nunt] *n* continente M

**contingency** [kun•TIN•jun•see] *n* contingencia F

**continual** [kun•TI•nyoo•ul] *adj* continuo M

**continually** [kun•TI•nyoo•u•lee] *adv* incesantemente

**continuation** [kun•TI•nyoo•AI•shn] *n* continuación F

**continue** [kun•TI•nyoo] *v* continuar

**contract** [*n.* KAHN•trakt *v.* kun•TRAKT] *n* contrato M; *vi* contraer

**contraction** [kun•TRAK•shn] *n*
contracción F

**contradict** [KAHN•tru•DIKT]
*vt* contradecir

**contradiction**
[KAHN•tru•DIK•shn] *n*
contradicción F

**contrary** [KAHN•TRE•ree] *adj*
*n* contrario; lo contrario M

**contrast** [*n* KAHN•trast *v*
kun•TRAST] *n* contraste M

**contribute** [kun•TRI•byoot] *vt*
*vi* contribuir

**contribution**
[KAHN•tri•BYOO•shn] *n*
contribución F

**contrive** [kun•TRUYV] *vi*
idear; inventar

**control** [kun•TROL] *vt*
dominar; sujetar

**controller** [kun•TRO•lur] *n*
director; interventor M

**controversy**
[KAHN•tru•VUR•see] *n*
controversia F

**convalescence**
[KAHN•vu•LE•suns] *n*
convalecencia F

**convalescent**
[KAHN•vu•LE•sunt] *adj n*
convaleciente MF

**convene** [kun•VEEN] *vt* reunir;
convocar

**convenience** [kun•VEE•nyuns]
*n* conveniencia F

**convenient** [kun•VEE•nyunt]
*adj* conveniente

**convent** [KAHN•vent] *n*
convento M

**convention** [kun•VEN•shn] *n*
convocación F

**converge** [kun•VURJ] *vi*
converger

**conversant** [kun•VUR•sunt] *adj*
conocedor M

**conversation**
[KAHN•vur•SAI•shn] *n*
conversación F

**converse 1** [kun•VURS] *vi*
conversar

**converse 2** [KAHN•vurs] *n*
recíproca F

**conversion** [kun•VUR•zhn] *n*
conversión F

**convert** [*n*. KAHN•vurt *v*.
kun•VURT] *n* converso M *vt*
convertir

**convex** [kahn•VEKS] *adj*
convexo M

**convey** [kun•VAI] *vt* llevar;
transmitir

**conveyer belt** [kun•VAI•ur ~ ]
*n* banda transportadora F

**convict** [*n*. kahn•vikt *v*.
kun•VIKT] *n* condenado M; *vt*
declarar culpable

**convince** [kun•VINS] *vt*
convencer

**convincing** [kun•VIN•sing] *adj*
convincente

**convoy** [KAHN•voi] *n*
convoy M

**coo** [koo] *vi* arrullar M

**cook** [kuk] *n* cocinero M

**cookie** [KU•kee] *n* bizcochito
M; galleta F

**cooking** [KU•king] *s* cocina M

**cool** [kool] *adj* fresco; *vt* enfriar;
*vt* enfriarse; ~ down\ clamarse
(person)

**coolness** [KOOL•nis] *n* fresco M

**coop** [koop] *n* caponera F

**cooperate** [ko•AH•pu•RAIT] *vi*
cooperar

**cooperation**
[ko•AH•pu•RAI•shn] *n*
cooperación F

**coordinate** [*n.* ko•AUR•di•nit
*v.* ko•AUR•di•NAIT] *v*
coordinar

**coordination**
[ko•AUR•di•NAI•shn] *n*
coordinación F

**cop** [kahp] *n* policía F (coll)

**cope** [kop] *vi* contender

**copious** [KO•pee•us] *adj*
copioso

**copper** [KAH•pur] *n* cobre M

**copy** [KAH•pee] *n* copía F

**copyright** [KAH•pee•RUYT] *n*
derechos de propiedad

**coral** [KAU•rul] *n* coral M

**cord** [kaurd] *n* cordón M

**corduroy** [KAUR•du•ROI] *n*
pana F

**cork** [kaurk] *n* corcho M

**corksrew** [KAURK•skroo] *n*
sacacorchos M

**corn** [kaurn] *n* semilla F

**corner** [KAUR•nur] *n* esquina F

**cornice** [KAUR•nis] *n* cornisa F

**coronation** [KAU•ru•NAI•shn]
*n* coronación F

**corporal** [KAUR•pu•rul] *adj*
corporal

**corporation**
[KAUR•pu•RAI•shn] *n*
corporación F

**corpse** [kaurps] *n* cadáver M

**correct** [ku•REKT] *adj* correcto;
*vt* corregir

**correction** [ku•REK•shn] *n*
corrección F

**correctly** [ku•REKT•lee] *adv*
correctamente

**correspond** [KAU•ri•SPAHND]
*vi* corresponder

**correspondence**
[KAU•ri•SPAHN•duns] *n*
correspondencia F

**correspondent**
[KAU•ri•SPAHN•dunt] *n*
correspondiente M

**corresponding**
[KAU•re•SPAHN•ding] *adv*
corrspondiente M

**corridor** [KAU•ri•daur] *n*
corredor M

**corrode** [ku•ROD] *vt* corroer

**corrosion** [ku•RO•zhn] *n*
corrosión F

**corrupt** [ku•RUHPT] *adj*
corrupto

**corruption** [ku•RUHP•shn] *n*
corrupción F

**Corsica** [KAUR•si•ku] *n*
Córcega

**cosmetic** [kahz•ME•tik] *adj n*
cosmético M

**cosmopolitan**
[KAHZ•mu•PAH•li•tn] *adj n*
cosmopolita F

**cost** [kaust] *n* coste; costo;
precio M; *vt* calcular el coste
de; at all ~s\ cueste lo que
cueste

**costume** [KAH•styoom] *n*
traje M

**cot** [kaht] *n* cabaña F

**cottage** [KAH•tij] *n* casita F

**cotton** [KAH•tn] *n* algodón M

**couch** [kouch] *n* sofa M

**cough** [kauf] *n* tos M; *vi* toser

**council** [KOUN•sl] *n* concilio M

**counsel** [KOUN•sl] *n* consejo M

**counselor** [KOUN•su•lur] *n* consejero M

**count** [kount] *vt vi* contar; numerar

**counter** [KOUN•tur] *n* tablero M

**counteract** [KOUN•tur•AKT] *vt* contrarrestar

**counterfeit** [KOUN•tur•FIT] *adj* falsificado

**counterpart** [KOUN•tur•PAHRT] *n* duplicado M

**countess** [KOUN•tis] *n* condesa F

**countless** [KOUNT•lis] *adj* incontable

**country** [KUHN•tree] *n* país M

**countryman** [KUHN•tree•mun] *n* paisano M

**county** [KOUN•tee] *n* condado M

**coup** [koo] *n* golpe meastro M

**couple** [KUH•pl] *n* pareja F

**coupon** [KOO•pahn] *n* cúpon F

**courage** [KU•rij] *n* valor M

**courageous** [ku•RAI•jus] *adj* valeroso

**courier** [KU•ree•ur] *n* mensajero M

**course** [kaurs] *n* curso M; in due ~\ a su debido tiempo; in the ~ of\ en el transcurso de, durante; of ~\ desde luege; por supuesto

**court** [kaurt] *n* corte M; *vt* cortejar; buscar (trouble)

**courteous** [KUR•tee•us] *adj* atento

**courtesy** [KUR•ti•see] *n* cortesía F

**courtyard** [KAURT•yahrd] *n* patio M

**cousin** [KUH•zin] *n* primo; prima M

**cove** [kov] *n* abra F

**covenant** [KUH•vu•nunt] *n* convenio M

**cover** [KUH•vur] *vt* cubrir

**coverage** [KUH•vu•rij] *n* cobertura F

**covering** [KUH•vu•ring] *n* cubierta F

**covert** [KO•vurt] *adj* cubierto

**covet** [KUH•vit] *vt* codiciar; desar

**cow** [kou] *n* vaca F

**coward** [KOU•urd] *n* cobarde M

**cowardice** [KOU•ur•dis] *n* cobardía F

**cowardly** [KOU•urd•lee] *adj* cobarde

**cowboy** [KOU•boi] *n* vaquero M

**cower** [KOU•ur] *vi* agacharse

**coy** [koi] *adj* modesta

**cozy** [KO•zee] *adj* cómodo

**crab 1** [krab] *n* cangrejo M

**crab 2** *vi* quejarse

**crack** [krak] *n* crujido M

**cracker** [KRA•kur] *n* galletas

**cradle** [KRAI•dl] *n* cuna F

**craft** [kraft] *n* arte M

**crafty** [KRAF•tee] *adj* astuto

**cram** [kram] *vt* rellenar

**cramp** [kramp] *n* calambre M

**cranberry** [KRAN•BE•ree] *n* arándano M

**crane** [krain] *n* grulla F

**crank** [krank] *n* manubrio M; manivela F

**cranky** [KRANG•kee] *adj* irritable

**crape** [kraip] *n* crespón M

**crash** [krash] *n* golpazo M; accidente M; *vt* estrellar; *vi* quebrar con estrépito

**crate** [krait] *n* canasta F; *vt* embalar

**crater** [KRAI•tur] *n* cráter M

**crave** [kraiv] *vt* suplicar; ansiar

**crawl** [kraul] *vi* arrastrarse

**crayfish** [KRAI•fish] *n* langosta F

**crayon** [KRAI•un] *n* barrita de color F

**craze** [kraiz] *n* manía F

**crazy** [KRAI•zee] *adj* loco

**creak** [kreek] *vi* crujir

**cream** [kreem] *n* crema F; *vt* batir (coll)

**creamy** [KREE•mee] *adj* cremoso

**create** [kree•AIT] *vt* crear

**creation** [kree•AI•shn] *n* creación F

**creative** [kree•AI•tiv] *adj* creador

**creator** [kree•AI•tur] *n* creado M

**creature** [KREE•chur] *n* criatura F

**credible** [KRE•di•bl]] *adj* creíble

**credit** [KRE•dit] *n* crédito M

**credit card** [KRE•dit KARD] *n* tarjeta de crédito F

**creed** [kreed] *n* credo M

**creek** [kreek] *n* abra F

**creep** [kreep] *vi* deslizarse

**crescent** [KRE•snt] *n* media luna F (moon)

**crest** [krest] *n* cresta F

**crevice** [KRE•vis] *n* hendidura F

**crew** [kroo] *n* equipo M

**crib** [krib] *n* comedero M

**cricket** [KRI•kit] *n* grillo M

**crime** [kruym] *n* crimen M

**criminal** [KRI•mi•nul] *adj* culpable; *n* criminal M

**crimson** [KRIM•sun] *adj* carmesí M

**cringe** [krinj] *vi* encogerse

**cripple** [KRI•pl] *n* cojo M

**crisis** [KRUY•sis] *n* crisis M

**crisp** [krisp] *adj* crespo

**criterion** [kruy•TEER•ree•un] *n* crierio M

**critic** [KRI•tik] *n* crítico M

**criticism** [KRI•ti•SI•zm] *n* crítica F

**criticize** [KRI•ti•SUYZ] *vt vi* criticar

**croak** [krok] *vi* graznido M

**crochet** [kro•SHAI] *n* hacer ganchillo

**crocodile** [KRAH•ku•DUYL] *n* cocodrilo M

**crook** [kruk] *n* curva F

**crooked** [KRU•kid] *adj* torcido

**crop** [krahp] *n* cultivo M; *vi* cortar; ~ up\ surgir

**cross** [kraus] *n* cruz F; *vt vi* cruzar; contariar (oppose); ~ off/out\ tachar

**crossfire** [KRAUS•fuyr] *n* fuego cruzado M

**crossroads** [KRAUS•rodz] *n* camino transveral M

**crossword (puzzle)** [KRAUS•wurd] *n* crucigrama F

**crow 1** [kro] *n* grajo; cuervo M

**crow 2** *vi* cacarear

**crowbar** [KRO•bahr] *n* palanca F

**crowd** [kroud] *n* pandilla F; *vt* amontonar; llenar; *vi* amontonarse; reunirse

**crown** [kroun] *n* corona F

**crucial** [KROO•shl] *adj* crítico

**crucifix** [KROO•зi•FIKS] *n* crucifijo M

**crude** [krood] *adj* crudo

**cruel** [krooul] *adj* cruel

**cruise** [krooz] *n* crucero M; *viu* hacer un crucero

**crumb** [kruhm] *n* miga F

**crumble** [KRUHM•bl] *vt* destrizar

**crunch** [kruhnch] *vt* mascar

**crusade** [kroo•SAID] *n* cruzada F

**crush** [kruhsh] *n* compresión F; *vt* aplastar; arrugar; have a ~ on\ estar perdido por

**crust** [kruhst] *n* corteza F

**crutch** [kruhch] *n* muleta F

**cry** [kruy] *n* grito M; *vi* llorar; gritar; to be a far ~ from\ distar much de (coll)

**crystal** [KRI•stl] *n* cristal M

**Cuba** [KYOO•bu] *n* Cuba

**Cuban** [KYOO•bun] *adj* cubano

**cube** [kyoob] *n* cubo M

**cubic** [KYOO•bik] *adj* cùbico M

**cucumber** [KYOO•kuhm•bur] *n* cohombro M

**cuddle** [KUH•dl] *n* abrazo; estrecho M; *vt* abrazar

**cue** [kyoo] *n* indicación F

**cuff** [kuhf] *n* puño M; *vt* abofetear; off the ~\ de improviso

**culminate** [KUHL•mi•NAIT] *vi* culminar

**culprit** [KUHL•prit] *n* culpable M

**cult** [kuhlt] *n* culto M

**cultivate** [KUHL•ti•VAIT] *vt* cultivar

**cultural** [KUHL•chu•rul] *adj* cultural

**culture** [KUHL•chur] *n* cultura F

**cumulative** [KYOO•myu•lu•tiv] *adj* cumulativo

**cunning** [KUH•ning] *adj* hábil

**cup** [kuhp] *n* taza F; copa F (prize)

**cupboard** [KUH•burd] *n* aparador M

**curate** [KYOO•rit] *n* coadjutor M

**curb** [kurb] *n* barandilla F

**curdle** [KUR•dl] *vt* cuajar

**cure** [kyoour] *n* cura F; *vt* curar

**curfew** [KUR•fyoo] *n* queda; toque de queda

**curiosity** [KYOOUR•ree•AH•si•tee] *n* curiosidad F

**curious** [KYOOUR•ree•us] *adj* curioso

**curl** [kurl] *n* rizo M; *vt* rizar, *vt* rizarse (hair)

**curly** [kurl] *adj* rizado

**currant** [KUH•runt] *n* grosella F

**currency** [KU•run•see] *n* curso M

**current** [KU•runt] *adj n* corriente; ~ events\ asuntas de actualidad *npl* M

**curse** [kurs] *n* madición F; *vt* maldecir; *vi* decir palabrotas

**curtail** [kur•TAIL] *vt* acortar

**curtain** [KUR•tn] *n* cortina F

**curve** [kurv] *n* curva F; *vt* encurvar; *vi* encorvarse

**cushion** [KU•shn] *n* cojín M

**custard** [KUH•sturd] *n* flan M

**custodian** [KUH•STO•dyun] *n*
custodio M

**custody** [KUH•stu•dee] *n*
guarda F

**custom** [KUH•stum] *n*
costumbre M

**customer** [KUH•stu•mur] *n*
cliente M

**cut** [kuht] *n* corte M; *v* cortar;
~ across; through\ atravesare;
~ back/down\ reducir; ~ in\
interrumpir; ~ out\ recortrar;
~ up\ cortar en pdeazos

**cute** [kyoot] *adj* lindo; listo

**cutlery** [KUHT•lu•ree] *n*
cuchillería F

**cutlet** [KUHT•lit] *n* chuleta F

**cycle** [SUY•kl] *n* ciclo M; *vi* ir
en bicicleta

**cyclical** [SIK•lih•kul] *adj* ciclico

**cyclone** [SUY•klon] *n* ciclòn M

**cynic** [SI•nik] *n* cínico M

**cynical** [SI•ni•kl] *adj* cìnico

**cypress** [SUY•pris] *n* ciprés M

**cyst** [sist] *n* quiste M

**czar** [zahr] *n* zar M

**Czech** [chek] *adj* checo

**Czechoslovakia**
[CHE•ko•slo•VAH•kee•uh] *n*
Checoslovaquia

# D

**dad** [dad] *n* papà M

**daffodil** [DA•fu•DIL] *n*
narciso M

**daily** [DAI•lee] *adj* diario

**dairy** [DAI•ree] *adj* lecherìa F

**daisy** [DAI•zee] *n* margarita F

**dam** [dam] *n* dique M; *vt*
embalsar

**damage** [DA•mij] *n* daño M; *vt*
dañare; estropear

**damaging** [DA•mij•ing] *adj*
prejudicial

**damp** [damp] *adj* húmedo; *n*
humidad F

**dampen** [DAM•pun] *vt* mojar

**dance** [dans] *vt vi* bailar; *n*
baile M

**dancer** [DAN•sur] *n*
bailador M

**dandelion** [DAN•di•LUY•un] *n*
amargón M

**dandruff** [DAN•druhf] *n*
caspa F

**danger** [DAIN•jur] *n*
peligro M

**dangerous** [DAIN•ju•rus] *adj*
peligroso

**dangle** [DANG•gl] *vt* colgar

**dare** [dair] *n* desafio M; *vt*
desafiar; *vi* attreverse a; I ~
say\ probablemente

**daredevil** [DAIR•de•vl] *n*
atrevido M

**daring** [DAI•ring] *adj* atrevido

**dark** [dahrk] *adj* obscuro M; in
the ~\ a oscuras

**darken** [DAHR•kn] *vt*
obscurecer

**darkness** [DAHRK•nis] *n*
obscuridad F

**darling** [DAHR•ling] *adj n*
querido M

**darn** [dahrn] *vt* zurcir

**dart** [dahrt] *n* dardo M; *vt*
lanzarse

**dash** [dash] *n* punta F; poquito
(small amount) *vi* precipitarse

**dashboard** [DASH•baurd] *n*
guardafango M

**data** [DAI•tu] *n* datos

**date1** [dait] *n* fecha F; to ~\
hasta la fecha; *vt* fechar; *vi*
datar

**date 2** [dait] (fruit) *n* dátril M

**daughter** [DAU•tur] *n* hija F

**daughter-in-law**
[DAU•tur•in•LAU] *s* nuera F

**daunt** [DAUN•ting] *vt* intimidar

**dawdle** [DAU•tur] *vi* perder el
tiempo

**dawn** [daun] *n* alba M

**day** [dai] *n* día M

**daybreak** [DAI•braik] *n*
amanecer M

**daydream** [DAI•dreem] *vi*
ensueño M

**daze** [daiz] *n* aturdimiento M; *vt*
aturdir

**dazzle** [DA•zl] *vt* encandilar

**dead** [ded] *adj* muerto; stop ~\
parar en seco; in the ~ of
night\ en plena noche; the ~\
los mertos

**deadline** [DED•luyn] *n* linea
vedada; fecha F

**deadly** [DED•lee] *adj* mortal

**deaf** [def] *adj* sordo

**deafen** [DE•fn] *vt* ensordecer

**deafening** [DE•fu•ning] *adj*
ensordecedor

**deal** [deel] *n* negociación F; *vt*
distribuir; ~ with\ tratar con

**dealer** [DEE•lur] *s*
comerciante M

**dealings** [DEE•lingz] *npl*
negocios F

**dean** [deen] *n* decano M

**dear** [deer] *adj* querido

**death** [deth] *n* muerte M

**debacle** [du•BAH•kl] *n*
deshielo M

**debase** [di•BAIS] *vt* rebajar

**debate** [di•BAIT] *n* debate M

**debauchery** [di•BAU•chu•ree]
*n* crápula F

**debit** [DE•bit] *n* debe M

**debt** [det] *n* deuda F

**debtor** [DE•tur] *n* deudor M

**debut** [DAI•byoo] *n* estreno M;

**decade** [DE•kaid] *n* década F

**decadence** [DE•ku•duns] *n*
decadencia F

**decadent** [DE•ku•dunt] *adj*
decadente

**decanter** [di•KAN•tur] *n*
garrafa F

**decay** [di•KAY] *n* decaimiento
M; decadencia F (tooth); *vi*
decaer; *vi* decaer (tooth)

**deceased** [di•SEEST] *adj*
muerto M

**deceit** [di•SEET] *n* engaño M

**deceitful** [di•SEET•ful] *adj*
engañoso

**deceive** [di•SEEV] *vt vi*
engañar

**December** [di•SEM•bur] *n*
diciembre M

**decency** [DEE•sn•see] *n*
decencia F
**decent** [DEE•sunt] *adj* decente
**deception** [di•SEP•shn] *n*
engaño M
**decide** [di•SUYD] *vt* decidir
**decimal** [DE•si•ml] *n* decimal
**decimate** [DE•si•MAIT] *vt*
diezmar
**decipher** [di•SUY•fur] *vt*
descifrar
**decision** [di•SI•zhn] *n*
decisión F
**decisive** [di•SUY•siv] *adj*
decisivo
**deck** [dek] *n* puente M
**declare** [di•KLAIR] *vt* declarar
**decline** [di•KLUYN] *n*
declive M
**decode** [dee•KOD] *vt* descifrar
**decompose** [DEE•kum•POZ] *vi*
descomponer
**decorate** [DE•ku•RAIT] *vt*
decorar
**decoration** [DE•ku•RAI•shn] *n*
decoración F
**decorum** [di•KAU•rum] *n*
decoro M
**decoy** [DEE•coi] *n* reclamo M
**decrease** [dee•CREES] *vt*
decrecer; disminuir
**decree** [di•KREE] *n* decreto M;
*vt* decretar
**decrepit** [di•KRE•pit] *adj*
decrépito
**dedicate** [de•di•KAIT] *vt*
dedicar
**dedication** [DE•di•KAI•shn] *n*
dedicación F
**deduct** [di•DUHKT] *vt* deducir;
substraer

**deduction** [di•DUHK•shn] *n*
deducción F
**deed** [deed] *n* acción F;
escritura F (legal)
**deem** [deem] *vt* estimar
**deep** [deep] *adj* hondo;
profundo; go off the ~ end\
enfadarse; be ~ in thought\
estar absorte en sus
pensiamentos; ~ freeze *n*\
congleador M
**deepen** [DEEP•in] *vt*
profundizar
**deer** [deer] *n* ciervo M
**deface** [di•FAIS] *vt* desfigurar
**defamation** [DE•fu•MAI•shn]
*n* difamación F
**defame** [di•FAIM] *vt* difamar
**default** [di•FAULT] *n* dejar de
cumplir
**defeat** [di•FEET] *n* derrota F
**defect** [*n*. DEE•fekt] *n*
defecto M
**defend** [di•FEND] *vt* defender
**defendant** [di•FEN•dunt] *n*
acusado M
**defense** [di•FENS] *n* defensa F
**defensive** [di•FEN•siv] *adj*
defensivo
**defer** [di•FUR] *vt* diferir
**defiance** [di•FUY•uns] *n*
desafiar F
**deficiency** [di•FI•shun•see] *n*
deficiencia F
**deficient** [di•FI•shunt] *adj*
deficiente
**deficit** [DE•fi•sit] *n* insuficie-
cia F
**defile** [di•FUYL] *vt* manchar
**define** [di•FUYN] *vt* definir

**definite** [DE•fi•nit] *adj*
definidio

**definitely** [DE•fi•nit•lee] *adv*
definidamente

**definition** [DE•fi•NI•shn] *n*
definición F

**deflate** [di•FLAIT] *vt* desinflar

**deflect** [di•FLEKT] *vt* desviar

**deformed** [di•FAURMD] *adj*
deformado

**defraud** [di•FRAUD] *vt*
defraudar

**defrost** [di•FRAUST] *vt* quitar
el hielo

**deft** [deft] *adj* diestro

**defy** [di•FUY] *vt* desafiar

**degenerate** [*adj.* di•JE•nu•rit *v.*
di•JE•nu•RAIT] *adj*
degenerado *vt* degenerar

**degrading** [di•GRAI•ding] *adj*
degradante

**degree** [di•GREE] *n* grado M

**dehydrate** [di•HUY•drait] *vt*
deshidratar

**deity** [DAI•i•tee] *n* deidad F

**dejected** [di•JEK•tid] *adj*
acongojado

**delay** [di•LAI] *n* tardanza F; *vt*
retardar dilatar

**delegate** [*n.* DE•li•gut *v.*
DE•li•GAIT] *n* delegado M; *vt*
delegar

**delegation** [DE•li•GAI•shn] *n*
delegación F

**delete** [di•LEET] *vt* borrar

**deliberate** [*adj.* di•LI•brut *v.*
du•LI•bu•RAIT] *adj*
deliberado; *vt* reflexionar

**delicacy** [DE•li•ku•see] *n*
delicadeza F

**delicate** [DE•li•kut] *adj*
delicado

**delicatessen** [DE•li•ku•TE•sun]
*n* fiambres

**delicious** [di•I I•shus] *adj*
delicioso

**delight** [di•LUYT] *n* encanto M

**delighted** [di•LUY•tid] *adj*
gozoso

**delightful** [di•LUYT•ful] *adj*
ameno

**delinquent** [di•LING•kwunt]
*adj n* delincuente M

**delirious** [di•LI•ree•us] *adj*
delirante

**deliver** [di•LI•vur] *vt* libertar

**delivery** [di•LI•vu•ree] *n*
entrega F

**deluge** [DE•lyooj] *n* diluvio M

**delusion** [di•LOO•zhn] *n*
delusión F

**demagogue** [DE•mu•GAHG] *n*
demagogo M

**demand** [di•MAND] *n*
demanda F; *vt* exigir; in ~\
muy popular; on ~\ a solicitud

**demanding** [di•MAN•ding] *adj*
exigente

**demeanor** [di•MEE•nur] *n*
conducta F

**demented** [di•MEN•tid] *adj*
demente

**demerit** [di•ME•rit] *n*
demérito M

**demobilize disarm**
[di•MO•bi•LUYZ] *vt*
desmovilizar

**democracy** [di•MAH•kru•see] *n*
democracia F

**democrat** [DE•mu•KRAT] *n*
demócrata F

**democratic** [DE•mu•KRA•tik]
*adj* democratico

**demolish** [di•MAH•lish] *vt*
demoler

**demonstrate**
[DE•mun•STRAIT] *vt*
demostrar

**demonstration**
[DE•mun•STRAI•shn] *n*
demostración F

**demonstrative**
[di•MAHN•stru•tiv] *adj*
demostrativo

**demoralize**
[di•MAU•ru•LUYZ] *vt*
desmoralizar

**demure** [di•MYOOR] *adj* serio

**den** [den] *n* guarida; caverna F

**denial** [di•NUYL] *n* negación F

**Denmark** [DEN•mahrk] *n*
Dinamarca

**denounce** [di•NOUNS] *vt*
denunciar

**dense** [dens] *adj* denso

**density** [DEN•si•tee] *n*
densidad F

**dent** [dent] *n* mella F

**dental** [DEN•tl] *adj* dental

**dentist** [DEN•tist] *n* dentista M

**deny** [di•NUY] *vt* negar

**depart** (leave; set out)
[di•PAHRT] *vi* partir; salir

**department** [di•PAHRT•munt]
*n* departamento M

**department store**
[dee•PART•mint STAUR] *n*
almacén M

**departure** [di•PAHR•chur] *n*
salida F

**depend** [di•PEND] *vi* pender;
depender

**dependable** [di•PEND•u•bl]
*adj* seguro

**depict** [di•PIKT] *vt* representar

**deplete** [di•PLEET] *vt* vaciar

**deplorable** [di•PLAU•ru•bl] *adj*
deplorable

**deplore** [di•PLAUR] *vt* deplorar

**deport** [di•PAURT] *vt* deportar

**depose** [di•POZ] *vt* deponer

**deposit** [di•PAH•zit] *n* depósito
M; *vt* depositar

**depot** [DEE•po] *n* estación F

**depreciate** [di•PREE•shee•AIT]
*vi* depreciar

**depress** [di•PRES] *vt* deprimir

**depressed** [di•PREST] *adj*
deprimido

**depression** [di•PRE•shn] *n*
depresión F

**deprive** [di•PRUYV] *vt*
despojar

**depth** [depth] *n* profundidad F

**deputy** [DE•pyu•tee] *n*
diputado M

**derail** [di•RAIL] *vi* descarrilar

**deranged** [di•RAINJD] *adj*
desarreglado

**deride** [di•RUYD] *vt* burlarse

**derive** [di•RUYV] *vt* derivar

**descend** [di•SEND] *vt vi*
descender

**descendant** [di•SEN•dunt] *n*
descendiente M

**descent** [di•SENT] *n* descenso M

**describe** [di•SKRUYB] *vt*
describir

**description** [di•SKRIP•shn] *n*
descripción F

**desert** [*n.* DE•zurt *v.* di•ZURT]
*n* desierto M; *vt* abandonar

**deserter** [di•ZUR•tur] *n*
desertor M

**deserve** [di•ZURV] *vt* merecer

**deserving** [di•ZUR•ving] *adj*
merecedor

**design** [di•ZUYN] *n* plan M; *vt*
diseñar

**designate** [DE•zig•NAIT] *vt*
indicar

**designer** [di•ZUY•nur] *n*
dibujante M

**desirable** [di•ZUY•ru•bl] *adj*
deseable

**desire** [di•ZUYUR] *n* deseo M

**desist** [di•SIST] *vi* desistir

**desk** [desk] *n* escritorio M

**desolate** [DE•su•lut] *adj*
desolado; *n* desolación

**despair** [di•SPAIUR] *n*
desesperación F

**desperate** [DE•sprut] *adj*
desesperado

**desperation** [DE•spu•RAI•shn]
*n* desesperaciòn F

**despicable** [di•SPI•ku•bl] *adj*
despreciable

**despise** [di•SPUYZ] *vt*
despreciar

**despite** [di•SPUYT] *prep* a
despecho de

**despondent** [di•SPAHN•dunt]
*adj* desalentado

**despot** [DE•sput] *n* déspota F

**dessert** [di•ZURT] *n* postres

**destination** [DE•sti•NAI•shn] *n*
destinación F

**destiny** [DE•sti•nee] *n* destino M

**destitute** [DE•sti•TOOT] *adj*
destituido

**destroy** [di•STROI] *vt* destruir

**destruction** [di•STRUHK•shn]
*n* destrucción F

**destructive** [di•STRUHK•tiv]
*adj* destructivo

**detach** [di•TACH] *vt* desatar

**detail** [DEE•tail] *n* detalle M; *vt*
detallar; destacar (mill)

**detain** [di•TAIN] *vt* detener

**detect** [di•TEKT] *vt* averiguar;
percibir

**detection** [di•TEK•shn] *n*
descubrimiento M

**detention** [di•TEN•shn] *n*
detención F

**deter** [di•TUR] *vt* detener;
apartar

**detergent** [di•TUR•junt] *n*
detergente M

**deteriorate**
[di•TEER•ee•aur•RAIT] *vi*
deteriorar

**determination**
[di•TUR•mi•NAI•shn] *n*
determinación F

**determine** [di•TUR•min] *vt*
determinar

**detest** [di•TEST] *vt* detestar

**detonate** [DE•tu•NAIT] *vt*
detonar

**detour** [DEE•toor] *n* desvío M

**detract** [di•TRAKT] *vt* detraer

**detrimental** [DE•tri•MEN•tl]
*adj* perjudicial

**devastate** [DE•vu•STAIT] *vt*
devastar

**devastating** [DE•vu•STAI•ting]
*adj* devastador

**develop** [di•VE•lup] *vt*
desenvolver

**development** [di•VE•lup•munt]
*n* desarrolo M

**deviate** [DEE•vee•AIT] *vi*
desviar

**device** [di•VUYS] *n*
dispositivo M

**devil** [DE•vl] *n* diablo M

**devious** [DEE•vee•us] *adj*
desviado

**devise** [di•VUYZ] *vt* planear

**devoid** [di•VOID] *adj* falto

**devote** [di•VOT] *vt* dedicar

**devoted** [di•VO•tud] *adj*
consagrado

**devotion** [di•VO•shn] *n*
devoción F

**devour** [di•VOUUR] *vt* devorar

**devout** [di•VOUT] *adj* devoto

**dew** [doo] *n* rocío M

**diabetes** [DUY•u•BEE•teez] *n*
diabetis M

**diabetic** [DUY•u•BE•tik] *adj n*
diabético M

**diagnose** [DUY•ug•NOS] *vt*
diagnosticar

**diagnosis** [DUY•ug•NO•sis] *adj*
*n* diagnosis M

**diagonal** [duy•AG•nl] *adj*
diagnoal

**diagram** [DUY•u•GRAM] *n*
diagrama F

**dial** [duyul] *n* muestra M; *vt*
marcar

**dialect** [DUY•u•LEKT] *n*
dialecto M

**dialog** [DUY•u•LAHG] *n*
diálogo M

**diameter** [duy•A•mi•tur] *s*
diámetro M

**diamond** [DUY•mund] *n*
diamante M

**diary** [DUY•u•ree] *n* diario M

**dice** [duys] (sing: die) *npl* dados

**dictate** [DIK•tait] *vt* dictar

**dictation** [dik•TAI•shn] *n*
dictado M

**dictator** [DIK•TAI•tur] *n*
dictador M

**dictatorship**
[dik•TAI•tur•SHIP] *n*
dictadura F

**dictionary** [DIK•shu•NE•ree] *n*
diccionario M

**did** [did] *pp* do hice hizo

**die** [duy] *vi* morir; ~ down\
disminuir; ~ out\ extinguirse

**diet** [DUY•ut] *n* dieta M; *vi*
estar a regimen

**differ** [DI•fur] *vi* diferir

**difference** [DI•fruns] *n*
diferencia F

**different** [DI•frunt] *adj*
diferente

**differentiate**
[DI•fu•REN•shee•ait] *vt*
diferenciar

**difficult** [DI•fi•kult] *adj* difícil

**difficulty** [DI•fi•kul•tee] *n*
dificultad F

**diffuse** [di•FYOOZ] *vt* difundir

**dig** [dig] *vt* cavar; excavar; ~
out\ extraer; ~ up\ desenterrar

**digest** [*n* DUY•jest *v.*
duy•JEST] *n* reumen; *vt vi*
digerir

**digestion** [duy•JES•chn] *n*
digestión F

**digit** [DI•jit] *n* dedo M

**dignified** [DIG•ni•FUYD] *adj*
dignificado

**dignify** [DIG•ni•FUY] *vt*
dignificar

**dignity** [DIG•ni•tee] *n* dignidad

**digress** [duy•GRES] *vt*
desviarse

**dilate** [DUY•lait] *vt* dilatar

**dilemma** [di•LE•mu] *n* dilema F

**diligence** [DI•li•juns] *n*
diligencia F

**diligent** [DI•li•junt] *adj*
diligente

**dilute** [duy•LOOT] *vt* diluir

**dim** [dim] *adj* obscuro; ~ the
headlights\ bajar los faros

**dimension** [di•MEN•shn] *n*
dimensión F

**diminish** [di•MI•nish] *vt vi*
disminuir

**dimple** [DIM•pl] *n* hoyuelo M

**din** [din] *n* fragor M

**dine** [duyn] *vi* comer

**diner** [DUY•nur] *n* comensal M

**dinghy** [DING•gee] *n*
chinchorro M

**dingy** [DIN•jee] *adj* manchado

**dining room** [DUY•ning ~ ] *n*
comedor M

**dinner** [DI•nur] *n* comida F

**dinosaur** [DUY•nu•SAUR] *n*
dinsaurio M

**diocese** [DUY•u•seez] *n*
diócesis M

**dip** [dip] *n* bajada F; *vt*
sumergir; *vi* bajar; ~ into\
hojear

**diploma** [di•PLO•mu] *n*
diploma F

**diplomacy** [di•PLO•mu•see] *n*
diplomacia F

**diplomat** [DI•plu•MAT] *n*
diplomático M

**diplomatic** [DI•plu•MA•tik] *adj*
diplomático

**dire** [duyur] *adj* horrendo

**direct** [di•REKT] *adj* directo; *vt*
dirigir

**direction** [di•REK•shn] *n*
dirección F; *npl* insturc-
ciones F

**directly** [di•REKT•lee] *adv*
directamente

**director** [di•REK•tur] *n*
director M

**directory** [di•REK•tu•ree] *n*
directorio M

**dirt** [durt] *n* tierra F

**dirty** [DUR•tee] *adj* sucio; ~
trick\ mala jugada; *vt* ensuciar

**disabled** [di•SAI•bld] *adj*
inutilizado

**disadvantage**
[DI•sud•VAN•tij] *n*
desventaja F

**disagree** [DI•su•GREE] *vi*
desconvenir

**disagreement**
[DI•su•GREE•munt] *n*
discordancia F

**disappear** [DI•su•PEEUR] *vi*
desaparecer

**disappoint** [DI•su•POINT] *vt*
deceptionar

**disappointing**
[DI•su•POIN•ting] *adj*
decepcionante

**disappointment**
[DI•su•POINT•munt] *n*
desilusión F

**disapprove** [DI•su•PROOV] *vi*
desaprobar

**disarm** [di•SAHRM] *vt vi*
desarmar

**disarray** [DI•su•RAI] *n*
desorden M

**disaster** [di•ZA•stur] *n*
desastre M

**disastrous** [di•ZA•strus] *adj*
desastroso

**disavow** [DI•su•VOU] *vt*
repudiar

**discard (release)**
[di•SKAHRD] *vt* descartarse;
abandonar

**discern** [di•SURN] *vt* discernir

**discharge** [*n.* DIS•charj *v.*
dis•CHARJ] *n* descarga F;
lanzamiento M; *vt* descargar

**disciple** [di•SUY•pl] *n* disípulo M

**discipline** [DI•si•plin] *n*
desciplina F; *vt* disciplinar;
castigar (punish)

**disclose** [di•SKLOZ] *vt*
descubrir

**disclosure** [dis•KLO•zhur] *n*
descubrimiento M

**discomfort** [di•SKUHM•furt] *n*
incomodidad F

**disconnect** [DI•sku•NEKT] *vt*
desunir; separar

**discord** [DI•skaurd] *n*
discordia F

**discount** [DI•skount] *n*
descuento M

**discourage** [di•SKU•rij] *vt*
descorazonar; desalentar;
disuadir

**discourse** [DIS•kaurs] *n*
discurso M

**discover** [di•SKUH•vur] *vt*
descubrir

**discovery** [di•SKUH•vu•ree] *n*
descubrimiento M

**discredit** [dis•KRE•dit] *n*
discrédito M

**discreet** [di•SKREET] *adj*
discreto

**discrepancy** [di•SKRE•pun•see]
*n* discrepancia F

**discretion** [di•SKRE•shn] *n*
discreción F

**discriminate**
[di•SKRI•mi•NAIT] *vi*
discernir; ~ between\
distinguir entre

**discuss** [di•SKUHS] *vt* discutir

**discussion** [di•SKUH•shn] *n*
discución F

**disdain** [dis•DAIN] *n*
menosprecio M

**disease** [di•ZEEZ] *n*
enfermedad F; ~d *adj* \ enfermo

**disengage** [DI•sin•GAIJ] *vt*
desembarazar; sacar

**disfigure** [dis•FI•gyur] *vt*
desfigurar

**disgrace** [dis•GRAIS] *n*
desgracia F; *vt* deshonorar

**disgraceful** [dis•GRAIS•ful] *adj*
deshonroso

**disgruntled** [dis•GRUHN•tld]
*adj* descontento

**disguise** [dis•GUYZ] *n*
disfraz M

**disgust** [dis•GUHST] *n*
repugnancia F

**disgusting** [dis•GUH•sting] *adj*
repugnante

**dish** [dish] *n* plato M; ~ out\
distribtuir; ~ up\ servir

**dishearten** [dis•HAHR•tn] *vt*
descorazonar

**dishevelled** [di•SHE•vld] *adj*
desgreñado

**dishonest** [dis•AH•nist] *adj*
fraudulento; poco honorado

**dishonor** [dis•AH•nur] *n*
deshonor M

**dishwasher** [DISH•WAH•shur]
*n* lavaplatos M

**disillusion** [DIS•i•LOO•zhn] *n*
desilusión F

**disinfect** [DI•sin•FEKT] *vt*
desinfectar

**disinfectant** [DI•sin•FEK•tunt]
*n* desinfectante M

**disintegrate**
[di•SIN•tu•GRAIT] *vi*
desintegrar

**disinterested** [dis•IN•tru•stid]
*adj* desinteresado

**disk** [disk] *n* disco M

**dislike** [di•SLUYK] *n* aversión;
antipatia F; *vt* tener aversión a

**dislocate** [DIS•lo•kait] *vt*
dislocar

**disloyal** [dis•LOI•ul] *adj*
pérfido M

**dismal** [DI•zml] *adj* triste;
sombrio

**dismay** [di•SMAI] *n* desmayo M

**dismiss** [dis•MIS] *vt* despedir

**dismissal** [dis•MI•sl] *n*
despido M

**dismount** [dis•MOUNT] *vi*
desmontar

**disobedient**
[DI•so•BEE•dee•unt] *adj*
desobediente

**disobey** [DI•so•BAI] *vt*
desobedecer

**disorder** [di•SAUR•dur] *n*
desorden M

**disorganized**
[di•SAUR•gu•NUYZD] *adj*
desorganizado

**disoriented**
[di•SAU•ree•EN•tud] *adj*
desorientado

**disown** [dis•ON] *vt* repudiar

**disparaging** [di•SPA•ru•jing]
*adj* detractor

**dispassionate** [di•SPA•shu•nit]
*adj* desapasionado

**dispel** [di•SPEL] *vt* dispersar

**dispense** [di•SPENS] *vt*
dispensar

**dispenser** [di•SPEN•sur] *n*
dispensador M

**disperse** [di•SPURS] *vt*
dispersar

**displace** [dis•PLAIS] *vt* dislocar

**display** [di•SPLAI] *n*
exhibición F

**displease** [dis•PLEEZ] *vt*
desplacer

**displeased** [dis•PLEEZD] *adj*
desagradable

**disposal** [di•SPO•zl] *n*
disposición F

**dispose** [di•SPOZ] *vt* disponer

**disposition** [DI•spu•ZI•shn] *n*
disposición F

**disprove** [dis•PROOV] *vt*
refutar

**dispute** [di•SPYOOT] *n*
desputar disputa F

**disqualify** [dis•KWAH•li•FUY]
*vt* inhabilitar

**disregard** [DIS•ree•GAHRD] *n*
• descuido M; *vt* desatender;
descuidar

**disreputable**
[dis•RE•pyu•tu•bl] *adj*
desacreditado

**disrespect** [DIS•ru•SPEKT] *n*
desacato M

**disrupt** [dis•RUHPT] *vt* romper; desgajar

**dissatisfy** [di•SAT•is•FUY] *vt* descontentar

**dissect** [duy•SEKT] *vt* disecar

**dissemble** [di•SEM•bl] *vt vi* disimular; fingir

**disseminate** [di•SE•mi•NAIT] *vt* diseminar

**dissent** [di•SENT] *n* disenso M

**dissimulate** [di•SI•myu•LAIT] *vt vi* disimular

**dissipate** [DI•si•PAIT] *vt* dispersar

**dissociate** [di•SO•shee•AIT] *vt* disociar

**dissolute** [DI•su•LOOT] *adj* disoluto M

**dissolve** [di•ZAHLV] *vt* disolver

**dissuade** [di•SWAID] *vt* disuadir

**distance** [DI•stuns] *n* distancia F; from a ~\ desde lejos; in the ~\ a lo lejos

**distant** [DI•stunt] *adj* distante

**distaste** [dis•TAIST] *n* disgusto M

**distill** [dis•TIL] *vt vi* destilar

**distillery** [dis•TI•lu•ree] *n* destilería F

**distinct** [dis•TINGKT] *adj* distinto

**distinguish** [di•STING•gwish] *vt* distinguir

**distort** [di•STAURT] *vt* torcer

**distract** [di•STRAKT] *vt* distraer

**distraught** [di•STRAUT] *adj* distraído

**distress** [di•STRES] *n* dolor M; pena F; *vt* afligir

**distribute** [di•STRI•byoot] *vt* distribuir

**distribution** [DI•stri•BYOO•shn] *n* distribución F

**district** [DI•strikt] *n* distrito M

**distrust** [dis•TRUST] *n* desconfianza F; *vt* desconfiar de

**distrustful** [dis•TRUST•ful] *adj* desconfiado

**disturb** [di•STURB] *vt* turbar; perturbar; molestar

**disturbance** [di•STUR•buns] *n* perturbación F

**disturbing** [di•STUR•bing] *adj* perturbador

**ditch** [dich] *n* trinchera F; *vt* abandonar (coll)

**ditto** [DI•to] *adv* ídem M

**dive** [duyv] *n* salto M; *vi* tirarse de cabeza

**diverge** [di•VURJ] *vi* divergir

**diverse** [di•VURS] *adj* diverso

**diversify** [di•VUR•si•FUY] *vt* diversificar

**diversity** [di•VUR•si•tee] *n* diversidad F

**divert** [di•VURT] *vt* desviar

**divide** [di•VUYD] *vt* dividir; *vi* dividirse

**divine** [di•VUYN] *adj* divino

**divinity** [di•VI•ni•tee] *n* divinidad F

**division** [di•VI•zhn] *n* división F

**divorce** [di•VAURS] *n* divorcio M; *vt* divorciarse de

**divulge** [di•VUHLJ] *vt*
divulgar; publicar

**dizzy** [DI•zee] *adj* mareado

**do** [doo] *vt vi* hacer; ~ away
with\ abolir; ~ without\ ver
con necesitar; ~ in\ agotar
(tire); mortar (kill)

**docile** [DAH•sul] *adj* dócil

**dock** [dahk] *n* maslo; dique M;
*vt* poner en dique

**doctor** [DAHK•tur] *n* doctor;
médico M

**doctorate** [DAHK•tu•rut] *n*
doctorado

**doctrine** [DAHK•trin] *n*
doctrina F

**document** [DAH•kyu•munt] *n*
documento M

**dodge** [dahj] *vt* esguince M; *vt*
esquivar

**doe** [do] *n* gama F

**dog** [daug] *n* perro M

**dogma** [DAUG•mu] *n* dogma F

**doings** [DOO•ings] *npl* hechos
M

**doll** [dahl] *n* muñeca F

**dollar** [DAH•lur] *n* dollar M

**dolphin** [DAHL•fin] *n* delfín M

**domain** [do•MAIN] *n*
heredad F

**dome** [dom] *n* cúpula F

**domestic** [du•ME•stik] *adj*
doméstico

**dominant** [DAH•mi•nunt] *adj*
dominante

**dominate** [DAH•mi•NAIT] *vt*
dominar

**domineering**
[DAH•mi•NEEU•ring] *adj*
dominante

**donate** [DO•nait] *vt* donar

**donation** [do•NAI•shn] *n*
donación F

**donkey** [DAHNG•kee] *n*
burro M

**donor** [DO•naur] *n* donador M

**doodle** [DOO•dl] *vi* borrajear

**doom** [doom] *n* condena F

**doomed** [doomd] *adj*
predestinado; *vt* ser
condenado a

**doomsday** [DOOMZ•dai] *n* día
del juicio final M

**door** [daur] *n* puerta F

**doorstep** [DAUR•step] *n*
escalón F

**dope** [dop] *n* droga F

**dormitory** [daur•mi•TAU•ree] *n*
dormitorio M

**dose** [dos] *n* dosis M

**dot** [daht] *n* punto M

**double** [DUH•bl] *adj* doble; on
the ~\ corriendo; *vt* doblar

**double vision** [DUH•bl VI•shn]
*n* doble vista F

**double-breasted** [-BRE•stid]
*adj* cruzado

**doubly** [DUH•blec] *adv*
doblemente

**doubt** [dout] *n* duda F; *vt* dudar

**doubtful** [DOUT•ful] *adj*
dudoso

**dough** [do] *n* masa F; dinero,
pasta (money) (coll)

**douse** [dous] *vt* rociar

**dove** [duhv] *n* palomo M

**down** [doun] *adv* abajo; come
~\ bajar; *vt* derribar; beber
(drink)

**down payment** [DOUN
PAI•mint] *n* pago al contado M

**downcast** [DOUN•kast] *adj* deprimido

**downpour** [DOUN•paur] *n* aguacero M

**downstairs** [DOUN•STAIURZ] *adj* escalera abajo F

**downward** [DOUN•wurd] *adj* descendente

**dowry** [DOUU•ree] *n* dote M

**doze** [doz] *vi* dormitar

**dozen** [DUH•zn] *n* docena F

**draft** [draft] *n* tiro M; bosquejar, reclutar (mil)

**drag** [drag] *vt vi* arrastrar; prolongar; *n* lata F (coll)

**dragon** [DRA•gn] *n* dragón M

**dragonfly** [DRA•gn•FLUY] *n* libélula F

**drain** [drain] *n* sumidero M; *vt* desaguar; apurar

**drama** [DRAH•mu] *n* drama M

**dramatic** [dru•MA•tik] *adj* dramático

**dramatist** [DRAH•mu•tist] *n* dramaturgo M

**dramatize** [DRAH•mu•TUYZ] *vt* dramatizar

**drape** [draip] *vt* colgar

**drapes** [draips] *npl* ropaje M

**drastic** [DRA•stik] *adj* drástico

**draw** [drau] *n* tiro M; *vt* tirar; ~ to\ atraer; ~ out\ sacar; ~ up\ pararse, redactar (legal)

**drawer** [draur] *n* cajón F

**drawing** [DRAU•ing] *n* dibujo M

**dread** [dred] *n* miedo M; *vt* temer

**dreadful** [DRED•ful] *adj* terrible; doloroso

**dream** [dreem] *n* sueño M; *vt* soñar

**dreamy** [DREE•mee] *adj* soñador

**dreary** [DREEU•ree] *adj* sombrío

**drench** [drench] *vt* remojar

**dress** [dres] *n* vestido M; *vt* vestir; *vi* vestirse

**dresser** [DRE•sur] *n* cómoda F

**dried** [druyd] *adj* seco

**drift** [drift] *n* deriva F; *vi* ir a la deriva

**drill** [dril] *n* taladro M; *vt* taladar; perforar

**drink** [dringk] *n* bebida F

**drip** [drip] *n* goteo M; *vi* gotear

**drive** [druyv] *n* paseo M; *vt* empujar; conducir; ~ at\ querer decir

**drivel** [DRI•vl] *n* baba F

**driver** [DRUY•vur] *n* conductor M

**drizzle** [DRI•zl] *n* llovizna F

**droop** [droop] *vi* inclinar

**drop** [drahp] *n* gota F; *vt* dejar caer; bajar; *vi* caer; ~ in on\ pasar por casa de; ~ out\ *vi* retirarse; *n* marginado M

**drought** [drout] *n* sequedad F

**drove** [drov] *n* manada F

**drown** [droun] *vt* ahogar; sumergir

**drowsy** [DROU•zee] *adj* adormecido

**drug** [druhg] *n* droga F

**drug addict** [DRUHG A•dikt] *n* adicto M

**druggist** [DRUH•gist] *n* droguero M

**drum** [druhm] *n* tambor M

**drummer** [DRUH•mur] *n* trambor M

**drunk** [druhngk] *adj* bebido; borracho M

**drunkenness** [DRUHNG•kn•nis] *n* embriaguez borrachera F

**dry** [druy] *adj* seco

**dryer** [DRUY•ur] *n* secador M

**dual** [dooul] *adj* dual M

**dubious** [DOO•byus] *adj* dudoso

**duchess** [DUH•chis] *n* duquesa F

**duck** [duhk] *n* pato M

**duct** [duhkt] *n* conducto; tubo M

**due** [doo] *adj* debido; ~ to\ debido a

**duel** [dooul] *n* duelo M

**duet** [doo•ET] *n* dueto M

**duke** [dook] *n* duque M

**dull** [duhl] *adj* embotado; romo; *vt* alivar (pain); entorpecer (mind)

**dumb** [duhm] *adj* mudo (mute); estúpido; tonto (stupid)

**dumbfound** [DUHM•found] *vt* confundir

**dummy** [DUH•mee] *n* mudo M

**dump** [duhmp] *v* descargar

**dunce** [duns] *n* tonto M

**dune** [doon] *n* duna F

**dung** [duhng] *n* estiércol M

**dungeon** [DUHN•jun] *n* calabozo M

**duplicate** [adj. n. DOO•pli•kut v. DOO•pli•KAIT] *adj n* duplicado; *vt* duplicar

**duplicity** [doo•PLI•si•tee] *n* duplicidad F

**durable** [DOOU•ru•bl] *adj* durable; duradero

**duration** [du•RAI•shn] *n* duración F

**dusk** [duhsk] *n* sombrío M

**dust** [duhst] *n* polvo M

**dustpan** [DUHST•pan] *n* pala F

**Dutch** [duhch] *adj* holandés

**duty** [DOO•tee] *n* deber M; on ~\ de servico; ~ free\ *adj* libre de impuestos

**duty-free** [DOO•tee FREE] *adj* libre de derechos

**dwarf** [dwaurf] *n* pigmeo M

**dwell** [dwel] *vi* habitar

**dwelling** [DWE•ling] *n* habitación F

**dwindle** [DWIN•dl] *vi* mermar; disminuirse

**dye** [duy] *n* tintura F; *vt* teñir

**dying** [DUY•ing] *adj* moribundo

**dynamic** [duy•NA•mik] *adj n* dinámico M

**dynamite** [DUY•nu•MUYT] *n* dinamita F

**dynasty** [DUY•nu•stee] *n* dinastía F

# E

**each** [eech] *adj* cada; ~ other\ uno a otro

**eager** [EE•gur] *adj* ansioso

**eagle** [EE•gl] *n* águila F

**ear** [eeur] *n* oreja F

**early** [UR•lee] *adj adv* temprano

**earn** [urn] *vt* ganar

**earnest** [UR•nist] *adj* serio; in ~\ en serio

**earring** [EEU•ring] *n* broquelillo M

**earth** [urth] *n* tierra F

**earthquake** [URTH•kwaik] *n* terremoto M

**ease** [eez] *n* descanso M; tranquilidad F; at~ !\ a gusto; ill at ~\ molesto; with ~\ facilamenta; *vt* clamar; alivar; *vi* calmarse

**easily** [EE•zi•lee] *adv* fácilmente

**east** [eest] *adj n* este M

**Easter** [EE•stur] *n* tiempo de Pascua M

**eastern** [EE•sturn] *adj* oriental

**eastward** [EEST•wurd] *adv* hacia el este

**easy** [EE•zee] *adj* fácil; take it ~\ no preocuparse; ~ going\ acomodadizo

**eat** [eet] *vt vi* comer

**ebb** [eb] *n* reflujo M

**ebony** [E•bu•nee] *adj* ébano M

**eccentric** [ek•SEN•trik] *adj n* excéntrico M

**ecclesiastic** [ee•KLEE•zee•A•stik] *adj* eclesiástico

**eclipse** [ee•KLIPS] *n* eclipse M

**ecology** [ee•KAH•lu•jee] *n* ecología F

**economic** [E•ku•NAH•mik] *adj* económico

**economical** [E•ku•NAH•mi•kl] *adj* económico

**economics** [E•ku•NAH•miks] *n* economía F

**economy** [ee•KAH•nu•mee] *n* economía F

**ecstasy** [EK•stu•see] *n* éxtasis M

**ecstatic** [ek•STA•tik] *adj* extático

**echo** [E•ko] *n* eco M; *vt* repetir; *vi* hacer eco

**edge** [ej] *n* filo; corte M; on ~\ nervioso

**edible** [E•di•bl] *adj* comestible

**edit** [E•dit] *vt* dirigir

**edition** [e•DI•shn] *n* edición F

**editor** [E•di•tur] *n* director M

**editorial** [E•di•TAU•ree•ul] *adj n* editorial F

**educate** [E•ju•KAIT] *vt* educar

**education** [E•ju•KAI•shn] *n* educación F

**educational** [E•ju•KAI•shu•nl] *adj* educativo

**eel** [eeul] *n* anguila F

**effect** [i•FEKT] *n* efecto M; *vt* efectural; take ~\ entrar en vigor

**effective** [i•FEK•tiv] *adj* efectivo

**efficiency** [i•FI•shun•see] *n* eficiencia F

**efficient** [i•FI•shunt] *adj* eficiente

**effort** [E•furt] *n* esfuerzo M

**egg** [eg] *n* huevo M

**eggplant** [EG•plant] *n* berenjena F

**ego** [EE•go] *n* ego M

**egotist** [EE•go•tist] *n* egotista M

**Egypt** [EE•jipt] *n* Egipto

**Egyptian** [ee•JIP•shn] *adj* egipcio

**eight** [ait] *num* ocho

**eighteen** [ai•TEEN] *num* dieciocho

**eighteenth** [ai•TEENTH] *num* octogésimo

**eighth** [aith] *num* octavo

**eighty** [AI•tee] *num* ochenta

**either** [EE•thur] *adj* uno y otro; entrambos

**eject** [ee•JEKT] *vt* echar

**elaborate** [*adj.* i•LA•brit *v.* i•LA•bu•RAIT] *adj* detallado; *vt* elaborar

**elastic** [i•LA•stik] *adj n* elástico M

**elated** [i•LAI•tid] *adj* gozoso

**elbow** [EL•bo] *n* codo M

**elder** [EL•dur] *adj n* mayor M

**elderly** [EL•dur•lee] *adj* mayor

**elect** [i•LEKT] *vt* elegir

**election** [i•LEK•shn] *n* elección F

**electric** [i•LEK•trik] *adj* eléctrico

**electricity** [i•LEK•TRI•si•tee] *n* electricidad F

**electrocute** [i•LEK•tru•KYOOT] *vt* electrocutar

**electronic** [i•LEK•TRAH•nik] *adj* electrónico

**elegance** [E•li•guns] *n* elegancia F

**elegant** [E•li•gunt] *adj* elegante

**element** [E•li•munt] *n* elemento M

**elementary** [E•li•MEN•tu•ree] *adj* elemental

**elephant** [E•lu•fint] *n* elefante M

**elevate** [E•lu•VAIT] *vt* elevar; levantar

**elevator** [E•li•VAI•tur] *n* elevador M

**eleven** [i•LE•vn] *num* once

**eleventh** [i•LE•vnth] *num* onceno

**elicit** [i•LI•sit] *vt* educir; sacar

**eligible** [E•li•ju•bl] *adj* elegible

**eliminate** [i•LI•mi•NAIT] *vt* eliminar

**elite** [i•LEET] *adj* lo mejor

**elk** [elk] *n* anta F

**elm** [elm] *n* olmo M

**elope** [i•LOP] *vi* fugarse

**eloquence** [E•lu•kwuns] *n* elocuencia F

**eloquent** [E•lu•kwunt] *adj* elocuente

**else** [els] *adv* más; otro; everybody ~\ todos los demás; nobody ~\ ningun otro; nothing ~\ nada más; somehwere ~\ en otra parte

**elsewhere** [ELS•waiur] *adv* en otra parte

**elude** [i•LOOD] *vt* eludir

**emaciated** [i•MAI•shee•AI•tid] *adj* flaco; demacrado

**emanate** [E•mu•NAIT] *vi* emanar

**emancipation** [i•MAN•si•PAI•shn] *n* emancipación F

**embankment** [em•BANGK•munt] *n* terraplén M

**embargo** [im•BAHR•go] *n* embargo M

**embarrass** [im•BA•rus] *vt* embarazar

**embarrassed** [im•BA•rust] *adj* embarazoso

**embarrassment**
[im•BA•rus•munt] *n*
embarazo M

**embassy** [EM•bu•see] *n*
embajada F

**embellish** [im•BE•lish] *vt*
embellecer

**embers** [EM•burz] *npl* ascuas F

**embezzle** [em•BE•zl] *vt*
desfalcar

**emblem** [EM•blum] *n*
emblema F

**embody** [im•BAH•dee] *vt*
encarnar

**embrace** [im•BRAIS] *n* abrazo M

**embroidery** [im•BROI•du•ree]
*n* bordado M

**embryo** [EM•bree•O] *n*
embrión F

**emerald** [E•mu•ruld] *adj n*
esmeralda F

**emerge** [i•MURJ] *vi* emerger

**emergency** [i•MUR•jun•see]
*adj* emergencia F

**emergency exit**
[ee•MUR•gin•cee EG•sit] *n*
salida de emergencia F

**emigrant** [E•mi•grunt] *n*
emigrante M

**emigrate** [E•mi•GRAIT] *vi*
emigrar

**eminence** [E•mi•nuns] *n*
eminencia F

**eminent** [E•mi•nunt] *adj*
eminente

**emissary** [E•mi•SE•ree] *n*
emisario M

**emission** [i•MI•shn] *n* emisión F

**emit** [i•MIT] *vt* emitir

**emperor** [EM•pu•rur] *n*
emperador M

**emphasis** [EM•fu•sis] *n*
énfasis M

**emphasize** [EM•fu•SUYZ] *vt*
dar énfasis a

**empire** [EM•puyur] *n* imperio M

**employ** [em•PLOI] *vt* emplear

**employee** [em•PLOI•YEE] *n*
empleado M

**employer** [em•PLOI•yur] *n*
dueño; obrero M

**employment** [em•PLOI•munt]
*n* empleo M

**empress** [EM•pris] *n*
emperatriz F

**empty** [EMP•tee] *adj* vacío; *vt*
vaciar; *vi* vaciarse

**emulate** [E•myu•LAIT] *vt*
emular

**enable** [e•NAI•bl] *vt* capacitar

**enact** [e•NAKT] *vt* establecer

**enamel** [i•NA•ml] *n* esmlate M

**enamored** [i•NA•murd] *adj*
enamorado

**encampment** [en•KAMP•munt]
*n* acampamento M

**enchant** [en•CHANT] *vt*
encantar

**enclose** [en•CLOZ] *vt* encerrar

**encompass** [en•KAHM•pus] *vt*
cercar

**encore** [AHN•kaur] *n* que se
repita

**encounter** [en•KOUN•tur] *n*
encuentro M; *vt* encontrar

**encourage** [en•KU•rij] *vt*
alentar

**encouragement**
[en•KU•rij•munt] *n* aliento M

**encroach** [en•KROCH] *vi*
usurpar

**encyclopedia**
[en•SUY•klo•PEE•dee•u] *n*
enciclopedia F

**end** [end] *n* fin; cabo M; *vt vi*
terminar; acabar; in the ~\ por
fin

**endanger** [en•DAIN•jur] *vt*
comprometer; arriesgar

**endearing** [en•DEEU•ring] *adj*
cariñoso

**endeavor** [en•DE•vur] *n*
esfuerzo; intento M; *vt*
enforzarse por

**ending** [EN•ding] *n* fin; final M

**endless** [END•lis] *adj*
interminable

**endorse** [en•DAURS] *vt*
endosar

**endurance** [en•DU•runs] *n*
resistencia F

**enemy** [E•nu•mee] *n* enemigo M

**energetic** [E•nur•JE•tik] *adj*
enérgico

**energy** [E•nur•jee] *n* energía F

**enforce** [en•FAURS] *vt* dar
fuerza a

**engage** [en•GAIJ] *vt* empeñar

**engaged** [en•GAIJD] *adj*
prometido

**engagement** [en•GAIJ•munt] *n*
noviazgo; compromismo M

**engaging** [en•GAI•jing] *adj*
agraciado

**engine** [EN•jin] *n* ingenio M

**engineer** [EN•ji•NEEUR] *n*
ingeniero M

**engineering**
[EN•ji•NEEU•ring] *n*
ingeniería F

**England** [ING•glund] *n*
Inglaterra F

**English** [ING•glish] *adj* inglés M

**engrave** [en•GRAIV] *vt* grabar

**engraving** [en•GRAI•ving] *n*
grabado M

**engulf** [en•GUHLF] *vt* engolfar

**enhance** [en•HANS] *vt*
engrandecer

**enigma** [i•NIG•mu] *n* enigma F

**enjoy** [en•JOI] *vt* gozar

**enjoyable** [en•JOI•u•bl] *adj*
agradable

**enlarge** [en•LAHRJ] *vt*
agrandar

**Enlightenment**
[en•LUY•tn•munt] *n*
movimiento filosòfico del
siglo xvii M

**enlist** [en•LIST] *vt* alistar;
enrolar

**enormous** [i•NAUR•mus] *adj*
enorme

**enough** [i•NUHF] *adj* bastante;
*excl* ¡basta!

**enrage** [en•RAIJ] *vt* enfurecer

**enrich** [en•RICH] *vt* enriquecer

**enroll** [en•ROL] *vt* alistar;
matricular

**enslave** [en•SLAIV] *vt*
esclavizar

**ensuing** [en•SOO•ing] *adj*
siguiente

**ensure** [en•SHOOUR] *vt*
asegurar

**entail** [en•TAIL] *vt* envolver

**enter** [EN•tur] *vt* entrar; entrar
en

**enterprise** [EN•tur•PRUYZ] *n*
emprendedor M

**enterprising**
[EN•tur•PRUY•zing] *adj*
emprendedor

**entertain** [EN•tur•TAIN] *vt*
divertir

**entertaining**
[EN•tur•TAI•ning] *adj*
entretenido

**entertainment**
[EN•tur•TAIN•munt] *n*
diversión F

**enthusiasm**
[en•THOO•zee•A•zm] *n*
entusiasmo M

**enthusiastic**
[en•THOO•zee•A•stik] *adj*
entusiástico

**enticing** [en•TUY•sing] *adj*
tentador

**entire** [en•TUYUR] *adj* entero;
*adv* enteramente

**entirety** [en•TUYUR•tee] *n*
totalidad F

**entitled** [en•TUY•tl] *adj*
intitulado

**entity** [EN•ti•tee] *n* entidad F

**entrance** [*n*. EN•truns *v*.
en•TRANS] *n* entrada F

**entry** [EN•tree] *n* entrada F

**enumerate** [i•NOO•mu•RAIT]
*vt* enumerar

**envelop** [en•VE•luhp] *vt*
envolver

**envelope** [EN•vu•LOP] *n*
envoltura F

**envious** [EN•vee•us] *adj*
envidioso

**environment**
[en•VUY•run•munt] *n*
ambiente M

**envoy** [EN•voi] *n* enviado M

**envy** [EN•vee] *n* envidia F; *vt*
envidiar

**epic** [E•pik] *adj* épico

**epidemic** [E•pi•DE•mik] *n*
epidémico M

**episode** [E•pi•SOD] *n*
episodio M

**epistle** [i•PI•sl] *n* epístola F

**epitaph** [E•pi•TAF] *n* epitafío M

**epitome** [e•PI•tu•mee] *n*
epitome M

**epoch** [E•puk] *n* época F

**equal** [EE•kwul] *adj* igual

**equality** [ee•KWAH•li•tee] *n*
igualdad F

**equally** [EE•kwu•lee] *adv*
igualmente

**equation** [ee•KWAI•zhn] *n*
ecuación F

**equator** [ee•KWAI•tur] *n*
ecuador M

**equip** [i•KWIP] *vt* equipar

**equipment** [i•KWIP•munt] *n*
equipo M

**equivalent** [i•KWI•vu•lunt] *adj*
*n* equivalente

**era** [E•ru] *n* era F

**eradicate** [i•RA•di•KAIT] *vt*
erradicar

**erase** [i•RAIS] *vt* borrar

**eraser** [i•RAI•sur] *n* goma de
borrar F

**erect** [i•REKT] *adj* derecho;
levantado

**erection** [i•REK•shn] *n*
erección F

**erode** [i•ROD] *vt* corroer

**erosion** [i•RO•zhn] *n*
corrosión F

**err** [er] *vi* errar; pecar (sin)

**errand** [E•rund] *n* misión F

**error** [E•rur] *n* error M

**erudite** [ER•yu•DUYT] *adj*
erudito

**erupt** [i•RUHPT] *vi* hacer erupción F

**eruption** [i•RUHP•shn] *n* erupción F

**escalate** [E•sku•LAIT] *vt* escalar

**escalator** [E•sku•LAI•tur] *n* escalera F

**escape** [e•SKAIP] *n* escape M; *vi* escaparse; *vt* evitar; have a narrow ~ /~ by the skin of one's teeth\ escapar por un pelo

**escort** [*n.* E•skaurt *v.* e•SKAURT] *n* acompañante M

**especially** [e•SPE•shu•lee] *adv* especialmente

**espionage** [E•spee•u•NAHZH] *n* espionaje M

**essay** [E•sai] *n* ensayo M

**essence** [E•suns] *n* esencia F

**essential** [e•SEN•shl] *adj* esencial

**essentially** [e•SEN•shu•lee] *adv* esencialmente

**establish** [e•STA•blish] *vt* establecer

**establishment** [e•STA•blish•munt] *n* establecimiento M

**estate** [e•STAIT] *n* estado M

**esteem** [e•STEEM] *n* estima F; *vt* estimar

**estimate** [*n.* E•sti•mut *v.* E•sti•MAIT] *n* estimación F

**estranged** [e•STRAINJD] *adj* extrañado

**eternal** [i•TUR•ul] *adj* eterno

**eternity** [i•TUR•ni•tee] *n* enternidad F

**ethic** [E•thik] *n* ético M

**ethical** [E•thi•kl] *adj* moral

**Ethiopia** [EE•thee•O•pee•u] *n* Etíopia

**ethnic** [ETH•nik] *adj* étnico

**etiquette** [E•ti•kut] *n* etiqueta F

**eulogy** [YOO•lu•jee] *n* elogio M

**euphemism** [YOO•fu•MI•zm] *n* eufemismo M

**Europe** [YOO•rup] *n* Europa

**European** [YU•ru•PEE•un] *adj* europeo

**euthanasia** [YOO•thu•NAI•zhu] *n* eutanasia F

**evacuate** [i•VA•kyoo•AIT] *vt* evacuar

**evade** [i•VAID] *vt* evadir

**evaluate** [i•VAL•yoo•AIT] *vt* evaluar

**evaporate** [i•VA•pu•RAIT] *vt* evaporar

**evasive** [i•VAI•siv] *adj* evasivo

**eve** [eev] *n* víspera F

**even** [EE•vn] *adj* igual; *vt* nivelar; *adv* aun, hasta, incluso; get ~ with\ desquitarse; ~ if\ aunque; ~ so\ aun; asi; not ~\ ni siquera

**evening** [EEV•ning] *n* tarde; F anochecer M

**evening gown** [EEV•ning GOUN] *n* vestido de noche M

**event** [i•VENT] *n* caso hecho M

**eventual** [i•VEN•choo•ul] *adj* eventual

**eventually** [i•VEN•choou•lee] *adv* eventualmente

**ever** [E•vur] *adv* siempre; ~ after/since\ desde entonces; hardly ~\ casi nunca

**evergreen** [E•vur•GREEN] *n*
pino M

**every** [E•vree] *adj* cada todo

**everybody** [E•vree•BUH•dee]
*pron* todos; cada uno

**everyday** [E•vree•DAI] *adj*
diario

**everything** [E•vree•THING]
*pron* todo

**everywhere** [E•vree•WAIUR]
*adv* dondequiera

**evict** [i•VIKT] *vt* desposeer

**evidence** [E•vi•duns] *n*
evidencia F

**evident** [E•vi•dunt] *adj* evidente

**evil** [EE•vl] *adj* malo; *n* mal M;
maldad F

**evoke** [i•VOK] *vt* evocar

**evolution** [E•vu•LOO•shn] *n*
evolución F

**evolve** [i•VAHLV] *vi*
desenvolver; desarrollar

**ewe** [yoo] *n* oveja F

**exact** [eg•ZAKT] *adj* exacto

**exaggerate** [eg•ZA•ju•RAIT]
*vt vi* exagerar

**exaggeration**
[eg•ZA•ju•RAI•shn] *n*
exageración F

**exalt** [eg•ZAULT] *vt* exaltar

**exam** [eg•ZAM] *n* exámen M

**examine** [eg•ZA•min] *vt*
examinar

**example** [eg•ZAM•pl] *n*
ejemplo M

**exasperate** [eg•ZA•spu•RAIT]
*vt* exasperar

**excavate** [EK•sku•VAIT] *vt*
excavar

**exceed** [ek•SEED] *vt* exceder

**excel** [ek•SEL] *vi* aventajar;
sobrepujar

**excellence** [EK•su•luns] *n*
excelencia F

**excellent** [EK•su•lunt] *adj*
excelente

**except** [ek•SEPT] *prep conj*
excepto

**exception** [ek•SEP•shn] *n*
excepción F

**exceptional** [ek•SEP•shu•nl]
*adj* excepcional

**excerpt** [EK•surpt] *n* cita F

**excess** [EK•ses] *adj* exceso M

**exchange** [eks•CHAINJ] *n*
cambio M

**excite** [ek•SUYT] *vt* excitar

**excited** [ek•SUY•tid] *adj*
acalorado

**exciting** [ek•SUY•ting] *adj*
excitante

**exclaim** [ek•SKLAIM] *vi*
exclamar

**exclamation point**
[EK•sklu•MAI•shn ~ ] *n*
punto de exclamación F

**exclude** [ek•SKLOOD] *vt*
excluir

**excrement** [EK•skri•munt] *n*
excremento M; mierdo (coll)

**excursion** [ek•SKUR•zhn] *n*
excursión F

**excuse** [ek•SKYOOS] *n*
excusa F

**execute** [EK•si•KYOOT] *vt*
ejecutar

**execution** [EK•si•KYOO•shn] *n*
ejecución F

**executioner**
[EK•si•KYOO•shu•nur] *n*
ejecutor M

**executive** [eg•ZE•kyu•tiv] *adj*
ejecutivo

**exemplary** [eg•ZEM•plu•ree]
*adj* ejemplar

**exemplify** [eg•ZEM•pli•FUY]
*vt* ejemplificar

**exempt** [eg•ZEMPT] *adj*
inmune

**exercise** [EK•sur•SUYZ] *n*
ejercicio M; *vt* ejercer; *vi*
hacer ejercicios

**exert** [eg•ZURT] *vt* ejercer

**exhale** [eks•HAIL] *vt* exhalar

**exhaust** [eg•ZAUST] *n* escape
M; descarga F; *vt* agotar

**exhausted** [eg•ZAU•stid] *adj*
fatigado

**exhaustion** [eg•ZAUS•chn] *n*
agotamiento M

**exhibit** [eg•ZI•bit] *n*
exhibición F

**exhilarating**
[eg•ZI•lu•RAI•ting] *adj*
alegrador

**exile** [EG•zuyl] *n* destierro M

**exist** [EG•zist] *vi* existir

**existence** [eg•ZI•stuns] *n*
existencia F

**exit** [EG•zit] *n* salida F; *vt* salir

**exodus** [EK•su•dus] *n* éxodo M

**exonerate** [eg•ZAH•nu•RAIT]
*vt* exonerar

**exotic** [eg•ZAH•tik] *adj* exótico

**expand** [ek•SPAND] *vt*
extender

**expansion** [ek•SPAN•shn] *n*
expansión F

**expect** [ek•SPEKT] *vt* esperar

**expectation**
[EK•SPEK•TAI•shn] *n*
espera F

**expedition** [EK•spu•DI•shn] *n*
expedición F

**expel** [ek•SPEL] *vt* expeler

**expend** [ek•SPEND] *vt*
expender

**expenditure** [ek•SPEN•di•chur]
*n* gasto M

**expense** [ek•SPENS] *n* gasto M

**expensive** [ek•SPEN•siv] *adj*
caro

**experience**
[ek•SPEEU•ree•uns] *n*
experiencia F; *vt* experimentar

**experienced**
[ek•SPEEU•ree•unst] *adj*
experimentado; a experto

**experiment** [ek•SPE•ri•munt] *n*
experimento M

**expert** [EK•spurt] *adj n*
experto M

**expire** [ek•SPUYUR] *vi* espirar

**explain** [ek•SPLAIN] *vt*
explicar

**explanation**
[EK•splu•NAI•shn] *n*
explicación F

**explode** [ek•SPLOD] *vt* volar;
estallar

**exploit** [*n.* EK•sploit *v.*
ek•SPLOIT] *n* proeza F; *vt*
explotar

**exploration** [EK•splu•RAI•shn]
*n* exploración F

**explore** [ek•SPLAUR] *vt vi*
explorar

**explorer** [ek•SPLAU•rur] *n*
explorador

**export** [*n.* EK•spaurt *v.*
ek•SPAURT] *n* exportación F;
*vt* exportar

**expose** [ek•SPOZ] *vt* exponer

**exposure** [ek•SPO•zhur] *n*
expuesto M
**express** [ek•SPRES] *adj*
expreso
**expression** [ek•SPRE•shn] *n*
expresión F
**expressive** [ek•SPRE•siv] *adj*
expresivo
**exquisite** [ek•SKWI•zit] *adj*
exquisito
**extend** [ek•STEND] *vt* extender
**extension** [ek•STEN•shn] *n*
extensión F
**extensive** [ek•STEN•siv] *adj*
extensivo
**extent** [ek•STENT] *n* alcance M
**exterior** [ek•STEEU•ree•ur] *adj*
*n* exterior M
**exterminate**
[ek•STUR•mi•NAIT] *vt*
exterminar
**external** [ek•STUR•nl] *adj*
externo M
**extinct** [ek•STINGKT] *adj*
destruido
**extinguish** [ek•STING•gwish]
*vt* extinguir
**extort** [ek•STAURT] *vt* arrancar
**extra** [EK•stru] *adj* extra *n*
suplemento MF

**extract** [*n.* EK•strakt *v.*
ek•STRAKT] *n* extracto
**extradite** [EK•stru•DUYT] *vt*
conceder la extradición
**extraordinary**
[ek•STRAU•di•NE•ree] *adj*
extraordinario
**extravagance**
[ek•STRA•vu•guns] *n*
exceso M
**extravagant**
[ek•STRA•vu•gunt] *adj*
gastador
**extreme** [ek•STREEM] *adj n*
extremo M
**extremist** [ek•STREE•mist] *adj*
*n* extremista M
**exuberant** [eg•ZOO•bu•runt]
*adj* exuberante
**exult** [eg•ZUHLT] *vi* exultar
**eye** [uy] *n* ojo M; keep an ~ on\
no perder de vista
**eyewitness** [UY•WIT•nis] *n*
testigo M
**eyeball** [UY•baul] *n* globo del
ojo M
**eyebrow** [UY•brou] *n* ceja F
**eyelash** [UY•lash] *n* pestaña F
**eyelid** [UY•lid] *n* párpado M
**eyesight** [UY•suyt] *n* vista F

# F

**fabric** [FA•brik] *n* tela F
**fabricate** [FA•bri•KAIT] *vt*
fabricar
**fabulous** [FA•byu•lus] *adj*
fabuloso

**facade** [fu•SAHD] *n*
fachada F
**face** [fais] *n* cara F; rostro M; in
the ~ of \ frente a; lose ~\
quedar mal; *vt* mirar haceia; *vi*

volverse; ~ up to\ enfrentarse con

**facet** [FA•sit] *n* faceta F

**facetious** [fu•SEE•shus] *adj* chistoso

**facilities** [tu•SI•li•tees] *npl* facilidad F

**facing** [FAI•sing] *prep* de cara a frente

**fact** [fakt] *n* hecho M; as a matter of ~/in ~\ en realidad; a decir verdad

**factor** [FAK•tur] *n* factor M

**factory** [FAK•tu•ree] *n* fábrica F

**faculty** [FA•kul•tee] *n* facultad F

**fad** [fad] *n* moda F

**fade** [faid] *vt* debilitarse; *vi* descolorarse

**fail** [fail] *vt* faltar; without ~\ sin falta; ~ to do\ dejar de hacer

**failure** [FAIL•yur] *n* fracaso M

**faint** [faint] *adj* débil; feel ~\ estar mareado

**fair 1** [faiur] *adj* propicio M; justo

**fair 2** [faiur] *n* feria F

**fairly** [FAIUR•lee] *adv* justamente (justly) bastante (rather)

**fairy** [FAIU•ree] *n* hada F

**fairy tale** [FAIR•ee tail] *n* cuento de hadas M

**faith** [faith] *n* fe F

**faithful** [FAITH•ful] *adj* fiel

**fake** [faik] *adj n vt* imitación F

**falcon** [FAL•kn] *n* halcón M

**fall** [faul] *n* caída F; *vi* caer; otoño (season); ~ down\ fracasar; ~ for\ enamorarse de

(coll); ~ out\ reñir (quarrel); ~ over\ caer(se)

**false** [fauls] *adj* falso

**falsify** [FAUL•si•FUY] *vt* falsear

**falter** [FAUL•tur] *vi* vacilar

**fame** [faim] *n* fama F

**famed** [faimd] *adj* famado

**familiar** [fu•MI•lyur] *adj* familiar

**familiarize** [fu•MI•lyu•RUYZ] *vt* familiarizar

**family** [FA•mu•lee] *n* familia F

**famine** [FA•min] *n* carestía F

**famished** [FA•misht] *adj* hambriento

**famous** [FAI•mus] *adj* famoso

**fan 1** [fan] *n* abanico; ventalle M; *vt* abanicar; soplar

**fan 2** [fan] *n* admirador; afficionado M

**fancy** [FAN•see] *adj* magín

**fang** [fang] *n* colmillo M

**fantastic** [fan•TA•stik] *adj* fantástico

**fantasy** [FAN•tu•see] *n* fantasía F

**far** [fahr] *adj* lejos; as ~ as\ hasta; as ~ as I know\ que yo sepa; by ~\ con mucho

**farce** [fahrs] *n* farsa F

**fare** [faiur] *n* pasajero M

**farewell** [faiur•WEL] *n* adiós M

**farm** [fahrm] *n* finca; hacienda F

**farmer** [FAHR•mur] *n* granjero M

**farming** [FAHR•ming] *n* cultivo M

**farther** [FAHR•thur] *adj* más lejos

**farthest** [FAHR•thist] *adj adv*
lo más lejos

**fascinate** [FA•si•NAIT] *vt*
fascinar

**fascinating** [FA•si•NAI•ting]
*adj* fascinando

**fascination** [FA•si•NAI•shn] *n*
fascinación F

**fascism** [FA•shi•zm] *n*
fascismo M

**fashion** [FA•shn] *n* modo M

**fashionable** [FA•shu•nu•bl] *adj*
a la moda

**fast 1** [fast] *adj* adelantado;
rapido; *adv* rápidamente;
firmemente; ~ asleep\
profundamente dormido

**fast 2** [fast] *vi* aunar; *n* ayuno M

**fasten** [FA•sun] *vt* afirmar

**fastidious** [fa•STI•dee•us] *adj*
exigente

**fat** [fat] *adj* gordo; grueso

**fatal** [FAI•tl] *adj* fatal

**fate** [fait] *n* destino M

**fateful** [FAIT•ful] *adj* funesto

**father** [FAH•thur] *n* padre M

**father-in-law**
[FA•thur•in•LAU] *n* suegro M

**fatherland** [FAH•thur•LAND]
*n* patria F

**fatherly** [FAH•thur•lee] *adj*
paternal

**fathom** [FA•thum] *n* braza F

**fatigue** [fu•TEEG] *n* fatiga F

**fatten** [FA•tun] *vt* engordar

**fatuous** [FA•chu•us] *adj* fatuo

**faucet** [FAU•sit] *n* espita F

**fault** [fault] *n* falta F

**faulty** [FAUL•tee] *adj*
defectuoso

**fauna** [FAU•nu] *n* fauna F

**favor** [FAI•vur] *n* favor M; *vt*
favorder; estar a favor de;
preferir

**favorable** [FAI•vru•bl] *adj*
favorable

**favorite** [FAI•vrit] *adj n*
favorito M

**fawn** [faun] *n* cervato M

**fear** [feeur] *n* miedo M

**fearful** [FEEUR•ful] *adj*
temeroso

**fearless** [FEEUR•lis] *adj* bravo

**feasible** [FEE•zu•bl] *adj*
factible

**feast** [feest] *n* fiesta F

**feat** [feet] *n* hecho M

**feather** [FE•thur] *n* pluma F

**feature** [FEE•chur] *n*
característica F; facción
(face); ~ film\ pelicula F

**February** [FE•broo•U•ree] *n*
febrero M

**federal** [FE•du•rul] *adj* federal

**federation** [FE•du•RAI•shn] *n*
federación F

**fee** [fee] *n* honorario M

**feeble** [FEE•bl] *adj* débil

**feed** [feed] *n* alimento M

**feel** [feeul] *v* tocar; sentir; do
you feel it's a good idea?\ ¿te
parece buena idea?; ~ as if\
tener la impressión de que; ~
hot/hungry\ tenar
calor/hambre; ~ like\ tener
ganas de

**feeling** [FEEU•ling] *n* sentido M

**feign** [fain] *vt* fingir

**fell** [fel] *pp* caído

**fellow** [FE•lo] *n* compañero M

**fellowship** [FE•lo•SHIP] *n*
confraternidad F

**felon** [FE•lun] *n* malvado M

**felt** [felt] *n* sentido M

**female** [FEE•mail] *adj* hembra F

**feminine** [FE•mi•nin] *adj*
femenino

**fence** [fens] *n* estacada F; *vt*
encerrar; dercar; i practica la
esgrima (sport)

**fencing** [FEN•sing] *n* esgrima F

**fend** [fend] *vi* defender

**fender** [FEN•dur] *n*
guardafuegos

**ferment** [*n.* FUR•ment *v.*
fur•MENT] v fermentar; *n*
fermento M

**fern** [furn] *n* helecho M

**ferocious** [fu•RO•shus] *adj*
fiero; feroz

**ferret** [FE•rit] *n* hurón F

**ferry** [FE•ree] *n* barca F

**fertile** [FUR•tl] *adj* fértil

**fertility** [fur•TI•li•tee] *n*
fertilidad F

**fertilize** [FUR•ti•LUYZ] *vt*
fertilizar

**fertilizer** [FUR•ti•LUY•zur] *n*
fertilizante M

**fervent** [FUR•vunt] *adj*
hirviente

**festival** [FE•sti•vl] *n* fiesta F

**festive** [FE•stiv] *adj* festivo

**fetch** [fech] *vt* ir por

**fetus** [FEE•tus] *n* feto M

**feud** [fyood] *n* disputa F

**feudal** [FYOO•dl] *adj* feudal

**fever** [FEE•vur] *n* fiebre M

**feverish** [FEE•vu•rish] *adj*
febricitante

**few** [fyoo] *adj* poco; quite a ~\
muchos

**fiancé** [fee•ahn•SAI] *n*
prometido M

**fiancée** [fee•ahn•SAI] *n*
prometida F

**fib** [fib] *n* mentirilla F

**fiber** [FUY•bur] *n* fibra F

**fickle** [FI•kl] *adj* vacilante

**fiction** [FIK•shn] *n* ficción F

**fiddle** [FI•dl] *n* violín F

**fidelity** [fi•DE•li•tee] *n*
fidelidad F

**fidget** [FI•jit] *vi* agitarse

**field** [feeuld] *n* campo M

**fiend** [feend] *n* demonio M

**fiendish** [FEEN•dish] *adj*
diabólico

**fierce** [feeurs] *adj* fiero

**fiery** [FUYU•ree] *adj* ardiente

**fifteen** [fif•TEEN] *num* quince

**fifteenth** [fif•TEENTH] *num*
decimoquinto

**fifth** [fifth] *num* quinto

**fiftieth** [FIF•tee•ith] *num*
quincuagésimo

**fifty** [FIF•tee] *num* cincuenta

**fig** [fig] *n* higo M

**fight** [fuyt] *n* lucha F; *vt vi*
luchar; disputar; ~ back\
defenderse; ~ off\ rechazar
(attack); luchar contra
(illness)

**figurative** [FI•gyu•ru•tiv] *adj*
figurativo

**figure** [FI•gyur] *n* figura F; *vt*
imaginar; ~ out\ explicarse; ~
of speech\ tropa M; figura F

**file 1** [fuyul] *n* fila F; *vt* archivar

**file 2** [fuyul] *n* lima F (tool) *vt*
limar

**fill** [fil] *vt* llenar; *vi* llenarse; ~
in\ rellenar; ~ up\ llenar
(auto)

**fillet** [fi•LAI] *n* filete M

**filling** [FI•ling] *n* relleno M;
~ station\ estación de servico

**film** [film] *n* película F

**filter** [FIL•tur] *n* filtro M

**filth** [filth] *n* suciedad F

**filthy** [FIL•thee] *adj* sucio

**fin** [fin] *n* aleta F

**final** [FUY•nl] *adj* final

**finally** [FUY•nu•lee] *adv* por fin

**finance** [fuy•NANS] *n* ciencia
F; *vt* financiar

**financial** [fuy•NAN•shl] *adj*
financiero

**finch** [finch] *n* pinzón M

**find** [fuynd] *n* encuentro M; *vt*
encontrar; ~ out\ enterarse de

**fine 1** [fuyn] *adj* fino; *adv* muy
bien

**fine 1** [fuyn] *n* multa F; *vt*
multar

**finger** [FING•gur] *n* dedo M

**fingerprint** [FING•gur•PRINT]
*n* huella digital F

**finish** [FI•nish] *n* término final M

**Finland** [FIN•lund] *n* Finlandia

**Finn** [fin] *n* finés

**Finnish** [FI•nish] *adj* finlandés

**fir** [fur] *n* abeto M

**fire** [fuyur] *n* fuego; incendio
M; *vt* disparar (bullet);
despidir (dismiss)

**fire station** [FUYUR
STAI•shn] *n* puesto de
bomberos M

**fireman** [FUYUR•man] *n*
bombero M

**fireplace** [FUYUR•plais] *n*
chimenea F

**firewood** [FUYUR•wud] *n*
leña F

**fireworks** [FUYUR•wurks] *npl*
fuegos artificiales M

**firm 1** [furm] *adj* duro; firme;
*adv* firmemente

**firm 2** [furm] *n* empresa F

**first** [furst] *adj* primero; ~ hand\
directament; ~ sight\ primera
vista; ~ of all\ ante todo

**first aid** [FURST AID] *n*
primeros auxilios

**first-class** [FURST•KLAS] *adj*
de primera clase F

**firsthand** [FURST•HAND] *adj*
*adv* de primera mano

**first name** [FURST NAIM] *n*
nombre de pila M

**fiscal** [FI•skl] *adj* fiscal

**fish** [fish] *n* pez; pescado M; *vt*
pescar

**fisherman** [FI•shur•mun] *n*
pesquero M

**fishing** [FI•shing] *n* pesca F; go
~\ ir de pesca

**fission** [FI•shn] *n* escisión F

**fissure** [FI•shur] *n*
hendimiento M

**fist** [fist] *n* puño M

**fit 1** [fit] *adj* propio; sano; *vt*
adaptar; sentar bien
(clothing); *vi* encajar (in
place)

**fit 2** *n* ataque M

**fitting room** [FI•ting ~ ] *n*
cuarto de prueba M

**five** [fuyv] *num* cinco

**fix** [fiks] *vt* fijar; reparar

**fixation** [fik•SAI•shn] *n*
fijación F

**fixed** [fikst] *adj* fijo

**fizz** [fiz] *n* efervescencia F

**flag** [flag] *n* bandera F

**flagpole** [FLAG•pol] *n* mástil M
**flagrant** [FLAI•grunt] *adj* flagrante
**flair** [flaiur] *n* aptitud F
**flake** [flaik] *n* copo M
**flame** [flaim] *n* flama F; *vi* llamear
**flamingo** [flu•MING•go] *n* flamenco M
**flammable** [FLA•mu•bl] *adj* flámeo
**flank** [flangk] *n* ijada F; flanco M
**flannel** [FLA•nl] *n* franela F
**flap** [flap] *n* falbalá F; *vi* ondear; *vt* sacudir; batir (wings)
**flare** [flaiur] *n* destello M
**flash** [flash] *n* llamarada F; *vi* brillar; *vt* despedir
**flashback** [FLASH•bak] *n* escena retrospectiva F
**flashlight** [FLASH•luyt] *n* linterna F
**flashy** [FLA•shee] *adj* ostentoso
**flask** [flask] *n* frasco M
**flat** [flat] *adj* plano
**flatten** [FLA•tn] *vt* allanar
**flatter** [FLA•tur] *vt* adular
**flattering** [FLA•tu•ring] *adj* adulado
**flattery** [FLA•tu•ree] *n* adulación F
**flaunt** [flaunt] *vt* desplegar
**flavor** [FLAI•vur] *n* sabor M; *vt* condimentar
**flaw** [flau] *n* brecha F
**flax** [flaks] *n* lino M
**flea** [flee] *n* pulga F
**fleck** [flek] *n* mancha F
**flee** [flee] *vt vi* huir
**fleece** [flees] *n* vellón F

**fleet** [fleet] *n* armada F
**flesh** [flesh] *n* carne F; in the ~\ en persona; one's own ~ and blood\ los de su sangre
**fleshy** [FLE•shee] *adj* carnoso
**flex** [fleks] *vt vi* doblar encorvar
**flexible** [FLEK•si•bl] *adj* flexible
**flicker** [FLI•kur] *vi* fluctuar
**flight** [fluyt] *n* vuelo M
**flimsy** [FLIM•zee] *adj* débil
**flinch** [flinch] *vi* vacilar
**fling** [fling] *vt* echar
**flint** [flint] *n* pedernal M
**flip** [flip] *n* golpe vivo M; *vt* dar un golpecito a
**flippant** [FLI•punt] *adj* impertinente
**flirt** [flurt] *n* flirteador M
**float** [flot] *vt* flotar
**flock** [flahk] *s* bandada F
**flog** [flahg] *vt* azotar
**flogging** [FLAH•ging] *n* azotes M
**flood** [fluhd] *n* diluvio M; *vt* inundar; *vi* inundarse
**floodlight** [FLUHD•luyt] *n* reflector M
**floor** [flaur] *n* boda F; *vt* derribar (knock down) confundir (amaze)
**flora** [FLAU•ru] *n* flora F
**florist** [FLAU•rist] *n* floricultor M
**floss** [flaus] *n* seda floja F
**flounder** [FLOUN•dur] *n* forcejeo M
**flour** [flouur] *n* harina F
**flourish** [FLU•rish] *vi* crecer
**flout** [flout] *vt* insultar
**flow** [flo] *n* flujo M; *vi* correr

**flower** [flouur] *n* flor F

**flown** [flon] *pp* vuelto

**flu** [floo] *n* gripe M

**fluctuate** [FLUHK•chu•AIT] *vi* fluctuar

**flue** [floo] *n* cañón M

**fluency** [FLOO•un•see] *n* fluidez F

**fluent** [FLOO•unt] *adj* fluido

**fluff** [fluf] *n* lanilla F

**fluid** [FLOO•id] *adj n* fluido M

**fluke** [flook] *n* uña F

**fluorescent** [flau•RE•sunt] *adj* fluorescente

**fluoride** [FLAU•ruyd] *n* fluoruro M

**flurry** [FLU•ree] *n* prisa M

**flush** [fluhsh] *vt* afluir; limpiar con agua; *vi* ruborizarse;

**fluster** [FLUH•stur] *vt* agitar

**flute** [floot] *n* flauta F

**flutter** [FLUH•tur] *vi* aletear

**fly 1** [fluy] *n* mosca F

**fly 2** *vi* volar; ir en avión; correr (rush) *vt* pilotar (airplane)

**flying saucer** [FLUY•ing SAU•sur] *n* nave spacial M

**foam** [fom] *n* espuma F

**focal** [FO•kl] *adj* focal

**focus** [FO•kus] *n* foco M

**fodder** [FAH•dur] *n* forraje M

**foe** [fo] *n* enemigo M

**fog** [fahg] *n* niebla F

**foil** [foiul] *n* laminita F

**fold** [fold] *n* doblez M; *vt* doblar; fracasar

**foliage** [FO•lee•ij] *n* follaje M

**folk** [fok] *adj* gente F

**follow** [FAH•lo] *vt vi* seguir; *adj* a siguiente; *prep* después de

**follower** [FAH•lo•ur] *n* seguidor M

**following** [FAH•lo•ing] *adj* siguiente

**folly** [FAH•lee] *n* tontería F

**foment** [FO•ment] *vt* fomentar

**fond** [fahnd] *adj* aficionado

**fondle** [FAHN•dl] *vt* acariciar

**food** [food] *n* comida F

**fool** [fooul] *n* tonto M

**foolish** [FOOU•lish] *adj* tonto necio

**foot** [fut] *n* pie M

**football** [FUT•baul] *n* fútbol M

**footpath** [FUT•path] *n* senda F

**footprint** [FUT•print] *n* huella F

**footstep** [FUT•step] *n* paso M

**for** [faur] *prep* para; por

**forage** [FAU•rij] *n* forrage M

**forbid** [faur•BID] *vt* prohibir

**force** [faurs] *n* fuerza F; *vt* forzar

**forceful** [FAURS•ful] *adj* poderoso

**forceps** [FAUR•seps] *npl* fórceps M

**ford** [faurd] *n* vado M

**forearm** [FAUR•ahrm] *n* antebrazo M

**forecast** [FAUR•kast] *n* pronóstico M

**forefather** [FAUR•fah•thur] *n* antepasado M

**forego** [faur•GO] *vt* preceder

**foreground** [FAUR•ground] *n* primer plano M

**forehead** [FAUR•hed] *n* frente M

**foreign** [FAU•run] *adj* extranjero

**foreigner** [FAU•ru•nur] *n*
extranjero M

**foreman** [FAUR•mun] *n*
encargado M

**foremost** [FAUR•most] *adj*
delantero

**forerunner** [FAUU•ruh•nur] *n*
predecesor M

**foresee** [faur•SEE] *vt* antever

**foreshadow** [faur•SHA•do] *vt*
prefigurar

**foresight** [FAUR•suyt] *n*
previsión F

**forest** [FAU•rist] *n* bosque M

**foretell** [faur•TEL] *vt* predecir

**forever** [fu•RE•vur] *adv*
siempre

**foreword** [FAUR•wurd] *n*
preámbulo M

**forfeit** [FAUR•fit] *vt* pérdida F

**forge 1** [faurj] *n* forja F; *vt*
fraguar; falsificar (copy)

**forge 2** *vi* avanzar; ~ ahead\
adelantarse rápidamente

**forget** [faur•GET] *vt vi*
olvidarse

**forgetful** [faur•GET•ful] *adj*
olvidado

**forgive** [faur•GIV] *vt* perdonar

**forgo** [faur•GO] *vt* abandonar

**fork** [faurk] *n* tenedor M

**forlorn** [faur•LAURN] *adj*
desolado

**form** [faurm] *n* forma F; *vt*
formar

**formal** [FAUR•ml] *adj* formal

**formality** [faur•MA•li•tee] *n*
formalidad F

**former** [FAUR•mur] *adj*
anterior pasado

**formidable** [FAUR•mi•du•bl]
*adj* formidable

**formula** [FAUR•myu•lu] *n*
fórmula F

**forsake** [faur•SAIK] *vt*
desamparar

**forsaken** [faur•SAI•kn] *adj*
abandonado

**fort** [faurt] *n* fortaleza F

**forth** [faurth] *adv* delante

**forthcoming**
[faurth•CUH•ming] *adj*
venidero

**fortification**
[FAUR•ti•fi•KAI•shn] *n*
fortificación F

**fortify** [FAUR•ti•FUY] *vt*
fortificar

**fortitude** [FAUR•ti•TOOD] *n*
fortaleza F

**fortnight** [FAURT•nuyt] *n*
quincena F

**fortress** [FAUR•tris] *n*
fortaleza F

**fortuitous** [faur•TOO•i•tus] *adj*
fortuito

**fortunate** [FAUR•chu•nut] *adj*
afortunado

**fortunately**
[FAUR•chu•nut•lee] *adv*
afortunadamente

**fortune** [FAUR•chun] *n*
fortuna F

**forty** [FAUR•tee] *num* cuarenta

**forward** [FAUR•wurd] *adj*
delantero

**fossil** [FAH•sl] *n* fósil M

**foul** [foul] *adj* repugnante;
sucio; *vt* ensuciar; ~ play\
jugada sucia

**found 1** [found] *pp* encontrado

**found 2** *vt* fundar

**foundation** [foun•DAI•shn] *n* fundación F

**founder** [FOUN•dur] *n* fundador M

**fountain** [FOUN•tun] *n* fuente F

**four** [faur] *num* cuatro

**fourteen** [faur•TEEN] *num* catorce

**fourth** [faurth] *num* cuarto

**fowl** [foul] *n* gallo M

**fox** [fahks] *n* zorro M

**fraction** [FRAK•shn] *n* fragmento M

**fracture** [FRAK•chur] *n* fractura F; *vt* fracturar; *vi* fracturarse

**fragile** [FRA•jul] *adj* frágil

**fragment** [FRAG•munt] *n* fragmento M

**fragrance** [FRAI•gruns] *n* fragancia F

**fragrant** [FRAI•grunt] *adj* fragante

**frame** [fraim] *n* armadura F; ~ of mind\ estado de ánimo; *vt* incriminar falsamente (coll)

**franc** [frangk] *n* franco M

**France** [frans] *n* Francia

**franchise** [FRAN•chuyz] *n* franqueza F

**frank** [frangk] *adj* sincero

**frantic** [FRAN•tik] *adj* frenético

**fraternal** [fru•TUR•nl] *adj* fraternal

**fraternity** [fru•TUR•ni•tee] *n* fraternidad F

**fraud** [fraud] *n* fraude M

**fraudulent** [FRAU•dyu•lunt] *adj* fraudulento

**frayed** [fraid] *adj* reñado

**freak** [freek] *adj* fenómeno

**free** [free] *adj* libre; ~ of charge\ gratis

**free speech** [FREE SPEECH] *n* libertad de palabra F

**free trade** [FREE TRAID] *n* librecambio M

**freedom** [FREE•dum] *n* libertad F

**freeze** [freez] *vt* helar

**freezer** [FREE•zur] *n* helador M

**freight** [frait] *n* carga F

**French** [french] *adj* francés

**french fries** [ ~ fruyz] *npl* papas fritas M

**frenzy** [FREN•zee] *n* locura F

**frequency** [FREE•kwun•see] *n* frecuencia F

**frequent** [*adj.* FREE•kwunt *v.* free•KWENT] *adj* frecuente

**fresh** [fresh] *adj* fresco; nuevo

**freshen** [FRE•shn] *vt* refrescar

**freshman** [FRESH•mun] *n* estudiante del primer año M

**freshness** [FRESH•nus] *n* frescura F

**freshwater** [FRESH•WAU•tur] *adj* de agua dulce M

**fret** [fret] *vi* rozar

**friar** [fruyur] *n* monje M

**friction** [FRIK•shn] *n* fricción F

**Friday** [FRUY•dai] *n* viernes M

**friend** [frend] *n* amigo

**friendly** [FREND•lee] *adj* amistoso

**friendship** [FREND•ship] *n* amistad F

**fright** [fruyt] *n* miedo M

**frighten** [FRUY•tn] *vt* dar
miedo
**frigid** [FRI•jid] *adj* frígido
**fringe** [frinj] *n* franja F
**frisk** [frisk] *vt* retozar
**frisky** [FRI•skee] *adj* alegre
**frivolous** [FRI•vu•lus] *adj*
frívolo
**frog** [frahg] *n* rana F
**frolic** [FRAH•lik] *vi* juguetear
**from** [fruhm] *prep* de desde; a
partir de (time, price, etc)
ségun (accroding to); take ~\
quitar
**front** [fruhnt] *adj* frente; *n* parte
delantera; fachada F
(building); in ~ of\ delante de
**front door** [FRUNT DAUR] *n*
puerta principal F
**frontier** [fruhn•TEER] *n*
frontera F
**frost** [fraust] *n* helamiento M
**froth** [frauth] *n* espuma F
**frown** [froun] *n* ceño M
**fruit** [froot] *n* fruto; fruta M
**fruitless** [FROOT•lis] *adj* inútil
**frustrate** [FRUH•strait] *vt*
frustrar
**frustration** [fruh•STRAI•shn] *n*
frustraciòn F
**fry** [fruy] *vt vi* saltear
**fudge** [fuj] *n* dulce de
chocolate F
**fuel** [fyooul] *n* combustible M
**fugitive** [FYOO•ju•tiv] *n*
fugitivo M
**fulfill** [ful•FIL] *vt* cumplir
**fulfillment** [ful•FIL•munt] *n*
cumplimiento M
**full** [ful] *adj* lleno; completo; at
~ speed\ a máxima velacidad;
in ~\ sin quitar

**full moon** [FUL MOON] *n* luna
llena F
**fumble** [FUHM•bl] *vt*
chapucear
**fumes** [fyoomz] *npl* humos
**fumigate** [FYOO•mi•GAIT] *vt*
fumigar
**fun** [fuhn] *adj* divertido; for ~\
en bruma; have ~\ divertirse;
make ~ of\ burlarse de
**function** [FUNGK•shn] *n*
función F; *vi* funcionar
**fund** [fuhnd] *n* fondo M
**fundamental**
[FUHN•du•MEN•tl] *adj*
fundamental
**funeral** [FYOO•nu•rul] *n*
entierro M
**fungus** [FUNG•gus] *n* hongo M
**funnel** [FUH•nl] *n* fonil M
**funny** [FUH•nee] *adj* cómico
**fur** [fur] *n* piel M
**furious** [FYOOU•ree•us] *adj*
furioso
**furnace** [FUR•nis] *n* horno M
**furnish** [FUR•nish] *vt* surtir;
proveer
**furniture** [FUR•ni•chur] *n*
muebles
**furry** [FU•ree] *adj* peludo
**further** [FUR•thur] *adj*
adelantado; a más lejano; *vt*
formentar
**furthermore**
[FUR•thur•MAUR] *adv*
además
**furthest** [FUR•thist] *adj adv*
más lejano
**furtive** [FUR•tiv] *adj* furtivo
**fury** [FYU•ree] *n* furia F

**fuse 1** [fyooz] *n* mecha F; *vt*
fundir
**fuse 2** *n* mecha F (of bomb)
**fusion** [FYOO•zhn] *n* fusión F
**fuss** [fuhs] *n* actividad F; jaleo
M; make a ~ of\ tratar con
mucha atención

**futile** [FYOO•tl] *adj* fútil
**future** [FYOO•chur] *adj* futuro
M; in ~\ en lo sucesivo
**fuzzy** [FUH•zee] *adj* velloso

# G

**gable** [GAI•bl] *n* hastial F
**gadget** [GA•jit] *n* mecanismo M
**Gaelic** [GAIU•lik] *adj n* gaélico
**gag** [gag] *n* mordaza F; *vt*
amordazar
**gage (gauge)** [gaij] *n* guante M
**gain** [gain] *n* ganancia F; *vt*
ganar
**gait** [gait] *n* andar M
**gale** [gaiul] *n* viento M
**gall** [gaul] *n* hiel M
**gallant** [GA•lunt] *adj* galante
**gallery** [GA•lu•ree] *n* gallería F
**galley** [GA•lee] *n* galera F
**gallon** [GA•ln] *n* galón F
**gallop** [GA•lup] *n* galope M; *vi*
galopar
**gallows** [GA•loz] *npl* horca F
**gamble** [GAM•bl] *n* juego M;
*vt vi* jugar; ~ on\ contar con
**game** [gaim] *n* juego M; *adj* a
valiente; ~ for\ listo para
**gang** [gang] *n* grupo M
**gangster** [GANG•stur] *n*
gangster M
**gangway** [GANG•wai] *n*
pasillo M

**gap** [gap] *n* boquete M; *n*
vacio M
**gape** [gaip] *vi* bostezar
**gaping** [GAI•ping] *adj*
bostezado
**garage** [gu•RAHZH] *n* garaje M
**garbage** [GAHR•bij] *n* basura F
**garden** [GAHR•dn] *n* jardín;
huerto M; *vi* trabajar en el
jardin; huerto
**gargle** [GAHR•gl] *vi* gargarizar
**gargoyle** [GAHR•goil] *n*
gárgola F
**garland** [GAHR•lund] *n*
guirnalda F
**garlic** [GAHR•lik] *n* ajo M
**garment** [GAHR•munt] *n*
vestido M
**garnish** [GAHR•nish] *v*
adornar; *n* aderzo M
**garrison** [GA•ri•sn] *n* presidio M
**garter** [GAHR•tr] *n* liga F
**gas** [gas] *n* gasolina F; fas M; *vt*
asfixiar con gas; *vi* charlar
(coll)
**gaseous** [GA•shus] *adj* gaseoso
**gasket** [GA•skit] *n* tomador M

**gasoline** [GA•su•LEEN] *n* gasolina F

**gasp** [gasp] *vi* boquear

**gate** [gait] *n* puerta F

**gather** [GA•thur] *vi* recoger; reunirse; *vt* reunir; acumularse (things)

**gathering** [GA•thu•ring] *n* recolección F

**gaudy** [GAU•dee] *adj* ostentoso

**gaunt** [gaunt] *adj* delgado

**gauntlet** [GAUNT•lit] *n* manopla F

**gauze** [gauz] *n* cendal M

**gay** [gai] *adj* animado; alegre; vivo; homosexual; gay (coll)

**gaze** [gaiz] *vt* mirar; *n* mirada F

**gazette** [gu•ZET] *n* periódico M

**gear** [geeur] *n* aparejo M

**gelatin** [JE•lu•tin] *n* gelatina F

**gem** [jem] *n* gema F

**gender** [JEN•dur] *n* género M

**gene** [jeen] *n* gen M

**general** [JE•nu•rl] *adj n* general M

**generalization** [JEN•ru•li•ZAI•shn] *n* generalización F

**generalize** [JE•nu•ru•LUYZ] *vt* generalizar

**generally** [JE•nu•ru•lee] *adv* generalmente

**generate** [JE•nu•RAIT] *vt* generar

**generation** [JE•nu•RAI•shn] *n* generación F

**generator** [JE•nu•RAI•tur] *n* generador M

**generosity** [JE•nu•RAH•si•tee] *n* generosidad F

**generous** [JE•nu•rus] *adj* generoso

**genetic** [ji•NE•tik] *adj* genético

**genial** [JEE•nyul] *adj* genial

**genital** [JE•ni•tl] *adj* genital

**genius** [JEE•nyus] *n* genio M

**gentle** [JEN•tl] *adj* dócil

**gentleman** [JEN•tl•mun] *n* caballero M

**gently** [JENT•lee] *adv* suavemente

**gentry** [JEN•tree] *n* gente culta

**genuine** [JE•nyoo•in] *adj* genuino

**geography** [jee•AH•gru•fee] *n* geografía F

**geology** [jee•AH•lu•jee] *n* geología F

**geometric** [JEE•u•ME•trik] *adj* geométrico

**geometry** [jee•AH•mu•tree] *n* geometría F

**germ** [jerm] *n* germen M

**German** [JER•mun] *adj* alemán

**Germany** [JER•mu•nee] *n* alemanía F

**germinate** [JER•mi•NAIT] *vi* germinar

**gesticulate** [je•STI•kyu•LAIT] *vi* manotear

**gesture** [JES•chur] *n* signo M

**get** [get] *vt* obtener; adquirir; encontrar (find); traer; buscar (fetch); comprender (understand); ~ ready\ prepararse; ~ along\ ir tirando; ~ along with\ llevarse bien con; ~ at\ llegar a; ~ away\ salir; escaparse; ~ out\ salir; ~ out of\ librarse de; ~ over\ reponerse de; ~ through\

pasar; terminar; ~ up\
levantarse; traje

**ghastly** [GAST•lee] *adj* horrible

**ghost** [gost] *n* espíritu;
fantasma M

**giant** [JUY•unt] *adj n* gigante M

**gibberish** [JI•bu•rish] *n*
farfulla M

**giddy** [GI•dee] *adj* mareado

**gift** [gift] *n* regalo M

**gifted** [GIF•tid] *adj* talentoso

**gigantic** [juy•GAN•tik] *adj*
gigantesco

**giggle** [GI•gl] *vi* reírse

**gilded** [GIL•did] *adj* dorado

**ginger** [JIN•jur] *n* jengibre M

**gingerbread** [JIN•jur•BRED] *n*
galleta F

**gingerly** [JIN•jur•lee] *adv*
cautelosamente

**gipsy** [JIP•see] *n* gitano M

**giraffe** [ji•RAF] *n* jirafa F

**girder** [GUR•dur] *n* viga F

**girdle** [GUR•dl] *n* cinto M

**girl** [gurl] *n* niña F

**girlfriend** [GURL•frend] *n*
novia F

**girth** [gurth] *n* cincha F

**gist** [jist] *n* substancia F

**give** [giv] *vt* dar; entregar
(deliver); regalar (present);
conceder (grant); *n* elasticidad
F; ~ away\ regalar; ~ back\
devolver; ~ in\ rendirse; ~
out\ distribuir; ~ up\ renunciar
a; ceder

**given** [GI•vn] *prep* dado

**glacier** [GLAI•shur] *n* glaciar M

**glad** [glad] *adj* alegre

**gladly** [GLAD•lee] *adv*
alegremente

**glamor** [GLA•mur] *n* encanto M

**glamorous** [GLA•mu•rus] *adj*
fascinador

**glance** [glans] *n* mirada F

**gland** [gland] *n* glándula F

**glare** [glaiur] *n* deslumbrante M

**glaring** [GLAIU•ring] *adj*
brillante

**glass** [glas] *n* vidrio M

**glasses** [GLA•siz] *npl* gafas F

**glassy** [GLA•see] *adj* cristalino

**glaze** [glaiz] *n* lustre M; *vt*
poner cristales a; vidrar

**gleam** [gleem] *n* destello M

**glean** [gleen] *vt* rebuscar

**glee** [glee] *n* alegría F

**glib** [glib] *adj* suelto

**glide** [gluyd] *vi* deslizarse

**glimmer** [GLI•mur] *n*
resplandor M

**glimpse** [glimps] *n* ojeada F

**glisten** [GLI•sn] *vi* brillar

**glitter** [GLI•tur] *v* resplandor M

**gloat** [glot] *vi* gozarse

**global** [GLO•bl] *adj* esférico

**globe** [glob] *n* globo M

**gloom** [gloom] *n* penumbra F

**gloomy** [GLOO•mee] *n* obscuro

**glorify** [GLAU•ri•FUY] *vt*
glorificar

**glorious** [GLAU•ree•us] *adj*
glorioso

**glory** [GLAU•ree] *n* gloria F;
esplendor M

**gloss** [glaus] *n* lustre M

**glossary** [GLAU•su•ree] *n*
glosario M

**glossy** [GLAU•see] *adj* lustroso

**glove** [gluhv] *n* guante M

**glow** [glo] *n* luz F; *vi* brillar

**glowing** [GLO•wing] *adj*
resplandeciente

**glucose** [GLOO•kos] *n*
glucosa F

**glue** [gloo] *n* cola F

**glum** [gluhm] *adj* malhumorado

**glut** [gluht] *n* hartazgo M

**glutton** [GLUH•tn] *n* glotón M

**gluttonous** [GLUH•tu•nus] *adj*
glotón

**gluttony** [GLUH•tu•nee] *n*
glotonería F

**gnarled** [nahrld] *adj* nudoso

**gnash** [nash] *vt* rechinar

**gnat** [nat] *n* mosquito M

**gnaw** [nau] *vt* roer

**go** [go] *vi* ir; irse; funcionar
(work); hacerse (become); ~
ahead\ adelante; ~ bad\
pasarse; ~ across\ cruzar; ~
away\ irse; ~ back\ volver; ~
back on\ falter a; ~ by\ pasar;
~ down\ bajar; ~ in\ entrar; ~
on\ seguir; ~ out\ salir; ~
over\ examinar; ~ through\
sufrir; ~ under\ hundirse; ~
without\ pasarse sin

**go-between** [GO bee•TWEEN]
*n* interponerse

**goal** [goul] *n* meta F

**goat** [got] *n* cabra F

**gobble** [GAH•bl] *vt* engullir

**goblin** [GAH•blin] *n* duende M

**God** [gahd] *n* Dios M

**goddaughter**
[GAHD•DAU•tur] *n* ahijada F

**goddess** [GAH•dis] *n* diosa F

**godfather** [GAHD•FAH•thur] *n*
padrino M

**godless** [GAHD•lis] *adj* sin
Dios

**godmother**
[GAHD•MUH•thur] *n*
padrina F

**godsend** [GAHD•send] *n*
chiripa F

**goggles** [GAH•glz] *npl* gafas
para el sol F

**gold** [gould] *n* oro M; *adj* de oro

**gold-plated** [GOLD•PLAI•tid]
*adj* vajilla de oro F

**golden** [GOL•dn] *adj* de oro

**goldfish** [GOLD•fish] *n* carpa
dorada F

**golf** [gahlf] *n* jugar al golf M

**gone** [gawn] *past adj* pasado

**gong** [gahng] *n* gong M

**good** [gud] *n* bien M; *adj*
bueno; ~ morning/afternoon/
evening\ ¡buenas días/tardes/
noches; as ~ as\ casi; do ~\
hacer bien; have a ~ time\
divertirse; it is ~ for you\ le
sentará bien; for ~\ para
siempre; it's no ~ .\ és inútil.

**good-looking** [GUD•LU•king]
*adj* hermoso; guapo

**goose** [goos] *n* ganso M

**gore** [gaur] *vt* acornear

**gorge** [gaurj] *n* garganta F

**gorgeous** [GAUR•jus] *adj*
magnífico

**gorilla** [gu•RI•lu] *n* gorila F

**gory** [GAU•ree] *adj* sangriento

**gospel** [GAH•spl] *n* evangelio M

**gossip** [GAH•sip] *n*
chismografía F; *vi* charlar;
comadrear

**gothic** [GAH•thik] *adj* gótico

**gourd** [gaurd] *n* calabaza F

**gout** [gout] *n* gota F

**govern** [GUH•vurn] *vt vi*
gobernar

**governess** [GUH•vur•nis] *n*
gobernadora F

**government** [GUH•vurn•munt]
*n* gobierno M

**governor** [GUH•vur•nur] *n*
gobernador M

**gown** [goun] *n* vestido M

**grab** [grab] *vt* agarrar

**grace** [grais] *n* gracia F

**graceful** [GRAIS•ful] *adj*
gracioso; elegante

**gracious** [GRAI•shus] *adj*
gracioso

**grade** [graid] *n* grado M; clase;
categoria F; *vt* clasificar

**grade school** [GRAID skool] *n*
escuela F

**gradual** [GRA•joo•ul] *adj*
gradual

**graduate** [n. GRA•joo•it v.
GRA•joo•AIT] v graduar

**graft** [graft] *n* injerto M

**grain** [grain] *n* grano M

**gram** [gram] *n* gramo M

**grammar** [GRA•mur] *n*
gramática F

**grammatical** [gru•MA•ti•kl]
*adj* gramatical

**granary** [GRAI•nu•ree] *n*
granero M

**grand** [grand] *adj* grande;
estupendo (coll)

**granddaughter**
[GRAN•DAU•tur] *n* nieta F

**grandeur** [GRAN•jur] *n*
grandeza F

**grandfather**
[GRAND•FAH•thur] *n*
abuelo M

**grandiose** [GRAN•dee•OS] *adj*
grandioso

**grandma** [GRAND•mah] *n*
abuela F

**grandparents**
[GRAND•PA•runts] *npl*
abuelos

**grandson** [GRAND•suhn] *n*
nieto M

**granite** [GRA•nit] *n* granito M

**grant** [grant] *n* concesión F; *vt*
conceder; donar (given)

**granule** [GRA•nyoo•ul] *n*
gránulo M

**grape** [graip] *n* uva F

**grapefruit** [GRAIP•froot] *n*
toronja F

**graph** [graf] *n* gráfica F

**graphic** [GRA•fik] *adj* gráfico

**grapple** [GRA•pl] *vi* aferrar

**grasp 1** [grasp] *vt* agarrar

**grasp 2** *n* asimiento M

**grass** [gras] *n* hierba F

**grasshopper** [GRAS•HAH•pur]
*n* saltamontes M

**grassy** [GRA•see] *adj* herboso

**grate** [grait] *n* reja F; *vt* rallar;
*vi* rechinar

**grateful** [GRAIT•ful] *adj*
agradecido

**grater** [GRAI•tur] *n* rallador M

**gratification**
[GRA•ti•fi•KAI•shn] *n*
satisfacción F

**grating** [GRAI•ting] *adj*
rechinante

**gratitude** [GRA•ti•TOOD] *n*
gratitud F

**gratuity** [gru•TOO•i•tee] *n*
propina F

**grave 1** [graiv] *adj* grave; serio

**grave 2** *n* sepultura F
**gravel** [GRA•vl] *n* arena F
**gravity** [GRA•vi•tee] *n* gravedad F
**gravy** [GRAI•vee] *n* salsa F
**gray** [grai] *adj n* gris M
**graze 1** [graiz] *vt vi* pacer (eat)
**graze 2** *vt* rozar; raspar; *n* rozadura F
**grease** [grees] *n* grasa F; *vt* engrasar
**great** [grait] *adj* gran M; *adj* grande; estupendo (coll)
**Great Britain** [~ bri•tn] *n* la Gran Bretaña F
**great-granddaughter** [GRAIT•GRAN•DAU•tur] *n* bisnieta F
**great-grandfather** [GRAIT•GRAND•FA•thur] *n* bisabuelo M
**great-grandmother** [GRAIT•GRAND•MU•thur] *n* bisabuela F
**great-grandparents** [GRAIT•GRAND•PAI•rintz] *npl* bisabuelos
**great-grandson** [GRAIT•GRAND•son] *n* bisnieto M
**greatness** [GRAIT•nis] *n* grandeza F
**Greece** [grees] *n* Grecia F
**greed** [greed] *n* ansia F
**greedy** [GREE•dee] *adj* ansioso
**Greek** [greek] *adj* griego
**green** [green] *adj n* verde
**greenhouse** [GREEN•hous] *n* invernáculo para plantas M
**Greenland** [GREEN•lund] *n* Groenlandia

**greet** [greet] *vt* saludar
**greeting** [GREE•ting] *n* saludo M
**grenade** [gru•NAID] *n* granada F
**grid** [grid] *n* reja F
**grief** [greef] *n* dolor M
**grievance** [GREE•vuns] *n* agravio M
**grieve** [greev] *vt* lastimar; afligir; *vi* afligirse; ~ for\ llorar
**grievous** [GREE•vus] *adj* doloroso
**grill** [gril] *n* parrillas F (cooking) *vt* asar a la parilla (cook on ~); interrogar (question)
**grille** [gril] *n* verja F
**grim** [grim] *adj* formidable
**grimace** [GRI•mus] *n* mueca F
**grime** [gruym] *n* mugre M
**grimy** [GRUY•mee] *adj* tiznado
**grin** [grin] *n* sonrisa F; *vt* sonreir
**grind** [gruynd] *vt* moler; ~ one's teeth\ hacer rechinar los dientes
**grinder** [GRUYN•dur] *n* molendero M
**grip** [grip] *n* agarro M; *vt* agarrar; captar la atención de (hold attention)
**gripe** [gruyp] *n* agarro M
**grisly** [GRIZ•lee] *adj* horroroso
**gristle** [GRI•sl] *n* cartílago M
**grit** [grit] *n* arena F; valor M (coll) ~ one's teeth\ acorcrazarse (coll)
**groan** [gron] *n* gemido M

**groceries** [GROS•reez] *npl* comestibles M

**grocery** [GROS•ree] *n* bodega F

**groin** [groin] *n* ingle M

**groom** [groom] *n* novio M

**groove** [groov] *n* ranura F

**grope** [grop] *vi* tentalear

**grotesque** [gro•TESK] *adj* grotesco

**grouch** [grouch] *n* enojo M; *vi* rezongar

**ground** [ground] *n* suelo M; terreno M (area); razón F (reason) *vt* varar

**ground floor** [GROUND FLAUR] *n* piso bajo M

**groundless** [GROUND•lis] *adj* infundado

**group** [groop] *n* grupo M

**grove** [grov] *n* bosquecillo M

**grovel** [GRAH•vl] *vi* sepear

**grow** [gro] *vt* crecer; cultiarse; *vt* cultivar; ~ up\ hacerse mayor

**growl** [grouul] *n* gruñido M

**growth** [groth] *n* crecimiento M

**grub** [gruhb] *n* larva F

**grubby** [GRUH•bee] *adj* gusaniento

**grudge** [gruhj] *n* resentimiento M

**grueling** [GROOU•ling] *adj* agotador

**gruff** [gruhf] *adj* rudo

**grumble** [GRUHM•bl] *vi* refunfuñar

**grumpy** [GRUHM•pee] *adj* malhumorado

**grunt** [gruhnt] *n* gruñido M; *vi* gruñir

**guarantee** [GA•run•TEE] *n* garantía F

**guard** [gahrd] *n* guardia F

**guardien** [GAHR•dee•un] *n* guardián M

**guerrilla** [gu•RI•lu] *n* guerrillero M

**guess** [ges] *n* conjetura F; *vt vi* adivinar; creer; ~ work\ *n* conjeturas *npl* F

**guest** [gest] *n* huésped (hotel); invitado M

**guestroom** [GEST•ROOM] *n* cuarto de respeto M

**guffaw** [guh•FAU] *vi* reír a carcajadas

**guidance** [GUY•duns] *n* guía F

**guide** [guyd] *vt* guiar; *n* guia MF

**guild** [gild] *n* gremio M

**guile** [guyul] *n* astucia F

**guillotine** [GI•lu•TEEN] *n* guillotina F

**guilt** [gilt] *n* culpa F

**guilty** [GIL•tee] *adj* culpable

**guinea pig** [GI•nee ~ ] *n* conejillo M

**guise** [guyz] *n* guisa F

**guitar** [gi•TAHR] *n* guitarra F

**gulf** [guhlf] *n* golfo M

**gulp** [guhlp] *n* trago M

**gullet** [GUH•lit] *n* gaznate M

**gullible** [GUH•li•bl] *adj* incauto

**gully** [GUH•lee] *n* cárcava F

**gum 1** [guhm] *n* goma F; *n* chicle M (chewing ~); *vt* engomar

**gum 2** *n* encia F (anat)

**gun** [guhn] *n* cañon M; pistola F; ~ down\ abatir a tiros

**gunfire** [GUHN•fuyur] *n* fuego de artillería M

**gunpowder** [GUHN•pou•dur] *n* pólvera F

**gunshot** [GUHN•shaht] *n* tiro M

**gurgle** [GUR•gl] *vi* borbolleo M

**gush** [guhsh] *n* chorro M

**gusset** [GUH•sit] *n* escudete M

**gust** [guhst] *n* racha F

**gut** [guht] *n* tripa F

**gutter** [GUH•tur] *n* arroyo M

**guy** [guy] *n* tipo M

**guzzle** [GUH•zl] *vt* engullir

**gym** [jim] *n* gimnasio M

**gymnasium** [jim•NAI•zce•um] *n* gimnasio M

**gymnast** [JIM•nust] *n* gimnasta F

**gymnastics** [jim•NA•stiks] *npl* himnasia F

**gypsy** [JIP•see] *n* gitano M

**gyrate** [JUY•rait] *vi* girar

# H

**habit** [HA•bit] *n* hábito M; costumbre F (clothing)

**habitual** [hu•BI•choo•ul] *adj* habitual

**hack** [hak] *vt* tajar; ~ to pieces\ cortar en pedazos

**hackneyed** [HAK•need] *adj* gastado

**haggard** [HA•gurd] *adj* macilento

**haggle** [HA•gl] *vi* altercado M

**hail** [haiul] *n* granizo M

**hailstone** [HAIUL•ston] *n* piedra de granizo F

**hair** [haiur] *n* pelo M

**hairbrush** [HAIUR•bruhsh] *n* cepillo M

**haircut** [HAIUR•kuht] *n* corte el pelo M

**hairdresser** [HAIUR•DRE•sur] *n* peluquero M

**hairless** [HAIUR•lis] *adj* calvo

**hairpin** [HAIUR•pin] *n* horquilla F

**hairstyle** [HAIUR•stuyul] *n* peinado M

**hairy** [haiur] *adj* cabelludo

**Haiti** [HAI•tee] *n* Haiti

**half** [haf] *n* mitad F; *adj* medio

**half-hearted** [-HAR•tid] *adj* indiferente

**half hour** [HAF OUR] *n* media hora F

**half-mast** [HAF•MAST] *adj* poner a media asta

**half-price** [HAF•PRUYS] *adj* medio precio M

**halfway** [HAF•WAI] *adj adv* medio

**hall** [haul] *n* vestíbulo M

**hallowed** [ha•lod] *adj* santo

**Halloween** [hah•lo•ween] *n* víspera de todos los santos F

**hallucination** [hu•loo•si•nai•shn] *n* alucinación F

**hallway** [haul•wai] *n* pasillo M

**halo** [HAI•lo] *n* halo M

**halt** [hault] *n* alto M
**halter** [HAUL•tur] *n* cabestro M
**halve** [hav] *vt* partir
**ham** [ham] *n* jamón M; *n*
raconista MF (theatrical)
**hamburger** [HAM•BUR•gur] *n*
hamburguesa F
**hamlet** [HAM•lit] *n* aldea M
**hammer** [HA•mur] *n* martillo M
**hammock** [HA•muk] *n*
hamaca F
**hamper** [HAM•pur] *n* cesta F
**hand** [hand] *n* mano F; on/at/by
~\ a mano; lend a ~\ echar
una mano; on the one ~.on
the other\ por un lado. por
otra; out of ~\ fuera de
control; *vt* dar; ~ down\ pasar;
~ over\ entregar; ~ out\
distribuir
**handbag** [HAND•bag] *n*
bolsa F
**handcuff** [HAND•kuhf] *n*
manilla F
**handful** [HAND•ful] *n* manojo M
**handicap** [HAN•dee•KAP] *n*
restricción F
**handicapped**
[HAN•dee•KAPT] *adj*
impedido
**handkerchief** [HANG•kur•chif]
*n* pañuelo M
**handle** [HAN•dl] *n* asa F
**handmade** [HAND•MAID] *adj*
hecho a mano M
**handshake** [HAND•shaik] *n*
apretón de manos M
**handwriting**
[HAND•WRUY•ting] *n*
escritura F
**handy** [HAN•dee] *adj* diestro

**hang** [hang] *vt* colgar;
suspender; ~ about\
holgazanear; ~ on\ resister;
esperar; ~ out\ tender; vivir; ~
up\ colgar (phone)
**hangar** [HANG•ur] *n* hangar M
**hanger** [HANG•ur] *n* barra F
**haphazard** [hap•HA•zurd] *adj*
casualidad F
**hapless** [HAP•lis] *adj*
descraciado
**happen** [HA•pn] *vi* ocurrir
**happening** [HA•pu•ning] *n*
suceso M
**happily** [HA•pi•lee] *adv*
felizmente
**happiness** [HA•pee•nis] *n*
felicidad F
**happy** [HA•pee] *adj* felíz
**harass** [hu•RAS] *vt* agotar
**harassment** [hu•RAS•munt] *n*
fatiga F
**harbor** [HAHR•bur] *n* puerto M
**hard** [hahrd] *adj* duro; dificil
(difficult) ~ of hearing\ duro
de oído; ~ up\ sin un cuarto
(coll)
**harden** [HAR•din] *vt* endurecer
**hardly** [HARD•lee] *adv* apenas
**hardship** [HAHRD•ship] *n*
opresión F
**hardware** [HAHRD•waiur] *n*
ferretería F
**hardy** [HAHR•dee] *adj* robusto
**hare** [haiur] *n* liebre M
**harm** [hahrm] *n* daño M; *vt*
hacer daño a (person); dañar
(thing)
**harmful** [HAHRM•ful] *adj*
dañoso

**harmless** [HAHRM•lis] *adj* salvo

**harmonica** [hahr•MAH•ni•ku] *n* armónica F

**harmonious** [hahr•MO•nee•us] *adj* armonioso

**harmonize** [HAHR•mu•NUYZ] *vt* armonizar

**harmony** [HAHR•mu•nee] *n* armonía F

**harness** [HAHR•nis] *n* arneses M

**harp** [hahrp] *n* arpa F

**harpoon** [hahr•POON] *n* arpón M

**harpsichord** [HARP•si•KAURD] *n* clavicordio M

**harsh** [hahrsh] *adj* rudo

**harvest** [HAHR•vist] *n* siega; cosecha F; *vt* cosechar

**haste** [haist] *n* prisa F

**hasten** [HAI•sn] *vt* apresurar

**hastily** [HAI•sti•lee] *adv* vivamente

**hat** [hat] *n* sombrero M

**hatch 1** [hach] *vt* incubar; empollar

**hatch 2** [hach] *n* ventanilla; escotilla (naut) F

**hatchet** [HA•chit] *n* destral M

**hate** [hait] *n* odio M; *vt* odiar

**hateful** [HAIT•ful] *adj* odioso

**hatred** [HAI•trid] *n* odio M

**haughty** [HAU•tee] *adj* orgulloso

**haul** [haul] *vt* tirar

**haunt** [haunt] *vt* frecuentar

**have** [hav] *aux verb* haber; *vt* tener; ~ something to

eat/drink etc.\ tomar; ~ to do\ tener que hacer

**haven** [HAI•vn] *n* fondeadero M

**havoc** [HA•vuk] *n* estrago M

**hawk** [hauk] *n* cernícalo M

**hay** [hai] *n* forraje M

**haystack** [HAI•stak] *n* montón de heno M

**hazard** [HA•zurd] *n* novatada F; *vt* arriesgar; aventurar (guess)

**hazardous** [HA•zur•dus] *adj* peligroso

**haze** [haiz] *n* calina F

**hazelnut** [HAI•zl•NUHT] *n* avellana F

**hazy** [HAI•zee] *adj* aneblado

**he** [hee] *pers pron* él

**head** [hed] *n* cabeza F

**headache** [HE•daik] *n* dolor de cabeza M

**headlight** [HED•luyt] *n* linterna F

**headline** [HED•luyn] *n* titulares M

**headphones** [HED•fonz] *npl* receptor M

**headquarters** [HED•KAUR•turz] *npl* cuartel general M

**headrest** [HED•rest] *n* apoyo M

**headstrong** [HED•straung] *adj* testarudo

**headway** [HED•wai] *n* marcha F

**heal** [heeul] *vt* curar

**health** [helth] *n* salud F

**healthy** [HEL•thee] *adj* sano M

**heap** [heep] *n* montòn F

**hear** [heeur] *vt* oír

**hearing** [HEEU•ring] *n* oído M

**hearsay** [HEEUR•sai] *n*
rumor M

**hearse** [hurs] *n* coche fúnebre M

**heart** [hahrt] *n* corazòn F; at ~\
en el fondo; by ~\ de
memoria; lose ~\
descorozonarse

**heart attack** [HAHRT a•TAK]
*n* ataque cardíaco M

**heartbeat** [HAHRT•beet] *n*
latido M

**heartbroken**
[HAHRT•BRO•kn] *adj*
acongojado

**hearth** [hahrth] *n* hogar M

**heartless** [HAHRT•lis] *adj* sin
corazón

**hearty** [HAHR•tee] *adj*
vigoroso

**heat** [heet] *n* calor M; *vt*
calentar; *vi* calentarse

**heater** [HEE•tur] *n* calentador M

**heather** [HE•thur] *n* brezo M

**heating** [HEE•ting]on *n*
calefacción F

**heave** [heev] *vt* levantar

**heaven** [HE•vn] *n* cielo M

**heavenly** [HE•vn•lee] *adj*
celestial

**heavily** [HE•vu•lee] *adv*
lentamente

**heavy** [HE•vee] *adj* pesado M

**heckle** [HE•kl] *vt* rastrillar

**hectic** [HEK•tik] *adj* héctico

**hedge** [hej] *n* valla F

**hedgehog** [HEJ•hahg] *n*
erizo M

**heed** [heed] *vt* atender; *n*
atención; take ~ of\ hacer
case de

**height** [huyt] *n* altura F

**heighten** [HUY•tn] *vt* elevar

**heir** [aiur] *n* heredero M

**heiress** [AIU•ress] *n* heredera F

**heirloom** [AIUR•loom] *n*
herencia F

**helicopter** [HE•li•KAHP•tur] *n*
helicóptero M

**hell** [hel] *n* infierno M

**hello** [hu•LO] *excl* hola

**helm** [helm] *n* timón M

**helmet** [HEL•mit] *n* casco M

**help** [help] *n* ayuda F; *vt vi*
ayudar

**helper** [HEL•pur] *n* ayudador M

**helping** [HEL•ping] *adj*
porción F

**helpless** [HELP•lis] *adj*
desvalido

**hem** [hem] *n* oria F; *vt* hacer un
dobladillo; ~ in\ encerrar

**hemisphere** [HE•mis•FEEUR]
*n* hemisferio M

**hemorrhage** [HE•mu•rij] *n*
hemorragia F

**hemorrhoids** [HE•mu•roidz]
*npl* hemorroides

**hen** [hen] *n* gallina F

**hence** [hens] *adv* desde; de aqui

**henceforth** [HENS•faurth] *adv*
de aquí

**hen-house** [HEN•hous] *n*
gallinero M

**her** [hur] *pers pron* la le

**herald** [HE•ruld] *n* heraldo M

**heraldry** [HE•rul•dree] *n*
heráldica F

**herb** [urb] *n* hierba F

**herbal** [UR•bl] *adj* herbario

**herd** [hurd] *n* rebaño M; *vt*
reunir

**here** [heeur] *adv* aquí

**hereby** [heer•BUY] *adv* por este medio

**hereditary** [he•RE•di•TE•ree] *adj* herediatrio

**heredity** [he•RF•di•tee] *n* herencia F

**herein** [heer•IN] *adv* incluso

**heresy** [HE•ru•sec] *n* herejía F

**herewith** [heeur•WITH] *adv* junto; con esto

**heritage** [HE•ri•tij] *n* herencia F

**hermit** [HUR•mit] *n* ermitaño M

**hernia** [HUR•nee•u] *n* hernia F

**hero** [HEEU•ro] *n* héroe M

**heroic** [hu•RO•ik] *adj* heroico

**heroin** [HE•ro•in] *n* heroìna F

**heroine** [HE•ro•in] *n* heroína F

**heroism** [HE•ro•I•zm] *n* heroismo M

**heron** [HE•run] *n* garza F

**herring** [HE•ring] *n* arenque M

**hers** [hurz] *poss pron* suyo; suya

**herself** [hur•SELF] *pron* ella misma

**hesitant** [HE•zi•tunt] *adj* vacilanté

**hesitate** [HE•zi•TAIT] *vi* vacilar

**hesitation** [HE•zi•TAI•shn] *n* vacilación F

**heterosexual** [HE•tu•ro•SEK•shoo•ul] *adj n* heterosexual M

**hexagon** [HEK•su•GAHN] *n* hexágono M

**hey** [hai] *excl* eh

**heyday** [HAI•dai] *n* colmo M

**hibernate** [HUY•bur•NAIT] *vi* invernar

**hibernation** [HUY•bur•NAI•shn] *n* hiemación F

**hiccup** [HI•kuhp] *n* hipo M; *vi* tener hipo

**hidden** [HI•dn] *adj* oculto; escondido

**hide 1** [huyd] *vt* esconder; ocultar

**hide 2** *n* pielo F; cuero M

**hideous** [HI•dee•us] *adj* feo horrible

**hiding** [HUY•ding] *n* escondimiento M

**hiding place** [HUY•ding PLAIS] *n* escondite M

**hierarchy** [HUYU•RAHR•kee] *n* jerarquía F

**high** [huy] *adj* alto

**high school** [HUY skool] *n* escuela secundaria F

**highlight** [HUY•luyt] *n* parte iluminada F

**highly** [HUY•lee] *adj* altamente

**highness** [HUY•nis] *n* altura F

**highway** [HUY•wai] *n* camino real M

**hike** [huyk] *vt* aumentar

**hilarious** [hi•LAU•ree•us] *adj* bullicioso

**hilt** [hilt] *n* puño M

**hill** [hil] *n* colina F

**hillside** [HIL•suyd] *n* ladera F

**hilltop** [HIL•tahp] *n* cima F

**hilly** [HI•lee] *adj* montuoso

**him** [him] *pers pron* lo; le

**himself** [him•SELF] *pron* él; él mismo

**hind** [huynd] *adj* trasero

**hinder** [HIN•dur] *vt* detener impedir

**hindrance** [HIN•druns] *n*
estorbo M

**Hindu** [HIN•doo] *adj*
hindú M

**hinge** [hinj] *n* gozne M; *vi*
depender de

**hint** *n* indicación F; *vt* dar a
entender; *vi* soltar una
indirecta; ~ at\ hacer alusión a

**hip** [hip] *n* cadera F

**hippopotamus**
[HI•pu•PAH•tu•mus] *n*
hipopótamo M

**hire** [huyur] *vt* alquilar

**his** [huiz] *poss adj* suyo; suya

**Hispanic** [hi•SPAN•ik *adj*
hispánico

**hiss** [his] *vi* sisear

**historian** [hi•STAU•ree•un] *n*
historiador M

**historic** [hi•STAU•rik] *adj*
histórico

**history** [HI•stu•ree] *n* historia F

**hit** [hit] *n* golpe M; *vt* golpear

**hitch** [hich] *vt* tirón M; *n*
prolema M (problem)

**hitherto** [HI•thur•TOO] *adv*
hasta aquí

**hive** [huyv] *n* colmena F

**hoard** [haurd] *n* acumulamiento
M; *vt* acumular

**hoarse** [haurs] *adj* ronco

**hoax** [hoks] *n* broma F

**hobble** [HAH•bl] *vi* cojear

**hobby** [HAH•bee] *n* tema F

**hobo** [HO•bo] *n* vagabundo M

**hockey** [HAH•kee] *n* hockey M

**hog** [hahg] *n* cerdo M; *vt*
acaparar (coll)

**hoist** [hoist] *vt* subir izar

**hold 1** [hold] *vt* tener; coger
(grasp); contener (contain);
mantenar (maintain); creer
(believe) *vi* mantinarse; *n*
asidero M, influencia F
(influence); ~ on to\ guaradar

**hold 2** [hold] *n* bodega F (naut)

**holder** [HOL•dur] *n* sostén M

**holding** [HOL•ding] *n*
tenencia F

**holdup** [HOLD•uhp] *n*
salteamiento M

**hole** [hol] *n* orificio M

**holiday** [HAH•li•DAI] *n*
fiesta F

**holiness** [HO•lee•nis] *n*
santidad F

**Holland** [hah•lund] *n* Holanda

**hollow** [hah•lo] *adj n* hueco

**holly** [hah•lee] *n* acebo M

**holocaust** [HAH•lu•kaust] *n*
holocausto M

**holster** [HOL•stur] *n*
pistolera F

**holy** [HO•lee] *adj* santo

**home** [hom] *n* hogar M

**homeland** [HOM•land] *n*
patria F

**homeless** [HOM•lis] *adj*
inhabitable

**homely** [HOM•lee] *adj* feo

**homemade** [HOM•MAID] *adj*
hecho en casa

**homesick** [HOM•sik] *n*
nostálgico M

**homeward** [HOM•wurd] *adv*
hacia casa

**homework** [HOM•wurk] *n*
tarea F

**homicide** [HAH•mi•SUYD] *n*
homicidio M

**homosexual**
[HO•mo•SEK•shoo•ul] *adj n*
homosexual; gay (coll)
**honest** [AH•nist] *adj* honrado
**honesty** [AH•ni•stee] *n*
honradez F
**honey** [HU•nee] *n* miel M
**honeymoon** [HU•nee•MOON]
*n* luna de miel F
**honk** [hahngk] *vi* tocar
**honor** [AH•nur] *n* honor M; *vt*
honorar
**honorable** [AH•nu•ru•bl] *adj*
honorable
**hood** [hud] *n* capucha F
**hoodlum** [HUD•lum] *n* matón F
**hoodwink** [HUD•wingk] *vt*
engañar
**hoof** [huf] *n* casco M
**hook** [huk] *n* gancho M;
anzuelo M (fishing); get off
the ~\ sacar a uno de un
apuro; *vt* enganchar; *vi*
engancharse
**hooky** [HU•kee] *n* ganchudo
**hoot** [hoot] *n* grito M
**hop** [hahp] *vt* saltar M
**hope** [hop] *n* esperanza F; *vt*
esperar
**hopeful** [HOP•ful] *adj*
esperanzado
**hopeless** [HOP•lis] *adj*
desesperado
**horizon** [hu•RUY•zn] *n*
horizonte M
**horizontal** [HAU•ri•ZAHN•tl]
*adj* horizontal
**hormone** [HAUR•mon] *n*
hormón F
**horn** [haurn] *n* cuerno M

**hornet** [HAUR•nit] *n*
avispón F
**horoscope** [HAU•ru•SKOP] *n*
horóscopo M
**horrible** [HAU•ri•bl] *adj*
horrible
**horrid** [HAU•rid] *adj* hórrido
**horrify** [HAU•ri•FUY] *vt*
horrorizar
**horror** [HAU•rur] *n* horror M
**horse** [haurs] *n* caballo M
**horseback** [HAURS•bak] *adj*
*adv* a caballo
**horsepower**
[HAURS•POU•wur] *n* fuerza
motriz ejercida por un
caballo F
**horseradish** [HAURS•RA•dish]
*n* rábano M
**horseshoe** [HAURS•shoo] *n*
herradura F
**hose** [hoz] *n* manga F
**hosiery** [HO•zhu•ree] *n*
calcetería F
**hospitable** [hah•SPI•tu•bl] *adj*
hospitalario
**hospital** [HAH•spi•tl] *n*
hospital M
**hospitality**
[HAH•spi•TA•li•tee] *n*
hospitalidad F
**host 1** [host] *n* hospedero M
**host 2** *n* hostia F (relig)
**hostage** [HAH•stij] *n* rehén M
**hostess** [HO•stis] *n* posadera F
**hostile** [HAH•stul] *adj* hostil
**hostility** [hah•STI•li•tee] *n*
hostilidad F
**hot** [haht] *adj* caliente; ~headed\
impetuso; ~ line\ teléfono rojo

**hot dog** |HAHT daug| *n*
salchicha F

**hot plate** |HAHT plait| *n*
plancha F

**hotel** |ho•TEL| *n* hotel M

**hot-tempered**
|HOT•TEM•purd| *adj*
exaltado

**hound** |hound| *n* lebrel M; *vt*
perseguir

**hour** |ouur| *n* hora F

**hourglass** |OUUR•glas| *n* reloj
de arena M

**hourly** |OUUR•lee| *adj adv* de
cada hora

**house** |n. hous v. houz| *n* casa
F; *vt* alojar; guardar (keep)

**housekeeper** |HOUS•KEE•pur|
*n* camarera F

**housekeeping**
|HOUS•KEE•ping| *n*
quehaceres domésticos

**housewife** |HOUS•wuyf| *n*
ama de casa F

**housework** |HOUS•wurk| *n*
quehaceres domésticos

**housing** |HOU•zing| *n*
albergue M

**hovel** |HUH•vl| *n* cobertizo M

**hover** |HUH•vur| *vi* cernerse

**how** |hou| *adv* cómo; ~ are
you?\ ¿cómo está Vd.? ~ do
you do\ much gusto; ~
many?\ ¿cuántos?; ~ often?\
¿cuántas veces?

**however** |hou•E•vur| *conj*
como; quiera' de cualquier
manera que

**howl** |houul| *n* aullido M

**hub** |huhb| *n* cubo M

**huddle** |HUH•dl| *vi*
amontonar

**hue 1** |hyoo| *n* color M

**hue 2** ~ **and cry** *n* clamor M

**huff** |huhf| *n* enfado M

**hug** |huhg| *n* abrazo M

**huge** |hyooj| *adj* grande enorme

**hull** |huhl| *n* corteza F

**hum** |huhm| *vt* zumbar

**human** |HYOO•mun| *adj n*
humano M

**human being** |HYOO•min
BEE•ing| *n* ser humano M

**humane** |hyoo•MAIN| *adj*
humano

**humanitarian**
|hyoo•MA•ni•TA•ree•un| *adj*
humanitario

**humanity** |hyoo•MA•ni•TEE| *n*
humanidad F

**human rights** |HYOO•min
RUYTS| *npl* derechos
humanos

**humble** |HUHM•bl| *adj*
humilde

**humid** |HYOO•mid| *adj*
húmedo

**humidity** |hyoo•MI•di•tee| *n*
humedad F

**humiliate** |hyoo•MI•lee•AIT| *v*
humillar

**humiliation**
|hyoo•MI•lee•AI•shn| *n*
humillación F

**humility** |hyoo•MI•li•tee| *n*
humildad F

**hummingbird**
|HUH•ming•BURD| *n*
colibrí M

**humor** |HYOO•mur| *n* humor M

**humorous** |HYOO•mu•rus| *adj*
cómico

**hump** [huhmp] *n* giba F; *vt*
encorbarse

**hunch** [huhnch] *n* joroba F

**hunchback** [HUHNCH•bak] *n*
jorobado M

**hundred** [HUHN•drud] *num*
cien; ciento M

**hundreth** [HUHN•druth] *num*
centésimo M

**Hungarian**
[HUNG•GAU•ree•un] *adj*
húngaro

**Hungary** [HUNG•gu•rce] *n*
Hungría

**hunger** [HUNG•gur] *n* hambre
M; *vi* ~ for\ tener hambre de

**hungry** [HUNG•gree] *adj*
hambriento; *adj* be ~\ tener
hambre

**hunt** [huhnt] *n* caza F; *vt vi*
cazar

**hunter** [HUHN•tur] *n* cazador M

**hurdle** [HUR•dl] *n* valla F

**hurl** [hurl] *vt* lanzar

**hurricane** [HU•ri•KAIN] *n*
huracán M

**hurried** [HU•reed] *adj*
precipitado

**hurriedly** [HU•red•lee] *adv*
apresuradamente

**hurry** [HU•ree] *n* prisa F; *vi*
apresuarar; dar prisa a

**hurt** [hurt] *vt* herir; lastimar; *n*
herida F; daño M (harm)

**hurtful** [HURT•ful] *adj*
dañoso

**husband** [HUHZ•bund] *n*
marido M

**hush** [huhsh] *n* silencio M; ~
up\ ocultar

**husk** [huhsk] *n* cáscara F

**husky** [HUH•skee] *adj* ronco

**hustle** [HUH•sl] *n* empujón M

**hut** [huht] *n* caseta F

**hutch** [huhch] *n* cofre M

**hyacinth** [HUY•u•SINTH] *n*
jacinto M

**hybrid** [HUY•brid] *adj n*
híbrido M

**hydrant** [HUY•drunt] *n* boca de
agua F

**hydraulic** [huy•DRAU•lik] *adj*
hidráulico

**hydrogen** [HUY•dru•jun] *n*
hidrógeno M

**hyena** [huy•EE•nu] *n* hiena F

**hygiene** [HUY•jeen] *n*
higiene F

**hymn** [him] *n* himno M

**hyphen** [HUY•fn] *n* guión M

**hypnosis** [hip•NO•sis] *n*
hipnosís M

**hypnotic** [hip•NAH•tik] *adj*
hipnótico

**hypnotize** [HIP•nu•TUYZ] *vt*
hipnotizar

**hypocrisy** [hi•PAH•kri•see] *n*
hipocresía F

**hypocrite** [HI•pu•KRIT] *n*
hipócrata F

**hypocritical** [HI•pu•KRI•ti•kl]
*adj* hipocrita

**hypothesis** [huy•PAH•thi•sis] *n*
hipotésis M

**hypothetical**
[HUY•pu•THIE•ti•kl] *adj*
hipotético

**hysterical** [hi•STE•ri•kl] *adj*
histérico

**hysterics** [hi•STE•riks] *npl*
ataque de nervios M

**I**

**I** [uy] *pers pron* yo
**ice** [uys] *n* hielo M
**ice cube** [UYS kyub] *n* cubito
 de hielo M
**ice skating** [UYS SKAI•ting] *n*
 patìn M
**ice-cream** [uys•KREEM] *n*
 helado M
**ice-skate** [UYS•skait] *vi* patinar
**iceberg** [UYS•burg] *n* iceberg M
**Iceland** [UYS•lund] *n* Islandia
**icing** [UYS•ing] *n* batido M;
 azúcar glaseado (cooking)
**icy** [UY•see] *adj* glacial
**idea** [uy•DEE•u] *n* idea F
**ideal** [uy•DEEUL] *adj n* ideal F
**idealism** [i•DEEUL•izm] *n*
 idealismo M
**idealistic** [uy•DEEU•LI•stik]
 *adj* idealista
**identical** [uy•DEN•ti•kl] *adj*
 idéntico
**identification**
 [uy•DEN•ti•fi•KAI•shn] *n*
 identificación F
**identify** [uy•DEN•ti•FUY] *vt*
 indentificar
**identity** [uy•DEN•ti•tee] *n*
 indentidad F
**ideology** [UY•dee•AH•lu•jee] *n*
 ideologia F
**idiot** [I•dee•ut] *n* idiota F
**idiotic** [I•dee•AH•tik] *adj* idiota
**idle** [UY•dl] *adj* ocioso; *vi*
 marchar en vacio (auto) *vt* ~
 away\ perder
**idol** [UY•dl] *n* ídolo M

**idolize** [UY•du•LUYZ] *vt*
 idolatrar
**if** [if] *conj* si
**ignite** [ig•NUYT] *vt* encender
**ignition** [ig•NI•shn] *n* ignición F
**ignorance** [IG•nu•runs] *n*
 ignorancia F
**ignorant** [IG•nu•runt] *adj*
 ignorante
**ignore** [ig•NAUR] *vt*
 desconocer
**ill** [il] *adj* enfermo
**ill at ease** [IL at EEZ] *adj*
 molesto
**ill will** *n* malquerencia F
**illegal** [i•LEE•gl] *adj* ilegal
**illegitimate** [I•li•JI•ti•mut] *adj*
 ilegítimo
**illicit** [i•LI•sit] *adj* ilìcito
**illiteracy** [i•LI•tu•ru•see] *n*
 analfabetismo M
**illiterate** [i•LI•tu•rut] *adj*
 analfabeto
**illness** [IL•nis] *n* enfermedad F
**illogical** [i•LAH•ji•kl] *adj*
 ilógico
**illuminate** [i•LOO•mi•NAIT] *vt*
 iluminar
**illusion** [i•LOO•zhn] *n* ilusión F
**illustrate** [I•lu•STRAIT] *vt*
 ilustrar
**illustration** [I•lu•STRAI•shn] *n*
 ilustración F
**illustrious** [i•LUH•stree•us] *adj*
 ilustre
**image** [I•mij] *n* imagen M

**imagery** [I•mu•jree] *n*
imaginería F

**imaginary** [i•MA•ji•NE•ree] *adj*
imaginario

**imagination** [i•MA•ji•NAI•зhn]
*n* imaginación F

**imaginative** [i•MA•ji•nu•tiv]
*adj* imaginativo

**imagine** [i•MA•jin] *vt* imaginar

**imbecile** [IM•bu•sil] *n*
imbécil M

**imitate** [I•mi•TAIT] *vt* imitar

**imitation** [I•mi•TAI•shn] *n*
imitación F

**immaculate** [i•MA•kyu•lut] *adj*
inmaculado

**immaterial** [I•mu•TEEU•ree•ul]
*adj* inmaterial

**immature** [I•mu•CHOOUR] *adj*
inmaturo

**immediate** [i•MEE•dee•ut] *adj*
inmediato

**immediately**
[i•MEE•dee•ut•lee] *adv*
inmediatamente

**immense** [i•MENS] *adj*
inmenso

**immerse** [i•MURS] *vt* sumergir

**immigrant** [I•mi•grunt] *n*
inmigrante M

**immigration** [I•mi•GRAI•shn]
*n* inmigración F

**imminent** [I•mi•nunt] *adj*
inminente

**immobile** [i•MO•bl] *adj*
inmóvil

**immobilize** [i•MO•bi•LUYZ] *vt*
inmovilizar

**immoral** [i•MAU•rl] *adj*
inmoral

**immorality** [I•mau•RA•li•tee] *n*
inmortalidad F

**immortal** [i•MAUR•tl] *adj*
inmortal

**immortality**
[i•MAUR•TA•li•tee] *n*
inmortalidad F

**immune** [i•MYOON] *adj*
inmune

**immunity** [i•MYOO•ni•tee] *n*
inmunidad F

**immunize** [I•myu•NUYZ] *vt*
inmunizar

**imp** [imp] *n* diablillo M

**impact** [*n.* IM•pakt *v.*
im•PAKT] *n* choque; impacto
M; *vi* impactarse

**impair** [im•PAIUR] *vt* debilitar

**impart** [im•PAHRT] *vt* impartir

**impartial** [im•PAHR•shl] *adj*
imparcial

**impassioned** [im•PASH•und]
*adj* apasionado

**impatience** [im•PAI•shns] *n*
impaciencia F

**impatient** [im•PAI•shnt] *adj*
impaciente

**impeach** [im•PEECH] *vt*
imputar

**impede** [im•PEED] *vt* impedir

**impediment** [im•PF•di•ment] *n*
impedimento M

**impel** [im•PEL] *vt* impeler

**imperative** [im•PE•ru•tiv] *adj*
imperativo

**imperfect** [im•PUR•fikt] *adj*
imperfecto

**imperial** [im•PEEU•ree•ul] *adj*
imperial

**imperious** [im•PEEU•ree•us]
*adj* imperioso

**impersonal** [im•PUR•su•nl] *adj*
impersonal

**impersonate**
[im•PUR•so•NAIT] *vt*
personificar

**impertinent** [im•PUR•ti•nunt]
*adj* impertinente

**impervious** [im•PUR•vee•us]
*adj* impenetrable

**impetuous** [im•PE•choo•us] *adj*
impetuoso

**impetus** [IM•pit•tus] *n* impetu M

**implant** [im•PLANT] *vt*
implantar

**implement** [*n.* IM•pli•munt *v.*
IM•pli•MENT] *n* herramiento
M; *vt* realizar

**implicate** [IM•pli•KAIT] *vt*
implicar

**implicit** [im•PLI•sit] *adj*
implícito

**implore** [im•PLAUR] *vt* implorar

**imply** [im•PLUY] *vt* implicar

**impolite** [IM•pu•LUYT] *adj*
impolítico

**import** [*n.* IM•paurt *v.*
im•PAURT] *n* importación F;
*vt* importar

**importance** [im•PAUR•tuns] *n*
importancia F

**important** [im•PAUR•tunt] *adj*
importante

**impose** [im•POZ] *vt* imponer

**imposition** [IM•po•SI•shn] *n*
imposición F

**impossible** [im•PAH•si•bl] *adj*
imposible

**impostor** [im•PAH•stur] *n*
impostor M

**impotent** [IM•pu•tunt] *adj*
impotente

**impress** [im•PRES] *vt* imprimir

**impression** [im•PRE•shn] *n*
impresión F

**impressive** [im•PRE•siv] *adj*
impresionante

**imprint** [*n.* IM•print *v.*
im•PRINT] *n* impresión F; *vt*
imprimir

**imprison** [im•PRI•zn] *vt*
encarcelar

**improbable** [im•PRAH•bu•bl]
*adj* improbable

**improper** [im•PRAH•pur] *adj*
impropio

**improve** [im•PROOV] *vt*
mejorar

**improvement**
[im•PROOV•munt] *n*
mejoramiento M

**improvise** [IM•pruh•VUYZ] *vt*
*vi* improvisar

**imprudent** [im•PROO•dunt] *adj*
imprudente

**impudent** [IM•pyu•dunt] *adj*
atrevido

**impulsive** [im•PUHL•siv] *adj*
impulsivo

**impunity** [im•PYOO•ni•tee] *n*
impunidad F

**impure** [im•PYUR] *adj* impuro

**impurity** [im•PYU•ri•tee] *n*
impureza F

**in** *prep adj n* en; ~ an hour\
dentro de una hor; ~ doing\ al
hacer; ~ so far as\ en cuanto
que; ~ the evening\ por la
tarde; ~ the rain\ baho la
lluvia; ~ the sun\ al sol; one ~
ten\ uno de cada diez; *adv*
dentro

**in love** (with) *adj* enamorado

**inability** [I•nu•BI•li•tee] *n*
incapacidad F

**inaccurate** [in•A•kyu•rut] *adj*
inexacto

**inactive** [in•AK•tiv] *adj*
inactivo

**inadequate** [in•A•du•kwit] *adj*
inadecuado

**inadvertent** [IN•ud•VER•tunt]
*adj* inadvertido

**inane** [i•NAIN] *adj* inane

**inanimate** [in•AN•uh•muht] *adj*
inanimado

**inappropriate**
[IN•u•PRO•pree•ut] *adj*
impropio

**inauguration**
[i•NAU•gyu•RAI•shn] *n*
inauguración F

**incapable** [in•KAI•pu•bl] *adj*
incapaz

**incense** [IN•sens] *n* incienso M

**incentive** [in•SEN•tif] *n*
incitativo M

**incessant** [in•SE•sunt] *adj*
incesante

**inch** [inch] *n* pulgada F

**incident** [IN•si•dunt] *n*
incidente M

**incidental** [IN•si•DEN•tl] *adj n*
incidental

**incite** [in•SUYT] *vt* incitar

**incline** [in•KLUYN] *n* declive M

**include** [in•KLOOD] *vt* incluir

**including** [in•KLOO•ding] *prep*
incluido

**income** [IN•kuhm] *n* ingreso M

**income tax** [IN•kum TAKS] *n*
impuesto M

**incomparable**
[in•KAHM•pra•bl] *adj*
incomparable

**incompatible**
[IN•kum•PA•ti•bl] *adj*
incompatible

**incompetent**
[in•KAHM•pu•tunt] *adj*
incometente

**incomplete** [IN•kum•PLEET]
*adj* incompleto

**inconsiderate**
[IN•kun•SI•du•rut] *adj*
inconsiderado

**inconsistent** [IN•kun•SIS•tnt]
*adj* inconsistente

**inconspicuous**
[IN•kun•SPI•kyoo•us] *adj*
poco visible

**inconvenient**
[IN•kun•VEE•nyunt] *adj*
incoveniente

**incorporate**
[in•KAUR•pu•RAIT] *vt*
incorporar

**incorrect** [IN•ku•REKT] *adj*
incorrecto

**increase** [*n.* IN•krees *v.*
in•KREES] *n* aumento M; *vt
vi* aumentar

**increasingly**
[in•KREE•sing•lee] *adv* en
aumento

**incredible** [in•KRE•di•bl] *adj*
increíble

**incredulous** [in•KRE•dyu•lus]
*adj* incrédulo

**incriminate** [in•KRI•mi•NAIT]
*vt* incriminar

**incur** [in•KUR] *vt* incurrir

**incurable** [in•KYOOU•ru•bl]
*adj* incurable

**incursion** [in•KUR•zjuhn] *n*
incursión F

**indebted** [in•DE•tid] *adj*
adeudado

**indecent** [in•DEE•sunt] *adj*
indecente

**indeed** [in•DEED] *adv*
realmente

**indefinite** [in•DE•fi•nit] *adj*
indefinido

**indemnity** [in•DEM•ni•tee] *n*
indemnidad F

**indent** [in•DEHNT] *vt* mellar

**independence**
[IN•du•PEN•duns] *n*
independencia F

**independent**
[IN•du•PEN•dunt] *adj*
independiente

**indestructible**
[IN•di•STRUHK•ti•bl] *adj*
indestructible

**index** [IN•deks] *n* indice M; *vt*
poner indice a

**India** [IN•dee•u] *n* India

**Indian** [IN•dee•un] *adj* indio

**indicate** [IN•di•KAIT] *vt* indicar

**indicator** [IN•di•KAI•tur] *n*
indicador M

**indication** [IN•di•KAI•shn] *n*
insinuación F

**indict** [in•DUYT] *vt* acusar

**indifferent** [in•DI•fu•runt] *adj*
indiferente

**indigenous** [in•DI•ji•nus] *adj*
indigena

**indigestion** [in•di•JES•chn] *n*
indigestión F

**indignant** [in•DIG•nunt] *adj*
indignado

**indigo** [IN•di•GO] *adj n*
indigo M

**indirect** [IN•di•REKT] *adj*
indirecto

**indiscreet** [IN•di•SKREET] *adj*
indiscreto

**indispensable**
[IN•di•SPEN•su•bl] *adj*
indispensable

**indisposed** [IN•di•SPOSD] *adj*
indispuesto

**indistinct** [IN•di•STINKT] *adj*
indistinto

**individual** [IN•di•VI•joo•ul] *adj*
individual

**indoctrinate**
[in•DAHK•tri•NAIT] *vt*
adoctrinar

**indoor** [IN•DAUR] *adj* interior

**induce** [in•DOOS] *vt* inducir

**induct** [in•DUHKT] *vt* instalar

**indulge** [in•DUHLJ] *vt*
satisfacer

**industrial** [in•DUH•stree•ul] *adj*
industrial

**industrious** [in•DUH•stree•us]
*adj* industrioso

**industry** [IN•duh•stree] *n*
industria F; aplicación F
(commitment)

**inebriated** [i•NEE•bree•AI•tid]
*adj* embriagar; borracho

**ineffective** [IN•u•FEK•tiv]] *adj*
ineficaz

**inequality**
[IN•ee•KWAH•li•tee] *n*
desigualdad F

**inevitable** [i•NE•vi•tu•bl] *adj*
inevitable

**inexpensive** [IN•ek•SPEN•siv]
*adj* barato; económico

**inexperienced**
[IN•ek•SPEEU•ree•unst] *adj*
inexperto

infallible [in•FA•li•bl] *adj*
infalible

infamous [IN•fu•mus] *adj*
infame

infancy [IN•fun•see] *n* infancia F

infant [IN•funt] *n* infante M

infantry [IN•fun•tree] *n*
infantería F

infect [in•FEKT] *vt* infectar

infection [in•FEK•shn] *n*
infección F

infectious [in•FEK•shus] *adj*
infeccioso

infer {in•FUR] *vt* inferir

inferior [in•FEEU•ree•ur] *adj n*
inferior M

infidelity [IN•fi•DE•li•tee] *n*
infidelidad F

infinite [IN•fi•nit] *adj* infinito

infinitive [in•FI•ni•tiv] *adj n*
infinitivo M

infinity [in•FI•ni•tee] *n*
infinidad F

infirmity [in•FUR•mi•tee] *n*
enfermedad F

inflame [in•FLAIM] *vt* inflamar

inflate [in•FLAIT] *vt* inflar

inflation [in•FLAI•shn] *n*
inflación F

inflection [in•FLEK•shn] *n*
inflexión F

inflict [in•FLIKT] *vt* infligir

influence [IN•FLOO•uns] *n*
influencia F

influenza [IN•floo•EN•zu] *n*
influenza F

influx [IN•fluhks] *n* flujo M

inform [in•FAURM] *vt* informar

informal [in•FAUR•ml] *adj*
familiar

information [IN•fur•MAI•shn]
*n* información F

infringe [in•FRINJ] *vt* infringir

infuriate [in•FYU•ree•AIT] *vt*
enfurecer

ingenious [in•JEE•nyus] *adj*
ingenioso

ingratitude [in•GRA•ti•TOOD]
*n* ingratitud F

ingredient [in•GREE•dee•unt *n*
ingrediente M

inhabit [in•HA•bit] *vt* habitar

inhale [in•HAIUL] *vt* inhalar;
aspirar

inherent [in•HE•runt] *adj*
inherente

inherit [in•HE•rit] *vt* heredar

inheritance [in•HE•ri•tuns] *n*
herencia F

inhibit [in•HI•bit] *vt* prohibir;
suprimir

inhuman [in•HYOO•mun] *adj*
inhumano

initial [i•NI•shl] *adj* inicial

initiate [i•NI•shee•AIT] *vt*
iniciar

inject [in•JEKT] *vt* inyectar

injure [IN•jur] *vt* dañar; herir;
perjudicar

injury [IN•ju•ree] *n* daño M;
herida F

injustice [in•JUH•stis] *n*
injusticia F

ink [ingk] *n* tinta F

inmate [IN•mait] *n* habitante M

inmost [IN•most] *adj* íntimo

inn [in] *n* fonda F

innate [i•NAIT] *adj* innato

inner [i•NUR] *adj* interior

innkeeper [IN•KEE•pur] *n*
fondista F

innocence [I•nu•suns] *n*
inocencia F

innocent [I•nu•sunt] *adj*
inocente

**innovation** [I•nu•VAI•shn] *n* innovación F

**innuendo** [IN•yoo•EN•do] *n* insinuación F

**inoculate** [i•NAH•kyu•LAIT] *vt* inocular

**inorganic** [IN•aur•GA•nik] *adj* inorgánico F

**inquire** [in•KWUY•ur] *vi* inquirir; preguntar

**inquiry** [in•KWU•ree] *n* pregunta F

**inquisition** [in•KWI•zi•shn] *n* inquisición F

**inquisitive** [in•KWI•zi•tiv] *adj* inquisitivo

**insane** [in•SAIN] *adj* insano

**insanity** [in•SA•ni•tee] *n* locura F

**insatiable** [in•SAI•shu•bl] *adj* insaciable

**inscription** [in•SKRIP•shn] *n* inscripción F

**insect** [IN•sekt] *n* insecto M

**insecticide** [in•SEK•ti•SUYD] *n* insecticida F

**insecure** [in•su•CYUR] *adj* inseguro

**insensitive** [in•SEN•si•tiv] *adj* insensible

**inseparable** [in•SE•pru•bl] *adj* inseparable

**insert** [IN•surt] *vt* inserir; *n* matera insertada

**inside** [in•SUYD] *adj* interior; *n* interior M; ~ out\ al revés; *adv* dentro; *prep* dentro de

**insight** [IN•suyt] *n* discernimiento M

**insignificant** [IN•sig•NI•fi•kunt] *adj* insignificante

**insipid** [in•SI•pid] *adj* insipido

**insist** [in•SIST] *vi* insistir

**insistent** [in•SI•stunt] *adj* insistente

**insolent** [IN•su•lunt] *adj* insolente

**insomnia** [in•SAHM•nee•u] *n* insomnio M

**inspect** [in•SPEKT] *vt* inspeccionar

**inspection** [in•SPEK•shn] *n* inspección F

**inspector** [in•SPEK•tur] *n* inspector M

**inspiration** [IN•spu•RAI•shn] *n* inspiración F

**inspire** [in•SPUY•ur] *vt* inspirar

**install** [in•STAUL] *vt* instalar

**installation** [IN•stu•LAI•shn] *n* instalación F

**instance** [IN•stuns] *n* ejemplo; caso M

**instant** [IN•stunt] *adj* instante; inmediato; instantáneo (food); *n* instante M

**instead** [in•STED] *adv* en vez de

**instigate** [IN•sti•GAIT] *vt* instigar

**instill** [in•STIL] *vt* instilar

**instinct** [IN•stingkt] *n* instinto M

**institute** [IN•sti•TOOT] *n* instituto M

**instruct** [in•STRUHKT] *vt* instruir

**instruction** [in•STRUHK•shn] *n* instrucción F

**instructor** [in•STRUHK•tor] *n* instructor M

**instrument** [IN•stru•munt] *n* instrumento M

**insufficient** [IN•su•FI•shunt]
*adj* insuficiente

**insulate** [IN•su•LAIT] *vt* aislar

**insulation** [IN•su•LAI•shn] *n*
insulflación F

**insult** [*n.* IN•suhlt *v.* in•SUHLT]
*n* insulto M; *vt* insultar

**insurance** [in•SHOOU•runs] *n*
aseguración F

**insure** [in•SHOOUR] *vt*
asegurar; ~ that\ aseguarse de
que

**intact** [in•TAKT] *adj* intacto

**integral** [IN•tu•grul] *adj*
integrante

**integrate** [IN•tu•GRAIT] *vt*
integrar; *vi* integrarse

**integration** [IN•tu•GRAI•shn]
*n* integración F

**integrity** [in•TE•gri•tee] *n*
integridad F

**intellectual** [IN•tu•LEK•chu•ul]
*adj n* intelectual

**intelligence** [in•TE•li•juns] *n*
inteligencia F

**intelligent** [in•TE•li•junt] *adj*
inteligente

**intend** [in•TEND] *vt* intentar

**intense** [in•TENS] *adj* intenso

**intensify** [in•TEN•si•FUY] *vt*
intensificar

**intensity** [in•TEN•si•tee] *n*
intensidad F

**intensive** [in•TEN•siv] *adj*
intenso

**intent** [in•TENT] *adj* intento M

**intention** [in•TEN•shn] *n*
intención F

**intentional** [in•TEN•shu•nl] *adj*
intencional

**intercept** [IN•tur•SEPT] *vt*
interceptar

**interchange** [*n.* IN•tur•chainj *v.*
in•tur•CHAINJ] *n* intercambio
M; *vi* intercambiar

**intercom** [IN•tur•KAHM] *n*
teléfonico interior M

**intercourse** [IN•tur•KAURS] *n*
trato carnal M

**interest** [IN•trust] *n* interés M;
ventaja F (advantage); *vt*
interesar

**interesting** [IN•tru•sting] *adj*
interesante

**interfere** [IN•tur•FEEUR] *vi*
interferir; ~ with\
entrometerse en

**interference**
[IN•tur•FEEU•runs] *n*
interferencia F

**interim** [IN•tu•rim] *adj*
intermedio

**interior** [in•TEEU•ree•ur] *adj n*
interior M

**interlock** [IN•tur•LAHK] *vi* unir

**intermediate**
[IN•tur•MEE•dee•ut]] *adj*
intermedio

**interminable**
[in•TUR•mi•nu•bl] *adj*
interminable

**intermission** [IN•tur•MI•shn] *n*
intermisión F

**intern** [IN•turn] *n* interno M

**internal** [in•TUR•nl] *adj* interno

**international**
[IN•tur•NA•shu•nl] *adj*
internacional

**interpret** [in•TUR•prit] *vt*
interpretar

**interpretation**
[in•TUR•pru•TAI•shn] *n*
interpretación F

**interpreter** [in•TUR•pri•tur] *n*
interpretado M

**interrogate** [in•TE•ru•GAIT] *vt*
interrogar

**interrogation**
[in•TE•ru•GAI•shn] *n*
interrogación F

**interrupt** [IN•tu•RUHPT] *vt vi*
interrumpir

**interruption** [IN•tu•RUHP•shn]
*n* interrupción F

**intersect** [IN•tur•SEKT] *vt*
cruzar

**intersection** [IN•tur•SEK•shn]
*n* intersección F

**intertwine** [IN•tur•TWUYN] *vt*
entretejer

**interval** [IN•tur•vl] *n* espacio M

**intervene** [IN•tur•VEEN] *vt*
intervenir

**intervention** [IN•tur•VEN•shn]
*n* intervención F

**interview** [IN•tur•VYOO] *n*
entrevista F; *vt* entrevistarse
con

**intestine** [in•TE•stin] *n*
intestino M

**intimacy** [IN•ti•mu•see] *n*
intimidad F

**intimate** [*adj.* IN•ti•mit *v.*
IN•ti•MAIT] *adj* intimo *vt*
intimidar

**into** [IN•too] *prep* en; dentro

**intolerable** [in•TAH•lu•ru•bl]
*adj* intolerable

**intolerance** [in•TAH•lu•runs] *n*
intolerancia F

**intolerant** [in•TAH•lu•runt] *adj*
intolerante

**intoxicated**
[in•TAHK•si•KAI•tid] *adj*
borracho

**intricate** [IN•tri•kut] *adj*
intrincado

**intrigue** [in•TREEG] *n* intriga F

**introduce** [IN•tru•DOOS] *vt*
introducir

**introduction**
[IN•tru•DUHK•shn] *n*
introducción F

**introvert** [IN•tru•VURT] *n*
introverso M

**intrude** [in•TROOD] *vi* imponer

**intruder** [in•TROO•dur] *n*
entremetido M

**intrusion** [in•TROO•zhn] *n*
intrución F

**intuition** [IN•too•I•shn] *n*
intuición F

**inundate** [I•nun•DAIT] *vt*
inundar

**invade** [in•VAID] *vt* invadir

**invalid** [*adj.* in•VA•lid *n.*
IN•vu•lid] *adj* inválido

**invaluable** [in•VA•lyu•bl] *adj*
inestimable

**invariably** [in•VA•ryu•blee] *adv*
invariablemente

**invasion** [in•VAI•zhn] *n*
invasión F

**invent** [in•VENT] *vt* inventar

**invention** [in•VEN•shn] *n*
invención F

**inventive** [in•VEN•tiv] *adj*
inventivo

**inventor** [in•VEN•tur] *n*
inventor M

**inventory** [IN•vun•TAU•ree] *n*
inventario M

**invest** [in•VEST] *vt vi* investir

**investigate** [in•VE•sti•GAIT]
*vt* investigar

**investigation**
[in•VE•sti•GAI•shn] *n*
investigación F

**investment** [in•VEST•munt] *n*
investidura F

**invigorating**
[in•VI•gu•RAI•ting] *adj*
vigorizador

**invincible** [in•VIN•si•bl] *adj*
invencible

**invisible** [in•VI•zi•bl] *adj*
invisible M

**invitation** [IN•vi•TAI•shn] *n*
invitación F

**invite** [in•VUYT] *vt* invitar

**inviting** [in•VUY•ting] *adj*
atractivo; atrayente

**invoice** [IN•vois] *n* fractura F

**invoke** [in•VOK] *vt* invocar

**involuntary**
[in•VAH•lun•TE•ree] *adj*
involuntario

**involve** [in•VAHLV] *vt*
envolver

**inward** [IN•wurd] *adj adv*
interno

**iodine** [UY•u•DUYN] *n* yodo M

**Iran** [i•RAN] *n* Irán M

**Iranian** [i•RAI•nyun] *adj* iranio
M

**Iraq** [i•RAK] *n* Irak M

**Ireland** [UYUR•lund] *n* Irlandia

**iris** [UY•ris] *n* arco iris M

**Irish** [UY•rish] *adj* irlandés

**iron** [UY•urn] *n* hierro M;
plancha F (appliance); *adj* de
hierro; *vt* planchar; ~ out\
allanar

**ironic** [uy•RAH•nik] *adj* irónico

**ironing** [UY•ur•ning] *n*
planchado M

**irony** [UY•ru•nee] *n* ironía F

**irrational** [i•RA•shu•nl] *adj*
irracional

**irregular** [i•RE•gyu•lur] *adj*
irregular

**irregularity**
[i•RE•gyu•LA•ri•tec] *n*
irregularidad F

**irrelevant** [i•RE•lu•vunt] *adj*
impertinente

**irreparable** [i•RE•pru•bl] *adj*
irreparable

**irreplaceable** [i•ri•PLAI•su•bl]
*adj* irreemplazable

**irresistible** [I•ru•ZI•stu•bl] *adj*
irresistible

**irresponsible**
[I•ri•SPAHN•su•bl] *adj*
irresponsable

**irrigate** [I•ri•GAIT] *vt* irrigar

**irrigation** [I•ri•GAI•shn] *n*
irrigación F

**irritable** [I•ri•tu•bl] *adj* irritable

**irritate** [I•ri•TAIT] *vt* irritar

**Islam** [iz•LAHM] *n* Islam

**island** [UY•lund] *n* isla F

**isolate** [UY•su•LAIT] *vt* aislar

**isolation** [UY•su•LAI•shn] *n*
aislamiento M

**issue** [I•shoo] *n* consecuencia F;
asunto, resultado M; at ~\ en
cuestión; take ~ with\
oponerse a; *vt* distribuir;
emitir; *vi* ~ from\ salir de

**it** *pron* él; ella; ello; ~ is hot\
hace calor; ~ is me\ soy; you;
far from ~\ ni mucho menos;
that's ~\ eso es; who is ~?\
¿quién es?

**Italian** [i•TAL•yun] *adj* italiano

**italic** [uy•TA•lik] *adj* itálico

**itch** [ich] *n* picazón F; *vi* picar

**itchy** [I•chee] *adj* sarnoso

**item** [UY•tum] *n* elemento M

**itemize** [UY•tu•MUYZ] *vt*
detallar

**itinerary** [uy•TI•nu•RE•ree] *n*
itinerario M
**its** [its] *poss pron* su; sus; suyo;
suyos

**itself** [it•SELF] *pron* él mismo
**ivory** [UY•vree] *n* marfil M
**ivy** [UY•vee] *n* hiedra F

# J

**jab** [jab] *n* pinchazo M; *vt*
pinchar
**jack** [jak] *n* barrilete M; ~ up\
alzar con gato
**jackal** [JA•kl] *n* chacal M
**jacket** [JA•kit] *n* chaqueta F
**jaded** [JAI•did] *adj* embotado
**jagged** [JA•gid] *adj* mellado
**jail** [jaiul] *n* cárcel M
**jam 1** [jam] *vt* interfir con; *vi*
obstruirse; *n* agolpamiento M
(people); embotellamiento M
(traffic)
**jam 2** *n* compota; mermelade F
**janitor** [JA•ni•tur] *n* portero M
**January** [JA•nyoo•E•ree] *n*
enero M
**Japan** [ju•PAN] *n* Japón M
**Japanese** [JA•pu•NEEZ] *adj*
japonés
**jar 1** [jahr] *n* tarro M
**jar 2** *vi* sonar mal; chillar; *vt*
sacudir
**jargon** [JAHR•gun] *n* jerga F
**jaundice** [JAUN•dis] *n*
ictericia F
**javelin** [JA•vu•lin] *n* jabalina F
**jaw** [jau] *n* mandíbula F
**jazz** [jaz] *n* jazz M
**jealous** [JE•lus] *adj* celoso
**jealousy** [JE•lu•see] *n* celos M

**jeans** [jeenz] *npl* pantalones M
**jeer** [jeeur] *vi* burlarse
**jelly** [JE•lee] *n* jalea F
**jellyfish** [JE•lee•FISH] *n*
medusa F
**jeopardize** [JE•pur•DUYZ] *vt*
arriesgar
**jerk** [jurk] *n* tirón F; *vt* sacudir
**jersey** [JUR•zee] *n* jersey M
**jest** [jest] *n* broma F; *vi* bromear
**jet 1** [jet] *n* chorro M; ~ lag\
cansancio M
**jet 2** *n* azabache M (mineral) ~
black\ de azabache; como el
azabache
**jetty** [JE•tee] *n* escollera F
**Jew** [joo] *n* judío M
**jewel** [jooul] *n* joya F
**jeweler** [JOOU•lur] *n* joyero M
**jewelry** [JOOUL•ree] *n* joyas
**Jewish** [JOO•ish] *adj* judaico
**jig** [jig] *n* giga F
**jiggle** [JI•gl] *vt* mover a
sacudidas
**jilt** [jilt] *vt* despedir; plantado
**jingle** [JING•gl] *n* tintín M
**job** [jahb] *n* trabajo M
**jockey** [JAH•kee] *n* jockey M
**jog** [jahg] *vi* correr
**join** [join] *vt* unir juntar; hacerse
socio de (club); *vi* empalmar

(roads, etc); confluir (river);
~ in\ participar en
**joint** [joint] *adj* nudillo; común;
*n* juntra F; articulación F
(anat); out of ~\ descoyuntado
**joint account** [JOINT
a•KOUNT] *n* cuenta
colectivo F
**joist** [joyst] *n* viga F
**joke** [jok] *n* chiste M
**joker** [JO•kur] *n* bromista M
**jolt** [jolt] *n* tumbo M
**jolly** [JAH•lee] *adj* festivo
**jot** [jaht] *vt* apuntar
**journal** [JUR•nl] *n* diario M
**journalism** [JUR•nu•LI•zm] *n*
periodismo M
**journalist** [JUR•nu•list] *n*
periodistico M
**journey** [JUR•nee] *n* viaje M
**jovial** [JO•vyul] *adj* alegre
**joy** [joi] *n* júbilo M
**joyful** [JOI•ful] *adj* jubiloso;
alegre
**jubilant** [JOO•bi•lunt] *adj*
jubiloso
**judge** [juhj] *n* juez M; *vt* juzgar
**judicial** [joo•DI•shl] *adj* judicial
**judicious** [joo•DI•shus] *adj*
juicioso
**jug** [juhg] *n* jarro M

**juggle** [JUH•gl] *vt* hacer trampas
**juggler** [JUH•glur] *n* juglar M
**juice** [joos] *n* jugo M
**juicy** [JOO•see] *adj* jugoso
**jukebox** [JOOK•bahks] *n*
gramófono M
**July** [ju•LUY] *n* julio M
**jump** [juhmp] *n* salto M; *vt vi*
saltar; ~ the gun\ obrar
prematuramente
**junction** [JUHNGK•shn] *n*
punto de unión M
**June** [joon] *n* junio M
**jungle** [JUHNG•gl] *n* manigua F
**junior** [JOO•nyur] *adj* menor
**junk** [juhngk] *n* junco M
**jurisdiction**
[JOOU•ris•DIK•shn] *n*
jurisdicción F
**juror** [JOOU•rur] *n* jurado M
**jury** [JOOU•ree] *n* jurado M
**just** [juhst] *adj* justo; he has ~
left\ acaba de marcharse
**justice** [JUH•stis] *n* justicia F
**justify** [JUH•sti•FUY] *vt*
justificar
**juvenile** [JOO•vu•NUYUL] *adj*
juvenil
**juxtapose** [JUHK•stu•POZ] *vt*
yuxtaponer

# K

**kaleidoscope**
[ku•LUY•du•SKOP] *n*
calidoscopio M

**kangaroo** [KANG•gu•ROO] *n*
canguro M
**keen** [keen] *adj* afilado; vivo
(mind, etc); afilado (edge);

agudo (eyesight); be ~ on\
gustarle a uno

**keep** [keep] *vt* guardar;
mantener (family); tener
(shop, animals); observar
(rules) ~ from\ impedir; ~
back\ retener; ~ out\ no dejar
entrar; ~ up with\ estar al día
en

**keeper** [KEE•pur] *n* guardia F

**keeping** [KEE•ping] *n* guarda F

**keepsake** [KEEP•saik] *n*
recuerdo M

**keg** [keg] *n* barril M

**kennel** [KE•nl] *n* perrera F

**Kenya** [KE•nyu] *n* Kenya

**kernel** [KUR•nl] *n* grano M

**kerosene** [KE•ru•SEEN] *n*
petróleo M

**ketchup** [KE•chup] *n* salsa de
tomate F

**kettle** [KE•tl] *n* caldera F

**key** [kee] *n* llave M

**keyboard** [KEE•baurd] *n*
teclado M

**key ring** [KEE ring] *n* llavero M

**khaki** [KA•kee] *adj* caqui M

**kick** [kik] *n* patada F; *vt* dar una
patada a *vi* dar patadas; ~ out\
ecahr a patadas (coll)

**kid** [kid] *n* cabrito M (goat);
cabritilla F (child, coll); *vt*
tomar el pelo a; *vi* bromear

**kidnap** [KID•nap] *v* secuestrar;
raptar

**kidnaping** [KID•na•ping] *n*
rapto M

**kidnapper** [KID•na•pur] *n*
raptor M

**kidney** [KID•nee] *n* riñon M

**kill** [kil] *vt* matar

**killer** [KI•lur] *n* matador M

**kiln** [kiln] *n* horno M

**kilogram** [KI•lu•GRAM] *n*
kilogramo M

**kilometer** [ki•LAH•mi•tur] *n*
kilometro M

**kilowatt** [KI•lu•WAHT] *n*
kilovoltio M

**kilt** [kilt] *n* falda corta F

**kin** [kin] *n* parientes

**kind** [kuynd] *adj* amable

**kindergarten**
[KIN•dur•GAHR•tn] *n* escueal
de párvulos F

**kindle** [KIN•dl] *vt* encender

**kindly** [KUYND•lee] *adj*
afectuoso

**kindness** [KUYND•nis] *n*
amabilidad F

**king** [king] *n* rey M

**kingdom** [KING•dum] *n*
reino M

**kinky** [KING•kee] *adj* chiflado

**kiss** [kis] *n* beso M; *vt* (vi)
besar(se)

**kit** [kit] *n* juego M

**kitchen** [KI•chn] *n* cocina F

**kitchen sink** [KI•chin SINK] *n*
fregadero M

**kite** [kuyt] *n* cometa F

**kitten** [KI•tn] *n* gatito M

**knack** [nak] *n* facilidad F

**knapsack** [NAP•sak] *n*
mochila F

**knead** [need] *vt* amasar

**knee** [nee] *n* rodilla F

**kneecap** [NEE•kap] *n* rótula F

**kneel** [neeul] *vi* arrodillarse

**knife** [nuyf] *n* cuchillo M

**knight** [nuyt] *n* caballero M

**knit** [nit] *vt vi* tejer

**knitting** [NI•ting] *n* calceta F
**knob** [nahb] *n* bulto M
**knock** [nahk] *n* golpe M; *vt*
  golpear; ~ about\ maltratar; *vi*
  rodar; ~ down\ derribar;
  atropellar; ~ off \ hacer caer
**knocker** [NAH•kur] *n*
  golpeador M
**knot** [naht] *n* nudo M

**know** [no] *vt* saber
**know-how** [NO•hou] *n*
  habilidad F
**know-it-all** [NO•it•AL] *n*
  sabidillo M
**knowledge** [NAH•lij] *n*
  conocimiento M
**knuckle** [NUII•kl] *n* nudillo M
**Korea** [ku•REE•u] *n* Corea M

# L

**lab** [lab] *n* laboratorio M
**label** [LAI•bl] *n* marca F
**labor** [LAI•bur] *n* trabajo M
**Labor Party** [LAI•bor PAR•tee]
  *n* partido laborista M
**labor union** [LAI•bor U•nyun]
  *n* asociación obrera F
**laboratory** [LA•bru•TAU•ree] *n*
  laboratorio M
**laborer** [LAI•bu•rur] *n*
  trabajador M
**lace** [lais] *n* cordón M; *vt* atar
**lack** [lak] *n* falta F
**lacquer** [LA•kur] *n* laca F
**ladder** [LA•dur] *n* escalera F
**ladle** [LAI•dl] *n* cucharón F
**lady** [LAI•dee] *n* dama F
**lag** [lag] *vi* rezagarse
**lagoon** [lu•GOON] *n* laguna F
**lair** [laiur] *n* yacija F
**lake** [laik] *n* lago M
**lamb** [lam] *n* cordero M
**lame** [laim] *adj* cojo
**lament** [lu•MENT] *vi*
  lamentarse

**laminate** [LA•mi•NAIT] *vt*
  laminar
**lamp** [lamp] *n* lampára F
**lampoon** [lam•POON] *n*
  libelo M
**lamp-post** [LAMP•post] *n*
  poste M
**lance** [lans] *n* lanza F
**land** [land] *n* tierra F; país m
  (country) *vi* desambarcar
  (from ship); aterrizar (from
  plane); caer (fall)
**landing** [LAN•ding] *n*
  desembarco M
**landlady** [LAND•LAI•dee] *n*
  propietaria F
**landlord** [LAND•laurd] *n*
  propietario M
**landmark** [LAND•mahrk] *n*
  señal M
**landowner** [LAND•O•nur] *n*
  hacendado M
**landslide** [LAND•sluyd] *n*
  derrumbamiento M
**lane** [lain] *n* camino M

**language** [LANG•gwij] *n*
lenguaje F

**languid** [LANG•gwid] *adj*
lánguido

**lantern** [LAN•turn] *n* linterna F

**lap 1** [lap] *n* falda F

**lap 2** *n* vuelta F (sport)

**lapel** [lu•PEL] *n* solapa F

**lapse** [laps] *n* lapso M

**larceny** [LAHR•su•nee] *n* robo M

**lard** [lahrd] *n* tocino gordo M;
manteca de cerdo

**large** [lahrj] *n* grande M' at ~\
en libertad

**largely** [LAHRJ•lee] *adv*
grandemente

**lark 1** [lahrk] *n* alondra F

**lark 2** *n* broma F (fun); *vi* andar
de juerga

**lash** [lash] *n* pestaña F (anat); *vt*
azotar; ~ out against\ atacar

**last 1** [last] *adj* último; ~
Monda el lunes pasado; have
the ~ word\ decir la última
palabra; the ~ straw\ el
colmo; *adv* por ultimo

**last 2** *vi* durar

**lasting** [LA•sting] *adj* duradero

**last name** [last naim] *n* nombre
de familia M

**latch** [lach] *n* pestillo M

**late** [lait] *adj* tarde; in ~ June\ a
fines de junio; the ~ Juan\ el
difunto Juan

**latent** [LAI•tunt] *adj* latente

**lather** [LA•thur] *n* espuma F

**Latin** [LA•tin] *adj n* latino M

**Latin America** [LA•tin
u•ME•ri•ku] *n* Ámerica
latina F

**latitude** [LA•ti•TOOD] *n*
latitud F

**latter** [LA•tur] *adj* más reciente

**lattice** [LA•tis] *n* celosía F

**Latvia** [LAHT•vee•u] *n*
Letonia M

**laugh** [laf] *n* risa; F *vi* reír

**laughter** [LAF•tur] *n* risa F

**launch** [launch] *n*
lanzamiento M

**launder** [LAUN•dur] *vt* lavar

**laundry** [LAUN•dree] *n*
lavadero M

**laurel** [LAU•rl] *n* laurel M

**lava** [LAH•vu] *n* lava F

**lavatory** [LA•vu•TAU•ree] *n*
lavabo M

**lavish** [LA•vish] *adj* dadivoso

**law** [lau] *n* regla; ley F

**law school** [LAW skool] *n*
escuela de derecho F

**law-abiding**
[LAW•a•BUY•ding] *adj*
observante de la ley

**lawful** [LAU•ful] *adj* legal

**lawn** [laun] *n* césped M

**lawn mower** [LAUN MO•wur]
*n* cortadora de césped F

**lawsuit** [LAU•soot] *n*
proceso M

**lawyer** [LAU•yur] *n* abogado;
procurador M

**lax** [laks] *adj* laxo

**laxative** [LAK•su•tiv] *n*
laxativo M

**lay** [lai] *v* derribar; tumbar;
acamar

**layer** [LAI•ur] *n* capa F

**layout** [LAI•out] *n*
planeamiento M

**lazy** [LAI•zee] *adj* perezoso

**lead 1** [leed] *n* plomo M

**lead 2** [led] *vt* primer lugar

**leader** [LEE•dur] *n* guía F

**leadership** [LEE•dur•SHIP] *n* dirección F

**leading** [LEE•ding] *adj* guía F

**leaf** [leef] *n* hoja F

**league** [leeg] *n* liga F

**leak** [leek] *n* filtración F

**lean** [leen] *adj* flaco

**leap** [leep] *n* salto M

**leap year** [LEEP YEER] *n* año bisiesto M

**learn** [lurn] *vt vi* aprender

**learning** [LUR•ning] *n* instrucción F

**lease** [lees] *n* arriendo M; *vt* arrendar

**leash** [leesh] *n* correa F

**least** [leest] *adj* mínimo

**leather** [LE•thur] *n* piel M

**leave** [leev] *n* licencia F

**Lebanon** [LE•bu•nahn] *n* Líbano M

**lecture** [LEK•chur] *n* lección F

**lecherous** [LE•chu•rus] *adj* lujurioso

**ledge** [lej] *n* anaquel M

**ledger** [LE•jur] *n* mayor M

**leech** [leech] *n* sanguijucla F

**leek** [leek] *n* puerro M

**leer** [leeur] *n* mirada F

**left 1** [left] *adj* izquierdo; *adv* a la izquierda; *n* izquierda F

**left 2** *pt pp* a leave puesto

**left-handed** [-HAN•did] *adj* mano izquierda F

**leftist** [LEF•tist] *adj n* izquierdista F

**left-overs** [LEFT•O•vurz] *npl* sobrante M

**left-wing** [LEFT•WING] *adj* de ala izquierda F

**leg** [leg] *n* pierna F

**legacy** [LE•gu•see] *n* legado M

**legal** [LEE•gl] *adj* legal M

**legalize** [LEE•gu•LUYZ] *vt* legalizar

**legend** [LE•jund] *n* leyenda F

**legendary** [LE•jun•DE•ree] *adj* legendario

**legible** [LE•ji•bl] *adj* legible

**legislation** [LE•jis•LAI•shn] *n* legislación F

**legislature** [LE•jis•LAI•chur] *n* cuerop legisladores M

**legitimate** [lu•JI•tu•mit] *adj* legitimo

**leisure** [LEE•zhur] *n* desocupación F

**lemon** [LE•mun] *n* limón M

**lemonade** [LE•mu•NAID] *n* limonada F

**lend** [lend] *vt* prestar

**length** [length] *n* longitud F

**lengthen** [LENG•thun] *vt* alargar

**lens** [lenz] *n* lente M

**Lent** [lent] *n* cuaresma F

**leopard** [LE•purd] *n* leopardo M

**leper** [LE•pur] *n* leproso M

**leprosy** [LE•pru•see] *n* lepra F

**lesbian** [LEZ•bee•un] *n* lesbiano M

**less** [les] *adj* menos; ~ and ~\ cada vez menos

**lessen** [LE•sn] *vt* aminorar

**lesser** [LE•sur] *adj* menor

**lesson** [LE•sn] n lección F

**let** [let] vt permitir; alquilar; ~ me do it\ déjame hacerlo; ~'s go!\ ¡vamos!; ~ on\ revelar; ~-down\ n desilusión F

**lethal** [LEE•thl] adj letal

**lethargy** [LE•thur•jee] n letargo M

**letter** [LE•tur] n carta F

**lettuce** [LE•tus] n lechuga

**level** [LE•vl] adj nivel M

**lever** [LE•vur] n palanca F

**levy** [LE•vee] n leva F

**lewd** [lood] adj lascivo

**liability** [LUY•u•BI•li•tee] n riesgo M

**liable** [LUY•u•bl] adj obligado

**liaison** [LEE•ai•ZAUN] n enlace M

**liar** [LUY•ur] n mentiroso M

**libel** [LUY•bl] n libelo M

**liberal** [LI•brul] adj n liberal M

**liberate** [LI•bu•RAIT] vt libertar

**liberation** [LI•bu•RAI•shn] n liberación F

**liberty** [LI•bur•tee] n libertad F

**librarian** [luy•BRE•ree•un] n bibliotecario M

**library** [LUY•BRE•ree] n biblioteca F

**Libya** [LI•bee•u] n Libia F

**license** [LUY•sns] n licencia F

**lick** [lik] vt lamer; dar una paliza a (defeat) n lametón M

**lid** [lid] n tapa F

**lie 1** [luy] vi echarse; quedarse (remain) ~ down\ acostarse

**lie 2** n mentira F; vi mentir

**lieutenant** [loo•TE•nunt] n teniente M

**life** [luyf] n vida F

**lifeboat** [LUYF•bot] n bote salvavidas M

**life expectancy** [LUYF ek•SPEK•ten•cee] n índice de longevidad F

**life jacket** [LUYF JA•ket] n cinturón salvidas M

**lifeless** [LUYF•lis] adj sin vida

**lifelike** [LUYF•luyk] adj que parece vivo

**lifelong** [LUYF•laung] adj de toda la vida

**life sentence** [LUYF SEN•tinz] n condena a cadena perpetua F

**lifestyle** [LUYF•stuyul] n moda de vivir F

**lift** [lift] n levantamiento M; vt levantar; robar (steal) vi disparse (fog); give a ~\ llevar a uno en su coche

**ligament** [LI•gi•mint] n ligadura F

**light** [luyt] adj luz F; bring to ~\ sacar a luz; come to ~\ salir a luz; vt encender; ~ up\ iluminar(se)

**lighten** [LUYT•tn] vt iluminar

**lighter** [LUY•tur] n encendedor M

**lighthouse** [LUYT•haus] n faro M

**lighting** [LUYT•ting] n iluminación F

**lightly** [LUYT•lee] adv ligeramente

**lightness** [LUYT•nis] n claridad F

**lightning** [LUYT•ning] n relámpago M

**likable** [LUY•ku•bl] adj amable

**like 1** [luyk] *adj* igual; parecido; como

**like 2** *vt* gustarle (a uno) I ~ sugar\ me gusta la azucar; would you ~?\ ¿quieres?

**likely** [LUYK•lee] *adj* probable

**likeness** [LUYK•nis] *n* semejanza F

**likewise** [LUYK•wuyz] *adv* parecidamente

**liking** [LUYK•ing] *n* deseo M

**limb** [lim] *n* miembro M; out on a ~\ aislado

**lime** [luym] *n* lima F

**limelight** [LUYM•luyt] *n* foco M

**limit** [LI•mit] *n* límite M; *vt* limitar

**limitation** [LI•mi•TAI•shn] *n* limitación F

**limousine** [LI•mu•ZEEN] *n* limousine M; limusina F

**limp** [limp] *adj* cojera

**line** [luyn] *n* línea F

**linen** [LI•nun] *n* lienzo M

**linger** [LING•gur] *vi* demorar

**lingerie** [LAHN•zhu•RAI] *n* ropa blanca F

**lingo** [LING•go] *n* jerga F

**linguistics** [ling•GWI•stiks] *n* linguístico M

**link** [lingk] *n* vínculo M

**lint** [lint] *n* hilas

**lion** [LUY•un] *n* león M

**lioness** [LUY•u•nes] *n* leona F

**lip** [lip] *n* labio M; give ~ service\ aprobar de boquilla

**lipstick** [LIP•stik] *n* lápiz labial M

**liquid** [LI•kwid] *adj n* líquido M

**liquidate** [LI•kwi•DAIT] *vt* liquidar

**liquor** [LI•kur] *n* licor M

**list** [list] *n* lista F; *vt* hacer una lista de

**listen** [LI•sn] *vi* escuchar

**listener** [LI•su•nur] *n* oyente M

**literal** [LI•tu•rl] *adj* literal

**literary** [LI•tu•RE•ree] *adj* literario

**literature** [LI•tu•RU•chur] *n* literatura F

**litigation** [LI•ti•GAI•shn] *n* litigación F

**litter** [LI•tur] *n* litera F

**little** [LI•tl] *adj* pequeño; a ~\ un poco; *adv* poco; ~ by ~\ poco a poco

**live 1** [liv] *vt vi* vivir

**live 2** [luyv ] *adj* vivo

**lively** [LUYV•lee] *adj* vivaz

**liver** [LI•vur] *n* hígado M

**livery** [LI•vu•ree] *n* librea F

**livestock** [LUYV•stahk] *n* ganado M

**livid** [LI•vid] *adj* lívido

**living** [LI•ving] *adj* viviente

**lizard** [LI•zurd] *n* lagarto M

**load** [lod] *n* carga F

**loaf 1** [lof] *n* pan M

**loaf 2** *vi* ~ about\ holgazanear

**loafer** [LO•fur] *n* cantonero; holgazán M

**loan** [lon] *n* préstamo M; *vt* prestar

**loathe** [loth] *vt* aborrecer

**loathsome** [LOTH•sum] *adj* aborrecible

**lobby** [LAH•bee] *n* pasillo M; *vt* hacer presión sobre

**lobe** [lob] *n* lóbulo M

**lobster** [LAHB•stur] *n* langosta F

**local** [LO•kl] *adj* local
**locality** [lo•KA•li•tee] *n* lugar M
**locate** [LO•kait] *vt* localizar
**location** [lo•KAI•shn] *n* lugar M
**lock** [lahk] *n* rizo M; *vt vi* cerrar(se) con llave
**locomotive** [LO•ku•MO•tiv] *n* locomotor M
**locust** [LO•kust] *n* langosta F
**lodge** [lahj] *n* casita F; *vt* alojar
**lodger** [LAH•jur] *n* huésped M
**lodgings** [LAH•jingz] *n* alojamiento M
**loft** [lauft] *n* ático M
**log** [lahg] *n* troza F; *vt* apuntar; recorrer (travel)
**logic** [LAH•jik] *n* lógica F
**logical** [LAH•ji•kl] *adj* lógico
**logo** [LO•go] *n* logo M
**loin** [loin] *n* ijada F
**loiter** [LOI•tur] *vi* rezagarse
**lollipop** [LAH•lee•PAHP] *n* palito M
**London** [LUHN•dn] *n* Londres M
**lone** [lon] *adj* solo
**loneliness** [LON•lee•nis] *n* soledad F
**lonely** [LON•lee] *adj* solo
**long 1** [laung] *adj* largo; how ~ is it?\ ¿cuánto tiene de largo? in the ~ run\ a la larga; *adv* largo/mucho tiemp; as ~ as\ mientras; before ~\ dentro de poco; so ~!\ ¡hasta luego!; so ~ as\ con tal que
**long 2** *vi* ~for\ anhelar
**longitude** [LAUN•ji•TOOD] *n* longitud F
**look** [luk] *n* mirada F; *vt* ~ at\ mirar; ~ after\ ocuparse de; ~ down on\ despreciar; ~ for\

buscar; ~ into\ investigar; ~ like\ parecerse a
**loom 1** [loom] *n* telar M
**loom 2** *vi* aparecerse
**loony** [LOO•nee] *adj* loco
**loop** [loop] *n* vuelta F
**loophole** [LOOP•houl] *n* abertura F
**loose** [loos] *adj* flojo; inmoral (morals); be at ~ ends\ no tener nada que hacer
**loosely** [LOOS•lee] *adv* flojamente
**loosen** [LOO•sn] *vt* soltar
**loot** [loot] *n* pillaje M; *vt* saquear
**lord** [laurd] *n* señor M
**lore** [laur] *n* saber M
**lose** [looz] *vt* perder
**loss** [laus] *n* pérdida F; be at a ~ for words\ no encontrar palabras
**lost** [laust] *adj* perdido; get ~\ perderse
**lot** [laht] *n* lote M; suerte F (fate); a ~ of\ muchos
**lotion** [LO•shn] *n* loción F
**loud** [loud] *adj* fuerte; ruidoso; out ~\ en voz alta
**loudspeaker** [LOUD•SPEE•kur] *n* altavoz F
**lounge** [lounj] *n* paseo M; *vi* repantigarse
**louse** [lous] *n* piojo M
**lout** [lout] *n* patán M
**lovable** [LUH•vu•bl] *adj* amable
**love** [luhv] *n* amor M; be in ~ with\ estar enamorado de; *vt* querer

**love affair** [LUV a•FAIR] *n* amores M

**lovely** [LUHV•lee] *adj* bello

**lover** [LUH•vur] *n* amante M

**low** [lo] *adj* bajo

**lower** [LO•ur] *adj* bajo

**lowly** [LO•lee] *adj* humilde

**loyal** [LOI•ul] *adj* fiel

**loyalty** [LOI•ul•tee] *n* fidelidad F

**lubricant** [LOO•bri•kunt] *n* lubricante M

**lubricate** [LOO•bri•KAIT] *vt* lubricar

**lucid** [LOO•sid] *adj* lúcido

**luck** [luhk] *n* suerte F; bad ~\ mala suerte

**luckily** [LUH•ku•lee] *adv* afortunadamente

**lucky** [LUH•kee] *adj* afortunado

**ludicrous** [LOO•di•krus] *adj* cómico

**lug** [luhg] *vt* asa F

**luggage** [LUH•gij] *n* equipaje M

**lukewarm** [LOOK•WAURM] *adj* tibio

**lull** [luhl] *n* memento de calma M

**lullaby** [LUH•lu•BUY] *n* arrullo M

**lumber** [LUHM•bur] *n* madera F

**lumberjack** [LUHM•bur•JAK] *n* leñador M

**luminous** [LOO•mi•nus] *adj* luminoso

**lump** [luhmp] *n* trozo M

**lunar** [LOO•nur] *adj* lunar

**lunatic** [LOO•nu•TIK] *n* loco demente M

**lunch** [luhnch] *n* almuerzo M; ~ hour\ *n* hora del almuerzo F

**lung** [luhng] *n* pulmón M

**lunge** [luhnj] *vi* irse a fondo

**lurch** [lurch] *n* tumbo M; *vt* tambalearse; leave in the ~\ dejar en la estacada

**lure** [loour] *n* engaño M; *vt* atraer

**lurid** [LU•rid] *adj* tempestuoso

**lurk** [lurk] *vi* esconderse

**luscious** [LUH•shs] *adj* delicioso

**lust** [luhst] *n* sensualidad F

**luster** [LUH•stur] *n* lustre M

**luxurious** [luhg•ZHU•ree•us] *adj* lujoso

**luxury** [LUHK•shu•ree] *adj* lujo M

**lying** [LUY•ing] *adj* falso mentiroso

**lynch** [linch] *vt* linchar

**lyric** [LEEU•rik] *adj* lírico M

**lyrical** [LEEU•ri•kl] *adj* lírico

# M

**macaroni** [MA•ku•RO•nee] *n* macarrones

**machine** [mu•SHEEN] *n* máquina F

**machine gun** [ma•SHEEN GUN] *n* ametrallar F

**machinery** [mu•SHEE•nu•ree] *n* maquinaria F

**mackerel** [MA•krul] *n*
escombro M

**mad** [mad] *adj* demente;
furioso; be ~ about\ estar loco
de; like ~\ como un loco

**madam** [MU•dam] *n* señora F

**madden** [MA•dn] *vt* enloquecer

**madly** [MAD•lee] *adv*
locamente

**madman** [MAD•man] *n* loco M

**madness** [MAD•nis] *n* locura F

**magazine** [MA•gu•ZEEN] *n*
revista F

**magic** [MA•jik] *adj* magia F

**magical** [MA•ji•kl] *adj*
mágico M

**magician** [ma•JI•shn] *n*
mágico M

**magistrate** [MA•ji•STRAIT] *n*
magistrado M

**magnet** [MAG•nit] *n* imán M

**magnetic** [mag•NE•tik] *adj*
magnético

**magnificence** [mag•NI•fi•suns]
*n* magnificencia F

**magnificent** [mag•NI•fi•sunt]
*adj* magnífico

**magnify** [MAG•ni•FUY] *vt*
agrandar

**magnifying glass**
[MAG•ni•FUY•ing GLAS] *n*
lente de aumento M

**magnitude** [MAG•ni•TOOD] *n*
magnitud F

**mahogany** [mu•HAH•gu•nee] *n*
caoba F

**maid** [maid] *n* doncella F

**maiden name** [MAI•dn NAIM]
*n* apellido de soltera M

**mail** [maiul] *n* correo M; *adj*
postal; de correos; *vt* echar al
correo; enviar por correo

**mailbox** [MAIUL•bahks] *n*
apartado M

**mailman** [MAIUL•man] *n*
cartero M

**maim** [maim] *vt* mutilar

**main** [main] *n* principal F; *adj*
primero; ~ course\ *n* vela
mayor F; in the ~\ en su
mayor parte

**mainland** [MAIN•land] *n*
continente M

**maintain** [main•TAIN] *vt*
mantener

**maintenance** [MAIN•tu•nuns]
*n* mantenimiento M

**majestic** [mu•JE•stik] *adj*
majestuoso

**majesty** [MA•ji•stee] *n*
majestad F

**major** [MAI•jur] *adj* mayor

**majority** [mu•JAU•ri•tee] *n*
mayoría F

**make** [maik] *vt vi* hacer;
fabricar (manufacture); ganar
(money); tomar (decision); ~
believe\ fingir; ~ off\ escarpe
con; *vi* arreglárselas; ~ over\
decer; ~ up\ formar; ~ up for\
compensar

**male** [maiul] *adj* macho M

**malice** [MA•lis] *n* malevolencia F

**malicious** [mu•LI•shus] *adj*
malévolo

**malign** [mu•LUYN] *vt* difamar

**malignant** [mu•LIG•nunt] *adj*
maligno

**malpractice** [mal•prak•tis] *n*
tratamiento erróneo M

**mallet** [MA•lit] *n* mazo M

**mammal** [MA•ml] *n* mamífero M

**mammoth** [MA•muth] *adj*
mamut M

**man** [man] *n* hombre M; ~ to
~\ de hombre a hombre; *vt*
guarnecer (de hombres)

**manage** [MA•nij] *vt* dirigir;
llevar; manejar

**management** [MA•nij•munt] *n*
administración F

**manager** [MA•ni•jur] *n*
director M

**mandate** [MAN•dait] *n*
mandato M

**mandatory**
[MAN•du•TAU•ree] *adj*
obligatorio

**mane** [main] *n* crin M

**maneuver** [mu•NOO•vur] *n*
maniobra F

**manhood** [MAN•hud] *n*
virilidad F

**mania** [MAI•nee•u] *n* manía F

**manicure** [MA•ni•KYUR] *n*
manicura F

**manifest** [MA•ni•FEST] *adj*
manifiesto M

**manipulate** [mu•NI•pyu•LAIT]
*vt* manipular

**mankind** [MAN•KUYND] *n*
humanidad F

**manner** [MA•nur] *n* manera F

**manor** [MA•nur] *n* feudo M

**manpower** [MAN•pouur] *n*
poder humano.M

**mansion** [MAN•shn] *n*
mansión F

**manslaughter**
[MAN•SLAU•tur] *n*
homicidio M

**mantelpiece** [MAN•tl•PEES] *n*
repisa de chimenea F

**manual** [MA•nyoo•ul] *adj n*
manual M

**manufacture**
[MA•nyu•FAK•chur] *n*
fabricar

**manufacturer**
[MA•nyu•FAK•chu•rur] *n*
fabricante M

**manure** [mu•NOOUR] *n*
abono M

**manuscript** [MA•nyu•SKRIPT]
*n* manuscrito M

**many** [ME•nee] *adj* muchos

**map** [map] *n* mapa M

**maple** [MAI•pl] *n* arce M

**mar** [mahr] *vt* estropear

**marathon** [MA•ru•THAHN] *n*
maratón F

**marble** [MAHR•bl] *n* mármol M

**march** [mahrch] *n* marzo M; *vt*
marchar

**mare** [maiur] *n* yegua F

**margarine** [MAHR•ju•rin] *n*
margarina F

**margin** [MAHR•jin] *n* margen M

**marginal** [MAHR•ji•nl] *adj*
marginal

**marigold** [MA•ri•GOLD] *n*
maravilla F

**marijuana** [MA•ri•WAH•nu] *n*
marihuana F

**marinate** [MA•ri•NAIT] *vt*
marinar

**marine** [mu•REEN] *adj n*
marino M

**mark** [mahrk] *n* marca F

**marker** [MAHR•kur] *n*
marcador M

**market** [MAHR•kit] *n*
mercado M

**marmalade** [MAHR•mu•LAID]
*n* mermelada F

**maroon** [mu•ROON] *adj*
castaño

**marriage** [MA•rij] *n*
matrimonio M

**married** [MA•reed] *adj* casado

**marry** [MA•ree] *vt* casar

**Mars** [mahrz] *n* Marte M

**marsh** [mahrsh] *n* pantano M

**marshal** [MAHR•shl] *n*
mariscal M

**marshy** [MAHR•shee] *adj*
húmedo

**martial** [MAHR•shl] *adj*
marcial

**martyr** [MAHR•tur] *n* mártir M;
*vt* martirizar

**marvel** [MAHR•vl] *n* maravilla F

**marvelous** [MAHR•vu•lus] *adj*
maravilloso

**mascara** [ma•SKA•ru] *n* tinte
para las pestañas M

**masculine** [MA•skyu•lin] *adj*
masculino

**mash** [mash] *vt* macerar

**mask** [mask] *n* antifaz F; *vt*
enmascarar

**mason** [MAI•sn] *n* francmasón M

**masquerade** [MA•sku•RAID] *n*
masarada F

**mass 1** [mass] *n* masa F;
montón M (great quantity)

**mass 2** *n* misa F (relig)

**massacre** [MA•su•kr] *n*
matanza F

**massage** [mu•SAHZH] *n*
masaje F

**massive** [MA•siv] *adj*
voluminoso

**mast** [mast] *n* mástil M

**master** [MA•stur] *adj n* amo
patrón M

**masterpiece** [MA•stur•PEES] *n*
obra maestra F

**mat** [mat] *n* estera F

**match** [mach] *n* fósforo M

**mate** [mait] *n* compañero M

**material** [mu•TEEU•ree•ul] *adj*
material

**materialist**
[mu•TEEU•ree•u•list] *n*
materialista F

**materialistic**
[mu•TEEU•ree•u•LI•stik] *adj*
materialista

**maternal** [mu•TUR•nl] *adj*
maternal

**mathematics**
[MA•thu•MA•tiks] *n*
matemática F

**matriculation**
[mu•TRI•kyu•LAI•shn] *n*
acción de matricularse

**matrimony** [MA•tri•MO•nee] *n*
matrimonio M

**matrix** [MAI•triks] *n* matriz F

**matter** [MA•tur] *n* substancia F;
as a ~ of fact\ en realidad; no
~\ no importa; what is the ~?\
¿qué pasa? *vi* importar; it
doesn't ~\ no importa

**mattress** [MA•tris] *n* colchón M

**mature** [mu•CHOOUR] *adj*
maduro M; *vt vi* madurar

**maturity** [mu•CHOOU•ri•tee] *n*
madurez F

**maximum** [MAK•si•mum] *adj*
*n* máximum M

**may** [mai] modal v poder; may
I smoke?\ ¿se permite fumar?

**May** [mai] *n* mayo M

**mayonnaise** [MAI•u•NAIZ] *n* salsa mahonesa F

**mayor** [MAI•yur] *n* alcalde M

**maze** [maiz] *n* laberinto M

**me** [mee] *pers pron* me; mí; hc knows ~\ me conoce; it's ~\ soy yo

**meadow** [ME•do] *n* prado M

**meager** [MEE•gr] *adj* magro

**meal** [meeul] *n* comida F

**mean 1** [meen] *vt* tener la intención de; querer

**mean 2** *adj* humilde tacaño

**meaning** [MEE•ning] *n* significación F

**meantime** [MEEN•tuym] *adv* entretanto

**meanwhile** [MEEN•wuyul] *adv* mientras

**measles** [MEE•zlz] *n* sarampión F

**measure** [ME•zhur] *n* medida F; *vt vi* medir; ~ up to\ estar a la altura de

**measurement** [ME•zhur•munt] *n* medición F

**meat** [meet] *n* carne M

**meatball** [MEET•baul] *n* albóndiga F

**mechanic** [mu•KA•nik] *n* mecánico M

**mechanical** [mu•KA•ni•kl] *adj* mecánico

**mechanism** [ME•ku•NI•zm] *n* mecanismo M

**medal** [ME•dl] *n* medalla F

**medallion** [mu•DAHL•yun] *n* medallón F

**meddle** [ME•dl] *vi* entrometerse

**media** [MEE•dee•u] *npl* media F

**mediate** [MEE•dee•AIT] *vt* mediar

**mediator** [MEE•dee•AI•tur] *n* mediador M

**medical** [ME•di•kl] *adj* médico M

**medicate** [ME•di•KAIT] *vt* medicinar

**medicine** [ME•di•sin] *n* medicina F

**medieval** [mi•DEE•vl] *adj* medieval

**mediocre** [MEE•dee•O•kr] *adj* mediocre

**meditate** [ME•di•TAIT] *vi* meditar

**medium** [MEE•dee•um] *adj* medio M

**meek** [meek] *adj* manso

**meet** [meet] *vt* encontrar; *vi* encontrarse; ~ with\ tropezar con

**meeting** [MEE•ting] *n* sesión asamblea F

**megaphone** [ME•gu•FON] *n* megáfono M

**melancholy** [ME•lun•KAH•lee] *adj* melancolía F

**melody** [ME•lu•dee] *n* melodía F

**melon** [ME•lun] *n* melón F

**melt** [melt] *vt* liquidar

**mellow** [ME•lo] *adj* blando

**member** [MEM•bur] *n* miembro M

**membership** [MEM•bur•SHIP] *n* sociedad F

**memo** [ME•mo] *n* nota F

**memoirs** [MEM•wahrz] *npl* memoria F

**memorial** [me•MAU•ree•ul] *adj*
conmemorativo

**memorize** [ME•mu•RUYZ] *vt*
aprender de memoria

**memory** [ME•mu•ree] *n*
memoria F

**menace** [ME•nus] *n* amenaza F;
*vt* amenzar

**menacing** [ME•nu•sing] *adj*
amenazador

**mend** [mend] *vt* reparar;
remediar

**menial** [MEEN•yul] *adj* servil

**menopause** [ME•nu•PAUZ] *n*
menopausia F

**menstruation**
[MEN•stroo•AI•shn] *n*
menstruación F

**mental** [MEN•tl] *adj* mental

**mentality** [men•TA•li•tee] *n*
mentalidad F

**mention** [MEN•chn] *vt*
mencionar; don't ~ it\ ¡no hay
de qué!; *n* mención F

**menu** [ME•nyoo] *n* menú F

**mercenary** [MUR•su•NE•ree]
*adj n* mercenario M

**merchandise**
[MUR•chun•DUYS] *n*
mercadería F

**merchant** [MUR•chunt] *n*
mercader M

**merciful** [MUR•si•ful] *adj*
misericordioso

**merciless** [MUR•si•lis] *adj*
implacable

**mercury** [MUR•kyu•ree] *n*
mercurio M

**mercy** [MUR•see] *n*
misericordia F; at the ~ of\ a
merced de

**mere** [meeur] *adj* simple

**merely** [MEEUR•lee] *adv*
meramente

**merge** [murj] *vt* unir

**merger** [MUR•jur] *n* unión F

**merit** [ME•rit] *n* mérito M; *vt*
merecer

**mermaid** [MUR•maid] *n*
sirena F

**merry** [ME•ree] *adj* alegre

**merry-go-round**
[MAI•ree•go•ROUND] *n*
tiovivo M

**mesh** [mesh] *n* malla F

**mesmerize** [MEZ•mu•RUYZ]
*vt* magnetizar

**mess** [mes] *n* desorden M; make
a ~\ chapucear; estropear

**message** [ME•sij] *n* mensaje M

**messenger** [ME•sin•jur] *n*
mensajero M

**messy** [ME•see] *adj*
desarreglado

**metal** [ME•tl] *n* metal M

**metallic** [mu•TA•lik] *adj*
metálico

**metaphor** [ME•tu•FAUR] *n*
metáfora F

**meteor** [MEE•tee•ur] *n*
meteoro M

**meteorology**
[MEE•tee•u•RAH•lu•jee] *n*
meteorología F

**meter** [MEE•tur] *n* medidor M

**method** [ME•thud] *n* método M

**meticulous** [mu•TI•kyu•lus] *adj*
meticuloso

**metric** [ME•trik] *adj* métrico

**metropolitan**
[ME•tru•PAH•li•tun] *adj*
metropolitano

**Mexican** [MEK•si•kun] *adj* mejicano

**Mexico** [MEK•si•KO] *n* Méjico M

**mice** [muys] *npl* ratones M

**microphone** [MUY•kru•FON] *n* micrófono M

**microscope** [MUY•kru•SKOP] *n* microscopio M

**microscopic** [MUY•kru•SKAH•pik] *adj* microscópico

**mid** [mid] *adj* medio

**middle** [MI•dl] *n* medio M; in the ~ of\ en medio de

**middle class** [ ~ KLAS] *n* de al clase media

**midnight** [MID•nuyt] *n* medianoche F

**midst** [midst] *n* centro M

**midwife** [MID•wuyf] *n* partera F

**might 1** [muyt] *modal v* poder

**might 2** *n* fuerza M

**mighty** [MUY•tee] *adj* poderoso

**migraine** [MUY•grain] *n* migraña F

**migrate** [MUY•grait] *vi* emigrar

**mild** [muyuld] *adj* blando

**mildew** [MIL•doo] *n* moho M

**mile** [muyul] *n* milla F

**militant** [MI•li•tunt] *adj n* militante

**military** [MI•li•TE•ree] *adj* los militares

**militia** [mi•LI•shu] *n* milicia F

**milk** [milk] *n* leche F

**mill** [mil] *n* molino M; *vt* moler; *vi* ~ about\ circular

**millennium** [mi•LE•nee•um] *n* milenio M

**million** [MIL•yun] *num* millón M

**millionaire** [MIL•yu•NAIUR] *n* millonario M

**mimic** [MI•mik] *n* mímico M

**mince** [mins] *vt* desmenuzar

**mind** [muynd] *n* mente F; be on one's ~\ preocuparle a uno; *vt* cuidar (look after); hacer caso de (heed); I don't mind\ no me molesta

**mindful** [MUYND•ful] *adj* atento

**mine 1** [muyn] *poss pron* el mío; la mía F

**mine 2** *n* mina F; *vt* extraer

**mineral** [MI•nu•rul] *adj n* mineral M

**mingle** [MING•gl] *vi* mezclar

**miniature** [MI•nu•CHUR] *adj n* miniatura F

**minimize** [MI•ni•MUYZ] *vt* disminuir

**minimum** [MI•ni•mum] *adj n* mínimo M

**mining** [MUY•ning] *n* minería F

**minister** [MI•ni•stur] *n* ministro M

**ministry** [MI•ni•stree] *n* ministerio M

**mink** [mingk] *n* visón F

**minor** [MUY•nur] *adj n* meno M

**minority** [muy•NAU•ri•tee] *n* minoridad F

**mint** [mint] *n* mina F

**minus** [MUY•nus] *prep* menos

**minute** [*adj.* muy•NOOT *n.* MI•nit] *adj* minuto M

**miracle** [MI•ru•kl] *n* milagro M

**miraculous** |mi•RA•kyu•lus|
*adj* milagroso

**mirage** |mi•RAHZH| *n* miraje M

**mirror** |MI•rur| *n* espejo M

**misanthrope** |MI•san•THROP|
*n* misántropo M

**misappropriation**
|mis•U•PRO•pree•AI•shn| *n*
malversación F

**misbehave** |MIS•bee•HAIV| *vi*
conducirse mal

**miscarriage** |MIS•KA•rij| *n*
aborto M

**miscellaneous**
|MI•su•LAI•nee•us| *adj*
misceláneo

**misconception**
|MIS•kun•SEP•shn| *vt* mala
interpretación F

**misconduct** |mis•KAHN•duhkt|
*n* mala conducta F

**misconstrue**
|MIS•kun•STROO| *vt* torcer
el sentido M

**miscount** |mis•KOUNT| *vt vi*
error de cuenta M

**mischief** |MIS•chif| *n*
travesura F

**mischievous** |MIS•chi•vus| *adj*
malo

**misdeed** |MIS•deed| *n*
fechoría F

**misdemeanor**
|MIS•du•MEE•nur| *n* mala
conducta F

**miser** |MUY•zur| *n* mísero M

**miserable** |MIZ•ru•bl| *adj*
miserable

**miserly** |MUY•zur•lee| *adj*
avaro

**misery** |MI•zu•ree| *n* miseria F

**misfire** |mis•FUYUR| *vi* fallar

**misfortune** |mis•FAUR•chun| *n*
infortunio M

**misgivings** |MIS•GI•vingz| *npl*
duda F

**mishap** |MIS•hap| *n* desliz F

**misinform** |MIS•in•FAURM| *vt*
informar mal

**misjudge** |mis•JUHJ| *vt* juzgar
mal

**misleading** |MIS•LEE•ding|
*adj* desencaminado

**misplace** |mis•PLAIS| *vt*
extraviar

**misprint** |MIS•print| *n* errata F

**Miss** |mis| *n* señorita F

**miss** *vt* errada F; *vt* erar; ~ the
point\ no comprender; ~ out\
omitir

**missile** |MI•sul| *n* arrojadizo M

**missing** |MI•sing| *adj* perdido

**mission** |MI•shn| *n* misión F

**missionary** |MI•shu•NE•ree| *n*
misionario M

**misspell** |mis•SPEL| *vt* escribir
con mala ortografía

**mist** |mist| *n* niebla F

**mistake** |mi•STAIK| *n*
equivocación F

**mistaken** |mi•STAI•kn| *adj*
equivocado

**mister** |MI•stur| *n* señor M

**mistreat** |mis•TREET| *vt*
maltratar

**mistress** |MI•strus| *n* ama F

**mistrust** |mis•TRUHST| *n*
desconfianza F

**misty** |MI•stee| *adj* brumoso

**misunderstand**
|mis•UHN•dur•STAND| *vt*
entender mal

**misunderstanding**
[mis•UHN•dur•STAN•ding] *n*
equivocación F

**misuse** [mis•YOOS] *n* abuso M

**mitigating** [MI•ti•GAI•ting] *adj*
mitigando

**mitten** [MI•tn] *n* guantes

**mix** [miks] *vt* mezclar

**mixture** [MIKS•chur] *n*
mezcla F

**moan** [mon] *n* gemido M; *vi*
gemir; quejarse (complain)

**moat** [mot] *n* foso M

**mob** [mahb] *n* tropel M; *vt*
acosar

**mobile** [MO•bl] *adj* móvil

**mobilize** [MO•bu•LUYZ] *vt*
movilizar

**mock** [mahk] *vt* mofar

**mockery** [MAH•ku•ree] *n*
burla F

**mode** [mod] *n* modo M

**model** [MAH•dl] *adj* modelo
M; *vt* modelar; *vi* ser maniquí
(fashion)

**moderate** [*adj. n.* MAH•du•rit
*v.* MAH•du•RAIT] *adj n*
moderado M; *vt* (*vi*)
moderar(se)

**moderation**
[MAH•du•RAI•shn] *n*
moderación F

**modern** [MAH•durn] *adj*
moderno

**modernize** [MAH•dur•NUYZ]
*vt* modernizar

**modest** [MAH•dist] *adj*
modesto

**modesty** [MAH•di•stee] *n*
modestia F

**modify** [MAH•di•FUY] *vt*
modificar

**moist** [moist] *adj* húmedo

**moisten** [MOI•sn] *vt* humectar

**moisture** [MOIS•chur] *n*
humedad F

**molar** [MO•lur] *n* molar M

**molasses** [mu•LA•sis] *n*
melaza F

**mold** [mold] *n* moho M; *vt*
moldear

**mole** [mol] *n* mola F

**molest** [mu•LEST] *vt* molestar

**molten** [MOL•tn] *adj* fundido

**mollusk** [MAH•lusk] *n*;
molusco M

**moment** [MO•munt] *n*
momento M

**momentary** [MO•mun•TE•ree]
*adj* momentáneo

**momentous** [mo•MEN•tus] *adj*
importante; grave

**monarch** [MAH•nahrk] *n*
monarca F

**monarchy** [MAH•nahr•kee] *n*
monarquía F

**monastery** [MAH•nu•STE•ree]
*n* monasterio M

**Monday** [MUHN•dai] *n* lunes M

**monetary** [MAH•nu•TE•ree]
*adj* monctario

**money** [MUH•nee] *n* dinero M;
~ order\ *n* giro postal M

**mongrel** [MAHN•grul] *n*
mestizo M

**monk** [muhngk] *n* monje M

**monkey** [MUHNG•kee] *n*
mono M

**monologue** [MAH•nu•LAHG]
*n* monólogo M

**monopolize**
[mu•NAH•pu•LUYZ] *vt*
monopolizar

**monopoly** [mu•NAH•pu•lee] *n*
monopolio M

**monotone** [MAH•nu•TON] *n*
monótono M

**monotonous** [mu•NAH•tu•nus]
*adj* monótono

**monotony** [mu•NAH•tu•nee] *n*
• monotonía F

**monsoon** [mahn•SOON] *n*
monzón F

**monster** [MAHN•stur] *n*
monstro M

**monstrosity**
[mahn•STRAH•si•tee] *n*
monstruosidad F

**monstrous** [MAHN•strus] *adj*
monstruoso

**month** [muhnth] *n* mes M

**monthly** [MUHNTH•lee] *adj n*
mensualmente

**monument** [MAH•nyu•munt] *n*
monumento M

**monumental**
[MAH•nyu•MEN•tl] *adj*
monumental

**moo** [moo] *n* mugido M

**mood** [mood] *n* humor M; be in
the ~\ to tener ganas de; in a
good/bad ~\ de buen/mal
humor

**moody** [MOO•dee] *adj*
malhumorado

**moon** [moon] *n* luna F

**moonlight** [MOON•luyt] *n* luz
de al luna F

**moor** [moour] *n* marjal M

**Moor** [moour] *n* moro M

**mop** [mahp] *n* aljofifa F; *vt*
fregar; ~ up\ limpiar

**mope** [mop] *vi* entristecer

**moral** [MAU•rul] *adj* moral

**morale** [mau•RAL] *n* moral M

**morality** [mu•RA•li•tee] *n*
moralidad F

**morbid** [MAUR•bid] *adj*
mórbido

**more** [maur] *adj* más; ~ and ~\
cada vez más; ~ or less\ más
o menos; once ~\ una vez
más; some ~\ más

**moreover** [mau•RO•vur] *adv*
además

**morgue** [maurg] *n* depósito de
cadaveres M

**morning** [MAUR•ning] *n*
mañana F

**Morocco** [mu•RAH•ko] *n*
Marruecos

**moron** [MAU•rahn] *n* atrasado
mental M

**morsel** [MAUR•sl] *n* bocado M

**mortal** [MAUR•tl] *adj n* mortal

**mortality** [maur•TA•li•tee] *n*
mortalidad F

**mortar** [MAUR•tur] *n*
mortero M

**mortgage** [MAUR•gij] *n*
hipotecar M; *vt* hipotecar

**mortify** [MAUR•ti•FUY] *vt*
mortificar

**mosaic** [mo•ZAI•ik] *n*
masaico M

**Moscow** [MAH•skou] *n*
Moscú M

**mosque** [mahsk] *n* mezquita F

**mosquito** [mu•SKEE•to] *n*
mosquito M

**moss** [maus] *n* musgo M

**most** [most] *adj adv* más for the
~ part\ en su mayor parte; *n*
la mayoría F; at ~\ a lo más;
make the ~ of\ provechar al
máximo

**mostly** [MOST•lee] *adv* en su
mayor parte

**moth** [mauth] *n* polilla F

**mother** [MUH•thur] *n* madre F

**mother-in-law**
[MUH•thur•in•LAU] *n*
suegra F

**motherhood** [MUH•thur•HUD]
*n* maternidad F

**motherly** [MUH•thur•lee] *adj*
maternal

**motif** [mo•TEEF] *n* motivo M

**motion** [MO•shn] *n*
movimiento M

**motivate** [MO•ti•VAIT] *vt*
motivar

**motivation** [MO•ti•VAI•shn] *n*
motivo M

**motive** [MO•tiv] *n* motivo M

**motor** [MO•tur] *n* motor M

**motorboat** [MO•tur•BOT] *n*
canoa automóvil F

**motorcycle** [MO•tur•SUY•kl] *n*
motocicleta F

**motto** [MAH•to] *n* mote M

**mound** [mound] *n* montón M

**mount 1** [mount] *vt vi* subir; *n*
montura F; ~ up\ aumentar

**mount 2** *n* monte M

**mountaineer**
[MOUN•tu•NEEUR] *n*
montañes M

**mountainous** [MOUN•tu•nus]
*adj* montañoso

**mourn** [maurn] *vt* lamentar

**mourning** [MAUR•ning] *n*
lamento M

**mouse** [mous] *n* ratón M

**moustache** [MUH•stash] *n*
bigote M

**mouth** [mouth] *n* boca F

**mouthful** [MOUTH•ful] *n*
bocado M

**mouthwash** [MOUTH•wahsh]
*n* enjuague M

**movable** [MOO•vu•bl] *adj*
movible

**move** [moov] *n* movimiento M;
*vt* mover; mudarse de (house);
conmover (with emotion); *vi*
moverse; ~ out\ irse; on the
~\ en movimiento; ~ along\
circular; ~ over\ apartarse

**movement** [MOOV•munt] *n*
movimiento M

**movie** [MOO•vee] *n* película F

**moving** [MOO•ving] *adj*
movimiento

**mow** [mo] *vt* apilar

**mucous** [MYOO•kus] *n*
mucoso M

**much** [muhch] *adj* mucho; ~ as\
por mucho que; ~ the same\
más o menos lo mismo; so ~\
tanto; too ~\ demasiado

**mud** [muhd] *n* barro M

**muddle** [MUH•dl] *n* embrollo M

**muddy** [MUH•dee] *adj* barroso

**muffin** [MUH•fin] *n* panecillo M

**muffle** [MUH•fl] *vt* mufla F

**mug** [muhg] *n* jarro M

**mule** [myooul] *n* burro M

**multiple** [MUHL•ti•pl] *adj n*
múltiple M

**multiplication**
[MUHL•ti•pli•KAI•shn] *n*
multiplicación F

**multiply** [MUHL•ti•PLUY] *vt*
multiplicar

**multitude** [MUHL•ti•TOOD] *n*
multitud F

**mumble** [MUHM•bl] *vt vi*
murmurar

**mummy** [MUH•mee] *n*
momia F

**mumps** [muhmps] *n* paperas F

**munch** [muhnch] *vt vi* mascar

**mundane** [muhn•DAIN] *adj*
mundano

**municipal** [myoo•NI•si•pl] *adj*
municipal

**municipality**
[myoo•NI•si•PA•li•tee] *n*
municipalidad F

**mural** [MYOOU•rul] *n*
mural M

**murder** [MUR•dur] *n* asesinato
M; *vt* aesinar

**murderer** [MUR•du•rur] *n*
asesino M

**murderous** [MUR•du•rus] *adj*
homicida

**murky** [MUR•kee] *adj* obscuro

**murmur** [MUR•mur] *n*
murmullo M

**muscle** [MUH•sl] *n* músculo M;
*vi* ~ in\ meterse por fuerza en
(coll)

**muscular** [MUH•skyu•lur] *adj*
muscular

**muse** [myooz] *n* meditación F;
*vi* meditar

**museum** [myoo•ZEE•um] *n*
museo M

**mushroom** [MUHSH•rum] *n*
hongo M

**music** [MYOO•zik] *n* música F

**musical** [MYOO•zi•kl] *adj*
musical

**musician** [myoo•ZI•shn] *n*
músico M

**Muslim** [MUHZ•lim] *adj*
muslime

**mussel** [MUH•sl] *n* mejillón F

**must** [muhst] *modal v* tener
que; you ~ go\ debes
marcharte

**mustache** [MUH•stash] *n*
bigote M

**mustard** [MUH•sturd] *n*
mostaza F

**muster** [MUH•stur] *vt* alistar

**musty** [MUH•stee] *adj* mohoso

**mute** [myoot] *adj n* mudo M

**mutilate** [MYOO•ti•LAIT] *vt*
mutilar

**mutiny** [MYOO•ti•nee] *n*
motín M

**mutter** [MUH•tur] *vt vi*
murmurar

**mutton** [MUH•tn] *n*
carnero M

**mutual** [MYOO•choo•ul] *adj*
mutuo

**muzzle** [MUH•zl] *n* hocico M

**my** [muy] *poss adj* mi; mis

**myself** [muy•SELF] *pron* yo
mismo

**mysterious** [mi•STEEU•ree•us]
*adj* misterioso

**mystery** [MI•stu•ree] *n*
misterio M

**mystic** [MI•stik] *n* místico M

**mystical** [MI•sti•kl] *adj* místico

**myth** [mith] *n* fábula F

**mythical** [MI•thi•kl] *adj* mítico

**mythology** [mi•THAH•lu•jee]
*n* mitología F

# N

**nab** [nab] *vt* agazapar

**nag** [nag] *vt* regañar; *vi* criticar

**nail** [naiul] *n* clavo M; *vt* clavar;
~ polish\ *n* esmalte para las
uñas M

**naive** [nuy•EEV] *adj* sencillo

**naked** [NAI•kid] *adj* desnudo;
to the ~ eye\ a simple vista

**nakedness** [NAI•kid•nis] *n*
desnudez F

**name** [naim] *n* nombre M; *vt*
nombrar

**namely** [NAIM•lce] *adv* esto es

**nap** [nap] *n* siesta F; *vi* echarse
un sueña

**napkin** [NAP•kin] *n* servilleta F

**narcotic** [nahr•KAH•tik] *adj n*
narcótico M

**narrate** [NA•rait] *vt* narrar

**narration** [na•RAI•shn] *n*
narración F

**narrative** [NA•ru•tiv] *adj*
narrativo

**narrator** [na•RAI•tur] *n*
narrador M

**narrow** [NA•ro] *adj* estrecho

**narrow-minded**
[NAI•ro•MUYN•did] *adj*
iliberal

**nasal** [NAI•zl] *adj* nasal

**nasturtium** [nu•STUR•shum] *n*
capuchina F

**nasty** [NA•stee] *adj* sucio

**nation** [NAI•shn] *n* nación F

**national** [NA•shu•nl] *adj*
nacional

**nationality** [NA•shu•NA•li•tee]
*n* nacionalidad F

**nationalize**
[NA•shu•nu•LUYZ] *vt*
nacionalizar

**native** [NAI•tiv] *adj* nativo

**Nativity** [nu•TI•vi•tee] *n*
nacimiento M

**natural** [NA•chrul] *adj* natural

**naturalize** [NA•chru•LUYZ] *vt*
naturalizar

**naturally** [NA•chru•lee] *adv*
naturalmente

**nature** [NA•chur] *n* natura F

**naughty** [NAU•tee] *adj* malo

**nausea** [NAU•zee•u] *n* náusea F

**nauseate** [NAU•zee•AIT] *vt*
dar náuseas

**nauseous** [NAU•shus] *adj*
asquerosamente

**naval** [NAI•vl] *adj* naval

**navel** [NAI•vl] *n* ombligo M

**navigate** [NA•vi•GAIT] *vt*
navegar

**navigation** [NA•vi•GAI•shn] *n*
navegación F

**navigator** [NA•vi•GAI•tur] *n*
navegante M

**navy** [NAI•vee] *adj* armada F

**near** [neeur] *adj* cercano; come
~\ acercarse; *prep* ~ to\ cerca
de; *vt* cercarse

**nearby** [neeur•BUY] *adj* cerca

**nearly** [NEEUR•lee] *adv*
cercanamente

**near-sighted** [NEEUR•suy•tid]
*adj* corto de vista

**neat** |neet| *adj* limpio; pulcro
**necessary** |NE•su•SE•ree| *adj*
  necesario
**necessity** |nu•SE•si•tee| *n*
  necesidad F
**neck** |nek| *n* cuello M; ~ and ~\
  parejos
**need** |need| *n* necesidad F
**needle** |NEE•dl| *n* aguja F
**needless** |NEED•lis| *adj*
  innecesario
**needy** |NEE•dee| *adj* necesitado
**negative** |NE•gu•tiv| *adj*
  negativo
**neglect** |ni•GLEKT| *vt*
  abandonar descuidar
**negligence** |NE•gli•juns| *n*
  negligencia F
**negligent** |NE•gli•junt| *adj*
  negligente
**negotiate** |ni•GO•shee•AIT| *vt*
  *vi* negociar
**negotiation**
  |ni•GO•shee•AI•shn| *n*
  negociación F
**Negro** |NEE•gro| *adj n* negro M
**neigh** |nai| *vi* relinchar
**neighbor** |NAI•bur| *n* vecino M
**neighborhood** |NAI•bur•HUD|
  *n* vecindad F
**neither** |NEE•thur| *adj*
  ninguno; ~.nor \ ni.ni.; *conj*
  tampoco
**nephew** |NE•fyoo| *n* sobrino M
**Neptune** |NEP•toon| *n*
  Neptuno M
**nerve** |nurv| *n* nervio M
**nervous** |NUR•vus| *adj*
  nervioso
**nest** |nest| *n* nido M; *vi* anidar;
  ~ egg\ *npl* ahorros M

**net** |net| *adj* red M
**Netherlands** |NE•thur•lundz|
  *npl* Países Bajos
**nettle** |NE•tl| *n* ortiga F
**network** |NET•wurk| *n* red M
**neurosis** |nu•RO•sis| *n*
  neurosis M
**neurotic** |nu•RAH•tik| *adj n*
  neurótico M
**neuter** |NOO•tur| *adj* neutro
**neutral** |NOO•trul| *adj* neutral
**neutrality** |noo•TRA•li•tee| *n*
  neutralidad F
**neutralize** |NOO•tru•LUYZ| *vt*
  neutralizar
**never** |NE•vr| *adv* nunca;
  jamás; ~ again\ nunca más; ~
  mind\ no te preocupes; no se
  preocupe
**nevertheless** |NE•vur•thu•LES|
  *adv* sin embargo
**new** |noo| *adj* nuevo
**newly** |NOO•lee| *adv*
  nuevamente
**news** |nooz| *n* noticia F
**newscast** |NOOZ•kast| *n*
  noticiario M
**newspaper** |NOOZ•pai•pur| *n*
  periódico M
**New Year** |NOO yeer| *n* año
  nuevo
**next** |nekst| *adj* próximo; ~ to\
  junto a; ~ to nothing\ casi
  nada
**next-door** |NEKST•DAUR| *adj*
  en la casa de al lado de
**nibble** |NI•bl| *vt* mordiscar
**nice** |nuys| *adj* simpático
**nicely** |NUYS•lee| *adv*
  finamente

**nick** [nik] *n* corte M; in the ~ of time\ justo a tiempo

**nickname** [NIK•naim] *n* apodo M

**nicotine** [NI•ku•TEEN] *n* nicotina F

**niche** [nich] *n* nicho M

**niece** [nees] *n* sobrina F

**night** [nuyt] *n* noche F

**nightclub** [NUYT•kluhb] *n* cabaret F

**nightfall** [NUYT•faul] *n* anochecer M

**nightingale** [NUY•ting•GAIUL] *n* ruiseñor M

**nightly** [NUYT•lee] *adj* nocturno

**nightmare** [NUYT•maiur] *n* pesadilla F

**nimble** [NIM•bl] *adj* ágil

**nine** [nuyn] *num* nueve

**nineteen** [nuyn•TEEN] *num* diecinueve

**ninety** [NUYN•tee] *num* noventa

**ninth** [nuynth] *num* noveno

**nipple** [NI•pl] *n* tetilla F

**nitrogen** [NUY•tru•jun] *n* nitrógeno M

**no** [no] *adv* no; *adj* ninguno; ~ entry\ prohibido el paso; ~ smoking\ se prohibe fumar; ~ way!\ ¡ni hablar!

**nobility** [no•BI•li•tee] *n* nobleza F

**noble** [NO•bl] *adj* noble

**nobody** [NO•bu•dee] *pron* nadie; ~ is there\ no hay nadie; he knows ~\ no conoce a nadie

**nocturnal** [nahk•TUR•nl] *adj* nocturno

**nod** [nahd] *n* saludo M; *vt* ~ one's head\ asentir con la cabeza; saludar (greeting)

**noise** [noiz] *n* ruido M

**noisy** [NOI•zee] *adj* ruidoso

**nominal** [NAH•mi•nul] *adj* nominal

**nominate** [NAH•mi•NAIT] *vt* nombrar

**nomination** [NAH•mi•NAI•shn] *n* nominación F

**nonchalant** [NAHN•shu•LAHNT] *adj* indiferente

**nonconformist** [NAHN•kun•FAUR•mist] *adj n* disidente M

**none** [nuhn] *pron adj* ninguno; nada; ~ of\ nada de; ~ of us\ ninguno de nosotros; I have ~\ no tengo nada

**nonentity** [NAHN•EN•ti•tee] *n* nada F

**nonsense** [NAHN•sens] *n* tontería F

**nonstop** [NAHN•STAHP] *adj* expreso

**noodles** [NOO•dlz] *npl* tallarines M

**noon** [noon] *n* mediodía M

**noose** [noos] *n* lazo M

**nor** [naur] *conj* ni; neither .~\ ni. ni.

**norm** [naurm] *n* norma F

**normal** [NAUR•ml] *adj* normal

**normally** [NAUR•mu•lee] *adv* normalmente

**north** [naurth] *adj* norte

**North America** [NAURTH
u•ME•ri•ku] *n* Norte América
**northern** [NAUR•thurn] *adj* del
norte
**Northern Ireland**
[NAUR•thurn UYUR•lend] *n*
Nortes Irlandés
**North Pole** [NAURTH POL] *n*
polo norte M
**northward**
[NAURTH•wurd(z)] *adv*
hacia el norte
**Norway** [NAUR•wai] *n*
Noruega
**Norwegian** [naur•WEE•jun] *adj*
noruego
**nose** [noz] *n* naríz F; *vi* ~
about\ curiosear
**nostalgia** [nah•STAL•ju] *n*
nostalgia F
**nostril** [NAH•stril] *n* ollar M
**nosy** [NO•zee] *adj* curioso
**not** [naht] *adv* no; ~ at all\
no.nada; de nada (after
thanks); ~ yet\ aún no; I do ~
know;\ no sé
**notable** [NO•tu•bl] *adj*
notable
**notably** [NO•tu•blee] *adv*
notablemente
**notary** [NO•tu•ree] *n* notario M
**notch** [nahch] *n* muesca F
**note** *n* nota F; *vt* notar
**notebook** [NOT•buk] *n*
libreta F
**noteworthy** [NOT•wur•thee]
*adj* notable
**nothing** [NUH•thing] *pron*
nada; ~ else\ nada más; ~
much\ por cosa

**notice** [NO•tis] *n* noticia F *vt*
notar; take ~ of\ prestar
atención a; hacer casa a
**noticeable** [NO•ti•su•bl] *adj*
notable
**notify** [NO•ti•FUY] *vt* notificar
**notion** [NO•shn] *n* noción F
**notoriety** [NO•tu•RUY•u•tee] *n*
notoriedad F
**notorious** [no•TAU•ree•us] *adj*
notorio
**notwithstanding**
[NAHT•with•STAN•ding] *adv*
sin embargo
**noun** [noun] *n* nombre M
**nourish** [NU•rish] *vt* nutrir
**nourishing** [NU•ri•shing] *adj*
nutritivo
**nourishment** [NU•rish•munt] *n*
nutrición F
**novel** [NAH•vl] *n* novela F; *adj*
nuevo
**novelist** [NAH•vu•list] *n*
novelista F
**novelty** [NAH•vul•tee] *n*
novedad F
**November** [no•VEM•bur] *n*
noviembre M
**novice** [NAH•vis] *n* novicio M
**now** [nau] *adv* ahora; ~ and
then\ de vez en cuando; just
~\ ahora mismo
**nowhere** [NO•waiur] *adv* en
ninguna parte
**noxious** [NAHK•shus] *adj*
nocivo
**nozzle** [NAH•zl] *n* lanza F
**nuance** [NOO•ahns] *n* matiz F
**nuclear** [NOO•klee•ur] *adj*
nuclear

**nucleus** [NOO•klee•us] *n* núcleo M
**nude** [nood] *adj n* nudo; desnudo M
**nudge** [nuhj] *n* codazo M
**nudist** [NOO•dist] *n* nudista F
**nudity** [NOO•di•tee] *n* desnudez F
**nuisance** [NOO•suns] *n* estorbo M
**null** [nuhl] *adj* nulo
**nullify** [NUH•li•FUY] *vt* anular
**numb** [nuhm] *adj* entumecido; *vt* entumecer
**number** [NUHM•bur] *n* número M; *vt* numerar
**numeral** [NOO•mu•rul] *n* numeral F

**numerous** [NOO•mu•rus] *adj* numeroso
**nuptial** [NUHP•shl] *adj* nupcial
**nurse** [nurs] *n* enfermero M
**nursery** [NUR•su•ree] *n* criadero M
**nursery rhyme** [NUR•sree RUYM] *n* cuentos para niños
**nurture** [NUR•chur] *vt* nutrir
**nut** [nuht] *n* nuez F
**nutcrackers** [NUHT•kra•kurz] *npl* cascanueces
**nutrition** [noo•TRI•shn] *n* nutrición F
**nutritious** [noo•TRI•shus] *adj* nutritivo
**nylon** [NUY•lahn] *n* nilón F
**nymph** [nimf] *n* ninfa F

# O

**oak** [ok] *n* roble M
**oar** [aur] *n* remo M
**oasis** [o•AI•sis] *n* oasis M
**oath** [oth] *n* juramento M
**oatmeal** [OT•meeul] *n* harina de avena F
**oats** [ots] *npl* avenas F
**obedience** [o•BEE•dee•uns] *n* obediencia F
**obedient** [o•BEE•dee•unt] *adj* obediente
**obese** [o•BEES] *adj* obeso
**obey** [o•BAI] *vt* obedecer
**obituary** [o•BI•choo•E•ree] *n* obituario M
**object** [*n.* AHB•jekt *v.* ub•JEKT] *n* objeto M; *vi* oponerse

**objection** [ub•JEK•shn] *n* objeción F
**objective** [ub•JEK•tiv] *adj n* objetivo M
**obligation** [AH•bli•GAI•shn] *n* obligación F
**obligatory** [u•BLI•gu•TAU•ree] *adj* obligatorio
**oblige** [u•BLUYJ] *vt* obligar
**obliging** [u•BLUY•jing] *adj* complaciente
**oblique** [o•BLEEK] *adj* oblicuo
**obliterate** [u•BLI•tu•RAIT] *vt* borrar
**oblivion** [u•BLI•vee•un] *n* olvido M

**oblivious** [u•BLI•vee•us] *adj*
desmemoriado M

**obnoxious** [ub•NAHK•shus]
*adj* ofensivo

**obscene** [ub•SEEN] *adj*
obsceno

**obscenity** [ub•SE•ni•tee] *n*
obscenidad F

**obscure** [ub•SKYOOUR] *adj*
obscuro

**obscurity** [ub•SKYU•ri•tee] *n*
obscuridad F

**observance** [ub•ZUR•vuns] *n*
observancia F

**observant** [ub•ZUR•vunt] *adj*
atento

**observation**
[AHB•sur•VAI•shn] *n*
observación F

**observatory**
[ob•SUR•vuh•TOR•ee] *n*
observatorio M

**observe** [ub•ZURV] *vt* observar

**observer** [ub•ZUR•vur] *adj*
observador M

**obsess** [ub•SES] *vt* obsesionar

**obsession** [ub•SE•shn] *n*
obsesión F

**obsessive** [ub•SE•siv] *adj*
obsesivo

**obsolete** [AHB•su•LEET] *adj*
anticuado

**obstacle** [AHB•stu•kl] *n*
impedimento M

**obstinacy** [AHB•sti•ni•cee] *n*
obstinación F

**obstinate** [AHB•sti•nit] *adj*
obstinado

**obstruct** [ub•STRUHKT] *vt*
obstruir

**obstruction** [ub•STRUHK•shn]
*n* obstrucción F

**obtain** [ub•TAIN] *vt* obtener

**obtuse** [ub•TOOS] *adj* obtuso

**obvious** [AHB•vee•us] *adj*
obvio

**obviously** [AHB•vee•us•lee] *adj*
obviamente

**occasion** [u•KAI•zhn] *n*
ocasión F

**occasional** [u•KAI•zhu•nl] *adj*
incidental

**occasionally**
[u•KAI•zhu•nu•lee] *adv* de
vez en cando

**occult** [u•KUHLT] *adj* oculto

**occupant** [AH•kyu•punt] *n*
ocupante M

**occupation** [AH•kyu•PAI•shn]
*n* ocupación F

**occupy** [AH•kyu•PUY] *vt*
ocupar

**occur** [u•KUR] *vi* hallarse;
encontrarse

**occurrence** [u•KU•runs] *n*
ocurrencia F

**ocean** [O•shn] *n* océano M

**octagon** [AHK•tu•GAHN] *n*
octágono M

**October** [ahk•TO•bur] *n*
octubre

**octopus** [AHK•tu•pus] *n*
pulpo M

**odd** [ahd] *adj* impar raro; the ~
one out\ la excepción; ~s and
ends\ *npl* retazos M

**oddity** [AH•di•tee] *n*
peculiaridad F

**odious** [O•dee•us] *adj* odioso

**odor** [O•dur] *n* olor M

**of** [uhv] *prep* de a en

**off** [auf] *adj* apartado; *adv* lejos; *prep* de desde; fuera (away from); be better ~\ estar mejor; be ~\ marcharse; day ~\ *n* día de asueta; día libre

**offend** [u•FEND] *vt* ofender

**offense** [u•FENS] *n* ofensa F

**offensive** [u•FEN•siv] *adj* ofensivo

**offer** [AU•fur] *n* oferta F; *vt* ofrecer

**offering** [AU•fu•ring] *n* ofrenda F

**offhand** [AUF•HAND] *adj* de improviso

**office** [AU•fis] *n* oficina F

**officer** [AU•fi•sur] *n* oficial M

**official** [u•FI•shl] *adj* oficial

**offspring** [AUF•spring] *n* vástago M

**offstage** [auf•STAIJ] *adj adv* de entre bastidores

**often** [AU•fn] *adv* a menudo; muchas veces; con frecuencia; how ~\ ¿cuántas veces?

**oil** [oiul] *n* accite M; *vt* lubricar

**oily** [OIU•lee] *adj* aceitoso

**ointment** [OINT•munt] *n* untura F

**old** [uld] *adj* viejo; how old is he?\ ¿cuántos años tiene?; he is ten years ~\ tiene diez años; ~ age\ *n* vejez F; ~ fashioned\ *adj* anticuado

**olive** [AH•liv] *adj n* olivo M

**omelet** [AHM•lit] *n* tortilla de huevos F

**omen** [O•mn] *n* presagio M

**ominous** [AH•mi•nus] *adj* ominoso

**omission** [o•MI•shn] *n* omisión F

**omit** [o•MIT] *vt* omitir

**omnipotent** [ahm•NI•pu•tunt] *adj* omnipotente

**omniscience** [ahm•NI•shents] *adj* omnisciencia F

**on** [ahn] *prep* en; sobre; encima de; a de; ~ foot\ a pie; ~ Monday\ el lunes; ~ the way\ de camino; *adv* endido; ~ and off\ de vez en cuando; ~ and ~\ sin cesar; and so ~\ y así sucesivamente; go ~\ continuar

**once** [wuhns] *adv* una vez; at ~ en seguida

**one** [wuhn] *adj n pron* uno; ~ another\ el uno al otro; ~ by ~\ uno a uno

**oneself** [wuhn•SELF] *pron* se si uno mismo si mismo

**one-sided** [WUHN•SUY•did] *adj* de un solo lado

**one-way** [WUHN•WAI] *adj* de una sola dirección

**onion** [UH•nyun] *n* cebolla F

**onlooker** [AHN•lu•kur] *n* espectador M

**only** [ON•lee] *adj* solo; único

**onslaught** [AHN•slaut] *n* arremetida F

**onward** [AHN•wurd] *adv* adelante

**ooze** [ooz] *vi* rezumarse

**opal** [O•pl] *n* ópalo M

**opaque** [o•PAIK] *adj* opaco

**open** [O•pn] *adj* abierto; público; *vt vi* abrir

**opening** [O•pu•ning] *adj* abertura F

**openly** [O•pn•lee] *adv* abiertamente

**open-minded** [O•pn•MUYN•did] *adj* de espíritu abierto

**opera** [AH•pru] *n* ópera F

**operate** [AH•pu•RAIT] *vt* dirigir

**operation** [AH•pu•RAI•shn] *n* operación F

**operator** [AH•pu•RAI•tur] *n* operador M

**opinion** [u•PI•nyun] *n* opinión F

**opinionated** [u•PI•nyu•NAI•tid] *adj* obstinado

**opponent** [u•PO•nunt] *n* oponente M

**opportune** [AH•pur•TOON] *adj* oportuno

**opportunist** [AH•pur•TOO•nist] *n* oportunista F

**opportunity** [AH•pur•TOON•ah•tee] *n* oportunidad F

**oppose** [u•POZ] *vt* oponer

**opposed** [u•POZD] *adj* opuesto

**opposite** [AH•pu•sit] *adj* opuesto

**opposition** [AH•pu•ZI•shn] *n* oposición F

**oppress** [u•PRES] *vt* oprimir

**oppression** [u•PRE•shn] *n* opresión F

**oppressive** [u•PRE•siv] *adj* opresivo

**opt** [ahpt] *vi* optar

**optical** [AH•pti•kl] *adj* óptico

**optician** [ahp•TI•shn] *n* óptico M

**optimism** [AHP•ti•MI•zm] *n* optimismo M

**optimist** [AHP•ti•mist] *n* optimista F

**optimistic** [AHP•ti•MI•stik] *adj* optimista

**option** [AHP•shn] *n* elección F

**optional** [AHP•shu•nl] *adj* facultativo

**opulence** [AH•pyu•luns] *n* opulencia F

**opulent** [AH•pyu•lunt] *adj* opulento

**or** [aur] *conj* o; ~ else\ si no; o bien

**oracle** [AU•ru•kl] *n* oráculo M

**orange** [AU•runj] *adj* naranja

**orator** [au•rai•tu.] *n* orador M

**oratory** [au•ru•tau•ree] *n* oratoria F

**orbit** [AUR•bit] *n* órbita F; *vt* orbitar

**orchard** [AUR•churd] *n* huerto M

**orchestra** [AUR•ku•stru] *n* orquesta F

**orchestral** [aur•KE•strul] *adj* de orquesta

**orchid** [AUR•kid] *n* orquidea F

**order** [AUR•dur] *n* orden M

**orderly** [AUR•dur•lee] *adj* ordenado

**ordinarily** [AUR•di•NE•ri•lee] *adv* ordinariamente

**ordinary** [AUR•di•NE•ree] *adj* usual

**ore** [aur] *n* mineral M

**oregano** [au•RE•gu•NO] *n* oregano M

**organ** [AUR•gn] *n* órgano M

organic [aur•GA•nik] *adj*
orgánico

organism [AUR•gu•NI•zm] *n*
organismo M

organization
[AUR•gu•ni•ZAI•shn] *n*
organizacíon F

organize [AUR•gu•NUYZ] *vt*
organizar

orgasm [AUR•ga•zm] *n*
orgasmo M

orgy [AUR•gee] *n* orgía F

oriental [AU•ree•EN•tl] *n*
oriental M

orientate [AU•ree•un•TAIT] *vt*
orientar

orientation
[AU•ree•un•TAI•shn] *n*
orientación F

orifice [AU•ri•fis] *n* oficina F

origin [AU•ri•jin] *n* origen M

original [u•RI•ji•nl] *adj n*
original M

originality [u•RI•ji•NA•li•tee] *n*
originalidad F

originally [u•RI•ji•nu•lee] *adv*
originalmente

originate [aur•RI•gi•NAIT] *vt*
originar

ornament [AUR•nu•munt] *n*
ornamento M

ornamental [AUR•nu•MEN•tl]
*adj* ornamental

ornate [aur•NAIT] *adj*
adornado

orphan [AUR•fn] *n* huérfano M

orphanage [AUR•fu•nij] *n*
orfandad F

orthodox [AUR•thu•DAHKS]
*adj* ortodoxo

oscillate [AH•si•LAIT] *vi*
oscilar

ostensible [ah•STEN•si•bl] *adj*
ostensible

ostentatious
[AH•stun•TAI•shus] *adj*
ostentoso

ostrich [AHS•trich] *n*
avestruz M

other [UH•thur] *adj* otro; ~
than\ de otra manera que; the
~ one\ el otro

otherwise [UH•thur•WUYZ]
*adv* otramente

otter [AH•tur] *n* oruga F

ought [aut] *aux v* deber

ounce [ouns] *n* onza F

our [ouur] *poss adj* nuestro

ours [ouurz] *poss pron* el
nuestro

ourselves [ouur•SELVZ] *pron
pl* nosotros mismos

oust [oust] *vt* desalojar

out *adv* fuera; ~ and ~ *adj* cien
por cien; ~ of doors\ fuera; ~
of order;\ estropeado; ~ of
place\ fuera de lugar; ~ of
sorts\ indispuesto; be ~\
equivocarse; be ~ of\
quedarse sin; made ~ of\
hecho de

outbreak [OUT•braik] *n*
erupción F

outburst [OUT•burst] *n*
arranque M

outcast [OUT•kast] *n*
desechado

outcome [OUT•kuhm] *n*
resultado M

outcry [OUT•cruy] *n* grito M

outdated [out•DAI•tid] *adj*
anticuado

**outdoor** [OUT•dauur] *adj* de fuera de casa

**outdoors** [out•DAUURZ] *adv* el aire libre

**outer** [OU•tur] *adj* exterior

**outfit** [OUT•fit] *n* equipo M

**outgoing** [OUT•go•ing] *adj* saliente

**outhouse** [OU•hous] *n* anejo M

**outing** [OU•ting] *n* paseo M

**outlaw** [OUT•lau] *n* bandido M

**outlet** [OUT•let] *n* salida F

**outline** [OUT•luyn] *n* perfil M

**outlive** [out•LIV] *vt* sobrevivir

**outlook** [OUT•luk] *n* vista F

**outmoded** [out•MO•did] *adj* anticuado

**outnumber** [out•NUHM•bur] *vt* ser más que

**output** [OUT•put] *n* rendimiento M

**outrage** [OUT•raij] *n* atropello M

**outrageous** [out•RAI•jus] *adj* ultrajante

**outright** [out•RUYT] *adj* sincero

**outset** [OUT•set] *n* comienzo M

**outside** [out•SUYD] *adj* exterior

**outsider** [out•SUY•dur] *n* forastero M

**outskirts** [OUT•skurts] *npl* borde M

**outspoken** [out•SPO•kn] *adj* claro

**outstanding** [out•STAN•ding] *adj* salidizo

**outward** [OUT•wurd] *adj* externo

**outwardly** [OUT•wurd•lee] *adv* exteriormente

**outweigh** [out•WAI] *vt* preponderar sobre

**oval** [O•vl] *adj n* oval M

**ovary** [O•vu•ree] *n* ovario M

**ovation** [o•VAI•shn] *n* ovación F

**oven** [UH•vn] *n* horno M

**over** [O•vr] *adj* arriba por encima; ~ and above\ por encima de; *adv* por encima; ~ and ~\ una y otra vez; ~ here\ por aquí; ~ there\ por allí; all ~\ por todas partes

**overall** [O•vur•AUL] *adj* completo; *adv* en conjunto

**overalls** [O•vur•aulz] *npl* pantalones de trabajo

**overbearing** [O•vur•BAIU•ring] *adj* dominador

**overboard** [O•vur•BAURD] *adv* al agua M

**overcast** [O•vur•kast] *adj* anublado

**overcharge** [O•vur•CHAHRJ] *vt* sobrecargar

**overcoat** [O•vur•KOT] *n* sobretodo M

**overcome** [O•vur•KUHM] *vt* subyugar

**overdo** [O•vur•DOO] *vt* excederse

**overdraw** [O•vur•DRAU] *vt* sobregirar

**overflow** [O•vur•FLO] *n* rebosadero M; *vt* rebosar

**overgrown** [O•vur•GRON] *adj* vicioso

**overhaul** [O•vur•HAUL] *vt*
reparar

**overhear** [O•vur•HEEUR] *vt*
oír

**overjoyed** [O•vur•JOID] *adj*
jubiloso

**overlap** [O•vur•LAP] *vt*
traslapar

**overlook** [O•vur•LUK] *vt*
repasar

**overnight** [O•vur•NUYT] *adj*
de noche; *adv* por la noche;
stay ~\ pasar la noche

**overpower** [O•vur•POU•ur] *vt*
predominar

**overrun** [O•vur•RUHN] *adj*
inundado

**overseas** [O•vur•ṢEEZ] *adj adv*
ultramarino

**oversee** [O•vur•SEE] *vt*
superintender

**overseer** [O•vur•SEE•ur] *n*
inspector M

**overshadow** [O•vur•SHA•do]
*vt* asombrar

**overstep** [O•vur•STEP] *vt* pasar

**overtake** [O•vur•TAIK] *vt*
alcanzar

**overthrow** [O•vur•THRO] *vt*
tumbar

**overtime** [O•vur•tuym] *n*
tiempo suplementario M

**overture** [O•vur•chur] *n*
prouesta F

**overweight** [O•vur•WAIT] *adj*
sobrepeso

**overwhelm** [O•vur•WELM] *vt*
sumergir

**overwhelming**
[O•vur•WEL•ming] *adj*
aplastante

**overwork** [O•vur•WURK] *vt*
fatigar

**owe** [o] *vt* deber; owing to a
cause de

**owl** [ouul] *n* búho M; lechuza F

**own** [on] *adj* propio; mismo; *vt*
poseer, tener; *vi* ~ up (to)\
confesar (coll); hold one's ~\
mantenerse firme; on one's ~\
por su cuenta

**owner** [O•nur] *n* dueño M

**ownership** [O•nur•SHIP] *n*
propiedad F

**ox** [ahks] *n* buey M

**oxygen** [AHK•si•jun] *n*
oxígeno M

**oyster** [OI•stur] *n* ostra F

# P

**pace** [pais] *n* paso M; *vi*
pasearse; keep ~ with\ andar
al mismo paso que

**Pacific** [pu•SI•fik] *adj* pacífico M

**pacify** [PA•si•FUY] *vt* pacificar

**pack** [pak] *n* paca F; *vt*
empaquetar

**package** [PA•kij] *n* paquete F

**packet** [PA•kit] *n* paquete F

**packing** [PA•king] *n*
empaque M

**pact** [pakt] *n* pacto; acuerdo M

**pad** [pad] *n* almohadilla F; *vt* rellenar

**padding** [PA•ding] *n* acolchado M

**paddle** [PA•dl] *n* canalete M

**padlock** [PAD•lahk] *n* candado M

**pagan** [PAI•gn] *adj n* pagano M

**page** [paij] *n* página F

**pail** [paiul] *n* colodra F

**pain** [pain] *n* dolor M; ~ in the neck\ pesado M (coll); be in ~\ tener dolores

**painful** [PAIN•ful] *adj* doloroso

**painless** [PAIN•lis] *adj* indoloro

**painstaking** [PAIN•STAI•king] *adj* afanoso

**paint** [paint] *n* pintura F; *vt vi* pintar

**paintbrush** [PAINT•bruhsh] *n* brocha F

**painter** [PAIN•tur] *n* pintor M

**painting** [PAIN•ting] *n* pintura F

**pair** [paiur] *n* pareja F; *vi* emparejarse

**pajamas** [pu•JA•muz] *npl* pijama F

**pal** [pal] *n* compañero; amigo M

**palace** [PA•lis] *n* palacio M

**palatable** [PA•li•tu•bl] *adj* sabroso

**palate** [PA•lit] *n* paladar M

**pale** [paiul] *adj* pálido

**Palestine** [PA•li•STUYN] *n* Palestina F

**palette** [PA•lit] *n* gocete M

**palm** [pahm] *n* palma F

**Palm Sunday** [PAHM SUN•dai] *n* Domingo de Ramos M

**palpable** [PAL•pu•bl] *adj* palpable

**paltry** [PAUL•tree] *adj* pobre M

**pamper** [PAM•pur] *vt* mimar

**pamphlet** [PAM•flit] *n* folleto M

**pan** [pan] *n* cazo M

**panacea** [PA•nu•SEE•u] *n* panacea F

**Panama** [PA•nu•MAH] *n* Panama

**pancake** [PAN•kaik] *n* hojuela F

**panda** [PAN•du] *n* panda F

**pane** [pain] *n* vidrio M

**panel** [PA•nl] *n* tablero M

**pang** [pang] *n* punzada F

**panic** [PA•nik] *n* pánico M; *vi* ser preso de pánico

**pansy** [PAN•zee] *n* trinitaria F

**pant** [pant] *vi* resollar

**panther** [PAN•thur] *n* pantera F

**panties** [PAN•teez] *npl* bragas

**pantry** [PAN•tree] *n* despensa F

**pants** [pants] *npl* pantalones M

**papa** [PAH•pu] *n* papá M

**papal** [PAI•pl] *adj* papal

**paper** [PAI•pur] *adj* papél M; documento M; on ~ \ en teoría;

**paperback** [PAI•pur•BAK] *n* libro en rústica M; *adj* en rústica

**par** [pahr] *n* equivalencia F

**parable** [PA•ru•bl] *n* parábola F

**parachute** [PA•ru•SHOOT] *n* paracaídas; *vi* lanzarse en paracaídas

**parade** [pu•RAID] *n* pompa F; *vi* desfilar; *vt* hacer alarde de

**paradise** [PA•ru•DUYS] *n* paraiso M

**paradox** [PA•ru•DAHKS] *n*
paradoja F
**paragraph** [PA•ru•GRAF] *n*
párrafo M
**Paraguay** [PA•ru•GWAI] *n*
Paraguay
**parakeet** [PA•ru•KEET] *n*
periquito M
**parallel** [PA•ru•LEL] *adj*
paralelo
**paralysis** [pu•RA•lu•sis] *n*
parálisis F
**paralyze** [PA•ru•LUYZ] *vt*
paralizar
**paranoid** [PA•ru•NOID] *adj*
paranoid
**paraphernalia**
[PA•ru•fu•NAIU•lyu] *n*
enseros M
**parasite** [PA•ru•SUYT] *n*
parásito M
**parasol** [PA•ru•SAUL] *n*
sombrilla F
**parcel** [PAHR•sl] *n* paquete M
**parchment** [PAHRCH•ment] *n*
pergamino M
**pardon** [PAHR•dn] *n* perdón F
**parent** [PA•rent] *n* padre M
**parenthesis** [pu•REN•thu•sis] *n*
paréntesis M
**parish** [PA•rish] *adj* parroquia F
**park** [pahrk] *n* parque M; *vt vi*
aprcar; ~ oneself\ *vr* instalarse
(coll)
**parking** [PAHR•king] *n*
estacionamiento M
**parking lot** [PAHR•king
LAHT] *n* parque dc
estacionamiento M
**parlance** [PAHR•luns] *n*
conversación F

**parliament** [PAHR•lu•munt] *n*
parlamento M
**parliamentary**
[PAHR•lu•MEN•tu•ree] *adj*
parlamentario
**parlor** [PAHR•lur] *n* sala de
recibimiento F
**parochial** [pu•RO•kee•ul] *adj*
parroquial
**parody** [PA•ru•dee] *n* parodia
F; *vt* parodiar
**parole** [pu•ROUL] *n* palabra de
honor F
**parrot** [PA•rut] *n* papagayo M
**parsley** [PAHR•slee] *n* perejil M
**parsnip** [PAR•snip] *n*
pastinaca F
**parson** [PAHR•sn] *n* párroco M
**part** [pahrt] *n* parte F; *adv* en
parte; *vt* separar; *vi* separarse;
on the ~ of\ por parte de; ~
with\ separarse de
**partial** [PAHR•shl] *adj* parcial
**partiality** [PAHR•shee•A•li•tee]
*n* parcialidad F
**partially** [PAHR•shu•lee] *adv*
parcialmente
**participant** [pahr•TI•si•punt] *n*
participante M
**participate** [pahr•TI•si•PAIT] *vi*
participar
**participation**
[pahr•TI•si•PAI•shn] *n*
participación F
**particle** [PAHR•ti•kl] *n*
partícula F
**particular** [pur•TI•kyu•lur] *adj*
particular
**particularly**
[pur•TI•kyu•lur•lee] *adv*
particularmente

**parting** [PAHR•ting] *n*
separacíon F

**partisan** [PAHR•ti•sun] *adj n*
partidario M

**partition** [pahr•TI•shn] *n*
división F

**partly** [PAHRT•lee] *adv* en
parte

**partner** [PAHRT•nur] *n*
consocio M

**partnership**
[PAHRT•nur•SHIP] *n*
consorcio M

**partridge** [PAHR•trij] *n*
perdiz M

**part-time** [pahrt•tuym] *adj
adv* tiempo incompleto M

**party** [PAHR•tee] *n* partido M

**pass** [pas] *n* paso; permiso M;
*vt vi* pasar; pasar por delante
de (in front of) aprobar
(approve, school); ~ down\
transmitir; ~ away\ morir; ~
out\ desmayarse (coll); make
a ~ at\ hacer proposiciones
amorosas a

**passage** [PA•sij] *n* pasaje (in
book); paso (voyage) M

**passenger** [PA•sin•jur] *n*
pasajero M

**passerby** [PA•sur•BUY] *n*
transeúnte M

**passion** [PA•shn] *n* pasión F

**passionate** [PA•shu•nit] *adj*
apasionado

**passive** [PA•siv] *adj* pasivo

**passport** [PAS•paurt] *n*
pasaporte F

**password** [PAS•wurd] *n*
contraseña F

**past** [past] *adj* pasado M; in
times ~\ en tiempos pasados;
*adv* por delante; *prep* más allá
de; go ~\ pasar

**pasta** [PAH•stu] *n* pasta F

**paste** [paist] *n* masa M; *vt*
pegar; joyas de imitación
(jewelry)

**pastel** [pa•STEL] *adj n* pastel M

**pasteurize** [PAS•chu•RUYZ] *vt*
pasterizar

**pastime** [PAS•tuym] *n*
pasatiempo M

**pastor** [PA•stur] *n* pastor M

**pastry** [PAI•stree] *n* pastelería F

**pastry shop** [PAI•stree
SHAHP] *n* pastelería F

**pasture** [PAS•chur] *n* pasto
pastura (f) M

**pat** [pat] *n* palmadita F; *vt* dar
palmaditas en

**patch** [pach] *n* remiendo M; *vt*
remediar

**pâté** [pa•TAI] *n* pastel de
carne M

**patent** [PA•tunt] *adj* patente M

**patent leather** [PA•tunt
LE•thur] *n* charol M

**paternal** [pu•TUR•nl] *adj*
paternal paterno

**paternity** [pu•TUR•ni•tee] *n*
paternidad F

**path** [path] *n* camino M

**pathetic** [pu•THE•tik] *adj*
patético

**pathology** [pa•THAH•lu•jee] *n*
patología F

**pathway** [PATH•wai] *n*
senda F

**patience** [PAI•shns] *n*
paciencia F

**patient** [PAI•shnt] *adj n*
paciente M
**patriot** [PAI•tree•ut] *n*
patriota F
**patriotic** [PAI•tree•AH•tik] *adj*
patriótico
**patriotism** [PAI•tree•u•TI•zm]
*n* patriotismo M
**patrol** [pu•TROUL] *n* patrulla
**patron** [PAI•trun] *n* patrono M;
mecenas (of the arts, etc);
cliente (customer) MF
**patronize** [PAI•tru•NUYZ] *vt*
patrocinar
**patter** [PA•tur] *n* galocha F
**pattern** [PA•turn] *n* ejemplo M
**pause** [pauz] *n* pausa F; *vi*
hacer una pausa
**pave** [paiv] *vt* pavimentar
**pavement** [PAIV•munt] *n*
pavimento M
**pavilion** [pu•VIL•yun] *n*
pabellón F
**paw** [pau] *n* garra F; *vi* tocar
con la pata; manosear
(person)
**pawn** [paun] *n* peón M
**pawnshop** [PAUN•shahp] *n*
casa de empeños F
**pay** [pai] *n* pago M; *vt* pagar
**pay off** *vt* pagar de un buque
**pay phone** [PAI FON] *n*
teléfono público M
**payable** [PAI•yu•bl] *adj*
pagable
**payment** [PAI•munt] *n* pago M
**pea** [pee] *n* guisante M
**peace** [pees] *n* paz F; ~ of
mind\ tranquilidad
**peaceful** [PEES•ful] *adj*
pacífico

**peacock** [PEE•cahk] *n* pavón M
**peach** [peech] *n* pérsico;
durazno M
**peak** [peck] *n* pico M
**peal** [peeul] *vt* repicar
**peanut** [PEE•nuht] *n*
cacahuete M
**peanut butter** [PEE•nut
BUH•tur] *n* pasta de
cacahuete F
**pear** [paiur] *n* pera F
**pearl** [purl] *n* perla F
**peasant** [PE•znt] *n* labrador M
**peat** [peet] *n* turba F
**pebble** [PE•bl] *n* guijarro M
**peck** [pek] *n* picotazo M; *vt*
picotear
**peculiar** [pi•KYOOU•lyur] *adj*
peculiar
**pedal** [PE•dl] *n* pedal M; *vi*
pedalear
**pedant** [PE•dunt] *n* pedante M
**pedantic** [pi•DAN•tik] *adj*
pedantesco
**peddle** [PE•dl] *vt* vender de
puerta a puerta
**pedestal** [PE•du•stl] *n*
pedestal M
**pedestrian** [pi•DE•stree•un] *n*
pedestre M
**pedigree** [PE•di•GREE] *adj*
genealogía F
**peek** [peek] *vi* atisbo M
**peel** [peeul] *n* telilla F; *vt* pelar;
*vi* pelarse
**peep** [peep] *vi* asomar; *n* mirada
furtiva F
**peephole** [PEEP•houl] *n*
mirilla F
**peer 1** [peeur] *n* par M
**peer 2** *vi* mirar; ~ at\ escudriñar

**peg** [peg] *n* clavija F; *vt* fijar

**pelt** [pelt] *n* pellejo M

**pellet** [PE•lit] *n* pelotilla F

**pen 1** [pen] *n* pluma F

**pen 2** *n* recinto M (enclosure)

**penal** [PEE•nl] *adj* penal

**penalty** [PE•nl•tee] *n* pena F

**penance** [PE•nuns] *n* penitencia F

**penchant** [PEN•chnt] *n* araña F

**pencil** [PEN•sl] *n* lápiz F

**pencil sharpener** [PEN•sil SHAR•pin•ur] *n* sacapuntas F

**pendant** [PEN•dnt] *n* medallón F

**pending** [PEN•ding] *adj* pendiente

**pendulum** [PEN•dyu•lum] *n* péndulo M

**penetrate** [PE•nu•TRAIT] *vt* penetrar

**penguin** [PENG•gwin] *n* pingüino M

**penicillin** [PE•ni•SI•lin] *n* penicilina F

**peninsula** [pu•NIN•su•lu] *n* península F

**penis** [PEE•nis] *n* pene M

**pennant** [PE•nunt] *n* flámula F

**penniless** [PE•nee•lis] *adj* sin dinero

**penny** [PE•nee] *n* centavo M

**pension** [PEN•shn] *n* pensión F

**pensive** [PEN•siv] *adj* pensativo

**people** [PEE•pl] *npl* gente F; *vt* poblar; ~ say\ se dice

**pepper** [PE•pur] *n* pimienta F

**peppermint** [PE•pur•mint] *n* menta F

**per** [pur] *prep* por

**perceive** [pur•SEEV] *vt* percibir

**percent** [pur•SENT] *adv* por ciento

**percentage** [pur•SEN•tij] *n* porcentaje M

**perception** [pur•SEP•shn] *n* percepción F

**perch** [purch] *n* perca F; *vi* posarse

**perennial** [pu•RE•nee•ul] *adj* perennal

**perfect** [*adj.* PUR•fikt *v.* pur•FEKT] *adj* perfecto; *vt* perfeccionar

**perfection** [pur•FEK•shn] *n* perfección F

**perfectly** [PUR•fikt•lee] *adv* perfectamente

**perforate** [PUR•fu•RAIT] *vt* perforar

**perform** [pur•FAURM] *vi* efectuar

**performance** [pur•FAUR•mns] *n* ejecución F

**perfume** [PUR•fyoom] *n* perfume M

**perhaps** [pur•HAPS] *adv* quizás; tal vez

**peril** [PE•ril] *n* peligro M

**perimeter** [pu•RI•mi•tur] *n* perímetro M

**period** [PEEU•ree•ud] *n* época; era F

**periodic** [PI•ree•AH•dik] *adj* periódico

**periodical** [PI•ree•AH•di•kl] *n* periódica F

**perish** [PE•rish] *vi* perecer

**perjury** [PUR•ju•ree] *n* perjurio M

perm [purm] *n* ondulación
permanente F

permanent [PUR•mi•nunt] *adj*
permanente

permeate [PUR•mee•AIT] *vt*
penetrar

permission [pur•MI•shn] *n*
permiso M

permit [*n.* PUR•mit *v.* pur•MIT]
*n* permiso M; *vt* permitir

perpendicular
[PUR•pn•DI•kyu•lur] *adj n*
perpendicular línea F

perpetrate [PUR•pu•TRAIT] *vt*
perpetrar

perpetual [pur•PE•choo•ul] *adj*
perpetuo

perplex [pur•PLEKS] *vt*
confundir

perplexed [pur•PLEKST] *adj*
perplejo

persecute [PUR•si•KYOOT] *vt*
perseguir

persevere [PUR•si•VEEUR] *vi*
perseverar

perseverance
[PUR•si•VEEU•rns] *n*
perseverancia F

Persian Gulf [PUR•zhn ~ ] *n*
golfo Pérsico M

persist [pur•SIST] *vi* persistir

persistence [pur•SI•stns] *n*
persistencia F

persistent [pur•SI•stnt] *adj*
persistente

person [PUR•sn] *n* persona F

personal [PUR•su•nl] *adj*
personal

personality [PUR•su•NA•li•tee]
*n* personalidad F

personnel [PUR•su•NEL] *n*
personal F

perspective [pur•SPEK•tiv] *n*
perspectiva F

perspiration
[PUR•spu•RAI•shn] *n*
transpiración F

perspire [pur•SPUYUR] *vi*
transpirar

persuade [pur•SWAID] *vt*
persuadir

persuasion [pur•SWAI•zhn] *n*
pesuasión F

persuasive [pur•SWAI•siv] *adj*
persuasivo

pertain [pur•TAIN] *vi*
pertenecer

pertinent [PUR•ti•nunt] *adj*
pertinente

perturb [pur•TURB] *vt*
perturbar

perverse [pur•VURS] *adj*
perverso

pervert [*n.* PUR•vurt *v.*
pur•VURT] *n* pervertido M

pessimism [PE•si•MI•zm] *n*
pesimismo M

pessimist [PE•si•mist] *n*
pesimista F

pessimistic [PE•si•MI•stik] *adj*
pesimista

pest [pest] *n* peste M

pester [PE•stur] *vt* molestar

pet [pet] *n* animal doméstico M;
favorito M; *adj* preferido; *vt*
acariciar

petal [PE•tl] *n* pétalo M

petition [pu•TI•shn] *n*
petición F

petrified [PE•tri•FUYD] *adj*
fosilizado

**petroleum** [pu•TRO•lee•um] *n*
petróleo M

**petty** [PE•tee] *adj* insignificante

**pew** [pyoo] *n* banco de iglesia M

**phantom** [FAN•tum] *n*
fantasma F

**pharmacist** [FAR•ma•sist] *n*
framacéutico M

**pharmacy** [FAHR•mu•see] *n*
farmacia F

**phase** [faiz] *n* fase F; *vt* ~ in\
introducir progresivamente; ~
out\ retirar progresivamente

**phenomenon**
[fu•NAH•mu•NAHN] *n*
fenómeno M

**philosopher** [fi•LAH•su•fur] *n*
filósofo M

**philosophical** [FI•lu•SAH•fi•kl]
*adj* filosófico

**philosophy** [fi•LAH•su•fee] *n*
filosifía F

**phone** [fon] *n* teléfono M; *vt vi*
llamar por teléfono

**phone call** [FON KAL] *n*
llamada F

**phonetics** [fu•NE•tiks] *n*
fonética F

**phony** [FO•nee] *adj* farsa

**photo** [FO•to] *n* fotografía F

**photograph** [FO•tu•graf] *n*
fotografía F

**photographer**
[fu•TAH•gru•fur] *n*
fotógrafo M

**photography** [fu•TAH•gru•fee]
*n* fotografía F

**phrase** [fraiz] *n* frase F; *vt*
expresar

**physical** [FI•zi•kl] *adj* físico

**physician** [fi•ZI•shn] *n* fisicó M

**physicist** [FI•zi•sist] *n* físico M

**physics** [FI•ziks] *n* física F

**physique** [fi•ZEEK] *n* físico M

**pianist** [pee•U•nist] *n* pianista F

**piano** [pee•A•no] *n* piano M

**pick 1** [pik] *n* pico M

**pick 2** *vt* escoger; recoger;
forzar (lock) ~ a fight\ buscar
camorra; ~ on\ meterse con; ~
out\ identificar; ~ up\ regoger;
*vi* mejorar

**picket** [PI•kit] *n* estaca F

**pickle** [PI•kl] *n* adobo M

**pickpocket** [PIK•PAH•kit] *n*
ratero M

**picnic** [PIK•nik] *n* partida del
campo F; *vi* merendar en el
campo

**picture** [PIK•chur] *n* pintura F

**picturesque** [PIK•chu•RESK]
*adj* pintoresco

**pie** [puy] *n* pastel M

**piece** [pees] *n* pedazo M;
peiza F

**pier** [peeur] *n* embarcadero M

**pierce** [peeurs] *vt* atravesar

**pig** [pig] *n* puerco M

**pigeon** [PI•jn] *n* pichón M

**pig-headed** [PIG•HE•did] *adj*
terco

**pigment** [PIG•munt] *n*
pigmento M

**pigsty** [PIG•stuy] *n* zahurda F

**pile** [puyl] *n* montón F; *vt*
amontonar; *vi* amontonarse; ~
it on\ exagerar; ~ up\
amontonar

**pilgrim** [PIL•grim] *n*
peregrinar M

**pilgrimage** [PIL•gri•mij] *n*
peregrinación F

**pill** [pil] *n* píldora F
**pillar** [PI•lur] *n* pilar M
**pillow** [PI•lo] *n* almohada F
**pillowcase** [PI•lo•KAIS] *n*
   funda de almohada F
**pilot** [PUY•lut] *n* piloto M
**pimp** [pimp] *n* rufián M
**pimple** [PIM•pl] *n* barro M
**pin** [pin] *n* clavillo M
**pinch** [pinch] *n* apuro M
**pine** [puyn] *n* pino M
**pineapple** [PUY•NA•pul] *n*
   ananás F
**pink** [pingk] *adj n* rosa F
**pinnacle** [PI•nu•kl] *n*
   pináculo M
**pint** [puynt] *n* cuartillo M
**pioneer** [PUY•u•NEEUR] *n*
   zapador M
**pious** [PUY•us] *adj* pío M
**pipe** [puyp] *n* tubo M
**pique** [peek] *n* pique M
**pirate** [PUY•rit] *adj* pirata F
**pistol** [PI•stl] *n* pistola F
**piston** [PI•stn] *n* pistón F
**pitch** [pich] *n* echada F; grado
   M (degree); tono M (music)
   camp M (sport); *vt* lanzar;
   armar; ~ in\ contribuir (coll)
**pitcher** [PI•chur] *n* jarro M
**pitchfork** [PICH•faurk] *n*
   horca F
**piteous** [PI•tee•us] *adj*
   lastimoso
**pitiful** [PI•ti•ful] *adj* compasivo
**pitiless** [PI•tee•lis] *adj*
   despiadado cruel
**pity** [PI•tee] *n* piedad F;
   compadecerse de
**pivot** [PI•vut] *n* espiga F; *n*
   cubo M; *vt* cubar

**placard** [PLA•kurd] *n* cartel M
**placate** [PLAI•kait] *vt* aplacar
**place** [plais] *n* lugar M; take ~\
   tener lugar; *vt* poner; colocar
**placid** [PLA•sid] *adj* plácido
**plague** [plaig] *n* plaga F
**plaid** [plad] *n* tartán M
**plain** [plain] *adj* plano
**plainly** [PLAIN•lee] *adv*
   claramente
**plaintiff** [PLAIN•tif] *n*
   demandante M
**plan** [plan] *n* plano M; *vt*
   planear
**plane** [plain] *adj* plano; *n* llano
   M
**planet** [PLA•nit] *n* planeta F
**plank** [plangk] *n* tablón F
**plant** [plant] *n* planta F; *vt*
   plantar
**plantation** [plan•TAI•shn] *n*
   plantación F
**plaque** [plak] *n* placa F
**plaster** [PLA•stur] *n* estuco M;
   *vt* enyesar; ~ of Paris\ yeso
   mate M
**plastic** [PLA•stik] *adj n*
   plástico M
**plate** [plait] *n* plato M; *vt*
   chapear
**plateau** [pla•TO] *n* mesa F
**plated** [PLAI•tid] *adj* dorado
**platform** [PLAT•faurm] *n*
   plataforma F
**platinum** [PLAT•num] *n*
   platino M
**platter** [PLA•tur] *n* platel M
**play** [plai] *n* juego M; *vt vi*
   jugar; desempeñar (a part);
   tocar (an instrument); ~ safe\
   no arriesgarse; ~ on words\

juego de palabras; ~ down\
minimizar

**playboy** [PLAI•boi] *n* joven
rico M

**player** [PLAI•ur] *n* jugador M

**playful** [PLAI•ful] *adj* juguetón

**playground** [PLAI•ground] *n*
patio de recreo M

**plaything** [PLAI•thing] *n*
juguete M

**playwright** [PLAI•ruyt] *n* autor
dramático M

**plea** [plee] *n* defensa F

**plead** [pleed] *vt* defender en
juicio

**pleasant** [PLE•znt] *adj*
agradable

**please** [pleez] *vt* agradar; *int*
por favor; do as you ~\ haz lo
que quieras

**pleased** [pleezd] *adj* contento

**pleasing** [PLEE•zing] *adj*
agradable

**pleasure** [PLE•zhur] *n* placer M

**pleat** [pleet] *n* doblez F

**pledge** [plej] *n* prenda F

**plentiful** [PLEN•ti•ful] *adj*
abundante

**plenty** [PLEN•tee] *adj*
abundancia F

**pliable** [PLUY•u•bl] *adj* flexible

**pliers** [PLUY•urz] *npl* alicates
F

**plight** [pluyt] *n* estado M

**plod** [plahd] *vi* afanarse

**plot** [plaht] *n* conspiración F

**plow** [plou] *n* arado M; *vi vt*
arar

**pluck** [pluhk] *vt* arrancar

**plug** [pluhg] *n* espita F

**plum** [pluhm] *n* ciruela F

**plumber** [PLUH•mur] *n*
plomero M

**plumbing** [PLUH•ming] *n*
fontanería F

**plume** [ploom] *n* pluma F

**plump** [pluhmp] *adj* gordo

**plunder** [PLUHN•dur] *vt*
despojar

**plunge** [pluhnj] *n* sumersión F;
salto M; *vt* hundir; sumergir;
*vi* ambullirse

**plunger** [PLUHN•jur] *n* buzo M

**plural** [PLOOU•rl] *adj n* plural F

**plus** [pluhs] *n* plus M; *prep*
más; *adj* positivo

**plush** [pluhsh] *n* peluche M

**ply** [pluy] *vt* plegar

**plywood** [PLUY•wud] *n*
contrachapado M

**pneumonia** [noo•MO•nyu] *n*
neumonia F

**poach** [poch] *vt* escalfar

**pocket** [PAH•kit] *n* bolsillo M;
*vt* poner en el bolsillo

**pocketbook** [PAH•kit•BUK] *n*
bolsa F

**pocketknife** [PAH•kit•NUYF]
*n* cortapluma F

**pod** [pahd] *n* cápsula F

**poem** [pom] *n* poema F

**poet** [PO•it] *n* poeta F

**poetic** [po•E•tik] *adj* poético

**poetry** [PO•e•tree] *n* poesía F

**point** [point] *n* punto M; lo
importante (meaning); to the
~\ pertinente; up to a ~\ hasta
cierto punto; ~ out\ señalar; *vi*
señalar

**pointed** [POIN•tid] *adj*
puntiagudo

**pointer** [POIN•tur] *n*
apuntador M

**pointless** [POINT•lis] *adj* sin
punta

**point of view** [POYNT uhv
VYOO] *n* punto de vista M

**poise** [poiz] *n* equilibrio M

**poison** [POI•zn] *n* veneno M

**poisoning** [POI•zu•ning] *n*
intoxicación F

**poisonous** [POI•zu•ŋus] *adj*
venenoso

**poke** [pok] *vt* picar

**poker** [PO•kur] *n* atizador M

**Poland** [PO•lund] *n* Polonia

**polar** [PO•lur] *adj* polar

**pole** [poul] *n* asta F

**Pole** [poul] *n* polaco

**police** [pu•LEES] *npl* policía F

**police officer** [ ~ aw•fi•sir] *n*
policía F

**police station** [ ~ STAI•shn] *n*
comisaría de policía F

**policeman** [pu•LEES•man] *n*
policía M

**policewoman**
[pu•LEES•WU•mun] *n* mujer
policía F

**policy** [PAH•li•see] *n* plan de
acción M

**Polish** [PO•lish] *adj* polaco

**polish** [PAH•lish] *n* pulimento M

**polite** [pu•LUYT] *adj* refinado

**politeness** [pu•LUYT•nis] *n*
cortesia F

**political** [pu•LI•ti•kl] *adj*
político

**politician** [PAH•li•TI•shn] *n*
político M

**politics** [PAH•li•TIKS] *n*
política F

**poll** [poul] *n* votación F; *vt*
obtener

**pollen** [PAH•ln] *n* polen M

**pollute** [pu•LOOT] *vt*
impurificar

**pollution** [pu•LOO•shn] *n*
ensuciamiento M

**polo** [PO•lo] *n* polo M

**Polynesia** [PAH•li•NEE•zhu] *n*
Polinesia

**pomp** [pahmp] *n* pompa F

**pompous** [PAHM•pus] *adj*
pomposo

**pond** [pahnd] *n* alberca F

**ponder** [PAHN•dur] *vt* ponderar

**pony** [PO•nee] *n* jaquita

**poodle** [POO•dl] *n* perro de
lanas M

**pool** [poool] *n* piscina F

**poor** [poour] *adj* pobre

**pop** [pahp] *n* tiro M; *vt* hacer
reventar; ~ in\ entrar; ~ out\
saltar; ~ up\ surgir

**pope** [pop] *n* papa M

**poplar** [PAHP•lur] *n* álamo M

**poppy** [PAH•pee] *n* amapola F

**populace** [PAH•pyu•lus] *n*
populacho M

**popular** [PAH•pyu•lur] *adj*
popular

**popularity**
[PAH•pyu•LA•ri•tee] *n*
popularidad F

**popularize**
[PAH•pyu•lu•RUYZ] *vt*
popularizar

**populate** [PAH•pyu•lur] *vt*
poblar

**population**
[PAH•pyu•LAI•shn] *n*
población F

**porcelain** [PAURS•lun] *n*
porcelana F

**porch** [paurch] *n* porche M

**porcupine** [PAUR•kyu•PUYN]
*n* puerco espín M

**pore 1** [paur] *n* poro M

**pore 2** *vi* ~ over\ estudiar
detenidamente

**pork** [paurk] *n* puerco M

**pornography**
[paur•NAH•gru•fee] *n*
pornografía F

**porous** [PAU•rus] *adj* poroso

**porpoise** [PAUR•pus] *n*
marsopa F

**porridge** [PAU•rij] *n* potaje M

**port 1** [paurt] *n* puerto M; ~ of
call\ puerto de escala

**port 2** *n* babor M (naut, left);
*adj* de babor

**portable** [PAUR•tu•bl] *adj*
portátil

**porter** [PAUR•tur] *n* portero M

**portfolio** [paurt•FO•lee•O] *n*
portilla F

**porthole** [PAURT•houl] *n*
porta F

**portion** [PAUR•shn] *n*
porción F

**portly** [PAURT•lee] *adj*
voluminoso

**portrait** [PAUR•trit] *n* retrato M

**portray** [paur•TRAI] *vt* retratar

**portrayal** [paur•TRAI•ul] *n*
retrato M

**Portugal** [PAUR•chu•gl] *n*
Portugal

**Portuguese** [PAUR•chu•geez]
*adj* portugués

**pose** [poz] *v* colocar; *n*
postura F

**position** [pu•ZI•shn] *n* posición
F; *vt* colocar

**positive** [PAH•zi•tiv] *adj*
positivo

**possess** [pu•ZES] *vt* poseer

**possession** [pu•ZE•shn] *n*
posesión F

**possibility** [PAH•si•BI•li•tee] *n*
posibilidad F

**possible** [PAH•si•bl] *adj*
posible

**possibly** [PAH•si•blee] *adv*
posiblemente

**post 1** [post] *n* poste M; *vt* fijar
(notice)

**post 2** *n* puesto M (place)

**post 3** *n* correo M (mail); *vt*
echar

**postage** [PO•stij] *n* sello M

**postal** [PO•stl] *adj* postal

**post date** [post DAIT] *n*
posfecha F

**poster** [PO•stur] *n* cartel M

**posterior** [pah•STEEU•ree•ur]
*adj n* posterior M

**posthumous** [PAH•styu•mus]
*adj* póstumo

**postman** [POST•man] *n*
cartero M

**post office** [POST AW•fis] *n*
oficina de correos F

**postpone** [post•PON] *vt*
suspender

**posture** [PAHS•chur] *vt*
postura F

**pot** [paht] *n* pote M

**potassium** [pu•TA•see•um] *n*
potasio M

**potato** [pu•TAI•to] *n* patata F

**potent** [PO•tunt] *adj* potente

**potential** [pu•TEN•shl] *adj n*
potencial F

**potentially** [pu•TEN•shu•lee]
*adv* potencialmente

**pothole** [PAHT•houl] *n*
hache M

**potion** [PO•shn] *n* poción F

**pottery** [PAH•tu•ree] *n*
ollería F

**pouch** [pouch] *n* saquito M

**poultry** [POUL•tree] *n*
pollería F

**pounce** [pouns] *vi* estarcir

**pound 1** [pound] *n* libra F

**pound 2** *vt* machacar (crush);
bombardear; *vi* golpear;
palpitar (heart)

**pour** [paur] *vt* echar; ~ out\
servir; *vi* fuilr; llover a cántros
(rain)

**pout** [pout] *vi* hacer mohínes

**poverty** [PAH•vur•tee] *n*
pobreza F

**powder** [POU•dur] *n* polvo M;
*vt* polvorear

**powdered** [POU•durd] *adj*
pulverizado

**power** [POU•ur] *n* poder M

**powerful** [POU•ur•ful] *adj*
poderoso

**powerless** [POU•ur•lis] *adj*
impotente

**practical** [PRAK•ti•kl] *adj*
práctico

**practical joke** [PRAK•ti•kul
JOK] *n* broma F

**practice** [PRAK•tis] *n* práctica
F; *vi* ejercitarse; *vt* hacer
ejercicios en

**prairie** [PRAIU•ree] *n* pradera F

**praise** [praiz] *n* loor M; *vt*
alabar

**prance** [prans] *vi* cabriolar

**prank** [prangk] *n* travesura F

**pray** [prai] *vi* rogar

**prayer** [praiur] *n* ruego M

**preach** [preech] *vt vi* predicar

**preacher** [PREE•chur] *n*
predicador M

**precarious** [pri•KA•ree•us] *adj*
precario

**precaution** [pree•KAU•shn] *n*
precaución F

**precede** [pri•SEED] *vt* preceder

**precedence** [PRE•si•duns] *n*
precedencia F

**precedent** [PRE•si•dunt] *n*
precendente M

**precious** [PRE•shus] *adj*
precioso

**precipitate** [pri•SI•pi•TAIT] *vt*
precipitar

**precipitation**
[pri•SI•pi•TAI•shn] *n*
precipitación F

**precise** [pri•SUYS] *adj* preciso

**precisely** [pri•SUYS•lee] *adv*
precisamente

**precision** [pri•SI•zhn] *n*
pecisión F

**preclude** [pri•KLOOD] *vt*
preventir

**precocious** [pri•KO•shus] *adj*
precoz

**predecessor** [PRE•di•SE•sur] *n*
predecesor M

**predestined** [pree•DES•tind]
*adj* predestino

**predicament** [pri•DI•ku•munt]
*n* predicamento M

**predicate** [PRE•di•kit] *adj n*
predicado M

**predict** [pri•DIKT] *vt* predecir

**prediction** [pri•DIK•shn] *n*
predicción F

**predisposed** [PREE•dis•POZD]
*adj* predisponado

**predominant**
[pri•DAH•mi•nunt] *adj*
predominante

**preface** [PRE•fus] *n* prefacio M

**prefer** [pri•FUR] *vt* preferir

**preferable** [PRE•fru•bl] *adj*
preferible

**preferably** [PRE•fru•blee] *adv*
preferiblemente

**preference** [PRE•fruns] *n*
preferencia F

**preferential** [PRE•fu•REN•shl]
*adj* preferente

**prefix** [PREE•fiks] *n* prefijo M

**pregnancy** [PREG•nun•see] *n*
preñez F

**pregnant** [PREG•nunt] *adj*
embarazada

**prejudice** [PRE•ju•dis] *n*
prejuicio M

**prejudiced** [PRE•ju•dist] *adj*
perjudicial

**preliminary** [pri•LI•mi•NE•ree]
*adj* preliminar

**prelude** [PRAI•lood] *n*
preludio M

**premature**
[PREE•mu•CHOOUR] *adj*
prematuro

**premier** [pre•MEEUR] *adj*
primero M

**premiere** [pri•MEEUR] *n*
primera F

**premise** [PRE•mis] *n* premisa F

**premium** [PREE•mee•um] *n*
premio M

**premonition** [PRE•mu•NI•shn]
*n* prenuncio M

**preoccupied**
[pree•AH•kyu•PUYD] *adj*
preocupado

**prepaid** [pree•PAID] *adj*
pagado por adelantado

**preparation** [PRE•pu•RAI•shn]
*n* preparación F

**prepare** [pri•PAIUR] *vt*
preparar

**preposition** [PRE•pu•ZI•shn] *n*
preposición F

**preposterous** [pri•PAH•stu•rus]
*adj* prepóstero

**prerequisite** [pri•RE•kwi•zit] *n*
requerido M

**prerogative** [pru•RAH•gu•tuv]
*n* privilegiado M

**prescribe** [pri•SKRUYB] *vt*
prescribir

**prescription** [pri•SKRIP•shn] *n*
prescripción F

**presence** [PRE•zns] *n*
presencia F

**present 1** [PRE•znt *adj*
presente; at ~\ actualmente;
for the ~\ por ahora

**present 2** *n* regalo M

**present 3** [pri•ZENT] *vt*
presentar; obsequiar; *n*
presentatción F

**presentable** [pri•ZEN•tu•bl] *s*
presentable

**presentation**
[PRE•zn•TAI•shn] *n*
presentación F

**presently** [PRE•znt•lee] *adv*
presentemente

**preserve 1** [pri•ZURV] *vt*
preservar

**preserve 2** (keep; maintain) *vi*
mantener

**president** [PRE•zi•dunt] *n*
presidente M

**press** [pres] *n* apretura F; *vt*
apretar; exprimir; *n* prensa F
(journalism); imprenta F
(printing) ~ conference *n*
rueda de prensa F

**pressing** [PRE•sing] *adj* urgente

**pressure** [PRE•shur] *n*
presión F

**prestige** [pre•STEEZH] *n*
prestigio M

**presumably** [pri•ZOO•mu•blee]
*adj* presumiblemente

**presume** [pri•ZOOM] *vt*
presumir

**presumption** [pri•ZUMP•shn]
*n* presunción F

**pretend** [pri•TEND] *vi*
aparentar

**pretension** [pri•TEN•shn] *n*
pretensión F

**pretentious** [pri•TEN•shus] *adj*
pretencioso

**pretext** [PREE•tekst] *n*
pretexto M

**pretty** [PRI•tee] *adj* lindo;
bonito

**prevail** [pri•VAIUL] *vi*
prevalecer

**prevailing** [pree•VAIU•ling]
*adj* prevaleciente

**prevalent** [PRE•vu•lunt] *adj*
reinante

**prevent** [pri•VENT] *vt* prevenir

**preventive** [pri•VEN•tiv] *adj*
impeditivo

**preview** [PREE•vyoo] *n* vista
antemano F

**previous** [PREE•vee•us] *adj*
previo

**prey** [prai] *n* presa F; *vi*
alimentarse de

**price** [pruys] *n* precio M

**priceless** [PRUYS•lis] *adj*
inapreciable

**prick** [prik] *vt* pinchar; ~ up
one's ears\ aguzar las orejas;
*n* pinchazo M

**pride** [pruyd] *n* orgullo M

**priest** [preest] *n* sacerdote M

**priesthood** [PREEST•hud] *n*
sacerdocio M

**prim** [prim] *adj* relamido

**primarily** [pruy•ME•ri•lee] *adv*
primariamente

**primary** [PRUY•me•ree] *adj*
primario

**primate** [PRUY•mait] *n*
primado M

**prime** [pruym] *adj* prima

**primer** [PRUY•mur] *n* pistón F

**primitive** [PRI•mi•tiv] *adj*
primitivo

**primrose** [PRIM•roz] *n*
vellorita F

**prince** [prins] *n* príncipe M

**princess** [PRIN•ses] *n*
princesa F

**principal** [PRIN•si•pl] *adj*
principal

**principle** [PRIN•si•pl] *n*
principio M

**print** [print] *n* impresión F; *vt*
imprimir

**printer** [PRIN•tur] *n*
impresor M

**printing** [PRIN•ting] *n*
estampación F
**prior** [PRUY•ur] *adj* anterior
**priority** [pruy•AU•ri•tee] *n*
prioridad F
**prism** [PRI•zm] *n* prisma F
**prison** [PRI•zn] *n* cárcel M
**prisoner** [PRI•zu•nur] *n*
prisionero M
**privacy** [PRUY•vu•see] *n*
. intimidad F
**private** [PRUY•vit] *adj* privado
**privation** [pruy•VAI•shn] *n*
privación F
**privilege** [PRIV•lij] *n*
privilegio M
**prize** [pruyz] *adj* premio M
**pro** [pro] *n* pro M
**probability**
[PRAH•bu•BI•li•tee] *n*
probabilidad F
**probable** [PRAH•bu•bl] *adj*
probable
**probably** [PRAH•bu•blee] *adv*
probablemente
**probation** [pro•BAI•shn] *n*
prueba F
**probe** [prob] *n* exploración F
**problem** [PRAH•blum] *n*
problema M
**procedure** [pru•SEE•jur] *n*
proceder M
**proceed** [pru•SEED] *vi*
proceder
**proceeding** [pru•SEE•ding] *adj*
proceder
**proceeds** [PRO•seedz] *npl*
beneficios M
**process** [PRAH•ses] *n* proceso M
**procession** [pru•SE•shn] *n*
procesión F

**proclaim** [pru•CLAIM] *vt*
proclamar
**procrastinate**
[pru•KRA•sti•NAIT] *vi*
aplazar
**procure** [pru•KYOOUR] *vt*
obtener
**prod** [prahd] *vt* punzar; *n*
empuje M
**prodigal** [PRAH•di•gl] *adj*
pródigo
**prodigy** [PRAH•di•jee] *n*
prodigio M
**produce** [PRO•doos] *n*
producto M
**producer** [pru•DOO•sur] *n*
productor M
**product** [PRAH•duhkt] *n*
producto M
**production** [pru•DUHK•shn] *n*
producción F
**productive** [pru•DUHK•tiv] *adj*
productivo
**profane** [pru•FAIN] *adj*
profano
**profession** [pru•FE•shn] *n*
profesión F
**professional** [pru•FE•shu•nl]
*adj n* profesional M
**professor** [pru•FE•sur] *n*
profesor M
**proficiency** [pru•FI•shn•see] *n*
pericia F
**profile** [PRO•fuyul] *n* perfil M
**profit** [PRAH•fit] *n* provecho M
**profitable** [PRAH•fi•tu•bl] *adj*
provechoso
**profound** [pru•FOUND] *adj*
profundo
**profuse** [pru•FYOOS] *adj*
profuso

**program** [PRO•gram] *n*
programa M

**progress** [*n.* PRAH•gres *v.*
pru•GRES] *n* progreso M; *vt*
progresar

**progressive** [pru•GRE•siv] *adj*
progresivo

**prohibit** [pru•HI•bit] *vt* prohibir

**prohibition** [PRO•hi•BI•shn] *n*
prohibición F

**project** [*n.* PRAH•jekt *v.*
pru•JEKT] *n* proyecto M; *vt*
proyectar

**projection** [pru•JEK•shn] *n*
proyección F

**proletariat** [PRO•lu•TA•ree•ut]
*n* proletariado M

**prolong** [pro•LAUNG] *vt*
prolongar

**promenade**
[PRAH•mu•NAHD] *n* paseo
M; *vt* pasear

**prominent** [PRAH•mi•nunt] *adj*
prominente

**promiscuous**
[pru•MI•skyoo•us] *adj*
promiscuo

**promise** [PRAH•mis] *n*
promesa F; *vt vi* prometer

**promising** [PRAH•mi•sing] *adj*
prometiente

**promote** [pru•MOT] *vt*
promover

**promoter** [pru•MO•tur] *n*
promotor M

**promotion** [pru•MO•shn] *n*
promoción F

**prompt** [prahmpt] *adj* pronto

**promptly** [PRAHMPT•lee] *adv*
prontamente

**prone** [pron] *adj* prono

**prong** [prahng] *n* gajo M

**pronoun** [PRO•noun] *n*
pronombre M

**pronounce** [pru•NOUNS] *vt*
pronunciar

**pronounced** [pru•NOUNST]
*adj* pronunciado

**pronunciation**
[pru•NUHN•see•AI•shn] *n*
pronunciación F

**proof** [proof] *n* prueba F

**prop** [prahp] *n* pilar M

**propaganda**
[PRAH•pu•GAN•du] *n*
propaganda F

**propel** [pru•PEL] *vt* propulsar

**propeller** [pru•PE•lur] *n*
propulsor M

**proper** [PRAH•pur] *adj* propio

**properly** [PRAH•pur•lee] *adv*
propiamente

**property** [PRAH•pur•tee] *n*
propiedad F

**prophecy** [PRAH•fi•see] *n*
profecia F

**prophesy** [PRAH•fi•SUY] *vt*
profetizar

**prophet** [PRAH•fit] *n* profeta F

**proportion** [pru•PAUR•shn] *n*
proporción F

**proposal** [pru•PO•zl] *n*
propuesta F

**propose** [pru•POZ] *vt* proponer

**proposition** [PRAH•pu•ZI•shn]
*n* proposición F

**proprietor** [pru•PRUY•u•tur] *n*
propiertario M

**prose** [proz] *n* prosa F

**prosecute** [PRAH•si•KYOOT]
*vt* proseguir

**prosecution** [PRAH•seh•KYOO•shun] *n*
presecución F

**prosecutor** [PRAH•seh•KYOO•tor] *n*
demandante M

**prospect** [PRAH•spekt] *n*
perspectiva F

**prospective** [pru•SPEK•tiv] *adj*
presunto

**prosper** [PRAH•spur] *vt*
prosperar

**prosperity** [prah•SPER•it•ee] *n*
prosperidad F

**prosperous** [PRAH•spur•us]
*adj* próspero

**prostitute** [PRAH•sti•TOOT] *n*
prostituta F

**prostrate** [PRAH•strayt] *adj*
postrado

**protect** [pro•TEKT] *vt* proteger

**protection** [pro•TEK•shun] *n*
protección F

**protective** [pro•TEK•tiv] *adj*
protector

**protector** [pro•TEK•tor] *n*
protector M

**protein** [PRO•teen] *n* proteína F

**protest** [PRO•test] *vt* protestar

**Protestant** [PRAH•tes•tahnt] *n*
protestante M

**protoplasm** [PRO•to•PLA•zm]
*n* protoplasma F

**protract** [pro•TRAKT] *vi*
alargar

**protrude** [pro•TROOD] *vi* sacar

**protuberance**
[pro•TOO•ber•uns] *n*
protuberancia F

**proud** [prowd *adj* orgulloso

**prove** [proov] *vt* probar

**proverb** [PRAH•vurb] *n*
proverbio M

**provide** [pro•VUYD] *vt* proveer

**providence** [PRAH•vi•dens] *n*
providencia F

**provider** [pro•VUY•dur] *n*
proveedor M

**province** [PRAH•vins] *n*
provincia F

**provincial** [pro•VIN•chal] *adj*
provincial

**provision** [pro•VIZH•un] *n*
provisión F

**proviso** [pro•VEE•zo] *n*
estipulación F

**provoke** [pro•VOK] *vt* provocar

**provost** [PRO•vost] *n*
preboste M

**prow** [prou] *n* proa M

**prowess** [PROU•es] *n* valor M

**prowl** [proul] *vt* rondar

**proximity** [prahk•SIM•it•ee] *n*
proximidad F

**proxy** [PRAHK•see] *n*
procuración F

**prude** [prood] *n* remilgada F

**prudence** [PROO•dens] *n*
prudencia F

**prudent** [PROO•dent] *adj*
prudente

**prune** [proon] *n* ciruela pasa F

**pry** [pruy] *vi* acechar

**psalm** [salm] *n* salmo M

**pseudonym** [SOO•do•NIM] *n*
seudónimo M

**psychiatrist** [su•KUY•a•trist] *n*
psiquiartra F

**psychiatry** [su•KUY•a•tree] *n*
psiquiatría F

**psychological**
[SUY•ko•LA•ji•kl] *adj*
psicológico

**psychologist** [suy•KA•lo•jist] *n* psicólogo M

**psychology** [suy•KA•lo•jee] *n* psicología F

**public** [PUH•blik] *n* público M

**publication** [PUH•bli•KAI•shn] *n* publicación F

**publicize** [PUH•bli•SUYZ] *vt* publicar

**publisher** [PUH•bli•shur] *n* publicador M

**pucker** [PUH•kur] *vt* plegar

**pudding** [PU•ding] *n* pudín M

**puddle** [PUH•dl] *n* poza F

**puff** [puhf] *n* resoplido M; *vt vi* soplar

**pug** [puhg] *n* barro M

**pull** [puhl] *vt* tirar de; sacar; ~ a fast one\ hacer una mala jugada; ~ down\ derribar; ~ off\ quitarse; ~ out\ sacar; ~ away\ alejarse (auto); ~ back\ retirarse; ~ in\ entrar; ~ through\ recobrar la salud; *n* tirón M; attracción F

**pulley** [PUHL•ee] *n* garrucha F

**pulp** [puhlp] *n* pulpa F

**pulpit** [PUHL•pit] *n* púlpito M

**pulsate** [PUHL•sait] *vt* pulsar

**pulsation** [puhl•SAI•shn] *n* pulsación F

**pulse** [puhlz] *n* pulso M

**pulverize** [PUHL•vur•UYZ] *vt* pulverizar

**pumice** [PUH•mis] *n* piedra pómez F

**pump** [puhmp] *n* bomba F; *vt* sacar con una bomba

**pumpkin** [PUHMP•kin] *n* clabaza F

**pun** [puhn] *n* juego de palabras M

**punch** [puhnch] *vt* remachar; *n* puñetazo; empuje M

**punctual** [PUHNK•tyoo•ul] *adj* puntual

**punctuation** [PUHNK•tyoo•AI•shn] *n* puntuación F

**puncture** [PUHNK•tyur] *vt* puntura F

**punish** [PUH•nish] *vt* castigar

**punishment** [PUH•nish•mint] *n* castigo M

**pup** [puhp] *n* perrito M

**pupil** [PYOO•pil] *n* estudiante M

**puppet** [PUH•pit] *n* muñeco M

**purchase** [PUR•chis] *n* compra F; *vt* comprar

**pure** [pyur] *adj* puro

**purgatory** [PUR•gi•TAUR•ee] *n* purgatorio M

**purge** [purj] *vt* purgar

**purify** [PYUR•i•FUY] *vt* purificar

**purity** [PYUR•i•tee] *n* pureza F

**purple** [PUR•pl] *adj* purpúreo

**purport** [pur•PORT] *vt* significar

**purpose** [PUR•pus] *n* fin objeto M

**purr** [pur] *vt* ronronear

**purse** [purs] *n* bolsa F

**pursue** [pur•SOO] *vt* perseguir

**pursuit** [pur•SOOT] *n* seguimiento M

**push** [push] *vt vi* empujar; *vt* apetar; *n* empuje M; ~ aide\ apartar; ~ back\ hacer retroceder

**put** [put] *vi* poner; expresar
(com); ~ across\ comunicar; ~
aside\ poner aparte; ~ away\
guardar; ~ back\ devolver; ~
down\ depositar; ~ in\
introducir; ~ off\ aplazar; ~
one's foot down\ mantenerse
firme; ~ out\ apagar
(extinguish); incomodar
**putrefy** [PYOO•tri•FUY] *vt*
pudrir

**putrid** [PYOO•trid] *adj* pútrido
**putter** [PUH•tir] *n* ponedor M
**putty** [PUH•tee] *n* masilla F
**puzzle** [PUH•zl] *n* perplejidad
F; *vt* dejar perplejo; *vi*
calentarse los sesos
**pylon** [PUY•lahn] *n* pilón F
**pyramid** [PEER•uh•MID] *n*
pirámide M

# Q

**quack** [kwak] *vt* graznar
**quadrant** [KWA•drant] *n*
cuadrante M
**quadrilateral**
[KWAH•dri•LA•tu•rl] *adj*
cuadrilátero
**quagmire** [KWAG•muyr] *n*
cenagal M
**quail** [kwail] *n* codorniz M
**quaint** [kwaint] *adj* pintoresco
**quake** [kwaik] *vi* temblar M; *n*
terremoto M (coll)
**qualification**
[KWA•li•fi•KAI•shn] *n*
calificación F
**qualify** [KWA•li•FUY] *vi*
calificar
**qualitative** [KWA•li•TAI•tiv]
*adj* cualitativo
**quality** [KWA•li•tee] *n*
calidad F
**qualm** [kwalm] *n*
remordimiento M

**quantitative**
[KWAHN•ti•TAI•tiv] *n*
cuantitativo M
**quantity** [KWAHN•ti•tee] *n*
cantidad F
**quarantine**
[KWAHR•in•TEEN] *n*
cuarentena F
**quarrel** [KWAH•rl] *n*
altercado M
**quarry** [KWAH•ree] *n* cantera F
**quart** [kwart] *n* cuarto M
**quarter** [KWAH•tur] *n* cuarto M
**quarterly** [KWAHR•tur•lee] *adj*
trimestral
**quartet** [kwar•TET] *n* grupo de
cuatro M
**quartz** [kwartz] *n* cuarzo M
**quaver** [KWAI•vur] *vi* temblar
**quay** [kway] *n* muelle M
**queen** [kween] *n* reina F
**queer** [kweer] *n* extraño
**quell** [kwell] *vt* reprimir
**quench** [kwench] *vt* extinguir

**query** |KWEER•ee| *n*
pregunta F
**quest** |kwest| *n* busca F
**question** |KWEST•shn| *n*
pregunta F; in ~\ en cuestiób;
out of the ~\ imposible;
without ~\ sinduda; *vt*
preguntar; interrogar (police,
etc)
**questionable**
|KWEST•shn•uh•bl| *adj*
cuestionable
**questionnaire**
|KWEST•shn•AIR| *n*
cuestionario M
**quibble** |KWIH•bl| *vt* sutilizar
**quick** |kwik| *adv* presto
**quicken** |KWIK•in| *vt* avivar
**quickly** |KWIK•lee| *adv*
vivamente
**quickness** |KWIK•nis| *n*
vivacidad F
**quicksand** |KWIK•sand| *n*
arena movediza F
**quicksilver** |KWIK•SIL•vur| *n*
mercurio M
**quid** |kwid| *n* quid M
**quiescence** |kwee•EH•sinz| *n*
quietud F
**quiet** |KWUY•it| *adj* callado; *vi*
calmarse

**quietly** |KWUY•it•lee| *adj*
tranquilamente
**quietness** |KWUY•it•nis| *n*
quietud F
**quilt** |kwilt| *n* colcha F
**quill** |kwill| *n* pluma F
**quince** |kwinz| *n* membrillo M
**quinine** |KWUY•nuyn| *n*
quinina F
**quintet** |kwin•TET| *n* grupo de
cinco M
**quintuplet** |kwin•TUH•plit| *n*
quintiplo M
**quip** |kwip| *vt* sarcasmo M
**quit** |kwit| *vt* dejar; renunciar
**quite** |kwuyt| *adv* totalmente
**quitter** |KWIH•tur| *n*
cobarde M
**quiver** |KWIH•vur| *vt* vibrar
**quixotic** |kwihk•ZAH•tik| *adj*
quijotesco
**quiz** |kwiz| *n* examen M; *vt*
interrogar
**quorum** |KWAUR•uhm| *n*
quórum M
**quota** (part; portion) |KWO•ta|
*n* cuota F
**quotation** |kwo•TAI•shn| *n*
citación F
**quote** |kwot| *vt* citar; *n* cita F
**quotient** |KWO•shnt| *n*
cociente M

# R

**rabbi** |RA•buy| *n* rabino M
**rabbit** |RA•bit| *n* conejo M
**rabble** |RA•bl| *n* chusma F

**rabid** |RA•bid| *adj* rabioso
**raccoon** |ra•KOON| *n*
mapache M

**race** |rais| *n* raza F; *vt* correr
regatear

**racer** |RAI•sur| *n* corredor M

**rack** |rak| *n* red M; *vt* ~ one's
brains\ devanarse los sesos

**racket** |RA•kit| *n* requeta F

**radiance** |RAI•dee•enz| *n*
brillo M

**radiant** |RAI•dee•ent| *adj*
radiante

**radiator** |RAI•dee•AI•tur| *n*
radiador M

**radical** |RA•di•kul| *adj* radical

**radio** |RAI•dee•O| *n* radio M

**radish** |RA•dish| *n* rábano M

**radius** |RAI•dee•is| *n* radio M

**raffle** |RA•fl| *n* rifa F

**raft** *n* balsa F

**rafter** |RAF•tur| *n* asna F

**rag** *n* trapo M

**rage** |raij| *n* rabia F; *vt* rabiar;
*vi* estar furioso

**ragged** |RA•gid| *adj* roto

**raid** |raid| *n* incursión F; ladrón
M; *vt* atacar (mil) hacer una
redada en (police)

**rail** |rail| *n* barra F

**railroad** |RAIL•rod| *n*
ferrocarril M

**railroad station** |~ STAI•shn|
*n* estación de ferrocarril F

**railway** |RAIL•wai| *n*
ferrocarril M

**rain** |rain| *n* lluvia F

**rainbow** |RAIN•bo| *n* arco
iris M

**raindrop** |RAIN•drahp| *n* gota
de lluvia F

**rainfall** |RAIN•fawl| *n* lluvia F

**rainy** |RAI•nee| *adj* lluvioso

**raise** |raiz| *vt* levantar; obtener
(wages); *n* aumento M

**raisin** |RAIZ•in| *n* pasa F

**rally** |RA•lee| *n* reunión F

**ram** |ram| *n* morueco M

**ramble** |RAM•bl| *vi* callejear

**rancid** |RAN•sid| *adj* rancio

**rancor** |RAN•kor| *n* rencor M

**random** |RAN•dom| *adj* azar M

**rang** |raing| *pp* sonado

**range** |rainj| *n* fila F; *vi*
extendaerse; variar (vary)

**rank** *n* categoría F; *vt* clasificar;
*vi* clasificarse; ~ and file\ la
masa

**ransack** |RAN•sak| *vt* saquear

**ransom** |RAN•som| *n* rescate M

**rant** |rant| *vt* delirar

**rap** |rap| *vt* golpear

**rape** |raip| *n* violación F; *vt*
violar

**rapid** |RAP•id| *adj* rápido

**rapt** |rapt| *adj* arrebatado

**rapture** |RAP•chur| *n* rapto M

**rare 1** |rair| *adj* raro

**rare 2** *adj* poco hecho

**rarity** |RAIR•i•tee| *n* rareza F

**rascal** |RA•skul| *n* bribón M

**rash** |rash| *adj* erupción F

**rasp** |rasp| *vt* raspar; *n*
escofina F

**raspberry** |RAZ•bur•ee| *n*
frambuesa F

**rat** *n* ratón M; *vi* ~ on\
debunciar

**rate** |rait| *n* grado M; velocidad
F; *n* precio M (price); *n* tipo
M (of interest); at any ~\ de
todas formas; at the ~ of\
razón de; at this ~\ así; *vt*

valorar; considerer; merecer
(deserve)

**rather** [RA•thur] *adv* bastante;
mejor dicho; *int* claro; I
would ~ not\ prefiero no

**ratify** [RA•ti•FUY] *vt* ratificar

**rating** [RAI•ting] *n* valuación F

**ratio** [RAI•she•O] *n* relación F

**rational** [RA•sha•nl] *adj*
racional

**rattle** [RAT•tl] *vt* agitar

**rattlesnake** [RAT•tl•SNAIK] *n*
crótalo M

**raucous** [RAW•kus] *adj* rauco

**ravage** [RA•vij] *vt* asolar

**rave** [raiv] *vi* delirar; ~ about\
entusiasmarse por

**raven** [RAI•vin] *n* cuervo M

**ravenous** [RA•vi•nis] *adj*
hambriento

**ravine** [ruh•VEEN] *n*
barranco M

**ravish** [RA•vish] *vt* arrebatar

**raw** *adj* crudo

**raw material** [RAW
muh•TEE•ree•ul] *n* materia
bruta F

**ray** [rai] *n* rayo M

**rayon** [RAI•on] *n* rayón M

**raze** [raiz] *vt* destruir

**razor** [RAI•zor] *n* navaja de
afeitar F

**react** [ree•AKT] *vi* reaccionar

**reaction** [ree•AK•shn] *n*
reacción F

**reactionary**
[ree•AK•shn•AIR•ee] *adj*
reaccionario

**reach** [reech] *vt* extender;
alcanzar; llegar a (arrive at);

*vi* extenderse; *n* alcance M;
within ~\ al alcance de

**read** [reed] *vt* leer; estudiar; *vi*
leer

**reader** [REE•dur] *n* lector M

**readily** [RED•i•lee] *adv*
prontamente

**readiness** [RED•i•nis] *n*
prontitud F

**reading** [REE•ding] *n* lectura F

**readjust** [REE•uh•JUST] *vt*
ajustar

**ready** [REH•dee] *adj* preparado;
get ~\ prepararse

**real** [reel] *adj* real; ~ estate *npl* \
bienes raíces M

**realism** [REEL•izm] *n*
realismo M

**realist** [REEL•ist] *n* realista F

**realistic** [reel•IS•tik] *adj* realista

**reality** [ree•A•li•tee] *n*
realidad F

**realization** [REEL•i•ZAI•shn] *n*
realización F

**realize** [REE•LUYZ] *vt*
comprender; realizar

**realm** [relm] *n* reino M

**really** [REEL•lee] *adj* realmente

**reap** [reep] *vt* segar

**reappear** [REE•uh•PEER] *vt*
reaparecer

**rear** [reer] *n* trasero M

**reason** [REE•zun] *n* razón F

**reasonable** [REE•zun•uh•bl]
*adj* racional

**reasonably** [REE•zun•uh•blee]
*adj* razonablemente

**reasoning** [REE•zun•ing] *n*
razonamiento M

**reassure** [REE•uh•SHUR] *vt*
tranquilizar

**rebate** [REE•bait] *n* rebaja F

**rebel** [REH•bl] *n* reblede M; *vi*
rebalarse

**rebellion** [ree•BEL•yin] *n*
rebelión F

**rebellious** [re•BEL•yis] *adj*
rebelde

**rebirth** [REE•burth] *n*
renacimiento M

**rebound** [REE•bound] *vi*
rebotar

**rebuild** [ree•BILD] *vt* reedificar

**rebuke** [ree•BYOOK] *vi*
increpar

**recall** [ree•KAUL] *vi* revivir; *n*
llamada F

**recede** [re•SEED] *vt* retroceder

**receipt** [re•SEET] *n* recibo M

**receive** [re•SEEV] *vt* recibir

**receiver 1** [re•SEE•vur] *n*
receptor M

**receiver 2** (telephone) *n*
auricular M

**recent** [REE•sent] *adv* reciente

**receptacle** [re•SEP•ti•kl] *n*
receptáculo M

**reception** [re•SEP•shn] *n*
recepción F

**recess** [REE•sess] *n* descanso
M; *n* hueco M

**recipe** [RE•si•pee] *n* receta F

**recipient** [re•SI•pee•int] *n*
receptor M

**reciprocal** [re•SI•pri•kl] *adj*
recíproco M

**reciprocate** [re•SI•pri•KAIT] *vt*
reciprocar

**recital** [ree•SUY•tl] *n* recital M

**recite** [ree•SUYT] *vt* recitar

**reckless** [REK•lis] *adj*
descuidado

**recklessness** [REK•lis•nis] *n*
indiferencia F

**reckon** [REK•kon] *vt* suponer

**reckoning** [REK•kon•ning] *n*
cuenta F

**reclaim** [ree•KLAIM] *vt*
reclamar

**recline** [ree•KLUYN] *vi* reclinar

**recluse** [REH•klooz] *n*
retirado M

**recognition** [RE•kuh•NI•shn] *n*
reconocimiento M

**recognize** [RE•kug•NUYZ] *vt*
reconocer

**recoil** [ree•KOYL] *vt*
retroceder

**recollect** [RE•ko•LEKT] *vi*
recordar

**recollection** [RE•ko•LEK•shn]
*n* recuerdo M

**recommend** [RE•ko•MEND] *vt*
recomendar

**recommendation**
[RE•ko•men•DAI•shn] *n*
recomendación F

**recompense** [RE•kom•PENZ]
*vt* recompensar

**reconcile** [RE•kun•SUYL] *vt*
reconciliar

**reconciliation**
[RE•kun•SI•lee•AI•shn] *n*
reconciliación F

**reconnaissance**
[re•KAHN•nai•zanz] *n*
reconocimiento M

**reconsider** [REE•kun•SI•dur] *vt*
repensar

**reconstruct**
[REE•kun•STRUKT] *vt*
reconstruir

**record** [n. RE•kord v. ri•KORD]
*vt* registrar; anotar; grabar

(mus); *n* documentación F,
expediente M; disco M (mus);
off the ~\ en confianza

**recount** [ree•KOUNT] *vt*
recontar; relatir

**recoup** [ree•KOOP] *vt* retener

**recourse** [REE•kors] *n*
recurso M

**recover** [ri•KUH•vur] *vt*
recobrar

**recovery** [ri•KUH•vree] *n*
recobro M

**recreation** [RE•kree•AI•shn] *n*
recreación F

**recruit** [re•KROOT] *vt* reclutar;
*n* recluta M

**rectangle** [REK•TAN•gl] *n*
rectángulo M

**rectify** [REK•ti•FUY] *vt*
rectificar

**rector** [REK•tur] *n* rector M

**recuperate** [ree•KOO•pur•AIT]
*vi* recuperar

**recur** [ri•KUR] *vt* recurrir

**red** [red] *adj* rojo

**redden** [RED•din] *vt* enrojecer

**redeem** (take off; detach)
[ri•DEEM] *vt* redimir

**redeemer** [ri•DEE•mur] *n*
redentor M

**redemption** [ri•DEM•shn] *n*
redención F

**redness** [RED•nis] *n* rojez F

**redress** [ree•DRES] *vt* resarcir

**reduce** [ree•DOOS] *vt* reducir

**reed** [reed] *n* caña F

**reef** [reef] *n* bajío M

**reek** [reek] *n* mal olor M

**reel** [reel] *n* aspa F

**re-enter** [REE•EN•tur] *vt*
reingresar F

**re-establish** [REE•a•STA•blish]
*vt* restablecer

**refer** [ree•FUR] *vt* referir

**referee** [RE•fur•EE] *n* arbitrar
M

**reference** [RE•fur•enz] *n*
referencia F

**refill** [REE•fill] *vt* rellenar

**refine** [ree•FUYN] *vt* refinar

**refined** [ree•FUYND] *adj*
refinado

**refinement** [ree•FUYN•mint] *n*
refinamiento M

**refinery** [ree•FUY•nur•ee] *n*
refinería F

**reflect** [ree•FLEKT] *vt* reflejar;
~ upon\ perjudicar

**reflection** [ree•FLEK•shn] *n*
reflexión F

**reflexive** [ree•FLEK•ziv] *adj*
reflexivo

**reform** [ree•FORM] *n* reforma
F; *vt* reformar; *vi* reformarse

**refraction** [re•FRAK•shn] *n*
refracción F

**refrain 1** [ree•FRAIN] *vt*
refrenar; *vi* abstenerse de

**refrain 2** *n* estribillo M

**refresh** [ree•FRESH] *vt*
refrescar

**refreshing** [ree•FRESH•ing] *adj*
refrescante

**refreshment** [rec•FRESH•mint]
*n* refrescadura F

**refrigeration**
[re•FRI•jur•AI•shn] *n*
refrigeración F

**refuge** [RE•fyudj] *n* refugio M

**refund** [REE•fund] *n* reembolso
M; *vt* reembolsar

**refusal** [ree•FYOO•sl] *n*
rechazamiento M

**refuse** [re•FYOOZ] *vt* repeler

**refute** [ree•FYOOT] *vi* refutar

**regain** [ree•GAIN] *vt* recuperar

**regal** [REE•gul] *adj* regio

**regalia** [ree•GAI•lee•uh] *n* regalías F

**regard** [ree•GARD] *vt* contemplar; mirar; *n* mirada F; atención (care); respeto M (esteem)

**regarding** [ree•GAR•ding] *adj* respecto de

**regime** [re•JEEM] *n* régimen M

**regiment** [RE•ji•mint] *n* regimiento M

**region** [REE•jin] *n* región F

**register** [RE•jis•tur] *vt* registrar; matricular; declarar (auto); certificar (birth)

**registration** [RE•jis•TRAI•shn] *n* registro M

**regret** [ree•GRET] *vt* lamentar; *n* pesar M

**regular** [RE•gyu•lur] *adj* regular

**regularly** [RE•gyu•lur•lee] *adv* regularmente

**regulate** [RE•gyu•LAIT] *vt* regular

**regulation** [RE•gyu•LAI•shn] *n* regulación F

**rehearsal** [ree•HUR•sul] *n* ensayo M

**rehearse** [ree•HURS] *vt* ensayar

**reign** [rain] *vt* reinar; *n* reinado M

**reimburse** [REE•im•BURS] *vt* reembolsar

**rein** [rain] *n* rienda F

**reindeer** [RAIN•deer] *n* reno M

**reinforce** [REE•in•FAURS] *vt* reforzar

**reiterate** [ree•I•tur•AIT] *vt* reiterar

**reject** [ree•JEKT] *vt* rechazar

**rejoice** [ree•JOIS] *vi* alegrar

**rejoicing** [ree•JOI•sing] *n* gozo M

**rejoin** [ree•JOIN] *vt* reunir

**rejuvenate** [ree•JOO•vi•NAIT] *vi* rejuvenecer

**relapse** [ree•LAPS] *vt* recaída F

**relate** [ree•LAIT] *vt* relatar

**related** [ree•LAI•tid] *adj* relatado

**relation** [ree•LAI•shn] *n* relación F

**relationship** [ree•LAI•shn•SHIP] *n* relación F

**relative** [RE•luh•tiv] *n* relativo

**relax** [ree•LAKS] *vt* relajar; *vi* relajarse

**relaxation** [ree•LAK•SAI•shn] *n* relajación F

**relay** [REE•lai] *n* parada F; *vt* retransmitir

**release** [ree•LEES] *n* libertad F; *vt* soltar; poner en libertad; strenar; publicar (news)

**relent** [ree•LENT] *vi* ablandarse

**relentless** [ree•LENT•les] *adj* implacable

**relevant** [RE•le•vint] *adj* pertinente

**reliability** [ree•LUY•uh•BI•li•tee] *n* veracidad F

**reliable** [ree•LUY•uh•bl] *adj* confiable

**reliance** [ree•LUY•ens] *n* confianza F

**relief** [ree•LEEF] *n* socorro M

**relieve** [ree•LEEV] *vt* remediar

**religion** [re•LI•jin] *n* religión F

**religious** [re•LI•jis] *adj* religioso

**relinquish** [re•LIN•kwish] *vt* abandonar

**relish** [RE•lish] *vt* saborear; *n* gusto M

**reluctant** [ree•LUK•tant] *adj* reluctante

**reluctantly** [ree•LUK•tant•lee] *adv* de mala gana

**rely** [ree•LUY] *vi* confiar

**remain** [ree•MAIN] *vi* quedar

**remainder** [ree•MAIN•dur] *n* resto M

**remains** [ree•MAINZ] *n* restos

**remark** [ree•MARK] *n* observación F

**remarkable** [ree•MAR•kuh•bl] *adj* observable

**remedy** [RE•mi•dee] *n* remedio M

**remember** [re•MEM•bur] *vi* recordar

**remind** [ree•MUYND] *vt* acordar

**reminder** [ree•MUYN•der] *n* recordativo M

**reminiscence** [RE•mi•NI•senz] *n* reminiscencia F

**remiss** [re•MIS] *adj* remiso

**remission** [re•MI•shn] *n* remisión F

**remit** [ree•MIT] *vt* remitir

**remnant** [REM•nent] *n* remanente M

**remodel** [ree•MO•dl] *vt* modelar

**remorse** [ree•MAURS] *n* remordimiento M

**remote** [ree•MOT] *adj* remoto

**removal** [ree•MOO•vl] *n* mudanza F

**remove** [ree•MOOV] *vt* remover

**removed** [ree•MOOVD] *adj* apartado

**renaissance** [RE•nai•SANZ] *n* renacimiento M

**render** [REN•dur] *vt* entregar

**renew** [re•NOO] *vt* renovar

**renewal** [re•NOO•wl] *n* renocación F

**renovate** [RE•no•VAIT] *vt* renovar

**renown** [ree•NOUN] *n* renombre M

**rent** [rent] *vt* arrendar; *n* alquiler M

**rental** [REN•tl] *n* renta F

**reopen** [ree•O•pin] *vt* reanudar

**repair** [ree•PAIR] *vt* reparar

**reparation** [RE•pur•AI•shn] *n* reparación F

**repay** [ree•PAI] *vt* restituir

**repeal** [ree•PEEL] *vt* derogar

**repeat** [ree•PEET] *vt* repetir

**repel** [re•PEL] *vt* repeler

**repent** [re•PENT] *vt* arrepentirse

**repetition** [RE•pi•TI•shn] *n* repetición F

**replace** [re•PLAIS] *vt* reponer

**replenish** [ree•PLE•nish] *vt* llenar

**replica** [RE•pli•kuh] *n* réplica F

**reply** [re•PLUY] *vi* responder

**report** [re•PAURT] *n* reportaje M; *vt* anunciar; *vi* presentar un informe

**reporter** [re•PAUR•tur] *n*
reportero M

**repose** [ree•POZ] *n* reposo M

**represent** [RE•pree•ZENT] *vt*
representar

**representation**
[RE•pree•ZEN•TAI•shn] *n*
representación F

**representative**
[RE•pree•ZEN•te•tiv] *n*
representate M

**repress** [re•PRES] *vt* reprimir

**reprimand** [RE•pri•MAND] *n*
reprimenda F

**reproach** [re•PROCH] *n*
reproche M; *vt* reprochar

**reproduce** [REE•pro•DOOS] *vt*
reproducir

**reproduction**
[REE•pro•DUK•shn] *n*
reprodución F

**reproof** [re•PROOF] *n*
repración F

**reprove** [re•PROOV] *vt*
reprobar

**reptile** [REP•tuyl] *n* reptíl M

**republic** [ree•PUH•blik] *n*
república F

**republican** [ree•PUH•bli•ken] *n*
republicano M

**repudiate** [re•PYOO•di•AIT] *vt*
repudiar

**repugnant** [ree•PUG•nent] *adj*
repugnante

**repulse** [ree•PULS] *vt* repulsar

**repulsive** [ree•PUL•siv] *adj*
repelente

**reputable** [RE•PYU•tuh•bl] *adj*
estimable

**reputation** [RE•pyu•TAI•shn] *n*
reputación F

**repute** [re•PYOOT] *vi* reputar;
*n* reputación F

**request** [re•KWEST] *n* ruego M

**require** [re•KWUYR] *vt*
requerir

**requirement**
[re•KWUYR•mint] *n*
requisito M

**rescue** [RES•kyoo] *vt* rescatar

**research** [REE•surch] *n*
rebusca F

**resemblance** [re•ZEM•blinz] *n*
parecido M

**resemble** [re•ZEM•bl] *vt*
parecerse

**resent** [re•ZENT] *vt* resentirse

**resentful** [re•ZENT•ful] *adj*
resentido

**reservation** [RE•zur•VAI•shn]
*n* reservación F

**reserve** [re•ZURV] *vt* reservar

**reside** [re•ZUYD] *vi* residir

**residence** [RE•zi•denz] *n*
residencia F

**residue** [RE•zi•DOO] *n*
residuo M

**resign** [ree•ZUYN] *vt* dimitir

**resignation** [RE•zig•NAI•shn]
*n* resignación F

**resist** [re•ZIST] *vt* resistir

**resistance** [re•ZI•stenz] *n*
resistencia F

**resolute** [RE•zo•LOOT] *adj*
resuelto M

**resolution** [RE•zo•LOO•shn] *n*
resolución F

**resolve** [re•ZOLV] *vt* resolver

**resonance** [RE•zo•nenz] *n*
resonancia F

**resonant** [RE•zo•nent] *adj*
resonante

**resort** [ree•ZAURT] *n* recurso M; *vi* ~ to\ recurrir a; as the last ~\ como último recurso

**resource** [REE•saurs] *n* recurso M

**respect** [re•SPEKT] *n* respeto M; with ~ to\ con respecto a; *vt* respetar

**respectable** [re•SPEK•tuh•bl] *adj* respetable

**respectful** [re•SPEKT•fl] *adj* respetuoso

**respective** [re•SPEK•tiv] *adv* respectivo

**respite** [RE•spit] *n* respiro M

**respond** [re•SPAHND] *vt* responder

**response** [re•SPAHNS] *n* respuesta F

**responsibility** [re•SPAHN•si•BI•li•tee] *n* responsabilidad F

**responsible** [re•SPAHN•si•bl] *n* responsable

**rest 1** [rest] *n* descanso M; pausa F; *vt* descansar

**rest 2** *n* resto M; lo demás; los otros; *vi* quedar

**restaurant** [RES•tuh•rant] *n* restaurante M

**restful** [REST•fl] *adj* reposado

**restitution** [RE•sti•TOO•shn] *n* restitución F

**restless** [REST•les] *adj* intranquilo

**restlessness** [REST•les•nes] *n* inquietud F

**restoration** [RES•tu•RAI•shn] *n* restauración F

**restore** [re•STAUR] *vt* restaurar

**restrain** [re•STRAIN] *vt* refrenar

**restrict** [re•STRIKT] *vt* restringir

**restriction** [re•STRIK•shn] *n* restricción F

**result** [re•ZUHLT] *n* resultado M

**resume** [RE•zoo•MAI] *vt* reasumir

**resuscitate** [re•SUS•si•TAIT] *vt* resucitar

**retail** [REE•tail] *n* venta al por menor F

**retailer** [REE•tai•lur] *n* detallista F

**retaliate** [ree•TA•lee•AIT] *vi* desquitarse

**retaliation** [ree•TA•lee•AI•shn] *n* desquite M

**retard** [ree•TARD] *vt* retardar

**retinue** [RE•ti•NOO] *n* comitiva F

**retire** [ree•TUYR] *vi* retirarse

**retirement** [ree•TUYR•mint] *n* retiro M

**retort** [ree•TAURT] *n* retorta F

**retract** [ree•TRAKT] *vt* retractar

**retreat** [ree•TREET] *n* retirada F

**retrieve** [ree•TREEV] *vt* recuperar

**retroactive** [RE•tro•AK•tiv] *adj* retroactivo

**return** [ree•TURN] *vi* volver; *vt* devolver; *n* vuelta F; in ~ for\ a cambio de, many happy ~s\ ¡ficeiz cumpeaños!

**return address** [ree•TURN a•DRES] *n* señas del remitente

**returns** (election) [ree•TURNZ (ee•LEK•shn)] *vi* resultados

**reunion** [ree•YOO•nyun] *n* reunión F

**reunite** [REE•yoo•NUYT] *vt* reunir

**reveal** [ree•VEEL] *vt* revelar

**revelation** [RE•vi•LAI•shn] *n* revelación F

**revelry** [RE•vil•ree] *n* jarana F

**revenge** [ree•VENJ] *n* venganza F

**revenue** [RE•vi•NOO] *n* provento M

**revere** [re•VEER] *vt* reverenciar

**reverence** [RE•vur•ens] *n* reverencia F

**reverend** [RE•vur•end] *adj* reverendo

**reverent** [RE•vur•ent] *adj* reverente

**reverse** [re•VERS] *n* lo inverso M; *vt* invertir; *vi* dar marcha atrás (auto)

**revert** [re•VERT] *vt* revertir

**review** [re•VYOO] *vt* revista F

**revile** [re•VUYL] *vt* ultrajar

**revise** [re•VUYZ] *vt* revisar

**revision** [re•VI•shn] *n* revisión F

**revival** [re•VUY•vul] *n* reavivamento M

**revoke** [re•VOK] *vt* revocar

**revolt** [re•VOLT] *vi* rebelarse; sublevarse; *vt* dar asco a; *n* sublevación F

**revolution** [RE•vo•LOO•shn] *n* revolución F

**revolutionary** [RE•vo•LOO•shn•AI•ree] *adj* revolucionario

**revolve** [re•VOLV] *vi* voltear

**reward** [re•WAURD] *n* premio M; recompensa F; *vt* recompensar

**rewrite** [re•RUYT] *vt vi* refundir

**rhetoric** [RE•tau•rik] *n* retórica F

**rheumatism** [ROO•muh•TIZM] *n* reumatismo M

**rhinoceros** [ruy•NOS•rus] *n* rinoceronte M

**rhubarb** [ROO•barb] *n* ruibarbo M

**rhyme** [ruym] *n* rima F

**rhythm** [RI•thim] *n* ritmo M

**rib** *n* costilla F

**ribbon** [RI•bin] *n* cinta F

**rice** [ruyz] *n* arroz M

**rich** [rich] *adj* rico

**richness** [RICH•nes] *n* riqueza F

**rid** [rid] *vt* librar; get ~ of\ decharcerse de

**riddle** [RI•dl] *n* enigma F

**ride 1** [ruyd] *vi* cabalgar; montar (horseback); ir; *vt* motar a; ir en; cn ablagata F; paseo en coche M (auto)

**ride 2** (bicycle) *vi* viajar en bicicleta

**ride 3** (horseback) *vi* montar

**rider** [RUY•dur] *n* ciclista (f) caballero M

**ridge** [rij] *n* espinazo M

**ridicule** [RI•di•KYUL] *vi* ridiculizar

**ridiculous** [ri•DI•kyu•lus] *adj* ridículo

**rifle** [RUY•fl] *n* rifle M

**rig** *n* equipo M; *vt* aprarehar; ~
up\ improvisar

**right** [ruyt] *adj* derecha; exacto;
justo; bueno; *n* dereco M
(entitlement); be in the ~\
tener razón; on the ~\ a la
dercha; put ~\ rectificar; *vt*
enderezar; corregir

**right away** [ ~ a•WAI ] *adj*
inmediamente

**righteous** [RUY•chus] *adj* recto

**righteousness** [RUY•chus•nes]
*n* rectitud F

**right-hand** [RUYT•hand] *adj*
de la mano derecha F

**rigid** [RI•jid] *adj* rígido

**rigidity** [ri•JI•di•tee] *n* rigidez F

**rigor** [RI•gor] *n* rigidez F

**rim** *n* borde M

**rind** [ruynd] *n* corteza F

**ring 1** [ring] *n* circulo, arco;
anillo (on finger); sortija (w/
jewel) F; *vt* rodear

**ring 2** *n* toque; tinteo M;
llamada F (phone, coll); *vt*
tocar

**rink** *n* patinadero M

**rinse** [rins] *vt* aclarar

**rip** [rip] *vt* rasgar; *vi* rasgarse;
let ~\ soltar; ~ off\ robar
(coll)

**ripe** [ruyp] *adj* maduro

**ripple** [RI•pul] *n* onda F

**rise** [ruys] *vi* subir; levantase;
sublevarse (rebel); *n* subida F;
altura F (land); give ~ to\
ocasionar

**risk** *n* riesgo M

**rite** [ruyt] *n* rito M

**ritual** [RI•chu•ul] *n* ritual M

**rival** [RUY•vl] *n* opuesto M

**rivalry** [RUY•vl•ree] *n*
rivalidad F

**river** [RI•vur] *n* río M

**road** [rod] *n* camino M; calle F;
on the ~ \ en camino

**roam** [rom] *vi* vagar

**roar** [ror] *vi* rugir; *n* rugido M;
~ with laugher\ reírse a
carcajadas

**roast** [rost] *vt* asar; *vi* asase; *adj*
*n* asado M; ~ beef\ *n* rosbif
M

**rob** [rahb] *vt* robar

**robber** [RA•bur] *n* ladrón M

**robbery** [RA•bree] *n* robo M

**robe** [rob] *n* ropaje M

**robin** [RA•bin] *n* petirrojo M

**robust** [ro•BUST] *adj* robusto

**rock 1** [rahk] *n* roca F; peñasco
M (boulder); on the ~s\ con
hielo; be on the ~s\
(relationship, etc) andar mal

**rock 2** *vt* mecer; sacudir (shake)
*vi* meerse; sacudirse; *n* música
rock F

**rocket** [RAH•kit] *n* cohete M

**rocking chair** [RAH•king
CHAIR] *n* mecedora F

**rocky** [RAH•kee] *adj* rocoso

**rod** [rahd] *n* barra F

**role** [rol] *n* parte F

**roll** [rol] *vi* rollo M; *vt* hacer
rodar; enrollar; virodar; ~
over\ dar una vuelta; ~ up\
enrollar

**Roman** [RO•man] *adj* romano

**romance** [ro•MANS] *n*
romance M

**romantic** [ro•MAN•tik] *adj*
romántico

**romanticism**
[ro•MAN•ti•SIZM] *n*
romanticismo M

**romanticist** [ro•MAN•ti•sist] *n*
autor romántico M

**room** [room] *n* cuarto M;
habtación F

**roommate** [ROOM•mait] *n*
copañero de cuarto M

**roomy** [ROO•mee] *adj*
espacioso

**roost** *n* percha; *vi* descansar F

**root 1** *n* raíz F; take ~ echar
raices

**root 2** *vt vi* ~ about\ hurgar; ~
for\ alenrar (coll); ~ out\
extirpar

**rope** [rop] *n* cuerda F

**rosary** [RO•suh•ree] *n* rosario M

**rose** [roz] *n* rosa F

**rosy** [RO•zee] *adj* rosado

**rot** [raht] *vt* pudrirs; *vt* pudir; *n*
putrefacción

**rotary** [RO•tuh•ree] *n* rotario M

**rotation** [ro•TAI•shn] *n*
rotación F

**rote** [rot] *adj* rutina F

**rotten** [RAH•tin] *adj*
putrefracto

**rough** [ruhf] *adj* rugoso; áspero;
malo (bad) brutal (violent);
*adv* duro; *vt* ~ it\ vivr sin
comodiades

**roughen** [RUHF•in] *vi* poner
áspero

**rough estimate** [RUHF
E•sti•MAIT] *n* a ojo de buen
cubero M

**roughly** [RUHF•lee] *adv*
rudamente

**round** [rond] *adj* redondo; *n*
circulo M; *prep* alrededor de;
~ about\ aproximadamente

**rouse** [rowz] *vt* despertar

**route** [root] *n* ruta F

**routine** [roo•TEEN] *n* rutina F

**row 1** [ro] *n* fila F

**row 2** *n* paseo; *vi* remar

**row 3** [rau] *n* ruido M; pelea F;
*vi* pelearse

**rubber** [RUH•bur] *n* goma F

**rubbish** [RUH•bish] *n* basura F

**rubble** [RUH•bl] *n* ripio M

**rub-down** [RUHB•doun] *vt*
frotar de arriba abajo

**ruby** [ROO•bee] *n* rubí M

**rudder** [RUH•dur] *n* timón M

**rude** [rood] *adj* rudo

**rueful** [ROO•ful] *adj* lamentable

**ruffian** [RUH•fee•in] *n* hombre
brutal M

**ruffle** [RUH•fl] *n* lechuguilla F

**rug** [ruhg] *n* alfrombra F

**rugged** [RUH•gid] *adj* rugoso

**ruin** [ROO•in] *n* ruina F

**rule** [rool] *n* regla F; costumbre
F (custom); domino M (gov);
as a ~\ por regla general; *vt*
gobernar; dominar; decretar; ~
out\ *vt* descartar; decidir
(decide)

**rum** *n* ron M

**rumble** [RUHM•bl] *vi* retumbar

**ruminate** [ROO•mi•NAIT] *vt*
rumiar

**rumor** [ROO•mur] *n* rumor M;
*vt* se dice que

**rump** [ruhmp] *n* obispillo M

**rumple** [RUHM•pl] *vt* arrugar

**run** [ruhn] *vi* correr; funcionar;
correrse (pol); *vt* tener
(house); in the long ~\ a la
larga; a ta ~\ corriendo; ~
across\ toparse con; ~ away\
escaparse; ~ down\ baja

corriendo; *vt* atropellar (auto);
~ out of\ quedar sin
**runaway 1** [RUHN•a•WAI] *n*
fugitivo M
**runaway 2** *vi* huir
**run-down** [run•doun] *adj* bajar
corriendo
**runner** [RUH•nur] *n* corredor
M; ~-up\ segundo sub
campeón
**running** [RUH•ning] *n*
carrera F
**runt** [ruhnt] *n* enano M
**rupture** [RUHP•chur] *vi*
rompersen ruptura F

**rural** [RUR•uhl] *adj* rural
**ruse** [rooz] *n* ardid M
**rush** [ruhsh] *vi* arrojarse
**rush-hour** [RUSH OUR] *n* hora
punta F
**russet** [RUH•sit] *adj* bermejo M
**Russia** [RUH•sha] *n* Rusia
**Russian** [RUH•shin] *adj* ruso
**rust** [ruhst] *n* moho M; *vt*
oxidar; *vi* oxidarse
**rustic** [RUH•stik] *adj* rústico
**rusty** [RUH•stee] *adj* mohoso
**rut** [ruht] *n* brama F
**ruthless** [ROOTH•les] *adj* cruel
**rye** [ruy] *n* centeno M

# S

**Sabbath** [SA•beth] *n* día de
descanso M
**saber** [SAI•bur] *n* sable M
**sabotage** [SA•bo•TAJ] *n*
sabotaje M
**sack** [sak] *n* saco M; get the ~\
ser despedido (coll); *vt*
despedir (coll)
**sacrament** [SA•kra•mint] *n*
sacramento M
**sacred** [SAI•krid] *adj* sagrado
**sacrifice** [SA•kri•FUYS] *n*
sacrificio M
**sad** *adj* triste
**sadden** [SA•din] *vt* entristecer
**saddle** [SAD•dl] *n* silla F
**sadistic** [sa•DIS•tik] *adj* sádico
**sadness** [SAD•nes] *n* tristeza F
**safe** [saif] *adj* salvo; seguro

**safely** [SAIF•lee] *adv*
seguramente
**safety** [SAIF•tee] *n* seguridad F
**safety pin** [SAFE•tee PIN] *n*
imperdible M
**saffron** [SA•frahn] *n* azafrán M
**sag** *vi* combar
**sagacious** [sa•GAI•shus] *adj*
sagaz
**sagacity** [sa•GA•si•tee] *n*
sagacidad F
**sage** [saij] *n* salvia F
**sail** *vi* navegar
**sailboat** [SAIL•bot] *n* buque de
vela M
**sailing** [SAI•ling] *n* náutica F
**sailor** [SAI•lur] *n* marinero M
**saint** *n* santo M
**saintly** [SAINT•lee] *adj*
santamente

**sake** [saik] *n* causa F

**salad** [SA•lid] *n* ensalada F

**sale** [sauil] *n* venta F; liquidación F; for ~\ se vende; on ~\ en venta

**salt** [salt] *n* sal F; *adj* salado; *vt* salar

**same** [saim] *adj* igual; ~ as\ igual que; mismo (que); (before noun) at the ~ time\ al mismo tiemp; *pron* the ~\ el mismo; la misma; los mismos; las mismas; do the ~ as\ hacer como; *adv* the ~\ de las misma manera; all the ~\ de todas formas

**sample** [SAM•pul] *n* mestra F; *vt* probar

**sand** [sand] *n* arena F; *vt* enarernar; ~s *npl* \ playa F

**sandwich** [SAND•wich] *n* bocadillo; sandwich M

**sane** [sain] *adj* cuerdo; razonable (act)

**sanely** [SAIN•lee] *adv* sensatamente

**sanitary** [SAN•i•TAIR•ee] *adj* higienico; santiario

**sanity** [SAN•it•ee] *n* cordura; F sensatez F

**Santa Claus** [SAN•tah KLAUZ] *n* Papá Noel M

**sap** [sap] *n* savia F; *vt* agotar

**sapphire** [SA•fuyr] *n* zafiro M

**sarcasm** [sar•KA•zum] *n* sarcasmo M; *adj* sarcástico

**satire** [SA•tuyr] *n* satira F

**satisfaction** [SA•tis•FAK•shun] *n* satisfacción

**satisfy** [SA•tis•FUY] *vt* satisfacer

**saturate** [SA•chu•RAIT] *vt* saturar empapar

**Saturday** [SA•tur•dai] *n* sábado

**sauce** [saus] *n* salsa F

**saucer** [SAU•sur] *n* platillo

**saunter** [SAUN•ter] *vi* deambular; pasearse

**sausage** [SAU•sej] *n* salchicha F

**savage** [SA•vej] *adj* salvaje; feroz; rabioso; *n* salvaje MF; *vt* atacar

**save** [saiv]; *vt* salvar; ahorrar (money, time); evitar (prevent); *n* parada F (sport); *prep* salvo, con excepción de

**savings** [SAI•vingz] *npl* ahorros M

**savior** [SAI•vyur] *n* salvador M

**savor** [say•vor] *n* sabor M; *vt* saborear

**saw** [sau] *n* sierra F; *vt* serrar

**say** [sai] *vt vi* decir; rezar; *n* have a ~\ expresar una opinión; have no ~ \ no tenr ni voz ni voto

**scab** [skab] *n* costra F

**scale 1** [skail] *n* escala F

**scale 2** *vt* escalar; ~ down\ reducir

**scan** [skan] *vt* escudriñar; echar un vistazo a; *vi* estar bien medil

**scandal** [SKAN•dal] *n* escándalo M; chismorreo M (gossip)

**Scandinavia** [SKAN•di•NAI•vee•uh] *n* Escandinavia; F

**Scandinavian** [SKAN•di•NAI•vee•uhn] *adj* *n* escandinavio

**scar** [skahr] *n* cicatriz F

**scarab** [SKA•rub] *n* escarabajo M

**scarce** [skairz] *adj* raro

**scare** [skair] *vt* asustar

**scarf** [skahrf] *n* bufanda F

**scarlet** [SKAHR•let] *n* de color escarlata M

**scary** [SKAIR•ee] *adj* medroso

**scathe** [skaith] *vt* perjudicar

**scatter** [SKA•tur] *vt* dispersar

**scavenger** [SKA•ven•jur] *n* basurero M

**scene** [seen] *n* esquema F; *n* escena F

**scenario** [suh•NAI•ree•o] *n* esquema F

**scenery** [SEE•nur•ee] *n* paisaje M

**scent** [sent] *n* olor M; perfume: *vt* presentir

**scepter** [SEP•tur] *n* cetro M

**schedule** [SKE•djool] *n* programa F; horario M (timetable; Behind ~\ con tetraso; on ~\ sin retraso; *vt* proyectar

**scheme** [skeem] *n* proyector M; *vi* hacer proyectos

**schist** [shist] *n* esquito M

**schism** [skizm] *n* cisma M

**scholar** [SKAH•lur] *n* escolar M

**scholarly** [SKAH•lur•lee] *adj* erudito

**scholarship** [SKAH•lur•ship] *n* erudicíon F

**scholastic** [sko•LAS•tik] *adj* escolástico

**school** [skool] *n* escuela F; facultad F; *adj* escolar; *vt* enseñar; ~ boy\ *n* colegial M,

~ girl\ *n* colegia F; *n* instrucción; ~ master/teacher\ *n* maestro; profesor M

**schooner** [SKOO•nur] *n* goleta F

**science** [SUY•enz] *n* ciencia F

**scientific** [SUY•yen•TI•fik] *adj* científico

**scientist** [SUY•yen•tist] *n* hombre de ciencia M

**scissors** [SI•surz] *n* tijeras

**scoff** [skoff] *n* mofa F

**scold** [skold] *vt* reñir

**scolding** [SKOL•ding] *n* regaño M

**sconce** [skahnz] *n* pantalia F

**scone** [skoan] *n* bizcocho M

**scoop** [skoop] *vt* cucharón F; *vt* ~ out\ excavar; ~ up\ recoger

**scope** [skoap] *n* alcance M

**scorch** [skorch] *vt* socarrar

**score** [skor] *n* cuenta F

**scorn** [skorn] *vt* desdeñar

**scorpion** [SKOR•pee•in] *n* escorpión F

**Scot** [skaht] *n* escocés M

**Scotland** [SKAHT•lind] *n* Escocia

**scoundrel** [SKOUN•drul] *n* bribón M

**scour** [skour] *vt* fregar

**scourge** [skurj] *n* azote M

**scout** [skout] *n* batidor M

**scowl** [skoul] *vt* expresar con el ceño

**scramble** [SKRAM•bl] *vt* gatea; ~ for\ pelearse para obtcer; *vt* revolver (eggs)

**scrap** [skrap] *n* fragmento M; *vt* desechar

**scrape** [skraip] *vt* raspar

**scraper** [SKRAI•pur] *n*
raspador M

**scratch** [skratch] *vt* rascadura F;
*n* raya F; Start from ~\
empezar sin nada; up to ~\ al
nivel requerido

**scrawl** [skraul] *vt* garabatear; *n*
garrapato

**scream** [skreem] *vi* gritar; *n*
grito M

**screech** [skreech] *vt* chillido M

**screen** [skreen] *n* pantalla F

**screw** [skroo] *vt* tornillo M

**screw-driver**
[SKROO•DRUY•vur] *n*
destornillador M

**scribble** [SKRIB•bl] *vt*
garrapatear

**scribe** [skruyb] *n* escribiente M

**script** [skript] *n* letra escritura F

**scripture** [SKRIP•chur] *n*
Sagrada Escritura F

**scroll** [skroll] *n* rollo M

**scrub** [skrub] *vt* fregar

**scruff** [skruf] *n* nuca F

**scruple** [SKROO•pl] *n*
escrúpulo M

**scrupulous** [SKROO•pyu•lus]
*adj* escrupuloso

**scrutinize** [SKROO•ti•NUYZ]
*vt* escrutar

**scrutiny** [SKROO•ti•nee] *n*
esrutinio M

**sculptor** [SKULP•tur] *n* escultor

**sculpture** [SKULP•tyur] *n*
escultura F

**scum** [skuhm] *n* espuma F

**scurrilous** [SKUR•ri•les] *adj*
chabacano

**scurry** [SKUR•ree] *vi* echar a
correr

**scythe** [suyth] *n* guadaña F

**sea** [see] *n* mar M; at ~\ en el
mar; by ~\ por mar

**seal 1** [seel] *n* sello M; *vt* sellar;
~ off\ acordonar

**seal 2** *n* foca F

**seam** [seem] *n* costura F

**seamstress** [SEEM•stres] *n*
costurera F

**sear** [seer] *vt* secar

**search** [surch] *vt* buscar; *n*
busqueda F; in ~ of\ en busca
de

**search warrant** [SURCH
WAHR•rent] *n* orden de
registro domiciliario M

**seasick** [SEE•sik] *adj* mareado

**season** [SEE•zon] *n* estación F;
*vt* sazonar

**seasonable** [SEE•zun•uh•bl]
*adj* tempestivo

**seasoning** [SEE•zun•ning] *n*
sazonamiento M

**seat** [seet] *n* asiento M; take a
~\ sentarse; *vt* sentar

**secede** [se•SEED] *vt* separarse

**secession** [se•SES•shn] *n*
secesión F

**seclude** [se•KLOOD] *vt* apartar

**seclusion** [se•KLOO•shn] *n*
retraimiento M

**second** [SE•kund] *adj* segundo

**secondary** [SE•kun•DAI•ree]
*adj* secundario

**second-hand** [SE•kund•HAND]
*adj* de segunda mano

**secondly** [SE•kund•lee] *adv* en
segundo lugar

**second-rate** [SE•kund•RAIT]
*adj* de segunda clase

secrecy [SEE•kruh•scc] *n*
secreto M

secret [SEE•kret] *n* secreto M

secretary [SE•kre•TAI•ree] *n*
secretario M

secrete [se•KREET] *vt* secretar

secretion [se•KREE•shn] *n*
secreción F

secretive [SE•kreh•tiv] *adj*
callado

sect [sekt] *n* sccta F

sectarian [sek•TAI•ree•in] *adj*
sectario

section [SEK•shun] *n* sección F

sector [SEK•tor] *n* sector M

secular [SE•kyu•lur] *adj* secular

secularize [SE•kyu•la•RUYZ]
*vt* secularizar

secure [se•KYUR] *vt* asegurar

security [se•KYU•ri•tee] *n*
seguridad F

sedan [se•DAN] *n* sedán M

sedate [se•DAIT] *adj* sereno

sedative [SE•duh•tiv] *n*
sedativo M

sedentary [SE•din•TAI•ree] *adj*
sedentario

sediment [SE•di•mint] *n*
sedimento M

sedition [se•DI•shn] *n*
sedimentación F

seditious [se•DI•shus] *adj*
sedicioso

seduce [se•DOOS] *vt* seducir

seducer [se•DOO•sur] *n*
seductor M

seduction [se•DUK•shn] *n*
seducción F

seductive [sc•DUK•tiv] *adj*
seductivo

see 1 [see] *vi* ver; comprender
(understand); notar (notice); ~
you later!\ ¡hasta luego!; ~
about\ ocuparse de; ~ off\
despedirse de

see 2 [see] *n* diócesis F

seed *n* semilla F; go to ~ granar

seek *vt* buscar

seem *vi* parecer

seep *vt* filtrar

seer [SEE•ur] *n* profeta F

seesaw [SEE•sau] *n*
columpio M

seethe [seeth] *vt* hervir

segment [SEG•ment] *n*
scgmento M

segregate [SE•gruh•GAIT] *vt*
segregar

seize [seez] *vt* coger; confiscar

seizure [SEE•shur] *n*
aprehensión F

seldom [SEL•dum] *adv*
raramente

select [se•LEKT] *vt* escoger;
seleccionar; *adj* selecto;
exclusivo

selection [se•LEK•shn] *n*
selección F

selective [se•LEK•tiv] *adj*
selectivo

self *n* yo; si mismo

self-centered [SELF•SEN•turd]
*adj* concentrado en sí mismo

self-confident
[SELF•KAHN•fi•dint] *adj*
seguro de sí mismo

self-conscious
[SELF•KAHN•shus] *adj*
consciente dc sí mismo

self-control [SELF•kun•TROL]
*adj* dominio de sí mismo

**self-defense** [SELF•di•FENS]
*n* defensa propia F

**selfish** [SEL•fish] *adj* egoísta F

**selfishness** [SEL•fish•nis] *n*
egoísmo M

**self-respect** [SELF•ree•SPEKT]
*n* respeto de sí mismo M

**self-taught** [SELF•TAUT] *adj*
autodidacto

**sell** *vt* vender; *vi* venderse; *n*
feca de caducidad

**semblance** [SEM•blenz] *n*
semejanza F

**semiannual** [SE•mee•AN•yul]
*adj* semestral

**semicolon** [se•mee•KO•lun] *n*
punto y coma M

**seminary** [SE•mi•NAI•ree] *n*
seminario M

**senate** [SE•nit] *n* senado M

**senator** [SE•ni•tur] *n*
senador M

**send** [send] *vi* mandar; enviar;
~ way\ despidir; ~ away for\
pedir; ~ for\ enviar a buscar;
~ off\ *n* despedida F

**sender** [SEN•dur] *n* remitente M

**senile** [SEE•nuyl] *adj* senil

**senility** [se•NI•li•tee] *n*
senectud F

**senior** [SEE•nyur] *n* mayor M

**seniority** [seen•YAUR•i•tee] *n*
mayor edad M

**sensations** [sen•SAI•shns] *n*
sensación F

**sense 1** [senz] *n* sentido M;
make ~\ *vt* tener sentido;
make ~ of\ comprender

**sense 2** (common) *n* sentido
común M

**senseless** [SENS•les] *adj*
insensible

**sensibility** [SENS•i•BI•li•tee] *n*
sensibilidad F

**sensible** [SEN•si•bl] *adj*
sensible

**sensitive** [SEN•si•tiv] *adj*
sensitivo

**sensitivity** [SEN•si•TI•vi•tee] *n*
sensibilidad F

**sensual** [SEN•shu•al] *adj*
sensual

**sentence** [SEN•tins] *n* oración
F; death ~\ *n* condena
perpetual F

**sentiment** [SEN•ti•mint] *n*
sentimiento M

**sentimentality**
[SEN•ti•men•TA•li•tee] *n*
sentimentalismo M

**sentinel** [SEN•ti•nel] *n*
centinela F

**separable** [SE•pruh•bl] *adj*
separable

**separate 1** [SEP•ret] *adj*
separado; independiente

**separate 2** [SE•puh•RAIT] *vt*
separar; *vi* separarse; *n*
separación F

**separately** [SE•prit•lee] *adv*
separadamente

**separation** [SE•puh•RAI•shn] *n*
separación F

**separatism** [SE•pruh•TI•zim] *n*
disidencia F

**September** [sep•TEM•bur] *n*
septiembre

**septic** [SEP•tik] *adj* séptico

**sepulcher** [SE•pul•kur] *n*
sepulcro M

**sequel** [SEE•kwel] *n* secuela F

**sequence** [SEE•kwens] *n*
serie F

**sequester** [see•KWES•tur] *vt*
secuestrar

**sequestration**
[SEE•kwes•TRAI•shɪɪ] *n*
secuestro M

**serenade** [SAIR•uh•NAID] *n*
serenata F

**serene** [suh•REEN] *adj* sereno

**serenity** [suh•RE•ni•tee] *n*
serenidad F

**sergeant** [SAR•jint] *n*
sargento M

**serial** [SEE•rec•ul] *n* seria F

**series** [SEE•reez] *n* seria F

**serious** [SEE•ree•us] *adj* serio

**seriously** [SEE•ree•us•lee] *adv*
seriamente

**seriousness** [SEE•ree•us•nes] *n*
seriedad F

**sermon** [SUR•min] *n* sermón M

**serpent** [SUR•pint] *n*
serpiente M

**serum** [SEER•uhm] *n* suero M

**servant 1** [SUR•vint] *n*
sirviente M

**servant 2** (civil) *n* siervo M

**serve** [surv] *vt* servir; ~\ servid
de; ~ purpose\ servir para el
caso; *n* saque M (tennis)

**service** [SUR•vis] *n* servico M;
*vt* revisar

**serviceable** [SUR•vi•suh•bl]
*adj* servible

**servile** [SUR•vuyl] *adj* servil

**servitude** [SUR•vi•TOOD] *n*
servidumbre M

**session** [SE•shun] *n* sesión F

**set** *n vt* poner; *vi* ponerse; *n*
serie F; colección F; *adj* fijo;

*n* decorado (thea); ~ about\ *vi*
*vt* empezar a; ~ back\
retardar; ~ off *vi* salr; *vt* ~
out\ poner en marcha; hacer
estallar; · the table\ poner la
mesa; ~ up\ *vt* establecer

**setting** [SET•ting] *n* escenario
M (thea); puesta F (sun);
engaste M (jewel)

**settle** [SET•tl] *vi* colocar; *vt*
areglar; *vi* posarse; ~down\
calmarse; ~ for\ aceptar; ~
up\ ajustar cuentas

**settlement** [SET•tl•mint] *n*
establecimiento M

**seven** [SE•vin] *num* siete

**seventeen** [SE•vin•TEEN] *num*
diecisiete

**seventeenth**
[SE•vin•TEENTH] *num*
decimoséptimo

**seventh** [SE•vinth] *num*
séptimo

**seventieth** [SE•vin•tee•eth]
*num* septuagésimo

**seventy** [SE•vin•tee] *num*
setenta

**sever** [SE•vur] *vt* partir

**several** [SE•vur•uhl] *adj* varios

**severe** [se•VEER] *adj* severo

**sew** [so] *vt* coser

**sewer** [SOO•ur] *n* cloaca F

**sewing** [SO•ing] *n* costura F

**sewing machine** [SO•ing
muh•SHEEN] *n* máquina de
coser F

**sex** [seks] *n* sexo M

**sexton** [SEKS•tin] *n* sacristán M

**sexual** [SEK•shoo•uhl] *adj*
sexual

**shabby** [SHA•bee] *adj* gastado

**shack** [shak] *n* casucha F
**shackle** [SHA•kl] *n* grillo M
**shad** *n* sábalo M
**shade** [shaid] *n* sombra F
**shadow** [SHA•do] *n* sombra F
**shaft** [shaft] *n* astil M; rayo M (light)
**shake** [shaik] *vt* sacudir; agitar; ~ hands with\ estrechar la mano a; *vi* tremblar
**shallow** [SHAL•lo] *adj* poco profundo
**sham** [sham] *n* farsa F; impostor M; *adj* falso; *vt* fingir
**shame** [shaim] *n* vergüenza; what a ~ !\ ¡qulastima!; *vt* avergonzar
**shampoo** [sham•POO] *n* champú
**shape** [shaip] *n* forma F; *vt* formar; determinar; *vi* fomarse; ~ up\ prometer
**share** [shair] *n* porción; F *vi* particpar; ~ in\ particpar en
**shark** [shark] *n* tiburón M
**sharp** [sharp] *adj* afilado; puntiagudo; *adv* en punto; *n* sotenido M (mus)
**shatter** [SHA•tur] *vt* hacer añicos; perturbar; *vi* hacerce añicos
**shave** [shaiv] *vt* afeitar; *vi* afeitarse; *n* afeitado M
**she** *pron* ella; *n* hembra F
**shear** [sheer] *vt* esquilar
**shed 1** [shed] *n* cobertizo M
**shed 2** *vt* perder; derramar
**sheet** [sheet] *n* sábna F; hoga F (paper)
**shelf** [shelf] *n* estate M

**shell** [shel] *n* concha F; *vt* desgranar
**shelter** [SHEL•tur] *n* reugio; abrigo M; *vt* abrigar; dar asilo a *vi* abrigarse
**shield** [sheeld] *n* escudo M; *vt* proteger
**shift** [shift] *vt* cambiar; cambiar de sito; *n* cambio M
**shine** [shuyn] *vi* brillar; *vt* scar brillo; *n* brillo M
**ship** [ship] *n* buque; barco; *vt* transportar; enviar
**shirt** [shurt] *n* camisa F
**shiver** [SHI•vur] *vi* temblar
**shock** [shahk] *n* choque M; *vt* escandilizar
**shoddy** [SHAH•dee] *n* falso
**shoe** [shoo] *n* zapato M
**shoelace** [SHOO•lais] *n* cordón de zapato M
**shoemaker** [SHOO•MAI•kur] *n* zapatero M
**shoot** *vt* fusilar
**shooter** [SHOO•tur] *n* tirador M
**shooting** [SHOO•ting] *n* tiro M
**shop** [shahp] *n* v tienda F; talk ~\ hablar de su trabajo; *vi* hacer compras; *n* comprador M
**shopkeeper** [SHAHP•KEE•pur] *n* tendero M
**shopper** [SHAH•pur] *n* comprador M
**shopping** [SHAH•ping] *n* compras F; go ~\ *vi* ir de compras
**shore** [shaur] *n* orilla F
**short** [shaurt] *adj* corto; bajo (person); a ~ time ago\ hace poco; be ~ of\ necesitar; in ~\ en resumen

**shortage** [SHAUR•tij] *n* falta F
**shortcoming** [SHAURT•KUH•ming] *n* defecto M
**shortcut** [SHAURT•kut] *n* atajo M
**shorten** [SHAUR•tin] *vt* acortar
**shortening** [SHAURT•ning] *n* manteca F
**shorthand** [SHAURT•hand] *n* taquigrafía F
**shortly** [SHAURT•lee] *adv* brevemente
**shot** [shaht] *n* tiro M; foto M (photog)
**shotgun** [SHAHT•gun] *n* escopeta de caza F
**should** [shud] *aux* deber; if he ~ come\ si viniese
**shoulder** [SHOL•dur] *n* hombro M; *vt* cargar con (responsibility); llevar a hombros (carry)
**shout** *vi* gritar; *n* grito M
**shove** [shuhv] *vt* empujar
**shovel** [SHUH•vl] *n* pala F
**show** [sho] *vi* mostrar; *n* demonstración F; exposición F; on ~\ expuesto; ~ up\ *vi* destacar
**shower** [SHOU•ur] *n* ducha F
**showy** [SHO•ee] *adj* vistoso
**shred** *vt* desgarrar; *n* pedazo M
**shrew** [shroo] *n* arpía F
**shrewd** [shrood] *adj* sagaz
**shrewish** [SHROO•ish] *adj* regañon
**shriek** [shreek] *n* chillido M
**shrike** [shruyk] *n* alcaudón M
**shrill** [shril] *adj* estridente
**shrimp** *n* camarón M

**shrine** [shruyn] *n* urna F
**shrink** *vt* disminuir
**shrinkage** [SHRIN•kij] *n* encogimiento M
**shrivel** [SHIRI•vll] *vt* arrugar
**shroud** *n* mortaja F; *vt* amortajar
**Shrove Tuesday** [SHROV TOOZ•dai] *n* martes de carneval M
**shrub** *n* arbusto M
**shrubbery** [SHRUB•bur•ee] *n* arbustos
**shrunk** *adj* encogado
**shudder** [SHUH•dur] *vi* temblar
**shuffle** [SHUH•fl] *vi* barajar
**shun** *vt* evitar
**shunt** *vt* desvío M
**shut** *vt* cerrar
**shutter** [SHUH•dur] *n* cerrador M
**shuttle** [SHUH•tl] *v* lanzadera F
**shy** [shuy] *adj* tímido
**shyness** [SHUY•nis] *n* timidez F
**sibyl** [SI•bil] *n* sibila F
**sick** [sik] *adj* enfermo
**sicken** [SI•kin] *vi* enfermar
**sickening** [SIK•ning] *adj* nauseabundo
**sickle** [SI•kil] *n* segur M
**sickly** [SIK•lee] *adj* enfermizo
**sickness** [SIK•nis] *n* enfermedad F
**side** [suyd] *n* lado M
**sideboard** [SUYD•baurd] *n* copero M
**sidetrack** [SUYD•trak] *n* apartadero M
**sidewalk** [SUYD•walk] *n* acera F

**sideways** [SUYD•waiz] *adj*
de lado

**siding** [SUY•ding] *n* adhesión a
un partido F

**siege** [seej] *n* sitio M

**sieve** [siv] *n* cedazo M

**sift** *vt* tamizar

**sigh** [suy] *vi* suspirar

**sight** [suyt] *n* vista F

**sightseeing** [SUYT•SEE•ing] *n*
turismo M

**sign** [suyn] *n* signo M

**signal** [SIG•nuhl] *n* señal M

**signalize** [SIG•nuh•LUYZ] *vi*
señalar

**signature** [SIG•nuh•CHUR] *n*
firma F

**signet** [SIG•nit] *n* sello M

**significance** [sig•NI•fi•kenz] *n*
importancia F

**significant** [sig•NI•fi•kent] *adj*
significante

**signify** [SIG•ni•FUY] *vt*
significar

**silence** [SUY•lens] *n* silencio M

**silencer** [SUY•len•sur] *n*
selenciador M

**silently** [SUY•lent•lee] *adv*
silenciosamente

**silhouette** [SIL•o•WET] *n*
silueta F

**silk** *n* seda F

**silken** [SILK•in] *adj* de seda

**sill** *n* umbral M

**silly** [SIL•lee] *adj* tonto

**silt** *n* sedimento M

**silver** [SIL•vur] *n* plata F

**silversmith** [SIL•vur•smith] *n*
platero M

**silverware** [SIL•vur•WAIR] *n*
plata labrada F

**similar** [SI•mi•lur] *adj* similar

**similarly** [SI•mi•lur•lee] *adv*
semejantemente

**similitude** [si•MI•li•TOOD] *n*
similitud F

**simmer** [SIM•mur] *vt* hervir

**simple** [SIM•pl] *adj* simple

**simpleton** [SIM•pl•tin] *n*
simplón M

**simplicity** [sim•PLI•ci•tee] *n*
simplicidad F

**simplification**
[SIM•pli•fi•KAI•shn] *n*
simplificación F

**simplify** [SIM•pli•FUY] *vt*
simplificar

**simulate** [SIM•yoo•LAIT] *vt*
simular

**simultaneous**
[SUY•muhl•TAI•nee•us] *adj*
simultáneo

**sin** *n* pecado M

**since** [sins] *adv* desde

**sincere** [sin•SEER] *adj* sincero

**sincerity** [sin•SAIR•i•tee] *n*
sinceridad F

**sinew** [SI•noo] *n* tendón M

**sing** [sing] *vi* cantar

**singe** [sinj] *vt* socarrar

**single** [SIN•gl] *adj* solo único

**single-handed**
[SIN•gl•HAN•did] *adj* manco

**singular** [SIN•gyu•lur] *adj*
singular

**sinister** [SI•ni•stur] *adj* siniestro

**sink** *vi* hundir; *n* fregadero M

**sinker** [SINK•kur] *n* plomo M

**sinless** [sin•les] *adj* puro

**sinner** [SIN•nur] *n* pecador M

**sinus** [SUY•nis] *n* seno M

**sip** *vt* beber a sorbos

**siphon** [SUY•fuhn] *n* sifón M

**sir** [sur] *n* señor

**sire** [suyr] *n* señor

**siren** [SUY•rin] *n* sirena F

**sirloin** [SUR•loin] *n*
solomillo M

**sister** [SIS•tur] *n* hermana F

**sister-in-law** [-in•LAU] *n*
cuñada F

**sit** *vi* sentar; asentar; *vi* sentarse;
~ up\ *vi* enderzarse

**site** [suyt] *n* sitio M

**sitting** [SIT•ting] *n* asentada F

**sitting-room** *n* sala F

**situate** [SI•choo•WAIT] *vt*
situado

**situation** [SI•choo•WAI•shn] *n*
situación F

**six** [siks] *num* seis

**sixteen** [siks•TEEN] *num*
dieciseis

**sixteenth** [siks•TEENTH] *num*
décimosexto

**sixth** [siksth] *num* sexto

**sixtieth** [SIKS•tee•ith] *adj*
sexagésimo

**sixty** [SIKS•tee] *num* sesenta

**size** [suyz] *n* medida F; *vt* ~ up\
juzgar

**sizzle** [SI•zul] *vi* freírse

**skate 1** [skait] *vi* patinar; *vi*
patinar

**skate 2** (ice) *n* patín M

**skate 3** (roller) *vi n* patín de
ruedas M

**skein** [skain] *n* madeja F

**skeleton** [SKEL•i•tin] *n*
esqueleto M

**skeptic** [SKEP•tik] *adj*
escéptico

**sketch** *n* boceto M

**skewer** [SKYOO•ur] *n*
brocheta F

**ski** [skee] *vi* esquiar; *n*
esquidor M

**skid** *vi* calzo M

**skill** [skil] *n* habilidad F

**skilled** [skild] *adj*
experimentado

**skillet** [SKI•lit] *n* cazo M

**skillful** [SKIL•ful] *adj* diestro

**skim** *vt* desnatar

**skin** *n* piel M; *vt* despellejar;
pelar

**skin-deep** [SKIN•DEEP] *adj*
superficial

**skinflint** [SKIN•flint] *n* avaro M

**skinny** [SKI•nee] *adj* flaco

**skip** *vi* brincar M; *vi* saltar; *n*
salto M

**skipper** [SKIP•pur] *n* saltador M

**skirt** [skurt] *n* falda F; *vt* rodear

**skit** *n* parodia F

**skittish** [SKI•tish] *adj*
asustadizo

**skulk** *vi* esconderse

**skull** [skul] *n* cráneo M

**skunk** *n* mofeta F

**sky** [skuy] *n* cielo M

**skylight** [SKUY•luyt] *n* luz del
cielo F

**skyscraper** [SKUY•SKRAI•pur]
*n* rascacielos M

**slab** *n* tabia F

**slack** [slak] *adj* flojo

**slacken** [SLAK•kin] *vt* aflojar

**slacker** [SLAK•kur] *n*
indolente M

**slag** *vi* grasa F

**slam** *vt* soltar; ~ the door\ dar
un portazo; *vi* cerrarse de
golpe; *n* golpe M

**slander** [SLAN•dur] *n* difamación F

**slang** [slang] *n* jerga F

**slant** *n* sesgo M; *vt* inclinar; presentar con parcialidad (information)

**slap** *n* palmada F

**slash** *vt* acuchillar

**slat** *n* tabililla F

**slate** [slait] *n* pizarra F

**slattern** [SLA•turn] *adj* descuidado

**slaughter** [SLAU•tur] *vt* matar

**slave** [slaiv] *n* esclavo M

**slavish** [SLAI•vish] *adj* servil

**slaw** [slau] *n* ensalada de col picada F

**slay** [slai] *vi* matar

**sledge** [slej] *n* trineo M

**sleek** *adj* liso

**sleep** *vi* dormir; *n* sueño; go to ~\ dormirse

**sleeper** [SLEE•pur] *n* durmiente M

**sleepiness** [SLEE•pee•nis] *n* somnolencia F

**sleeping** [SLEE•ping] *adj* durmiente

**sleepless** [SLEEP•les] *adj* insomne

**sleepy** [SLEE•pee] *adj* soñoliento'

**sleet** *n* agaunieve F

**sleeve** [sleev] *n* manga F

**sleigh** [slai] *n* trineo' M

**sleight** [sluyt] *n* destreza F

**sleuth** [slooth] *n* sabueso M

**slice** [sluys] *n* rebanada F; *vt* cortar; rebanar

**slick** [slik] *adj* diestro

**slicker** [SLI•kur] *n* alisador M

**slide** [sluyd] *vi* resbalar

**slight** [sluyt] *adj* ligero

**slightly** [SLUYT•lee] *adj* ligeramente

**slim** *adj* delgado

**slime** [sluym] *n* baba F

**sling** [sling] *n* honda F

**slink** *vi* escurrirse

**slip** *n* resbalón M

**slipper** [SLIP•pur] *n* zapatilla F

**slippery** [SLIP•pree] *adj* resbaladizo

**slit** *n* abertura F

**slither** [SLI•thur] *vi* bajar

**sliver** [SLI•vur] *n* raja F

**slobber** [SLAH•bur] *vi* babar

**slogan** [SLO•gen] *n* frase F

**sloop** *n* balandra F

**slop** [slahp] *n* lodo blando M

**slope** [slop] *n* bajada F

**small** [small] *adj* pequeño

**smart** [smart] *adj* elegante; inteligente; *vi* escocer; *vi* arreglarse

**smash** [smash] *vt* romper; hacer pedazos; *vi* romperse

**smell** [smel] *n* olor; *vt vi* oler

**smile** [smuyl] *n* sonrisa F; *vi* sonreírse

**smoke** [smok] *n* humo M; *vt vi* fumar

**snack** [snak] *n* tentempié M

**snail** [snayul] *n* caracol M

**snake** [snaik] *n* serpiente F

**snap** [snap] *vt* romper; *vi* romperse; ~ at\ intentar morder; *n* chasquido M

**snare** [snayr] *n* trampa F

**sneak** [sneek] *n* solpón M; *vi* ~ entrar furtivamente; ~ out\ salir furtivamente

**sneer** [sneer] *n* sonrisa de
desprecio

**sneeze** [sneez] *n* estorundo M;
*vi* estorundar

**sniff** [snif] *vt* oler; *vi* aspirar por
la nariz

**snort** *vt* resoplar

**snout** *n* trompa F

**snow** [sno] *n* nieve F

**snowball** [SNO•bahl] *n* bola de
nieve F

**snowdrift** [SNO•drift] *n* nieve
acumulada F

**snowfall** [SNO•fahl] *n* nevada F

**snowflake** [SNO•flaik] *n* copo
de nieve M

**snowplow** [SNO•plou] *n*
limpianieves M

**snub** [snuhb] *vi* reprender

**snuff** [snuhf] *n* moco M

**snuffle** [SNUHF•fl] *vi* gangear

**snug** [snuhg] *adj* cómodo

**so** *adv conj adj pron* así; de este
modo; ~ am I\ yo tambien; ~
as to\ para ~ far\ *adv* hasta
ahora; ~ far as I know\ que
yo sepa; ~ much\ tanto; ~
that\ para que; and ~ on\ ys
así sucesivaments; if ~\ si es
así; I think ~\ creo que si; or
~\ más o menos

**soak** [sok] *vi* empapar

**soap** [sop] *n* jabón M

**soar** [saur] *vi* volar

**sob** [sahb] *vi* sollozar

**sober** [SO•bur] *adj* sobrio

**soberly** [SO•bur•lee] *adv*
sobriamente

**sobriety** [so•BRUY•i•tee] *n*
sobriedad F

**sociable** [SO•shuh•bl] *adj*
sociable

**social** [SO•shuhl] *adj* social

**socialism** [SO•shuh•LIZM] *n*
socialismo M

**socialist** [SO•shuh•list] *n*
socialista F

**society** [so•SUY•i•tee] *n*
sociedad F

**sociology** [SO•shee•AH•lo•gee]
*n* sociología F

**sock** [sahk] *n* calcetín M

**socket** [SAH•kit] *n* encaje M

**sod** [sahd] *n* césped M

**soda** [SO•duh] *n* soda F

**sodium** [SO•dee•um] *n* sodio M

**sofa** [SO•fuh] *n* sofá M

**soft** [sauft] *adj* suave

**soften** [SAUF•fin] *vi* ablandar

**softness** [SAUFT•nis] *n*
blandura F

**soil** *n* tierra F; *vt* ensuciar; *vi*
ensuciarse

**sojourn** [SO•jurn] *n* estancia F

**solace** [SAH•les] *n* consuelo M

**solar** [SO•lur] *adj* solar

**solder** [SAH•dur] *n* soldadura F

**soldier** [SOL•jur] *n* soldado M

**sole** (of shoe) [sol] *n* suela F

**solecism** [SAH•lu•SI•zm] *n*
solecismo M

**solemn** [SAH•lim] *adj* solemne

**solemnity** [so•LEM•ni•tee] *n*
solemnidad F

**solemnize** [SAH•lem•NUYZ] *vi*
solemnizar

**solicit** [suh•LI•sit] *vt* solicitar

**solicitation** [so•LI•ci•TAI•shn]
*n* solicitación F

**solicitor** [so•LI•ci•tur] *n*
procurador M

**solicitous** [so•LI•si•tus] *adj*
solícito

**solid** [SAH•lid] *adj* sólido

**solidarity** [SAH•li•DAIR•i•tee]
*n* solidaridad F

**solidify** [so•LI•di•FUY] *vi*
solidificar

**solidity** [so•LI•di•tee] *n*
solidez F

**soliloquy** [suh•LIL•o•kwee] *n*
soliloquio M

**solitary** [SAH•li•TAI•ree] *adj*
solitario

**solitude** [SAH•li•TOOD] *n*
soledad F

**solo** [SO•lo] *adj* solo

**solstice** [SOL•stis] *n* solsticio M

**solution** [so•LOO•shn] *n*
solución F

**solve** [sahlv] *vt* resolver

**solvent** [SAHL•vint] *n*
solvente M

**somber** [SAHM•bur] *adj*
obscuro

**some** [suhm] *adv* un; algún;
cierto

**somebody** [SUHM•buh•dee]
*pron n* alguien

**somehow** [SUHM•how] *adv* de
algún modo

**someone** [SUHM•wuhn] *pron*
alguien

**somersault** [SUHM•ur•SALT]
*n* dar saltos mortales

**something** [SUHM•thing] *n*
algo

**sometime** [SUHM•tuym] *adv*
*adj* algún día M

**sometimes** [SUHM•tuyms] *adv*
*adj* a veces

**somewhat** [SUHM•wuht] *adv*
algo alguna cosa F

**somewhere** [SUHM•wair] *adv*
*n* en alguna parte

**somnolent** [SAHM•nuh•lint]
*adj* soñoliento

**son** [suhn] *n* hijo M

**son-in-law** [SUHN•in•LAU] *n*
yerno M

**sonata** [so•NAH•tuh] *n*
sonata F

**song** [saung] *n* canto M;
canción F

**song-bird** [SAUNG•burd] *n*
pájaro M

**sonnet** [SAH•nit] *n* soneto M

**sonorous** [sah•NUH•ruhs] *adj*
sonoro

**soon** *adv* pronto

**soot** [sut] *n* hollín M

**soothe** [sooth] *vt* aliviar

**soothsayer** [SOOTH•SAI•ur] *n*
adivino M

**sooty** [SUT•tee] *adj* holliniento

**sop** [sahp] *vt* ensopar

**sophisticated**
[so•FI•sti•KAI•tid] *adj*
sofisticado

**sophistication**
[so•FI•sti•KAI•shn] *n*
sofisticación F

**sophomore** [SAUF•mor] *n*
estudiante de segundo año M

**soporific** [SAH•po•RI•fik] *adj*
soporífero

**soprano** [so•PRA•no] *n*
soprano M

**sorcerer** [SAUR•sir•rur] *n*
hechicero M

**sordid** [SAUR•did] *adj* sórdido

**sore** [saur] *adj* penoso; *n* llaga F

**sorrow** [SAH•ro] *n* dolor M
**sorrowful** [SAH•ro•ful] *adj* afligido
**sorry** [SAH•ree] *adj* pesaroso; be ~\ sentirlo; ~! ¡perdón!
**sort** *n vt* clase especie clasificar F
**soul** [sol] *n* alma F
**sound 1** [sound] *n* sueño M; *vt* sonar
**sound 2** *adj* sano; lógico; seguro
**soundless** [SOUND•les] *adj* silencioso
**soundproof** [SOUND•proof] *adj* a prueba de sonido
**soup** [soop] *n* sopa F
**sour** [SOU•ur] *adj* ácido
**source** [saurs] *n* origen M
**south** *adj* sur
**South America** [SOUTH u•ME•ri•ku] *n* América del Sur F
**southeast** [south•EEST] *adj* sudeste
**southerner** [SUHTH•thur•nur] *n* del sur
**southward** [SOUTH•wurd] *adv* situado hacia el sur
**southwest** [south•WEST] *adv* sudoeste
**souvenir** [SOO•ven•NEER] *n* recuerdo M
**sovereign** [SAHV•rin] *n* soberano M
**Soviet** [SO•vee•it] *adj* soviet
**sow** [sou] *n* cerda F
**space** [spais] *n* espacio M
**spacious** [SPAI•shus] *adj* espacioso
**spade** [spaid] *n* laya F

**span** *n* extensión F; *vt* extenderse sobre
**spangle** [SPANG•gl] *n* destello M
**Spaniard** [SPAN•yurd] *n* español M
**spaniel** [SPAN•yuhl] *n* perro M
**Spanish** [SPA•nish] *n* español M
**spank** *vt* zurrar
**spanking** [SPANK•king] *n* azote M
**spar** [spahr] *vi* adiestrar
**spare** [spair] *vt n* ahorrar; *adj* de reserva
**spark** [spahrk] *n* chispa F
**sparkle** [SPAHR•kl] *vi* chispear
**sparkling** [SPAHRK•kling] *adj* chispeante
**spark plug** *n* bujía F
**sparrow** [spair•ro] *n* gorrión F
**sparse** [spahrs] *adj* esparcido
**spasm** [SPA•zim] *n* espasmo M
**spatter** [SPA•tur] *vt* salpicar
**spawn** [spaun] *n* huevas
**speak** [speek] *vi* hablar
**speaker** [SPEE•kur] *n* orador M
**spear** [speer] *n* lanza F
**special** [SPE•shul] *adj* especial
**specialist** [SPE•shuh•list] *n* especialista F
**specialize** [SPE•shuh•LUYZ] *vi* especializar
**species** [SPEE•sheez] *n* especie F
**specific** [spuh•SI•fik] *adj* específico
**specify** [SPE•si•FUY] *vt* especificar
**specimen** [SPE•si•min] *n* espécimen M

**specious** [SPEE•shus] *adj*
especioso

**speckle** [SPE•kl] *vt* manchar

**spectacle** [SPEK•ti•kl] *n*
espectáculo M

**spectacular**
[spek•TAK•kyu•lur] *adj*
espectacular

**spectator** [SPEK•TAI•tur] *n*
espectador M

**specter** [SPEK•tur] *n* espectro M

**spectrum** [SPEK•trum] *n*
espectro M

**speculate** [SPEK•kyu•LAIT] *vi*
especular

**speculation**
[SPEK•kyu•LAI•shn] *n*
especulación F

**speculative** [SPEK•kyu•luh•tiv]
*adj* especulativo

**speculator** [SPEK•kyu•LAI•tur]
*n* especulador M

**speech** *n* habla F

**speed** *n* rapidez F

**speedily** [SPEED•di•lee] *adv*
rápidamente

**speed limit** [SPEED LI•mit] *n*
límite de velocidad M

**speedway** [SPEED•wai] *n*
autopista F

**speedy** [SPEED•dee] *adv*
rápido

**spell 1** [spel] *vi* hechizar
(magic)

**spell 2** *vt vi* escribir

**spell 3** *n* período

**spellbound** [SPEL•bound] *adj*
hechizado

**spelling** [SPEL•ling] *n*
deletreo M

**spend** *vt* gastar; pasar (time
etc); *vi* gastar dinero

**spendthrift** [SPEND•thrift] *n*
derrochardor M

**spew** [spyoo] *vi* vomitar

**sphere** [sfeer] *n* esfera F

**spherical** [SFEER•i•kl] *adj*
esférico

**spice** [spuys] *n* picante M

**spider** [SPUY•dur] *n* araña F

**spigot** [SPI•git] *n* espiche M

**spike** [spuyk] *n* pincho M

**spill** [spil] *vt* despedir; *vi*
derramarse; ~ over\
desbordarse

**spin** *vt* hilar; *n* vuelta F

**spinach** [SPI•nich] *n* espinaca F

**spinal** [SPUY•nl] *adj* espinal

**spinal column** [SPUY•nl
KAH•lim] *n* espina dorsal F

**spinal cord** [SPUY•nl KAURD]
*n* médula espinal F

**spinner** [SPI•nur] *n* hilador M

**spinning wheel** [SPIN•ning
WEEL] *n* torno para hilar M

**spinster** [SPIN•stur] *n*
solterona F

**spiral** [SPUY•rl] *adj* espiral

**spire** [spuyr] *n* espira F

**spirit** [SPI•rit] *n* espíritu M; *vt* ~
away\ hacer desaparecer

**spirited** [SPI•ri•tid] *adj* vivo

**spiritual** [SPI•ri•chul] *adj*
espiritual

**spiritualism**
[SPI•ri•chuh•LI•zm] *n*
espiritualismo M

**spirituality**
[SPIR•i•choo•A•li•tee] *n*
espiritualidad F

**spit 1** *vi* espetar

**spit 2** *n* asador M (roasting)
**spite** [spuyt] *n* despecho M
**splash** *vt* salpicar
**spleen** *n* bazo M
**splendid** [SPLEN•did] *adj* espléndido
**splendor** [SPLEN•dor] *n* brillo M
**splice** [spluys] *vt* juntar
**splint** *n* astilla F
**splinter** [SPLIN•tur] *n* astilla F
**split** *vt* partir; ~ up\ separarse; ~ one's sides\ caerse de risa; *n* hendidura
**spoil** *vt* deteriorar
**spoke** [spok] *n* rayo M
**spokesperson** [SPOKS•PUR•sin] *n* portavoz F
**sponge** [spuhnj] *n* esponja F; *vi* ~ off\ vivir a costa de
**sponge cake** [SPUHNJ caik] *n* bizcocho M
**sponger** [SPUHN•jur] *n* parásito M
**sponsor** [SPAHN•sur] *n* garante M
**spontaneity** [SPAHN•tuh•NAI•i•tee] *n* espontaneidad F
**spontaneous** [spahn•TAI•nee•us] *adj* espontáneo
**spook** *n* fantasma F
**spool** *n* carrete M
**spoon** *n* cuchara F
**spoonful** [SPOON•ful] *n* cucharada F
**sport** [spaurt] *n* deporte M; be a good ~\ ser buen perdedor; *vt* lucir

**sportsman** [SPAURTS•mun] *n* deportista F
**spot** [spaht] *n* mancha F; *vt* manchar; on the ~\ en el lugar; in a · \ en un apuro
**spotted** [SPAH•tid] *adj* manchado
**spouse** [spous] *n* esposo M
**spout** *vt* echar
**sprain** *n* torcedura F
**sprawl** [spraul] *vi* arrastrarse
**spray** [sprai] *vt* esparcir; *n* ramo M
**sprayer** [SPRAI•ur] *n* pulverizador M
**spread** [spred] *vt* extender; *vi* extenderse; *n* extensión F
**spree** *n* juerga F
**sprightly** [SPRUYT•lee] *adv* animado
**spring** *n* primavera F
**sprinkle** [SPRINK•kl] *vt* salpicar
**sprint** *vi* correr a toda velocidad
**sprout** *n* retoño M
**spruce** [sproos] *n* picea F
**spun** *pp* spin hilado
**spur** *n* espuela F
**spurn** *vt* desdeñar
**spurt** *n* borbotón M
**spy 1** [spuy] *n* espía F
**spy 2** *vi* espiar
**squabble** [SKWAH•bl] *vi* disputar; *n* disputa F
**squadron** [SKWAH•druhn] *n* escuadra F
**squalid** [SKWAH•lid] *adj* escuálido
**squall** [skwahl] *n* racha F
**squander** [SKWAHN•dur] *vt* derrochar

**square** [skwair] *n* cuadrado M; town ~\ plaza F; *adj* cuadrado; all ~\ iguales; *vi* areglar;

**squash** [skwahsh] *vt* estrujar

**squat** [skwaht] *vi* agacharse

**squawk** [skwahk] *vi* graznar

**squeak** [skweek] *vi* chillar

**squeal** [skweel] *vi* chillar

**squeamish** [SKWEE•mish] *adj* remilgado

**squeeze** [skweeze] *vt* apretar

**squelch** [skwelch] *vt* aplastar

**squint** [skwint] *vi* bizcar; *n* estrabismo M

**squire** [skwuyr] *n* escudero M

**squirm** [skwirm] *vi* retorcerse

**squirrel** [skwirl] *n* ardilla F

**squirt** [skwirt] *vi* jeringar

**stab** *vt* herir

**stability** [stuh•BI•li•tee] *n* estabilidad F

**stabilize** [STAI•bi•LUYZ] *vt* estabilizar

**stable 1** [STAI•bl] *adj* estable

**stable 2** *n* establo M

**stack** [stak] *n* pila F

**stadium** [STAI•dee•um] *n* estadio M

**staff** [staf] *n* barra F

**stag** *n* ciervo M

**stage** [staij] *n* escena F

**stage door** [staij daur] *n* puerta por donde entran F

**stage fright** [staij fruyt] *n* miedo al público M

**stagger** [STAG•gur] *vi* vacilar

**stagnant** [STAG•nint] *adj* estancado

**staid** *adj* grave

**stain** *n* mancha F; *vt* manchar

**stainless** [STAIN•lis] *adj* limpio

**stair** *n* escalera F

**stake** [staik] *n* estaca F; at ~\ en juego; *vt* estacar

**stale** [stail] *adj* pasado

**stalk 1** [stauk] *vi* acercarse; *vt* seguir

**stalk 2** *n* tallo M

**stall 1** [stal] *n* establo M

**stall 2** *vt* parar; *vi* pararse

**stallion** [STAHL•yun] *n* caballo padre M

**stalwart** [STAL•wurt] *adj* fornido

**stamina** [STA•mi•nuh] *n* vitalidad F

**stammer** [STAM•mur] *vi* tartamudear

**stamp** *n* estampa F; *vt* patear (feet) estampar (press); ~ out\ acabar

**stampede** [stam•PEED] *n* estampica F

**stanch** *vt* estancar

**stand** *vt* estar levantarse; *n* parada ; ~ a chance\ tener una posibilidad; ~ one's ground\ mantenerse firm; *n* posición F; ~ back\ retroceder; ~ by\ estar preparado

**standardization** [STAN•dir•di•ZAI•shn] *n* reducción F

**standardize** [STAN•dir•DUYZ] *vt* unificar

**standing** [STAN•ding] *n* posición F

**stanza** [STAN•zuh] *n* estancia F

**staple 1** [STAI•pl] *adj* principal

**staple 2** *vt* sujetar

**star** [stahr] *n* estrella F
**starboard** [STAHR•baurd] *n* estribor M
**starch** *n* almidón M
**starchy** [STAHR•chee] *adj* amiláceo
**stark** [stahrk] *adj* tiso rígido
**start** [stahrt] *vi* empesar; poner en marcha; *vi* empezr (startle); *n* príncipio M
**starting** [STAHR•ting] *n* comienzo M
**starting point** [STAHR•ting POINT] *n* punto de partida M
**startle** [STAHR•tl] *vi* asustar
**starvation** [stahr•VAI•shn] *n* hambre M
**starve** [stahrv] *vi* morir de hambre
**state** [stait] *n* estado M
**stately** [STAIT•lee] *adj* majestuoso
**statement** [STAIT•mint] *n* declaración F
**stateroom** [STAIT•room] *n* camarote M
**statesman** [STAITS•min] *n* estadista F
**static** [STA•tik] *adj* estático
**station** [STAI•shin] *n* estación F
**stationary** [STAI•shi•NAI•ree] *adj* estacionario
**stationery** [STAI•shun•NAI•ree] *npl* papelería F
**statistics** [stuh•TI•stiks] *n* estadísticos
**statue** [STA•choo] *n* estatua F
**status** [STA•tus] *n* estado legal M

**statute** [STA•choot] *n* ley decreto (m) F
**staunch** *adj* estanco M
**stay** [stai] *vi* sostener; quedar; ~ put\ mantenarse firme; ~ in\ quedar en casa
**stead** [sted] *n* servicio M
**steadfast** [STED•fast] *adj* firme
**steadily** [STED•i•lee] *adj* firmemente
**steadiness** [STE•dee•nes] *n* firmeza F
**steady** [STE•dee] *adj* firme
**steak** [staik] *n* biftec
**steal** [steel] *vt* robar
**stealth** [stelth] *n* disimulo M
**steam** [steem] *n* vapor M
**steamboat** [STEEM•bot] *n* buque de vapor M
**steam engine** [STEEM EN•jin] *n* máquina de vapor F
**steamer** [STEE•mur] *n* vapor M
**steamship** [STEEM•ship] *n* buque de vapor M
**steed** *n* corcel M
**steel** *n* acero M
**steep 1** *adj* alto
**steep 2** *vt* empapar
**steeple** [STEE•pl] *n* capitel M
**steer 1** *vt* gobernar
**steer 2** *n* buey M
**stem** *n* tallo M
**stencil** [STEN•sul] *n* estarcido M
**stench** *n* peste M
**stenographer** [ste•NAH•gruh•fur] *n* estenógrafo M
**step** *n* estufa F; *vi* ir; ~ down\ retirarse; in ~ \ de acuerdo con; out of ~\ en desacuerdo con

**stepchild** [STEP•chuyld] *n* hijastro M

**stepdaughter** [STEP•DAU•tur] *n* hijastra F

**stepfather** [STEP•FA•thur] *n* padrastro M

**stepladder** [STEP•LA•dur] *n* escala F

**stepmother** [STEP•MUH•thur] *n* madrastra F

**stepson** [STEP•suhn] *n* hijastro M

**stereo** [STAIR•ree•O] *n* esterio M

**stereotype** [STAIR•ree•o•TUYP] *n* estereotipo M

**sterile** [STAIR•ruyl] *adj* estéril

**sterility** [stair•RI•li•tee] *n* esterilidad F

**sterilize** [STAIR•ri•LUYZ] *vt* esterilizar

**sterling** [STUR•ling] *n* esterlina F

**stern** [sturn] *adj* duro

**stethoscope** [STETH•uh•SKOP] *n* estetoscopio M

**stevedore** [STEEV•dor] *n* estibador M

**stew** [stoo] *vt* guisado M; *vt vi* guisar

**steward** [STOO•wurd] *n* camarero M

**stewardess** [STOO•wur•des] *n* camarera F

**stick** [stik] *n* palo M; *vt* pegar; *vi* pegarse; ~ to\ aferrrarse a; ~ up for\ defender (coll)

**stiff** [stif] *adj* rígido

**stiffen** [STIF•fin] *vt* atiesar

**stiffness** [STIF•nes] *n* tiesura F

**stifle** [STUY•fl] *vt* sofocar

**stigma** [STIG•muh] *n* estigma F

**stilt** *n* zanco M

**still 1** [stil] *adv* quieto; *adv* a pesar; de eso

**still 2** *n* alambique M

**stillness** [STIL•nis] *n* quietud F

**stimulant** [STIM•yoo•lint] *n* estimulante M

**stimulate** [STIM•yoo•LAIT] *vt* estimular

**stimulation** [STIM•yoo•LAI•shn] *n* estímulo M

**stimulus** [STIM•yoo•lus] *n* estímulo M

**sting** *vt* picar

**stinginess** [STIN•jee•nes] *n* avaricia F

**stingy** [STIN•jee] *adj* avaro

**stink** *vi* oler

**stipend** [STUY•pend] *n* estipendio M

**stipulate** [STIP•yoo•LAIT] *vt* estipular

**stir** [stur] *vt* bullir; *vi* moverse; *n* agitación

**stirring** [STUR•ring] *n* emocionante M

**stirrup** [STUR•rip] *n* estribo M

**stitch** *n* puntada F

**stock** [stok] *n* tronco M; *vt* abastecer

**stockade** [stah•KAID] *n* estacada F

**stockbroker** [STAHK•BRO•kur] *n* bolsista F

**Stock Exchange** [STAHK eks•CHAINJ] *n* Bolsa de valores F

**stockholder** [STAHK•HOL•dur] *n* accionista F

**stocking** [STAHK•king] *n* calceta F

**stock market** [STAHK MAHR•kit] *n* mercado de bolsas M

**stockroom** [STAHK•room] *n* almacén M

**stocky** [STAHK•kee] *adj* rechoncho

**stoic** [STO•ik] *n* estoico M

**stoicism** [STO•i•SIZM] *n* stoicismo M

**stoke** [stok] *vt* atizat

**stole** [stol] *n* estola F

**stolid** [STAH•lid] *adj* impasible

**stomach** [STUH•mik] *n* estómago M

**stomachache** [STUH•mik•AIK] *n* dolor del estómago M

**stone** [ston] *n* piedra F

**stonework** [STON•wurk] *n* obra de sillería F

**stony** [STO•nee] *adj* pedregoso

**stool** *n* taburetc M

**stool pigeon** [STOOL PI•jin] *n* ganchio M

**stoop** *n* abatimiento M

**stop** [stahp] *vt* parar; detener; *n* parada F

**stoppage** [STAH•pij] *n* detención F

**stopper** [STAH•pur] *n* tapon M

**stopwatch** [STAHP•wahtch] *n* cronógafo M

**storage** [STOR•aij] *n* almacenamiento M

**store** [stor] *n* tienda; provisión F; *vt* poner cn reserva; ~ up\ *vt* acumular

**storekeeper** [STOR•KEE•pur] *n* guardamlacén M

**stork** *n* cigüeña F

**storm** [staurm] *n* tempestad F

**stormy** [STAUR•mee] *adj* tempestuoso

**story 1** [STAU•ree] *n* historia F

**story 2** *n* piso M (of house)

**stout** *adj* sólido

**stove** [stov] *n* estufa F

**stow** [sto] *vt* apretar

**straddle** [STRAD•dl] *vi* esparrancarse

**straggle** [STRAG•gl] *vt* desbandarse

**straight** [strait] *adj* recto

**straighten** [STRAI•tin] *v* arreglar

**straightforward** [STRAIT•FAUR•wurd] *adj* derecho

**straightway** [strait•wai] *adv* inmediatamente

**strain** *n* tirantez F

**strainer** [STRAI•nur] *n* coladero M

**strait** *n* estrecho M

**strand** *n* costa F; *vi* embarrancar

**strange** [strainj] *adj* extraño

**strangeness** [STRAINJ•nes] *n* extrañeza F

**stranger** [STRAIN•jur] *n* extraño M

**strangle** [STRAN•gl] *vt* estrangular

**strangulate**
   [STRAN•gyu•LAIT] *vt* apretar
**strangulation**
   [STRAN•gyu•LAI•shn] *n*
   estrangulación F
**strap** *n* tira F; *vt* atar con
   correa
**strategic** [struh•TEE•jik] *adj*
   estratégico
**strategy** [STRA•ti•jee] *n*
   estrategia F
**stratosphere**
   [STRA•to•SFEER] *n*
   estratosfera F
**straw** (drinking) [strau] *n*
   paja F
**strawberry** [STRAU•bair•ree] *n*
   fresa F
**stray** [strai] *vi* desviarse
**streak** [streek] *n* raya F
**stream** [streem] *n* corriente M
**streamer** [STREE•mur] *n*
   flámula F
**streamlined** [streem•luynd] *adj*
   aerodinámico
**street** *n* calle F
**streetcar** [STREET•kahr] *n*
   tranvia F
**strength** *n* fuerza F
**strengthen** [STRENGTH•en] *vi*
   fortalecer
**strenuous** [STREN•yoo•us] *adj*
   estrenuo
**stress** [stres] *n* presión F
**stretch** [strech] *vt* extender
**stretcher** [STRECH•chur] *n*
   estirador M
**strew** [stroo] *vt* esparcir
**strict** [strikt] *adj* estricto
**stride** [struyd] *vi* a pasos largos

**strident** [STRUY•dint] *adj*
   estridente
**strife** [struyf] *n* lucha F
**strike** [struyk] *vt* golpear; *vi*
   golpear; declararse enhuelga
   (go on strike); *n* huelga F (of
   workers)
**striker** [STRUY•kur] *n*
   golpeador M
**striking** [STRUY•king] *adj*
   notable
**string** *n* cordón M
**strip 1** *n* faja F
**strip 2** (clothes) *vt* desnudar
**stripe** [struyp] *n* raya F
**strive** [struyv] *vi* esforzarse
**stroke 1** [strok] *n* golpe M
**stroke 2** (medical) *n* ataque M
**stroll** [strol] *vi* pasear
**strong** [straung] *adj* fuerte
**stronghold** [STRAUNG•hold]
   *n* fortaleza F
**strongly** [STRAUNG•lee] *adj*
   fuertemente
**structural** [STRUK•chur•ul] *adj*
   estructural
**structure** [STRUK•chur] *n*
   estructura F
**struggle** [STRUH•gl] *vi* luchar
**strut** [struht] *n* riostra F
**stub** [stuhb] *n* tocón M
**stubble** [STUHB•bl] *n*
   rastrojo M
**stubborn** [STUHB•born] *adj*
   obstinado
**stubbornness**
   [STUHB•born•nes] *n*
   obstinación F
**stucco** [STUH•ko] *n* estuco M
**stuck-up** [STUH•KUHP] *adj*
   tieso

stud 1 [stuhd] *n* poste M

stud 2 *n* acaballadero M (animal)

student [STOO•dint] *n* estudiante M

studio [STOO•dee•o] *n* estudio M

study [STUH•dee] *vi* estudiar

stuff [stuhf] *n* material F; *vt* rellenar; disecar; atiborrar

stuffing [STUHF•fing] *n* relleno M

stuffy [STUH•fee] *adj* sofocante

stumble [STUHMB•bl] *vi* tropezar

stump [stuhmp] *n* tocón M

stun [stuhn] *vt* aturdir

stunt 1 [stuhnt] *n* hazaña F

stunt 2 *vt* impedir el crecimiento

stupefy [STOO•pi•FUY] *vt* atontarse

stupendous [stoo•PEN•dus] *adj* estupendo

stupid [STOO•pid] *adj* estúpido

stupidity [stoo•PI•di•tee] *n* estupidez F

stupor [stoo•pur] *n* estupor M

sturdy [stur•dee] *adj* fornido

sturgeon [stur•jun] *n* esturión F

stutter [stuh•tur] *vi* tartamudear

sty [stuy] *n* orzuelo M

style [stuyl] *n* estilo M; *vt* diseñar

stylish [STUY•lish] *adj* elegante

subcommittee [SUB•ko•MI•tee] *n* subcomisión F

subconscious [sub•KAHN•shus] *adj* subconsciente

subdivision [SUB•di•VI•shn] *n* subdivisión F

subdue [sub•DOO] *vt* sojuzgar

subject [SUB•jekt] *n* sujeto M

subjection [sub•JEK•shn] *n* sometimiento M

subjective [sub•JEK•tiv] *adj* subjetivo

subjugate [SUB•juh•GAIT] *vt* subyugar

subjunctive [sub•JUNK•tiv] *adj* subjuntivo

sublet [SUB•LET] *vt* subarrendar

sublime [sub•LUYM] *adj* sublime

submarine [SUB•muh•REEN] *n* submarino M

submerge [sub•MURJ] *vt* sumergir

submission [sub•MI•shn] *n* sumisión F

submit [sub•MIT] *vt* someter

subordinate [suhb•BAUR•di•nit] *adj* subordinado

subpoena [suh•PEE•nuh] *n* citación F

subscribe [suhb•SKRUYB] *vt* subscribir

subscriber [suhb•SKRUY•bur] *n* firmante M

subscription [sub•SKRIP•shn] *n* firma F

subsequent [SUB•se•kwent] *adj* subsecuente

subservient [sub•SUR•vee•ent] *adj* subordinado

subside [suhb•SUYD] *vi* menguar

**subsidize** [SUHB•si•DUYZ] *vt*
subvencionar

**subsist** [suhb•SIST] *vt* subsistir

**substance** [SUHB•stenz] *n*
substancia F

**substantial** [stuhb•STAN•shul]
*adj* substancial

**substantive** [SUHB•stan•tiv]
*adj* substantivo

**subterranean**
[SUHB•tur•RAI•nee•yen] *adj*
subterráneo

**subtle** [SUH•tl] *adj* sutil

**subtract** [suhb•TRAKT] *vt*
substraer

**subtraction** [suhb•TRAK•shn]
*n* substracción F

**suburb** [SUH•burb] *n*
suburbio M

**suburban** [suh•BUR•ban] *adj*
suburbano

**subversive** [suhb•VUR•siv] *adj*
subversivo

**subway** [SUHB•wai] *n*
metropolitano M

**succeed** [suhk•SEED] *vi*
suceder

**success** [suhk•SES] *n* éxito M

**successful** [suhk•SES•fl] *adj*
próspero

**succession** [suhk•SES•shn] *n*
sucesión F

**succor** [SUHK•or] *n* socorro M;
*vt* socorrer

**succulent** [SUHK•yoo•lint] *adj*
suculento

**succumb** [suh•KUM] *vi*
sucumbir

**such** [suhch] *adj* tal; *adv* tan; ~
and ~\ tal o cual; ~ as it is\
tal como es

**suck** [suhk] *vt* chupar; ~ up\
absorber

**suction** [SUHK•shn] *n*
succión F

**sudden** [SUH•din] *adj*
inesperado

**suddenly** [SUH•din•lee] *adv* de
repente

**suddenness** [SUH•din•nes] *n*
brusquedad F

**suds** [suhdz] *n* jabonaduras

**sue** [soo] *vt* demandar

**suet** [SOO•it] *n* sebo M

**suffer** [SUH•fur] *vi* sufrir

**suffering** [SUHF•fring] *n*
sufrimiento M

**suffice** [suh•FUYS] *vi* bastar

**sufficiency** [suh•FI•shen•see] *n*
suficiencia F

**sufficient** [suh•FI•shent] *adj*
suficiente

**suffocate** [SUH•fo•KAIT] *vt*
sofocar

**suffocation** [SUH•fo•KAI•shn]
*n* sofocación F

**suffrage** [SUH•frij] *n* sufragio M

**suffuse** [suh•FYOOZ] *vt* teñir

**sugar** [SHUH•gur] *n* azúcar M

**sugar bowl** [SHUH•gur BOL]
*n* azucarera F

**suggest** [sug•JEST] *vt* sugerir

**suggestion** [sug•JES•shn] *n*
sugestión F

**suggestive** [sug•JES•tiv] *adj*
sugestivo

**suicide** [SOO•i•SUYD] *n*
suicidio M

**suit** [soot] *n* traje m; *vt* convenir

**suitcase** [SOOT•kais] *n*
maleta F

**suite** [sweet] *n* (rooms)
apartamento M; *n* (of
furniture) séquito M

**sulk** [suhlk] *vi* enfurruñarse; *npl*
enfurruñamiento MF

**sullen** [suh•LEN] *adj* resentido;
*adv* con resentimiento

**sultan** [suhl•TIN] *n* sultán M

**sum** [suhm] *n* suma F; *vt*
evaluar

**summarize**
[SUHM•may•RUYZ] *vt*
resumir

**summary** [SUHM•muh•ree] *n*
sumario F; resumen M

**summer** [SUHM•mur] *n*
verano M

**summit** [SUHM•mit] *n* cumbre
F

**summon** [SUH•mun] *vt* llamar;
(meeting) convocar

**summons** [SUH•munz] *n*
llamada F

**sun** [suhn] *n* sol M; *vr* to ~
oneself \ tomar el sol

**sunbathe** [SUHN•baith] *vi*
tomar el sol

**sunbeam** [SUHN•beem] *n* rayo
de sol M

**sunburn** [SUHN•birn] *n*
quemadura de sol F

**Sunday** [SUHN•dai] *n*
domingo M

**sunflower** [SUHN•flouur] *n*
girasol M

**sunglasses** [SUHN•glah•sez]
*npl* gafas de sol F

**sunlight** [SUHN•luyt] *n* luz de
sol F

**sunny** [SUHN•nee] *adj* de sol;
(place) soleado; it is ~\ hace
sol

**sunshine** [SUHN•shuyn] *n*
sol M

**super** [SOO•pur] *adj* estupendo

**superb** [soo•PURB] *adj*
espléndido

**superficial** [SOO•pur•FI•shul]
*adj* superficial

**superhuman**
[SOO•pur•HYOO•mun] *adj*
sobrehumano

**superintendent**
[SOO•pur•in•TEN•dunt] *n*
director M; (police)
comisario M

**superior** [soo•PEE•ree•ur] *adj*
superior; *n* superior M

**superlative** [soo•PUR•la•tiv] *adj*
superlativo; *n* superlativo M

**supermarket**
[SOO•pur•MAHR•ket] *n*
supermercado M

**supernatural**
[SOO•pur•NA•chur•el] *adj*
sobrenatural

**supersede** [SOO•pur•SEED] *vt*
reemplazar; suplantar

**superstition**
[SOO•pur•STI•shun] *n*
superstición F

**supervise** [SOO•pur•VUYZ] *vt*
supervisar

**supervision** [SOO•pur•VI•zhun]
*n* supervisión F

**supper** [SUH•pur] *n* cena F

**supplment** [SUH•pluh•munt] *n*
supplemento M; *vt* completar,
aumentar

**supply** [SUH•pluy] *n*
suministrador M; *vt* proveer;
(feed) alimentar; (need)
satisfacer

**support** [suh•PAURT] *vt*
sostener; (endure) soportar;
aguantar; (fig) apoyar; *n*
apoyo M

**suppose** [suh•POZ] *vt* suponer;
(think) creer

**suppress** [suh•PRES] *vt*
suprimir

**supreme** [suh•PREEM] *adj*
supremo

**sure** [shoor] *adj* seguro; cierto;
*vi* make ~\ asegurarse; *adv*
¡claro!

**surf** [surf] *n* oleaje M

**surface** [SUR•fas] *n* superficie
F; *adj* superficial; de la
superficie; *vi* salir al la
superficie; (appear) emerger

**surge** [surj] *vi* encresparse;
(crowd) moverse en tropel; *n*
oleada F; (electric)
sobretensión F

**surgeon** [SUR•jun] *n* sirujano M

**surgery** [SUR•jur•ee] *n*
cirugiá F

**surgical** [SUR•ji•kul] *adj*
quirúgico

**surly** [SUR•lee] *adj* áspero

**surmount** [sur•MOUNT] *vt*
superar

**surname** [SUR•naim] *n*
apellido M

**surpass** [SUR•pas] *vt*
sobrepasar; exceder

**surplus** [SUR•plus] *n* excedente
M *adj* excedente

**surprise** [sur•PRUYZ] *n* spresa
F; *adj* sopredente; *vt*
soprender

**surrealism** [sur•REE•lizm] *n*
surrealismo M

**surrender** [sur•REN•dur] *vt*
entregar; *vi* entregarse; *n*
entrega F; (military)
rendición F

**surrpetitious** [SU•rep•TI•shus]
*adj* clandestino

**surround** [su•ROUND] *vt*
rodear; *n* borde M

**surrounding** [su•ROUN•ding]
*adj* circudante

**surroundings**
[su•ROUN•dingz] *npl*
aleredores M

**survey** [n. SIR•veh v. sir•VEH]
*n* inspección F; informe M;
(view) vista de conjunto F; *vt*
examinar; hacer una encuesta
de

**survival** [sur•VUY•vul] *n*
supervivencia F

**survive** [sur•VUYV] *vt*
sobrevivir

**survivor** [sur•VUY•vur] *n*
sobreviviente M

**susceptibility**
[suh•SEP•ti•BI•li•tee] *n*
susceptibilidad F

**susceptible** [suh•SEP•ti•bl] *adj*
susceptible

**suspect** [suh•SPEKT] *vt*
sopechar

**suspend** [sus•SPEND] *vt*
suspender

**suspenders** [sus•SPEN•durz]
*npl* suspendedores M

**suspense** [suhs•SPENS] *n*
suspensión F

**suspicion** [suhs•SPI•shn] *n*
sospecha F

**sustain** [suh•STAIN] *vt* sostener

**sustenance** [SUH•ste•nens] *n* sostenimiento M

**suture** [SOO•chur] *n* sutura F

**swab** *n* estropajo M

**swagger** [SWAG•gur] *vi* contonearse

**swain** *n* zagal M

**swallow 1** [SWAH•lo] *vt* tragar

**swallow 2** *n* deglución F

**swamp** *n* pantano M

**swan** [swahn] *n* cisne M

**swap** [swahp] *vt* cambiar

**swarm** [swaurm] *n* hormiguero M

**swarthy** [SWAUR•thee] *adj* atezado

**swat** *vt* golpear

**swathe** [swath] *n* faja F

**sway** [swai] *vi* oscilar

**swear** [swair] *vi* jurar

**sweat** [swet] *vi* exudar; *n* sudor M

**sweater** [SWET•tur] *n* suéter M

**Swede** [sweed] *n* sueco M

**Sweden** [SWEED•din] *n* Suecia F

**Swedish** [SWEED•dish] *adj* sueco

**sweep** *vt* barrer

**sweeper** [SWEEP•pur] *n* barrendero M

**sweeping** [SWEEP•ping] *adj* arrebatador

**sweet** *adj* dulce

**sweetbread** [SWEET•bred] *n* mojellas F

**sweeten** [SWEET•tin] *vt* endulzar

**sweetness** [SWEET•nis] *n* dulzura F

**sweet potato** [SWEET po•TAI•to] *n* batata F

**swelter** [SWEL•tur] *vi* sofocar

**swell** [swel] *vi* inflar; hincharse

**swelling** [SWEL•ing] *n* hinchazón M

**swerve** [swurv] *vi* desviar

**swift** *adj* veloz

**swiftness** [SWIFT•nes] *n* velocidad F

**swim** *vi* nadar

**swimmer** [SWIM•mur] *n* nadador M

**swimming** [SWIM•ming] *n* natación F

**swimming pool** *n* piscina F

**swimsuit** [SWIM•soot] *n* traje de baño M

**swindle** [SWIN•dl] *vi* estafar

**swindle** [SWIN•dl] *n* estafa F

**swing** *vt vi* oscilar; *n* balanceo M; in full ~\ en plena actividaad

**swipe** [swuyp] *vi* golpear

**swirl** *vi* arremolinarse

**Swiss** *n* suizo M

**switch** *n* látigo M

**switchboard** [SWICH•baurd] *n* cuadro de distribución M

**Switzerland** [SWIT•zur•land] *n* Suiza

**swivel** [SWI•vul] *vi* girar

**swoon** *vi* desmayarse

**swoop** *vi* barrer

**sword** [swaurd] *n* espada F

**sycamore** [SI•ki•MAUR] *n* sicómoro M

**syllable** [SI•li•bl] *n* sílaba F

**syllogism** [SI•lo•JIZM] *n* silogismo M

**symbol** [SIM•buhl] *n*
símbolo M
**symbolic** [sim•BAH•lik] *adj*
simbólico
**symmetrical** [sim•ME•tri•kuhl]
*adj* simétrico
**sympathetic**
[SIM•puh•THE•tik] *adj*
simpático
**sympathy** [SIM•puh•thee] *n*
simpatía F
**symphony** [SIM•fo•nee] *n*
sinfonía F
**symptom** [SIMP•tum] *n*
síntoma F
**symptomatic**
[SIMP•to•MA•tik] *adj*
sintomático
**synagogue** [SI•nuh•GAHG] *n*
sinagoga F

**synchronize** [SIN•kro•NUYZ]
*vi* sincronizar
**syndicate** [SIN•di•kit] *n*
sindicatura F
**synonym** [SI•ni•NIM] *n*
sinónimo M
**synonymous**
[si•NAHN•ni•mus] *adj*
sinónimo
**syntax** [SIN•taks] *n* sintaxis F
**synthesis** [SIN•thuh•sis] *n*
sintesis F
**Syria** [SEE•ree•uh] *n* Siria
**Syrian** [SEE•ree•yen] *n* sirio M
**syringe** [sir•RINJ] *n* jeringa F
**syrup** [SEER•rup] *n* jarabe M
**system** [SIS•tim] *n* sistema M
**systematic** [SIS•te•MA•tik] *adj*
del sistema

# T

**tab** *n* pestaña F
**table** [TAI•bl] *n* mesa F
**tablet** [TAB•lit] *n* tableta F
**tableware** [TAI•bl•WAIR] *n*
servicio de mesa M
**tabloid** [TAB•bloid] *n*
tableta F
**tabular** [TAB•yoo•lar] *adj*
tabular
**tacit** [TA•sit] *adj* tácito
**taciturn** [TA•si•TURN] *adj*
taciturno
**tack** [tak] *n* tachuela F; *vt*
sujetar con tachuelas
**tackle 1** [TAK•kl] *vi* atar

**tackle 2** (fishing) *n* avíos de
pescar M
**tact** [takt] *n* tacto M
**tactical** [TAK•ti•kul] *adj* táctico
**tactics** [TAK•tiks] *n* táctica F
**tactile** [TAK•tul] *adj* táctil
**tachometer** [ta•KAH•me•tur] *n*
tacómetro M
**tadpole** [TAD•pol] *n*
renacuajo M
**taffeta** [TA•fit•tuh] *n* tafetán M
**tag** *n* cinta F; *vt* poner etiqueta a
**tag along** *vi* andar detrás de;
seguir
**tail** *n* cola F; *vt* seguir (coll)

**tailor** [TAI•lur] *n* sastre M
**taint** *n* corrupción F
**take** [taik] *vt* tomar; agarrar;
llevar; ~ advantage of \
aprovechar; ~ after\ parecerse
a; ~ away\ quitar; ~ back\
retirar; ~ in\ achicar; ~ off \
quitarse; ~ out\ sacar; ~ over\
tomar el poder; ~ part\
participar; ~ place\ tener
lugar; ~ up\ decidarse a; ~ up
with\ trabar amistad con; ~
off \ *n* despegue M
**talcum** [TAL•kum] *n* talco M
**tale** [tail] *n* cuento M
**talent** [TAL•int] *n* talento M
**talk** [tauk] *vi* hablar; ~ about\
hablar de; ~ over\ discutir; *n*
conversación F
**talkative** [TAUK•uh•tiv] *adj*
hablador
**talker** [TAU•kur] *n* orador M
**talking** [TAU•king] *n*
parlante M
**tall** [tal] *adj* alto
**tallow** [TA•lo] *n* sebo M
**tally** [TA•lee] *vt* sumar
**tam o' shanter** [TAM o
SHAN•tur] *n* boina escocesa F
**tame** [taim] *adj* dócil
**tamper** [TAM•pur] *vt* meter
**tan** *n* tanino M
**tandem** [TAN•dim] *n*
tándem M
**tangent** [TAN•jent] *n*
tangente M
**tangerine** [TAN•juh•REEN] *n*
tangerino M
**tangible** [TAN•juh•bl] *adj*
tangible
**Tangiers** [tan•JEERZ] *n* Tánger

**tangle** [TANG•gl] *vt* enredar
**tank** *n* tanque M
**tanker** [TANK•kur] *n* buque
cisterna M
**tannery** [TAN•nur•ree] *n*
tenería F
**tantalize** [TAN•tuh•LUYZ] *vi*
atormentar
**tantrum** [TAN•trum] *n*
pataleta F
**tap** *n vt* canilla sangrar F
**tap** *vt* sacar
**tape** [taip] *n* esparadrapo M; *vt*
atar con cinta; grabar (record)
**tape recorder** *n* manetiofón M
**taper** [TAI•pur] *vt* disminuir
**tapestry** [TA•pe•stree] *n*
tapiz M
**tar** *n* brea F; *vt* alquitranar
**tardy** [TAR•dee] *adj* tardo
**tare 1** [tair] *n* tara F
**tare 2** *n* destarar
**target** [TAR•git] *n* blanco M
**tariff** [TAIR•rif] *n* tarifa F
**tarnish** [TAR•nish] *vt* deslustrar
**tarpaulin** [tar•PO•lin] *n* tela
embreada F
**tarry** [TAIR•ree] *vi* tardar
**tart 1** *adj* acre
**tart 2** *n* tarta F
**tartar** [TAR•tur] *n* tártaro M
**task** *n* tarea F
**tassel** [TA•suhl] *n* borla F
**taste** [taist] *vi* saborear; *n* sabor;
gusto M; ~ of\ saber a
**tasteless** [TAIST•les] *adj*
insulso
**tasty** [TAI•stee] *adj* sabroso
**tattered** [TAT•turd] *adj* roto
**tattle** [TAT•tl] *vt* revelar

**tattle-tale** [TAT•tl•TAIL] *n* parloteo M

**tattoo** [tat•TOO] *n* retreta F

**taught** [taut] *pp* enseñado

**taunt** *vt* provocar

**tavern** [TA•vurn] *n* taberna F

**tax 1** [taks] *n* impuesto M; *vt* imponer contribuciones a

**tax 2** (income) *n* impuesto de utilidades M

**taxi** [TAK•see] *n* taxi M

**taxpayer** [TAKS•PAI•ur] *n* contribuyente M

**tea** [tee] *n* té M

**teacup** [TEE•kup] *n* taza de té F

**teach** [teech] *vt* enseñar

**teacher** [TEE•chur] *n* maestro M

**teaching** [TEE•chǐng] *n* instrucción F

**teakettle** [TEE•ket•tl] *n* tetera F

**teal** [teel] *n* trullo M

**team** [teem] *n* equipo M

**teamwork** [TEEM•wurk] *n* trabajo de equipo M

**tea party** [TEE PAHR•tee] *n* té M

**teapot** [TEE•pot] *n* tetera F

**tear 1** [tair] *vt* rasgar

**tear 2** [teer] *n* lágrima F

**tease** [teez] *vi* fastidiar

**teaspoon** [TEE•spoon] *n* cucharilla F

**technical** [TEK•ni•kul] *adj* técnico

**technician** [tek•NI•shn] *n* técnico M

**tedious** [TEE•dee•is] *adj* tedioso

**teem** *vi* engendrar M

**teens** [teenz] *npl* jovenes

**teethe** *vi* endentecer

**telegram** [TEL•le•GRAM] *n* telegrama M

**telegraph** [TEL•le•GRAF] *n* telégrafo M

**telephone** [TEL•le•FON] *n* teléfono M; *vt* llamar

**telephone number** [TEL•le•FON NUM•bur] *n* número de teléfono M

**telephone operator** [TEL•le•FON AH•pur•RAI•tur] *n* telefonista F

**telescope** [TEL•le•SKOP] *n* telescopio M

**televise** [TEL•le•VUYZ] *vi* televisar

**television** [TEL•le•VI•shn] *n* televisión F

**television set** [TE•li•VI•shn SET] *n* televisión F

**tell** [tel] *vt* decir; contrar; ~ off\ *vt* reprender

**teller** [TEL•lur] *n* relator M

**telling** [TEL•ling] *adj* notable

**telltale** [TEL•tail] *n* chismoso M

**temerity** [te•MAIR•ri•tee] *n* temeridad F

**temper** [TEM•pur] *n* temple M

**temperament** [TEM•pur•ment] *n* constitución F

**temperance** [TEM•prens] *n* templanza F

**temperate** [TEM•pret] *adj* templado

**temperature** [TEM•pruh•CHUR] *n* temperatura F

**tempest** [TEM•pest] *n* tempestad F

**tempestuous** [tem•PES•chus] *adj* tempestuoso

**temple** [TEM•pl] *n* templo M

**temporal** [TEM•pruhl] *adj* temporal

**temporary** [TEM•po•RAI•ree] *adj* temporal

**temporize** [TEM•po•RUYZ] *vi* adaptarse

**tempt** *vt* tentar

**temptation** [tem•TAI•shn] *n* tentación F

**tempting** [TEMP•ting] *adj* tentador

**ten** *num* diez

**tenable** [TEN•uh•bl] *adj* sostenible

**tenacious** [ten•AI•shus] *adj* tenaz

**tenacity** [ten•A•si•tee] *n* tenacidad F

**tenant** [TEN•nant] *n* arrendatario M

**tend** *vi* cuidar; *vt* conducir (a machine)

**tendency** [TEN•den•cee] *n* tendencia F

**tender 1** [TEN•dur] *adj* tierno

**tender 2** *vt* ofrecer; *n* oferta F

**tenderloin** [TEN•dur•LOIN] *n* filete M

**tenderness** [TEN•dur•nes] *n* terneza F

**tendon** [TEN•din] *n* tendón M

**tendril** [TEN•dril] *n* zarcillo M

**tenement** [TEN•ne•mint] *n* vivienda F

**tennis** [TEN•nis] *n* tenis M

**tenor** [TEN•nor] *n* tenor M

**tense 1** [tenz] *adj* tenso; *vi* ~ up\ tensarse; *n* tensión F

**tense 2** *n* tiempo M

**tension** [TEN•shun] *n* tensión F

**tent** *n* cabaña F

**tentative** [TEN•tuh•tiv] *adj* tentativo

**tenth** *num* décimo

**tenuous** [TEN•yoo•us] *adj* tenue

**tepid** [TE•pid] *adj* tibio

**term** [turm] *n* término M; período M; *vt* llamar; on bad ~s\ en malas ralaciones; good ~s\ buenas relaciones

**terminal** [TUR•min•nl] *n* término M; *adj* terminal; final

**terminate** [TUR•min•NAIT] *vt* terminar

**terrace** [TAIR•res] *n* terraza F

**terrain** [TAIR•rain] *n* terreno M

**terrestrial** [tair•RES•stree•ul] *adj* terrestre

**terrible** [TAIR•uh•bl] *adj* terrible

**terrific** [tuhr•RIF•fik] *adj* terrífico

**terrify** [TAIR•ri•FUY] *vt* aterrar

**territory** [TAIR•ri•TAU•ree] *n* teritorio M

**terror** [TAIR•ror] *n* terror M

**terrorize** [TAIR•ro•RUYZ] *vt* aterrorizar

**terse** [turz] *adj* terso

**test** *n* prueba F; *vt* probar; examinar

**testament** [TES•tuh•mint] *n* testamento M

**testify** [TES•ti•FUY] *vt* testificar

**testimony** [TES•ti•MO•nee] *n* testimonio M

**test tube** [test toob] *n* tubo de ensayo M

**tether** [TE•thur] *vt* cuerda F

**text** [tekst] *n* texto M

**textbook** [TEKST•bok] *n* libro de texto M

**textile** [TEKS•tuyl] *npl* textil

**texture** [TEKS•chur] *n* textura F

**than** *conj prep* que

**thank** *vt* dar gracias

**thankful** [THANK•ful] *adj* agradecido

**thankfully** [THANK•fuh•lee] *adv* con gratitud

**thankless** [THANK•les] *adj* desagradecido

**thanklessness** [THANK•les•nes] *n* desagradecimiento M

**that** *pron conj adj adv* ese; esa; aquel; ~ is\ es decir; ~ is\ hy por eso; like ~\ asi; *adv* tan

**thatch** [thach] *n* techo M

**thaw** [thau] *vi* deshelar

**the** [thuh] *adv prep* el; la; lo; los; las

**theater** [THEE•i•tir] *n* teatro M

**theatrical** [thee•A•trik•kl] *adj* teatral

**theft** *n* robo M

**their** [thair] *pron* su; sus

**theirs** [thairz] *pron* suyo; suya

**them** *adj pron* los; las; les

**theme** [theem] *n* tema F

**themselves** [them•SELVZ] *pron* se

**then** *adv* entonces; now and ~\ de vez en cuando; since ~\ desde entonces; *adj* de entonces

**theology** [thee•AH•lo•gee] *n* teología F

**theorem** [THEE•or•em] *n* teorema F

**theoretical** [THEE•o•RE•tik•kl] *adj* teórico

**theory** [THEE•or•ree] *n* teoría F

**therapeutic** [THAIR•uh•PYOO•tik] *adj* teraéutica

**there** [thair] *prep* allí; ahí; ~ are/is\ hay; ~ he is\ ahí está; down ~\ ahí arriba; up ~\ ahí abajo

**thereabouts** [THAIR•uh•BOUTZ] *prep* por allí

**thereafter** [thair•AF•tur] *adv* después

**thereby** [thair•BUY] *prep* por allí

**therefore** [thair•FAUR] *prep* por eso

**therein** [thair•IN] *prep* allí dentro

**thereof** [thair•UHV] *prep* de eso

**thereon** [thair•AHN] *adv* encima

**thereupon** [THAIR•uh•PAHN] *adv* sobre esto

**thermal** [THUR•muhl] *adj* termal

**thermometer** [thur•MAH•me•tur] *n* termómetro M

**thermostat** [THUR•mo•STAT] *n* termostato M

**these** [theez] *pl* estos; estas

**thesis** [THEE•sis] *n* tesis M

**they** [thai] *pron* ellos; ellas

**thick** [thik] *adj* espeso grueso
**thicken** [THIK•kin] *vt* espesar
**thickness** [THIK•nes] *n*
espesor M
**thief** [theef] *n* ladrón M
**thigh** [thuy] *n* muslo M
**thimble** [THIM•bl] *n* dedal M
**thin** *adj* delgado; *adv*
ligeramente; *vt* adelgazar;
diluir; ~ out\ hacer menos
denso
**thing** [thing] *n* cosa F; for one
~\ en primer lugar; just the ~\
exactamente lo que se
necesita; poor ~\ ¡pobrecito!
**think** *vi* pensar; I ~ so\ creo que
sí; ~ over\ pensar bien; ~ up\
idear; inventar
**thinker** [THINK•kur] *n*
pensador M
**thinking** [THINK•king] *n*
pensamiento M
**thinly** [THIN•lee] *adj*
delgadamente
**thinness** [THIN•nes] *n*
delgadez F
**third** [thurd] *num* tercero
**thirdly** [THURD•lee] en tercer
lugar
**thirst** [thurst] *n* sed M; be
thirsty\ tener sed
**thirteen** [thur•TEEN] *num* trece
**thirteenth** [thur•TEENTH] *num*
décimotercio
**thirtieth** [THUR•tee•eth] *num*
trigésimo
**thirty** [THUR•tee] *num* treinta
**this** *pron adj adv* este; esta
**thistle** [THIS•tl] *n* cardo M
**thong** *n* correa F
**thorn** *n* espina F

**thorough** [THUR•ro] *adj*
completo
**thoroughbred**
[THUR•ro•BRED] *adj* de pura
raza
**thoroughfare**
[THUR•ro•FAIR] *n* vía
pública F
**thoroughly** [THUR•ro•lee] *adj*
completamente
**those** [thoz] *pron* esos; esas
**thou** tú
**though** [tho] *adv* aunque
**thought** [thaut] *n* pensamiento M
**thoughtful** [THAUT•fl] *adj*
meditativo
**thoughtfulness**
[THAUT•fl•nes] *n*
consideración F
**thoughtless** [THAUT•les] *adj*
inconsiderado
**thoughtlessness**
[THAUT•les•nes] *n*
inadvertencia F
**thousand** [THOU•zund] *num*
mil
**thousandth** [THOU•zundth]
*num* milésimo
**thrash** *vt* trillar
**thread** [thred] *n* hilo M
**threadbare** [THRED•bair] *adj*
raído M
**threat** [thret] *n* amenaza F
**threaten** [THRET•tin] *vt*
amenazar
**threatening** [THRET•ning] *adj*
amenaza
**three** *num* tres
**threshing** [THRESH•ing] *n*
trilla F

**threshold** [THRESH•hold] *n* umbral M

**thrice** [thruys] *adv* tres veces

**thrift** *n* economia F

**thrill** [thril] *n* espeluznante M; *vi* emocionarse

**thrive** [thruyv] *vt* adelantar

**throat** [throt] *n* garganta F

**throb** [thrahb] *vi* latir

**throne** [thron] *n* trono M

**throng** *n* multitud F

**throttle** [THRAH•tl] *n* gaznate M

**through** [throo] *prep* por

**throw** [thro] *vi* tirar

**throw out** [thro out] *vi* echar fuera

**throw up** [thro uhp] *vi* vomitar

**thrush** [thruhsh] *n* tordo M

**thrust** [thruhst] *vt* empujar

**thug** [thuhg] *n* criminal M

**thumb** [thuhmb] *n* pulgar M

**thump** [thuhmp] *vi* aporrear

**thunder** [THUHN•dur] *n* trueno M

**thunderbolt** [THUHN•dur•BOLT] *n* centella F

**thunderclap** [THUHN•dur•KLAP] *n* trueno gordo M

**thundering** [THUHN•dring] *adj* atronador

**thunderous** [THUHN•drus] *adj* atronador

**thunderstorm** [THUHN•dur•STAURM] *n* tronada F

**Thursday** [THURZ•dai] *n* jueves M

**thus** [thuhs] *adv* así; ~ far\ *adv* hasta ahora

**thwart** *vt* desbaratar

**thyme** [tuym] *n* tomillo M

**tiara** [tee•AHR•uh] *n* tiara F

**tibia** [TI•bee•uh] *n* tibia F

**tick 1** [tik] *n* garrapata F

**tick 2** *vi* hacer tictac

**tick 3** (insect) *n* rezno M

**ticket** [TIK•kit] *n* billete M

**ticket office** [TIK•kit AW•fis] *n* despacho de billetes M

**tickle** [TIK•kl] *vt* cosquillear

**tidal** [TUY•dl] *adj* ola

**tide** [tuyd] *n* marea F

**tidiness** [TUY•dee•nes] *n* orden M

**tidings** [TUY•dings] *npl* nuevas F

**tidy** [TUY•dee] *adj* aseado; *vt vi* ordenar

**tie** [tuy] *n* corbata F

**tier** [teer] *n* fila F

**tie-up** [TUY•uhp] *vt* atar

**tiger** [TUY•gur] *n* tigre M

**tight** [tuyt] *adj* tieso

**tighten** [TUY•tin] *vt* tupir

**tightness** [TUYT•nes] *n* impermeabilidad F

**tightwad** [TUYT•wahd] *n* cicatero M

**tigress** [TUY•gris] *n* tigresa F

**tile** [tuyl] *n* teja F

**tilt** *vt* inclinar; *n* inclinación F

**till 1** [til] *prep* hasta

**till 2** *n* cajón M

**timber** [TIM•bur] *n* madera F

**time** [tuym] *n* tiempo M; ~ off\ tiempo libre; at ~s\ a veces; for the ~ being\ por ahora; in no ~\ en un abrir de un año; *vt* elegir el momento

**timekeeper** [TUYM•KEE•pur] *n* mercador del tiempo M

**timely** [TUYM•lee] *adj* temprano

**timepiece** [TUYM•pees] *n* reloj M

**timer** [TUY•mur] *n* contador M

**timetable** [TUYM•TAI•bl] *n* horario M

**timid** [TI•mid] *adj* tímido

**tin** *n* estaño M; *adj* lata; ~ foil\ *n* papel de estaño

**tincture** [TINK•chur] *n* tintura F

**tinder** [TIN•dur] *n* yesca F

**tinfoil** [TIN•foil] *n* hoja de estaño F

**tinge** [tinj] *vt* teñir

**tingle** [TING•gl] *vi* hormiguear

**tinkle** [TINK•kl] *vi* retiñir

**tinned** [tind] *adj* estañado

**tinsel** [TIN•sul] *n* lama F

**tint** *n* tinte M;

**tiny** [TUY•nee] *adj* pequeñito

**tip 1** *n* ápice M

**tip 2** *n* extremo M

**tipsy** [TIP•see] *adj* calamocano

**tiptoe** [TIP•to] *adj* de puntillas

**tirade** [TUY•raid] *n* diabtriba F

**tire 1** [tuyr] *n* llanta F; spare ~\ llanta extra F

**tire 2** *vi* cansar

**tired** [tuyrd] *adj* cansado

**tiredness** [TUYRD•nes] *n* cansancio M

**tireless** [TUYR•les] *adj* incansable

**tiresome** [TUYR•sum] *adj* cansado

**tissue** [TI•shyoo] *n* tisú M

**tissue-paper** [-PAI•pur] *n* papel de seda M

**tithe** [tuyth] *n* diesmo M

**title** [TUY•tl] *n* título M

**titular** [TI•choo•lur] *adj* perteneciente

**to** [too] *prep* a; give it ~ me\ dámelo; I don't want ~\ no quiero; ~ and fro\ de aquí para allá

**toad** [tod] *n* sapo M

**toast** [tost] *n* tostada F; *vt* brindar por

**tobacco** [tuh•BAK•ko] *n* tabaco M

**tobacconist** [tuh•BAK•ko•nist] *n* fabricante de tabaco M

**toboggan** [tuh•BAUG•gin] *n* tobogán M

**today** [too•DAI] *adv* hoy

**toe** [to] *n* dedo del pie M

**toenail** [TO•nayul] *n* uña de un dedo F

**together** [too•GE•thur] *prep* junto

**toil** *vi* trabajar

**toilet** [TOI•let] *n* baño M

**toilet paper** [ ~ PAI•pur] *n* papel higiénico M

**token** [TO•kin] *n* señal M

**tolerable** [TAH•lur•uh•bl] *adj* tolerable

**tolerance** [TAH•luh•rens] *n* tolerancia F

**tolerant** [TAH•luh•rent] *adj* tolerante

**tolerate** [TAH•luh•RAIT] *vi* tolerar

**toll 1** [tol] *n* peaje M

**toll 2** *n* pontazgo M

**toll-bridge** [TOL•brij] *n* puente donde se paga pontazgo M

**tomato** [to•MAI•to] *n* tomate M

**tomb** [toomb] *n* tumba F

**tombstone** [TOOMB•ston] *n* piedra sepulcral F

**tomcat** [TAHM•kat] *n* gato M

**tomorrow** [too•MAH•ro] *adv* mañana

**ton** [tuhn] *n* tonelada F

**tone** [ton] *n* sonido M

**tongs** [taungz] *n* tenazas

**tongue** [tuhng] *n* lengua F

**tongue-tied** [TUHNG•tuyd] *adj* mudo

**tonic** [TAH•nik] *n* tónico M

**tonight** [too•NUYT] *adv* esta noche

**tonnage** [TUH•nij] *n* tonelaje M

**tonsil** [TAHN•sil] *n* tonsila F

**tonsillitis** [TAHN•si•LUY•tis] *n* amigdalitis M

**tonsure** [TAHN•shur] *n* tonsura F

**too** *adv* también; ~ many\ *adj* demasiados; ~ much\ de masiado

**tool** *n* instrumento M

**tooth** *n* diente M

**toothache** [TOOTH•aik] *n* dolor de diente M

**toothpaste** [TOOTH•paist] *n* pasta dentífrica F

**toothpick** [TOOTH•pik] *n* mondadientes M

**top** [tahp] *n* lo alto M; cima F; from ~ to bottom\ de arriba abajo; on ~ of\ encima de

**topaz** [TO•paz] *n* topacio M

**topcoat** [TAHP•kot] *n* abrigo M

**topic** [TAH•pik] *n* asunto M

**topmost** [TAHP•most] *adv* más alto

**topography** [tah•PAH•grah•fee] *n* topografía F

**topple** [TAH•pl] *vi* derribar

**topsy-turvy** [TAHP•zee•TUHR•vee] *adj* lo de arriba abajo

**torch** *n* antorcha F

**torment** [taur•MENT] *vt* atormentar

**tormentor** [taur•MEN•taur] *n* atormentador M

**tornado** [taur•NAI•do] *n* tornado M

**torpedo** [taur•PEE•do] *n* torpedo M

**torpid** [TAUR•pid] *adj* tórpido

**torrent** [TAUR•rint] *n* torrente M

**torrid** [TAUR•rid] *adj* tórrido

**tortoise** [TAUR•tus] *n* tortuga F

**tortuous** [TAUR•choo•us] *adj* tortuoso

**torture** [TAUR•chur] *n* tortura F

**torturer** [TAUR•chur•rur] *n* atormentador M

**toss** *vt* echar el aire

**tot** [taht] *n* chiquitín M

**total** [TO•tl] *n adj* total M

**totalitarian** [to•TA•li•TAI•ree•yen] *adj* totalitario

**totality** [to•TA•li•tee] *n* totalización F

**totally** [TO•tuh•lee] *adv* totalmente

**totter** [TAH•tur] *vi* vacilar

**touch** [tuhch] *vi* tocar; *n* toque M; in ~ with\ ponerse en contacto con; ~ down\

aterrizar; ~ and go\ incerto; dudoso

**touching** [TUHCH•ching] *adj* tocante

**touchy** [TUH•chee] *adj* susceptible

**tough** [tuhf] *adj* fuerte duro

**toughen** [TUH•fin] *vt* endurecer

**toughness** [TUHF•nis] *n* endurencimiento M

**tour** [taur] *n* viaje M

**tourist** [TAUR•rist] *n* turista F

**tournament** [TAUR•nuh•mint] *n* torneo M

**tow** [to] *n* v estopa remolcar F

**towards** [TOO•wahrdz] *prep* hacia

**towel** [TOW•wuhl] *n* toalla F

**tower** [TOW•wur] *n* torre M

**towing** [TO•wing] *n* remolque M

**town** [toun] *n* ciudad F

**township** [TOUN•ship] *n* municipio M

**toxic** [TAHK•sik] *adj* tóxico M

**toxin** [TAHK•sin] *n* toxina F

**toy** [toi] *n* juguete M; *vi* ~ with\ jugar con

**trace** [trais] *n* v pisada delinear F

**tracer** [TRAI•sur] *n* trazador M

**trachea** [TRAI•kee•uh] *n* tráque M

**track** [trak] *n* carril M

**tract** [trakt] *n* terreno M

**tractable** [TRAK•tuh•bl] *adj* manejable

**traction** [TRAK•shn] *n* tracción F

**tractor** [TRAK•tur] *n* tractor M

**trade** [traid] *n* comercio; negocio M; *vt vi* comerciar

**trade school** [TRAID SKOOL] *n* escuela industrial F

**trade union** [TRAID YOON•yun] *n* asociación de obreros F

**trademark** [TRAID•mahrk] *n* marca de fábrica F

**trader** [TRAI•dur] *n* comerciante M

**tradesman** [TRAIDZ•man] *n* mercader M

**trading** [TRAI•ding] *n* comercio M

**tradition** [truh•DI•shn] *n* tradición F

**traffic** [TRAF•fik] *n* tráfico M

**tragedy** [TRA•ji•dee] *n* tragedia F

**tragic** [TRA•jik] *adj* trágico

**trail** *n* pista F; *vt* seguir la pista de

**trailer** [TRAI•lur] *n* remolque M

**train** *n* tren M; express ~\ *n* tren rápido M; *vt* adiestrar; eduar; *vi* adiestrarse (sport)

**trainer** [TRAI•nur] *n* amaestrado M

**training** [TRAI•ning] *n* instruccíon F

**trainman** [TRAIN•man] *n* ferroviario M

**trait** *n* rasgo M

**traitor** [TRAI•tor] *n* traidor M

**trajectory** [truh•JEK•to•ree] *n* trayectoria F

**tram** *n* tranvia F

**tramp** *n* vagabundo M; *vt* recorrer a pie; *vi* andar con pasos pesados

**trample** [TRAM•pl] *vi* pisar

**trance** [trans] *n* rapto M

**tranquil** [TRAN•kwil] *adj* tranquilo

**tranquillity** [tran•KWIL•li•tee] *n* tranquilidad F

**transact** (terminate; conclude) [tranz•AKT] *vt* negociar

**transaction** [tranz•AK•shn] *n* despacho M

**transcend** [tran•SEND] *vt* sobrepujar

**transcribe** [tran•SCRUYB] *vt* transcribir

**transept** [TRAN•sept] *n* crucero M

**transfer** [TRANS•fur] *vt* transferir

**transform** [trans•FAURM] *vt* transformar

**transformation** [TRANS•faur•MAI•shn] *n* transformación F

**transformer** [trans•FAUR•mur] *n* transformador M

**transfusion** [trans•FYOO•shn] *n* transfuión F

**transgress** [trans•GRES] *vt* transgredir

**transgression** [trans•GRE•shn] *n* transgresión F

**transient** [TRAN•zee•int] *adj* transitorio

**transit** [TRANS•zit] *n* tránsito M

**transition** [trans•ZI•shn] *n* transición F

**transitive** [TRANS•zi•tiv] *adj* transcendente

**translate** [tran•SLAIT] *vt* traducir

**translation** [trans•SLAI•shn] *n* traducción F

**translator** [trans•SLAI•tur] *n* traductor M

**translucent** [trans•LOO•sent] *adj* trasluciente

**transmission** [trans•MI•shn] *n* transmisión F

**transmit** [trans•MIT] *vt* transmitir

**transmitter** [trans•MI•tur] *n* transmisor M

**transom** [TRANS•sum] *n* traviesa F

**transparent** [trans•PAIR•rent] *adj* transparente

**transpiration** [TRANS•pi•RAI•shn] *n* transpiración F

**transpire** [tran•SPUYR] *vi* transpirar

**transplant** [trans•PLANT] *vt* trasplantar

**transport** [TRANS•port] *vt* transportar

**transpose** [trans•POZ] *vt* transponer

**transverse** [trans•VURS] *adj* transverso

**trap** *n* trampa F

**trap-door** [trap•DAUR] *n* trampa F

**trapeze** [tra•PEEZ] *n* trapecio M

**trappings** [TRAP•pings] *n* jaeces

**trash** *npl* basura F

**travel** [TRA•vul] *vi* viajar

**travel agency** [TRA•vul AI•jin•cee] *n* agencia de viajes F

**traveler** [TRA•vuh•lur] *n*
viajero M

**traveling** [TRA•vuh•ling] *adv*
de viaje

**traverse** [tra•VURS] *vt*
atravesar

**travesty** [TRA•ve•stee] *n*
disfraz M

**tray** [trai] *n* bandeja F

**treacherous** [TRE•chur•us] *adj*
traidor

**treachery** [TRE•chur•ree] *n*
traición F

**tread** [tred] *n* paso M; *vi* andar;
*vt* pisar

**treason** [TREE•zun] *n*
traición F

**treasure** [TRE•shur] *n* tesoro M

**treasurer** [TRE•shuh•ur] *n*
tesorero M

**treasury** [TRE•shuh•ree] *n*
tesoro M

**treat** [treet] *vt* tratar

**treatise** (dissertation; essay)
[TREE•tis] *n* tratado M

**treatment** [TREET•mint] *n*
trato M

**treaty** [TREE•tee] *n* tratado M

**treble** [TRE•bl] *adj* triple

**treble clef** *n* de tiple M

**treble voice** [TRE•bl VOIS] *n*
triple M

**tree** *n* árbol M; family ~ *n\*
árbol geneslógico M

**trefoil** [TREE•foil] *n* trébol M

**trellis** [TRE•lis] *n* espaldera F

**tremble** [TREM•bl] *vi* temblar

**tremendous** [tre•MEN•dus] *adj*
tremendo

**tremor** [TRE•mur] *n* tremor M

**tremulous** [TRE•myu•lus] *adj*
trémulo

**trench** *n* foso M

**trench coat** [TRENCH KOT] *n*
trinchera F

**trend** *n* tendencia F; á la ultimá
(coll)

**trespass** [TRES•pas] *n*
infracción F

**trespasser** [TRES•pa•sur] *n*
transgresor M

**tress** [tres] *n* trenza F

**trestle** [TRE•sl] *n* asnilla F

**trial** [truyl] *n* prueba F

**triangle** [TRUY•an•gl] *n*
triángulo M

**tribe** [truyb] *n* tribu M

**tribulation** [TRI•byu•LAI•shn]
*n* tribulación F

**tribunal** [truy•BYOO•nl] *n*
tribunal M

**tribune** [TRI•byoon] *n* tribuno M

**tributary** [TRI•byu•TAI•ree] *n*
tributario M

**trick** [trik] *n* treta F; play a ~
on\ gastar una broma

**trickery** [TRIK•ree] *n* fraude M

**trickle** [TRIK•kl] *vi* escurrir

**tricky** [TRIK•kee] *adj* trapacero

**trifle** [TRUY•fl] *n* friolera F

**trigger** [TRI•gur] *n* gatillo M

**trill** [tril] *vt* trinar

**trim** *adj* aseado; *vt* cortar;
recortar; adornar

**trinket** [TRINK•kit] *n* joya F

**trio** [TREE•o] *n* trío M

**trip 1** *n* viaje M

**trip 2** *vi* tropezar; *vt* hacer
tropezar

**triple** [TRIP•pl] *adj* triple

**tripod** [TRUY•pod] *n* trípode M

**trite** [truyt] *adj* trillado

**triumph** [TRUY•uhmf] *n* triunfo M

**triumphant** [truy•UHM•fint] *adj* triunfal

**triumphantly** [truy•UHM•fint•lee] *adj* triunfalmente

**trivial** [TRI•vee•ul] *adj* trivial

**trolley** [TRAH•lee] *n* tranvía F

**trombone** [trahm•BON] *n* trombón M

**troop** *n* tropa F

**trooper** [TROOP•pur] *n* soldado M

**trophy** [TRO•fee] *n* trofeo M

**tropic** [TRAH•pik] *adj* tropical; ~s\ *npl* trópico

**trot** [traht] *vi* trotar; *n* trote M

**trouble** [TRUH•bl] *n* disturbio M; be in ~\ estar en un apuro; make ~\ armar un lio; *vt* molestar; preocupar

**trouble maker** [TRUH•bl MAI•kur] *n* agitador M

**troublesome** [TRUH•bl•suhm] *adj* penoso

**trough** [trahf] *n* comedero M

**trousers** [TROU•zurz] *n* pernera F

**trousseau** [troo•SO] *n* ajuar de novia M

**trowel** [TROU•wl] *n* trulla F

**truant** [TROO•int] *n* novillero M

**truce** [troos] *n* tregua F

**truck** [truhk] *n* carretilla F

**trudge** [truhj] *vt* andar

**true** [troo] *adj* verdadero

**truly** [TROO•lee] *adj* verdaderamente

**trump** [truhmp] *vt* triunfar

**trumpet** [TRUHM•pit] *n* trompeta F

**trunk** [truhnk] *n* tronco M

**trust** [truhst] *vt* confiar; *n* en confianza F

**trustee** [TRUHS•stee] *n* fideicomisario M

**trustworthy** [TRUHST•wur•thee] *adj* fiable

**trusty** [TRUH•stee] *adj* fiel

**truth** [trooth] *n* verdad F

**truthful** [TROOTH•fl] *adj* veraz

**truthfulness** [TROOTH•fl•nes] *n* veracidad F

**try** [truy] *vt n* probar; prueba F

**trying** [TRUY•ying] *adj* de prueba

**tub** [tuhb] *n* batea F

**tube** [toob] *n* tubo M

**tubercular** [too•BUR•kyu•lur] *adj* tuberculoso

**tuberculosis** [too•BUR•kyu•LO•sis] *n* tuberculosis M

**tubing** [TOO•bing] *n* tubería F

**tuck** [tuk] *n* alforza F

**Tuesday** [TOOZ•dai] *n* martes M

**tuft** [tuhft] *n* penacho M

**tug** [tuhg] *vt* tirar de

**tuition** [TOO•i•shn] *n* enseñanza F

**tulip** [TOO•lip] *n* tulipán M

**tulle** [tool] *n* tul M

**tumble** [TUHM•bl] *n* tumbo M

**tumbler** [TUHM•blur] *n* volteador M

**tumor** [TOO•mur] *n* tumor M

**tumult** [TUH•muhlt] *n* tumulto M

**tumultuous**
[tuh•MUHL•choo•us] *adj*
tumultuoso

**tun** *n* tonel M

**tuna** [TOO•nuh] *n* tuna F

**tune** [toon] *n* melodía F, *vi*
atinar; be in ~\ estar afinado

**tunic** [TOO•nik] *n* túnica F

**tuning** [TOO•ning] *n*
afinación F

**tunnel** [TUH•nuhl] *n* túnel M

**turbid** [TUR•bid] *adj* turbio

**turbine** [TUR•buyn] *n*
turnbina F

**turbulent** [tur•BYU•lint] *adj*
turbulento

**turf** *n* césped M

**turgid** [TUR•jid] *adj* turgente

**Turk** *n* turco M

**turkey** [TUR•kee] *n* pavo M

**Turkey** [TUR•kee] *n* Turquia F

**Turkish** [TUR•kish] *adj* turco
turquesco

**turmoil** [TUR•moil] *n* tumulto M

**turn** *vt* volver; hacer girar; dar
vueltas a; *vi* girar; ~ against\
volverse; ~ off\ cerrar; ~ on\
abrir; ~ up\ *vi* aparecer; *vt*
encontrar (find)

**turnip** [TURN•ip] *n* nabo M

**turnover** [TUR•NO•vur] *vt*
voltereta F

**turntable** [TURN•TAI•bl] *n*
placa giratoria F

**turpentine** [TUR•pin•TUYN] *n*
trementina F

**turpitude** [TUR•pi•TOOD] *n*
torpeza F

**turquoise** [TUK•koiz] *n*
turquesa F

**turret** [TUR•rit] *n* torrecilla F

**turtle** [TUR•tl] *n* tortuga F

**tusk** [tuhsk] *n* colmillo M

**tutor** [TOO•tur] *n* preceptor M

**tuxedo** [tuk•SEE•do] *n* traje de
esmoquing M

**twang** *n* sonido vibrante M

**tweed** *n* paño M

**tweezers** [TWEE•zurz] *npl*
pinzas F

**twelfth** *num* duodécimo

**twelve** [twelv] *num* doce

**twentieth** [TWEN•tee•ith] *num*
vigésimo

**twenty** [TWEN•tee] *num* veinte

**twice** [twuyz] *num* dos veces

**twig** *n* ramita F

**twilight** [TWUY•luyt] *n*
crepúscolo M

**twin** *n* gemelo M

**twine** [twuyn] *n* cordel M

**twinge** [twinj] *n* punzada F

**twinkle** [TWINK•kl] *n*
centelleo M

**twinkling** [TWINK•kling] *n*
centelleante M

**twirl** *vt* retorcer

**twist** *vt* torcer

**twitch** [twich] *vt* temblor M

**twitter** *vi* gorjeo M

**two** [too] *num* dos

**tympani** [TIM•puh•nee] *n*
tambor M

**type** [tuyp] *n* tipo M

**typewriter** [TUYP•RUY•tur] *n*
máquina de escribir F

**typhoid** [TUY•foid] *adj*
tifoldeo M

**typhoon** [tuy•FOON] *n* tifón M

**typhus** [TUY•fus] *n* tifo M

**typical** [TI•pi•kl] *adj* típico

**typist** [TUY•pist] *n*
mecanógrafo M
**typography**
[tuy•PAH•gruh•fee] *n*
tipografía F

**tyrannical** [teer•RA•ni•kl] *adj*
tiránico
**tyranny** [TEER•ri•nee] *n*
tiranía F
**tyrant** [TUY•rent] *n* tirano M

# U

**udder** [UH•dur] *n* ubre M
**ugliness** [UH•glee•nes] *n*
fealdad F
**ugly** [UH•glee] *adj* feo
**ulcer** [UHL•sur] *n* úlcera F
**ulceration** [UHL•sur•RAI•shn]
*n* ulceración F
**ulterior** [uhl•TEE•ree•ur] *adj*
ulterior
**ultimate** [UHL•ti•mit] *adj*
último
**ultimately** [UHL•ti•mit•lee] *adj*
finalmente
**umbilicus** [uhm•BI•li•kus] *n*
ombligo M
**umbrage** [UHM•brij] *n*
sombra F
**umbrella** [uhm•BREL•luh] *n*
paraguas F
**umpire** [UHM•puyr] *n* árbitro M
**un-** [uhn] des; in; no; sin
**unable** [uhn•AI•bl] *adj* incapaz
**unaccountable**
[UHN•a•KOUN•tuh•bl] *adj*
inexplicable
**unaccustomed**
[UHN•a•KUH•stumd] *adj*
desacostumbrado
**unacknowledged**
[UHN•ak•NAH•lejd] *adj* no
reconocido

**unaffected** [UHN•a•FEK•ted]
*adj* sencillo
**unanimity**
[YOO•nuh•NI•mi•tee] *n*
unanimidad F
**unanimous** [yoo•NA•ni•mus]
*adj* unánime
**unapproachable**
[UHN•a•PRO•chuh•bl] *adj*
inaccesible
**unarmed** [uhn•ARMD] *adj*
desarmado
**unassailable**
[UHN•a•SAIL•luh•bl] *adj*
inexpugnable
**unassuming**
[UHN•uh•SOO•ming] *adj*
modesto
**unattractive**
[UHN•uh•TRAK•tiv] *adj* poco
atractivo
**unavailable**
[UHN•uh•VAI•luh•bl] *adj* no
disponible
**unavoidable**
[UHN•uh•VOI•duh•bl] *adj*
inevitable
**unaware** [UHN•uh•WAIR] *adj*
desprevenido

**unawares** [UHN•uh•WAIRZ]
*adj* inadvertidamente

**unbalanced** [uhn•BAL•cnzd]
*adj* desequilibrado

**unbearable** [uhn•BAI•ruh•bl]
*adj* insufrible

**unbecoming**
[UHN•bee•KUH•ming] *adj*
impropio

**unbelievable**
[UHN•bee•LEE•vuh•bl] *adj*
increíble

**unbeliever** [UHN•bee•LEE•vur]
*n* incrédulo M

**unbending** [uhn•BEN•ding] *adj*
inflexible

**unbiased** [uhn•BUY•esd] *adj*
imparcial

**unbounded** [uhn•BOUN•ded]
*adj* ilimitado

**unbreakable**
[uhn•BRAI•kuh•bl] *adj*
irrompible

**unbroken** [uhn•BRO•ken] *adj*
entero

**unburden** [uhn•BUR•den] *vt*
descargar

**unbutton** [uhn•BUH•ten] *vt*
desabotonar

**uncanny** [uhn•KA•nee] *adj*
misterioso

**unceasing** [uhn•SEE•sing] *adj*
incesante

**uncertain** [uhn•SUR•ten] *adj*
incierto

**unchangeable**
[uhn•CHAIN•juh•bl] *adj*
inmutable

**unchanged** [uhn•CHAIN•jed]
*adj* inalterado

**uncivil** [uhn•SI•vil] *adj* incivil

**unclaimed** [uhn•KLAI•med] *adj*
no reclamado

**uncle** [UHN•kl] *n* tío M

**unclean** [uhn•KLEEN] *adj*
sucio

**uncomfortable**
[uhn•KUHM•faur•tuh•bl] *adj*
incómodo

**uncommon** [uhn•KAH•men]
*adj* poco común

**uncompromising**
[uhn•KAHM•pro•MUY•zing]
*adj* inflexible

**unconcerned**
[uhn•KUHN•surnd] *adj*
indiferente

**unconditional**
[UHN•kun•DI•shuh•nl] *adj*
incondicional

**unconquered**
[uhn•KAHN•kurd] *adj*
inconquistado

**unconscious** [uhn•KAHN•shus]
*adj* inconsciente

**unconsciousness**
[uhn•KAHN•shus•nes] *n*
inconcienia F

**uncontrollable**
[UHN•kuhn•TRO•luh•bl] *adj*
irrefrenable

**uncontrolled**
[UHN•kuhn•TROLD] *adj* sin
freno

**unconventional**
[UHN•kuhn•VEN•shuh•nl] *adj*
original

**uncork** [uhn•KAURK] *vt*
descorchar

**uncouth** [uhn•KOOTH] *adj*
toscamente

**uncover** [uhn•KUH•vur] *vt*
descubrir

**unction** [UHNK•shun] *n*
unción F

**unctuous** [UHNK•shus] *adj*
untuoso

**uncultured** [uhn•KUL•churd]
*adj* inculto

**undeceive** [UHN•dee•SEEV] *vt*
desengañar

**undecided**
[UHN•dee•SUY•ded] *adj*
indeciso

**undeniable**
[UHN•dee•NUY•uh•bl] *adj*
innegable

**under** [UHN•dur] *prep* bajo;
debajo de

**underbrush**
[UHN•dur•BRUSH] *n*
maleza F

**undercarriage**
[UHN•dur•KAI•rij] *n* soporte
inferior M

**underclothes**
[UHN•dur•klothz] *n* ropa
interior F

**underestimate**
[UHN•dur•ES•ti•MAIT] *vt*
desestimar

**undergo** [UHN•dur•GO] *vt*
experimentar

**undergraduate**
[UHN•dur•GRA•joo•wait] *n*
estudiante de universidad M

**underground**
[UHN•dur•GROUND] *adj*
subterráneo

**underhanded**
[UHN•dur•HAN•ded] *adj*
secreto

**underline** [UHN•dur•LUYN] *vt*
subrayar

**underlying**
[UHN•dur•LUY•ing] *adj*
subyacente

**undermine** [UHN•dur•MUYN]
*vt* minar

**underneath** [uhn•dur•NEETH]
*prep* debajo

**underpay** [UHN•dur•PAI] *vt*
pagar poco

**undersell** [UHN•dur•SEL] *vt*
vender a bajo precio

**undershirt** [UHN•dur•SHURT]
*n* camiseta F

**undersigned**
[UHN•dur•SUYND] *n*
infrascrito M

**undersized** [UHN•dur•SUYZD]
*adj* pequeño

**understand**
[UHN•dur•STAND] *vi*
comprender; entender

**understandable**
[UHN•dur•STAN•duh•bl] *adj*
comprensible

**understanding**
[UHN•dur•STAN•ding] *n*
conocimiento M

**understate** [UHN•dur•STAIT]
*vt* decir menos de lo que hay

**understudy**
[UHN•dur•STUH•dee] *n*
suplente M

**undertake** [uhn•dur•TAIK] *vt*
emprender

**undertaken**
[UHN•dur•TAI•ken] pp
emprenado

**undertaker** [UHN•dur•TAI•kur]
*n* empresario M

**undertaking**
[UHN•dur•TAI•king] *n*
empresa F

**undertow** [UHN•dur•TO] *n*
resaca F

**underwear** [UHN•dur•WAIR]
*n* ropa interior F

**underworld**
[UHN•dur•WURLD] *n* este
mundo M

**underwrite** [UHN•dur•RUYT]
*vt* subscribir

**undeviating**
[UHN•DEE•vee•AI•ting] *adj*
directo

**undo** [uhn•DOO] *vt* deshacer

**undress** [uhn•DRES] *vi vt*
desnudar

**undue** [uhn•DOO] *adj* indebido

**undulate** [UHN•joo•LAIT] *vi*
ondular

**undying** [uhn•DUY•ing] *adj*
imperecedero

**unearned** [uhn•URN•ed] *adj*
inmerecido

**unearth** [uhn•URTH] *vt*
desenterrar

**uneasy** [uhn•EE•zee] *adj*
intranquilo

**uneducated**
[uhn•ED•joo•KAI•ted] *adj*
inculto

**unemployed**
[UHN•em•PLOID] *adj*
desocupado

**unemployment**
[UHN•em•PLOI•ment] *n*
desocupación F

**unending** [uhn•EN•ding] *adj*
inacable

**unequal** [uhn•EE•kwel] *adj*
desigual

**uneven** [uhn•EE•ven] *adj*
desigual

**unexpected**
[UHN•ek•SPEK•tid] *adj*
inesperado

**unfair** [uhn•FAIR] *adj* injusto

**unfaithful** [uhn•FAITH•ful] *adj*
infiel

**unfasten** [uhn•FAS•sin] *vt*
desabrochar; (clothing)
desatar

**unfit** [uhn•FIT] *adj* inadecuado;
no apto

**unfold** [uhn•FAULD] *vt*
desdoblar; (fig) revelar

**unfortunate**
[uhn•FAUR•tchoo•net] *adj*
desgraciado

**unfriendly** [uhn•FREND•lee]
*adj* poco amistoso; frio

**ungrateful** [uhn•GRAIT•ful]
*adj* desgradecido

**unhappy** [uhn•HA•pee] *adj*
infeliz; triste

**unhappiness** [uhn•HA•pee•nes]
*n* tristeza F

**unhealthy** [uhn•HEL•thee] *adj*
enfermizo; (unsanitary)
malsano

**unicorn** [YOO•nee•kaurn] *n*
unicornio M

**uniform** [YOO•ni•faurm] *adj*
uniforme; *n* uniforme M

**unimportant**
[UHN•im•PAUR•tant] *adj*
insignificante

**union** [YOO•nyuhn] *n* unión F

**unique** [yoo•NEEK] *adj* único

**unison** [YOO•ni•suhn] *n* al unisóno

**unit** [YOO•nit] *n* unidad F

**unite** [yoo•NUYT] *vt* unir; *vi* unirse

**United Kingdom** *n* Reino Unido M

**United Nations** *n* Orginazación de las Naciones Unidas

**United States** *npl* Estados Unidos M

**universe** [YOO•ni•vers] *n* universo M

**universal** [YOO•nee•VER•sal] *adj* universal

**university** [YOO•nee•VER•see•tee] *n* universidad F; *adj* universitario

**unjust** [uhn•JUHST] *adj* injusto

**unkind** [uhn•KUYND] *adj* poco amable; cruel

**unkindess** [uhn•KUYND•nes] *n* falta de amabilidad F

**unknown** [uhn•NOHN] *adj* desconocido

**unless** [uhn•LES] *conj* a menos que; a no ser que

**unlike** [uhn•LUYK] *adj* diferente; *prep* a diferencia de

**unlikely** [uhn•LUYK•lee] *adj* improbable

**unlimited** [uhn•LIM•i•tud] *adj* ilimitado

**unload** [uhn•LOHD] *vt* descargar

**unlock** [uhn•LAHK] *vt* abrir

**unlucky** [uhn•LUH•kee] *adj* desgraciado

**unmarried** [uhn•MA•reed] *adj* soltero; ~ mother\ madre soltera

**unnatural** [uhn•NA•chur•el] *adj* no natural; anormal

**unnecessary** [uhn•NE•si•SAI•ree] *adj* innecesario

**unnoticed** [uhn•NOH•tisd] *adj* in advertido

**unofficial** [uhn•oh•FI•shul] *adj* no oficial

**unpack** [uhn•PAK] *vt* desempaquetar; *vi* deshacer la maleta

**unpleasant** [uhn•PLEH•zunt] *adj* desagreable

**unpopular** [uhn•PAH•pyoo•lur] *adj* impopular

**unpredictable** [uhn•pree•DIK•tuh•bul] *adj* imprevisible

**unqualified** [uhn•KWAH•li•FUYD] *adj* sin titulo; (absolute) absoluto

**unravel** [uhn•RA•vul] *vt* desenredar; deshacer; *vi* desenredarse

**unreal** [uhn•REEL] *adj* irreal

**unrealistic** [uhn•REE•uh•LIS•tik] *adj* poco realista

**unreasonable** [uhn•REE•sohn•uh•bl] irrazonable

**unsuccessful** [UHN•suhk•SES•fl] *adj* infructuoso

**unsuitable** [uhn•SOO•tuh•bl] *adj* impropio

**unsuspected** [UHN•suh•SPEK•ted] *adj* insospechado

**unsuspecting**
[UHN•suh•SPEK•ting] *adj*
descuidado

**unthinkable**
[uhn•THIN•kuh•bl] *adj*
inconcebible

**unthinking** [uhn•THIN•king]
*adj* irreflexivo

**untidiness** [uhn•TUY•dee•nes]
*n* desaseo M

**untie** [uhn•TUY] *vt* desatar

**until** [uhn•TIL] *prep* hasta; *conj*
hasta que

**untimely** [uhn•TUYM•lee] *adj*
intempestivo

**untiring** [uhn•TUYR•ring] *adj*
incansable

**unto** [UHN•too] *prep* hacia

**untold** [uhn•TOLD] *adj* no
dicho

**untouched** [uhn•TUCHD] *adj*
intacto

**untrained** [uhn•TRAIND] *adj*
inexperto

**untried** [uhn•TRUYD] *adj* no
probado

**untroubled** [uhn•TRUH•bld]
*adj* quieto

**untrue** [uhn•TROO] *adj*
contrario

**unused** [uhn•YOOSD] *adj* no
usado

**unveil** [uhn•VAIL] *vt* descubrir

**unwarranted**
[uhn•WAH•ren•ted] *adj*
injustificado

**unwary** [uhn•WAI•ree] *adj*
descuidado

**unwashed** [uhn•WASHD] *adj*
sucio

**unwelcome** [uhn•WEL•kom]
*adj* indeseable

**unwholesome** [uhn•HOL•sum]
*adj* malsano

**unwieldy** [uhn•WEEL•dee] *adj*
pesado

**unwilling** [uhn•WIL•ling] *adj*
reacio

**unwillingness**
[uhn•WIL•ling•ncs] *n*
renuencia F

**unwind** [uhn•WUYND] *vt*
devanar

**unwise** [uhn•WUYZ] *adj*
imprudente

**unworthy** [uhn•WUR•thee] *adj*
indigno

**unwrap** [uhn•RAP] *vt*
desenvolver

**unyielding** [uhn•YEEL•ding]
*adj* inflexible

**up** [uhp] *adv* arriba; ~ here\
aqui arriba; ~ to\ hasta; be ~
against\ engrentarse con; be ~
to\ tramar; what's ~?\ ¿qué
pasa?

**up-to-date** [UHP•too•DAIT]
*adj* hasta la fecha

**upbraid** [uhp•BRAID] *vt*
reconvenir

**upgrade** [uhp•GRAID] *n*
cuesta F

**upheaval** [uhp•HEE•vul] *n*
solevamiento M

**uphill** [UHP•hil] *adj* cuesta
arriba

**uphold** [uhp•HOLD] *vt*
mantener

**upholster** [uh•POL•stur] *vt*
tapizar

**upholstery** [uh•POL•stree] *npl* tapicería F

**upkeep** [UHP•keep] *n* manutención F

**uplift** [uhp•LIFT] *vt* levantar

**upon** [uh•PAHN] *prep* sobre; encima

**upper** [UH•pur] *adj* alto superior

**upright** [UHP•ruyt] *adj* derecho

**uprising** [UHP•ruy•zing] *n* levantamiento M

**uproar** [UHP•ror] *n* gritería F

**upset** [uhp•SET] *vt* volcar; *n* trastorno M

**upshot** [UHP•shot] *n* resultado final M

**upside** [UHP•suyd] *n* lado superior M; ~ down\ *adv* al revés

**upstairs** [uhp•STAIRZ] arriba

**upstart** [UHP•start] *n* advenedizo M

**upward** [UHP•wurd] *adv* ascendente

**uranium** [yur•AI•nee•um] *n* uranio M

**urban** [UR•bin] *adj* urbano

**urchin** [UR•chin] *n* bribonzuelo M

**urge** [urj] *vt* insistir; *n* impulso M

**urgency** [UR•jen•see] *n* urgencia F

**urgent** [UR•jent] *adj* urgente

**urgently** [UR•jent•lee] *adv* urgentemente

**urinate** [YUR•in•NAIT] *vi* orinar

**urine** [YUR•rin] *n* orina F

**urn** *n* urna F

**us** [uhs] *per pron* nosotros

**usage** [YOO•sej] *n* trato M

**use** [yooz] *n vt* uso M; *vt* emplear; it's no ~\ es inútil; no sirve para nada; make ~ of \ servirse de; ~ up\ agotar, consumir

**used car** [YOOZD KAHR] *n* coche usado M

**useful** [YOOS•ful] *adj* útil

**usefulness** [YOOS•ful•ness] *n* utilidad F

**useless** [YOOS•les] *adj* inútil

**uselessness** [YOOS•les•nes] *n* inutilidad F

**usher** [UH•shur] *n* portero M

**usual** [YOO•zjuh•ul] *adj* usual

**usually** [YOO•zj·wuh•lee] *adv* ususalmente

**usurer** [YOO•zjhoo•rur] *n* usurero M

**usurp** [yoo•SURP] *vt* usurpar

**usury** [YOO•zjhur•ee] *n* usura F

**utensil** [yoo•TEN•sul] *n* utensilio M

**utility** [yoo•TI•li•tee] *n* utilidad F

**utilize** [YOO•ti•LUYZ] *vt* utilizar

**utmost** [UHT•most] *adj* sumo

**utter 1** [UHT•tur] *vi* prunciar

**utter 2** *adj* completo

**utterly** [UHT•tur•lee] *adv* totalmente

**utterance** [UHT•tur•anz] *n* articulación F

**U-turn** [YOO•turn] *n* vuelta F

**uvula** [YOO•vyu•luh] *n* úvula F

# V

**vacancy** [VAI•ken•see] *n* vacancia F

**vacant** [VAI•kint] *adj* vacante

**vacate** [VAI•kait] *vi* evacuar

**vacation** [vai•KAI•shn] *n* vacación F

**vaccinate** [VAK•zin•NAIT] *vt* vacunar

**vaccine** [vak•SEEN] *n* vacuno M

**vacillate** [VA•sil•LAIT] *vi* vacilar

**vacuum** [VA•kyum] *n* vacuo M; ~ cleaner\ *n* aspiradora F

**vagabond** [VA•guh•BAUND] *n* vagabundo M

**vague** [vaig] *adj* vago

**vain** *adj* vano; inútil

**valentine** [VA•len•TUYN] *n* Valentín M

**valet** [va•LAIT] *n* planchador M

**valiant** [VA•lee•ent] *adj* valiente

**valid** [VA•lid] *adj* válido

**validity** [va•LI•di•tee] *n* validez F

**valise** [va•LEES] *n* maleta F

**valor** [VA•lor] *n* valentía F

**valorous** [VA•lo•rus] *adj* valeroso

**valuable** [VAL•yoo•bl] *adj* valioso

**value** [VAL•yoo] *n* valor M; market ~ \ *n* valor mercadil M

**valve** [vahlv] *n* válvula F

**valley** [VAL•lee] *n* valle M

**van** *n* carramato M

**vane** [vain] *n* veleta F

**vanilla** [vuh•NIL•luh] *n* vainilla F

**vanish** [VA•nish] *vi* desaparecer

**vanity** [VA•ni•tee] *n* vanidad F

**vanquish** [VAN•kwish] *vt* vencer

**vantage** [VAN•tij] *n* ventaja F

**vapid** [VA•pid] *adj* evaporado

**vapor** [VAI•por] *n* vapor M

**vaporize** [VAI•po•RUYZ] *vt* vaporizar

**variable** [VAIR•ree•uh•bl] *adj* variable

**variance** [VAIR•ree•ens] *n* variación F

**variation** [VAIR•ree•AI•shn] *n* variación F

**varied** [VAIR•reed] *adj* vario

**variegated** [VAI•re•GAI•ted] *adj* abigarrado

**variety** [vuh•RUY•i•tee] *n* variedad F

**various** [VAIR•ee•us] *adj* vario

**varnish** [VAR•nish] *n* barniz M

**vary** [VAIR•ree] *vt* variar

**vase** [vaiz] *n* florero M

**vast** *adj* vasto

**vastness** [VAST•nis] *n* vastedad F

**vat** *n* tina F

**vault** *n vi* bóveda F

**vaunt** *vt vi* jactancia F; cripta F (tomb); sótano M (jump) *vt vi* saltar

**veal** [veel] *n* ternera F

**veer** *vi* virar

**vegetable** [VE•je•tuh•bl] *n*
vegetal M

**vegetarian** [VE•je•TAI•ree•en]
*n* vegetariano M

**vegetate** [VE•je•TAIT] *vi*
vegetar

**vegetation** [VE•je•TAI•shn] *n*
vegetación F

**vehemence** [VEE•him•menz] *n*
vehemencia F

**vehicle** [VEE•hi•kl] *n* vehículo M

**veil** [vail] *n* velo M; *vt* velar

**vein** [vain] *n* nervio M

**vein** [vain] *vi* prunciar

**velocity** [ve•LAH•si•tee] *n*
velocidad F

**velvet** [VEL•vit] *n* velludo M

**vendor** [VEN•dur] *n* vendedor M

**veneer** [vuh•NEER] *n* chapa F;
apariencia F

**venerable** [VE•nur•uh•bl] *adj*
venerable

**venerate** [VE•nur•RAIT] *vt*
venerar

**veneration** [VE•nur•RAI•shn]
*n* veneración F

**vengeance** [VEN•jenz] *n*
venganza F

**venison** [VE•ni•sun] *n* venado M

**venom** [VE•nuhm] *n* veneno M

**venomous** [VE•nuh•mus] *adj*
venenoso

**vent** *n* abertura F; *vt* hacer un
agujero en; desahogar (coll);
give ~ to\ dar salida a

**ventilate** [VEN•ti•LAIT] *vt*
ventilar

**ventilation** [VEN•ti•LAI•shn] *n*
ventilación F

**ventilator** [VEN•ti•LAI•tur] *n*
ventilador M

**venture** [VEN•chur] *n* ventura
F; *vt* arriesgar; *vi* atreverse

**venue** [VEN•yoo] *n*
jurisdicción F

**verandah** [vur•AN•duh] *n*
pórtico M

**verb** [vurb] *n* verbo M

**verbal** [VER•bul] *adj* verbal

**verbose** [vur•BOS] *adj* verboso

**verdict** [VUR•dikt] *n* veredicto M

**verge** [vurj] *n* borde M; ~ on\
acercarse a

**verification**
[VAI•ri•fi•KAI•shn] *n*
verificación F

**verify** [VAI•ri•FUY] *vt* verificar

**veritable** [VAI•rih•ti•bl] *adj*
verdadero

**vermin** [VUR•min] *n* bicho M

**vernacular** [vur•NAK•kyu•lur]
*adj* vernáculo

**verse** [vurz] *n* verso M

**versed** [vurzd] *adj* versado

**version** [VUR•shin] *n* versión F

**vertebra** [VUR•ti•bruh] *n*
vértebra F

**vertical** [VURT•ti•kl] *adj*
vertical

**vertigo** [VUR•ti•GO] *n*
vértigo M

**very** [VAIR•ree] *adv* muy; ~
much\ muchísimo; ~ well\
muy bien; the ~ first\ el
primero de todos; *adj* mismo;
the ~ thing\ exactamente lo
que hace falta

**vespers** [VE•spurz] *n* Véspero M

**vessel** [VE•sul] *n* vasija F

**vest** *n* chaleco M; *vt* conferir

**vestibule** [VE•sti•BYUL] *n*
vestíbulo M

**vestige** [VE•stij] *n* vestigio M
**vestigial** [ve•STI•jul] *adj*
rudimentario
**vestment** (official attire)
[VEST•mint] *n* vestidura F
**vestry** [VES•stree] *n* sacristía F
**veteran** [VE•tur•rin] *n*
veterano M
**veterinarian**
[VE•truh•NAI•ree•en] *n*
veterinario M
**veterinary** [VE•truh•NAI•ree]
*adj* veterinario
**veto** [VEE•to] *n* veto M
**vex** [veks] *vt* vejar
**via** [VEE•yuh] *prep* vía
**viaduct** [VUY•uh•DUKT] *n*
viaducto M
**vial** [vuyl] *n* redoma F
**viands** [VEE•endz] *n* vianda F
**viaticum** [vee•A•ti•kum] *n*
viático M
**vibrate** [VUY•brait] *vi* vibrar
**vibration** [vuy•BRAI•shn] *n*
vibración F
**vice** [vuys] *n* vicio M
**vicinity** [ve•SIN•i•tee] *n*
vecindad F
**vicious** [VI•shus] *adj* vicioso
**victim** [VIK•tim] *n* víctima F
**victor** [VIK•tur] *n* vencedor M
**victorious** [vik•TAU•ree•us] *adj*
victorioso
**victory** [VIK•tree] *n* victoria F
**victuals** [VIK•chulz] *npl*
vitualla F
**vie** [vuy] *vi* emular; rivalizar
**view** [vyu] *vi* vista F; in my ~\
a mijuicio; in ~ of\ en vista
de; on ~\ expuesto, with a ~

to\ con miras a; *vt* ver; visitar;
considerar
**vigil** [VI•jil] *n* vigilia F
**vigilant** [VI•ji•lint] *adj* vigilante
**vigor** [VI•gur] *n* vigor M
**vigorous** [VI•gur•us] *adj*
vigoroso
**vile** [vuyl] *adj* vil
**villa** [VI•luh] *n* villa F
**village** [VI•lij] *n* pueblo M
**villager** [VI•li•jur] *n* lugareño M
**villain** [VI•lin] *n* bribón M
**villainous** [VI•lin•nis] *adj*
villano
**villainy** [VI•lin•nee] *n* villanía F
**vim** *n* fuerza F
**vindicate** [VIN•di•KAIT] *vt*
vindicar
**vindictive** [vin•DIK•tiv] *adj*
vindicativo
**vine** [vuyn] *n* parra F
**vinegar** [VI•ni•gur] *n* vinagre M
**vineyard** [VIN•yurd] *n* viña F
**vintage** [VIN•tij] *n* vendimia F
**violate** [VUY•o•LAIT] *vt* violar
**violation** [VUY•o•LAI•shn] *n*
violación F
**violence** [VUY•o•lens] *n*
violencia F
**violent** [VUY•o•lent] *adj*
violento
**violet** [VUY•o•let] *n* violeta F
**violin** [VUY•o•lin] *n* violin F
**violinist** [VUY•o•LI•nist] *n*
violinista F
**viper** [VUY•pur] *n* víbora F
**virgin** [VUR•jin] *n* virgen F
**virginity** [vur•JI•ni•tec] *n*
virginidad F
**virile** [VEER•rl] *adj* viril

**virility** [vur•RI•li•tee] *n*
virilidad F

**virtual** [VUR•choo•ul] *adj*
virtual

**virtually** [VUR•chuh•lee] *adj*
virtualmente

**virulence** [VEER•yoo•lenz] *n*
virulencia F

**virus** [VUY•rus] *n* virus M

**visa** [VEE•zuh] *n* visado M

**visage** [VI•sej] *n* rostro M

**viscera** [VI•suh•ruh] *npl*
vísceras F

**viscosity** [vi•SKAH•si•tee] *n*
viscosidad F

**visibility** [VI•si•BI•li•tee] *n*
visibilidad F

**visible** [VI•si•bl] *adj* visible

**vision** [VI•shin] *n* vista F

**visionary** [VI•shin•NAI•ree] *adj*
visionario

**visit** [VI•zit] *n* visita F; *vt* visitar

**visitation** [VI•zi•TAI•shn] *n*
visitación F

**visitor** [VI•zi•tur] *n* visitante M

**visor** [VUY•zur] *n* visera F

**vista** [VI•stuh] *n* vista F

**visual** [VI•zjhoo•ul] *adj* visual

**visualize** [VI•zjhoo•LUYZ] *vt*
hacer visible

**vital** [VUY•tl] *adj* vital M

**vitality** [vuy•TA•li•tee] *n*
vitalidad F

**vitamin** [VUY•tuh•min] *n*
vitamina F

**vitreous** [VI•tree•us] *adj* vitreo

**vitriol** [VI•tree•ol] *n* vitriolo M

**vivacious** [vuy•VAI•shus] *adj*
vivaz

**vivacity** [vuy•VA•si•tee] *n*
vivacidad F

**vivid** [VI•vid] *adj* vívido

**vocabulary**
[vo•KA•byu•LAI•ree] *n*
vocabulario M

**vocal** [VO•kul] *adj* vocal

**vocation** [vo•KAI•shn] *n*
vocación F

**vogue** [vog] *n* moda F

**voice** [voiz] *n* voz F

**void** *adj* vacío

**volatile** [VAH•li•tl] *adj* volátil

**volcanic** [vol•KA•nik] *adj*
volcánico

**volcano** [vol•KAI•no] *n*
volcán M

**volt** *n* voltio M

**voltage** [VOL•tej] *n* voltaje M

**volume** [VAHL•yoom] *n*
volumen M

**voluntary** [VAH•lun•TAI•ree]
*adj* voluntario

**volunteer** [VAH•lun•TEER] *n*
voluntario M

**voluptuous** [vuh•LUP•shus]
*adj* voluptuoso

**volley** [VAH•lee] *n* descarga F

**vomit** [VAH•mit] *vt* vomitar

**voracious** [vor•RAI•shus] *adj*
voraz

**vote** [vot] *n* voto M; *vt* votar

**voter** [VO•tur] *n* votante M

**voting** [VO•ting] *n* votación F

**vouch** *vi* testificar

**voucher** [VOU•chur] *n*
garante M

**vow** [vou] *n* promesa F; *vi* jurar

**vowel** [VOU•wul] *n* vocal M

**voyage** [VOI•ij] *n* viaje por
mar M

**vulgar** [VUL•gur] *adj* vulgar

**vulgarity** [vul•GAI•ri•tee] *n*
vulgaridad F
**vulnerable** [VUHL•nur•uh•bl]
*adj* vulnerable

**vulture** [VUHL•chur] *n*
cóndor M

# W

**wad** [wahd] *n* pelota F
**waddle** [WAH•dl] *vi* anadeo M
**wade** [waid] *vi* andar sobre
agua
**wafer** [WAI•fur] *n* hostia F
**waffle** [WAH•fl] *n* barquillo M
**waft** [wahft] *vt* mecer
**wag** *vi* menear
**wage** [waij] *n* paga F
**wager** [WAI•jur] *vt* apostar
**wagon** [WAG•gin] *n* carreta F
**waif** *n* golfillo M
**wail** *vi* lamentar
**waist** *n* talle M
**wait** *vi* esperar
**waiter** [WAI•tur] *n* mozo M
**waiting** [WAI•ting] *n* espera F
**waiting-room** *n* antesala F
**waitress** [WAI•tres] *n* moza F
**waive** [waiv] *vt* renunciar
**wake 1** [waik] *vt* despertar; *vi*
dispertarse
**wake 2** *n* estela F
**waken** [WAI•kin] *vt* despertar
**walk** [wauk] *vi* andar; caminar;
ir a pie; ~ out\ salir; ~ out on\
abandonar; ~ of life\ clase
social
**walnut** [WAHL•nut] *n* nogal M
**waltz** [wahlz] *n* vals M
**wall** [waul] *n* pared F

**wallet** [WAU•lit] *n* mochila F
**wallflower**
[WAUL•FLOU•wur] *n*
alhelí M
**wallop** [WHAH•lop] *vt* pegar
**wallow** [WHAH•lo] *vi*
revolcarse
**wan** *adj* pálido
**wand** *n* vara F
**wander** [WAHN•dur] *vi* vagar
**wanderer** [WAHN•dur•rur] *n*
viajero M
**wane** (decrease; lessen) [wain]
*vi* menguar
**want** [wahnt] *aux verb* querer;
*vi* ~ for\ carecer de; *n*
necesidad F; falta F (lack)
**wanton** [WAHN•tin] *adj*
travieso
**war** [waur] *n* guerra F; at ~\ en
guerra
**warble** [WAUR•bl] *vt*
murmurar
**ward** [waurd] *n* guarda F
**warden** [WAUR•din] *n*
guardián M
**wardrobe** [WAUR•drob] *n*
armario M
**ware** [wair] *n* mercancías
**warehouse** [WAIR•houz] *n*
almacén M

**warlike** |WAUR•luyk| *adj*
belicoso

**warm** |wahrm| *adj* caliente

**warmth** |wahrmth| *n* calor M

**warn** |waurn| *vt* avisar

**warning** |WAUR•ning| *n*
aviso M

**warp** |waurp| *vt* urdir

**warrant** |WAUR•rint| *n*
autorización F

**warrior** |WAUR•yur| *n*
guerrero M

**wart** |waurt| *n* verruga F

**wary** |WAIR•ree| *adj* cauto

**wash** *vt* lavar; *vi* lavarse; *n*
lvado M; ~ out\ *vt* enjuagar

**washer** |WAH•shur| *n* lavado M

**washing** |WAH•shing| *n*
lavado M

**washing-machine**
|WAH•shing muh•SHEEN| *n*
lavadora F

**wasp** |wahsp| *n* avispa F

**waste** |waist| *vt* devastar; *adj*
desecho; yermo; ~ away\
consumirse

**wasteful** |WAIST•fl| *adj*
asolador

**waste-paper basket**
|WAIST•PAI•pur BA•skit| *n*
cesto M

**watch** |wach| *vt n* reloj M; *vt*
mirar; *n* vigilancia F; on the
~\ alerta; ~ out\ tener cuidado

**watchman** |WACH•mun| *n*
guardián M

**water** |WA•tur| *n* agua M; by
~\ pormar; in hot ~\ en un
apuro (coll); ~ down\ diluir

**water sports** |WA•tur
SPAURTS| *n* deportes
acuáticos

**watercolor** |WA•tur•KUH•lur|
*n* acuarela F

**waterfall** |WA•tur•FAL| *n*
cascada F

**waterproof** |WA•tur•PROOF|
*adj* impermeable

**watertight** |WA•tur•TUYT|
*adj* estanco

**waterway** |WA•tur•WAI| *n*
canal M

**watery** |WA•tur•ree| *adj* acuoso

**wave** |waiv| *n* ola F

**wavelength** |WAIV•length| *n*
longitud de onda F

**wavy** |WAIV•vee| *adj* ondoso

**wax** |waks| *n* cera F; *vt* cerar

**way** |wai| *n* vía F

**waylay** |WAI•lai| *vt* aguardar
emboscado

**wayward** |WAI•wurd| *adj*
díscolo

**we** |wee| *pers pron* nosotros

**weak** |week| *adj* débil

**weaken** |WEE•kin| *vt* debilitar

**weakly** |WEEK•lee| *adj* débil

**wealth** |welth| *n* riqueza F

**wealthy** |WEL•thee| *adj* rico

**wean** |ween| *vt* despechar

**weapon** |WE•pun| *n* arma F

**wear** |wair| *vt* llevar; degastar
(damage); ~ off\ desaprecer;
~ and tear\ *n* desgaste M

**weariness** |WEE•ree•nes| *n*
cansancio M

**wearisome** |WEE•ree•suhm|
*adj* cansado

**weary** |WEE•ree| *adj* cansado

**weasel** |WEE•zul| *n*
comadreja F

**weather** |WE•thur| *n* tiempo M

**weather conditions** [WE•thur kun•DI•shns] *n* condiciones de tiempo

**weave** [weev] *vt* tejer; *n* tejedor M

**web** *n* tejido M

**webbing** [WEB•bing] *n* tejido M

**wed** *vt* casarse

**wedded** [WED•ded] *adj* casado

**wedding** [WED•ding] *n* boda F

**wedge** [wej] *n* calza F

**Wednesday** [WENS•dai] *n* miércoles

**weed** *n* hierba F

**weedy** [WEE•dee] *adj* algoso

**week** *n* semana F

**weekday** [WEEK•dai] *n* día de la semana M

**weekly** [WEEK•lee] *adj* semanal

**weep** *vi* llorar

**weeping** [WEE•ping] *adj* llanto

**weevil** [WEE•vul] *n* gorgojo M

**weigh** [wai] *vt* pesar

**weight** [wait] *n* peso M

**weighty** [WAI•tee] *adj* pesado

**welcome** [WEL•kum] *n* bien venido

**weld** *vt* soldar

**welfare** [WEL•fair] *n* bienestar M

**welt** *n* ribete M

**well 1** [wel] *adj* bien; *int* bueno

**well 2 (oil)** *n* fuente M

**well-being** [WEL•BEE•ing] *n* bienestar M

**well-to-do** [WEL•too•DOO] *adj* acomodado

**west** *n* oeste M

**western** [WES•turn] *adj* occidental

**westerner** [WES•tur•nur] *n* habitante del oeste M

**westward** [WEST•wurd] *adj* al oeste

**wet** *adj* mojado, get ~\ mojarse

**whack** [wak] *vt* pegar

**whale** [wail] *n* ballena F

**wharf** [warf] *n* embarcadero M

**what** [waht] *int* qué; ~ about me?\ ¿y yo?; ~ for?\ ¿para que?; ~ is it?\ ¿qué es?

**whatever** [waht•EV•vur] *pron* cualquier

**wheat** [weet] *n* trigo M

**wheel** [weel] *n* rueda F

**wheelbarrow** [WEEL•BAIR•ro] *n* carretilla de mano F

**wheelchair** [WEEL•chair] *n* silla de ruedas F

**wheezy** [WHEE•zee] *adj* asmático

**when** [wen] *adv conj* cuando

**whenever** [wen•EV•vur] *adv* cuando quiera

**where** [wair] *prep* donde; ~ are you going?\ ¿adónde vas?

**whereabouts** [WAIR•uh•BOUTZ] paradero

**whereas** [wair•AS] *prep* considerando

**whereby** [wair•BUY] *prep* por donde

**wherefore** [WAIR•for] *adv* por lo que

**wherever** [wair•EV•vur] *prep* dondequiera

**wherewithal** [WAIR•with•AL] *n* con lo qual

**whet** [wet] *vt* afilar

**whether** [WE•thur] *adv* si

**which** [wich] cuál

**whichever** [wich•EV•vur] *pron*
cualquiera

**whiff** [wif] *n* soplo M

**while** [wuyl] *n* rato M; *adv*
durante

**whim** [wim] *n* antojo M

**whimper** [WIM•pur] *vt* gemir

**whimsical** [WIM•si•kl] *adj*
caprichoso

**whine** [wuyn] *vi* gemir

**whip** [wip] *n* látigo M

**whipping** [WIP•ping] *n*
azotamiento M

**whir** [wur] *vi* zumbar

**whirl** [wurl] *vi* girar

**whirlpool** [WURL•pool] *n*
vorágine M

**whirlwind** [WURL•wind] *n*
torbellino M

**whisk** [wisk] *vt n* barrer
cepillo M

**whisker** [WIS•kur] *n* patilla F

**whiskey** [WIS•kee] *n* whisky M

**whisper** [WIS•pur] *vi* susurrar

**whistle** [WIS•sl] *vi* silbar

**whit** [wit] *n* pizca F

**white** [wuyt] *adj* blanco

**whiten** [WUY•tin] *vi* blanquear

**whiteness** [WUYT•nis] *n*
blancura F

**Whitsuntide** [WIT•zun•tuyd] *n*
Pascua de Pentecostés F

**whittle** [WIT•tl] *vt* dar forma

**whiz** [wiz] *vi* zumbar

**who** [hoo] *pron* que; quien;
el/la/los/las que (particular
person)

**whole** [hol] *adj* todo

**wholesale** [HOL•sail] *n* al por
mayor M

**wholesome** [HOL•sum] *adj*
sano

**wholly** [HOL•lee] *adv*
totalmente

**whom** [hoom] *pron* quien; a
quien

**whomever** [hoom•EV•vur]
*pron* quienesquiera

**whoop** [woop] *n* grito M

**whore** [hor] *n* puta F

**whose** [hooz] *pron* cuyo; cuya

**why** [wuy] *adv* por qué

**wick** [wik] *n* mecha F

**wicked** [WIK•kid] *adj* malo

**wickedness** [WIK•kid•nes] *n*
maldad F

**wicker** [WIK•kur] *n* mimbre M

**wicket** [WIK•kit] *n* postigo M

**wide** [wuyd] *adj* ancho

**wide awake** [WUYD
uh•WAIK] *adj* muy despierto

**widely** [WUYD•lee] *adv*
extensamente

**widespread** [wuyd•spred] *adv*
extendido

**widow** [WI•do] *n* viuda F

**widower** [WI•do•wur] *n*
viudo M

**width** *n* anchura F

**wield** [weeld] *vt* ejercer

**wife** [wuyf] *n* esposa F

**wig** *n* peluca F

**wild** [wuyld] *adj* salvaje

**wile** [wuyl] *vt* atraer

**wilt** *vt* secar

**wily** [WUY•lee] *adj* astuto

**will** [wil] *vi* querer; *n* voluntad F

**willful** [WIL•ful] *adj*
voluntarioso

**willing** [WIL•ling] *adj* deseoso

**willingly** [WIL•ling•lee] *adj* voluntariamente

**willingness** [WIL•ling•nis] *n* buena voluntad F

**willow** [wil•lo] *n* sauce M

**win** *vt* ganar

**wInce** [winz] *vt* cejar

**winch** *n* manubrio M

**wind1** [wind] *n* viento M

**wind 2** [wuynd] *vt* enrollar; dar cuerda a (clock); *vi* serpentear (road); ~ up\ termini; concluir

**windfall** [WIND•fal] *n* suerte F

**winding** [WUYN•ding] *n* arrollamiento M

**windmill** [WIND•mil] *n* molino de viento M

**window** [WIN•do] *n* ventana F

**window shade** [WIN•do SHAID] *n* transparente M

**windowsill** [WIN•do•SIL] *n* antepecho M

**windshield** [WIND•sheeld] *n* parabrisas

**windy** [WIN•dee] *adj* ventoso

**wine** [wuyn] *n* vino M

**wine cellar** [WUYN SEL•lur] *n* bódega F

**wineglass** [WUYN•glas] *n* taza de vino F

**wing** *n* ala F

**winged** [WING•gid] *adj* alado

**wink** *vi* pestañear

**winner** [WIN•nur] *n* ganador M

**winning** [WIN•ning] *adj* triunfo

**winter** [WIN•tur] *n* invierno M

**wintry** [WIN•tree] *adj* de invierno

**wIpe** [wuyp] *vt* limpiar

**wiper** [WUY•pur] *n* frotador M

**wire** [wuyr] *n* alambre M

**wireless** [WUYR•les] *adj* inalámbrico

**wiry** [WUYR•ree] *adj* de alambre

**wisdom** [WIZ•dom] *n* sabiduría F

**wise** [wuyz] *adj* sensato

**wiseacre** [WUYZ•AI•kur] *n* sabihondo M

**wisecrack** [WUYZ•krak] *n* agudeza F

**wish** *n* deseo M; *vi* desear

**wistful** [WIST•ful] *adj* anhelante

**wit** *n* ingenio M

**witch** [wich] *n* bruja F

**with** *prep* con; be ~ it\ estar al día (coll)

**withdraw** [with•DRAU] *vt* retirar

**withdrawal** [with•DRAU•wul] *n* retiro M

**withdrawn** [with•DRAUN] *adj* retirado

**wither** [WITH•thur] *vi* secar

**withhold** [with•HOLD] *vt* detener

**within** [with•THIN] *prep* dentro

**without** [with•THOUT] *prep* sin

**withstand** [with•STAND] *vt* resistir

**witness** [WIT•nes] *n* testigo M

**witticism** [WIT•ti•SI•zm] *n* agudeza F

**witty** [WIT•tee] *adj* ingenioso

**wizard** [WIZ•zurd] *n* brujo M

**woe** [wo] *n* dolor M

**wolf** *n* lobo M

**woman** [WUH•man] *n* mujer F

**womanhood**
[WUH•min•HUD] *n*
feminidad F
**womanly** [WUH•min•lee] *adj*
femenino
**womb** [woom] *n* útero M
**won** *pp* ganado
**wonder** [WUN•dur] *n*
admiración F
**wonderful** [WUN•dur•fl] *adj*
admirable; maravilloso
**wonderfully**
[WUN•dur•ful•lee] *adv*
maravillosamente
**wont** [wahnt] *adj* acostumbrado
**woo** *vt* galantear
**wood** [wud] *n* madera F
**woodland** [WUD•land] *n*
bosque M
**woodpecker** [WUD•PEK•kur]
*n* picaposte M
**woodwork** [WUD•wurk] *n*
enmaderamiento M
**woof** [wuf] *n* trama F (wool)
**woolen** [WUH•lin] *n* lanudo
**woolly** [WUH•lee] *adj* de lana
**word** [wurd] *n* palabra F
**wore** [waur] *pp* llevado
**work** [wurk] *n* trabajo M; *vt*
hacer trabajar; manejar; *vi*
trabajar
**workday** [WURK•dai] *n* día de
trabajo M
**worker** [WURK•ur] *n*
trabajador M
**working** [WUR•king] *n*
trabajo M
**workman** [WURK•man] *n*
obrero M
**workmanship**
[WURK•man•SHIP] *n* arte en
el trabajo M

**workshop** [WURK•shop] *n*
taller M
**world** [wurld] *n* mundo M
**worldly** [WURLD•lee] *adj*
mundano
**worm** [wurm] *n* gusano M
**worry** [WUR•ree] *vi*
preocuparse; *vt* molestar
(bother); *n* preocupación F
**worse** [wurz] *adj* peor
**worship** [WUR•ship] *vt*
reverenciar
**worshipper** [WUR•ship•pur] *n*
adorador M
**worst** [wurst] *adj* lo peor
**worth** [wurth] *n* valor M
**worthless** [WURTH•les] *adj*
sin valor
**worthy** [WUR•thee] *adj* valioso
**wound** [woond] *n* lesión F
**wrangle** [RAN•gl] *vi* altercar
**wrap** [rap] *vt* envolver
**wrapper** [RAP•pur] *n*
envolvedor M
**wrapping paper** [RAP•ping
PAI•pur] *n* cubierta F
**wrath** [rath] *n* ira F
**wreath** [reeth] *n* corona F
**wreck** [rek] *n* choque M
**wrench** [rench] *n* torcimiento M
**wrest** [rest] *vt* torcer
**wrestle** [RES•tl] *vi* luchar
**wretch** [retch] *n* miserable M
**wretched** [RETCH•chid] *adj*
infeliz
**wring** [ring] *vt* retorcer
**wrinkle** [RINK•kl] *n* arruga F
**wrist** [rist] *n* muñeca F
**writ** [rit] *n* escrito M
**write** [ruyt] *vt* escribir
**writer** [RUY•tur] *n* escritor M

**writhe** [ruyth] *vi* torcer
**writing** [RUY•ting] *n* escritura F
**wrong** [rong] *adj* malo; erróneo

**wrought iron** [ROUT l•urn] *n*
hierro forjado M
**wry** [ruy] *adj* torcido

# X

**X-ray** [EKS•rai] *n* radiográfico M
**xenophobe** [ZEE•no•fob] *n*
xenófobo M
**xylography**
[zuy•LAHG•gruh•fee] *n*
xilografía F

**xylophone** [ZUY•luh•FON] *n*
xilófono M

# Y

**yacht** [yaht] *n* yate M
**yank** *vt* dar un tirón
**yard** [yahrd] *n* yarda F
**yardstick** [YAHRD•stik] *n* vara
de medir F
**yawn** [yaun] *vi* bostezar; *n*
bostezo M
**yea** [yai] sí
**year** [yeer] *n* año M; be ten ~s
old; tener diez años
**yearn** [yurn] *vi* anhelar
**yearning** [YUR•ning] *n*
anhelo M
**yeast** [yeest] *n* levadura F
**yell** [yel] *vi* gritar
**yellow** [YEL•lo] *adj* amarillo
**yeoman** [yo•min] *n* hombre
libre M
**yes** *adj n* sí

**yesterday** [YES•tur•dai] *adv*
ayer
**yet** *adv* todavía
**yield** [yeeld] *vt* rendir
**yielding** [YEEL•ding] *adj* flojo
**yoke** [yok] *n* yugo M
**yolk** [yok] *n* yema F
**yonder** [YON•dur] *adv* aquel
**yore** [yaur] *adv* otro tiempo
**you** [yoo] tú; usted; with ~\
contigo; I know ~\ conozco;
you can't \ no se puede
**young** [yung] *adj* joven
**youngster** [YUNG•stur] *n* el
más joven M
**your; yours** [yor yorz] tu tus;
de usted; de ustedes
**yourself** [yor•SELF] tú; ti usted
**youth** [yooth] *n* juventud F

**youthful** [YOOTH•fl] *adj* joven

**Yuletide** [YOOL•tuyd] *n*
Pascua de Navidad F

# Z

**zeal** [zeel] *n* celo M

**zealot** [ZE•lot] *n* fanático M

**zealous** [ZE•lus] *adj* ardiente

**zebra** [ZEE•bruh] *n* cebra F

**zenith** [ZEE•nith] *n* zenit M

**zephyr** [ZE•fur] *n* céfiro M

**zeppelin** [ZE•pi•lin] *n*
zepelín M

**zero** [ZEE•ro] *n* cero M

**zest** *n* bizna F

**zigzag** [ZIG•zag] *n* zigzag M

**zinc** [zink] *n* cinc M

**zip** *vt* silbar

**zipper** [ZIP•pur] *n*
releampago M

**zither** [ZITH•thur] *n* cítara F

**zodiac** [ZO•dee•ak] *n* zodíaco M

**zodiacal** [zo•DUY•i•kl] *adj*
zodiacal

**zone** [zon] *n* zona F

**zoo** *n* parque zoológico M

**zoological**
[ZOO•uh•LAH•jik•kl] *adj*
zoológico

**zoology** [zoo•AH•lo•gee] *n*
zoología F

**zoom** *vi* aumentar